CURRENT ISSUES
AND CONTROVERSIES
IN POLICING

MICHAEL D. WHITE

John Jay College of Criminal Justice,
City University of New York

PEARSON

Boston ■ New York ■ San Francisco
Mexico City ■ Montreal ■ Toronto ■ London ■ Madrid ■ Munich ■ Paris
Hong Kong ■ Singapore ■ Tokyo ■ Cape Town ■ Sydney

Editor-in-Chief, Social Sciences: *Karen Hanson*
Series Editor: *Dave Repetto*
Series Editorial Assistant: *Liz DiMenno*
Marketing Manager: *Kelly May*
Production Supervisor: *Beth Houston*
Editorial Production Service: *Pine Tree Composition, Inc.*
Composition Buyer: *Linda Cox*
Manufacturing Buyer: *Megan Cochran*
Electronic Composition: *Pine Tree Composition, Inc.*
Cover Administrator: *Elena Sidorova*

For related titles and support materials, visit our online catalog at www.ablongman.com.

Between the time website information is gathered and then published, it is not unusual for some sites to have closed. Also, the transcription of URLs can result in typographical errors. The publisher would appreciate notification where these errors occur so that they may be corrected in subsequent editions.

Library of Congress Cataloging-in-Publication Data

White, Michael D. (Michael Douglas)
    Current issues and controversies in policing / Michael D. White.
        p. cm.
    ISBN 0-205-47005-X
    1.   Police—United States. 2.   Police administration—United States.   I. Title.
    HV8141.W435 2007
    363.20973—dc22

                                                                2006017166

Printed in the United States of America

10 9 8   16 15 14 13 12 11

CONTENTS

Preface   xiii

PART ONE   Selection, Recruitment, and Training

CHAPTER ONE

Recruitment and Selection   1

   THE TRADITIONAL APPROACH   1
       The First Fifty Years of Professional Policing   1
       Reforming the Police: Recruitment and Selection
       as a First Step   2
       The Emergence of Selection Procedures: Elements
       of a Standard Process   3

   CURRENT ISSUES AND CONTROVERSIES   10
       Recruitment   10
       Basic Requirements   13
       Selection Tests   19
       Other Current Issues in Recruitment and Selection   20

   SUMMARY   23

   KEY TERMS   24

   DISCUSSION QUESTIONS   24

   REFERENCES   24

   APPENDIX *Scholar's Perspective:* **The Challenge of Police Recruitment,
   by Heath Grant   27**

CHAPTER TWO

Training the Police   31

CRAFT VERSUS PROFESSION   34
Policing as a Craft   34
Policing as a Profession   35
Finding the Middle Ground: Reducing the Gap between the Academy and the Street   35
The Need for Training and Education   36

POLICE ACADEMY TRAINING   36
Historical Perspective   36
The Traditional Academy Model   38
Shortcomings of the Traditional Academy Training   41

FIELD TRAINING OFFICER PROGRAMS   43
The San Jose Model   43
The Benefits of an FTO Program   43
Performance Evaluation of Rookies   44
Selecting the Field Training Officers   45
An Example of an FTO Program   45

IN-SERVICE TRAINING   46
Specialized Training   46
Management Training   47

CURRENT ISSUES   47
Changing the Traditional Police Academy Pedagogy: Andragogy   47
Training in Community/Problem-Oriented Policing   48
Multicultural/Diversity Training   49
Stress Management Training   51
Domestic Violence Training   53
Training in Handling the Mentally Ill   53
Training in Communication and Writing   55
Technology and Training   56
Counterterrorism Training   56

SUMMARY   57

KEY TERMS   57

DISCUSSION QUESTIONS   58

REFERENCES   58

APPENDIX *Scholar's Perspective:* Police Training in America, by Maria (Maki) Haberfeld   61

PART TWO   **New Philosophies and Strategies**

CHAPTER THREE

Developing the Professional Policing Model   **67**

THE ORIGINS OF PROFESSIONAL POLICING: SIR ROBERT PEEL
AND THE METROPOLITAN LONDON POLICE   **67**

The Impetus for Change in London   67

Sir Robert Peel and the Metropolitan Police Act of 1829   68

The Need for Development of Professional Policing
in the United States   69

U.S. POLICING IN THE NINETEENTH CENTURY   **71**

Who Became Police Officers and How Did They Get the Job?   71

The Activities of the Nineteenth-Century U.S. Police Officer   72

Corruption and Brutality   72

REFORMING THE POLICE   **73**

A First Attempt at Reform   73

A Second Effort at Police Reform   74

CRACKS IN THE FOUNDATION OF THE PROFESSIONAL
POLICE MODEL   **76**

A Partial Success   76

Signs of Trouble: Prohibition and the Wickersham Commission   77

The Police Subculture and the Working Personality   78

The 1950s and 1960s: National Crisis and the Police   79

The Research Revolution   84

Fallout from the 1960s: Policing Comes Full Circle   86

SUMMARY   **87**

KEY TERMS   **88**

DISCUSSION QUESTIONS   **88**

REFERENCES   **88**

APPENDIX *Scholar's Perspective:* **Populism, Politics, and the Struggle
for Police Professionalism in the United States, by Anders Walker**   **90**

CHAPTER FOUR

New Policing Philosophies and Strategies   **93**

PROBLEM-ORIENTED POLICING   **93**

Theoretical Foundations   93

The Basic Elements of Problem-Oriented Policing: The SARA Model   96
Characteristics of the Problem-Oriented Police Department   98
Diffusion: How Widespread Is Problem-Oriented Policing?   99
Research on the Effectiveness of Problem-Oriented Policing   99
Limitations and Questions   101

COMMUNITY-ORIENTED POLICING   102
Theoretical Foundations   102
Core Features of Community Policing   103
Diffusion   107
Research on the Effectiveness of Community Policing   108
Limitations and Questions   110

COMPSTAT   112
Background   112
The Stages of CompStat   112
The Six Core Components   115
Diffusion and Impact of CompStat   117

ZERO TOLERANCE POLICING   118
The Principles of Zero Tolerance Policing   118
The Impact of Zero Tolerance Policing   119

**COP, POP, COMPSTAT, AND ZERO TOLERANCE:
SIMILARITIES AND DIFFERENCES   120**

SUMMARY   121

KEY TERMS   122

DISCUSSION QUESTIONS   122

REFERENCES   122

APPENDIX *Scholar's Perspective:* **The Brooklyn North Neighborhood Safety Project,
by Nancy Jacobs, Heath Grant, Wendy Rowe, and Jessica Saunders   124**

PART THREE   Police Management and Operations

CHAPTER FIVE

The Police Organization   128

THE POLICE BUREAUCRACY   128
Bureaucracy and the Police   128
The Quasi-Military Style of Policing   132

Civil Service   134

Police Unions   135

FUNCTION AND STRUCTURE OF THE POLICE ORGANIZATION   138

Functions of the Police   138

Structure of the Police Organization   140

Supervision and Leadership   146

CURRENT ISSUES IN POLICE MANAGEMENT AND ORGANIZATION   150

Alternative Organizational Methods   150

Manpower and Resource Shortages   152

Militarization of the Police   154

SUMMARY   156

KEY TERMS   156

DISCUSSION QUESTIONS   157

REFERENCES   157

APPENDIX *Scholar's Perspective:* **Restructuring of the City of Paterson, New Jersey, Police Department, by Michael C. Walker   159**

CHAPTER SIX

Police Field Work   164

POLICE AND THE LAW   164

Key Legal Principles and Issues from the Bill of Rights: Search, Seizure, and Arrest   165

Current Issues and Controversies Involving the Law   169

DISCRETION AND DECISION MAKING   173

Defining and Discovering Discretion   173

The Context of Police Decision Making   174

The Factors that Influence Police Decisions   175

Understanding the Complexity of Police Decision Making   177

Building on What We Know: Increasing the Rationality of Police Decision Making   178

NEW (AND SOME OLD) CRIME PROBLEMS   179

Drugs and Gangs   179

Policing Domestic Violence   183

Police and the Mentally Ill   185

Identity Theft and Computer Crime   188

Terrorism   193

SUMMARY   195

KEY TERMS   195

DISCUSSION QUESTIONS   196

REFERENCES   196

APPENDIX *Scholar's Perspective:* The Police and Sex Offenders,
by Karen J. Terry   201

CHAPTER SEVEN

Measuring Police Performance   204

THE UNCLEAR POLICE MANDATE   205

TRADITIONAL MEASURES OF POLICE PERFORMANCE   206
    The Numbers Game   207
    Summary   216

NEW MEASURES OF POLICE PERFORMANCE   216
    At the Department Level   216
    At the Individual Officer Level   223

SUMMARY   230

KEY TERMS   231

DISCUSSION QUESTIONS   231

REFERENCES   231

APPENDIX *Practitioner's Perspective:* Measuring Police Officer Performance
in the NYPD, by Anthony J. Raganella   233

PART FOUR   Police Misconduct and Accountability

CHAPTER EIGHT

Police Misconduct   237

DEFINING AND MEASURING POLICE MISCONDUCT   238
    Police Crime   238
    Occupational Deviance   239

Corruption   239

Abuse of Authority   239

U.S. POLICING AND MISCONDUCT: HISTORY, PREVALENCE, AND CONSEQUENCES   240

The History of U.S. Policing and Misconduct   240

How Prevalent Is Police Misconduct Today?   241

The Consequences of Police Misconduct   241

THEORETICAL FRAMEWORKS FOR UNDERSTANDING POLICE MISCONDUCT   242

The Rotten Apple Theory   242

Structural Explanations   243

THE PERSISTENT PROBLEMS FOR POLICE   247

Abuse of Authority   247

Corruption   253

Prejudice and Discrimination   256

SUMMARY   260

KEY TERMS   261

DISCUSSION QUESTIONS   261

REFERENCES   262

APPENDIX *Scholar's Perspective:* **Police Pursuit: Policies and Training, by Geoffrey P. Alpert   266**

CHAPTER NINE

Police Accountability: Internal Mechanisms   269

INTERNAL CONTROL MECHANISMS   269

Careful Recruitment and Selection of Personnel   269

Police Training   272

Supervision   273

Administrative Guidance   275

Internal Affairs   279

Integrity Tests   281

Early Warning Systems   282

Accreditation   284

Changing the Subculture   285

The Central Role of the Chief   286

SUMMARY   287

KEY TERMS   288

DISCUSSION QUESTIONS   288

REFERENCES   288

APPENDIX *Scholar's Perspective:* Early Warning Systems: Responding to the Problem Police Officer, by Samuel Walker, Geoffrey P. Alpert, and Dennis J. Kenney   291

CHAPTER TEN

Police Accountability: External Mechanisms   295

EXTERNAL CONTROL MECHANISMS   295
    Criminal Law: Prosecuting the Police   295
    Civil Litigation: Suing the Police   299
    Judicial Intervention   304
    Special Investigations   307
    U.S. Department of Justice Consent Decrees   312
    Citizen Oversight   314
    Public Interest Groups, the Media, and the Public   318

SUMMARY   319

KEY TERMS   320

DISCUSSION QUESTIONS   320

REFERENCES   320

APPENDIX *Scholar's Perspective:* Supercession of the Camden, New Jersey, Police Department, by Carmen V. LaBruno   323

PART FIVE   The Future of Policing

CHAPTER ELEVEN

Technology and the Police   327

STAGES OF TECHNOLOGICAL ADVANCEMENT   327
    The First Stage: 1881–1945   328

The Second Stage: 1946–1959   328
The Third Stage: 1960–1979   328
The Fourth Stage: 1980–Present   329

CRIME SCENE INVESTIGATION   329
Historical Perspective   330
The Locard Principle and Physical Evidence   330
Basic Procedures in Crime Scene Investigation   334
The Realities of Crime Scene Investigation   336

CRIME ANALYSIS   337
Historical Perspective   337
Crime Analysis in the Twenty-First Century   337
Geographic Information Systems (GIS)   339

OTHER TECHNOLOGICAL ADVANCES   341
Computers and the Internet   341
Global Positioning Systems (GPS)   342
Closed Circuit Television (CCTV)   343
NIBRS   343
Biometrics   344
Cold Case Squads   344
Less-than-Lethal Weapons   345
Imaging   345

SUMMARY   346

KEY TERMS   347

DISCUSSION QUESTIONS   347

REFERENCES   347

APPENDIX *Scholar's Perspective:* **Crime Mapping—A Tool for Law
Enforcement, by Jennifer B. Robinson   349**

CHAPTER TWELVE

―――――

Next Steps and Challenges for Police   **353**

THE FUTURE OF POLICING   353
Recruitment and Selection   353
Training the Police   355
New Philosophies and Strategies   356
Organizational Issues   358

Police Field Work   359

Measuring Police Performance   360

Police Deviance and Responding to It   361

Technology   362

SUMMARY   **363**

KEY TERMS   **363**

DISCUSSION QUESTIONS   **364**

REFERENCES   **364**

APPENDIX *Scholar's Perspective: COPS* **and** *CSI:* **Reality Television?**
by Michael Hallett   **365**

Index   369

PREFACE

∎ ∎ ∎ ∎ ∎

When a thing ceases to be a subject of controversy,
it ceases to be a subject of interest.
—William Hazlitt

The distinction between the past, present, and future
is only a stubbornly persistent illusion.
—Albert Einstein

INTRODUCTION

This book examines the major issues and controversies facing police officers today and is guided by two overriding themes: (1) the central role of change in policing and (2) the importance of history for framing the discussion of today's issues. With regard to the first theme, policing as an institution is resistant to change. In fact, many argue that promoting conformity and maintaining the status quo are central—though unstated—objectives in U.S. policing. If policing is indeed focused on resisting change, the question then becomes: Why do we need a book devoted entirely to current issues and controversies in policing? In response to that question, consider the following recent events:

- In 2002, Commissioner Ray Kelly of the New York Police Department (NYPD) stated that "the integration of counter terrorism into our mission ranks as one of the most important changes in our history" (NYPD, 2002, p. 1).
- On November 30, 2004, Amnesty International published a report on the Taser and, citing more than 70 deaths of suspects after being "tased," called for a moratorium on its use by police in the United States.
- In April 1999, the Attorney General of the state of New Jersey admitted that citizens traveling on the New Jersey Turnpike had been stopped and/or searched based only on the color of their skin. In August 2002 and January 2003, New Jersey settled racial profiling claims in the amounts of $250,000 and $775,000, respectively.
- Police shootings of black males in Cincinnati and St. Petersburg sparked riots and civil disorder. Although reminiscent of the tumultuous 1960s, the incidents occurred in 1996 (St. Petersburg) and 2001 (Cincinnati).

■ In 2002, William Bratton referred to CompStat as a "sea change in the way the New York Police Department does business (McDonald, 2002, p. xiii)." In July 2003, Weisburd and colleagues reported that CompStat and similar programs have been adopted or are in planning stages in more than half of all U.S. police departments with more than 100 sworn officers.

Also, think about these questions: Should police officers be required to have a college degree? Is it important for a police department to be racially representative of the community it serves? Are problem and community-oriented philosophies of policing the latest fad, or are they here to stay? Should community satisfaction with the police be considered a measure of police performance? Is it possible for a police department to effectively police itself, and if so, how?

Clearly, and despite police officers' affinity for the status quo, policing is a dynamic and ever-changing field. In simple terms, change plays a vital role in policing. Changes in norms and culture, economy, politics, technology, and the law, among many other things, help to transform the environment in which the police work. Given these challenges, perhaps Vollmer was not too far off the mark when he said—in frustration—that police are expected to "have the wisdom of Solomon, the courage of David, the strength of Samson, the patience of Job, the leadership of Moses, the kindness of the Good Samaritan, the faith of Daniel, the diplomacy of Lincoln, the tolerance of the Carpenter of Nazareth, and finally, an intimate knowledge of every branch of the natural, biological, and social sciences" (Vollmer, cited in Bain, 1939).

But, and here we get to the second overriding theme of the book, police officers do not have to start from scratch when confronting the issues and controversies of today. History provides an excellent starting point for police when struggling with and crafting responses to "new" problems. Many of the controversial topics that have emerged in policing over the last decade are by no means new. This is an important point, and one that may represent a saving grace for an institution that cannot possibly employ people with all of the qualities of Job, Solomon, Moses, etc. For example, issues of proper training, education, and police performance were addressed by Robert Peel in the original *Peel's Principles.* One need only to consider the professionalism movement led by August Vollmer, as well as the Commissions led by Wickersham, Knapp, Christopher, and Mollen, to place issues of police misconduct and accountability in historical context. Although issues of technology are revolutionizing some aspects of policing, technology has always played a role in police work: Consider the transition to automobile patrol and the adoption of the two-way radio. The Patriot Act and changes in constitutional law present new challenges for the police, but this is an institution that effectively adapted to the due process revolution of the 1960s.

In simple terms, history offers important lessons for addressing the issues and controversies of the twenty-first century. In my view, there is a wealth of institutional knowledge that has accumulated over the first 150 years of professional policing in the United States, and it would be a mistake to ignore that knowledge, even in a book called *Current Issues and Controversies.* In many ways, this book is not so much about the new issues and problems facing the current generation of police officers as it is about how old problems have re-emerged—or never left—and continue to present challenges for police. This historical context is an important and guiding theme throughout the book, one that shapes and frames each issue, and that provides a backdrop that is critically important for fully understanding the challenges and problems that face the twenty-first-century police officer.

OVERVIEW OF CONTENTS

Within the context of these two themes—the importance of change and history—this book examines five general areas of policing:

1. Selection, Recruitment, and Training
2. New Philosophies and Strategies
3. Police Management and Operations
4. Police Misconduct and Accountability
5. The Future of Policing

In each general area, chapters are devoted to specific issues and topics that have emerged in recent years. Each chapter is grounded in a historical context, describing how the issue has emerged and how it has affected policing in the past. Naturally, the book emphasizes the challenges and problems posed by these issues for police today. In each chapter, a specific issue is given special attention in a *Practitioner's* or *Scholar's Perspective* appendix, where leaders in the field offer their views and opinions on the topic.

The first section examines many of the contemporary issues on the front-end of policing, with chapters devoted to Selection, Recruitment, and Training. In Chapter 1, selection and recruitment issues discussed include basic requirements for being a police officer, college education, affirmative action, and building a representative police department. Chapter 2 deals with a range of training issues, such as the debate over policing as a craft or profession, the traditional training approach, and areas where training has been altered and improved in recent years (including field training programs).

Part 2 examines New Philosophies and Strategies and begins with a chapter on the traditional police model (Chapter 3). This chapter, in particular, lays important historical groundwork that enhances the treatment of new philosophies described in subsequent chapters. These include community, problem-oriented, and zero tolerance policing and CompStat, discussed in Chapter 4. Each new philosophy is discussed in terms of its theoretical foundation, basic concepts, and diffusion, with particular attention paid to the state-of-knowledge regarding effectiveness.

Part 3 examines contemporary issues related to Police Management and Operations. Chapter 5 discusses the police organization, in particular its bureaucratic nature and quasi-military style. Special attention is paid to the police subculture and the "cops as soldiers" mentality. Chapter 6 tackles the diverse issues associated with police fieldwork and discretion, most notably the law, critical decisions, the emergence of forensics and crime scene investigation, and the addition of terrorism to the police mandate. Law-related issues include recent changes in constitutional law (i.e., Fourth and Fifth Amendment protections) and the Patriot Act, and critical decisions include handling domestic violence and the mentally ill. Chapter 7 examines the issue of police performance at the individual officer and department level, describing traditional measures as well as those that have been developed more recently.

Part 4 covers issues related to Police Misconduct and Accountability. Chapter 8 examines police misconduct, first describing the major theoretical explanations and then addressing the major persistent problems: abuse of authority, corruption, and discrimination, including racial profiling. Recent scandals are described to illustrate the specific misconduct problems. Chapters 9 and 10 address the primary accountability mechanisms in place to prevent and control misconduct: Chapter 9 examines internal mechanisms including internal affairs, supervision, administrative policy, and early warning systems; Chapter 10 looks at external mechanisms such as the law, citizen oversight, civil litigation, and consent decrees.

The final section considers the Future of Policing. Chapter 11 is devoted to technology with specific coverage of NIBRS, less-than-lethal weapons, and the impact of forensics and DNA testing. Chapter 12 considers next steps and challenges for the police. In particular, the chapter examines the permanence of community and problem-oriented policing, as well as police efforts to handle manpower and budget shortages, and the roles of contracting services, civilianization, and consolidation.

FINAL THOUGHTS

I have two final parting comments before the reader begins the book. First, my original motivation for writing this book came from a lack of alternatives. There are plenty of *introduction to policing* textbooks at the undergraduate level and a wealth of readers and edited volumes at the graduate level. But when it comes to undergraduate study of the police that goes beyond the introductory level, there is very little to choose from, and I hope this book starts to fill that gap. Second, by its very nature, this book, or at least parts of it, may be obsolete or outdated in short order. New issues will emerge—or re-emerge—in the next few years that are not sufficiently covered here. Recall the two overriding themes of the book—the central role of change for police and the importance of history—and bear in mind that this text represents a snap-shot of the state of affairs in policing during the first part of the first decade in the twenty-first century. Change will continue, and history will offer us a guide.

REFERENCES

Bain, R. (1939). The policeman on the beat. *Science Monthly, 48,* 5.

McDonald, P.P. (2002). *Managing police operations: Implementing the New York crime control model—CompStat.* Stamford, CT: Wadsworth.

New York City Police Department. (2002). *Training bureau: 2002 annual report.* New York: Author.

Weisburd, D., Mastrofski, S.D., McNally, A.M., Greenspan, R., & Willis, J.J. (2003). Reforming to preserve: CompStat and strategic problem solving in American policing. *Criminology and Public Policy, 2* (3), 421–456.

ACKNOWLEDGMENTS

My name may be the only one on the cover but there is no way I could have finished this book on my own. The list of people I must thank is rather long so please bear with me. First, I would like to offer my appreciation to the staff at Allyn and Bacon including Liz DiMenno, Dave Repetto, Beth Houston, and Jennifer Jacobson. I would also like to thank Patty Donovan at Pine Tree Composition. I owe a debt of gratitude to my colleagues who increased the value of the book exponentially by offering their thoughts in the *Scholar's* and *Practitioner's Perspective* appendixes. Thanks to Dr. Heath Grant, Dr. Maki Haberfeld, Dr. Anders Walker, Dr. Nancy Jacobs and colleagues, Michael Walker, Director of the Paterson (NJ) Police Department, Dr. Karen Terry, Lieutenant Anthony Raganella, New York City Police Department, Drs. Sam Walker, Geoff Alpert and Dennis Kenney, Chief Carmen LaBruno, Hoboken (NJ) Police Department, Dr. Jennifer Robinson and Dr. Michael Hallett. Thanks also to the reviewers: Tod W. Burke, Radford University; Doug Davenport, Truman State University; Chris Menton, Roger Williams University; and Dan Okada, California State University–Sacramento.

In the other—and more important—part of my life, I would like to thank my wife, Alyssa and my children, Devon, Gabrielle, and Logan, for their patience and understanding as I hunched over my computer for months at a time writing this book. In reality, this college professor/author gig is what I do to pass the time when I can't be with them. Without question, their love and support is the source of my determination and drive.

Last, I would like to offer my gratitude to Dr. James J. Fyfe. Jim died as I was writing this book though he continues to be the inspiration for it. Over the past 15 years I got to know Jim as a mentor, colleague, and friend, and nearly everything I know about policing I know because of him. Jim is sorely missed by many—me included—and this book is for him.

RECRUITMENT AND SELECTION

This first chapter addresses current issues related to the recruitment and selection of police personnel. This area has experienced dramatic changes over the approximately 150 years of professional policing in the United States. During the first fifty years, recruitment and selection were dominated by the political nature of policing. Employment in the police department was a reward given by local politicians to their friends and supporters. At the beginning of the twentieth century, the leaders of the professionalism movement—men like August Vollmer—sought to implement rigid hiring standards to ensure that only the most qualified, morally incorruptible applicants were selected for employment. The standards set by Vollmer and others during the 1920s and 1930s are still in place in many departments across the United States today, but contemporary police departments now face new challenges such as a shortage of qualified applicants and pressure to hire more minority and female officers.

This chapter examines recruitment and selection issues over time, tracing the early developments from no standards at all to the efforts of the professional movement. The basic elements of a traditional selection process are described for the reader. The chapter then focuses on the current controversies in this area, including the push to field a representative police department (i.e., diversity), affirmative action, changes in basic requirements (especially residency and educational requirements), psychological testing, job-relevant physical testing, and the problems with mass hiring. The chapter concludes with a discussion of the Police Corps program and its efforts to draw college-educated men and women into law enforcement.

THE TRADITIONAL APPROACH

The First Fifty Years of Professional Policing

Professional policing began to emerge in the United States in the 1840s and 1850s. The New York City Police Department was formally created in 1845, following a series of riots and civil disorder. Often referred to as the **"political era" of policing**, police departments during the last half of the nineteenth century were intrinsically linked to local politics, and politicians heavily influenced all aspects of the administration and operation of the police department. During this time, there were essentially no recruitment efforts by departments and no selection process or preservice standards. Entrance into the police department was either awarded as part of the *spoils system* (i.e., political patronage) or based on a monetary payment (Grant & Terry, 2005). For example, during the Tammany Hall reign in New York City, joining the NYPD required a $300 payment to City Hall (Berman, 1987). There was no shortage of people interested in working for the police department because it paid substantially more than regular factory jobs: Most big city police officers received an annual salary of $900, compared to just $450 for factory positions (Walker & Katz, 2002).

Moreover, there were no preservice standards as we know them. No background checks were completed. There were no minimum standards for health, physical condition, education, intelligence, eyesight, or moral character. Jobs in the police department were given to men regardless of these seemingly critical issues. The lack of selection standards was compounded by little or no preservice training and virtually no supervision. "New officers were generally handed a badge, a baton, and a copy of the department rules (if one existed), and were sent out on patrol" (Walker & Katz, 2002, p. 29). Police departments were highly decentralized, with each precinct acting independently as its own mini-police department. Also, the lack of communication system meant that patrol officers were on their own during their shift, with supervisors having little or no capability to monitor their activities or performance. Finally, since employment in the police department was a political patronage position, elections often resulted in widespread turnover in the department as the newly elected leaders removed their predecessors' appointments and replaced them with their own. A police officer's job was secure only so long as his political contact remained in office. For example, in Cincinnati in 1880, 219 of the 295 members of the police department were fired the day after a local election. Given the lack of selection standards, training, and supervision, as well as the spoils system for gaining employment, it is not surprising that this political era of policing was characterized by corruption, brutality, and inefficiency.

Reforming the Police: Recruitment and Selection as a First Step

Though there were early efforts at reforming the police (i.e., the Progressives during the 1880s), significant change did not begin to occur until after the start of the twentieth century. Yet, an important development took place in 1883 that laid much of the groundwork for later reform efforts, particularly those directed at recruitment and selection. In 1883 at the federal level, the **Pendleton Act** was passed to reduce corruption in the presidential administration of Ulysses S. Grant (Grant & Terry, 2005). The Pendleton Act "established objective criteria for hiring public officials and made it unlawful to dismiss civil employees for political reasons" (Grant & Terry, 2005, p. 49). Although the Pendleton Act affected employment standards at the federal level, it was soon followed by similar legislation at the local and state levels across the United States.

Successful efforts to professionalize the police began to crystallize during the early 1900s when a small group of police chiefs developed and implemented innovations in their police departments. During what is commonly referred to as the **reform**

era of policing, these police chiefs took significant steps to professionalize the police and isolate them from political influence. **August Vollmer,** chief of the Berkeley Police Department from 1905 to 1932 and founder of the School of Criminology at the University of California at Berkeley, is widely considered the leader of this professionalism movement. The professionalism movement included a wide range of issues aimed at improving policing (see Chapter 3 for a more thorough discussion of the professionalism movement), but setting minimum standards for health, education, intelligence, and moral character was a centerpiece of the agenda. Vollmer, in particular, pushed for stringent recruitment and selection procedures, including clean background (no criminal record), college-level education, and intelligence and psychiatric testing of applicants.

Efforts to professionalize the police at the local level were facilitated by the development of the Federal Bureau of Investigation (FBI) and Director **J. Edgar Hoover's** emphasis on professional law enforcement. Hoover placed tremendous emphasis on selection standards and training, garnering an image of his special agents as the quintessential crime fighters—well trained, educated, honest, efficient, and impartial. Hoover's success in capturing numerous "Public Enemy Number 1s," the creation of the FBI National Training Academy (which offered training for police officers from around the country), the creation of the FBI Crime Laboratory, and his emphasis on crime statistics (i.e., creation of the Uniform Crime Reports, UCR) secured the FBI's image as the "paragons of the profession," and the FBI soon became the standard that local police departments sought to meet.

During this reform era of policing, recruitment efforts by police were minimal at best simply because there was no need. Jobs in the police department still paid better than other blue-collar positions. In many ways, the effort to professionalize the police increased interest in policing among the public, particularly as Hoover's FBI began garnering headlines with the captures of "Machine Gun" Kelly, "Pretty Boy" Floyd, "Baby Face" Nelson, Ma Barker, Bonnie Parker and Clyde Barrow, and John Dillinger. As interest in policing increased, departments were able to institute selection standards, weed out those inappropriate for law enforcement, and hire the best, most qualified applicants for the position. Although many police departments continued to struggle throughout the mid-1900s (see Chapter 3), **professionalism** had become the universal goal in law enforcement, with stringent selection standards playing a central role.

The Emergence of Selection Procedures: Elements of a Standard Process

Throughout the twentieth century, police departments began developing their own procedures for identifying and selecting new police officers. Although there certainly has been variation in the processes that have been put in place across the United States, there are some basic, standard elements that have been employed by the police. These common selection elements can be separated into two categories: minimum qualifications and selection tests.

Minimum Qualifications.   All police departments have traditionally had certain minimum qualifications that an individual must possess before being considered for a position as a police officer. These minimum requirements are laid out below. Current issues and controversies surrounding several of these requirements are described later in the chapter.

Citizenship   All police departments require that officers be citizens of the United States. Many departments, such as the LAPD and NYPD, allow legal aliens to begin the application process but require citizenship before the applicant can begin working (if hired).

Age   All police departments have minimum age requirements although there is some minor variation in the specified age. The most commonly cited age minimum is 21, and this is used by both the LAPD and the NYPD. Other police departments allow younger applicants to begin the application process, however. The Atlanta Police Department sets its minimum age at 20; the Miami-Dade Police Department requires that applicants be a minimum of 19 years of age. There is considerable debate over the appropriate age minimum that should be required for employment as a police officer. Given the tremendous responsibility of the job, many experts have argued that even 21 is too low a minimum age, and many departments have responded by raising their age requirement (Walker & Katz, 2002). The basic issue is, When does one possess the emotional maturity necessary to be a police officer? Departments that maintain the 21-year-old (or younger) requirement typically argue that maturity is not always tied to age and that the department will make judgments about who is ready and who is not. Recall that the minimum age to join the U.S. military is 18.

Traditionally, police departments have also had maximum age requirements, typically 35. The age limit was put in place because of the sometimes physically strenuous nature of policing and to prevent individuals from retiring and earning pensions after only a few years on the job (Walker & Katz, 2002). Federal laws that ban age discrimination put an end to the practice of maximum age limits for most police departments, although as recently as 1994, 12 percent of local departments still had age limits in place (Langworthy, Hughes, & Sanders, 1995).

Driver's License   Automobile patrol has been a central feature of U.S. policing for more than sixty years. As a result, all police departments require that applicants possess a valid driver's license, or be eligible to receive one (and possess it prior to the start of employment). Also, the driver's license must be issued from the state in which the applicant will work.

Health   Police departments have traditionally maintained basic minimum requirements regarding physical and mental health. For example, the Miami-Dade Police Department requires that applicants meet minimum county medical standards. Most departments require applicants to receive and pass a physical exam by a licensed physician prior to hiring. Serious physical conditions that will inhibit a person's performance on the job may serve as a disqualifier. Many departments also have basic standards regarding eyesight and hearing. The Atlanta Police Department requires no less than 20/100 vision in each eye (uncorrected), with 20/20 corrected vision. Nearly 90 percent of police departments use some form of psychological testing to identify those who are too unstable for employment in law enforcement (i.e., serious mental disorders) or who are unsuitable for the job (often based on a psychologist's clinical judgment). The issue of psychological testing of recruits is discussed later in the chapter.

Height and Weight   As recently as thirty years ago, the vast majority of police departments had minimum height requirements, typically 5 feet 8 inches tall (President's Commission on Law Enforcement and Administration of Justice, 1967). The rationale for the height requirement was that police officers needed to be physically imposing and able to overcome resistance from suspects. Some law enforcement agencies, particularly state police agencies, had height requirements that sometimes exceeded 6 feet (the rationale being that the applicant had to be tall enough to aim a shotgun over the roof of the patrol car).

Height requirements were challenged in a number of lawsuits that alleged the standards discriminated against women and minorities (Hispanics and Asians). The foundation of these lawsuits rested on several important federal laws:

1. The Civil Rights Act of 1964, which prohibits employment discrimination on the basis of race, color, religion, gender, or national origin (and the 1972 Equal Employment Opportunity Act, which extended the provisions of the Civil Rights Act to state and local governments).
2. The **Uniform Guidelines on Employee Selection Standards (1978),** which state that any hiring practice that has an "adverse impact" on women and minorities is illegal unless it is directly related to an employee's ability to do the job.

Although departments no longer have specific height requirements, many still require that an applicant's height and weight be proportional. The Miami-Dade Police Department, for example, has such a standard. Departments rely on medically and federal government-approved measures to assess the proportionality of height and weight. Ironically, though police departments have traditionally maintained requirements for height and weight among applicants, few have enforced weight standards among their rank and file. Essentially, one had to meet a weight requirement when applying, but not when on the job. This too has been changing recently as numerous departments have instituted annual or semiannual fitness proficiency tests for their police officers.

Criminal Record   All police departments have standards regarding prior criminal conduct by applicants though there is some variation in those standards. Nearly all police departments (95 percent) refuse to hire any applicant who has been convicted of a felony, but only 75 percent reject applicants because of a juvenile conviction (Griesinger, Slovak, & Molkup, 1979). Departments appear much more tolerant of misdemeanor convictions and of arrests not resulting in conviction:

- 30 percent reject applicants with juvenile or adult misdemeanor convictions.
- 20 percent reject those with an adult felony arrest with no conviction.
- 25 percent reject those with a juvenile (felony or misdemeanor) arrest but no conviction. (Grant & Terry, 2005; Griesinger et al., 1979)

Some police departments are more specific with their standards regarding criminal conduct. The NYPD, for example, lists the following factors as cause for disqualification:

- Any conviction for an offense that is punishable by one or more years' imprisonment (felony).
- Any repeated convictions of an offense that indicates a disrespect for the law, a lack of good moral character, or disposition toward violence and disorder.
- Discharge from employment, where such discharge indicates poor behavior and/or an inability to adjust to discipline.
- A dishonorable discharge from the armed forces.
- Persons convicted of a petit larceny.
- Persons convicted of any domestic violence offense. (http://www.nyc.gov/html/nypd)

The rationale for disqualifying applicants based on past criminal, immoral, and improper conduct is both philosophical and practical. From a philosophical standpoint, police officers are entrusted with tremendous power and authority, and only those with the most impeccable, unimpeachable ethics should be given that power. Prior criminal conduct suggests that an individual has shown poor judgment and may have a lack of ethical standards. In many cases, departments look far beyond criminal conduct to assess an individual's moral character. Issues also considered include financial history; drug use and alcoholism; and problems with authority and prejudicial attitudes with regard to race, religion, sexual identity, and gender. From a practical perspective, police officers carry firearms as part of their duties. In many states, individuals convicted of a crime are prohibited from owning or carrying firearms, which then makes it impossible for them to be a police officer.

Residency   Many police departments also have **residency requirements:** The officer must live within the boundaries of the jurisdiction where he or she works. Oftentimes, the applicant can begin the application process as a nonresident but must move to the jurisdiction prior to be hired. The residency requirement issue emerged from several of the Presidential Commissions during the 1960s that highlighted the disconnect between police and communities as a contributing factor in the riots and disorders of that decade (Grant & Terry, 2005). Several of the commissions recommended that police officers be required to live where they work so they gain an increased understanding of the community and its problems and could then interact with residents on a personal level. Approximately 25 percent of police departments require their officers to reside in the city or county, and another 40 percent have a more relaxed requirement (i.e., must live in the state) (Bureau of Justice Statistics, 2000). In recent years, however, residency requirements have become quite controversial and police unions have lobbied hard for their removal (see p. 15 in this chapter discussing the current controversies surrounding residency requirements).

Education   Police departments have traditionally required that applicants possess a high school diploma or GED. However, the push for police officers to have a college education can be traced back to August Vollmer and the professionalism movement. The President's Commission on Law Enforcement and the Administration of Justice (1967) stated that "the ultimate aim of all police departments should be that all personnel with general enforcement powers have baccalaureate degrees" (p. 109). The Law Enforcement Assistance Administration was created by the federal government in the 1960s to facilitate greater levels of education for police and included the development of a grant program (**Law Enforcement Education Program**) to ease the financial burden for interested officers. The issues surrounding the current push for college-educated police officers will be discussed in greater detail later in the chapter.

Veteran's Preference or Prior Work Experience   Most police departments give preferential treatment to veterans or those with prior work experience in law enforcement. Oftentimes the preferential treatment for veterans is given in the form of additional points on a civil service exam or by streamlining the application process in some way. The rationale for giving special consideration to veterans (and those with prior experience) is that their prior experience and training will put them a step ahead of other recruits: They have already been trained in the use of firearms, they are familiar with military regimentation and discipline, and they understand and respect authority. Or, quite simply, veterans have put their lives on the line to defend our country and should be rewarded for their efforts and sacrifice. Importantly, the preference given to veterans or those with prior law enforcement experience does not translate into a higher rank upon hiring. It is very rare for a person to be hired by a police department at a rank higher than patrol officer (except at the chief or commissioner level). There is very little lateral movement or promotions across agencies (i.e., a sergeant leaving the Newark, New Jersey, Police Department for New York will still begin at the patrol officer rank for the NYPD).

Selection Tests.   Applicants who possess the basic minimum requirements are then faced with a series of specific tests that are designed to identify the most appropriate and qualified for the job of police officer. Police departments vary in the types of tests that are used and in the order in which they are given, but there are several commonly used measures, including a written test, a physical agility test, a background check, and an oral interview.

Written Test   Typically, the first step in a selection process involves some sort of written exam. Many police departments use a standard civil-service-type exam, while others either create their own or hire an outside company to create one (Grant & Terry, 2005). The purpose of the exam at this early stage is to assess each candidate's basic skills in reading, writing, comprehension, logic, memory, and perhaps mathematics. It is unusual for a police department to employ an exam that tests knowledge of the law, police work, or general criminal justice knowledge. Since police departments have traditionally received many more applicants than open positions, this first exam often serves as an initial screener: The department sets a minimum score and only those applicants who receive grades above that score progress in the application process. Unfortunately, this type of exam often serves to eliminate applicants who are non-native English speakers because of the exam's emphasis on reading and writing (and often it is a timed exercise) (Grant & Terry, 2005). Departments can avoid this problem by offering non-native recruits additional time or by offering preparatory courses (National Crime Prevention Council, 1995).

Physical Agility   Most police departments also use physical fitness or agility tests early in the application process as an additional screener. Traditionally, physical agility tests have focused on speed and upper body strength and have included activities such as push-ups, sit-ups, pull-ups, long jump, and timed short distance running. For example, during the mid-1990s the New Jersey State Police required recruits to do the following: timed shuttle run, vertical jump, sit-ups, push-ups, and pull-ups. Physical agility tests came under scrutiny in the 1970s for being unrelated to the actual skills required for employment and for discriminating against female recruits (i.e., **Civil Rights Act of 1964**). Recent changes in physical agility and fitness tests are discussed in the next section.

Background Check   Nearly all police departments employ some sort of background check that delves into the recent history of each applicant. Since this process, if done thoroughly, is costly and time-intensive, departments often wait until the applicant pool has been reduced by earlier (and cheaper) tests such as the physical and written exams. At a minimum, departments check an applicant's criminal history to determine if he or she has been arrested or convicted, and if so, for what crime. Oftentimes, a police department will examine a range of other factors that give an indication of the applicant's "moral character" (Fagin, 2003). A thorough background check may involve:

- Interviewing former employers
- Interviewing references provided by the applicant
- Interviewing family members and neighbors
- Interviewing co-workers
- Examining prior employment history
- Examining financial/spending patterns
- Examining school performance

- Examining for indications of prejudice or discrimination
- Examining for indications of drug and excessive alcohol use
- Examining for indications of violence or anger issues
- Examining for indications of not getting along with others

The background investigation is viewed by many as the most important stage of the application process. Although it is very difficult to predict who will be a good police officer, a thorough background investigation can uncover patterns of problem behavior and serve to identify those who are not appropriate for police work. Two problems have emerged in recent years in this area for police departments. First, it is very important that officers assigned to conduct background investigations be unbiased and professional. Anthony Bouza (1972) argued that in the 1970s the background investigation process for NYPD applicants was heavily influenced by the "biases of the investigating sergeant" (p. 120). Second, when departments engage in "mass hirings," the background investigation process is often expedited, increasing the likelihood that problem individuals will be hired (the relationship between mass hirings and problem police officers is discussed later in the chapter).

Oral Interview   Nearly all police departments employ a face-to-face interview with applicants. Again, because of the time and resources required, this stage usually occurs near the end of the application process. Although the format varies, the oral interview usually involves multiple interviewers (three to five), lasts 30 to 60 minutes, and covers a range of topics. The interview is typically semistructured, giving the applicant an opportunity to respond to open-ended and scenario-based questions. The interviewers may also ask the applicant to explain or elaborate on issues that arose in the background investigation (i.e., explaining a juvenile arrest). Often, this stage of the process is used to measure a variety of skills including communication, reasoning, composure, appearance, ability to think quickly, and demeanor. Many of these skills will be assessed by asking the applicant what he or she would do in a given situation, such as responding to emergencies, handling combative or abusive suspects, using discretion, and uncovering problem behavior among fellow officers. Some departments employ a format that is adversarial or even combative (i.e., to measure poise and composure), while others rely on a more traditional or informal style. Although this stage is generally recognized to be very important in making hiring decisions, Doerner (1997) examined the relationship between interview scores and job performance and found "a persistent inability of this selection technique to isolate suitable candidates" (p. 784).

Making Hiring Decisions: Variation in the Scoring System.
Police departments employ several different methods for rating the applicants who proceed through their recruitment and selection process. For most police departments, there are certain automatic disqualifiers such as discovering a prior felony conviction that was not disclosed or failing the psychological exam because of a serious mental disorder. In addition, some departments require that an applicant receive a passing score on each

selection test. Under this approach, a failing score at any given stage results in the applicant's removal from the selection process. Alternatively, other police departments make hiring decisions according to an overall score, based on the cumulative performance at each stage. Under this approach, failure at one stage would not result in automatic disqualification. An applicant may still be hired if he or she performs poorly on one test but excels in all others. For example, an applicant may fail to perform the minimum number of pull-ups but excel in all other areas and, as a result, may still be offered a job. Or consider the applicant who performs well in all tests but fails a timed short-distance run because he or she tripped. Both scoring approaches are commonly used by police departments to make their hiring decisions.

CURRENT ISSUES AND CONTROVERSIES

Recruitment

Diversity: Building a Representative Police Department.   Policing has traditionally been a profession for white males. Martin (1980) conducted the first thorough study of women in policing and found that the occupational culture had a decidedly masculine tone, with those women who were able to "break and enter" the occupation limited to a few special assignments (i.e., working with juveniles). Similarly, minorities, particularly African Americans, have traditionally been underrepresented among police departments. Some researchers have linked this under-representation to the long history of conflict between the police and the African American community and the negative attitudes of police held by young African Americans, while other research has highlighted discrimination in the police selection process (Alex, 1969; Kappeler, Sluder, & Alpert, 1998; Wilson Huang & Vaughn, 1996). Skolnick and Fyfe (1993) suggest that the lack of minority representation among police departments in Los Angeles and Milwaukee, in combination with populations that had become heterogeneous quickly, may have contributed to the brutality and discrimination scandals that plagued those departments during the 1980s and 1990s.

As a result, police departments have come under increasing pressure from community groups, professional organizations, and their constituents to hire more female and minority police officers. The Commission on Accreditation for Law Enforcement (CALEA) recommends in its *Standards for Law Enforcement Agencies* that the composition of the police department reflect the composition of the community. Walker and Katz (2002) describe an **equal employment opportunity (EEO) index** that determines the extent to which the community reflects the department (this index is calculated by dividing the percentage of a minority group on the police force by the percentage of the minority in the local community, with 1.0 indicating representativeness). Such a measure allows departments to track their efforts to create a representative police force over time.

Motivations for Becoming a Police Officer.   As departments continue in their efforts to attract officers—especially females and minorities—research on motivations for becoming a police officer has become increasingly important. Simply put, recruitment efforts that are specifically tailored to attract specific types of officers (i.e., female and minority officers) seem more likely to be successful.

A fair amount of research on the police has examined reasons for entering the field. Much of the early work during the 1950s and 1960s addressed motivations for becoming a police officer among white males, since women and racial minorities did not enter the field in significant numbers until the 1970s. Although some early research indicated that individuals who entered policing were more likely to have authoritarian personalities, seeking power and control, most of the research from that time highlighted the desire for job security as a primary motivating factor (Harris, 1973; McNamara, 1967; Niederhoffer, 1969; Rankin, 1957). In later work, Lester (1983) also found pay and security to be primary reasons why recruits entered policing. The desire to help people and the nature of police work have also emerged as often-cited reasons for entering policing (Cumming, Cumming, & Edell, 1965; Raganella & White, 2004).

Do Motivations Differ by Race and Gender?   Much of the research has reported similar motivations among men and women who become police officers. Meagher and Yentes (1986) state that, "the reasons expressed by male and female police officers for career selection do not markedly differ" (p. 321). Women are no more likely than men to enter policing because of a desire for power or authority (Powers, 1983). Job security and helping others are the most commonly cited reasons for females entering policing (Charles, 1982). Milton (1972) concluded that salary was the major attraction for policewomen in her study, followed by the opportunity to perform a useful service. Nearly half of the female police officers in Ermer's (1978) study cited salary as their primary motivator, followed by the opportunity to help others. Bridges (1989) found that men and women ranked salary and opportunity for advancement equally.

There is less research examining motivations for entering police work among minorities, and the findings regarding racial differences are mixed. Reiss (1967) found only minor differences between black and white officers: Black officers were more interested in economic benefits, were slightly more attracted to opportunities to help others, but were less influenced by family and friends. More recent research examining motivations for becoming a police officer among NYPD recruits found that influences are remarkably similar, regardless of race and gender, and that the most influential factors are altruistic and practical, for example, the opportunity to help others, job security, and benefits (Raganella & White, 2004).

Affirmative Action.   **Affirmative action** came about in 1965 as a result of presidential Executive Order 11246, which required that all federal agencies develop written plans to take positive steps to remedy past discrimination (Walker & Katz, 2002). Affirmative action plans are now also required for all private companies that receive federal funding. The rationale behind affirmative action is that simply eliminating discrimination is not enough—the government is required to take additional steps to atone for past practices. Walker and Katz (2002) note that an affirmative action plan typically includes several parts:

1. A census of current employees
2. Identification of underutilization or concentrations of minorities and women
3. Development of a recruitment plan to correct any underutilization

Underutilization is typically defined as employing fewer women or minorities than would be expected based on their representation in the labor market (U.S. Equal Employment Opportunity Commission, 1974).

The most controversial aspect of affirmative action involves the use of **quotas:** rigid rules that dictate hiring practices. A number of discrimination suits against police departments were settled through consent decrees that included hiring quotas. For example, in 1980 the LAPD signed a consent decree requiring that 45 percent of all new recruits would be African American and 20 percent would be women (Walker & Katz, 2002). Supporters of quota systems argue that they are necessary to make up for past hiring practices and that they are successful in improving minority and female representation in police departments. Martin (1990) found that police departments with court-ordered affirmative action plans had a higher percentage of female officers than departments with voluntary or no affirmative action plans. Hochstedler (1984) found that hiring quotas were significantly correlated with improvements in minority hiring.

The two primary arguments against affirmative action are that it amounts to reverse discrimination and that it has created lower hiring standards for minority and female applicants. With regard to the first issue, opponents argue that quotas involve discrimination against whites and males, in violation of the Civil Rights Act of 1964. The U.S. Supreme Court has failed to issue a ruling that decisively addresses this reverse discrimination argument. In a 1987 case, the Court upheld a voluntary plan in Santa Clara, California (Johnson v. Transportation Agency, 480 US 616, 1987). Since that time, however, the Court has generally been opposed to race-based preferences; for example, in the late 1990s the Court upheld California's Proposition 209, which eliminated any form of affirmative action in the state. Nevertheless, the Court has occasionally supported plans that were clearly defined as temporary and were to be removed once representation is achieved.

Second, opponents argue that affirmative action has produced differential standards for hiring; specifically, the standards have been lowered for female and minority applicants in order to meet the quotas. The extent to which this is true is unknown and likely varies by police department. However, the intent of affirmative action is NOT to lower standards for female and minority recruits. Rather, the foundation of the principle is that departments should more aggressively recruit minorities and females to find those who are qualified: Essentially, the qualified candidates are out there, but the department may have to look and work harder to find them. How police departments implement their affirmative action plans may lead to lower standards to meet the quota, but that is the decision of the department and does not reflect the true spirit of affirmative action.

Based on the theoretical foundation of affirmative action, a department that fails to identify the required number of qualified minority applicants should NOT hire individuals who fail to meet the minimum standards. Rather, the department should suspend the hiring process to do more recruiting or reduce the overall number of applicants hired so the quota percentage is achieved. Consider the following scenario. Department X has funding to hire 200 new officers, and its court-ordered affirmative action quota dictates that 30 percent—or 60—of the new hires should be black. If the department has identified only 50 qualified black applicants, the department can reduce the entire recruit class from 200 to 165 recruits, and the quota will be met (50 is 30 percent of 165). The leftover money can be set aside for the next recruit class or to pay for officer overtime to make up for any temporary manpower shortage.

Basic Requirements

Over the last several years, police departments have modified, removed, and/or added a number of basic requirements for employment as a police officer. Some of these changes have occurred either as a result of technological advances or because of changes in the nature of law enforcement in the twenty-first century. Others have occurred as part of a continuing effort to professionalize policing.

Alcohol and Drug Testing. Many police departments now require that applicants submit to a urinalysis to test for drug and alcohol use. The drug testing can occur at any point in the application process, but given its cost, it usually occurs near the end of the process just before hiring decisions are made. Some police departments will hire medical staff to conduct the drug testing on site; others simply require applicants to submit a sample to their own physician as part of a more general physical examination. There are clear limitations to the use of drug testing during the application stage: Illegal drugs and alcohol remain in the body for a relatively short period of time; results can be inaccurate (i.e., false positives); and results can be faked (i.e., using someone else's urine). Nevertheless, urinalysis sends a clear message to applicants that illegal drug use and excessive drinking will not be tolerated by the department. Importantly, an increasing number of police departments are beginning to conduct drug testing of active police officers.

New Knowledge. Law enforcement in the twenty-first century has become increasingly advanced and complex, forcing police officers to acquire new knowledge and skills in a range of diverse areas. Perhaps the clearest example of this involves technological advances, particularly police departments' reliance upon computers. The computerization of police data—including crime and arrest data, personnel data, fingerprint data, use of force data, and early warning systems—means that departments must employ police officers who have an ability to understand and use computers. In many areas of the country, patrol cars are equipped with laptop computers that allow officers instant access to criminal history databases, motor vehicle records, and stolen vehicle and warrant or "wanted" databases. In addition, about one-third of all police departments use some sort of crime mapping software to conduct crime analysis (i.e., CompStat or similar strategies [see Chapter 4]). Applicants who are well-versed in the use of computers are highly sought after by police departments.

Second, knowledge of the law and legal issues is critical to police work. The law is not static: It is constantly changing as a result of case law at the state and federal levels. Recent rulings have addressed critical issues involving the Fourth, Fifth, and Sixth Amendments, including search and seizure, *Miranda* warnings, and right to counsel (i.e., the Patriot Act). The largest police departments employ a legal staff to stay on top on changes in the law and then to inform the rank and file of those changes through memos and in-service training. However, the vast majority of police departments are small and cannot afford a legal staff. As a result, the individual police officer is responsible for acquiring and understanding changes in the law. Although the police academy provides basic knowledge of constitutional law, criminal procedure, criminal and civil law, and rules of evidence, an individual who has prior knowledge in this area (i.e., college degree in criminal justice) is a step ahead of his or her fellow applicants.

Third, police departments have placed increasing emphasis on hiring officers who can speak and understand foreign languages. Given the current concerns involving terrorism, applicants who are fluent in Middle Eastern or Arabic languages are highly sought after at the local, state and federal levels of law enforcement. In fact, other basic requirements such as prior work experience may be waived in lieu of fluency in a foreign language. In a more traditional sense, however, police departments that have large ethnic populations in their jurisdiction must have officers who understand the cultures and who are fluent in any native languages. For example, law enforcement agencies in South Florida, Texas, and Southern California actively recruit applicants who are fluent in Spanish. Cities in the Northwest, such as Portland and Seattle, have large Asian populations and, as a result, need police officers who are fluent in Chinese, Japanese, and Korean.

Last, the widespread adoption of community and problem-oriented philosophies of policing (see Chapter 4) require that officers be proactive, seek out the assistance of the community, and employ a problem-solving process to the challenges they face on their beats. Communication and interpersonal skills have become critical, as have analytic and critical thinking ability. Officers are now being asked to identify the patterns or links between calls for service, to isolate the underlying problems, to think about creative and innovative solutions to those problems, and then to assess their impact. In many police departments throughout the country, the days of routine, isolated car patrol interspersed with quickly handling calls for service are over. In those places, the reactive "just-the-facts-ma'am" officer has been replaced with the proactive, critical, "outside-the-box" thinker who enlists the aid of the community to identify problems and implement solutions.

Residency.   Many police departments have traditionally required their officers to live inside the city limits of the jurisdiction where they work. The rationale for the residency requirement, as mentioned previously, is that it affords the officer the opportunity to understand the issues in the community, and in a sense, to become more connected to the area. If the officer has a vested interest in the well-being of the community and is knowledgeable about the issues and challenges because he or she lives there, this person will become a better police officer. There are a number of other arguments in favor of the residency requirement. First, requiring officers to live in the community may improve citizen-police relations, as residents see officers off duty and on a personal level. In effect, having police officers as neighbors through the town or city will personalize peoples' impressions of the police, based on the informal and positive contacts that would naturally occur. Second, police officers make good neighbors and may even deter crimes from occurring. If potential criminals know that a police officer lives on the street or in the apartment building, they may decide to not commit a crime because of the increased risk of arrest. In fact, the Jacksonville (FL) Sheriff's Office allows police officers to take their marked patrol cars home while off-duty because they believe the presence of marked patrol cars through the city—in driveways, parking lots, shopping centers, movie theaters, etc.— will have a deterrent effect on crime.

There are a number of arguments against residency requirements, and police departments have come under increasing pressure to lift them, in many cases from police unions and police officers themselves. First, some departments have considered lifting the requirement because of the current shortage of qualified applicants. Some departments are looking to eliminate as many barriers to employment as possible to increase the size of the qualified applicant pool. Second, opponents argue that the requirement is an infringement on the officer's right to choose where to live. Outside of political office, there are few other occupations that place such a restriction on employees. In some cases, an officer may be required to live in the actual precinct where he or she works. What if an officer has an opportunity for promotion but it involves re-assignment to another part of the city? Should the officer be forced to move to the other precinct (uprooting his or her family) or be forced to pass on a career opportunity? Third, the residency requirement may place an undue financial burden on the police officer. Officers who start off earning $35,000 to $40,000 a year will struggle to make ends meet in cities such as New York, Boston, Chicago, or Los Angeles, especially if they have families. Moreover, officers who are required to live in large cities like those mentioned above are then forced to struggle with big-city problems such as traffic, poor public schools, crime, pollution, and noise.

Fourth, opponents also argue that the residency requirement may lead officers to burn out more quickly because they are unable to get away from the stress and pressure of the job because they live where they work (Walker & Katz, 2002). Also, officers while off duty may often be approached by neighbors to handle problems: a loud radio, a barking dog, teenagers on the corner, car alarms, and crime. In effect, the officer is never off duty. Fifth, there is also the possibility that officers may become too familiar with their neighbors. It is more difficult to arrest one's neighbor than a stranger. Police exercise tremendous discretion, and there is at least the potential that officers' relationships with citizens may influence how they resolve encounters with people they know on a personal level.

Last, there is no empirical evidence to suggest that a residency requirement improves police officer performance, citizen perceptions of the police, or police officer perceptions of the community. In New York, for example, a study found that officers who lived outside of the city received fewer citizen complaints than those who lived in the city (NYCCCRB, 1993). Murphy and Worrall (1999) conducted a national survey of public attitudes on the matter and found that officers who are subject to residency requirements would be viewed less favorably than officers who are not. Nevertheless, there is still a push by some to maintain residency requirements. In a report examining the issue in Los Angeles, the American Civil Liberties Union of Southern California (ACLU, 1994) found that 83 percent of officers in the LAPD lived outside of the city, creating the appearance of an "outside hired force" (p. i) (see also Walker & Katz, 2002). The federal government even created a special program—called *Homes for Peace Officers and Firefighters*—that offered a variety of incentives, such as loans with no down payments, to encourage police officers to live where they work.

College-Educated Police Officers.   The debate over whether police officers should be college educated is not new. As far back as the 1920s, August Vollmer advocated for a college-educated police force. The issue reemerged at a variety of points during the twentieth century, including recommendations by the National Commission on Law Observance & Enforcement [Wickersham Report] (1931), and the President's Commission on Law Enforcement and the Observance of Justice (1967). In the 1970s, the **Law Enforcement Assistance Administration (LEAA)** created the Law Enforcement Education Program (LEEP), which for more than a decade provided money and opportunities for police officers to attend college. In 1985, a federal court upheld a Dallas Police Department requirement that applicants have at least 45 college credits with a C average or better. By 1990, over 70 percent of local police departments had education incentive programs in place that provide tuition reimbursement and/or salary increases for officers who take college classes (Carter, Sapp, & Stephens, 1989).

Despite these efforts, as recently as 1997 only 2 percent of police departments required a four-year college degree for applicants, with an additional 25 percent requiring some college (Bureau of Justice Statistics, 2000). Although the number of police departments requiring a four-year degree has continued to increase since 1997, in most jurisdictions applicants still only need a high school diploma to apply for a position as a police officer.

Arguments against a College Degree Requirement   There are a number of persuasive arguments against a college degree requirement. The major arguments against requiring a college degree are that it unnecessarily limits an already thin applicant pool and that it has a disproportionate negative impact on minorities. With regard to the first argument, most police departments are actively recruiting officers and/or are operating understaffed. Since policing has traditionally been an occupation for the working class, opponents argue that the requirement will unduly prohibit a large number of otherwise eligible candidates from applying. With regard to the second argument, Bureau of Statistics (1997) data indicate that in 1998, 25 percent of white Americans received a four-year college degree, compared to 15 percent of African Americans, and 8 and 12 percent of Hispanic Americans (Mexican and Puerto Rican origin, respectively). The basic issue is whether minorities and whites have an equal opportunity to attend college and receive a four-year degree. If they do not have an equal opportunity, then the college degree requirement has a disparate negative impact on minority populations, and in effect, short circuits efforts to build a diverse, representative police department (see earlier section on diversity). However, in 1991, the **Police Executive Research Forum** published a discussion paper on the issue and concluded that "there appears to be an adequate pool of both minority and majority college-educated men and women interested in police employment" (Carter & Sapp, 1991, p. 27).

There are two other arguments against requiring applicants to have a four-year college degree. First, opponents of the college requirement argue that a college education does not provide the skills needed to perform the job. In police lore, we often hear of the seasoned veteran telling the rookie that the first thing he or she needs to do is forget everything he or she just learned in the academy. Police officers traditionally argue that academy training does not prepare recruits for the street because policing is a craft "in which learning comes exclusively through experience intuitively processed by individual officers" (Bayley & Bittner, 1984, p. 35). In other words, learning the skills necessary to become a good police officer comes exclusively from experience on the job. From this perspective, police officers are viewed as skilled laborers who bring specialized skills and training to their trade, much like plumbers and electricians (Crank 1990). From this perspective, the education and skills provided by a four-year college degree are simply unrelated to the job.

Second, there is no consistent empirical evidence to suggest that college-educated police officers outperform non-college-educated police officers (Sherman, 1978; Walker & Katz, 2002). Cao and Huang (2000) examined citizen complaint rates among officers with different levels of education and found no difference in those rates. Other research has shown that college-educated officers are at greater risk of becoming frustrated by the work and having lower levels of job satisfaction, which may lead to higher turnover rates (Dantzker, 1995). Yet, much of the research conducted in this area has suffered from a number of methodological problems that limit the conclusions that can be drawn.

Arguments in Favor of a College-Degree Requirement   Alternatively, there are compelling arguments supporting the college-degree requirement. Dating back to Vollmer, the emphasis on college education for police officers is based on the assumption that the occupation is a complex profession, where skills and knowledge necessary to do the job successfully can be learned in a classroom setting, not solely through on-the-job training. Similarly, the movement for college-educated police officers is an integral part of the effort to professionalize policing (a movement that can also be traced back to Vollmer and others during the early twentieth century). Also, over the last half century, our society has become increasingly educated and it is necessary for police to keep pace with the greater public (from 1960 to 1998, the percentage of people graduating from college more than tripled).

Many of the other arguments in favor of a college degree requirement are more practical but equally persuasive. Proponents argue that college-educated applicants will be older, more mature, and more well-rounded. During college, people are likely to interact with others who look and act differently, as well as adhere to different belief systems. This exposure to other cultures and customs will lead to greater tolerance and understanding among police when they interact with people who are different from them. Moreover, those who study criminal justice at college will bring with them a more in-depth knowledge of the system, its various components, how it functions, as well as the prevailing theories on the causes of crime. Educational backgrounds in psychology, government, sociology, public management, communications, business, and the natural sciences would also benefit police officers in various aspects of the job. Also, as departments have moved toward problem-oriented styles of policing, critical thinking and analytic skills have become centrally important, and both of these skills are often developed and improved in the college classroom.

Perhaps more importantly, two critical features of police work involve communication and writing. Police officers have interactions with people on a daily basis, from encounters with their bosses and colleagues to informal contacts with citizens and formal encounters with victims and suspects. The ability to communicate effectively is absolutely vital to police work, particularly when there is a potential for violence: The officer who communicates effectively can deescalate a situation (what is sometimes called verbal judo), while the officer with poor communication skills may be faced with an increasingly aggravated and combative suspect. Report writing is another critical function of policing. Paperwork is a large and unheralded part of policing, but it plays a central role in the formal activity of the department. Reports serve as the official measure of police effectiveness (both among individual officers and at the department level), and they also serve as the foundation for additional formal action by other system players (i.e., the district attorney filing charges). For example, officers who are called to the witness stand to testify in a criminal prosecution will often rely on their notes and reports to recall specific events, document and identify evidence, and provide support for the course of action that was taken.

As the debate over the college-degree requirement continues, with most departments opting not to institute the condition, the actual picture that emerges among recruits is quite different. Simply put, departments that do not have a college requirement often select and hire recruits who have college degrees. In 1993, less than 1 percent of police departments required a four-year degree, with an additional 12 percent requiring some level of college credit (Terry & Grant, 2003). However, by 1988, 65 percent of police officers in the United States had some college education, and 23 percent had a four-year degree (Carter et al., 1989). Moreover, promotion and salary increases are tied to a college education in many police departments.

Selection Tests

Physical Testing: Making It More Job Relevant.   Police departments have been forced to modify their physical agility testing because traditional tests were challenged in terms of their job relevance, as well as their discriminatory impact on female applicants. The **Equal Employment Opportunity Commission (EEOC)** guidelines for sex discrimination prohibit denying employment to a woman because of characteristics that are attributable to women as a class (Grant & Terry, 2005). Police departments must also demonstrate that the tests measure skills that are relevant to the job. The question becomes How relevant are traditional physical tests such as sit-ups and push-ups to police work? Many departments now employ physical agility exams that test the skills often used by a police officer, such as an obstacle course, climbing a wall, performing a "dummy drag" (dragging a 150-pound dummy a certain distance), and running. Some jurisdictions have different minimum standards for male and female applicants (i.e., longer times and/or shorter distances for women), while others employ the same standards.

Polygraph Tests.   The federal Polygraph Protection Act prohibits employers from using lie detectors as a pre-employment screener; however, police departments are considered exempt from this rule (Walker & Katz, 2002). About half of all local police departments use a polygraph, or lie detector, test as part of the applicant selection process (Grant & Terry, 2005). Despite the portrayals in television and movies, the polygraph does not actually make a determination about whether the person being tested is lying. Rather, the polygraph measures physiological characteristics of the individual—breathing, blood pressure, pulse rate, and perspiration—as he or she is asked a series of questions. Generally speaking, changes in any of the above vital signs are seen as an indication of deception, or lying. Police departments ask about a range of different issues during a polygraph, including criminal behavior, drug and alcohol use, and other questionable or deviant activities. However, the polygraph examiner's assessment of the physiological changes in the individual is inherently subjective, and for that reason polygraph results are inadmissible in court. The Board on Behavioral, Cognitive, and Sensory Sciences (2003) estimates that the polygraph has an accuracy rate of 80 to 90 percent. Given the potential for error, departments should be careful not to make hiring decisions based solely on the results of a polygraph examination. Technological innovation has led to the development of a range of other lie detection mechanisms, such as the voice stress analyzer, facial thermal imaging, and even magnetic resonance imaging (MRI), although none of these are in widespread use in police selection processes.

Psychological Testing.   Approximately 80 percent of local police departments use some sort of psychological test as a screening mechanism for recruits. The overall goal of psychological testing is to assess recruits' personality and attitudes, and importantly, to identify those with mental disorders. A number of common psychological tests are employed, including the ***Minnesota Multiphasic Personality Inventory (MMPI)*** and the *California Psychological Inventory (CPI)*. The *MMPI* is composed of over 550 questions assessing a person's attitudes, beliefs, and ideas. Both the *CPI* and *MMPI* are deemed by psychologists to be reliable and valid.

Two separate issues can be measured through a psychological or personality test: stability and suitability. The first issue, stability, focuses on whether the recruit is mentally stable, free of serious mental disorders. Although serious mental disorders (personality disorders, schizophrenia, etc.) can often be managed effectively with medication and treatment, individuals suffering from mental illness are screened out of law enforcement for a number of reasons, including the tremendous authority of the job, as well as the frequency of high-stress encounters with citizens and suspects (Grant & Terry, 2005). Generally, very few recruits are deemed to be unstable as a result of a psychological test.

The second issue, suitability, is more complex and involves an assessment of whether the individual is suitable for policing. This is often a clinical judgment made by a licensed psychologist or psychiatrist, based on either in-person testing or from reviewing test results. The issue of suitability involves an inherent prediction about how someone will perform as a police officer. Unfortunately, research has shown that neither psychological test scores nor clinical assessments accurately predict police officer performance. Wright, Doerner, and Speir (1990) examined the relationship among pre-employment scores on the *MMPI* and the *CPI* and performance ratings during field training among Tallahassee (FL) police officers and found no correlation. The Independent Commission on the Los Angeles Police Department (1991), which investigated the LAPD in the wake of the Rodney King beating, offered strong conclusions about the effectiveness of psychological testing:

> This initial screening can identify obvious social misfits in the grossest sense, but cannot test for more subtle abnormalities which may make an individual ill-suited to be a police officer, such as poor impulse control and the proclivity toward violence. (p. 110)

Other Current Issues in Recruitment and Selection

Predicting and Measuring Police Officer Performance.   The problems associated with psychological test scores and police performance stem from the larger challenges of predicting police performance and developing objective measures that capture good performance. Chapter 7 deals with the issue of police performance, including how it has traditionally been measured by counting things—tickets, arrests, etc.—and some new, alternative ways of measuring performance. A major theme of that chapter is that there is a lack of consensus over the best ways to measure performance, both at the individual officer and department levels. Overreliance on crime and arrest statistics promotes an aggressive and legalistic style of policing that does not jibe with the community and problem-oriented philosophies of policing that have enjoyed widespread adoption in the United States. Standard performance evaluations used by police departments are typically vague, subjective, and often are not filled out thoughtfully or seriously by supervisors. In Chapter 9, we see that there are numerous examples of corrupt and brutal officers who received excellent performance evaluations from their supervisors. Simply put, how can psychological tests and experts in the field be expected to predict who will be good police officers if there is no clear definition of good policing? Doerner (1997) concluded that "a holistic scheme for identifying and pinpointing the qualities that make one a suitable police officer still eludes administrators" (p. 784). Until the qualities of a good police officer and good policing are more clearly and empirically defined, our ability to predict police performance will be necessarily limited.

Mass Hiring.   Police departments who have engaged in **mass hiring**—hiring a large number of officers at one time—have frequently experienced problems with those officers down the road. The primary problem with mass hiring is that the large number of recruits prevents the department from completing all of the recruitment and selection tests, most importantly comprehensive background investigations. Perhaps the best example of this problem is the Washington, DC, Metropolitan Police Department in the late 1980s. In 1989, the department hired 1,800 new officers. Background checks were not completed at all or were completed after hiring. One former academy instructor later said, "We swore in entire classes—hundreds of people—without background checks," and former Chief of Police Isaac Fulwood said, "Hire them now, we'll fire them later" (Carlson, 1993, p. 28). Nearly 100 of the officers from the 1989 and 1990 recruit classes were subsequently arrested on criminal charges ranging from shoplifting to murder. Quite simply, the need to hire police officers quickly cannot supercede the need for a deliberate and comprehensive recruitment and selection process. The consequences of hiring individuals who are unsuitable for policing and who engage in illegal actions may include, at the very least, scandal, deterioration in police-community relations, and civil litigation.

Police Corps.   The Federal Office of the Police Corps and Law Enforcement Education—and the **Police Corps** program—was established as part of the Violent Crime Control and Law Enforcement Act of 1994. "The overall goal of the program is to address violent crime by helping local and state law enforcement agencies increase the number of officers with advanced education and training who serve on community patrol" (Pate, 2005, p. 336). A number of states have developed Police Corps programs with guidance from the federal office. College students who are accepted into the program can receive up to $15,000 to pay for college (originally the cap was $30,000), provided they serve a minimum of four years as a police officer in a designated law enforcement agency. The selection standards of the Police Corps program are generally more stringent than local requirements, including attendance at a four-year accredited college or university, and the positions are highly competitive.

The Police Corps training is much more intensive than traditional academy training. The training lasts 16 to 24 weeks and requires participants to live in a dorm-like setting during the week (with most weekends off).

> The Police Corps Act provides funding for basic law enforcement training that is to go well beyond the "minimum standards" training available to police officers in many states. This training is intended to teach the knowledge, skills, and attitudes essential to serve effectively on community patrol; to develop the physical, moral, and analytical capabilities of the participants; and to teach self-discipline and organizational loyalty. Police Corps training places special emphasis on leadership, integrity, effective communication, understanding of social context, problem solving in multicultural settings, and commitment to the principles embodied in the U.S. Constitution, including respect for the dignity of all people. (Pate, 1995, p. 336)

Upon graduation, the Police Corps cadet is assigned to a participating law enforcement agency and deployed to sectors or beats where he or she is likely to be most effective. In some programs, such as Florida, Police Corps graduates receive higher salaries than officers who attend the standard basic training program. If a Police Corps graduate fails to complete the required four years of law enforcement service (or prior to that, fails to graduate from college), he or she must repay all funds received from the program with interest (Pate, 2005).

The Police Corps has been the subject of both praise and criticism. Skolnick and Fyfe (1993) note that the program holds tremendous promise: "Over time, the entry into police ranks of substantial numbers of PCC officers would redefine policing as respectable and appropriate work for people who have taken the time and effort to pursue education beyond high school" (p. 262). Moreover, the influx of college-educated officers would potentially reduce insularity among the police; even if most of the cadets left after their four-year stint, the side effect would be an increasing number of professionals who have a comprehensive understanding of policing (Skolnick & Fyfe, 1993).

Alternatively, others have criticized the Police Cadet Corps training because it is highly militarized, similar to boot camp training in the armed forces. Many have pointed out that this type of military-style training—where cadets perceive themselves as soldiers in a war—flies directly in the face of the tenets of community policing. Can officers trained like soldiers in a boot camp reasonably be expected to then serve as effective community police officers? The answer to this question remains unknown; in fact, little research has been conducted to compare Police Corps officers to other officers to determine if there are differences in performance. Last, other critics have focused on the tremendous cost of the program and the small number of officers who complete it: In 1997, the Police Corps spent $54 million, yet put only 246 officers on the street (Pate 1995).

SUMMARY

This chapter examines the issues of police recruitment and selection using a two-fold discussion. First, the chapter outlines the traditional approach taken by police departments, by tracing the historical development of recruitment and selection from the start of professional policing in the United States through the turn of the twentieth century—i.e., the first fifty years of policing when recruitment and selection standards were nonexistent. The chapter then traces the traditional recruitment and selection model that we know today, as it emerged during the professionalism movement and continued to develop through the twentieth century. This section focuses specifically on basic requirements for employment, such as age, citizenship, health, and criminal record, as well as standard components of police selection tests. These include written tests, background investigations, physical agility tests, and oral interviews.

The second part of the chapter addresses a wide range of current recruitment and selection issues that have emerged as controversial in some respect. These include:

- Diversity in recruitment, or building a representative police department (and the role of affirmative action)
- Basic requirements for employment
  - alcohol and drug testing
  - new knowledge (computers, foreign languages, problem-solving)
  - residency requirements
  - college education
- Selection tests
  - physical testing
  - polygraph
  - psychological testing
- Other issues
  - predicting and measuring police officer performance
  - mass hiring
  - Police Corps

Overall, the chapter highlights this first early stage of policing as a critically important step for police departments. Although, in some cases, local police departments employ vastly different approaches to recruitment and selection, a few common themes emerge. First, generally speaking, there is a real shortage of qualified and interested applicants, particularly minority and female applicants. Police departments are now required to devote a significant amount of resources to active and aggressive recruitment to find their next generation of police officers. Second, for a variety of reasons—legal, technological, and philosophical—the path to selecting and hiring the next generation of police officers is changing rapidly. As these changes continue to occur, police departments will find it increasingly difficult to find, select, train, and field professional police officers. This chapter highlights many of the challenging issues associated with the first part of that process, recruitment and selection. The next chapter focuses on the second part of that process—training.

KEY TERMS

Affirmative action
CPI
Civil Rights Act of 1964
Equal Employment Opportunity Commission (EEOC)
Equal employment opportunity (EEO) index
Hoover, J. Edgar
Law Enforcement Assistance Administration (LEAA)
Law Enforcement Education Program (LEEP)
Mass hiring
Minnesota Multiphasic Personality Inventory (MMPI)

Pendleton Act
Police Executive Research Forum
Professionalism movement
Police Corps
Political era of policing
Quotas
Reform era of policing
Residency requirements
Spoils system
Uniform Guidelines on Employee Selection Standards (1978)
Vollmer, August

DISCUSSION QUESTIONS

1. Describe the recruitment and selection process among U.S. police departments during the last half of the nineteenth century (i.e., the first fifty years of policing).

2. Describe how August Vollmer and J. Edgar Hoover contributed to changes in recruitment and selection practices during the first half of the twentieth century.

3. List and describe five basic minimum requirements employed by most police departments.

4. Discuss the role of affirmative action in police recruitment and selection. Do you favor the use of quotas? Explain your position.

5. Describe the major arguments for and against residency requirements for police.

6. Describe the major arguments for and against a college-degree requirement for police.

7. What is the Police Corps? What are the major advantages it offers for local law enforcement? What are its major weaknesses?

REFERENCES

Alex, N. (1969). *Black in blue: A study of the Negro policeman.* New York: Appleton-Century-Crofts.
American Civil Liberties Union (ACLU) of Southern California. (1994). *From the outside in: Residency patterns within the Los Angeles Police Department.* Los Angeles: Author.

Bayley, D.H., & E. Bittner (1984). Learning the skills of policing. *Law and Contemporary Problems, 47,* 35–59.

Berman, J.S. (1987). *Police administration and progressive reform: Theodore Roosevelt as police commissioner of New York.* New York: Greenwood Press.

Board on Behavioral, Cognitive, and Sensory Sciences and Education. (2003). *The polygraph and lie detection.* Washington, DC: National Academies Press.

Bouza, A.V. (1972, March). The policeman's character investigation: Lowered standards or changing times? *Journal of Criminal Law, Criminology, and Police Science, 63,* 120–124.

Bridges, J. (1989). Sex differences in occupational values. *Sex Roles, 3/4,* 205–211.

Bureau of Justice Statistics. (2000). *Law enforcement management and administrative statistics, 1997.* Washington, DC: Government Printing Office.

Cao, X., & Huang, X. (2000). Determinants of citizen complaints against police abuse of power. *Journal of Criminal Justice, 28* (2), 203–213.

Carlson, T. (1993). D.C. blues: The rap sheet on the Washington police. *Policy Review, 63,* 26–33.

Carter, D.L., & Sapp, A.D. (1991). *Police education and minority recruitment: The impact of a college requirement.* Washington, DC: Police Executive Research Forum.

Carter, D.L., Sapp, A.D. & Stephens, D.W. (1989). *The state of police education.* Washington, DC: Police Executive Research Forum.

Charles, M.T. (1982). Women in policing: The physical aspect. *Journal of Police Science and Administration, 10* (2), 194–205.

Crank, J.P. (1990). Police: Professionals or craftsmen? An empirical assessment of professionalism and craftsmanship among eight municipal police agencies. *Journal of Criminal Justice, 18,* 333–349.

Cumming, E., Cumming, I., & Edell, L. (1965). Policemen as philosopher, guide and friend. *Social Problems, 12,* 266–268.

Dantzker, M.L. (1995, December). Do college education requirements for police create an over-education problem? *Subject to Debate, 9,* 4.

Doerner, W.G. (1997). The utility of the oral interview board in selecting police academy admissions. *Policing, 20* (4), 784.

Ermer, V.B. (1978). Recruitment of female police officers in New York City. *Journal of Criminal Justice, 6,* 233–246.

Fagen, J.A. (2003). *Criminal justice.* Boston, MA: Allyn and Bacon.

Griesinger, G.W., Slovak, J.S., & Molkup, J.J. (1979). *Civil service systems: Their impact on police administration.* Washington, DC: Government Printing Office.

Grant, H.B., & Terry, K.J. (2005). *Law enforcement in the 21st century.* Boston: Allyn and Bacon.

Harris, R.N. (1973). *The police academy: An inside view.* New York: John Wiley and Sons.

Hochstedler, E. (1984, June). Impediments to hiring minorities. *Journal of Police Science and Administration, 12,* 233.

Independent Commission on the Los Angeles Police Department. (1991). *Report of the independent commission on the Los Angeles Police Department.* Los Angeles: Independent Commission on the Los Angeles Police Department.

Kappeler, V.E., Sluder, R.D., & Alpert, G.P. (1998). *Forces of deviance: Understanding the dark side of policing.* Prospect Heights, IL: Waveland Press.

Langworthy, R., Hughes, T., & Sanders, B. (1995). *Law enforcement recruitment, selection and training: A survey of major police departments in the U.S.* Highland Heights, KY: Academy of Criminal Justice Sciences.

Lester, D. (1983). Why do people become police officers: A study of reasons and their predictions of success. *Journal of Police Science and Administration, 11* (2), 170–174.

Martin, S.E. (1980). *Breaking and entering.* Berkeley: University of California Press.

Martin, S.E. (1990). *On the move: The status of women in policing.* Washington, DC: The Police Foundation.

McNamara, J.H. (1967). Uncertainties in police work: The relevance of police recruits' backgrounds and training. In D.J. Bordua (Ed.), *The police: Six sociological essays.* New York: John Wiley and Sons.

Meagher, S., & Yentes, N. (1986). Choosing a career in policing: A comparison of male and female perceptions. *Journal of Police Science and Administration, 14* (4), 320–327.

Milton, C. (1972). *Women in policing.* Washington, DC: The Police Foundation.

Murphy, D.W., & Worrall, J.L. (1999). Residency requirements and public perceptions of the police in large municipalities. *Policing, 22* (3), 327–342.

National Commission on Law Observance and Enforcement [Wickersham Report]. (1931). *Report on lawlessness in law enforcement.* Washington, DC: Government Printing Office.

National Crime Prevention Council. (1995). *Lengthening the stride: Employing peace officers from newly arrived ethnic groups.* Washington, DC: Author.

New York City Civilian Complaint Review Board (NYCCCRB). (1993). *Annual report 1993.* New York: Author.

Niederhoffer, A. (1969). *Behind the shield: The police in urban society.* Garden City, NY: Doubleday & Company.

Pate, A. (2005). Police corps. In L. Sullivan & M.S. Rosen (Eds.), *Encyclopedia of law enforcement, Volume 1: State and local* (pp. 336–337). Thousand Oaks, CA: Sage Publications.

Powers, M.T. (1983). Employment motivation for women in policing. *Police Chief, 50,* 60–63.

President's Commission on Law Enforcement and Administration of Justice. (1967). *Task force report: The police.* Washington DC: U.S. Government Printing Office.

Raganella, A.J., & White, M.D. (2004). Race, gender and motivation for becoming a police officer: Implications for building a representative police department. *Journal of Criminal Justice, 32,* 501–513.

Rankin, J.H. (1957). Preventive psychiatry in the Los Angeles Police Department. *Police, 28.*

Reiss, A.J., Jr. (1967). Career orientations, job satisfaction and the assessment of law enforcement problems by police officers. In the President's Commission on Law Enforcement and Administration of Justice (Ed.), *Studies in crime and law enforcement in major metropolitan areas: Field surveys III* (Vol. 2). Washington, DC: U.S. Government Printing Office.

Sherman. L.W. (1978). *The quality of police education.* San Francisco: Jossey-Bass.

Skolnick, J.H., & Fyfe, J.J. (1993). *Above the law: Police and the excessive use of force.* New York: Free Press.

Terry, K.J., & Grant, H.B. (2003). The roads not taken: Improving the use of civilian complaint review boards and implementation of the recommendations from investigative commissions. In D.J. Brown & K.J. Terry (Eds.), *Policing and minority communities: Bridging the gap* (pp. 160–182). Upper Saddle River, NJ: Prentice-Hall.

Walker, S., & Katz, C.M. (2002). *The police in America: An introduction.* New York: McGraw Hill.

Wilson Huang, W.S., & Vaughn, M.S. (1996). Support and confidence: Public attitudes toward the police. In T.J. Flanigan & D.R. Longmire (Eds.), *Americans view crime and justice: A national public opinion survey.* Newbury Park, CA: Sage Publications.

Wright, B.S., Doerner, W.G., & Speir, J.C. (1990). Pre-employment psychological testing as a predictor of police performance during the FTO program. *American Journal of Police, IX* (4), 65–84.

U.S. Bureau of Statistics. (1997). *Local Police Departments, 1997.* Washington, DC: Government Printing Office.

U.S. Equal Employment Opportunity Commission. (1974). *Affirmative action and equal employment.* Volume 1. Washington, DC: Government Printing Office.

■ ■ ■ ■ ■

SCHOLAR'S PERSPECTIVE

The Challenge of Police Recruitment

Heath Grant, Ph.D.*
John Jay College of Criminal Justice

Throughout the history of policing, most major incidents or scandals involving the police have led to public outcry about the recruitment process for police officers. If the police department required more education in its recruits, officers may have had the necessary critical thinking skills to avoid a misuse of force. If there were only more women represented in the upper ranks of the department, there would be far fewer citizen complaints. If the officers on patrol only represented the demographics of the beats they policed, there would be less of the mistrust between police and community that invariably makes the police less able to do their job effectively. While on the surface recruitment might seem to be the simple solution to many problems, the reality is that it is difficult to identify the characteristics of the "ideal" officer, and there are many conflicting empirical findings related to the value of requirements in the areas of education, diversity, gender, legal knowledge, and residency.

As a result, the fact that the recruitment standards vary significantly depending on the area being policed should not be surprising. Every department in the United States has its own standards, although most require that a prospective recruit have at a minimum no prior felony convictions; have a valid driver's license; be at least 21 years of age; and pass a series of phases including a written exam, medical exam, interview, physical agility test, and psychological screening. What should recruitment standards look like given that few would argue that the job of a police officer includes responding to stressful situations, quick decision making, good judgment, solid ethics, and an ability to interact professionally with members of the community? How do the common solutions of education, diversity, and residency really impact the ability of the officers to do each of these things?

EDUCATION

Although the push for higher educational standards for police officers began with August Vollmer's early efforts to professionalize police, it was not until the last

*Assistant Professor, John Jay College of Criminal Justice. Ph.D. Graduate Center, City University of New York, 2004.

decade that educational standards became readily apparent across U.S. police departments. By the year 2001, educational standards were nearly double the standards of 1990 (US DOJ, 1992, 2001); however, even at this time less than 23.8 percent of all police agencies required some level of college education.

Findings on the impact of education on police performance are mixed in the empirical literature. Although some studies have found educational standards did not make a difference in the number of complaints filed against officers (Smith, 2000), other studies have found that there are fewer complaints against more educated officers (Carter & Sapp, 1988). Still other studies have evidenced a correlation between education and such characteristics of a good officer as observation and stress management (Molden, 1999).

DIVERSITY

Unquestionably the biggest push in the area of recruitment has consistently been the need to diversify police forces nationally. Although early police reform efforts in this area focused on women and African Americans, this has inevitably changed along with the immigration trends of the country. The huge surge in the number of Hispanics in certain parts of the country has resulted in some major departments struggling with the ability to communicate with the communities they are trying to reach. The representation of minorities in police forces nationally has improved significantly (Grant & Terry, 2005); however, many authors have argued that there is still a need to improve the representation in the higher ranks of departments.

The logic of having departments that represent the communities they police is clear: By sharing ethnic or cultural backgrounds, it is assumed that officers would be better able to relate to the citizens in their assigned beat or district. However, here again, the evidence is not solid that this alone will be the answer to all problems of police/community relations. Some studies have actually indicated that citizen complaints by minority citizens against minority officers can actually be higher than those against their counterparts (Alpert & Dunham, 1992). Other studies have indicated that African American officers are equally as likely to use force, controlling for all other variables.

Having recruitment officers who represent the communities the department is trying to attract is an important ingredient in successful efforts (Milgram, 2002). The fraternal organizations have experimented with mentorships for minority applicants through the recruitment process with varying degrees of success to provide positive role models to interested citizens. To overcome language barriers, some departments have provided pay incentives to officers with a second-language competency and the use of language labs to encourage such study. In the meantime some departments have turned to the extensive use of translators in certain situations.

Many of the traditional efforts of recruitment such as internships, cadet programs, and college open houses are important methods. However, in communities where there is traditionally a lack of trust between residents and the police, even these efforts may not be enough. Long-term partnerships with key community leaders in these areas may first be necessary to begin to make the profession of policing more attractive to citizens who have only had negative perceptions of the police.

RESIDENCY

The intention of recruiting officers who are better able to know and understand their beats has also led many commissions and reform advocates to argue for residency requirements. Some departments require officers to live within the communities they police for this reason, at least beginning with the time of appointment. Although residency requirements may ensure that officers are more in touch with the communities they serve, there can also be the corresponding dangers associated with possible decreased objectivity in handling the situational demands of the job (Grant & Terry, 2005).

WHERE DO WE GO FROM HERE WITH RECRUITMENT?

Many police scholars and practitioners argue that there is nothing new to explore with respect to the question of recruitment. It is thought that everything that can be tried has been, and any change to recruitment strategy by itself will not make a significant difference in the type and quality of the officers it attracts.

Police departments need to include recruitment efforts within an overall strategic plan related to diversity and professional standards. Too often, recruitment offices work in isolation within police departments, and thus tend to rely on the same processes of recruitment with often less than desirable results. Departments develop a concrete vision of who the "ideal" candidate will be, and then ensure that recruitment efforts are supported with the necessary training, concrete policies, opportunities for mentorship, and other forms of professional development necessary to develop an environment of integrity and skill.

Involvement of community and business leaders in strategic planning for recruitment and professional development can help departments gain an understanding of what obstacles might exist to attracting residents in their community to the profession of policing. Some possible considerations might include negative perceptions of police officers, a high incidence of criminal records within the target population of recruits, fear of ostracism from other community support networks, or not having permanent residence. Working with community leaders around such issues, departments can match recruitment efforts to the underlying issues of the community their potential pools of recruits come from. While no single strategy will create an immediate difference in the type of officers departments recruit, through long-term strategic planning efforts, more significant and sustainable change can result.

REFERENCES

Alpert, G.P., & Dunham, R.G. (1992). *Policing urban america,* 2nd edition. Prospect Heights, IL: Waveland Press.

Carter, D., & Sapp, A. (1988). *The state of police education: Critical findings.* Washington, DC: Police Executive Research Forum.

Grant, H., & Terry, K. (2005). *Law enforcement in the 21st century.* Boston: Allyn and Bacon.

Milgram, D. (2002). Recruiting women to policing: Practical strategies that work. *The Police Chief* (69), 31–34.

Molden, J. (1999, January). College degrees for police applicants. *Law and Order,* 21–22.

Smith, B.W. (2003). The impact of police officer diversity on police-caused homicides. *Policy Studies Journal,* 31(2), 147–162.

U.S. Department of Justice, Bureau of Justice Statistics. (1992). Local Police Departments. Washington, DC: Author.

U.S. Department of Justice, Bureau of Justice Statistics. (2001). Local Police Departments. Washington, DC: Author.

CHAPTER 2

TRAINING THE POLICE

"Ignorance of police duties is no handicap
to a successful career as a policeman."
—Charles Reith (1975).

This chapter builds on the groundwork laid in the first chapter and discusses current issues related to the training of police personnel. Academy training provides the formative knowledge and experience for new officers, and as such represents a critical first step in fielding professional and skilled officers. Officers who leave the academy ill-prepared for the realities of police work would seem to be at greater risk of performing poorly during the initial weeks and months on the street, even if under the guidance of a field training sergeant. Poor performance among new officers has potential negative implications for police–community relations, civil liability, and the department's impact on crime. Alternatively, recruits who are better prepared for police work seem more likely to take initiative and engage in positive behavior, earning the respect of the community, co-workers, and supervisors.

Much like recruitment and selection, police training has changed dramatically in recent years. The emphasis on police training over the last several decades has sought to disprove Reith's (1975) observations noted above. This chapter presents the issues surrounding police training in the context of a larger debate over the appropriate foundation for such instruction; specifically, the controversy over education versus training. This foundational issue is tied to the perception of policing as a profession or as a craft. After introducing the reader to this larger controversy, the chapter addresses the three general areas of police training: academy training, field or probationary training, and in-service training. The primary focus of the chapter involves the training of new police officers, although there is some brief discussion of training for specialized units and management positions.

With regard to academy training, the chapter traces its development historically, focusing specifically on the prevailing model that emerged and continues to exist in many jurisdictions today. The shortcomings and problems with this academy training model are described as well. The next part of the chapter describes the development of field officer training, including its historical origins, content, and objectives. The traditional pitfalls of field officer training programs are explored, as are methods for avoiding them. The next part of the chapter is devoted to in-service training, where veteran personnel are periodically trained to maintain their current skills (i.e., firearms training) or are introduced to new information, skills, and techniques.

Finally, numerous current issues and controversies in training are described, including community and problem-oriented policing, policing a multicultural society, counterterrorism training, communication and "verbal judo," less-than-lethal weapons, and policing the mentally ill. The chapter also describes an alternative teaching approach called *andragogy,* or adult learning. First, however, it is useful to consider the skills required to be an effective police officer and how departments can go about imparting those skills to recruits. August Vollmer offers an interesting perspective on this issue.

VOLLMER'S ASSESSMENT OF THE POLICE: UNREALISTIC EXPECTATIONS OR NECESSARY SKILLS?

The citizen expects police officers to have the wisdom of Solomon, the courage of David, the strength of Samson, the patience of Job, the leadership of Moses, the kindness of the Good Samaritan, the strategical training of Alexander, the faith of Daniel, the diplomacy of Lincoln, the tolerance of the Carpenter of Nazareth, and finally, an intimate knowledge of every branch of the natural, biological, and social sciences. If he had all these, he might be a good policeman! (August Vollmer, cited in Bain, 1939)

Vollmer's quote above clearly reflects his frustration with the unrealistic expectations among the public regarding the police. Yet, those familiar with policing recognize that the average patrol officer will, at times throughout his or her career, be called upon to demonstrate all of the skills described above. As a result, it is incumbent upon police departments to provide adequate training in all of these areas to ensure that officers are properly prepared. Haberfeld (2002) begins her book on police training by highlighting the skills described by Vollmer and demonstrating how those skills can be developed and/or enhanced by police training. Before going any further, it is useful to summarize Haberfeld's discussion as an illustration of the central importance of police training (excerpted from Haberfeld, 2002, pp. 4–13).

- *The Wisdom of Solomon*
Decisions by police officers are likely to have profound implications for the people with whom they come in contact and for the officers themselves. They often affect people's liberty and personal safety. Some decisions determine whether people—citizens and officers—live or die . . .
    One of the most important benefits of training is that it confers "wisdom" by instilling in officers the importance of acting on facts and by providing and enhancing the skills necessary to develop the facts. Even more fundamentally, effective training incorporates the norms and values of the organization into all curricula . . .
- *Courage of David and Strength of Samson*
Danger is a central theme of police work. Thinking about it and preparing for danger are critical objectives of police and corrections training. Law enforcement trainers cannot *teach* courage. Officers are not *trained* to be brave. But they are given tools which, when understood and properly utilized, enable them to perform acts of bravery that present an illusion of courage.

It is the responsibility of law enforcement training to promote officer courage by developing physical and informational prowess. Training that does not meet both objectives fails to meet its responsibility to the officers it develops and nurtures.

- *Leadership of Moses*

In most walks of life, levels of education and training are society's yardsticks by which it measures one's suitability to lead and by which it distinguishes leaders from followers. Law enforcement agencies throughout the United States have focused substantial attention and resources on developing *leadership training* curricula.

. . . The failure to develop the leadership skills of law enforcement officers leaves many officers unprepared for managing "street" situations as they arise.

- *Patience of Job and Faith of Daniel*

For it is no exaggeration to suggest that suffering—widely perceived (and usually correctly so) by law enforcement officers as undeserved—is an occupational reality and, for some, a daily burden. . . . Law enforcement officers are subjected to stress with a frequency and to a degree that most citizens would not and could not tolerate.

Recruits must learn to recognize the signs and symptoms of stress. They must be taught that some manifestations of the consequences of job-related stress are the norm, not the exception. . . . These notions can be taught in basic academy training and should be reinforced regularly in in-service training.

- *Kindness of the Good Samaritan*

Citizens expect courtesy and respect from their police officers. Even in the face of adversity, citizens expect police officers to display good spirits and self-control. No matter how insulting, provocative, or intimidating members of the public may be, police officers are supposed to remain "calm, cool, and collected."

Police officers are only human—they need help to master self-control in the face of adversity. Appropriate training can go a long way toward providing officers with hard-to-acquire coping skills.

- *Strategical Training of Alexander*

The analogy of the law enforcement officer to the soldier is buttressed by the fact that law enforcement personnel suffer from "battle fatigue syndrome" as much as soldiers do.

Unchecked cynicism evolves into what will be referred to as *moral corruption*. The emergence of stress management training and secondarily, employee assistance programs are the only tangible indications that some law enforcement agencies recognize and are attempting to address the serious problems presented by moral corruption.

- *Diplomacy of Lincoln*

Every day on the job, law enforcement officers confront situations that would challenge the negotiating abilities of even the most highly trained and experienced diplomats.

The more difficult challenge to trainers is to develop curricula that produce law enforcement personnel who are trained in the diplomatic arts of reasoning and persuasion. Only when officers possess effective communication skills can they substitute the power of persuasion for physical power and thereby reduce the risk of physical injury to themselves and the people with whom they must deal.

- *Tolerance of the Carpenter of Nazareth*
Understanding the customs and mores of the citizen groups with which a police officer comes in contact can go a long way toward enabling that officer to interpret properly information and actions critical to sound, often on-the-spot decision making.

Beginning in the mid-1980s, diversity training was incorporated into most law enforcement training curricula. . . . Teaching officers how to enable one's views and beliefs to coexist with the different views and beliefs of other citizens—and other officers—is one of the greatest challenges to law enforcement training.

- *Intimate Knowledge of Every Branch of the Sciences*
As many professions have evolved into subgroups of highly trained specialists, law enforcement officers have evolved into ever-broadening generalists, who must instantly answer a wide range of difficult questions and take prompt and correct action:

  - How should one evacuate people from a building flattened by a terrorist's bomb?
  - Is the person before me suffering from cocaine shock, or is he a common drunk?
  - Does the prisoner who says she's going to kill herself mean it?
  - How does one talk to a juvenile who may have killed his parents?
  - How does one effectively use laptop computers, video cameras, recording devices, and cell phones to better patrol, control, and investigate?

CRAFT VERSUS PROFESSION

Central to the issue of police training is the debate over whether the occupation is a craft where the primary skills are learned through on-the-job training, or a profession where skills are first passed on to recruits through an academically oriented academy curriculum (i.e., education) and supplemented by later field experience. In simpler terms, are police officers more like plumbers and electricians, where the required skills are learned through on-the-job training, or more like a doctors and lawyers where skills are learned in an educational environment followed by supervised field experience (i.e., residency)?

Policing as a Craft

Although most scholars recognize its importance, police officers argue that "training given in police academies is universally regarded as irrelevant to 'real' police work" (Bayley & Bittner, 1984, p. 35). In other words, learning the skills necessary to become a good police officer comes exclusively from experience on the job (Bayley & Bittner, 1984). From this perspective, police officers are viewed as skilled laborers who bring specialized skills and training to their trade, much like plumbers and electricians (Bumgarner, 2002).

There are a number of issues that suggest that policing is more a **craft than profession.** Wilson (1968) argues that policing is a craft because of four defining features: the importance of on-the-job learning, a generalist work ethic, a lack of deference to authority, and the existence of oral traditions (see also Bumgarner, 2002; Crank 1990; Stinchcombe, 1980). In fact, the U.S. Department of Education has traditionally classified law enforcement training programs under the "trade and industrial" category (Calhoun & Finch, 1982).

Policing as a Profession

Alternatively, many scholars and police leaders argue that policing is a profession, with education as a central feature of the occupation. Classroom training (and college education) served as a foundation of the early professionalism movement, led by August Vollmer and other progressive police chiefs (Walker & Katz, 2002). Radelet and Carter (1994), Crank, Payn, and Jackson (1993), and Capps (1998) argue that policing possesses the key features of a profession, including a specialized body of knowledge and skills, accreditation through a professional organization, an orientation toward clients or service, considerable discretion given to members, and a primary objective other than profit.

The increasing emphasis on college education for police officers is based on the assumption that the occupation is a profession, where skills and knowledge necessary to do the job successfully can be learned in a classroom setting, not solely through on-the-job training. Although the research on the impact of college education on officer performance is mixed, the arguments for requiring a four-year degree are compelling. (see Chapter 1).

Finding Middle Ground: Reducing the Gap between the Academy and the Street

Although there is little agreement on whether policing is a craft or profession, most agree that current academy training has significant limitations and often leaves new officers ill-prepared for actual police work (Dantzker 2000a, 2000b; Doerner, Horton, & Smith, 2003; Stinchcombe & Terry, 1995). Some experts argue that reducing the gap between the academy and police work on the street simply requires developing more relevant academy training programs. Bayley and Bittner (1984, p. 55) argue that even if policing is a craft where formative experiences occur on the street, learning can be "accelerated and made more systematic" by relevant academy training. They argue that academy training must bring the reality of police work into the academy, by teaching it more like an internship than an introductory college course (Bayley & Bittner, 1984). "What is needed in police training . . . is frank discussion, with case studies of the realities of field decision" (Bayley & Bittner, 1984, p. 55).

The Need for Training and Education

There has been tension between the roles of training and education in policing since the 1960s. Although this training/education debate stems from the earlier debate about the occupation as a craft or profession, the nature, format and content of early criminal justice programs at colleges and universities exacerbated the tension. More specifically, as college-level criminal justice programs spread throughout the United States during the 1960s, 1970s, and 1980s, many were structured as "policing" programs focusing more on the "how-to" (how to search, how to arrest) than the "why" (why do police arrest, why do they use force) (Palmiotto, 2003). As such, many police departments and training centers came to view these early criminal justice programs as competitors.

Yet, as criminal justice programs have continued to develop and become more well-established, this perceived overlap or competition between training and education has begun to disappear. In fact, most scholars and police leaders recognize the importance of both training and education in policing. Haberfeld (2002) argues that both training and education play important roles in policing, and each should shape the early experiences of new police officers. Training in a police academy will continue to provide officers with the basic skills need to perform daily police functions, such as writing tickets, handling suspects and victims, search and seizure, arrest, and use of force. Education, whether it occurs at a university or as part of an academically oriented academy component, can provide very different and equally useful skills, such as a broader understanding of the criminal justice system, how it functions, and the causes of crime. Perhaps the different and important roles of both training and education were summarized best by the President's Commission on Law Enforcement and the Administration of Justice (1967, p. 127): "The trained man has developed skills and attitudes needed to perform a complex task. The educated man has developed his capacity to judge the worth, the performance, and the excellence of human action."

POLICE ACADEMY TRAINING

Most police cadets complete a minimum of only 400 hours of basic training before becoming a sworn officer. An exceptionally well-trained cadet will receive only about 800 hours. Attorneys, on the other hand, receive over 9,000 hours of instruction and doctors over 11,000 hours. Even embalmers with 5,000 hours, and barbers, with 4,000 hours, receive more training than police officers. . . . The concern over the inadequacy of police basic training programs has resulted in one police scholar observing, "Doctors bury their mistakes, while lawyers send theirs to jail." Unfortunately, untrained police officers do a little of both (Edwards, 1993, p. 23).

Historical Perspective

Professional policing in the United States has developed through three distinct periods or eras: the political era, the reform era, and the community era (Kelling & Moore, 1988; each of these eras is discussed in greater detail in Chapter 3). The political era, which represents approximately the first seventy years of policing (from the mid-nineteenth century to the early twentieth), was marked by very little professionalism, as police were essentially political appointees with no training and no pre-service or in-service standards of conduct. New officers learned how to do the job from more senior personnel because there was, generally speaking, no formalized training process. However, there is some evidence to indicate that the New York Police Department (NYPD) employed basic training as early as 1853 (Palmiotto, 2003). Called the City of New York Training School, the school was developed as a unit within the police department, although the content and nature of the training was limited to military drills, local and criminal law, and department rules (Palmiotto, 2003). Fosdick (1920) states:

> Because of the varied use of the term "school," it is difficult to determine when the New York institution was first inaugurated. If a single instructor, a number of students, and a certain amount of time devoted to instruction constitute a school, then the New York department has been equipped with a school for half a century. In early times, however, the instruction was of the most elementary kind. Police recruits were taught for a period of thirty days by a sergeant specifically detailed for that purpose, and in addition the students were sent out on patrol during certain hours of the day and night. (p. 299)

The second era of policing, the reform era, was marked by a widespread effort to professionalize policing, and formalized training was a central feature of that effort. By 1914, the NYPD had expanded its training to twelve weeks and offered four different types of training: recruit, refresher, specialized, and pre-promotion (Palmiotto, 2003). A number of other police departments followed suit and implemented training programs in the first part of the twentieth century, including Berkeley, Philadelphia, Los Angeles, Wichita, and New Orleans (Palmiotto, 2003). The creation of state police agencies during the 1930s in nearly every state—and the emphasis those agencies placed on training—also motivated local police departments to continue to adopt formalized training programs. Despite this push for formal training, as recently as 1965, less than 20 percent of all police departments provided training to police officers (Chappell, Lanza-Kaduce, & Johnston, 2005).

The third era of policing, the community era, began as a result of the riots and civil disorder of the 1950s and 1960s. A number of presidential commissions linked the police and tensions between police and minority communities to the civil disorder, and police came under significant pressure to change their approach to the community. As the impersonal style of the professional model came under fire (perhaps best illustrated by Sergeant Joe Friday's "just the facts ma'am"), community and problem-oriented philosophies of policing emerged and were widely adopted.

During this time, formalized police training also continued to evolve, specifically with the shift toward **state-mandated training.** In 1959, the New York State Legislature created the first state-mandated police training program in the United States (Palmiotto, 2003), requiring that a recruit receive 80 hours of training prior to becoming a police officer anywhere in the state of New York. California quickly followed suit and created its own commission on **Peace Officer Standards and**

Training (POST), which established rules and regulations for police training and certified and monitored training facilities throughout the state. Finally, in 1967, the President's Commission on Law Enforcement and Administration of Justice recommended that all states establish a POST commission. The POST commissions were to perform two important functions:

1. To establish mandatory minimum training standards (recruit and in-service), to approve curricula and instructors, and to monitor training facility compliance with state standards.
2. To certify police officers who successfully completed the required training. (Bennett & Hess, 1996)

By the mid-1980s, every state had mandated police training, though many of the larger departments continued to operate their own training academies. Finally, in 1979 four police organizations—the International Association of Chiefs of Police (IACP), the National Organization of Black Law Enforcement Executives (NOBLE), the National Sheriff's Association (NSA), and the Police Executive Research Forum (PERF)—came together and created the **Commission on Accreditation for Law Enforcement (CALEA).** CALEA developed standards designed to professionalize the police (there are 944 standards) and a process for accrediting law enforcement agencies (CALEA is discussed in greater detail in Chapter 9). A number of the standards deal directly with recruit training:

- Establish a training committee.
- Establish policies for remedial training.
- Maintain records of each training class.
- Provide for the operation and administration of training academies, if necessary.
- Provide suitable classrooms, office space, physical training capacities, and a library in academy facilities.
- Provide a written directive for agency personnel trained by an outside academy describing the relationship between the agency and the outside academy.
- Require instructors to have lesson plans, performance objectives, instructional techniques, testing and evaluation techniques, and resources available for use. (CALEA, 1994, pp. 33-2, 33-4)

The Traditional Academy Model

Types of Police Academies. Haberfeld (2002) states that there are currently three basic types of police academies: agency, regional, and college-sponsored.

Agency schools are generally found in large municipal areas or are established for the state police or highway patrol. *Regional academies* handle the training functions for both large and small departments located in a designated geographical area. *College-sponsored training academies,* which operate on the premises of postsecondary institutions, particularly community colleges, allow a person to take police training and earn college credit. (Haberfeld, 2002, p. 58).

Haley (2003) describes an expanded typology of police academies, although the types are often not mutually exclusive: State Police/Highway Patrol Academy, Centralized POST Academy, Municipal Police Academy, Sheriff/County Police Academy, Private Academy, Specialized Academy, Regional Academy, College/University Academy, and Citizen Police Academy. There are at least three important distinguishing features of the nine academy types: first, whether the academy is resident or non-resident (i.e., do recruits live at the academy); second, are the recruits full-time or part-time; and third, are the academy instructors and staff full-time or part-time (Haley, 2003). All types of academies provide at least the minimum training required by the state, and in many cases they will offer more extensive training than is mandated by the POST.

Functions and Foundations. The police academy experience serves a number of basic functions for new recruits. First, the academy provides formal training for new officers. This formal training includes both technical skills, such as self-defense and use of weapons, and knowledge, such as criminal and constitutional law and community policing (Walker & Katz, 2002). Second, the academy experience serves as a process for weeding out those who are either ill-prepared or unqualified to become police officers. Last, Walker and Katz (2002, p. 410) state, "it is a rite of passage that socializes recruits into the police culture. This subculture includes a strong ethos of identification with the profession, the department, and fellow officers." CALEA (1994, p. 33-1) states that training serves three purposes:

> First, well-trained officers are generally better prepared to act decisively and correctly in a broad spectrum of situations. Second, training results in greater productivity and effectiveness. Third, training fosters cooperation and unity of purpose.

Haberfeld (2002) argues that a number of philosophical planks serve as the foundation for modern police training including:

- Motivation plus acquired skills lead to positive action.
- Learning is a complex phenomenon that depends on a number of factors.
- Improvement on the job is a complex function involving the individual, the workforce, and the work environment.
- Training is the tripartite responsibility of the department, trainer, and trainee.
- Training is a continuous process that serves as a vehicle for constant updating knowledge, attitudes, and skills.
- Training is a continuous process and method for consistent improvement in the capacity of individual officers to act as a team. (pp. 41–42)

Style and Content. The format of training in the academy can vary notably. Traditionally, academy training has relied on the pedagogical approach to teaching, which is lecture-based with the instructors acting as "talking heads." However, academies are increasingly employing other methods and formats for teaching, including those that are more adult-centered (i.e., andragogy) and scenario-based (see the *Current Issues* section on page 47 for more in-depth discussion of both of these methods). More and Wegener (1996) state that, regardless of the training format employed, an effective program typically includes seven different actions:

1. *Preparing:* Select the right topics for the trainees and their needs.
2. *Motivating:* Get attention, promote interest, create desire.
3. *Presenting:* Use interactive techniques and multimedia.
4. *Reviewing:* Summarize, review, and conclude.
5. *Applying:* Blend theory with practice.
6. *Testing:* Evaluate knowledge through testing.
7. *Reinforcing:* Provide positive support for proper performance.

The length of academy training has increased considerably over the last half century and still varies quite a bit from agency to agency. Frost and Seng (1984) reported that academy training increased from an average of 342 hours in 1952 to 633 hours in 1982. The Bureau of Justice Statistics surveyed 12,000 law enforcement agencies in 1993 and found that departments required 640 hours of training for recruits, 425 classroom hours and 215 field training hours (Edwards, 1993).

Despite the variation in length and content, police academy curricula tend to share several common features. Thibault et al. (1998) state that training programs can be categorized into six general content areas:

1. Administrative procedures: Such as quizzes, exams, and note-taking.
2. Administration of justice: Such as the history of law enforcement, probation and parole, social services, and police organization.
3. Basic law: Constitutional and criminal law, juvenile law, and civil liability.
4. Police procedures: Patrol, mental illness, criminal investigation, accident investigation, domestic violence, and interviews and interrogation.
5. Police proficiency: Firearm training, self-defense, arrest techniques, and courtroom testimony.
6. Community relations: Minority groups, victim/witness services, crime prevention, and media relationships.

Of course, as time has passed and new issues and challenges emerged, the topics covered in the academy have necessarily increased. Haberfeld (2002) provides an overview of the Washington, DC, Metropolitan Police Department training curriculum as an illustration of a typical academy program. The recruit training is 26 weeks in length, including two weeks on the street:

- Orientation and personnel issues, 40 hours
- Level 1: Organization of the Department, 49 hours

- Level 1–2: DC Code, Part I, 44 hours
- Level 1–3: DC Code, Part II, 44 hours
- Level 4: Criminal Procedure, Part I, 41 hours
- Level 5: Criminal Procedure, Part II, 59 hours
- Level 6: Investigative Patrol Techniques, 58 hours
- Level 7: Handling Property, 25 hours
- Level 8: Unique Patrol Situations, 26 hours
- Level 9: Traffic Regulations, 18 hours
- Level 10: Traffic Enforcement, 36 hours
- Level 11: Use of Force, Firearms, 68 hours
- Level 12: Vehicle Skills Training, 42 hours
- Level 13: First Responder, 33 hours
- Level 14: Use of Force, Defensive Tactics, 85 hours
- Level 15: Behavioral Sciences, 37 hours
- Level 16: Civil Disturbance, 35 hours
- Level 17: Physical Training, 52 hours. (p. 63)

Shortcomings of the Traditional Academy Training

Police, academics, and researchers generally agree that the traditional academy training model has a number of limitations. This recognition is perhaps best illustrated by the fact that most police departments now follow up academy training with a field training program (described later). In general, the field training program is intended to fill the gaps between the academy training and the "real world" of policing. A number of scholars have been more specific in their critique of police academy training. Walker and Katz (2002) state that many training programs still do not provide enough (or any) coverage of critical police issues such as discretion, ethics, and the use of informants. Also, the lecture format that is traditionally employed is not an effective way to teach police officers about issues such as domestic violence and mental illness. Thibault et al. (1998) identified a number of common deficiencies in academy training programs:

1. *Program Content:* Failure to adequately cover human relations, communications, adult versus juvenile behavior, and other topics.
2. *Quality Control of Instructors:* Training personnel pulled from the field often do not know how to teach.
3. *Training Facilities:* Facilities are often old and outdated.
4. *Training Equipment:* Teaching is primarily lecture-based.
5. *Part-Time Personnel:* Instructors often perform training duties only on a part-time basis.
6. *Part-Time Attendance:* Part-time students often cannot devote their full attention to the training.
7. *Training before Power:* Recruits often are granted police powers prior to graduation.

8. *Follow-up Evaluation:* Follow-up of police officer performance is rarely done.
9. *Field Training Officers and Programs:* FTO programs often fail to prepare officers for "solo performance." (pp. 315–316)

More and Wegener (1996) describe ten cardinal errors to be avoided when designing a training curriculum:

1. Trying to teach too much.
2. Trying to teach too fast.
3. Lack of communication concerning training plans.
4. Failure to recognize individual differences.
5. Failure to provide practice time.
6. Failure to show other employees the big picture.
7. Failure to give positive reinforcement.
8. Intimidating employees.
9. Lack of common vocabulary.
10. The Pygmalion effect: Expectations must be realistic and appropriate.

Several scholars have identified the quasi-militaristic structure of academy training as problematic because it contributes to an *us versus them* **mentality.** Skolnick and Fyfe (1993) argue that the "cops as soldiers" mentality leads to frustration among officers when they realize they are in a war against crime they cannot win. For some officers, that frustration leads to withdrawal and cynicism; for others, it leads them to take out their frustrations on "the enemy."

In a similar vein, the overemphasis on danger during academy training is seen as a limitation of the current model. Kappeler, Sluder, and Alpert (1998) state that:

> An inordinate amount of attention and misinformation concerning the dangers of police work is disseminated to police recruits at police academies. . . . most police training curricula overemphasize the potential for death and injury and further reinforce the danger notion by spending an inordinate amount of time on firearms skills, dangerous calls, and "officer survival." The training orientation often resembles preparation for being dropped behind enemy lines on a combat mission. (p. 92)

Although Kappeler et al. (1998) are careful to acknowledge the real danger inherent in policing, their point is well taken. In the traditional basic law enforcement training program, very little time is spent on developing intellectual skills such an understanding of community relations, ethical considerations, and specific critical issues (the underlying issues associated with mental illness and domestic violence, for example), while large blocks of time—90 percent according to Chappell et al. (2005)—are devoted danger-related skills (officer safety, use of firearms, etc.) (Kappeler et al., 1998). Bayley (1976) explains very clearly the consequences of the emphasis on danger: "The possibility of armed confrontation shapes training, patrol preoccupations, and operating procedures. It also shapes the relationship between citizen and policeman by generating mutual apprehension" (p. 171).

FIELD TRAINING OFFICER PROGRAMS

The San Jose Model

As mentioned previously, **field training officer (FTO) programs** were created as a result of the perceived limitations of academy training. In 1967, the President's Commission on Law Enforcement and the Administration of Justice recommended a period of supervised training following graduation from the academy. The field training officer program would bridge the gap between the academy and the realities of policing, allowing officers to apply what they had learned in the classroom environment to police work on the street under the guidance of a veteran officer. The first FTO program was developed by the San Jose, California, Police Department in 1972 and has since served as the model for hundreds of other police departments. The San Jose model involves a mentoring approach that is fourteen weeks long, three four-week periods of training followed by a two-week evaluation period (Haberfeld, 2002). The recruit is assigned to a different training officer during each four-week period to ensure variation in style and approach, and rookies are evaluated on a weekly basis. As the weeks progress, the rookie assumes a greater level of independence and takes on more job responsibilities. By 1986, two-thirds of surveyed police departments had a FTO program in place, with more than half indicating that their program modeled the San Jose program (McCampbell, 1986).

The Benefits of an FTO Program

There are a number of advantages for police departments that operate an FTO program. McCampbell's (1986) survey of 300 police departments found that FTO programs fulfilled a number of organizational needs including standardized training for recruits; standardized evaluations that would validate agency hiring, retention, and termination decisions; and reduced civil liability. Molden (1987) identified four benefits of an FTO program:

- A structured, standardized learning experience that prepared rookies for patrol.
- The application of academy training to real-life situations on the job.
- Exposure of rookies to veteran officers who can serve as mentors and role models.
- Documented evaluation of rookie performance that can support agency decisions regarding retention, termination, assignment, and can offer protections against civil liability.

Haberfeld (2002) states:

> . . . recruits who participate successfully in an FTO program will, as a consequence of having been trained under standardized conditions, have improved self-image, perform better, and be better able to contribute to the safety and welfare of citizens. Conversely,

incompetent, ill-suited candidates will be discovered and terminated, thereby reducing agency liability. Discrimination and liability charges can be defended successfully with records generated during the training cycle. . . . Standardized training and evaluation enables agencies to better predict performance outcomes. (p. 79)

Finally, in order to receive accreditation from CALEA, a law enforcement agency must have a field training officer program in place.

Performance Evaluation of Rookies

A critical component of a FTO program involves the evaluation process. The procedures for evaluating a rookie should be consistent, structured and objective. Rookies should be evaluated regularly, usually daily by their training officers. Feedback to the rookie regarding performance—specifically, areas where improvement is needed—is essential for an effective program. In order to accurately assess rookie performance, a number of police departments have conducted a task analysis of the patrol function to capture the breadth of responsibilities involved in the job (Doerner et al., 2003). This task analysis then produces a list of functions relevant to the position—also called a **behaviorally anchored rating scale (BARS)**—that can be used to provide structured and consistent training and evaluation (Doerner et al., 2003). Many police departments have used this approach to create a daily evaluation tool—typically called a **daily observation report (DOR)**—that training officers complete at the end of each day to assess the rookie's performance.

Doerner et al. (2003) describe the DOR used by the Tallahassee (FL) Police Department that assesses rookies on a range of areas including:

- Appearance and attitude
- Knowledge of laws, policies, and procedures
- Relationships
- Technical skills such as driving, use of the radio, interviewing, and use of force
- Report writing
- Control of conflict
- Patrol procedures and investigative techniques
- Problem/solving and decision making

On the first part of the DOR, rookies are rated on each of the skills using a seven-point Likert scale: 1–3 below average, 4 satisfactory, and 5–7 above average. The second part of the evaluation includes seven open-ended, narrative questions where the training officer describes specific instances of officer performance (good and bad), and the topics covered during the day. The DOR provides training officers with a simple, straightforward evaluation tool that adequately captures the field training experience and rookie performance on a daily basis.

Selecting the Field Training Officers

A second critical piece of an effective FTO program involves the selection of the best, most-qualified training officers. "Since these officers form the backbone of the program, there is a need for careful selection, training, and retention of experienced senior patrol officers for FTO assignment" (Doerner et al., 2003, p. 213). FTO officers should have exemplary work histories, including a clean record with Internal Affairs, excellent performance evaluations, with good communication and report writing skills. Often departments employ standardized selection criteria for the FTO position that may include a written test, recommendations from supervisors and an oral interview.

Field training officers undergo their own training prior to becoming an FTO and received periodic in-service updates. In many jurisdictions, a new FTO completes two 40-hour blocks of training called "Instructor's Techniques School" and "Preparation for Becoming a Field Training Officer" (Doerner et al., 2003). The Techniques course focuses on teaching style, methods of delivery, and student assessment, while the FTO preparation course introduces the officer to the concepts and structure of the field training program (Doerner et al., 2003). Most departments test their field training officers annually to ensure competency, and they may also receive additional training as new issues, techniques, and challenges emerge (Haberfeld, 2002).

Importantly, the FTO position should be a sought-after assignment that qualified veteran officers voluntarily compete for, rather than a mandatory assignment to an officer who may not want the position. The department can often provide a number of incentives to draw the best applicant pool. Incentives can include pay raises, access to additional or new equipment, departmental certification and acknowledgement, and participation in other types of police training. The overall goal is for the field training officers to be among the best police officers in the department who can then pass on their skills and knowledge to the new officers coming out of the academy.

An Example of an FTO Program

Haberfeld (2002) summarizes the content and structure of a number of FTO programs, and it is useful to do the same here. The FTO program below is for a department of 500 sworn officers that has been modeled after the original San Jose program.

- *Phase I:* This phase lasts 28 days with a concentration on training (90 percent) and a small portion on evaluation of individual work (10 percent). The evaluation criteria are simply positive or negative. The focus on training in this phase is a result of the high potential for liability since the officer has just left the academy.
- *Phase II:* Phase II lasts 28 days. The rookie is assigned to a different shift and area of the city with a new FTO. This phase is evenly split between training and

evaluation. This phase does involve "solo performance." The officer is rated on a numerical scale.

- *Phase III:* Phase III lasts 28 days. This phase is 90 percent individual work (and evaluation) and 10 percent training. The rookie is again assigned to a new area with a new FTO.
- *Phase IV:* Phase IV lasts two weeks. The officer is assigned to the FTO from Phase I, and the rookie is in plainclothes. This phase is 100 percent individual work and evaluation. This is the last stage in which the rookie is evaluated.
- *Phase V:* Phase V lasts two weeks. The officer is assigned to the traffic division and spends time learning accident and driving while intoxicated (DWI) investigation techniques.
- *Phase IV:* Phase VI lasts two weeks. The officer is assigned to a community-oriented police officer in the area where he or she will be permanently assigned.
- *Evaluation:* The FTO completes a daily observation report for the rookie. FTOs meet every other Friday with the FTO Sergeant to discuss the officer's progress. The FTO submits a final evaluation and recommendation to the FTO Sergeant, and the FTO Sergeant and Lieutenant make the decision regarding the officer "graduating" the program. (Haberfeld, 2002, pp. 82–84)

IN-SERVICE TRAINING

Most states now require that police officers receive periodic **in-service training** throughout their careers. Traditionally, in-service training has focused on specialized skills such as requalifying at the gun range, pursuit driving, and the usage of other nonlethal weapons (batons, mace, etc.). However, any topic or issue can be the subject of in-service training. Other areas that have recently been the focus of this type of training include changes in criminal or constitutional law, domestic violence, handling the mentally ill, **counterterrorism,** youth gangs, and **community policing.** "Continuing police training throughout a police officer's career enables the officer to function more efficiently and safely, and is considered important in curtailing civil liability actions against an officer and his department" (Palmiotto, 2003, p. 15). Also, CALEA (1994) has several standards regarding in-service training of police:

- Maintain a written directive that requires all sworn personnel to complete an annual retraining program, including legal updates and firearms requalification.
- Have a written directive that governs roll-call training.

Specialized Training

Officers assigned to specialized units will receive additional training in the skills and knowledge required for their specific responsibilities. Depending on the size of the department, there may be any number of specialized units that require officers to possess unique skills. Just a few examples include tactical units such as SWAT, narcotics, highway patrol, community policing, detective work (homicide, burglary, white collar, or organized crime), domestic violence, juvenile and gang, and specialized units to handle the mentally ill (several of these are discussed in the next section).

Management Training

Officers who receive promotions and are assigned to supervisory and management levels of the department will also receive specialized training. At the supervisory levels (i.e., sergeant and lieutenant), departments typically provide internal training to newly promoted officers. At higher supervisory levels, departments may employ internal training or send their personnel to external training programs. There are a number of leadership training programs developed by the West Point Military Academy, the FBI National Academy, the IACP, and a host of private consultants (Haberfeld, 2002). There are a number of theories that guide leadership training, as well as a range of instructional approaches. Given that supervisors and management play a crucial role in setting the tone of both the informal and formal working environments, ensuring that these department leaders receive appropriate and effective training is absolutely critical. The actual content and structure of this specialized management training goes beyond the scope of this book and interested readers should consult Haberfeld (2002) and Palmiotto (2003) for more detail.

CURRENT ISSUES

A number of current issues and controversies have emerged in the area of police training over the last decade. The remainder of the chapter is devoted to describing some of these contemporary issues.

Changing the Traditional Police Academy Pedagogy: Andragogy

Many scholars argue that the behavioral and militaristic environment in most police training academies hinders the learning experience (Ortmeier, 1997). Birzer (2003, p. 32) notes the paradox for police who "work in a democratic society but are trained and learn their jobs in a very paramilitary, punitive, and authoritarian environment."

Andragogy has emerged as an effective adult learning technique in a variety of fields (Brookfield, 1986; Caffarella, 1993; Merriam & Caffarella, 1999). Andragogy highlights self-directed learning with the instructor playing a facilitating role, rather than the traditional lecture-based **pedagogy.** Under the andragogical approach, students participate in "self-directed group discussions and active debate," while the instructors ". . . manage the classroom by allowing participants to share their experiences and knowledge . . . integrate new knowledge, and . . . provide strategies that will allow transfer of learning back to the job" (Birzer, 2003, pp. 34–35).

Proponents of the andragogical approach for police training argue that it (1) draws on trainees' past experiences, (2) treats trainees as adults, (3) adapts to the needs of participants, and (4) fosters critical thinking and creativity (Birzer & Tannehill, 2001). This method of instructional format would seem to match calls from police scholars to bring the realities of police work into the academy through critical discussion, role plays, and interaction between recruits and instructional staff.

Training in Community/Problem-Oriented Policing

As problems with the traditional, professional model of policing emerged in the 1960s and 1970s (see the next chapter), two new and related philosophies of policing emerged: community-oriented policing (COP) and **problem-oriented policing (POP).** During the 1980s and 1990s, departments adopted these new philosophies, either separately or in tandem (see Chapter 4 for an in-depth discussion of these new approaches). Both COP and POP represent a significant shift in how police officers carry out their day-to-day responsibilities. Quite simply, the days of routine patrol, responding to calls for service, and handling those calls as quickly as possible to be available for additional calls are over. The adoption of community and problem-oriented policing has serious implications for police training: If either approach is to be successfully implemented, training must play a central role in introducing officers to the concepts and framework and garnering their support for its adoption.

Haberfeld (2002) notes that training in COP and POP has generally been ineffective. One problem associated with community policing is that in many departments it has not been fully adopted. At its heart, COP represents a departmentwide shift in philosophy, approach, and techniques. During the 1990s, the federal government, through the Office of Community-Oriented Police Services, made a significant amount of funding available to departments who would adopt COP. Unfortunately, the adoption of COP in many departments translates into one or a small number of officers assigned to a specialized unit. COP and POP training in these departments is pointless since only the few specially assigned officers are responsible for engaging in the new approach. Haberfeld (2002) also states that training problems also occur with the timing, content, and intensity of the message: For example, COP training is too short and occurs at the end of the academy (conveying the perception that it is unimportant); training does not properly develop key skills such as problem solving and communication; and officers do not understand the cultural norms of the communities in which they work.

One example of community policing training where there has been some success involves the development of **regional community policing institutes (RPIs).** As a result of funding through the federal COPS office, 35 RPIs were developed throughout the United States to provide a centralized and uniform training center for community policing for all police officers in the area. Although the RPIs were funded for only one year (1997), nearly all of the RPIs still exist today. The New Jersey Regional Community Policing Institute developed an 80-hour block of training that has since been incorporated to regional police academies throughout the state. The curriculum, shown below, covers a range of topics and is intended to immerse every new police recruit in the state of New Jersey into a theoretical, conceptual and practical understanding of community policing.

THE NEW JERSEY REGIONAL COMMUNITY POLICING INSTITUTE TRAINING CURRICULUM
- Module 101—Orientation to Community Policing
  - Definitions and history of COP
  - Philosophy and concepts
- Module 102—Cultural Diversity in Community Policing
  - Tools to learn, practice, and implement an appreciation of diversity
- Module 103—Community Organizing and Partnerships
  - Key steps in building effective community policing partnerships
- Module 104—Conflict Resolution in Community Policing
  - Basic understanding of crisis and conflict resolution
- Module 105—Crime Prevention in Community Policing
  - Basic concepts of crime prevention as they relate to community policing
  - Information about the capstone project
- Module 106—Community Resources and Services
  - Police officer's roles of referral and networking with public and nonprofit agencies
  - Introduction and familiarization with the range of services and agencies
- Module 107—Problem-Solving Strategies in Community Policing
  - Components of problem solving
  - The SARA model
- Module 108—Strategic Planning in Community Policing
  - The value and role of strategic planning
- Module 109—Community Policing Program/Management/Research Skills
  - Methods of design, implementation, and evaluation of community policing
  - The Capstone Project is discussed
- Module 110—Ethical Issues in Community Policing
  - Historical perspective of police integrity
  - Ethics in the context of the new roles and responsibilities

Multicultural/Diversity Training

Diversity training for police is not a new issue. In the 1940s, the International City Management Association (ICMA) published a manual titled *The Police and Minority Groups.* The importance of diversity training for police emerged during the 1960s when police actions were linked to several of the riots that occurred during that decade. The Kerner Commission (1968), in particular, identified poor police community relations as one of several root causes of the riots. Yet, despite sixty years of training, the police–community relationship in many areas is still antagonistic and tense (i.e., us vs. them mentality). Recent civil disturbances in Cincinnati and St. Petersburg (FL) highlight the continuing tension in many communities throughout the United States. Moreover, the widespread adoption of community policing—and the recognition that the best hopes for crime reduction lie with a police–community partnership—has forced police departments to place a renewed emphasis on multicultural or diversity training for police, and a number of new training models have emerged in this area.

Haberfeld (2002) points to the Shusta et al. (1995) book, titled *Multicultural Law Enforcement,* as a critical resource in providing an overall framework for training police to understand and be sensitive to diversity. Since the early 1990s, the state of California has mandated diversity training (Champion & Hooper, 2003). California law (section 13519.4) states, "the course or courses of instruction and the guidelines shall stress understanding and respect for racial and cultural differences, and development of effective, noncombative methods of carrying out law enforcement duties in a racially and culturally diverse environment."

The central theme of diversity training is that police officers will be more effective if they are able to secure community support and that police officers will be better able to secure that support if they have an understanding of the culture of the residents (especially the marginalized groups). Gould (1997) offers a number of important considerations when implementing diversity training:

- One should remember that teaching diversity also means the "unteaching" of some already existing culturally insensitive attitudes and behaviors.
- A change in behavior will not generally result from sitting through one cultural diversity course.
- For the training to have its greatest effect, it should be tailored to meet the needs of officers as well as the community.
- The training of experienced officers should include the training of administrators in the same classroom setting.
- Experienced officers' training should include more time for venting of frustrations centering on the cultural diversity training.
- Cultural diversity training should begin early in an officer's career.
- The training should be reinforced throughout an officer's career.
- The training should be aimed toward explanation and discovery concerning cultural differences rather than appearing to place blame for police–community conflict on the individual officer. (pp. 354–355)

The curriculum in cultural diversity training tends to cover a wide range of topics including police prejudices and assumptions about minorities, race and culture, inter-ethnic relations, minority integration, cultural evolution, human rights, and police ethics and behavior (Grant & Terry, 2005). Haberfeld (2002) has developed a training model called *Multicultural Close-Contact Training* (MCC). Designed to be incorporated into academy training, the MCC model "explores the pervasive influence of culture, race and ethnicity on daily encounters, contacts and interaction between police officers and civilian employees of police organizations and other community members" (Haberfeld, 2002, p. 195). The model uses different instructional techniques—lectures, videos, and guest lecturers—and includes nine modules on a range of topics:

- Module 1—Multicultural Communities: Race, Ethnicity, and Crime
  - Challenges for police and society, prejudice in policing, police knowledge of cultural groups.
- Module 2—The Changing Law Enforcement Agency: Interaction with the Society
  - Victims and offenders, myths and realities, women in policing.
- Module 3—Past—Present—and the Past Again?
  - History of profiling, laws and court decisions, recruitment, discrimination in employment decisions, reverse discrimination.
- Module 4—Cultural Awareness or Cultural Ignorance?
  - Cultural awareness, coping with frustration, tolerance vs. prejudice.
- Module 5—Inter- and Intra-Cross-Cultural Communications
  - Language barriers and power, attitudes and power, nonverbal communication, cross-gender communication.
- Module 6—Case Studies
  - African Americans, Asian/Pacific Americans, Latino/Hispanic Americans, Middle Eastern Americans, American Indians.
- Module 7—Hate and Bias Crime: History and Priorities
  - Historical perspectives, the impact of ignorance, law enforcement responses, individual discretion.
- Module 8—Agitation versus Accommodation
  - Work habits and practices, sensitive peacekeeping.
- Module 9—Professionalism and Peacekeeping Strategies in a Diverse Society
  - Leadership in professionalism, professionalism, ethnic and minorities, peacekeeping strategies, controlling the multicultural law enforcer.

Stress Management Training

There is no question that policing is a stressful occupation. As an illustration, simply recall Vollmer's assessment in the beginning of this chapter of the skills required for the job. Moreover, policing has traditionally been a male-dominated occupation characterized by a degree of *machismo* where officers are discouraged from discussing their feelings and emotional issues. Oglesby (1991) identifies two general categories of stresses:

External—unfavorable court decisions, police media coverage, lack of community support, increase in violent crime, increased disrespect for law and order, and the increased potential to become the victim of an assault which may be fatal.

Internal—struggle for increased salary and benefits, highly competitive promotional practices, limited career advancement, affirmative action, sexual harassment, lack of administrative support, policies which adversely affect morale, rotating shifts, excessive paperwork, and poor quality, outdated, and limited equipment.

As a result, research has consistently shown that police officers tend to have elevated levels of alcoholism, divorce, suicide, and a variety of physical ailments such as heart disease, high cholesterol, and high blood pressure. For example, while the national divorce rate is 40 percent, the rate for police officers is between 60 and 75 percent. In response to these issues, a number of police departments have developed programs to provide support, counseling, and **stress management** to their officers. Generally, officers can be recommended for a support or employee assistance program, but the decision ultimately rests with the individual officer. These programs generally acknowledge that stress cannot be eliminated and work toward developing officers' ability to successfully handle it. A number of different types of programs have been developed:

- *Stress inoculation:* Focus is on creating a lifestyle that resists the effects of stress and techniques, including relaxation methods, exercise, eating healthy, getting enough sleep, and developing a network of family and friends for support.
- *Police family stress reduction units:* Training is provided to police families to develop an increased awareness and understanding of stressors in police officers' lives. The training also helps families develop stress management techniques.
- *Peer support:* Some departments have developed formal groups of fellow officers who provide support and advice to their colleagues, typically following a traumatic incident.
- *Critical incident stress debriefing teams:* This is a unit within the police department that provides emergency counseling and psychological services to officers suffering from posttraumatic stress syndrome following a critical incident.
- *Early warning mental health programs:* The original program was developed for sergeants in the LAPD to help them detect mental health problems among officers under their supervision. Training focuses on helping sergeants identify early warning signs and introducing them to crisis intervention techniques and procedures and resources for referral to other programs.
- *Police stress unit:* These units are formed by nonprofit organizations outside of the police department, either because the department could not afford to create its own unit or officers were unwilling to seek out help from department-based units (i.e., the stigma). Units are typically staffed with volunteers and licensed counselors who offer services in a range of areas including marital and family problems, financial issues, alcoholism and drug abuse and job-related issues (i.e., shootings, injuries, etc.). (Champion & Hooper, 2003, pp. 318–320)

Haberfeld (2002) acknowledges the importance of these types of programs but argues that they often are missing one critical piece: "the need to express one's frustrations, fears, dissatisfaction and an overall sense of injustice" (p. 129). The need for this type of "venting" is critical for all police officers, not just those who experience traumatic events. Haberfeld (2002) describes a new approach called *Feelings-Inputs-*

Tactics (FIT) that builds on existing department resources but adds this missing component. Participation in the program is mandatory for all officers thereby eliminating the stigma often faced by those who seek out help. Much like CompStat meetings, the FIT sessions occur on a regular basis and each officer takes turns discussing their feelings (i.e., venting their frustrations). Other officers offer suggestions and advice, and the meeting is facilitated by a professional. Haberfeld (2002) states that the program should be introduced at the academy, so officers become familiar with it and are more accepting once on the job. The overall goal of the FIT model is to reduce the stigma of participation in such programs, to create a formal mechanism for all officers to express their emotions, and eventually, to reach the point where officers are admired as much for their psychological self-defense as for their physical (Haberfeld, 2002).

Domestic Violence Training

Conventional wisdom about the appropriate police response to domestic violence has changed dramatically over the last few decades, from mediation and less formal responses (i.e., a private matter not requiring police intervention) in the 1960s and 1970s to an increasing move toward mandatory arrest (particularly for felony cases) in the 1980s and 1990s. Criticisms of mandatory arrest—that it disempowers the victim, it fails to deter future offenses (and may lead to an increase in violence for some), it has led police to rely on dual arrest (police arresting both parties), and continued problems with victim recanting—have caused many jurisdictions to move toward more comprehensive team approaches that coordinate law enforcement and prosecutorial objectives with efforts to meet victims' needs (see Chapter 6 for more detail).

As the police response to domestic violence has changed, so too has the need for police training in this area. Over the last twenty years, police departments have been forced to revise or enhance domestic violence training to incorporate changes in state law, to reflect changing definitions of domestic violence (beyond husband on wife violence), to reflect changing departmental policies, to identify signs or indicators of abuse, and to ensure that officers are knowledgeable about available services for victims and offenders. Moreover, many departments have incorporated a theoretical component to their academy training, providing officers with a basic understanding of the history and causes of domestic violence, the reasons why a victim may choose to stay in an abusive relationship, and the role the criminal justice system can play in ending the violence (through formal arrest and prosecution, assisting and providing services to the victim, and mandating the batterer to attend counseling).

Training in Handling the Mentally Ill

Teplin (1986, 1990) reported that approximately 7 to 10 percent of police–citizen encounters involved a mentally ill person. In a recent Bureau of Justice Statistics survey (1999), it was estimated that 238,000 mentally ill offenders were incarcerated in

U.S. prisons and jails in 1998, representing 16 percent of all state prison and local jail inmates and 7 percent of federal prisoners. Given that the police represent the "front-line" contact between criminal justice and mentally ill, it is safe to assume that the majority of the mentally ill in prison had an encounter with the police. Barring major shifts in policy regarding mental health issues and services, the mentally ill will continue to be channeled into the criminal justice system and, as a result, will continue to find themselves coming to the attention of the police.

Mentally ill individuals—or consumers (the term preferred by the Alliance for the Mentally Ill)—present a serious challenge for the police, particularly since the behavior leading to police involvement is typically either noncriminal or relatively minor. There are a number of issues that can be addressed in training to reduce the risk that encounters with consumers are handled inappropriately. First, unfortunately, police officers—as well as society in general—hold many misconceptions about the mentally ill, particularly that they are usually violent and uncontrollable (Grant & Terry, 2005). These misconceptions have sometimes led to violent and tragic encounters between police and mentally disturbed individuals. Proper training can eliminate these misconceptions. Second, patrol officers should be trained to recognize the indicators that a person is mentally ill and in crisis. Proper police training—both in the academy and in-service—can educate police about these indicators. The likelihood of a violent outcome is greatly increased if the officer does not recognize that the individual is in crisis.

Third, once the officer recognizes the nature of the encounter, he or she must handle the situation differently than an encounter with a non-mentally ill suspect. The consumer may not follow verbal commands and may be acting in an irrational manner. The consumer may curse or spit at the officer. The properly trained police officer will recognize that the consumer is in crisis and will not take these behaviors as an affront to his or her authority (i.e., contempt of cop). Instead, well-trained officers will understand the nature of the encounter, show tolerance and patience, and engage in nonthreatening actions to try to alleviate the crisis (family and friends can be a valuable resource in reducing the crisis). Last, police should be trained in the options that are available to end the encounter with the consumer (i.e., informal disposition, referral, arrest, hospitalization), when each disposition is appropriate, and what resources are available in the community. In handling situations involving consumers in crisis, knowledge and training are the police officer's best weapons, and in many cases (but not all) will be the only weapons needed to resolve the encounter.

A number of jurisdictions have developed new approaches to handle the mentally ill finding their way into the justice system. The Memphis, Tennessee, Police Department, in partnership with the University of Tennessee Medical Center, has created a **Crisis Intervention Team (CIT)** comprised of officers who have gone through 40 hours of intensive training on appropriate responses to the mentally ill (Vickers, 2000; see Chapter 6 for a more detailed discussion). Dispatchers in Memphis route calls that likely involve the mentally ill to the nearest CIT-trained officer. Nontrained patrol officers can also request a CIT officer if needed. The Memphis program has been adopted in a number of other jurisdictions around the country.

The goals of CIT are to provide immediate response to and management of situations where the mentally ill are in a state of crisis; prevent, reduce or eliminate injury to both the consumer and the responding police officer; find appropriate care for the consumer; and establish a treatment program that reduces recidivism (Vickers, 2000, p. 2).

Training in Communication and Writing

Two of the most important skills for a police officer to develop are his or her communication and writing skills. A patrol officer spends a good portion of the day talking to people: supervisors, colleagues, business owners and residents, community and church leaders, victims, witnesses, suspects, and other officials in the criminal justice system. Police must also complete reports that will withstand the scrutiny of supervisors, lawyers, and judges. Often, the prosecution of a suspect will depend tremendously on the reports completed by the officer months before. Communication skills were important in the traditional, reactive model of policing, but they are absolutely critical in community-oriented policing.

> The community police officer is required to demonstrate more than physical abilities. He or she must also be proficient in effective communication skills (oral and written) and interpersonal skills (multicultural communication, collaboration and creativity, conflict resolution, and crisis intervention). Within the context of community policing, these skills are essential (Champion & Hooper, 2003, p. 246).

Importantly, effective oral and written communication skills can be taught through training and practice. Realistic, scenario-based training with debriefings afterwards is often the best vehicle for enhancing police officers' writing and verbal skills. Many departments have incorporated "verbal judo" into their training, which teaches officers how to use language—both oral and body—to de-escalate potentially violent encounters. In their scenario-based training text, Reynolds and Mariani (2002) argue that effective communication skills can benefit police by helping to create a professional image, by serving as the first line of defense in potentially violent encounters, and by helping officers advance their career (i.e., effective communication skills are required for promotion to supervisory and management level ranks). Reynolds and Mariani (2002) also offer a number of guidelines for effective communication, such as:

- Avoiding language that triggers fear, anxiety, or inferiority.
- Appreciating and using body language effectively.
- Appreciating the power of courteousness.
- Learning to use words as a problem-solving tool and to inform others of the procedures you are following.
- Using words to foster cooperation.
- Monitoring your own thoughts and putting yourself in the other person's place.

Technology and Training

As technological innovations have been incorporated into everyday police work, departments have been forced to enhance training to ensure that officers have the skills and knowledge to use those innovations effectively. Basic computer skills are essential for police officers, as most patrol cars are equipped with either laptop computers or mobile digital terminals (MDTs). The adoption of CompStat and geomapping of crime patterns means that police must have staff with the skills to properly carry out that crime analysis. Many police departments have adopted a variety of less-than-lethal weapons to supplement the traditional police tools, such as the Taser, extendable baton, mace, and bean-bag gun. Police must be trained in the proper use of these weapons before carrying them on the street. Inadequate training (or no training) puts departments at risk of civil litigation should an officer misuse a weapon. Other examples of technological innovations that have impacted policing include aerial surveillance (i.e., helicopters and planes), the use of infra-red equipment, crime scene investigation (i.e., DNA), and computer-based training simulation (i.e., FATS). Quite simply, as technology changes policing, departments must keep pace by properly training officers to take advantage of those tools.

Counterterrorism Training

Traditional police training has not given much attention to terrorism and counterterrorist techniques, and it was not until after the attacks on September 11, 2001 that local police departments throughout the United States began to see terrorism prevention and response as part of their mandate. In fact, prior to 2001 the literature on policing terrorism in the United States in scant. However, in 1996 Congress enacted the Anti-terrorism and Effective Death Penalty Act to improve law enforcement agencies' ability to fight terrorism (National Institute of Justice, 1999). In response to the Act, NIJ sponsored research in 1997 to assess technology needs of state and local law enforcement agencies to effectively accomplish the goals laid out by Congress. Interviews with nearly 200 individuals representing 138 agencies showed that most agencies cited intelligence, communications, and explosives-related technology as areas for needed enhancement, though improved training for officers was frequently mentioned.

In the wake of the September 11, 2001 attacks, policing terrorism moved to the forefront for local, state, and federal law enforcement agencies across the United States. Despite major changes in federal law enforcement (i.e., creation of the Department of Homeland Security), patrol officers in local police agencies still represent the first line of defense in preventing, detecting, and responding to terrorism.

The New York Police Department (NYPD) is excellent example of how counterterrorism has been incorporated into police training. New York City is home to a host of buildings, bridges, and infrastructure that remain high-level targets for terrorist events (i.e., Empire State Building, Brooklyn Bridge, United Nations, financial district, Times Square, etc.). Commissioner Kelly notes, "the integration of counter terrorism into our mission ranks as one of the most important changes in our history" (NYPD, 2002: 1). The July 2002 recruit class (the first post-9/11 class) and subsequent classes received extensive training in counterterrorism and intelligence as part of their academy curriculum, with daily exercises on terrorism and disaster response. In-service training was also provided to thousands of other officers in the department. To illustrate the point, the 2003 recruit class graduated from the Police Academy shortly after Christmas, and the first assignment for all 1,500 new officers was patrol in Times Square on New Year's Eve.

SUMMARY

This chapter emphasizes the central role of training in fielding an effective and professional police force. The discussion of police training occurs within the context of the larger debate over whether policing should be considered a craft or a profession, and the implications of that debate for education and training of officers. The chapter presents a detailed discussion of two types of training, academy training of recruits and field training programs for new officers, and provides brief discussion of a third type, in-service training. Academy and FTO programs are described in terms of their historical development, theoretical foundations, functions, and limitations. In particular, the limitations of the traditional police academy training model provide a nice segue into the discussion of current issues and controversies in police training. A wide range of issues are presented including alternative teaching styles (adult learning or andragogy), community and problem-oriented policing, diversity or multicultural training, stress management, dealing with domestic violence and the mentally ill, the importance of oral and written communication, technology, and the incorporation of counterterrorism into the police mandate. In sum, policing continues to change in a number of ways, from changes in police philosophy, techniques and responsibilities to new tools brought about by technological innovation. Each change has implications for training, and a result, the state of affairs in police training and education is also constantly changing.

KEY TERMS

Andragogy
Behaviorally anchored rating scale (BARS)
Commission on Accreditation in Law
 Enforcement (CALEA)
Community policing
Counterterrorism
Craft vs. profession
Crisis intervention team (CIT)
Daily observation report (DOR)
Diversity training

Field training officer (FTO) programs
In-service training
Peace Officer Standards and Training
 (POST)
Pedagogy
Problem-oriented policing (POP)
Regional community policing institute (RPI)
State-mandated training
Stress management
Us versus them mentality

DISCUSSION QUESTIONS

1. Describe the debate over whether policing is a craft or profession. Which argument do you find more persuasive?

2. What are some of the limitations of the traditional police academy training model?

3. What is andragogy? How is it different from pedagogy?

4. Describe a typical FTO program in terms of its form, function, and organization.

5. What is diversity training? Why is it important?

6. How has technology influenced police training?

7. Are communication and writing skills important for police? Why or why not?

REFERENCES

Bain, R. (1939). The policeman on the beat. *Science Monthly, 48,* 5.

Bayley, D.H. (1976). *Forces of order: Police behavior in Japan and the United States.* Berkeley: University of California Press.

Bayley, D.H., & Bittner, E. (1984). Learning the skills of policing. *Law and Contemporary Problems, 47,* 35–59.

Bennett, W.B., & Hess, K.M. (1996). *Management and supervision in law enforcement* (2nd ed.). St. Paul, MN: West Publishing.

Birzer, M.L. (2003). The theory of andragogy applied to police training. *Policing: An International Journal of Police Strategies and Management, 26*(1), 29–42.

Birzer, M.L., & Tannehill, R. (2001). A more effective training approach for contemporary policing. *Police Quarterly, 4*(2), 233–252.

Brookfield, S. (1986). *Understanding and facilitating adult learning.* San Francisco: Jossey-Bass.

Bumgarner, J. (2002). An assessment of the perceptions of policing as a profession among two-year and four-year criminal justice and law enforcement students. *Journal of Criminal Justice Education, 13*(2), 313–334.

Bureau of Justice Statistics. (1999). *Prison and jail inmates at mid-year 1998.* Washington, DC: Government Printing Office.

Caffarella, R.S. (1993). Self-directed learning. In S. Merriam (Ed.), *An update on adult learning theory, new directions for adult and continuing education.* San Francisco: Jossey-Bass.

Calhoun, C.C., & Finch, A.V. (1982). *Vocational education: Concepts and operations.* Belmont, CA: Wadsworth.

Capps, L.E. (1998, July). CPR: Career-saving advice for police officers. *FBI Law Enforcement Bulletin,* 14–18.

Champion, D.H., & Hooper, M.K. (2003). *Introduction to American policing.* New York: McGraw-Hill.

Chappell, A.T., Lanza-Kaduce, L., & Johnston, D.H. (2005). Law enforcement training: Changes and challenges. In R.G. Dunham & G.P. Alpert (Eds.), *Critical issues in policing* (5th ed). Prospect Heights, Ill: Waveland Press.

Commission on Accreditation for Law Enforcement (CALEA). (1994). Standards. Fairfax, VA: Commission on Accreditation for Law Enforcement.

Crank, J.P. (1990). Police: Professionals or craftsmen? An empirical assessment of professionalism and craftsmanship among eight municipal police agencies. *Journal of Criminal Justice, 18,* 333–349.

Crank, J.P., Payn, B., & Jackson, S. (1993). The relationship between police belief systems and attitudes toward police practices. *Criminal Justice and Behavior, 20,* 199–221.

Dantzker, M.L. (2000a). Police academies and their curriculum: Beginning the exploration. *Police Forum, 10*(2), 8–11.

Dantzker, M.L. (2000b). Comparing police academy curricula: Toward a national curriculum. *Police Forum, 10*(3), 4–7.

Doerner, W.G., Horton, C., & Smith, J.L. (2003). The field training officer program: A case study approach. In M.J. Palmiotto (Ed.), *Police and training issues.* Upper Saddle River, NJ: Prentice-Hall.

Edwards, T.D. (1993). State police basic training programs: An assessment of course content and instructional methodology. *American Journal of Police, 12,* 23–45.

Fosdick, R. (1920). *American police system.* New York: The Century Company.

Frost, T.M., & Seng, M.J. (1984). Police entry level curriculum: A third year perspective. *Journal of Police Science and Administration, 12,* 251–259.

Gould, L.A. (1997). Can an old dog be taught new tricks? Teaching cultural diversity to police officers. *Policing, 20,* 339–356.

Grant, H.B., & Terry, K.J. (2005). *Law enforcement in the 21st century.* Boston: Allyn and Bacon.

Haberfeld, M.R. (2002). *Critical issues in training.* Upper Saddle River, NJ: Prentice-Hall.

Haley, K. (2003). Police academy management: Procedures, problems, and issues. In M.J. Palmiotto (Ed.), *Police and training issues.* Upper Saddle River, NJ: Prentice-Hall.

Kappeler, V.E., Sluder, R.D., & Alpert, G.P. (1998). *Forces of deviance: Understanding the dark side of policing.* Prospect Heights, IL: Waveland Press.

Kelling, G., & Moore, M. (1988). From political to reform to community: The evolving strategy of police. In J. Greene & S. Mastrofski (Eds.), *Community policing: Rhetoric or reality.* New York: Praeger.

McCampbell, M.S. (1986). *Field training for police officers: State of the art.* Research in Brief. Washington, DC: National Institute of Justice.

Merriam, S.B., & R.S. Caffarella (1999). *Learning in adulthood* (2nd ed.). San Francisco: Jossey-Bass.

Molden, J.B. (1987). Training field training officers. *Law and Order, 35*(1), 22.

More, H.W., & Wegener, W.F. (1996). *Effective police supervision* (2nd ed.). Cincinnati, OH: Anderson Publishing.

National Advisory Commission on Civil Disorders. (1968). *Report of the National Advisory Commission on Civil Disorders.* New York: Bantam Books.

National Institute of Justice. (1999). *Inventory of state and local law enforcement technology needs to combat terrorism.* Research in Brief. Washington, DC: Office of Justice Programs, National Institute of Justice.

New York City Police Department (NYPD). (2002). *Training bureau: 2002 annual report.* New York: Author.

Oglesby, E.W. (1991). Review of the third edition, *Introduction to Law Enforcement and Criminal Justice,* by Wrobleski, W.M. & Hess, K.M.

Ortmeier, P.J. (1997). Leadership for community-policing: A study to identify essential officer competencies. *The Police Chief, LXIV* (10), 88–96.

Palmiotto, M.J. (2003). An overview of police training through the decades: Current issues and problems. In M.J. Palmiotto (Ed.), *Police and training issues.* Upper Saddle River, NJ: Prentice-Hall.

President's Commission on Law Enforcement and Administration of Justice. (1967). *Task force report: The police.* Washington DC: US Government Printing Office.

Radelet, L.A., & D.L. Carter (1994). *The police and the community.* New York: Macmillan.

Reith, C. (1975). *The blind eye of history: A study of the origins of the present police era.* Montclair, NJ: Patterson Smith.

Reynolds, J., & Mariani, M. (2002). *Police talk: A scenario-based communications workbook for police recruits and officers.* Upper Saddle River, NJ: Prentice-Hall.

Skolnick, J.H. & Fyfe, J.J. (1993). *Above the law: Police and the excessive use of force.* New York: Free Press.

Shusta, R.M., Levine, D.R., Harris, P.R., & Wang, H.Z. (1995). *Multicultural law enforcement: Strategies for peacekeeping in a diverse society.* Upper Saddle River, NJ: Prentice Hall.

Stinchcombe, J.B. (1980). Beyond bureaucracy: A reconsideration of the professional police. *Police Studies, 3,* 49–60.

Stinchcombe, J.B., & W.C. Terry, III (1995). A study of state certification exam results for Florida police and correctional recruits in relation to grade-level equivalency. *Criminal Justice Policy Review, 7,* 223–243.

Teplin, L. (1986). *Keeping the peace: Parameters of police discretion in relation to the mentally disordered.* Washington, DC: Government Printing Office.

Teplin, L. (1990). The prevalence of severe mental disorder among male urban jail detainees: Comparison with the epidemiological catchment area program. *American Journal of Public Health, 80* (6), 663–669.

Thibault, A.T., Lynch, L.M., & McBride, R.B. (2001). *Proactive police management,* 5th ed. Upper Saddle River, NJ: Prentice Hall.

Vickers, B. (2000). *Memphis, Tennessee, Police Department's Crisis Intervention Team.* Practitioner Perspectives. Washington, DC: Bureau of Justice Assistance.

Walker, S. & C.M. Katz (2002). *The police in America: An introduction.* New York: McGraw-Hill.

Wilson, J.Q. (1968). *Varieties of police behavior.* Cambridge, MA: Harvard University Press.

Yoder, N.M. (1942). *The selection and training of public safety personnel in American municipalities.* Columbus, OH: Ohio State University, unpublished Ph.D. dissertation.

■ ■ ■ ■ ■

SCHOLAR'S PERSPECTIVE
Police Training in America

Maria (Maki) Haberfeld, Ph.D.*
Professor, John Jay College of Criminal Justice

Despite the growing popularity of the Community Oriented Policing movements in the last two decades, it is impossible to understand the nature of police training in the twenty-first century without looking at the history of policing throughout the ages. The way police departments were and, to a large extent are still, trained is predicated upon a certain rather controversial theme that can be easily verified by examining police training modules and their content throughout the entire country. This theme is a premise that police forces, throughout the history, served and protected the ruler, the king, the politician, and never the public. The safety and security of the public was always secondary to the safety and security of the ruler, king, politician, etc. One cannot lead a prosperous life—as a ruler, leader, king, or politician—if the status quo is disrupted in one way or another. A happy public is a quiet public. The Roman emperors knew how to keep the public compliant: give them bread and games, this will make them happy and—just in case it will not—establish a strong police force.

The acceptance of this premise will allow for a better understanding of how and why police forces were and are trained and will foster the transition to the concepts that are being introduced in police academies around the country in the last ten or fifteen years in a slow but nevertheless consistent attempt to enable the officer to take upon a new role—one of serving and protecting the public.

BASIC ACADEMY TRAINING

The term *police academy* usually refers to three main types of police academies in the United States: agency (also referred to as in-house), regional, and college-sponsored. Agency schools are generally found in large municipal areas or are established for the state police or highway patrol. Regional academies handle the training

---

*Professor, John Jay College of Criminal Justice. BA—Hebrew University of Jerusalem—MA, Institute of Criminology, Hebrew University of Jerusalem, MPhil—John Jay College of Criminal Justice, Ph.D.—City University of New York Graduate Center.

functions for both large and small departments located in a designated geographical area. The college-sponsored training academies operate on the premises of postsecondary institutions, particularly community colleges. These college-sponsored academies allow a person to take police training and earn college credit (Thibault, Lynch, & McBride, 1998).

It was in California in 1959 that a training council first established the Police Officers Standards and training guidelines. Although this was state and not federal initiative, within approximately four years, many states throughout the country had developed their own standards for training (Christian & Edwards, 1985).

In 1967, the President's Commission on Law Enforcement and Administration of Justice recommended that Peace Officer Standards and Training (POST) commission be established in every state. These POST commissions or boards were empowered to set mandatory minimum requirements and appropriately funded so that they might provide financial aid to governmental units for the implementation of established standards. The two important charges of the POST commissions were:

- Establishing mandatory minimum training standards (at both the recruit and in-service levels), with the authority to determine and approve curricula, identify required preparation for instructors, and approve facilities acceptable for police training.
- Certifying police officers who have acquired various levels of education, training, and experience necessary to adequately perform the duties of the police service. (Bennett & Hess, 1996)

On average, departments require 640 training hours of their new officer recruits, including 425 classroom training hours and 215 field training hours. The length of the training varies from academy to academy with police departments getting as little as 8 weeks of training to as much as 32 weeks. Contentwise, each academy is encouraged to add on to the basic minimum hours required by the state's POST, and it is up to each and every agency to decide what and how much should and will be added.

Over the last few decades, the percentage of time devoted to military drill and the overall paramilitary orientation went down but was replaced by a rise in the time devoted to general physical fitness, while the time devoted to firearms training remained about the same. Today, newer topics have been added and covered in police training and will be discussed further on. Nationally, most training programs can be divided according to the following areas:

1. Administrative procedures: Includes quizzes, graduation, and instruction on note taking.
2. Administration of justice: Includes history of law enforcement, police organization, probation, probation, parole, and social services.
3. Basic law: Includes constitutional law, offenses, criminal procedure, vehicle and traffic law, juvenile law and procedures, and civil liability.

4. Police procedures: Includes patrol observation, crimes in progress, field notes, intoxication, mental illness, disorderly conduct, domestic violence, police communication, alcoholic beverage control, civil disorder, crowd and riot control, normal duties related to traffic enforcement including accidents and emergency vehicle operations, criminal investigations, including interviews and interrogations, control of evidence, and various kinds of cases, such as burglary, robbery, injury, sex crime, drugs, organized crime, arson, and gambling.
5. Police proficiency: Includes normal firearm training, arrest techniques, emergency aid, courtroom testimony and demeanor, and bomb threats and bombs.
6. Community relations: Includes psychology for police, minority groups, news media relationships, telephone courtesy, identification of community resources, victim/witness services, crime prevention, officer stress awareness, law enforcement family, and police ethics. (Thibault et al., 1998)
7. In the aftermath of 9/11 most of the police academies added some type of counter-terrorism and crisis management training, which vary in terms of length and content almost by each and every agency in the country.

The critical issues with regard to the basic academy training can be summarized in two words: length and content.

It is extremely difficult to revise any type of training, both in length and in content, without a close cooperation from the given state's POST commission and major support from the local politicians. Nevertheless, each and every academy director can easily "move around" certain topics and change the allocation of hours. Of course, the mandatory minimum required by the local POST cannot be disregarded or compromised; however, most of the academies do add additional hours of training to the minimum required and make an honest attempt to include more community-oriented topics such as topics of instruction related to communication skills, diversity awareness, and social sciences. Still, in order to truly change the officer's orientation and skew it more effectively toward community-oriented theme requires more than is presently done at the basic level. Some of these deficiencies are addressed during the Field Training Officer Program and other in-service developmental training.

Field Training Officer Programs

Begun in 1972, the San Jose Model FTO program is the most widely recognized program of its kind. It is emulated by law enforcement agencies throughout the country that are seeking to achieve several key organizational objectives, primarily the improvement of recruit officer training.

The San Jose program was developed in response to an incident that occurred in the early spring of 1970. A recruit police officer was involved in a serious traffic accident while negligently operating a police vehicle on duty. A passenger in the other vehicle was killed and the officer was seriously injured. The officer was dismissed by the city. A review of his personnel record revealed serious inadequacies in the department's recruit training and evaluation procedures. The incident led San

Jose Police Department managers to conclude that the process by which rookie officers acquired practical on-the-job knowledge and skills needed to be formalized. What emerged from San Jose's experience was the concept of the FTO program.

The original San Jose FTO model is a mentoring-type model, designed to provide a practical, information bridge from the training academy to the job. San Jose's model is fourteen weeks long: three four-week periods of training, followed by a two-week evaluation period. Upon graduation from the training academy, a recruit is immediately assigned to the FTO program. Training occurs on each of the three work-day shifts and is concentrated in two districts. The FTO team working with the recruit-trainee plans days off and study time well in advance. The recruit-trainee is assigned to a different FTO for each training period. This enables the trainee to be exposed to various styles of police work and to ensure that he or she will not be penalized because of personality clash with a single FTO (Johnson, 1995). Each FTO provides specific training consistent with a curriculum developed for the program; each FTO evaluates the trainee's abilities and developing skills and knowledge.

FTO programs have been implemented by hundreds of law enforcement agencies across the United States. The original San Jose program has been modified by many agencies to suit their own needs and objectives; many other agencies have developed their own unique programs.

The most important incentive for implementation of an FTO program is accreditation. The Commission on Accreditation for Law Enforcement Agencies, Inc. (CALEA) requires all police agencies seeking accreditation to have a formal FTO program. But there are other important reasons for agencies to establish FTO programs, some of which have to do with the awareness of the fact that the basic academy training did not provide the officers with all the necessary tools and skills needed on the streets, especially in the case of regional training, and the additional screening mechanism that provides the agency with the last opportunity to make sure that the newly hired officer is actually suited to wear the agency's uniform and properly subscribe to its mission statement.

SPECIALIST AND DEVELOPMENTAL TRAINING

On of the more prominent events that highlighted the need for specialized training can be traced to the early 1960s. In August 1966, an incident occurred in Austin, Texas, that, contrary to other incidents, pushed law enforcement toward assessment of its capabilities in handling high-risk situations. After killing his wife and mother, Charles Whitman went to the rooftop of the University of Texas and began a shooting spree, killing fifteen people and wounding thirty others. This event contributed to the establishment of special police teams to handle high-risk situations.

As for today, when one analyzes the themes of police specialized training, it appears that the new trends, such as the increase in violent crimes, high-technology crimes, the increased number of high-risk repeat offenders (an outcome of prison overcrowding), the overall sophistication of criminal element, diversity-related issues, and a host of additional problems that create the need for a specialized and developmental training approach, generate, at best, what could be defined as a "post-hoc training" approach.

Thibault et al. (1998) identified some of the newer topics that have been covered recently in police training. They are:

1. Stress training
2. Dealing with terrorist activity
3. Domestic crisis intervention
4. AIDS awareness
5. Domestic violence training
6. Stalking
7. Tactical operations
8. Diversity
9. Bias crimes
10. American with Disabilities Act
11. Computer/video simulation
12. Interactive teleconferencing/cable TV

Though the range of the newer topics is pretty impressive, the concept of post-hoc training is probably more valid than ever before, with agencies trying to train their officers in a host of post-disaster-related concepts, when the training in its content and length is still not adequate and not always customized for the local realities, especially with regard to terrorist activities and critical incident management training.

SUPERVISORY AND MANAGEMENT TRAINING

Advanced police training is not a luxury but a must in the United States today. The officers who are trained in advanced police courses are a special group of people, chosen to handle administrative and tactical/operational situations beyond the scope of basic police activity, with particular, relatively new, orientation toward the needs and desires of the communities they serve. Uniqueness, complexity, unpredictability, and the possible consequences of each and every situation necessitate advanced training.

Numerous organizations—law enforcement, academics, and other private entities—offer advanced training for police supervisors. A number of those organizations, such as the FBI National Academy, Federal Law Enforcement Training Center (FLETC), a number of academic institutions with well-developed criminal justice majors, or the International Association of Chiefs of Police, offer a valuable contribution to advanced training, by combining practical law enforcement approach with the academic "touch." However, the access to these training opportunities is relatively limited, for a number of reasons such as cost, human resources (personnel who cannot be spared to attend the National Academy, which requires a long absence from the force), political interference, ignorance about existing opportunities, and lack of mandatory requirements. Moreover, the quality both in length and in content of the advanced training modules varies dramatically, based on the agency and/or the organization that offers the training. For example, executive leadership training, which has gained popularity in recent years, can vary in length from a few day's modules through the entire semester or even advanced degree offerings.

THE FUTURE

As we move on the continuum of democratic policing, from serving the rulers and the politicians to addressing the needs and wants of the local communities, the more global events interfere with the natural progression of police training. As more and more agencies make attempts at introducing the more progressive and democratic values into police training, the globalization and internationalization of crime, with particular emphasis on the proliferation of terrorist activities and various crisis-management-related themes, the move toward more human rights—community-oriented training—is hampered and threatened by the more militaristic approach toward the "war against terrorism" that, of course, will be fought by our law enforcement agencies that are not yet equipped (training wise) with all the necessary tools.

REFERENCES

Bennett, W.W., & Hess, K.M. (1996). *Criminal investigation.* St. Paul, MN: West.
Christian, K.E., & Edwards, S.M. (1985). Law enforcement standards and training councils: A human resource for planning force in the future. *Journal of Police Science and Administration, 13,* 1–9.
Haberfeld, M.R. (2002). *Critical issues in police training.* Upper Saddle River, NJ: Prentice Hall.
Johnson, G. (1995). San Jose: A commitment to excellence. *The Trainer, 3* (1), 31–38.
Thibault, E.A., Lynch, L.M., & McBride, R.B. (1998). *Proactive police management* (2nd ed.). Englewood Cliffs, NJ: Prentice Hall.

■ ■ ■ ■ ■

CHAPTER 3

DEVELOPMENT OF THE PROFESSIONAL POLICING MODEL

This chapter takes a step back in time and retraces the development and implementation of professional policing in the United States, from approximately the mid nineteenth century through the 1970s. Although there is a long history of more informal law enforcement elsewhere in the world and in the United States during colonial times, the emphasis of this chapter is on the professional police model that has dominated law enforcement for most of the twentieth century. Kelling and Moore (1991) state that U.S. policing has gone through three separate and distinct eras: the political era, the reform era, and the community era. Chapter 3 describes in some detail the first two of those eras and sets the stage for the third, which is discussed in the next chapter.

This chapter begins with a discussion of events in London during the late 1830s, specifically the creation of the London Metropolitan Police Department and the early principles laid out by Sir Robert Peel. Peel's London police model laid the foundation for the U.S. police agencies that developed over the next two decades. The U.S. translation of the London model differed in important ways, however, as characterized by the vastly different experiences among police in the two countries during the last half of the nineteenth century. The poor state of affairs in U.S. policing during the political era set an important context for the reform era and the birth of the professional model. The foundation and elements of the professional model are described and traced through the 1960s, when serious questions began to emerge regarding its impact on police community relations and its ability to control crime. The chapter ends with a discussion of several watershed events that spurred a rethinking of how police should go about conducting their business and led to the emergence of new philosophies of policing such as community and problem-oriented policing.

THE ORIGINS OF PROFESSIONAL POLICING: SIR ROBERT PEEL AND THE LONDON METROPOLITAN POLICE

The Impetus for Change in London

A number of events and changes occurred in London during the first part of the nineteenth century that led to the creation of the first professional police department. First, London experienced tremendous population growth, in large part due to a boom in industry. From 1750 to 1820, the population doubled, and the Industrial Revolution led to a large increase in the number of factories, tenements, and businesses (Uchida, 2005). Second, the industrialization and urbanization of London led to a host of problems, including substantial increases in poverty, public health problems, ethnic conflict (particularly over jobs), and crime. The informal constable-watch system that provided law enforcement in London was simply unable to handle all of these new problems.

Third, a number of riots occurred during the time that highlighted the need for more social control: food riots, the Gordon riots (1780) between Irish immigrants and English citizens, and the Peterloo Massacre (1819), where armed soldiers clashed with unemployed protestors (resulting in eleven dead and hundreds injured). The Peterloo Massacre, in particular, underscored the dangers of using the military to handle civil disorders (Champion & Hooper, 2003). Last, Henry Fielding, an author and magistrate in London, organized a volunteer force of plainclothes detectives—called the **Bow Street Runners**—who gained widespread support for their crime control efforts, especially when they foiled a plot to assassinate several government officials (Champion & Hooper, 2003). The success and popularity of the Bow Street Runners demonstrated to the government and citizens how a nonmilitary force could effectively combat crime.

Sir Robert Peel and the Metropolitan Police Act of 1829

In response to dramatic increases in crime and related problems, **Sir Robert Peel,** England's Home Secretary, proposed before Parliament the "**Metropolitan Police Act of 1829,**" which called for the creation of a full-time, professional police force called the London Metropolitan Police. The force was to be composed of civilians who would be appointed and paid by the community. Peel faced substantial resistance to his plan both in Parliament and among the citizens. As a result, he crafted his approach very carefully to gain the necessary support. To ensure that the police force would not serve as an occupying military force, his police officers—called "Bobbies" after Peel—were unarmed except for a small concealed truncheon, wore distinctive uniforms including the trademark top hats, and were responsible for crime prevention (Klockars, 1983). Nevertheless, Peel did adopt a quasi-military organizational structure and appointed two former military officers as police commissioners (the success of the British military was indisputable at the time).

More generally, Peel organized his department along a number of basic principles that served as the basis for modern policing as it is known today. Peel's principles were:

- Prevention of crime is the basic mission of the police.
- The police must be stable, efficient, and organized along military lines.
- The police must be under governmental control.
- The distribution of crime news is absolutely essential.
- The deployment of police strength both by time and area is essential.

- No quality is more indispensable to a policeman than a perfect command of temper; a quiet, determined manner has more effect than violent action.
- Good appearance demands respect.
- The securing and training of proper persons is at the root of efficiency.
- Police must have the full respect of the citizenry.
- A citizen's respect for the law develops his respect for the police.
- Cooperation of the public decreases as the use of force increases.
- Police must render impartial enforcement of the law.
- Physical force is used only as the last resort.
- The police are the public and public are the police.
- Police represent the law.
- Police headquarters should be centrally located and easily accessible to the people.
- Policemen should be hired on a probationary business.
- The absence of crime and disorder is the test of police efficiency. (Champion & Hooper, 2003, pp. 61–62)

Clearly, a number of the basic principles laid out by Peel have tremendously influenced the development of professional policing in the United States. Although elements of the professional model—discussed in the upcoming pages—strayed from Peel's initial principles, the development and widespread adoption of community policing represents a return to those concepts. More than 170 years ago, Peel stressed the importance of crime prevention as a central goal of the police, as well as the critical importance of positive police-community relations. Four of Peel's principles deal exclusively with the public, their relationship with police, and their role in combating crime. Peel also describes the importance of avoiding excessive use of force and the impact that such force would have on the police community relationship. Peel highlights the importance of keeping the public informed, of rigid selection standards and training, and also hints at targeted patrol (i.e., hot spots). Finally, while the traditional police model that has developed over the better part of the twentieth century focuses on measuring police effectiveness through numbers (number of crimes, number of arrests, etc.), Peel argued that effectiveness is evidenced by the *absence* of crime.

The Need for and Development of Professional Policing in the United States

Policing in Colonial America.   Much like Great Britain, the American colonies employed a variety of more informal methods of policing during the seventeenth, eighteenth, and early nineteenth centuries. Many of the larger cities had organized watch systems where members of the community volunteered to patrol neighborhoods under the guidance of constables and sheriffs. Participation in the watch patrol was viewed as an obligation to the community, although many avoided participation by paying someone else to take their place. Problems with the volunteer system led several cities to employ full-time, paid watchmen (Grant & Terry, 2005). Two other common versions of law enforcement were vigilante committees and slave patrols. Vigilante committees were common in rural parts of the country and involved volunteers taking on all aspects of the criminal justice system, from arrest and prosecution to punishment. **Slave patrols** were established in the South during the mid-1700s to punish slaves who committed crimes or simply disobeyed their masters.

> Often mounted on horseback and carrying whips, the slave patrols enforced laws that prohibited literacy and commerce among slaves. The slave patrols also made sure that slaves were not in possession of weapons or ammunition and had the power to search "Negro houses" to ensure that such laws were not being violated. Even though slaves were not considered full citizens, they were capable of being held criminally responsible for their "crimes," particularly actions such as being away from their masters without carrying passes. (Grant & Terry, 2005, p. 46)

In many places in the South, the slave patrols became quite formalized and even took on an organized structure with a chain of command. Despite their initial narrow and racist focus, many consider these slave patrols to be the precursor of the modern police department (Grant & Terry, 2005). Although slave patrols disappeared following the Civil War, the Jim Crow laws and "black codes" that emerged in states throughout the South continued to give policing racist overtones throughout the nineteenth and early twentieth centuries.

The Development of U.S. Professional Policing.   As large cities in the United States began to feel the effects of urbanization and industrialization, they experienced the same problems that had forced London to create Peel's Metropolitan Police Force. Given their recent history with military occupation (i.e., the American Revolution), many U.S. cities were very reluctant to consider a full-time, professional police force, despite numerous riots and increases in crime throughout the 1830s. In 1844, after visiting London and observing the London police, city officials in New York created the first formal police department in the United States. Other large cities, such as Boston, Chicago, and Philadelphia, quickly followed suit.

U.S. cities did not adopt the Peel model of policing wholesale; rather, they chose selectively from their London counterparts. Miller's (1977) comparison of the London and New York Police Departments illustrates the important differences and provides the necessary background to understand the problems that emerged in U.S. policing. First, while the British Bobbies were representatives of the Crown, U.S. police officers were tied to local and municipal governments. As a result, London police officers could rely on institutional authority while New York police had to rely much more on their own individual authority. The decision to "localize" U.S. police departments stemmed from concerns over creating a federal police force. Second, the London Police Force was highly centralized with most of the decision-making power resting in headquarters. The New York Police Department (and other U.S. departments) was highly *decentralized,* with each local precinct essentially operating as an independent police department.

Third, because U.S. policing was tied to local governments, police officers were tremendously influenced by local politics. In fact, in most jurisdictions, police officers were simply "hired guns" who served the interests of local ward leaders and councilmen. The London police were able to avoid getting involved in local politics because of their link to the national government. Fourth, Peel made a conscious decision to not give his police officers firearms. While New York and many other cities tried to follow suit, the prevalence of guns and gun crime in the United States forced cities to arm their officers quickly. Quite simply, an armed criminal element posed too great a danger to an unarmed police force. Last, while the London force sought to control officer discretion and decision-making power, the U.S. police exercised tremendous discretion in carrying out their duties.

U.S. POLICING DURING THE NINETEENTH CENTURY

The first era of U.S. policing—called the **political era** by Kelling and Moore (1991)—was far from memorable. Walker and Katz (2002) sum up the state of affairs concisely and accurately:

> In the United States, however, politics influenced every aspect of American policing in the nineteenth century. Inefficiency, corruption, and lack of professionalism were the chief results. (p. 29)

The problems experienced during this first period of **professional policing** can be summarized best by considering who became police officers and how they got the job, what their duties were and how they were carried out, and prevalence of brutality and corruption as central features in American policing during this time.

Who Became Police Officers and How Did They Get the Job?

As mentioned briefly in Chapters 1 and 2, no preservice or selection standards were employed by police departments during this time, nor was there any formal police training. There were no minimum standards for education, health, or moral code. "Officers were selected entirely on the basis of their political connections" (Walker & Katz, 2002, p. 29). Criminal convictions, poor eyesight, lack of education, and serious physical ailments did not hinder an appointment as a patrol officer if one was connected to the current local politicians in power. In many places, jobs within the police department could be purchased as well: In New York, an appointment to the NYPD could be received with a $300 payment to Tammany Hall. Because of the inherent political ties, there was also tremendous turnover in U.S. policing. When a local political leader lost a reelection bid, all of his appointments to the police department were also in jeopardy of losing their jobs because the incoming political leader would fire them and fill the positions with his own supporters. The **Pendleton Act of 1883** was passed by the U.S. Congress to specifically eliminate this type of "spoils system" and political patronage. Although the Pendleton Act applied to federal employees only, states and local municipalities quickly adopted similar laws to attempt to control political appointments at the lower levels of government.

The Activities of the Nineteenth-Century U.S. Police Officer

Much like the police officer today, the primary technique of the nineteenth century officer was routine patrol. However, patrol in the nineteenth century accomplished little in the way of crime prevention or investigation. Patrol was on foot and officers were required to patrol regardless of temperature and weather conditions. Beats were often very large with police spread thin. In Chicago, patrol beats were three to four miles long (Walker & Katz, 2002). Officers were essentially on their own with little chance of getting backup or assistance from other officers if they got into trouble. Also, there was no systematic method for citizens to call the police when a crime had occurred. Typically, the only way to report a crime was to find an officer on patrol or to go to the local station house. Finally, there was very little supervision of patrol officers because sergeants had no way to keep tabs on their officers. Early efforts to establish call boxes where officers would be required to check in at given locations during given points of time were easily sabotaged and/or evaded.

> Supervision was weak or nonexistent. Officers easily evaded duty and spent much of their time in saloons and barber shops. Rain, snow, and extremely hot weather were powerful incentives for officers to avoid patrolling. Sergeants also patrolled on foot and found it nearly impossible to keep track of the officers under their command. (Walker & Katz, 2002, p. 30)

Police officers in the nineteenth century also served two other basic functions. First, given their ties to local politicians, officers often served the interests of their local political "sponsors," whatever those interests may be. In many cases, this involved police officers' ignoring illegitimate activities that benefited "their" politician, such as gambling and prostitution, or cracking down on the interests, both legitimate and illegitimate, of rival politicians. Second, police officers during the nineteenth century played a large role in providing social services to the homeless, needy, and poor; in providing overnight lodging; finding and returning lost children; conducting code enforcement; and checking boilers (Monkkonen, 1981). The roles and responsibilities of early U.S. police far exceeded the crime control mandate that was highlighted in later years.

Corruption and Brutality

Given what we now know about early U.S. policing—no preselection standards, no training, no supervision, and strongly tied to local politics—it is not at all surprising that corruption and brutality were commonplace. The reliance on physical force certain stems from the characteristics of policing described above: tremendous authority given to individuals with questionable backgrounds, no training, and no supervision or accountability. Yet, there were other issues that contributed to the problem. First, police officers knew they had little chance of receiving assistance from fellow police officers because of the lack of a communication system and the isolated nature of the work. As a result, the officer's ability to resolve each citizen encounter without injury or death to himself centered on the ability to engender cooperation, and many officers used physical force to gain that compliance. Second, if an officer made an arrest, he would have to walk the arrestee back to the precinct house, which may be several miles away. Many officers chose to handle encounters more informally, by distributing punishment (i.e., street justice) to the offender on the spot, thereby saving the long walk back to the precinct house and the requisite paperwork. Last, despite the very clear mandate about the use of force set forth in Peel's principles, U.S. police departments provided little in the way of guidance for officers in using force and were even less likely to subsequently punish an officer for brutality. Quite simply, there were generally no consequences for an officer who used excessive force and little recourse for the victim of that force.

Corruption was also a central feature of early U.S. policing. In many cases, the corrupt activities of police officers were directly related to the protection of the interests of local politicians. There were also plenty of the more traditional examples of police corruption: taking payoffs from gambling and prostitution operations, shaking down peddlers and business owners, and charging for police protection (Uchida, 2005). Corruption pervaded entire police departments, from the office of the chief down to the beat patrolmen. Several historians note that police corruption was part of a broader corruption epidemic within city governments. Haller (1976) argues that corruption was one of the primary functions of local government, and the police were only one part of the problem. Other scholars argue that police corruption served important social objectives. For example, U.S. society was very conservative and rigid during this period, and police corruption allowed for a social outlet in the form of drinking, gambling, and prostitution. Regardless, by 1880, there were calls for widespread reform of the police.

REFORMING THE POLICE

A First Effort at Reform

The poor state of affairs during the last part of the nineteenth century led to two formal efforts to reform policing. The first effort, begun around 1880, involved a group of middle and upper class educated Protestants called the "Progressives." The **Progressives** viewed big-city political machines as the central problem that needed to be addressed. "By eliminating machine politics from government, all facets of social services, including the police, would improve" (Uchida, 2005, p. 29). The Progressives pursued a number of initiatives that directly involved reforms of the police:

1. The police departments should be centralized, with more power and authority resting with the chief and less power at the local precinct houses.

2. The quality of police personnel should be upgraded through rigid selection standards, training, and discipline.
3. The police function should be narrowed to include crime control only; the social service functions should be delegated to other city agencies.
4. Police departments should be autonomous from political control. (Uchida, 2005)

The Progressive reform movement lasted for about thirty years, and it mostly failed to achieve any measurable positive change in the state of policing. There were, however, a few minor successes, such as the move toward using civil service for police and the creation of police commissions to investigate misconduct (i.e., the Lexow Committee in New York). Fogelson (1977) states that the Progressives failed to achieve their reforms because of their inability to defeat the big-city political machines. Successful efforts to defeat the political machines were only temporary (i.e., as illustrated by Theodore Roosevelt's short tenure as Police Commissioner in New York), as either new political leaders gained control or the old machine was able to reassert itself. Also, the police themselves resented the Progressives because they viewed them as outsiders with little understanding of police work or the problems that face police officers.

A Second Effort at Police Reform

Following the failed Progressive reform effort, a small group of police chiefs began their own efforts at reforming the profession. This reform effort was led by **August Vollmer** (considered the "father" of the modern professionalism movement), Richard Sylvester, and O.W. Wilson. In many ways, the objectives of this new reform effort mirrored the earlier efforts of the Progressives:

- Police should be involved in crime fighting only (with minimal or no involvement in social services).
- Officers should be experts in their work (the professional crime fighter).
- The police should be autonomous from political control.
- The department should be administratively efficient with centralized command and appropriate and effective use of police personnel.
- Qualified chief executives must be appointed; professionalism must flow from the chief's office.
- Departments should employ rigid selection standards, including minimum standards for intelligence, health, and moral character.
- Police officers should be college-educated.
- Departments should develop specialized units to handle specific crime problems; officers in those units should have proper training and expertise in the specific crime problems.

Because of their leadership positions within law enforcement, these reformers were able to overcome resistance by rank-and-file police officers and implement many of their initiatives. Vollmer, in particular, initiated a number of innovations in the Berkeley, California, Police Department including college-level police education programs (Vollmer founded the Criminology program at the University of California, Berkeley), bicycle and automobile patrols, scientific crime detection, and intelligence and psychiatric testing of applicants. The timeline below demonstrates Vollmer's progressiveness:

1906:   Vollmer initiates a red light signal system to reach officers on beats from headquarters; he also installs telephones in call boxes and creates a police record system.

1908:   Vollmer adds two motorcycles to patrol and begins a police school.

1909:   Vollmer is officially named chief of police in Berkeley; he convinces town trustees to appoint a Bertillon expert and purchase fingerprinting equipment; he also creates a *modus operandi* file system.

1911:   All patrol officers are using bicycles.

1914:   Three privately owned automobiles are authorized for patrol use. By 1917, Berkeley PD has the first fully motorized police force.

1915:   Vollmer establishes a central office for police reports.

1916:   Vollmer urges Congress to establish a national fingerprinting bureau; he also begins annual lectures on police procedures and convinces a biochemist to install and direct a crime laboratory.

1917:   Vollmer recruits college students for part-time police positions; he also begins consulting for police departments around the country.

1918:   Vollmer initiates testing to measure mental, physical, and emotional fitness of police recruits; he employs a psychiatrist to run the examinations.

1919:   Vollmer begins testing delinquents and using psychology to predict delinquent behavior; he implements a juvenile program to reduce delinquency.

1921:   Vollmer guides the development of the first "lie detector" and begins developing radio communications between patrol cars; he also initiates handwriting analysis.

1931:   Vollmer authors the Wickersham Commission Report highlighting the use of the "third degree" and other forms of police misconduct, as well as laying out a roadmap for reform. (Peak, 2000, p. 26)

The reform efforts of these police leaders were facilitated by technological advances that helped shape the professional model of policing. Three innovations, in particular, came together to lay the foundation for the reactive, incident-driven style of policing. First, in 1877, the invention of the telephone meant that citizens were able to call police headquarters to report a crime or other type of emergency. Second, the invention of the automobile in the early 1900s allowed police departments to begin using motorized patrol. The use of automobiles allowed for more efficient patrol and greater coverage, as well as quicker response times. Moreover, as the United States was transformed into an "automobile society," police departments were forced to adopt car patrol simply to keep up with the rest of the country. Third, the invention of the two-way radio in the 1930s completed the communication network:

- Police officers engage in preventive patrol throughout the city in automobiles.
- Citizens call police headquarters on the telephone to report a crime.
- Headquarters dispatches a patrol car to the location of the call for service through the two-way radio.
- The police officer responds quickly in his or her automobile.

The two-way radio also allowed for much greater supervision of police officers because it offered a mechanism for headquarters to have continuous contact with patrol cars. Also, as mentioned in Chapter 2, the emergence of the Federal Bureau of Investigation (FBI) under **J. Edgar Hoover** helped solidify the professional model of policing as the standard that local departments sought to achieve. Hoover was able to successfully characterize his special agents as the prototypical crime fighters. Hoover's emphasis on rigid selection standards, proper training and education, honesty, efficiency and impartiality, scientific crime analysis, and use of crime statistics epitomized the professional model of policing. Hoover was also the first to declare a "war on crime," and his success in tracking down Public Enemy Number 1, was well-publicized across the United States. Of course, as time passed, a number of controversies surrounded Hoover and his approach to law enforcement, including an exaggeration of the FBI's role in catching several of the infamous criminals (i.e., public enemies), the manipulation of crime data to exaggerate the FBI's impact on crime, avoidance of white-collar and organized crime (focusing on the single offender), and violation of civil rights (i.e., spying on political figures and celebrities and maintaining secret files on them).

CRACKS IN THE FOUNDATION OF THE PROFESSIONAL POLICE MODEL

A Partial Success

Clearly, the leaders of the professional police reform movement did not achieve all of their objectives. There is still an ongoing debate about whether policing is a craft or a profession, as well as over the importance of academy training (see Chapter 2). Many departments have only recently begun to employ rigorous screening and selection procedures. Only a small percentage of police departments today require recruits to possess a four-year college degree before applying for a position as a police officer.

Also, Vollmer's emphasis on scientific crime detection went mostly unnoticed and has only recently become a central focus in law enforcement. And last, although the crime-fighting role became the central focus of police, they continued to be heavily involved in service-related and order maintenance activities. Wilson's (1968) seminal study of police showed that officers spent only about 10 percent of their time on law enforcement-related activities.

Yet, the professional movement accomplished a number of important objectives. Perhaps most important, the professional model became the goal of the law enforcement community. Quite simply, the principles of the professional model became the standard that police departments sought to achieve. Also, most police departments were able to limit the amount of political influence on their operation and functioning; certainly, the days of serving the whims and interests of local politicians had ended. Most police departments also became highly specialized, creating units to handle a range of specific crime problems, such as narcotics, vice, juvenile, and specialized detective units (homicide, burglary, robbery, etc.). And finally, the reactive, incident-driven style of the professional model—defined by automobile patrol, the telephone, and the two-way radio—became the dominant method of police patrol for the next fifty years.

Signs of Trouble: Prohibition and the Wickersham Commission

In 1919, the **Volstead Act** and Eighteenth Amendment to the United States Constitution were passed by Congress. The Act declared that the manufacture, sale, and transportation of alcohol was illegal in the United States. Over the next fourteen years, until it was repealed, Prohibition was enormously unpopular and placed police officers in the very difficult position of enforcing a nearly unenforceable law. The difficulty of enforcing Prohibition, the adversarial relationship it created among police and the community, and officers' own beliefs regarding alcohol led many police to either ignore alcohol violations or to take bribes to allow bootleggers to continue their activities. Organized crime also became increasingly powerful during Prohibition as it seized control of the illegal alcohol market. The gang wars that resulted from competition over this market—best illustrated by the rise of Al Capone in Chicago—led to numerous violent murders and placed significant pressure on police because of their inability to abate the violence.

Although the professional model became the ideal, many police departments continued to struggle with corruption and brutality scandals. These persistent problems were exposed in 1931 by The National Commission on Law Observance and Enforcement (also known as the **Wickersham Commission**). Created by President Herbert Hoover in 1929, the Wickersham Commission conducted a national study of the criminal justice system. Although the Commission published a total of fourteen reports, the *Report on Lawlessness in Law Enforcement* captured national attention with its depiction of police misconduct, specifically the use of the "third degree." The report (National Commission on Law Observance and Enforcement, 1931) concluded that, "the third degree—the inflicting of pain, physical or mental, to extract confessions or statements—is extensively practiced" (p. 1). The report also detailed widespread brutality and illegal detention, search, and seizure. The Wickersham Commission findings clearly illustrated that, despite the principles of the professional model, a significant number of police officers still engaged in the type of illegal and brutal behavior that characterized the earlier political era.

The Police Subculture and the Working Personality

The **professional model** produced a complete transformation of the U.S. police officer. The political era police officer was an individual walking the streets of his beat in preventive patrol, with many service and social welfare responsibilities, who was very approachable to the public. The new, professional-model police officer was an individual riding around in a patrol car, isolated from the community, responding to calls for service, while emphasizing the crime-fighting role and downplaying the other roles. The isolation from the community created by this new style of policing has been linked to the development of a **police subculture,** defined by a distinct working personality and an antagonistic, "us versus them" mentality.

Westley's (1970) study of police in Gary, Indiana, "sought to isolate and identify the major social norms governing police conduct, and to describe the way in which they influence police action in specific situations" (p. viii). Based on his interviews with police, Westley (1970) concluded that a distinct subculture existed, defined by secrecy, solidarity, violence, negative attitudes toward the public, and perceived negative attitudes of the community toward them (more than 70 percent of officers said they believed that the public was hostile toward them; see Chapter 8 for a more complete discussion of the police subculture). Officers indicated that they viewed the public as the enemy and that they believed it was acceptable to lie to protect each other from public criticism (Westley, 1970). Westley argued that police resentment of the public developed because of the selective nature of police-citizen encounters: The majority of citizen interactions with the police occur because something negative has happened. Bittner (1974) put this best stating that police work involves "something-that-ought-not-to-be-happening-and-about which-someone-had-better-do-something-now."

Skolnick (1966) further defined the police subculture in his classic study of police in Westville (a.k.a. Oakland, California). Skolnick (1966) argued that police had a distinct working personality defined by the danger and authority of police work, producing both isolation from the rest of society and group solidarity. Police also developed a "perceptual shorthand" or mental list of characteristics that indicated a suspect was dangerous—known as a symbolic assailant (Skolnick, 1966). Neiderhoffer (1967) argued that the subculture was characterized by cynicism and authoritarianism, which emphasizes aggression, superstition, and a tendency to stereotype. Later research linked the police subculture and its various elements to problem police behavior—such as corruption, racial profiling, and brutality—and argued that reducing tension between the police and the public hinges upon breaking down the barriers produced by the police subculture (see Skolnick & Fyfe, 1993).

The 1950s and 1960s: National Crisis and the Police

The work of Skolnick, Westley, and Neiderhoffer demonstrated that the police–community relationship was in a far worse state than suggested by Sergeant Joe Friday's "just the facts ma'am" impersonal and professional persona. Prior to the tumultuous events of the 1950s and 1960s, the relationship between the police and public was characterized by tension, antagonism, and resentment. Unfortunately, during the 1950s and 1960s a number of events and movements came together to create a national crisis, forcing confrontations between police and citizens, and highlighting the inherent limitations of the professional model of policing.

Due Process Revolution. Beginning in the 1950s, the United States Supreme Court, led by liberal Chief Justice Earl Warren, handed down a number of rulings protecting the rights of the accused, a **due process revolution** of sorts, and placing tremendous pressure on police to alter their field practices. The Supreme Court rulings also highlighted continuing problems with police practices regarding basic constitutional rights, such as protections against illegal search and seizure, self-incrimination, the right to due process, freedom of speech, and the right to counsel. Below is a brief review of several—though certainly not all—of the most important cases.

Mapp v. Ohio, 367 U.S. 643 (1961) In 1957, Cleveland police officers forcibly entered the house of Dolree Mapp without a search warrant (although they waved a piece of paper they claimed was a warrant, there was no record anywhere of a search warrant being processed or approved). The police were searching for a suspect they believed was in the house, and when they could not find him, they arrested Mapp for possession of obscene material. Mapp was convicted, but she appealed the conviction and the case was eventually heard by the U.S. Supreme Court. In 1961, the Court issued its ruling and overturned Mapp's conviction. The Court applied the "**exclusionary rule**" (a principle from the *U.S. v. Weeks* case [1914] that dealt with federal prosecutions) stating the evidence seized illegally (without a search warrant or probable cause) cannot be used in court proceedings. The Court stated:

> The right to be secure against rude invasions of privacy by state officers is constitutional in origin, we can no longer permit that right to remain an empty promise. We can no longer permit it to be revocable at the whim of any police officer who, in the name of law enforcement itself, chooses to suspend its enjoyment. (*Mapp v. Ohio,* 367 U.S. 643 (1961))

The Supreme Court applied the exclusionary rule to local and state police through the Fourteenth Amendment, which says that no state may deprive one of its citizens of due process (Walker & Katz, 2002). The *Mapp* ruling was critically important for police because, first, it set a minimal national standard for search and seizure—with consequences for violation of that standard—and second, the case set a precedent for the U.S. Supreme Court as a mechanism for holding local police accountable for their actions (Walker & Katz, 2002). Later rulings by the Court created a number of exceptions to the exclusionary rule, including the good faith exception (evidence is still admissible if the search and arrest lacked probable cause but the police could not have known), the public safety exception (concern for public safety outweighs adherence to the rules), and the inevitability of discovery exception (the illegally seized evidence would have been found anyway).

Gideon v. Wainwright, *372 U.S. 335 (1963)*   Clarence Earl Gideon was arrested and charged with a felony in Florida, but was unable to afford legal counsel. In Florida at the time, legal counsel was appointed to indigent suspects in capital cases only. As a result, when Gideon requested that the court appoint an attorney, his request was denied. Gideon subsequently defended himself and was convicted. The U.S. Supreme Court agreed to hear his case, and in a unanimous ruling in 1963, overturned his conviction and the ruling in an earlier case (*Betts v. Brady,* [1942], where the court ruled that indigency alone was not sufficient grounds for requiring court-appointed counsel). The Court ruled that the Sixth Amendment obligates that federal, state, and local governments provide legal counsel for those who cannot afford it if the case is serious enough that jail might result (felonies). Later rulings expanded this right to counsel to those charged with misdemeanors as well.

Miranda v. Arizona, *384 U.S. 436 (1966)*   On March 3, 1963, an 18-year-old girl was abducted and raped in Phoenix, Arizona. During the course of the investigation, Ernesto Miranda was identified in a police lineup by the victim, was subsequently arrested, and after interrogation, confessed to the crime. Miranda was convicted and sentenced to a long prison term. Although Miranda was never advised of his constitutional rights, the Arizona Supreme Court ruled in Miranda's appeal that since he had been arrested previously he knowingly waived his rights. In 1966, the U.S. Supreme Court ruled in favor of Miranda, stating that in order to ensure a suspect's Fifth Amendment right against self-incrimination, the police must advise the suspect of his or her constitutional rights. Of course, those rights include the right to remain silent, notification that anything the suspect says (giving up the right to remain silent) can be used in court, the right to an attorney, and the right to a court-appointed attorney if the suspect cannot afford his or her own legal counsel. Ruling that the atmosphere inside a police station is inherently coercive and may induce suspects to give up their protection against self-incrimination, the Court said, "when an individual is taken into custody or otherwise deprived of his freedom by the authorities in any significant way and is subjected to questioning, the privilege against self-incrimination is jeopardized." The Court has wrestled with the reading of Miranda rights in a number of cases over the last twenty-five years—especially the difference between an interview (when advisement of Miranda rights is not necessary) and an interrogation—but the Court has generally upheld the original ruling.

Terry v. Ohio, *392 U.S. 1 (1968)*   In October 1963, a Cleveland detective witnessed two men standing near a jewelry store. The detective observed the suspects as they continued to move up and down the street and look into the windows of the jewelry store. When they were joined by a third man, the detective suspected that they were either about to rob the store or were casing it for a later robbery. The detective approached the suspects, identified himself as a police officer, and because he suspected that they might be armed, he conducted a "pat-down" search over the clothes of one of the suspects (John Terry). Two of the three men were armed with revolvers and were subsequently arrested and prosecuted for carrying concealed weapons. Both were convicted and appealed their case to the U.S. Supreme Court. In 1968, the Court upheld the convictions and acknowledged the constitutionality of "stop and frisk" searches that do not meet the probable cause standard. The Court stated that whenever a police officer stops an individual based on suspicion and prevents him or her from walking away (defined as a seizure), the officer is permitted to conduct an over-the-clothes protective search for weapons that may pose a threat to the officer. The Court also distinguished between this type of stop and search and arrest (a Terry stop is NOT an arrest), but stated that the Terry stop is governed by the Fourth Amendment and requires reasonableness (*Terry v. Ohio,* 392 U.S. 1 (1968)).

The Civil Rights and Anti-War Movements, Riots, and Disorder.   The 1950s and 1960s were characterized by two important social movements—the **civil rights movement** and the anti–Vietnam War movement—that defined the turbulence of the era and thrust the police as agents of social control into conflict with demonstrators. The civil rights movement had begun in the South during the 1950s as a concerted effort to achieve equality in all aspects of life for African Americans. Although the techniques used by civil rights advocates were primarily nonviolent, such as sit-ins, boycotts, and peaceful demonstrations (i.e., civil disobedience), they led to direct confrontations with the police. The police soon became the symbol of an oppressive government that would not grant equal rights and justice to black citizens.

In the early 1960s, the frustrations among African Americans escalated to violence, riots, and disorder in a number of U.S. cities, and in many cases, the incident that sparked the violence involved the police. On July 16, 1964, a white New York City police officer shot and killed a black teenager. Protestors demanding that action be taken against the officer marched to police headquarters, when rioting broke out. The riots continued for two days, resulting in one death, 100 injuries, 500 arrests, and millions of dollars in property damage (Walker & Katz, 2002). In the Watts riot in Los Angeles the following year, 34 people were killed, 1,000 were injured, and 4,000 were arrested. In Detroit in 1967, disorder lasted for almost a week, resulting in 43 deaths and $40 million in property damage. In 1966, there were 43 riots in major urban centers across the United States. The riots in Watts and Newark were sparked by routine traffic stops by police, and the Detroit riot began after a police raid of an after-hours bar. The role of police in the riots and disorder was highlighted by the findings of the Kerner Commission (see below) and placed police in the national spotlight for their negative relationship with minority communities.

Police also found themselves in sometimes violent confrontations (though nothing on the scale of the riots described above) with anti-war and other types of "against-the-establishment" demonstrations. There were numerous large and mostly peaceful demonstrations against the U.S. involvement in the Vietnam war. There were also various other types of demonstrations, many on college campuses, involving acts of civil disobedience. Unfortunately, their order maintenance responsibilities forced the police into confrontations with demonstrators and resulted in police again becoming the symbol of a repressive federal government.

Crime.   A central tenet of the professional model involved the police focusing solely on crime fighting and their being experts at that work. With the development of the reactive, incident-driven style of policing, for fifty years citizens had been told to call the police—"the experts"—when crime occurred. Citizens began to take for granted that when crime occurred, they could call the police, the police would arrive quickly, ensure their safety, and then locate the criminal and bring him or her to justice. These expectations were reinforced through the publicity surrounding the FBI's success with Public Enemy number 1 and portrayals of the police by Hollywood (Sergeant Joe Friday in *Dragnet*).

During the 1960s, crime skyrocketed. The crime rate per 100,000 citizens more than doubled from 1960 to 1970. Drug use also became much more open and widespread. As the crime rate increased throughout the decade, the media and the public in general became more critical of the police and their inability to curtail it. Quite simply, the public had been trained for five decades to think that crime was the sole responsibility of the police, and when police were unable to reduce the crime rate, the public was understandably upset and critical.

The failure of the police to reduce crime, coupled with the other events described here, led to serious questions about the prevailing style of policing. These issues also, without question, served to exacerbate the strained relationship between the police and the communities they served, and reinforced the "us versus them" mentality that had been documented earlier by Westley, Skolnick, and Niederhoffer.

Presidential Commissions and New Law Enforcement Agencies.   As a result of the turbulent events described above and the role of police in those events, the White House and Congress initiated a number of Commissions and created new law enforcement agencies to assist the police during these difficult times. Several of the most important are described below.

President's Commission on Law Enforcement and the Administration of Justice
President Lyndon B. Johnson created this commission to specifically investigate the potential impact of the criminal justice system—and its various components—on controlling crime. The Commission's report, called "The Challenge of Crime in a Free Society," focused primarily on the police and sponsored the seminal work of Donald Black and Albert Reiss, who observed patrol officers at work (Walker & Katz, 2002). The Commission's report described in some detail the complex nature of policing and the importance of recognizing and controlling police discretion. The report touted most of the critical elements of the professional model, including more

stringent recruitment and selection standards, better and longer training (400 hours minimum), and improved supervision and management (Walker & Katz, 2002). The Commission made a number of other specific recommendations such as:

- Establishing citizen advisory committees in minority neighborhoods.
- Recruiting more minority police officers.
- Establishing clear and straightforward mechanisms for filing citizen complaints.
- Moving toward a college-educated police force.
- Establishing police standards commissions in every state.
- Involving the police in community planning.
- Producing more scholarly research on the police.

This very important commission and its report set the agenda for police for the next thirty years, and importantly, it specifically highlighted the importance of research in moving police toward their long-sought-after goal of professionalism.

The National Advisory Commission on Civil Disorders (The Kerner Commission)
After devastating riots in Atlanta, Detroit, and Newark, President Lyndon B. Johnson created the **Kerner Commission** to study the causes of the riots. The Commission's report identified a number of social and community problems that contributed to the violence: institutional racism, unemployment, discrimination in jobs and housing, inadequate social services, and unequal justice. The report also concluded that hostility and tension between police and minority communities played a central role in the riots. The report identified four specific problems related to the police:

1. Police conduct was often brutal and abusive, particularly against minority suspects.
2. Training and supervision were inadequate.
3. Police–community relations and mechanisms for receiving citizen complaints against the police were poor.
4. The employment of black police officers lagged far behind the growth of the black population. (National Advisory Commission on Civil Disorders, 1967)

Importantly, the Kerner Commission questioned some of the basic tenets of the professional model, noting that "many of the serious disturbances took place in cities whose police are among the best led, best organized, best trained, and most professional in the country" (National Advisory Commission on Civil Disorders, 1967, p. 301). The report specifically discussed the negative impact of car patrol, aggressive crime-fighting tactics, and frequent stop and frisks on police–community relations.

Law Enforcement Assistance Administration and Law Enforcement Education Program In 1968, Congress passed the Omnibus Crime Control and Safe Streets Act, which established the Law Enforcement Assistance Administration (LEAA). The

LEAA was created to offer funding and guidance to local jurisdictions and states with regard to crime prevention and control (Champion & Hooper, 2003). Over the next fifteen years, the LEAA provided over $8 billion in funding to towns, cities, and states to combat crime. Despite the huge sum of money, there was little overall impact on crime, and the LEAA is generally considered to be a failure (Champion & Hooper, 2003). The LEAA did, however, place strong emphasis on scholarly research. It funded a number of important research projects, and it also required police departments to hire program evaluators for initiatives created with LEAA money. Also, from 1968 to 1976, the Law Enforcement Education Program (LEEP), a federally funded program, provided approximately $200 million in financial aid to students studying criminal justice in college.

American Bar Association, "Standards Relating to the Urban Police Function"   In 1973, the American Bar Association published its report examining the police role and police standards and tactics in urban centers. The report evaluated a number of police programs, identifying several that were successful, and made policy recommendations for improving policing. The report also highlighted the complex role of the police and concluded that police officers spend the majority of their time in order-maintenance activities rather than fighting crime. The ABA report also acknowledged the need for police discretion but stressed that it must be controlled rather than unfettered.

New Federal Law Enforcement Agencies   The 1960s were also marked by assassinations of a number of important political and social movement leaders including President John F. Kennedy, Senator Robert Kennedy, and Martin Luther King, Jr. These assassinations and the overall increase in gun crimes during the 1960s led Congress to pass a number of more restrictive and punitive gun laws and to create the Bureau of Alcohol, Tobacco, and Firearms (BATF). The BATF was given authority to enforce many of the firearms laws and was also responsible for monitoring the sale, licensing, and carrying of firearms. In response to increased drug use, in 1972 President Richard Nixon created the Drug Enforcement Administration (DEA) to enforce drug laws and combat drug dealers and drug-related crime.

The Research Revolution

Public and media scrutiny of the police, as well as the findings of the commissions described above, led to a wealth of social research examining the police. The LEAA was responsible for funding much of this research, and in 1970 the Ford Foundation created the Police Foundation with a $30-million grant. A number of seminal research studies built on the early work of Skolnick, Westley, and Niederhoffer and helped redefine our understanding of the police and the fundamental limitations of the professional model. Several of these research studies are described below.

James Q. Wilson's Varieties of Police Behavior. In 1968, Wilson published his groundbreaking study of police in eight communities. The book, *Varieties of Police Behavior,* categorized departments based on their style of policing, as watchmen, legalistic, or service. Wilson (1968) critically evaluates each style, offering insights on the advantages and drawbacks of each approach. Wilson (1968) also devotes a chapter to police discretion, including the factors that influence officer decision making and the need for controlling that discretion. Until this point, police departments were typically viewed as monolithic, ministerial agencies that varied little in their approach and style. Last and perhaps most importantly, Wilson (1968) was among the first scholars to report that police officers spent only a small amount of their time engaged in law enforcement-related activities (Wilson concluded that 10 percent of police work involved "crime fighting" and law enforcement).

The Kansas City Preventive Patrol Study. Perhaps no research study has influenced policing more than the **Kansas City Preventive Patrol Study,** conducted in 1972–1973. Funded by the newly created Police Foundation, the study (Kelling, Pate, Dieckman, & Brown, 1974) sought to test a number of basic assumptions of the professional model, including the potential impact of preventive patrol on crime, fear of crime, and response time. Importantly, the study employed a strong research design where fifteen city beats were matched on a number of relevant factors (crime levels, population size, calls for service, etc.) and assigned one of three levels of patrol:

1. *No preventive patrol:* Police only entered these beats in response to specific calls for service; there would be no routine, preventive patrol.
2. *Standard preventive patrol:* These beats were assigned to receive the standard or typical amount of preventive patrol.
3. *Saturated preventive patrol:* These beats were to receive two to three times the average level of preventive patrol.

The assigned patrol levels were maintained for a period of several months, and afterwards researchers examined the crime data from police and surveyed residents on a number of relevant issues (residents were unaware of the research study). The study produced a number of significant findings that, quite simply, shook the professional model at its core:

- The areas with saturated preventive patrol did NOT experience less crime.
- The areas with no preventive patrol did NOT experience an increase in crime.
- Citizens' fear of crime in areas with saturated preventive patrol was NOT reduced; citizens' fear of crime in areas with no preventive patrol did NOT increase.
- Citizen's attitudes toward the police did NOT improve in the areas with saturated patrol.
- Faster response times did NOT lead to increases in arrests; few calls involved crimes in progress, and most crime victims did not call the police immediately. (Kelling et al., 1974)

The conclusions of the study represented a serious challenge to the professional model of policing. The value of preventive patrol and rapid response time with regard to crime prevention and suppression, citizen fear of crime, and citizen attitudes toward the police are core components of the model. With the events of the 1950s and 1960s as a backdrop, the Kansas City study led many practitioners and scholars to begin to think about new ways for police to go about their daily business.

Other Research Studies.   Also in the early 1970s, the RAND Corporation conducted an important study of criminal investigation and detective work. The study challenged many of the basic assumptions about the work of detectives and success of criminal investigations. The study found that follow-up criminal investigations are often unproductive, that most crimes are solved based on information obtained by the first responder (patrol officer, not the detective), and that most detective work is boring, routine, and primarily involves paperwork (Greenwood, 1975). Other research continued to examine important police issues such as discretion and how to control it, the police subculture, the complex police role, and use of deadly force and how to control it.

Finally, from 1977–1979 research studies were carried out in Newark, New Jersey, and Flint, Michigan, to test the impact of foot patrol on crime, fear of crime, and officer attitudes. Both studies employed similar designs (and questions) used in the Kansas City study, but the results were notably different:

- Crime levels did NOT decrease in foot patrol areas (similar to the Kansas City study).
- Citizen fear of crime DID decrease in foot patrol areas.
- Citizen attitudes toward the police DID improve in foot patrol areas.
- Officers assigned to foot patrol had higher levels of job satisfaction.
- Officers assigned to foot patrol had higher levels of perceived personal safety. (Police Foundation, 1981)

Although foot patrol did not result in a decrease in crime, its impact on fear of crime and attitudes toward the police were still important. Scholars argued that if residents are less fearful, the informal community controls that hold a neighborhood together and resist the intrusion of crime and disorder may be maintained. Also, coming out of the 1960s, police departments were desperate for ways to improve their relationships to the community, and foot patrol seemed to offer a logical and inexpensive way to do just that.

Fallout from the 1960s: Policing Comes Full Circle

This chapter documented how the early U.S. police officer was transformed from a version of the British Bobbie—on foot patrol with prevention of crime as a central goal—to the completely reactive, incident-driven officer responding to calls for service by automobile. The due process revolution, the role of police in the riots and disorder of the 1960s, the dramatic increases in crime, and the explosion of social research all set the table for a complete rethinking of the police and their role. Within five years of the Kansas City study's being published, Herman Goldstein published his seminal piece on problem-oriented policing. Three years later, Wilson and Kelling (1982) published their piece on "broken windows" and began the discourse on community-oriented policing. Both problem- and community-oriented policing represented a fundamental shift in philosophy away from the professional model, producing significant changes to the police role and how police effectiveness should be measured. These new philosophies of policing, along with more recent innovations such as CompStat and Zero Tolerance policing, are the subject of the next chapter.

SUMMARY

This chapter has served as the requisite chapter on police history, and as such has traced the development of professional policing in our society. Although the focus of this chapter—and the entire book—is policing in the United States, the origins of our police model lie with Sir Robert Peel and the London Metropolitan Police Force. The chapter traces events in London during the early part of the nineteenth century that led to discussion of a professional police force, most notably industrialization, urbanization and their by-products, and describes in some detail the principles underlying Peel's police model. As similar problems emerged in the United States, city officials turned to the Peel model, but borrowed selectively. This selective adoption led to a vastly different early experience with policing in the United States.

Much of the chapter describes the first two eras of professional policing: the political and reform eras. The key players, major events, and changes in policing are summarized for each period. Particular attention is paid to the second major effort at reform, led by police chiefs such as August Vollmer. The principles defined by Vollmer and others laid the foundation for the professional police model that dominated U.S. law enforcement throughout the better part of the twentieth century. This model is defined by a focus on crime fighting, police being experts in their work, autonomy from political control, rigorous selection and training standards, bureaucratic efficiency, and specialization.

As we entered the 1950s and 1960s, it became evident that the professional model had more than its fair share of limitations. The due process revolution, the police role in riots and disorder, substantial increases in crime, numerous presidential commissions, and deep-seated hostility between police and minority communities all served to put the spotlight on police. These events also served to foster an explosion in scholarly research that produced a new understanding of the police, their complex roles and activities. The Kansas City Preventive Patrol Study, in particular, produced findings that seriously challenged the philosophical underpinnings of the professional model. Importantly, the events of the 1960s and the research that followed set the stage for a rethinking of police: By the early 1980s both community policing and problem-oriented policing had become viable alternatives to the professional model that were garnering attention and research funding. Both are described in detail in the next chapter.

KEY TERMS

Bow Street Runners
Civil rights movement
Due process revolution
Exclusionary rule
Gideon v. Wainright
Hoover, J. Edgar
Kansas City Preventive Patrol Study
Kerner Commission
Mapp v. Ohio
Metropolitan Police Act of 1829
Miranda v. Arizona
Peel, Robert

Pendleton Act of 1883
Political era of policing
Police subculture
President's Commission on Law Enforcement and the Administration of Justice
Professional model
Progressives
Slave patrols
Terry v. Ohio
Vollmer, August
Volstead Act
Wickersham Commission

DISCUSSION QUESTIONS

1. Describe Peel's principles that governed the creation of the London Metropolitan Police Force.

2. What were some basic differences between the London police force and early U.S. police departments?

3. Describe U.S. policing during the last half of the nineteenth century (1850–1900).

4. What are the key components of the professional model of policing, developed by Vollmer and others?

5. Describe the events of the 1950s and 1960s that put police under a national spotlight.

6. Why is the Kansas City Preventive Patrol study important? Describe the key findings.

REFERENCES

Bittner, E. (1974). Florence Nightingale in pursuit of Willie Sutton: A theory of the police. In H. Jacob (Ed.), *The potential for reform of criminal justice* (pp. 1-25). Beverly Hills, CA: Sage.
Champion, D.H., & Hooper, M.K. (2003). *Introduction to American policing.* New York: McGraw Hill.
Fogelson, R. (1977). *Big-city police.* Cambridge, MA: Harvard University Press.
Gideon v. Wainright, 372 U.S. 335 (1963).

Grant, H.B., & Terry, K.J. (2005). *Law enforcement in the 21st century.* Boston: Allyn and Bacon.

Greenwood, P. (1975). *The criminal investigation process.* Santa Monica, CA: Rand.

Haller, M. (1976). Historical roots of police behavior: Chicago, 1890–1925. *Law & Society Review.* 10, 303–324.

Kelling, G.L., Pate, T., Dieckman, D., & Brown, C.E. (1974). *The Kansas City preventive patrol experiment.* Washington, DC: The Police Foundation.

Kelling, G.L.Z., & Moore, M.H. (1991). From political to reform to community: The evolving strategy of the police. In J.R. Greene & S.D. Mastrofski (Eds.), *Community policing: Rhetoric or reality.* New York: Praeger.

Klockars, C.B. (1983). *Thinking about police: Contemporary readings.* New York: McGraw-Hill.

Mapp v. Ohio, 367 U.S. 643 (1961).

Miller, W.R. (1977). *Cops and bobbies: Police authority in New York and London, 1830–1870.* Chicago: University of Chicago Press.

Miranda v. Arizona, 384 U.S. 436 (1966).

Monkkonen, E.H. (1981). *Police in urban America, 1860–1920.* Cambridge, UK: Cambridge University Press.

National Advisory Commission on Civil Disorders (1967). *Report of the National Advisory Commission on Civil Disorders.* New York: Bantam Books.

National Commission on Law Observance and Enforcement [Wickersham Report]. (1931). *Report on lawlessness in law enforcement.* Washington, DC: Government Printing Office.

Niederhoffer, A. (1967). *Behind the shield: The police in urban society.* Gordon City, NY: Anchor Books.

Peak, K.J. (2000). *Policing America: Methods, issues, challenges* (3rd ed.). Upper Saddle River, NJ: Prentice-Hall.

Police Foundation. (1981). *The Newark foot patrol experiment.* Washington, DC: The Police Foundation.

Skolnick, J.H. (1966). *Justice without trial: Law enforcement in a democratic society.* New York: John Wiley.

Skolnick, J.H., & Fyfe, J.J. (1993). *Above the law: Police and the excessive use of force.* New York: Free Press.

Terry v. Ohio, 392 U.S. 1 (1968).

Uchida, C. (2005). The development of the American police: An historical overview. In R.G. Dunham & G.P. Alpert (Eds.), *Critical issues in policing: Contemporary readings* (pp. 20–40). Long Grove, IL: Waveland Press.

Walker, S., & Katz, C.M. (2002). *The police in America: An introduction.* New York: McGraw Hill.

Westley, W. (1970). *Violence and the police.* Cambridge, MA: MIT Press.

Wilson, J.Q. (1968). *Varieties of police behavior.* Cambridge, MA: Harvard University Press.

Wilson, J.Q., & Kelling, G.L. (1982). *Broken windows: Police and neighborhood safety.* Atlantic Monthly. 249 (March), 29–38.

SCHOLAR'S PERSPECTIVE

Populism, Politics, and the Struggle for Police Professionalism in the United States

Anders Walker*

John Jay College of Criminal Justice

Chapter 3, "Development of the Professional Policing Model," provides a succinct history of police reform in the United States. Dr. White shows, for example, how policing evolved from informal watch systems, vigilante committees, and slave patrols to more formal organizations. He explains, in particular, how city officials in New York and Boston borrowed from policing models in England to help quell rioting and disorder in the first half of the nineteenth century. White goes on to show how the U.S. model differed from the English model, due largely to its ties to local politics and absence of centralized state control. This lack of centralized control, White maintains, led invariably to amateurism, political corruption, and, beginning in the 1880s, recurring attempts at police reform. These attempts were led first by Progressives at the close of the nineteenth century, then by police officials like August Vollmer through the 1930s, and, finally, by the federal government in the 1960s and 1970s.

Although one might conclude that policing has evolved over time to become more professional, centralized, and effective, White suggests an alternative conclusion, which is that professionalism has struggled, consistently, in the United States, and continues to do so today. To take just a few examples, White shows that although Progressives like Theodore Roosevelt struggled mightily to professionalize police in the 1890s, they failed to break the political machines that dominated police hiring, thereby inviting a return to corruption. Similarly, although police chiefs like August Vollmer called for renewed efforts at professionalism in the 1920s and '30s, these efforts seem to have had more success at changing the technologies of policing than actually transforming police procedure, because problems with police brutality, illegal detention, and search and seizure continued well into the 1960s. Indeed, White suggests that one of the outcomes of reform efforts, beginning in the 1960s and continuing through the end of the twentieth century, were attempts to rethink profession-

---

*Assistant Professor, John Jay College of Criminal Justice. B.A. Wesleyan University, 1994; J.D./M.A. Duke University, 1998; Ph.D. Yale University, 2003.

alism generally and to come up with alternative less formal models, like community, or problem-oriented, policing, popular in the 1980s and 1990s.

That police departments in the United States began to consider community policing in the 1980s, in many ways a return to preprofessional models popular in the early decades of the nineteenth century, is ironic. Yet, it points to three larger themes in U.S. history: localism, popular rule, and an aversion to centralized authority. Traces of these three interconnected themes can be found as early as the colonial era, when Americans mounted a revolution against the centralized authority of the British crown in favor of local popular control. This resentment of centralized authority continued, arguably, through the founding and into the Early Republic. The existence of slavery in the South contributed to it, as southern leaders fought against centralized authority and in favor of states' rights, largely to preserve their property. Massive waves of immigration to northern cities also contributed to it, as legions of new immigrants fractured notions of a common, national identity, often fueling the rise of powerful political machines at the local level.

Indeed, it is no surprise that even though city officials in the North turned to British models of professionalism in the 1840s, these models ultimately failed. Unable to draw authority from a centralized, unified state, police officials remained closely tied to local, democratic, populist rule. Corruption, consequently, retained a decidedly democratic flair. As immigrant communities began voting, police departments became political extensions of those communities, highly responsive to local needs, but brutal in the exercise of power against aliens and resistant to any kind of centralized control or reform (Walker, 1977). Progressives, although well-intentioned, sought invariably to contain the cultural, ethnic, and religious diversity of such communities and failed. Their attempts to professionalize police, which would have made it easier to control immigrants, arguably failed as well (Walker, 1977).

It is no accident, in other words, that Prohibition, a Progressive, Protestant-led campaign to control the rapidly expanding immigrant (primarily Catholic) population, led to rampant police corruption. Local police, particularly when drawn from local, Catholic communities, sided with their own. This was also true, incidentally, for labor. Just as Catholic communities led to Catholic police, so too did working-class communities lead invariably to working-class police (Johnson, 1976). As waves of strikes rolled across the country in the early decades of the twentieth century, corporations struggled to break ties between local police and striking workers. One solution, popular in states like Pennsylvania, was the formation of centralized, professional, state police (Walker, 1977). Another solution was the formation of private police forces, like the Pinkerton Detective Agency (Walker, 1977).

As elites struggled to break ties between local politics and police, so too did police reformers. Perhaps the most famous of these was August Vollmer, who took inspiration from the military in reforming Berkeley, California's police department. Among other things, Vollmer recommended a shift in hiring away from working-class communities and toward college graduates (Vollmer, 1921). Despite Vollmer's success in reforming Berkeley's police department, however, he failed to professionalize police departments nationwide. This was true in rural areas, where locally elected sheriffs dominated law enforcement. It was also true in cities like Chicago, Philadelphia, New York, and Los Angeles. In fact, Vollmer served as chief of the Los Angeles police for a year, only to abandon his post in despair (Walker, 1998). Arguably, this was not a problem for the majority of Americans. As long as local police were drawn from local communities, wide levels of police discretion (and a lack of adherence to centrally mandated professional standards or rules) seemed not to be a topic of particular popular concern.

However, the impact on unpopular disenfranchised minorities was brutal. (Williams & Murphy, 1990). Perhaps the greatest victims of such brutality were African Americans. In the South, African Americans lacked the right to vote and, by extension, the ability to control local police departments. This led to a recurring problem of torture and abuse that continued well into the twentieth century, not to mention a string of early Supreme Court decisions that sought to intervene in local affairs and improve police procedure (Klarman, 2000). Police treatment of blacks in the North and West, where blacks were often blocked, informally, from joining departments, was arguably not much better. This became obvious in the 1960s, when forceful arrests led to wide-scale rioting in urban centers.

Not surprisingly, one of the outcomes of minority/police tension in the 1960s was community policing (Williams & Murphy, 1990). Arguably, this had always been the answer to policing in the United States.[1] Indeed, it is what differentiated the United States from centralized, professional forces in countries like England, and it is what makes an understanding of White's chapter relevant for today.

REFERENCES

Johnson, B.C. (1976). Taking care of labor: The police in American politics. *Theory and Society, 3,* 89.
Kelling, G.L., & Moore, M.H. (1988). The evolving strategy of policing. *Perspectives on Policing, 4.* Washington, DC: National Institute of Justice.
Klarman, M.J. (2000). The racial origins of modern criminal procedure. *Michigan Law Review,* 99.
Vollmer, A. (May 1920 – February 1921). Practical method for selecting policemen. *Journal of American Institute of Criminal Law and Criminology, 11,* 571.
Walker, S. (1977). *A critical history of police reform: The emergence of professionalism.* Lexington, MA: Lexington Books.
Walker, S. (1998). *Popular justice: A history of American criminal justice.* New York: Oxford University Press.
Williams, H., & Murphy, P.V. (1990). The evolving strategy of police: A minority view. *Perspectives on Policing, 13.* Washington DC: National Institute of Justice.

[1]This contradicts what George L. Kelling and Mark H. Moore (1988) argue. Kelling and Moore divide policing in the United States into three eras: political, professional, and community. I see more continuity, hence my argument that U.S. police have always operated at the community level. Indeed, this is what made them political during the nineteenth century, and it is what hindered professionalism during the first half of the twentieth century. What they see as a new development, namely community policing, I see as a return to old forms.

■ ■ ■ ■ ■

CHAPTER 4

NEW POLICING PHILOSOPHIES AND STRATEGIES

The last chapter described the development and basic elements of the professional model of policing, typified by its reactive and incident-driven style of automobile patrol. The events of the 1950s, 1960s, and 1970s underscored the fundamental problems with this model of policing and set the stage for new approaches to police organization and operation. Following serious questions that arose from those tumultuous times—and the scholarly research on police that followed—a number of researchers and practitioners began to think more broadly about the police role in society and how officers should go about their daily activities. The results of the Kansas City Preventive Patrol study demonstrated quite clearly that the prevailing model was not achieving its basic objectives, leaving the field ripe for innovation.

Fortunately, those innovations were quick in coming, and they serve as the focus of this chapter. In 1979, just five years after publication of the Kansas City findings, Herman Goldstein published an article on "problem-oriented policing." In 1982, Wilson and Kelling published their seminal piece on "broken windows" and began the discussion of "community policing." This chapter describes in detail these innovations, including their theoretical foundations, basic elements, diffusion, research examining their effectiveness, and limitations. The chapter then turns attention to more recent innovations, including CompStat and zero tolerance policing, and describes these approaches in the same manner. The chapter concludes with a review of the basic similarities and differences between the various new approaches.

PROBLEM-ORIENTED POLICING

Theoretical Foundations

In 1979, Herman Goldstein published an article in the scholarly journal *Crime and Delinquency,* titled "Improving Policing: A Problem-Oriented Approach." The overall goal of problem-oriented policing is to solve persistent community problems. In order to do this, Goldstein (1979) states that police should begin to view their workload differently; instead of thinking about general categories of crime, they should focus on specific types of crime and then develop strategies to address those crime types. Goldstein's argument focuses on the fundamental weakness of the professional model: its reactive, incident-driven style. Specifically, police officers drive around their sectors on routine patrol, waiting for calls for service. When they receive a call, they respond and deal with the call as quickly as possible, so they can get back on patrol and be available for the next call for service. Goldstein (1979) argues that this reactive approach fails to address the underlying condition that caused the problem, and as a result, police will find themselves back at the same address or location in the near future because the underlying condition still persists. Goldstein (1979) states that police are prisoners of their communications system because it keeps them in a reactive stance and limits any serious planning about community problems. Consider the following diagram:

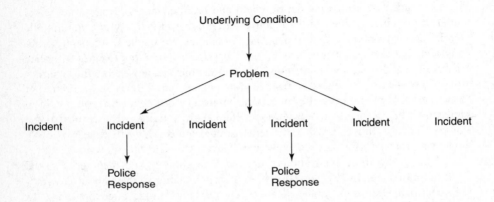

There is an **underlying condition** that is the root cause of the problem. The problem leads to several incidents, and some of those incidents result in a police response. Under the traditional reactive model, the police response is short term and addresses the specific incident. However, the underlying condition is not addressed, and it will continue to produce problems, incidents, and occasional police responses. The underlying conditions that cause problems can involve any number of things, including characteristics of people (offenders, victims, others), the social setting in which people interact, and the physical environment. "**Problem-oriented policing** involves getting police officers and departments to think outside of the box, recognizing connections across like incidents that they may not have been able to see when responding to a seemingly random incident from an incident-based, reactive perspective" (Grant & Terry, 2005, p. 308).

A number of scholars have employed a dental analogy to illustrate the theoretical foundation of problem-oriented policing. Consider this example.

> One morning you wake up with a toothache. You take aspirin and the toothache goes away. Several hours later the pain returns. You schedule an appointment with the dentist, who upon examination discovers a cavity. The dentist fills the cavity and you go on your

way. However, several days later, the pain returns and you make another appointment with the dentist. The dentist this time discovers an infection in the root of the tooth requiring a root canal. After the procedure is completed, the pain is gone. (example borrowed from Reitzel, Leeper Piquero, & Piquero, p. 420, 2005)

In the analogy, the pain from the toothache would be the incident generating a response, or calls for service. The aspirin and first visit to the dentist are the responses, or actions taken by police to temporarily resolve the incident. In both instances, the aspirin and the first dentist visit did not resolve the underlying condition, which was the root infection; consequently, the pain returned (i.e., more calls for service). Finally, in the second visit to the dentist, the underlying condition was identified was addressed. Once the underlying condition was addressed, there was no more pain (i.e., no more calls for service).

The central thrust of problem-oriented policing involves officers recognizing that a problem exists (possibly through repeated calls for service from the same location), identifying the underlying condition that is causing the problem, and then developing a strategy—through a problem-solving process—to address that underlying condition. The problems that arise may appear unrelated or different, but they stem from the same underlying condition. Consider the following police example (with the toothache example as a frame of reference).

An apartment complex changes ownership and the new owner is negligent in "upkeep" of the building and physical grounds. The grass goes uncut for long periods of time and street lights and other lighting fixtures that burn out are not replaced. Tenants' calls regarding repairs to interior and exterior fixtures go unanswered. Trash begins to collect near the complex. The physical deterioration may lead to a social deterioration. Groups of unruly youths may begin hanging around the complex. There may be vandalism, harassment of tenants, noise complaints, even a burglary, and several of these "incidents" come to the attention of the police.

The reactive, incident-driven police officer will respond to the calls for service, handle each one individually and move on to the next call. The problem-oriented police officer would handle this very differently. He or she would identify the problem, perhaps by recognizing the physical deterioration of the complex or simply by taking note of the increasing number of calls for service to that location. Once the problem is identified, the officer would investigate to determine the underlying condition that is causing the problems. In this case, the officer would determine that there had been a change in ownership and that the new owner was delinquent in many of his or her responsibilities. The officer would then devise a strategy to address this underlying condition. The officer could enforce building codes, pressure the owner to make repairs, install new lighting and security fixtures, or address other specific issues.

Problem-oriented policing operates under two basic assumptions. First, problem solving is a strategy that can be employed by all officers in the department as a normal part of their routine, daily responsibilities (Reitzel et al., 2005). Problem-oriented policing is a department-wide strategy; all field officers are to be engaged in the process. Problem-oriented policing does not involves the creation of additional specialized units or even any additional resources. It simply involves a redefining of how currently assigned officers engage in their daily activity. Second, problem-oriented policing assumes that this type of problem-solving activity can be effective in identifying underlying conditions, fashioning effective responses, and ultimately, eliminating the underlying condition and reducing repeat calls for service (Reitzel et al., 2005).

The Basic Elements of Problem-Oriented Policing: The SARA Model

The **SARA** problem-solving **model** serves as the backbone of problem-oriented policing. SARA is an acronym for *scanning, analysis, response,* and *assessment.* SARA represents the problem-solving model that each officer in a problem-oriented police department should employ. In *scanning,* the officer examines his or her beat and seeks to identify a problem. This is the critical stage where the officer recognizes that a series of seemingly unrelated incidents are actually related and caused by the same problem. Scanning can involve simply patrolling an area and noticing changes over time, or it can involve an assessment of recent calls for service or other types of activity.

The second stage, *analysis,* is often considered the heart of the problem-solving model because any mistakes that are made at this stage will lead to inefficient or inappropriate responses at later stages. Analysis involves the officer collecting information and examining the data that have been collected. Importantly, officers are encouraged to gather information from a range of sources, both within and outside the criminal justice system. Valid information sources may include fellow officers, police data (calls for service, arrests, crime reports, stop and frisk data, etc.), residents and business owners in the area, other criminal justice actors (i.e., probation department, district attorney), and officials in other city agencies (e.g., sanitation, housing authority, parks and recreation).

The overall objective of this goal is identification of the underlying condition that is the root cause. This stage of the problem-solving process represents a substantial adjustment for police officers because it is diametrically opposite of what they are used to doing: responding to and handling individual calls as quickly as possibly (in very busy jurisdictions, sometimes doing no more than "triaging" the incidents). The analysis stage often involves a focus on a conceptual framework called the "**crime triangle,**" which emphasizes how crime events should be broken down into core elements: victims, offenders, and problem areas (i.e., opportunity) (Grant & Terry, p. 309, 2005). The underlying condition should be analyzed in these terms to produce a comprehensive understanding of the underlying condition and the problem it creates.

The third stage, *response,* involves building on the analysis of the second stage and developing a strategy to address the underlying condition. Again, officers are encouraged to think broadly about potential responses. Although law enforcement remains a central and often-used response, the nature of the underlying condition may require a multifaceted strategy involving a range of different "partners," many of whom may be outside the criminal justice system. Often, the sources of information at the analysis stage may also be appropriate partners for the response: residents and business owners, church and community leaders, other criminal justice officials, and representatives from other city agencies.

The final stage, *assessment,* involves the officer evaluating the effectiveness of the response. Quite simply, did it work? Has the underlying condition been addressed? Has the problem been eliminated? This is an activity that is new for many police officers. Under the traditional, reactive model, officers generally spend little time thinking about whether their actions have solved the larger problem that led to the incident. In most cases, they do what is necessary to address the immediate issue that led to the call for service, but once that was accomplished, the officer moved on to the next call. Depending on the nature of the underlying condition and the response, the officer may be able to engage in assessment almost immediately following implementation of the response. Changes in the physical environment (lighting, security cameras, picking up trash, painting over graffiti, etc.) and in calls for service can be observed right away. Other changes may be longer term in scope and duration such as changes in the social environment (i.e., rebuilding the sense of community). Importantly, if the officer determines that the response is not effective, he or she is to craft a new response—building on lessons learned from the first effort—and then assess the impact of the second strategy.

In the apartment complex example described above, we can think about the officer's activities at each stage of SARA. The officer's scanning may have focused on the repeated calls for service to the complex or just observation of the physical and social deterioration over time. At the analysis stage, the officer would speak with residents of the complex, review the calls for service, crime reports, and arrest information, and also speak to the owner. The officer would then identify the change in ownership and the subsequent delinquency of the new owner in properly managing the complex as the underlying condition. The officer's response could include targeted and frequent patrols of the area, code enforcement and pressure on the owner to fix lighting and improve the physical condition of the building, coordinating with the sanitation department for trash pickup, and meeting with residents (perhaps convincing them to organize a neighborhood watch). Assessment would involve the officer speaking with residents, noting any changes in the physical and social environment of the complex and monitoring calls for service to the complex.

Although the SARA model is a four-step procedure, the problem-solving process is intended to be both interactive and reciprocal (Scott, 2000). That is, the process is constantly in operation, and the various stages will often link back to one another. For example, assessment of a response may lead back to the development of other responses, but it may also suggest the need for further analysis and/or scanning (Reitzel et al., 2005). Also, experts recognize that the problem-solving process may produce solutions that are not necessarily transferable to other problems and other jurisdictions (Reitzel et al., 2005). In fact, a central element of problem-oriented policing is that the problem-solving process should produce a solution that is specifically tailored to the identified problem and underlying condition. That being said, police departments are well advised to keep a running file of all the underlying conditions that are identified and the solutions that are crafted—both those that are effective and ineffective. This file will serve as a continually growing source of institutional knowledge about what works for specific problems, and while officers may not be able to adopt previously tested solutions "wholesale," at the very least they will not have to start from scratch. Instead, they will have a baseline source of information from which they can "spring board" and craft (and test) their own unique, specifically tailored responses.

Characteristics of the Problem-Oriented Police Department

Given that problem-oriented policing represents a fundamental shift in how both individual officers and the department as a whole function, there are a number of key, defining features that characterize the department that has successfully implemented this strategy. Eck and Spelman (1987) note that there are at least seven defining features:

1. Problem solving will be the standard method of policing, not just an occasionally used tactic.
2. Problem-solving efforts will focus on problems of the public, not police administration.
3. When problems are taken on, police will establish precise, measurable objectives.
4. Police managers will constantly look for ways to get all members of the department involved in solving problems.
5. Officers should consistently undertake thorough analysis using data from many sources, both internal and external to the police agency.
6. Officers will engage in an uninhibited search for solutions to all problems they take on.
7. All members of the department will be involved in problem solving.

Like any other police initiative, successful implementation hinges on several key factors. First, there must be support for problem-oriented policing from the top of the organization down through the chain of command. If line officers sense that support for problem-oriented policing is halfhearted among their supervisors and the chief, they will not take it seriously. The culture of police is deeply entrenched in the traditional reactive model, and it is often difficult to change that culture. Second, there must be accountability for officers: Those who do not engage in the process must be held accountable while those that do engage in problem solving should be rewarded for their efforts. Third, there must be changes in how individual police performance is measured. The traditional approach—simply counting arrests, tickets, etc.—no longer applies for the problem-oriented police officer because, in many cases, arrest may not be the best course of action. Also, the additional time that officers spend engaged in the various components of the SARA model will necessarily limit their time for producing numbers. Last, problem-oriented policing is more likely to be successful if the department actively engages other stakeholders in the initiative, particularly the residents, business owners, church and community leaders, and other city agencies.

Diffusion: How Widespread Is Problem-Oriented Policing?

It is difficult to estimate how many police departments across the country have adopted problem-oriented policing. Because problem-solving is a central component of community policing (see the next section), one could argue that all departments seriously engaged in community policing are also engaged in problem-oriented policing. Also, CompStat, at least as it is applied in New York, incorporates many of the basic elements of the problem-solving process, including analysis, response, and assessment (see the later discussion of CompStat). In fact, one could make a persuasive argument that CompStat is actually problem-oriented policing with a technological flare: The scanning is done with computer-aided statistics and crime mapping, rather than by individual officers. A recent study by Weisburd et al. (2003) shows that CompStat has been widely adopted by police departments across the country (primarily large departments), although there appear to be adaptations to the original model in many of those jurisdictions.

Since 1993, the Police Executive Research Forum (PERF) has given awards to individual officers or entire departments in recognition of successful problem-solving efforts. Called the *Herman Goldstein Award for Excellence in Problem-Oriented Policing,* PERF awards officers/departments who demonstrate innovation in addressing persistent problems and who can show that crime, disorder, or other public safety problems have been successfully addressed (and of course, awardees must also keep with the basic principles laid out by Goldstein) (Reitzel et al., 2005). On its website, PERF lists all applicants for the award by year: From 1993 through 2003, there were approximately 640 applicants. In sum, although exact estimates of the prevalence of problem-oriented policing are elusive, there is evidence to suggest that a substantial number of police departments in the United States have adopted the strategy either in its entirety or just specific components, and either formally or informally.

Research on the Effectiveness of Problem-Oriented Policing

Problem-oriented policing has been studied in numerous jurisdictions, and a growing body of evidence suggests that it can be effective in reducing crime, disorder, and related problems. A few studies are described below.

Newport News, Virginia.   In the mid-1980s, the National Institute of Justice, the research arm of the U.S. Department of Justice, funded an evaluation of problem-oriented policing in Newport News, Virginia. The police department targeted two specific problems to address with the problem-oriented approach: burglaries in the Briarfield Apartment complex and vehicle thefts in the Newport News Shipyards

(Eck & Spellman, 1987). In effect, the department conducted the scanning phase of the model for the officers. In the first case, burglaries in the apartment complex, the assigned detective conducted a survey of residents and discovered that both burglaries and physical problems with the complex were viewed as the most problematic (analysis). Police coordinated with other city agencies to clean up the complex, trash was hauled away, abandoned appliances and cars were removed, and potholes were filled (response). The evaluation showed that reports of burglaries dropped by 35 percent following the response (assessment) (Eck & Spelman, 1987).

In the second case, stolen vehicles from the shipyards, the officer engaged in analysis and discovered that the majority of thefts occurred in a few parking areas. The officer interviewed workers and was able to identify a small number of suspects. The officer also interviewed several convicted felons to ascertain what specific characteristics made some cars more attractive than others for theft, and this information was passed along to workers and security to craft a theft prevention plan. The evaluation determined that auto thefts in the shipyards declined by 55 percent following implementation of the problem-solving initiative (Eck & Spelman, 1987). This early effort in Newport News and the evaluation indicating its effectiveness signaled to other police departments around the country that problem-oriented policing was a viable alternative to the traditional reactive model.

Jersey City, New Jersey. Two separate problem-solving initiatives were implemented in Jersey City. The first initiative focused on public housing, the second more generally on violence. In the public housing initiative, problem-solving teams in six developments were created to identify high-priority problems that included drugs, graffiti, and loitering (Green-Mazerolle, Ready, Terrill, & Waring, 1999). Responses were crafted for each of the identified problems, and the evaluation results showed that: (1) there was a negative correlation between problem-solving activities and calls for service and (2) the decreases in calls for service were greatest in the areas where problem-solving activities were targeted (Green-Mazerolle & Terrill, 1997).

In the second initiative focusing on violence, "violent crime places were matched into twelve pairs with one member of each pair allocated to treatment (i.e., problem solving) conditions in a randomized block field experiment and the other member not allocated to treatment (i.e., the control group)" (Reitzel et al., 2005, p. 425). Officers in the treatment sites engaged in the problem-solving process, identifying a wide range of problems (physical and social disorder, crime, etc.) and implementing a diverse set of responses. Results from an evaluation showed that crime and disorder decreased significantly in the targeted areas (Braga et al., 1999).

Boston. In the early 1990s, Boston experienced an explosion in youth violence and homicide (scanning). In response, a coalition of federal, state, and local agencies implemented the Boston Gun Project, a problem-solving initiative aimed at reducing the prevalence of youth violence (Walker & Katz, 2002). During the analysis phase, researchers and team members discovered that much of the violence was gang-related and was driven by a strong illegal gun market (Kennedy, 1997). The Boston

Gun Project involved a number of activities that targeted the supply and demand for guns.

> Gang members were told that drug markets would be shut down, warrants would be served, the street would swarm with law enforcement officials (including federal presence), bed checks would be performed on probationers, rooms would be searched by parole officers, unregistered cars would be taken away, and disorder offenses such as drinking in public would be pursued. (response—Walker & Katz, 2002, p. 227)

Two years after the project began, youth gang homicides dropped by 70 percent (assessment), fear of crime among residents in the targeted areas dropped by 21 percent, and the percentage of residents having faith in the police to prevent crime increased by 33 percent (Kennedy, 1997). Following the success of the project in Boston, the federal government has funded similar youth gun interdiction programs in 27 other cities including Chicago, Baltimore, New York, Los Angeles, and Rochester.

Richmond, California.   In 1995, after becoming one of the most violent cities in the United States (per capita), the Richmond, California, Police Department implemented a multifaceted problem-solving strategy called the *Comprehensive Homicide Initiative* (White, Fyfe, Campbell, & Goldkamp, 2003). The initiative was developed after the department conducted an extensive review of homicide and violence over the previous several years, as well as a survey of residents and community summits (scanning). Much of the violence was linked to drug dealing, gang activity, and firearms (analysis). Although a significant portion of the initiative involved preventive components, much of it involved targeted and specific enforcement efforts (response)—in tandem with collaboration from other city agencies and the community—focusing on drug, gun, and gang-related violence (White et al., 2003). Annual totals of homicides dropped significantly in the years following the initiative (1996–1998), specifically those in the targeted areas, but it was unclear whether this drop was caused by the problem-solving strategy or if it simply reflected more general crimes patterns in the state and nation. In order to resolve this question, researchers used sophisticated time series analysis to compare homicide trends from 1985 through 1998 in Richmond to 75 other California cities (all cities the same size as Richmond or larger) and discovered that few other cities experienced the same decline as Richmond (White et al., 2003). This evidence suggested that the decline in homicide in Richmond was relatively unique and supported the theory that the problem-solving initiative caused the decrease.

Limitations and Questions

Despite the review of effective problem-oriented initiatives described above, there is additional evidence suggesting that the approach has limitations. Some experts argue that departments that adopt problem-oriented policing often do not fully implement it and equate the strategy with a long line of passing fads that eventually fall by the wayside (Manning, 2005). The police culture is notoriously resistant to change, and problem-oriented policing represents a significant and fundamental shift in the police paradigm. Others have argued that the typical rank and file officer does not have the necessary skill-set to engage in the problem-solving process. The adoption of problem-oriented policing must begin with a substantial retraining of the entire police force in the basic theory, concepts, and expectations of the strategy. This training has often not occurred, leaving officers wondering how they are supposed to go about implementing the new approach. Also, the department itself must be reorganized to support the problem-solving activities of patrol officers. In order to successfully engage in the SARA model, officers must be freed up from racing from one call for service to the next. The problem-solving model requires time and energy, and officers will be unable to successfully engage in it if they remain "slaves to the communications system."

Finally, recent research in San Diego suggests that "full scale POP [problem-oriented policing] is rare" (Cordner & Biebel, 2005, p. 178). The San Diego Police Department (SDPD) has been a strong advocate of problem-oriented policing for more than a decade, yet research suggests that officers rarely engage in the formal SARA model or crime triangle (Cordner & Biebel, 2005). Cordner and Biebel (2005) draw a distinction between everyday problem-solving—which officers frequently engage in—and formal problem-oriented policing with the SARA model (which they do not). There is also some indication that officers in the SDPD have experienced a degree of fatigue with regard to problem-oriented policing that may affect their willingness and ability to engage in the full-fledged problem-solving model.

Despite proponents' arguments that all officers in the department should be engaged in the problem-solving model, the evidence suggests that more realistic expectations may be appropriate. The successful studies described here tended to focus on one large problem (homicide, gun violence, burglaries) and engage a large number of officers in the problem-solving model for that problem. The evidence indicating that problem-oriented policing can be effective when implemented in a targeted manner is compelling. However, there is scant evidence supporting the notion that the model has been adopted and implemented throughout a police department and that the entire rank and file has successfully engaged in the SARA model. Quite simply, the department-wide implementation approach may be impractical and ineffectual, while the more targeted approach—with an emphasis on the rank and file engaging in everyday problem-solving and targeting large problems in groups—seems more feasible and promising.

COMMUNITY-ORIENTED POLICING

Theoretical Foundations

The idea of **community-oriented policing** emerged from two philosophical understandings. First, by the 1970s it had become evident that it was unrealistic to expect the police to deal with the crime problem by themselves. This realization became clear during the 1960s when crime rates increased significantly and the police were unable to control crime. Also, criminological research on the causes of crime began to focus on a range of different causal factors within the family, school, and neighborhood that far exceeded the mandate of the police. If the primary causes of crime involve broken homes, poor parenting, delinquent peers, and poor educational systems, what could the police reasonably be expected to accomplish in terms of crime prevention? Scholars and practitioners began focusing on a cooperative effort among police and the community as a more viable approach to dealing with the crime problem.

Second, in 1982 Wilson and Kelling published their seminal piece called "Broken Windows" in *Atlantic Monthly*. In this article, Wilson and Kelling (1982) make a crucial link between disorder and crime and describe how this link impacts the social fabric of the neighborhood. Their argument centers of the proverbial **broken window,** which, if left unrepaired, sends a message that no one cares about the appearance of the property. In practical terms, the broken window is a metaphor for disorder and indicates that there is a breakdown in the informal social controls that govern behavior in the neighborhood. No one cares so nobody fixed it. The unrepaired broken window will soon draw other signs of disorder: other broken windows, graffiti, broken and unrepaired lighting fixtures, untended lawns and landscaping, and abandoned vehicles. The physical disorder may be followed by social disorder. Families move out of the area, youths begin hanging out on street corners and harassing passersby, and prostitutes and drug dealers begin appearing. The single unrepaired broken window can spark this downward spiral of deterioration. The spread of disorder in the area is facilitated by the fear it creates. Residents begin to avoid spending time outside; they become unconcerned about who is standing on street corners; they become less likely to get involved in community activities; and they become less likely to call the police. The decline in the sense of community and the increasing level of disorder makes the area vulnerable to criminal activity and predatory behavior (Wilson & Kelling, 1982).

Wilson and Kelling (1982) argued that because of this link between disorder, social cohesion, and crime, police should focus their efforts on disorder and the **quality of life offenses** in neighborhoods, and they should work with the community to accomplish this. Quite simply, police can effectively address problems with physical and social disorder: They can remove drunks, aggressive panhandlers, kids on street corners, prostitutes, and open-air drug dealing. They can pressure business owners and tenants to improve the physical environment—improve lighting, cut the grass, paint over graffiti, and fix the broken windows. As police reduce the level of disorder, residents' fear will decrease and the informal social controls will begin to take hold in the community again. Finally, the absence of disorder and the strengthened social cohesion will prevent the spread of serious crime into the area.

Core Features of Community Policing

Police–Community Partnership.   Community policing seeks to build on the theoretical foundation of broken windows by expanding the police mandate and including the community as a partner in crime prevention. "Community policing seeks to broaden the police role to include such issues as fear of crime, order maintenance, conflict resolution, neighborhood decay and social and physical disorder as basic functions of the police" (Walker & Katz, 2002, p. 205). The central argument for community policing is that the best way for police to address disorder and community decay—and, as a result, crime—is to build a collaborative relationship with the residents of the community. This collaborative relationship will provide police with greater access to information and, in turn, will make the police more responsive to community needs (Walker & Katz, 2002).

Bayley (1994) states that two elements are necessary to build a successful partnership: consultation and mobilization. Consultation between police and residents often occurs in community meetings or forums, but can also occur more informally during encounters on the street. The more formal meetings serve a number of purposes:

1. They allow citizens to convey their problems and concerns to police.
2. They allow police to instruct citizens about crime and disorder in the community.
3. They allow citizens to voice any complaints they have about the police.
4. They allow police to describe their past and current activities and to discuss the success of those initiatives. (Bayley, 1994)

Recall that in many places the police and community have had very poor relationships, marked by tension, antagonism, and general unwillingness to cooperate with one another. Chapter 3 described in some detail the police subculture and police working personality, and this component of community policing represents a fundamental shift away from the isolation and "us versus them" mentality that has traditionally characterized the police. "Regardless, a distinctive characteristic of the police under community policing is that the police seek to reposition themselves so that they become an integral part of community life rather than remain distant and alienated from the community as in years past" (Walker & Katz, 2002, p. 206).

According to Bayley (1994), a second key component of the police–community partnership involves mobilization by the residents in an organized manner. The community plays an active role in preventing crime, and this typically occurs through neighborhood or block watches. This mobilization serves a number of objectives. First, it conveys to those interested in crime that the informal social norms of the neighborhood are strong and will resist intrusion (Bayley, 1994). This may or may not produce a deterrent effect. Although this mobilization is recognized as a critical feature in the development of a police–community partnership, there is little evidence to suggest that neighborhood watches prevent crime (Bennett, 1994). Second, and perhaps more importantly, the mobilized community becomes additional eyes and ears—and sources of information—for the police.

Organizational Change.   Community policing represents a significant change in the focus and operation of a police department, and if it is to be successfully implemented, organizational change must occur in several critical areas. These changes are necessary to ensure that officers engage in community-policing activities and to make the department more flexible and amenable to forming a partnership with the community (Walker & Katz, 2002). The first organizational change that must occur involves the structure of the department. Community policing requires that the department become more decentralized, with fewer levels of management and less specialization (Walker & Katz, 2002). Patrol officers require a greater level of discretion to meet with and respond to community needs, and like problem-oriented policing, they need time away from responding to calls for service to accomplish these tasks. Accordingly, managers in the department must play a larger support role in assisting line officers to respond to community needs. Also, community policing requires that officers remain in the same assignments for extended periods of time so they can build the requisite relationships and foster trust among residents and business owners. Frequent reassignment of officers to different beats serves as a barrier to the relationship-building process.

Second, there must be a change in the organizational culture. Most police departments have become wedded to the traditional reactive model, particularly the focus on crime fighting. Community policing involves a recognition that the other police responsibilities—service related functions and order maintenance, for example—are just as important and warrant attention (Cordner, 2005). Also, Chapter 3 described in some detail the traditional "us versus them" view of the community among many police. In Van Maanen's (1978) classic piece called "The Asshole," he argues that

> police tend to view their occupational world as comprised exhaustively of three types of citizens:
>
> 1. Suspicious persons: Those whom the police have reason to believe may have committed a serious offense;
> 2. Assholes: Those who do not accept the police definition of the situation;
> 3. Know nothings: Those who are not either of the first two categories but are not police and therefore, according to police, cannot know what the police are about. (p. 223)

None of the above categories is particularly positive, but community policing requires that police change their view of the third category from "know nothings" to valuable partners whose needs must be met by the police. In many cases, this is a difficult transition.

Problem Solving. Problem solving is a third important feature of community policing. As a result of the police/community partnership, neighborhood problems will be identified and subsequently, police and the community work together to address the problems. Much like problem-oriented policing, the goal of problem solving involves addressing the underlying conditions that are causing the problem. In practical terms, the problem-solving component of community policing does not necessarily follow the formal SARA model, and it is essential that the police and community collaborate in the problem solving process (in problem-oriented policing, the officer engages in the SARA model without direct community involvement, though the community may become part of the response) (Cordner, 2005). Perhaps most important, the problems are identified by the community residents themselves, and together with police, solutions are crafted through a problem-solving process.

Programmatic Elements of Community Policing.   There is no set list of programs or elements that are to be employed when adopting community policing. However, there are clearly some common characteristics from department to department. Cordner (2005) notes that there are four major dimensions of community policing, and he describes the typical elements in each:

- *Philosophical dimension:* The central ideas behind the philosophy.
  - *Citizen input:* Citizens have input in police policies and decisions, usually achieved through town meetings.
  - *Broad police function:* Emphasis on order maintenance, social service, resolving conflict, solving problems, and reducing fear (moving beyond the focus on crime fighting).
  - *Personal service:* Tailoring police functions to local norms, values, and individual needs.
- *Strategic dimension:* The operational concepts that translate philosophy into action.
  - *Re-oriented operations:* Less reliance on car patrol, more emphasis on face-to-face interaction through foot patrol, bicycle patrol; also greater emphasis on disorder and minor offenses (i.e., broken windows).
  - *Geographic focus:* Permanent assignments for officers; focus on holding officers accountable for what occurs in smaller areas (not entire beats or sectors).
  - *Prevention emphasis:* Proactive and preventive orientation; identify underlying conditions to solve current problems and prevent future ones; officers play a social welfare role, especially for juveniles.
- *Tactical dimension:* Programs, practices, and behaviors.
  - *Positive interaction:* Seize opportunities for positive encounters with citizens, either during calls for service or while on patrol; positive interaction builds trust, familiarity, and confidence.
  - *Partnerships:* Community participation in its own protection; this can occur on an individual level or by groups of residents creating more formal organizations; police can facilitate by finding common interests for residents to rally around.
  - *Problem solving:* Includes community input; typically involves problem identification, analysis of the problem; search for a response, and implementation and assessment of the problem; emphasis on a broad range of solutions (not just criminal law).

- *Organizational dimension:* Changes in administration, management, and supervision to support community policing.
  - *Structure:* Decentralized, despecialized, team approach (groups of officers assigned together), civilianization (increased use of non-sworn personnel).
  - *Management:* Greater emphasis on strategic planning, positive supervision (not punitive, more like coaching), mentoring of young officers, empowering officers to show creativity and imagination.
  - *Information:* Avoidance of traditional performance measures (arrests, tickets, etc.), program evaluation, crime analysis, geographic information systems (GIS). (pp. 402–414)

Diffusion

Title 1 of the 1994 Violent Crime Control and Law Enforcement Act, called the "Public Safety Partnership and Community Policing Act," created the Office of Community Oriented Policing Services, otherwise known as the **COPS Office,** and authorized it to spend $9 billion on grants to state and local law enforcement agencies to facilitate the implementation of community policing (Roth, Roehl, & Johnson, 2004). Given the widespread availability of federal funding to support community policing, research indicates that its adoption has been extensive across the United States among both small and large police departments. Maguire and Katz (1997) examined the adoption of community policing in more than 1,600 police agencies. Roth et al. (2004) conducted surveys of police departments in the United States in 1996, 1998, and 2000. The researchers asked police departments about the extent of their use of four basic tenets of community policing: partnership building, problem solving, prevention, and supportive organizational changes. Across these tenets, Roth et al. (2004) queried about the use of no fewer than 40 different tactics, and by 2000, results demonstrate how community policing has taken hold in the United States:

- Partnership building
  - Large agencies—80.1%
  - Small agencies—42.7%
- Problem solving
  - Large agencies—86.5%
  - Small agencies—59.7%
- Prevention
  - Large agencies—76.9%
  - Small agencies—49.5%
- Supportive organizational changes
  - Large agencies—66.0%
  - Small agencies—45.2%

These results do suggest that elements of community policing are more common in large agencies, and the authors caution that the results are self-reported by police and may not reflect actual police practice. Nevertheless, much like the professional model became the goal of police agencies throughout most of the twentieth century, it would appear that community policing has taken over as the benchmark for twenty-first-century law enforcement agencies.

Research on the Effectiveness of Community Policing

Given the shift toward community policing in recent years and the use of federal money to facilitate that shift, there is a substantial body of research examining the impact of community policing. The general findings on the effectiveness of community policing are presented here in two ways. First, Cordner (2005) reviewed more than 60 evaluations of community policing initiatives, and his general conclusions are presented here. Second, one specific initiative, the **Chicago Alternative Policing Strategy (CAPS),** is described in some detail. The CAPS initiative represents perhaps the most extensive and ambitious application of community policing to date.

General Findings.   In his review, Cordner (2005) notes that evaluations of community policing have focused almost exclusively on its tactical aspects—examining its impact on crime, fear of crime, disorder, calls for service, community relations, police officer attitudes, and police officer behavior. While these are clearly important issues to study, research has virtually ignored the effects of philosophical, strategic, and organizational changes on those same outcomes (Cordner, 2005). Cordner's (2005) review of the impact of the tactical aspects of community policing are described below.

- *Crime:* The evidence is mixed. Overall, a slight majority of the studies have detected crime decreases, giving reason for optimism, but evaluation design limitations prevent us from drawing any authoritative conclusions.
- *Fear of crime:* Again the evidence is mixed, but it leans more heavily in the positive direction. The now widely accepted view that community policing helps reduce levels of fear of crime and increases perceptions of safety seems reasonably well founded, although some efforts have failed to accomplish fear reductions.
- *Disorder:* The impact of community policing on disorder, minor crime, incivilities, and signs of crime has not been subjected to careful testing as frequently as its impact on crime and fear. The available evidence suggests, though, that community policing, and especially foot patrol and problem solving, helps reduce levels of disorder, lending partial support to the "broken windows" thesis.
- *Calls for service:* Community policing might reduce calls for service in several ways: Problem solving might address underlying issues that generate calls, collaboration might increase call referrals to other government agencies; foot patrols and mini-stations might receive citizen requests directly, thus heading off calls to central dispatch; and workload management might find alternative

responses for some types of calls. Although the ability of the last approach (workload management) to reduce the volume of calls dispatched to sworn units for immediate response has clearly been demonstrated (McEwen, Connors, & Cohen, 1986), the rest of the evidence on the effects of community policing on calls for service is mixed.

■ *Community relations:* The vast majority of the studies that have looked at the impact of community policing on citizen's attitudes toward the police have uncovered positive effects. Clearly, citizens generally appreciate mini-stations in their neighborhoods, foot patrols, problem-solving efforts, and other forms of community policing.

■ *Police officer attitudes:* A clear majority of the studies that have investigated the effects of community policing on officer's job satisfaction, perceptions of the community and other related attitudes have discovered beneficial effects . . . especially if they are volunteers or members of special units. What is somewhat less certain, however, is (1) whether the positive effects of community policing on officers will survive the long term and (2) whether these benefits are as universal when *all* officers are required to engage in community policing.

■ *Police officer behavior:* Significant anecdotal evidence suggests that foot patrol, problem solving, permanent assignment, mini-stations, and other features of community policing lead to changes in some officers' behavior, but these behavioral effects have only been lightly documented thus far. Evidence also suggests that many officers resist changing their behavior. (pp. 414–417)

The Chicago Alternative Policing Strategy (CAPS) Program.   CAPS leaders estimated that it would take up to five years to fully implement the program. Although the initiative was established citywide, five districts (each with approximately 500,000 residents) served as the focus of the evaluation. The CAPS program was implemented based on six guiding principles:

1. The program would involve the entire police department and city.
2. Officers would be assigned to permanent beat assignments.
3. Officers would receive substantial training in the principles, objectives, and strategies of community policing.
4. There would be a high level of community involvement, citizen input, and partnership with the police.
5. There would be a close link between the police and other city agencies.
6. Crime analysis, especially geographic analysis of crime patterns, would play an important role. (Skogan & Hartnett, 1997)

Through regular meetings between police and citizens, a wide range of problems were identified. Drug dealing was the most commonly cited problem, but many of the other most prominent issues involved disorder-type problems: youth problems, abandoned cars, noise problems, litter and garbage, youth curfews, public drinking and loitering, and abandoned buildings (Skogan & Hartnett, 1997). Based on the issues that arose in specific neighborhoods, police and residents engaged is a multitude of approaches to alleviate the problems.

The evaluation of CAPS, much like Cordner's review above, indicated that findings were mixed. Some goals were achieved while others were not. Importantly, results indicate that police did engage in a significant amount of problem solving, and in the evaluated districts there was less crime, less fear of crime, less gang activity, and more positive attitudes toward the police (Skogan & Hartnett, 1997). The evaluation suggested that community policing could be successfully implemented on a department-wide scale in a major urban police agency (Walker & Katz, 2002). Perhaps the most disappointing finding involved the lack of citizen involvement in certain poor, high-crime areas. In particular, Latinos, low-income households, and those without high school diplomas were not engaged by the CAPS program (Walker & Katz, 2002).

Limitations and Questions

Despite some promising results from the CAPS evaluation and more generally from Cordner's review of current research, there are some well-defined problems with community policing. Going back to the CAPS evaluation, program leaders were confronted with a number of significant obstacles during implementation of the program. First, the public presented strong opposition to two elements of the program, funding revenue to be generated through a proposed tax increase and the closing of several precinct houses (Walker & Katz, 2002). Second, the rank and file of the department was not overly supportive of the initiative, especially young, white male officers. Third, CAPS struggled with freeing up officers' time to engage in community policing activities: As one of the largest cities in the United States, citizens in Chicago place a tremendous number of calls for service. Last, given the new philosophy and officer activities, the police department struggled with supervision issues (recall that community policing requires officers to be given more discretion) and performance evaluation issues (Walker & Katz, 2002).

A number of other problems or limitations associated with community policing have been raised by scholars, researchers, and practitioners. In large part because of the availability of federal funding, many departments have adopted community policing without careful planning. Departments that expand too rapidly without garnering cooperation from the community, without retraining the rank and file, and without considering the organizational implications of the initiative are doomed for failure. Others have raised the question of whether it is appropriate for police to be engaged as community organizers and involved in non-law-enforcement-related activities (Walker & Katz, 2002). Also, in many police departments where there is a long history of corruption, brutality, and other deviant behavior, the increased discretion for line officers and problems with maintaining supervision and accountability may pose very serious problems for police leadership. Also, how will community policing take hold in crime-ridden, impoverished areas where there is no sense of community, certainly no community consensus, and no desire among the residents of the area to work with the police? Can there be community policing if there is no community?

Manning (1984) argues that community policing rests on ten major assumptions and that these assumptions are "largely untested and untestable."

1. People desire to see police officers in their local areas of residence and business on a regular and casual basis.
2. The more police they see, the more they will be satisfied with police practices.
3. The more police they see (to some unknown limit), the more secure they will feel.
4. People yearn for personal contact of a nonadversarial character with police.
5. The public is more concerned about crime than disorder.
6. There is a single public, a single public mood, and a "common good" that is known and coherently represented.
7. People are dissatisfied with current police practices.
8. Previous policing schemes have been shown to have failed.
9. Public satisfaction as measured in polls is a valid index of "public opinion."
10. The police are responsible for defending, defining, expanding, and shaping the common good of the community by active means.
11. Community policing best meets the above needs.

Greene and Mastrofski (1988) boil down the discussion of community policing to one simple question: Is it reality or rhetoric? More specifically, Does community policing represent something new, or is it a way to appear progressive and innovative without abandoning traditional policing? The answer to this question is complex and, to some extent, still unknown. Manning (2005), however, is skeptical:

> Community policing would require a change in the uses of the law; in the standards used to apply the law and order enforcement; in the overall contracts governing police and the public and the degree of centralization, structure, hierarchy and formalization of such matters as recruitment, evaluation, promotion and rewards in police departments. The implications of this argument are that, short of making changes in the direction indicated, much of the political rhetoric about community policing is ideology, yearning for the past, and a wish to respond to projected public "demands." (p. 32)

Yet, the results of the CAPS evaluation and Cordner's (2005) review would seem to indicate that there is some "reality," especially for the potential of tactical elements to influence important outcomes such as crime, fear of crime, and citizen and police attitudes.

COMPSTAT

Background

CompStat, or computer-driven crime statistics, emerged as the centerpiece of the New York Police Department Crime Control Model during the mid 1990s. Prior to delving into the discussion of CompStat and its various components, it is useful to review the context in which the model emerged. This background provides an important foundation for understanding the development and diffusion of the CompStat model. First, during the late 1980s and early 1990s, major urban centers in the United States experienced substantial increases in violent crime and homicide, mostly as a result of the crack cocaine epidemic and turf battles over control of its highly profitable drug market. At the height of the crime surge, New York City experienced more than 2,000 homicides in one year.

Second, soon-to-be mayor Rudolph Guiliani seized the increase in crime as a major issue in his mayoral platform, promising to abandon the then-current community-policing approach for a return to more traditional crime-fighting. Once elected, Guiliani and Commissioner **William Bratton** adopted a zero tolerance approach (see next section) characterized by a crackdown on quality of life and order maintenance offenses.

Third, crime in the New York City transit system was rampant. Ridership dropped off substantially in large part due to violent crime, robberies in particular, and the significant amount of disorder—trash, graffiti, homelessness, and aggressive panhandling. As head of the New York Transit police, William Bratton (with Jack Maple) developed the CompStat model and targeted three specific problems: reducing robberies (there were 30 to 40 per day), eliminating disorder, and reducing fare evasion (turnstile jumping, which was costing the transit system between $80,000 and $120,000 per day). After success in the Transit police and a brief stop in Boston, Bratton returned to New York as Commissioner of the NYPD and brought CompStat with him.

The Stages of CompStat

CompStat represents a vastly different approach to the management of police operations and involves a return to the principle that police have the ability to prevent and reduce crime (recall that following the 1960s and 1970s there were serious questions about the police ability to control crime). In simple terms, CompStat involves the use of computer-generated statistics to analyze crime problems and develop appropriate responses. Under this model, timely analysis of data becomes the foundation for police management and operations—the "engine" that drives the department (McDonald 2002) CompStat involves a five-stage process:

1. Specific objectives
2. Timely and accurate intelligence
3. Effective strategies and tactics

4. Rapid deployment of personnel and resources
5. Relentless follow-up and assessment (p. 10)

Specific Objectives. The identification of specific and measurable objectives is a critical first part of the CompStat model. The identification of objectives—and communication of those objectives to the rest of the department—sends a message that the leadership is committed to addressing these serious issues. All subsequent work that the department engages in is directed at achieving these objectives. McDonald (2002) recommends that the department select approximately five objectives that can be reached within one year, or other reasonable period of time. Bratton identified seven objectives when he came to the NYPD:

1. Reducing the number of guns on the street.
2. Curbing youth violence.
3. Driving drug dealers out of New York.
4. Breaking the cycle of domestic violence.
5. Reclaiming public space.
6. Reducing auto-related crime.
7. Rooting out corruption and building integrity in the NYPD. (McDonald, 2002)

Accurate and Timely Intelligence. The second critical stage of CompStat involves information. This information is used to direct and focus the entire department's crime-fighting efforts.

> If the police are to respond effectively to crime and criminal events, officers at all levels of the organization must have accurate knowledge of when particular types of crimes are occurring, how and where the crimes are being committed, and who the criminals are. The likelihood of an effective police response to crime increases proportionally as the accuracy of this intelligence increases. (NYPD, 1995, p. 2)

The most important feature of this CompStat step is a data system in which police officers record accurate data in a timely fashion, which can then be analyzed in nearly real time. Data come from a host of sources including the department's management information system (MIS), intelligence and field interrogation reports, informants, information from private security and other public agencies, and citizens. The second important feature of this stage is **geographic crime analysis** (i.e., GIS, or pin-mapping) that provides visible pictures of problems across the city and within precincts over time. The computer mapping and data analysis seek to identify two trends:

1. Hot spots: Series of crimes occurring in one general location.
2. Crime patterns: Same types of crime occurring in several locations.

As the quote above suggests, all officers in the department should have access to this information, and ideally, updated data will be available for review on a daily basis.

Effective Tactics.   The third stage of CompStat, effective tactics, seeks to utilize the information from stage two and to develop appropriate and effective responses.

> Effective tactics are prudently designed to bring about the desired result of crime reduction, and they are developed after studying and analyzing the information gleaned from our accurate and timely crime intelligence. In order to avoid merely displacing crime and quality of life problems, and in order to bring about permanent change, these tactics must be comprehensive, flexible, and adaptable to the shifting crime trends we identify and monitor. (NYPD, 1995, p. 2)

There are a number of key points in this stage. First, the tactics are designed based on a careful analysis of the available data, which represents a significant move away from the traditional, reactive style of policing. In effect, intelligence and data have replaced calls for service as the engine driving the department. Second, there is a conscious effort to eliminate problems, not simply displace them. Third, the effective tactics are developed at the now-famous CompStat meetings, where officers are gathered together to examine problems, develop solutions, and return to discuss the potential impact of previously employed tactics. At these twice-weekly meetings, which sometimes are quite adversarial, patrol commanders are "called to the carpet" for the problems that emerge in their areas and for their ability or inability to respond to those problems. For example, if the data show a rash of purse snatchings in the 75th precinct over the last two weeks, officers at the CompStat meeting will develop a response to the problem. At the next meeting, the command staff will call the commander forward to report on his or her progress in dealing with the purse-snatching problem. If the problem has not been addressed, new solutions will be sought. There is a strong emphasis on accountability: Failure to respond effectively to a problem has led to the reassignment of patrol commanders.

These meetings are unique in a couple of other ways as well. First, under the traditional approach each specialized unit operates almost independently with little interaction and virtually no information sharing. The CompStat meetings bring together officers from all relevant units and remove the traditional barriers to information sharing, such as time, distance, and different objectives (McDonald, 2002). Second, under this model, patrol is the central focus of the police effort. Patrol is held accountable for crime in a given area while investigation and other specialized units are aligned to support patrol activity.

Rapid Deployment of Personnel and Resources.   Once the tactics have been identified, the next stage of CompStat involves implementation.

> Once a tactical plan has been developed, an array of personnel and other necessary resources are promptly deployed. Although some tactical plans might involve only patrol personnel, for example, experience has proven that the most effective plans require that personnel from several units and enforcement functions work together to address the problem. A viable and comprehensive response to a crime or quality of life problem generally demands that patrol personnel, investigators and support personnel bring their expertise and resources to bear in a coordinated effort. (NYPD, 1995, p. 2)

Key points at this stage include the prompt deployment of resources, utilizing personnel from many different units, and applying the expertise of those personnel in a coordinated and targeted effort. Given that the CompStat meetings are held regularly, patrol commanders will be expected to report back within days on the relative success of the tactics, and the commander will be held accountable for those results (or lack thereof). In fact, some have pointed to this accountability as perhaps the most critical element of CompStat: Failure to address the identified problem will result in negative consequences for the commander (whether that involves a "dressing down" at the meeting, re-assignment, or something in between).

The tactics that are deployed during CompStat, at least with the New York experience, tend to be traditional law enforcement and crime-control activities. These include additional patrol, targeted sweeps, surveillance, and use of undercover officers and informants. That being said, it is feasible that the resources of other city agencies could be brought to bear if the particular problem called for it. Other agencies that could play a role include federal law enforcement (Drug Enforcement Agency [DEA], Federal Bureau of Investigation [FBI], etc.), Probation and Parole, District Attorney's Office, Housing and Transit Authority, and Sanitation.

Relentless Follow-up and Assessment. The final step of the CompStat model is the element that, more than likely, seems most unnatural to police officers: follow-up and assessment.

> As in any problem-solving endeavor, an on-going process of rigorous follow-up and assessment is absolutely essential to ensure that the desired results are actually being achieved. This evaluation component also permits us to assess the viability of particular tactical responses and to incorporate the knowledge we gain in our subsequent tactics development efforts. By knowing how well a particular tactic worked on a particular crime or quality of life problem, and by knowing which specific elements of the tactical response worked most effectively, we are better able to construct and implement effective responses for similar problems in the future. The follow-up and assessment process also permits us to re-deploy resources to meet newly identified challenges once a problem has abated. (NYPD, 1995, p. 2)

Clearly, the CompStat model recognizes the critical importance of assessing the impact of their deployed tactics. This final assessment piece helps the department to determine if the problem has been successfully addressed, allowing them to target another problem and reassign resources. If the problem persists, new or modified tactics can be designed, deployed, and then assessed. Finally, the CompStat model recognizes the importance of not "re-inventing the wheel" every time a problem is identified. Rather, the evaluation component allows the department to maintain a record of successful tactics that can be drawn upon when the same or similar problems emerge in different areas—or re-emerge in the same area.

The Six Core Components

In their study of CompStat, Weisburd et al. (2003) identify six key features of the strategy. These core components include mission clarification, internal accountability, geographic organization of command, organizational flexibility, data-driven problem identification and assessment, and innovative problem solving. Although some of these components are self-evident from the description of the CompStat stages above, they warrant special attention because they are, in large part, responsible for the popularity and success of the CompStat model in New York.

1. *Mission Clarification:* Top management is responsible for clarifying and exalting the core features of the department's mission. . . . Mission clarification includes a demonstration of management's commitment to specific goals for which the organization and its leaders can be held accountable, such as reducing crime by ten percent in a year.

2. *Internal Accountability:* Internal accountability must be established so that people in the organization are held directly responsible for carrying out organizational goals. Internal accountability in CompStat establishes middle managers as the central actors in carrying out the organizational mission, and it holds them directly accountable for the actions of their subordinates.

3. *Geographic Organization of Operational Command:* Organizational power is shifted to the commanders of geographic units. . . . Operational command is focused on the policing of territories, so central decision-making authority on police operations is delegated to commanders with territorial responsibility (i.e., precincts).

4. *Organizational Flexibility:* Middle managers are not only empowered with the authority to make decisions in responding to problems, but they are also provided with the resources necessary to be successful in their efforts. CompStat requires that the organization develop the capacity and the habit of changing established routines to mobilize resources when and where they are needed for strategic application.

5. *Data-Driven Problem Identification and Assessment:* CompStat requires that data are made available to identify and analyze problems and to track and assess the department's response. Data are made available to all relevant personnel on a timely basis and in a readily usable format.

6. *Innovative Problem-Solving Tactics:* Middle managers are expected to select responses because they offer the best prospects of success. . . . Innovation and experimentation are encouraged; use of best available knowledge about practices in expected. (Weisburd et al., 2003, pp. 427–429)

The core features of the original CompStat model in New York represent a substantial deviation from the traditional professional model. Terms like "data-driven," "innovative problem solving," "organizational flexibility," and "geographic organization" are foreign to the model of policing that dominated most of the twentieth century. These core components seem even more remarkable considering they were applied to the largest police department in the United States, with over 40,000 sworn personnel. The next section describes the adoption of this CompStat model elsewhere and whether the original model has remained intact, as well as the impact of the approach.

Diffusion and Impact of CompStat

Diffusion. Although CompStat was created just over a decade ago in New York, recent research indicates that it "has spread widely and quickly across larger American police agencies" (Weisburd et al., 2003, p. 444). A survey of large police departments (with 100 or more sworn officers) in 1999 found that one-third had implemented CompStat or a similar data-driven strategy and that another one-quarter were in the planning stages to implement such a program (Weisburd et al., 2003). Just five years after it was developed, more than half of large police departments in the United States were using CompStat (or a version of it) or would be soon. The diffusion of CompStat certainly rivals that of community policing, especially since there is no federal "CompStat agency" (like the COPS office) that provides federal funding and promotes the strategy.

There are several reasons for the widespread diffusion of CompStat. First, Weisburd et al. (2003) note that police departments were already using many of the elements of CompStat before it was officially developed, such as problem solving and crime mapping. Second, the NYPD has traditionally played a leadership role in U.S. policing, and other departments around the country have often turned to New York as a model to emulate. Third, Weisburd et al. (2003) note that CompStat is popular because, in many ways, it represents a refocus on crime for the police. Many police departments never fully embraced community policing because of its emphasis on working with the community and on addressing disorder. "Rather, it [CompStat] preserves—indeed, claims to reinvigorate—the traditional hierarchical structure of the military model of policing, a structure that has been attacked by a powerful reform wave over the last two decades" (Wesiburd et al., 2003, p. 446). Last, CompStat has been adopted across the country for its potential to reduce crime. The adoption of CompStat in New York coincided with dramatic decreases in crime, and the originators of the model have touted CompStat as the driving force behind that decline (see the next section for more detail).

The adoption of CompStat has been much less common in smaller police departments across the country. Many small departments lack the technology and resources to sufficiently analyze crime on a nearly real-time basis. Also, smaller departments do not have the luxury of threatening middle managers with reassignment if they fail to effectively respond to a problem because there may be only one middle manager and nowhere else to reassign him or her. Finally, in many rural and small-town jurisdictions, there simply is not enough crime—hot spots and crime patterns, in particular—to justify the adoption of CompStat.

Impact. There are at least two important ways to think about the impact of CompStat: first, what impact has it had on the function and operations of police departments; and second, what impact has it had on crime. In New York, the implementation of CompStat led to a complete refocus of the NYPD, and it has revolutionized how the department responds to crime. The twice-weekly CompStat meetings define and shape the operations of the department through analysis of crime data and brainstorming to develop responses. It seems less clear that other departments who have adopted CompStat have applied all of the components of the original model (see above), or that they have experienced the dramatic shift in police operations as a result (Weisburd et al., 2003).

The second way to think about the impact of CompStat involves its potential to control crime. From 1993 through 1997, the number of felony criminal complaints in New York dropped by more than 40 percent, including a 60 percent drop in homicides, a 12 percent drop in rape, a 48 percent drop in robbery, and a 46 percent drop in burglary (Green, 1999). William Bratton, former Mayor Guiliani, and others have pointed to CompStat—in conjunction with zero tolerance policing (see next section)—as the reason for the dramatic decline in crime. New Orleans and Minneapolis have also reported significant drops in crime following the adoption of CompStat (Walsh, 2001). In 1996, CompStat won the *Innovations in American Government* award from the Ford Foundation and the John F. Kennedy School of Government at Harvard University.

However, other researchers question the causal link between CompStat and the crime reductions in New York. During that same time, crime decreases were documented nationally and in many places where CompStat had not been embraced. Criminologists point to a number of factors for the overall crime decrease in the 1990s, including the maturation of drug markets, the aging and demographics of the country (i.e., baby boomers), declining unemployment rates and a healthy economy, and the mass incarceration of drug offenders. Green (1999) compared New York to San Diego, which employed a community policing approach and achieved comparable reductions in crime. In short, the actual impact of CompStat on crime in both New York and elsewhere remains a subject of great debate. Criminologists almost universally agree that changes in crime patterns are rarely caused by one factor, but it seems clear that CompStat has the potential to make a significant contribution to crime control. The next few years will offer more definitive evidence about the size and nature of that contribution.

ZERO TOLERANCE POLICING

The Principles of Zero Tolerance Policing

A fourth strategy of policing that has emerged over the last twenty years is called **zero tolerance policing.** Like community policing, zero tolerance is based on the broken windows theory, and as a result, it calls for police to focus on disorder and minor crime (i.e., quality of life offenses).

> It is characterized by interventions that aggressively enforce criminal and civil laws and that are conducted for the purpose of restoring order to communities. It is believed that through aggressive enforcement of disorder, residents will be more inclined to care for their community, which will increase order, which in turn will lead to a reduction in the fear of crime and ultimately signal to potential criminals that law breaking will not be tolerated. (Walker & Katz, 2002, p. 228)

Zero tolerance policing is distinctive in several ways. First, there is no partnership between the community and the police in zero tolerance policing. From the zero tolerance perspective, the community is likely unable to possess the strong institutions and social cohesiveness to effectively partner with police in crime control efforts (Walker & Katz, 2002). Second, there is no emphasis on identifying the underlying conditions or engaging in any sort of problem-solving process in the zero tolerance model. It simply involves a law enforcement response to low-level offenders such as fare-beaters, prostitutes, vagrants and loiterers, and aggressive panhandlers. Third, zero tolerance is place-specific: It involves targeting disorder and crime is specific neighborhoods (i.e., the aggressive panhandlers on subway platforms). Last, zero tolerance does not involve any sort of innovation like the three previously described strategies (POP, COP, and CompStat). It simply involves a back-to-the basics approach that focuses on low-level crime and disorder (Walker & Katz, 2002). Greene (2000: 318) states that:

> Zero tolerance policing has its roots in the suppressive aspect of policing. In some respects it returns the police to a more traditional stance *vis-à-vis* law enforcement, a direction that is actively supported within many American police departments.

The Impact of Zero Tolerance Policing

The most well-known application of zero tolerance policing occurred in New York City during the 1990s. Bratton and Guiliani implemented the zero tolerance philosophy in conjunction with the CompStat model to address the social and physical disorder of the city. As mentioned previously, there were significant crime reductions in New York during the 1990s, but the role that zero tolerance and CompStat played in that decrease remains unknown. However, the level of disorder in targeted areas of New York City has clearly decreased substantially. The subways, Times Square, and Central Park, for example, look and feel very different now than they did in the late 1980s. As a result, there would seem to be a more plausible link between the level of disorder and zero tolerance policing. An evaluation of zero tolerance policing in Chandler, Arizona, similarly found that the strategy produced clear reductions in levels of disorder and minor offenses, but there was no clear impact on more serious crime (Katz, Webb, & Schaefer, 2001).

Green (1999) questions the value of zero tolerance, given its consequences. The number of citizen complaints filed with the Civilian Complaint Review Board (CCRB) in New York City increased more than 60 percent between 1992 and 1996. Joel Berger, a civil rights attorney in New York, notes that civil rights claims against the police increased by 75 percent from 1994 to 1998. In 1996, Amnesty International (1996) published a report concluding that police brutality and excessive force was widespread in the NYPD and that the deviant behavior was most frequent in minority and poor neighborhoods. In 1997, Abner Louima was sodomized and beaten in an NYPD precinct house in Brooklyn (see Chapter 8 for more discussion of the Louima case). Green (1999) links the "hyperaggressive crime-control tactics" of zero tolerance to these indicators of police problem behavior and tension between police and minority neighborhoods, noting that San Diego experienced significant decreases in crime without the concomitant increase in civilian complaints. Concluding that the effectiveness and long-term impact of zero tolerance policing remains unknown, Walker and Katz (2002) highlight a number of potential problems with the strategy including:

- Its impact on police community relations (because of overly aggressive officers).
- Its potential to increase crime in the long run (as arrest records for targeted individuals hinder their ability to find and maintain employment).
- Its disproportionate impact on poor and minority communities.

COP, POP, COMPSTAT, AND ZERO TOLERANCE: SIMILARITIES AND DIFFERENCES

There are some very clear similarities and differences among the four strategies described in this chapter. It is useful to think about those commonalties and defining features in order to crystallize our understanding of each. A number of the distinctive features of zero tolerance policing were mentioned above: no community involvement, no problem solving, and strictly traditional law enforcement activities. At least foundationally, though, zero tolerance and community policing share the broken windows theory. Community policing, problem-oriented policing, and CompStat represent a new approach to police organization and operations, and all share an emphasis on the problem solving process. In fact, many argue that problem-oriented policing is a central feature of community policing. Building partnerships with the community, the most important feature of community policing, is not a requisite component of problem-oriented policing or CompStat, however (especially as implemented in New York). McDonald (2002) argues, however, the CompStat is compatible with a community policing approach, where the CompStat process would function as the core problem-solving component in conjunction with building community partnerships, focusing on broken windows, etc. Although CompStat is a problem-solving approach, it differs from problem-oriented policing in that the scanning and assessment is done during the CompStat meetings by middle managers, not by line officers (as is POP). CompStat is most distinctive because of its data-driven nature, with crime analysis determining the operations of the department.

The four strategies also differ in the amount of empirical support for their impact. CompStat, at least in New York, have clearly revolutionalized how the NYPD conducts its daily business. One of the critiques of community policing, and to a lesser extent problem-oriented policing, is that many departments have failed to fully embrace the true spirit of these approaches (and in effect, they are nothing more than "window dressing"). With regard to their impact on crime and disorder, there is at least some evidence supporting a positive impact for each. With zero tolerance, the impact seems to be limited to disorder and quality-of-life issues. The evidence of an impact on crime seems strongest for problem-oriented policing, although the exact role of CompStat in New York and other places remains unknown.

Finally, Greene (2000) compares these four strategies and the traditional professional model along twelve dimensions, including the focus of policing, forms of intervention, range of police activity, amount of discretion at the line level, focus of the police culture, locus of decision-making, communication flow, range of community involvement, linkage with other agencies, type of organization and command focus, implications for organizational change/development, and measurement of success. Although the results of this work are too lengthy to document here, there are clearly some important differences among the various approaches along these important organizational and structural dimensions. In sum, although there are certainly instances where CompStat, community, problem-oriented, and zero tolerance policing represented little more than buzz words to secure grant funding or placate the community, it seems clear that there has been wave of innovation in U.S. policing in recent years. In fact, David Bayley (1994), a noted police scholar, remarked that "the last decade of the twentieth century may be the most creative period in policing since the modern police officer was put onto the streets of London in 1829" (p. 101).

SUMMARY

Historically, this chapter picked up as the United States came out of the tumultuous 1960s with serious concerns about the state of policing and the traditional, professional model. These concerns were reinforced by the seminal police research conducted during the 1960s and 1970s, particularly the Kansas City Preventive Patrol study. As the limitations of the professional model became clear, scholars, researchers, and practitioners began thinking about new ways in which the police could be organized and how they could accomplish their objectives on a daily basis. This chapter describes the four major strategies that emerged from the 1970s through the 1990s: problem-oriented policing, community policing, CompStat, and zero tolerance policing. These new strategies represent a revolution in U.S. policing, as focus has shifted away from the professional model toward one or more of these new approaches.

Each new strategy was described in detail, focusing on the theoretical foundation, basic elements and tactics, diffusion, and research supporting its effectiveness. Very clearly, these four strategies are not mutually exclusive, and in fact, in many ways they build upon each other and can be used in a variety of different combinations. This is perhaps best illustrated through the discussion of similarities and differences at the end of the chapter. Importantly, evidence on the effectiveness of these new approaches is mostly "not in." There is some empirical support for problem-oriented and community policing, but contradictory findings have also emerged to prevent definitive conclusions from being drawn. In short, COP and POP have worked in some places, but not in others. Despite its relatively short history, Comp-Stat has spread quickly among large police departments in the United States, although there is some evidence suggesting that components of the CompStat model were widely used prior to the coining of the term in New York. Although the adoption of CompStat has coincided with crime decreases in several cities, the exact contribution of CompStat to the reduction remains unknown. Finally, there is some evidence to suggest that zero tolerance policing can effectively reduce disorder and quality of life offenses, but there is little empirical support for its purported impact on more serious crime. And, at least in New York, the approach has appeared to play a contributing role in straining police community relations through over-aggressive tactics.

KEY TERMS

Bratton, William
Broken windows
Chicago Alternative Policing Strategy
   (CAPS)
Community-oriented policing
CompStat
COPS office

Crime triangle diffusion
Geographic crime analysis
Problem-oriented policing
Quality of life offenses
SARA model
Underlying condition
Zero tolerance policing

DISCUSSION QUESTIONS

1. Describe the SARA model and each of its components.

2. What is the broken windows theory? How does it relate to policing?

3. What are the key elements of community policing?

4. What are the six important features of the CompStat model?

5. What is zero tolerance policing? How is it different from COP and POP?

6. Do COP and POP work? What does the research tell us?

REFERENCES

Amnesty International. (1996). *Police brutality and excessive force in the New York City Police Department.* New York: Amnesty International.
Bayley, D. (1994). *Police for the future.* New York: Oxford Press.
Bennett, T. (1994). Community policing on the ground: Developments in Britain. In D. Rosenbaum (Ed.), *The challenge of community policing.* Thousand Oaks, CA: Sage.
Braga, A.A., Weisburd, D.L., Waring, E.J., Mazerolle, L.G., Spellman, W., & Gajewski, G. (1999). Problem-oriented policing in violent crime places: A randomized controlled experiment. *Criminology, 37,* 541–580.
Cordner, G. (2005). Community policing: Elements and effects. In R.G. Dunham & G.P. Alpert (Eds.), *Critical issues in policing* (5th ed.). Long Grove, IL: Waveland Press.

Cordner, G., & Biebel, E.P. (2005). Problem-oriented policing in practice. *Criminology and Public Policy, 4*(2), 155–180.

Eck, J., & Spelman, W. (1987). *Problem-solving: Problem-oriented policing in Newport News.* Research in Brief. Washington, DC: National Institute of Justice.

Goldstein, H. (1979). Improving policing: A problem-oriented approach. *Crime and Delinquency, 25,* 236–258.

Grant, H.B., & Terry, K.J. (2005). *Law enforcement in the 21st century.* Boston: Allyn and Bacon.

Green, J.A. (1999). Zero tolerance: A case study of police policies and practices in New York City. *Crime and Delinquency, 45* (2), 171–187.

Greene, J.R. (2000). Community policing in America: Changing the nature, structure and function of the police. In Horney (Ed.), *Policies, processes, and decisions of the criminal justice system, criminal justice 2000.* Volume 3. Washington, DC: Government Printing Office.

Greene, J.R., & Mastrofski, S.D. (1988). *Community policing: Rhetoric or reality.* New York: Praeger.

Green-Mazerolle, L., Ready, J., Terrill, W., & Waring, E. (1999). Problem-oriented policing in public housing: The Jersey City evaluation. *Justice Quarterly, 17*(1), 129–155.

Green-Mazerolle, L., & Terrill, W. (1997). Problem-oriented policing in public housing: Identifying the distribution of problem places. *Policing, 20,* 235–255.

Katz, C.M., Webb, V.J., & Schaefer, D.R. (2001). An assessment of the impact of quality-of-life policing on crime and disorder. *Justice Quarterly, 18*(4), 825–877.

Kennedy, D. (1997). *Juvenile gun violence and gun markets in Boston.* Washington, DC: National Institute of Justice.

Maguire, E.R., & Katz, C.M. (1997). *Community policing, loose coupling and sensemaking in American police agencies.* Presented at the annual meeting of the American Society of Criminology in San Diego, California.

Manning, P.K. (1984). Community-based policing. *American Journal of Police, 3,* 205–277.

Manning, P.K. (2005). Problem-solving? *Criminology and Public Policy, 4* (2), 149–154.

McDonald, P.P. (2002). *Managing police operations: Implementing the New York crime control model—CompStat.* Belmont, CA: Wadsworth.

McEwen, J.T., Connors III, E.F., & Cohen, M.I. (1986) *Evaluation of the differential police responses field test.* Washington, DC: National Institute of Justice.

New York City Police Department. (1995). *The CompStat process.* New York: Office of Management Analysis and Planning, New York City Police Department.

Reitzel, J.D., Leeper Piquero, N., & Piquero, A.R. (2005). Problem-oriented policing. In R.G. Dunham & G.P. Alpert (Eds.), *Critical issues in policing* (5th ed.; pp. 419–431). Long Grove, IL: Waveland Press.

Roth, J.A., Roehl, J., & Johnson, C.C. (2004). Trends in community policing. In W.G. Skogan, (Ed.), *Community policing: Can it work?* Belmont, CA: Wadsworth.

Scott, M. (2000). *Problem-oriented policing: Reflections on the first 20 years.* Washington, DC: U.S. Department of Justice, COPS Office.

Skogan, W.G., & Hartnett, S.M. (1997). *Community policing, Chicago style.* New York: Oxford University Press.

Van Maanen, J. (1978). The asshole. In P.K. Manning, & J. Van Maanen (Eds.), *Policing: A view from the street.* Santa Monica: Goodyear Publishing.

Walker, S., & Katz, C.M. (2002). *The police in America: An introduction.* New York: McGraw-Hill.

Walsh, W.F. (2001). CompStat: An analysis of an emerging police managerial paradigm. *Policing: An International Journal of Police Strategies and Management, 24* (3), 347–362.

Weisburd, D., Mastrofski, S.D., McNally, A.M., Greenspan, R., & Willis, J.J. (2003). Reforming to preserve: CompStat and strategic problem-solving in American policing. *Criminology and Public Policy, 2,* 421–456.

White, M.D., Fyfe, J.J., Campbell, S.P., & Goldkamp, J.S. (2003). The police role in preventing homicide: Considering the impact of problem-oriented policing on the prevalence of murder. *Journal of Research in Crime and Delinquency, 40* (2), 194–225.

Wilson, J.Q., & Kelling, G.L. (1982). Broken windows: The police and neighborhood safety. *Atlantic Monthly, 249,* 29–38.

SCHOLAR'S PERSPECTIVE

The Brooklyn North Neighborhood Safety Project*

Nancy Jacobs, Ph.D.†
Heath Grant, Ph.D.
Wendy Rowe
Jessica Saunders

INTRODUCTION

The Brooklyn North Neighborhood Safety Project was built on the premise that the continued suppression of crime (i.e., maintaining level of success from prior intensive enforcement efforts) requires the mobilization and organization of community residents to be proactive forces for change with regard to crime and related quality of life concerns. Research has shown the long-term benefits of engaging police and residents together as collaborative partners. Within such a relationship, they can work toward the proper identification of neighborhood problems, development of the most appropriate strategies to ameliorate them, and recruitment of additional partners necessary for the comprehensive implementation of those strategies.

In seeking to develop a police/community collaborative problem-solving capability within Brooklyn North, the NYPD and CCNYC jointly developed a plan to mobilize residents in both organized and unorganized communities throughout the

*This contribution is part of a larger evaluation of the Brooklyn North project conducted by the Criminal Justice Research and Evaluation Center (CJREC), John Jay College of Criminal Justice. The final report was submitted to the City of New York in 1999.

†Nancy Jacobs is the Executive Director of the Criminal Justice Research and Evaluation Center (CJREC), John Jay College of Criminal Justice. She received her Ph.D. in Political Science from Columbia University in New York.

Heath Grant, Ph.D. is an Assistant Professor in the Department of Law, Police Science and Criminal Justice Administration, John Jay College of Criminal Justice. He received his Ph.D. from the Graduate Center, City University of New York.

Wendy Rowe is a Research Assistant at the Criminal Justice Research and Evaluation Center (CJREC), John Jay College of Criminal Justice.

Jessica Saunders is a Senior Research Assistant at the Criminal Justice Research and Evaluation Center (CJREC), John Jay College of Criminal Justice.

command, and then funnel them into a series of intensive workshops focusing on the requisite skill development for collaborative problem-solving. Knowing that training is often not enough, the Neighborhood Safety Project sought to develop an appropriate mechanism for the application of these skills within each participant's own neighborhood or block, thereby fostering the creation of police/community partherships. To serve this need, the Neighborhood Safety Project hired a full-time Community Coordinator to provide follow-up technical assistance to groups funded by the Reisenbach Foundation to implement community improvement projects in their target areas.

1. *Outreach and Recruitment Activities*

The first component of the Project involved mobilizing a sufficient resident base for the participation in the Neighborhood Safety Leadership Institute training workshops. The CCNYC and the NYPD collaborated on this activity, reviewing both crime and community organization data, and then creating several vehicles for recruiting NSLI participants. The Project surpassed its original objective, recruiting seventy-nine individuals from ten targeted community areas in Brooklyn North.

2. *The Neighborhood Safety Leadership Institute (NSLI)*

The NSLI workshop series was well received by both police and resident participants, with most individuals reporting satisfaction with both the training content and delivery. All ten Brooklyn North precincts had participants attending at least one of the workshops, with varying rates of participant retention across the ten components. The majority of participants reported that they were only "partially prepared" to implement community projects following the NSLI, pointing to the need for intensive follow-up technical assistance. Twenty-one groups from Brooklyn North received Reisenbach funding for community involvement projects, of which the evaluation examined thirteen closely.

3. *Follow-up Technical Assistance Activities*

Despite varying levels of technical assistance and police collaboration across these sites, the neighborhood groups produced an impressive array of activities and preliminary outcomes. Many police and residents reported increased communication; although this was largely in the form of information sharing rather than collaboration on problem identification, strategy selection, and action plan development as presented in the CCNYC collaborative problem-solving model.

The largest constraint on the Neighborhood Safety Project was the lack of sufficient resources to support full-time follow-up technical assistance from the Community Coordinator, and for precinct and Community Affairs officers to engage in activities of collaboration that would have resulted in true community-police partnerships throughout Brooklyn North. The original target area alone was an ambitious undertaking, but because resources were stretched to include the Manhattan Model Block initiatives, the Neighborhood Safety Project was left unable to provide ongoing, intensive technical assistance to each of the resident groups graduating from its training institute. In the absence of sufficient follow-up, research and practical experience has shown that skill retention is often tenuous.

4. *Police—Community Collaboration*

Community Affairs officers reported difficulties in committing sufficient time to working with the Brooklyn North neighborhood groups. As noted above, this is reflected in the types of collaboration reported by both police and residents. One of the major barriers noted was insufficient priority being placed on working with the sites by precinct commanding officers. While the current evaluation design lacked the resources to interview commanding officers or command-level personnel to verify these concerns, these responses do point to a need for further investigation of this possible organizational disjuncture. It is important to point out, however, that the movement of policing practice beyond an interaction and referral nature, toward increasing police/community partnership takes a substantial amount of time that is beyond the scope of the Neighborhood Safety Project. Such a level of collaboration thus is not a reasonable expectation for this project.

What can be expected from a project such as this one, however, is the beginnings of a skill transference that exposes police personnel to new ways of looking at problems and collaborating with the community. Past research on organizational transformation within police departments stresses the importance of pilot projects such as this one, ultimately leading to changes in practice as future replications are conducted with transfer the new skills to more and more personnel as resources allow (Sackmann, 1991; Chan, 1996).

Although the resources for this project were somewhat limited for such a purpose, important lessons can be learned through both its successes and constraints. The NYPD's growth over the last ten years demonstrates an increasing attention to the importance of community organizing and collaboration for controlling crime and disorder. The COMPSTAT model looks at crime complaint statistics as the bottom-line measure of precinct and department success, and as an accountability mechanism. The restructuring and the focus on quality of life issues as apparent in SAT COM Brooklyn North, represents further movement in this area. Current activities such as the Neighborhood Safety and Model Blocks initiatives are thus additional efforts designed to ultimately produce organizational change at the same time as crime is reducing throughout the city.

The level of officer participation at the focus groups is an important indicator of the fact that the Community Affairs officers attached a great deal of importance to the project, and saw potential in similar efforts in the future. In fact, those officers that reported a more regular involvement with the Brooklyn North neighborhoods groups were also the ones to view the project overall as being helpful in the day-to-day tasks for doing their jobs. The officers also noted the need to include beat and commanding officers in future initiatives, demonstrating some knowledge of the need to include all key stakeholders in the collaborative problem-solving process. Similar recommendations were also obtained about participation from agencies such as Probation and the District Attorney's office.

5. *Community Crime-Related Outcomes*

Crime trends were examined for each of the thirteen blocks examined in this study between January 1998 and January 1999. Given that there were different levels of activity, technical assistance, and police/community collaboration across the 13 neighborhood areas, there was an expectation that there would also be differential levels of crime. Recognizing that the numbers are small given the unit of analysis (neighborhood blocks), some evidence was provided for a greater crime reduction/ maintenance in the intensive sites. Although both the intensive and non-intensive sites exhibited overall crime reductions between January and June 1998 (the pre-test period), beginning in June the crime index in the non-intensive sites climbed 50% (from 14 to 28) and then fluctuated randomly for the post-analysis period. In the intensive sites however, there was an immediate 75% increase in the crime indicators between July and August, followed by a continued reduction reaching 85% by November (from 28 to 4). We can speculate that the initial rise may be due to the increased resident and police activity in the areas, followed by a suppression effect immediately following this attention.

Overall, the outcomes illustrated throughout this report paint the picture of a successful pilot demonstration for the CCNYC and the NYPD. The ambitiousness of the project design speaks to the commitment of both partners to the vision of organizing targeted neighborhoods and blocks throughout the city for crime and quality of life reduction.

WORKS CITED

Sackmann, S. (1991). *Cultural knowledge in organizations.* Newbury, CA: Sage

Chan, J. (1996). "Changing police culture," *British Journal of Criminology, 36*(1), 109–134.

CHAPTER 5

THE POLICE ORGANIZATION

The first four chapters of this book have examined a range of issues that affect the police department, though much of the focus has centered on the individual police officer (i.e., selection and recruitment, training, and various forms of policing, from the professional model to community policing and CompStat). This chapter takes a step back and examines the police organization itself, including how it is structured, how it functions, and, of course, current issues in this area of police study. The chapter is divided into three parts.

The first part examines the police department as a bureaucratic and quasi-military organization. Although police departments share some common features with other bureaucracies, some features are unique to policing. The roles of civil service and the police union are also addressed. Finally, the advantages and disadvantages of the police bureaucracy are described.

The second part of the chapter examines the structure and function of the typical police department, beginning with a discussion of the complex and sometimes contradictory roles and responsibilities. The structural components that are discussed include field services and administration, as well as supervision and leadership.

The final section of the chapter delves into current issues involving the organization of policing such as consolidation, civilianization, contracting for police services, and the increasing militarization.

THE POLICE BUREAUCRACY

Bureaucracy and the Police

Although there are more than 17,000 law enforcement agencies in the United States, the vast majority are organized in much the same way, with a hierarchical command structure and authoritarian management style (Walker & Katz, 2002). The police department is a bureaucratic organization similar to universities and private-sector corporations. Walker and Katz (2002) note that "the bureaucratic form of organization exists because it is the most efficient means that has been developed for organizing and directing many different activities in the pursuit of a common goal" (p. 466). As a bureaucracy, the police department shares in common many features with these other bureaucracies. According to Perrow (1972), the defining features of a **bureaucracy** include the following:

- It is a complex organization performing many different tasks in pursuit of a common goal.
- The different tasks are grouped into separate divisions or bureaus.
- The organizational structure is hierarchical or pyramidal, with a clear division of labor between workers, first-line supervisors, and chief executives.
- Responsibility for specific tasks is delegated to lower-ranking employees.
- There is a clear chain of command that indicates who is responsible for supervising each employee.
- There is a clear unity of command, so that each employee answers to one and only one supervisor.
- Written rules and regulations are designed to ensure uniformity and consistency.
- Information flows up and down through the organization according to the chain of command.
- There are clear career paths by which personnel move upward through the organization in an orderly fashion. (see also Walker & Katz, 2002, pp. 466–467)

Key Features of the Police Bureaucracy

Multiple Tasks The police bureaucracy performs a number of basic tasks to achieve its organizational objectives. These organizational objectives will be discussed in greater detail in the next section of this chapter, but to briefly summarize, they include enforcing the law, maintaining order, preventing crime, protecting constitutional rights, and providing basic emergency services. The police engage in a range of activities to achieve these objectives, mostly notably patrol, traffic, and investigation. Patrol, often called the backbone of the police organization, is the central activity of the department that involves the majority of its personnel and resources. The manner in which this task is carried out can vary substantially, as we now know from the previous two chapters describing the professional model, community and problem-oriented policing, zero tolerance, and CompStat. The size of the department will determine the degree of specialization utilized to accomplish these objectives.

The Pyramid-Shaped Hierarchy A **hierarchical organization** is characterized by several layers of command, with the amount of authority increasing at the upper levels of the department. This is often referred to as the chain of command, or order of authority. Police departments sometimes vary in the number and type of ranks depending on their size, but typical ranks include patrol officer, sergeant, lieutenant, captain, deputy chief, and chief. The pyramidal shape emerges because of the number of personnel at each layer of command: The largest number of personnel are assigned at the bottom level—patrol officers—with fewer numbers assigned at each subsequent level. For example, a department with 50 sworn officers may have 40 patrol officers, five sergeants, two lieutenants, two captains, and one chief.

The majority of the department's service delivery—the tasks that are carried out to achieve organizational objectives—occurs at the line level. In simpler terms, the lowest ranking officers in the department (patrol officers) are responsible for patrol, traffic, and investigation. At the supervisory levels, each member is responsible for a clearly defined number of lower level officers, and each supervisor is responsible for ensuring that communication flows smoothly from the lower levels to the higher levels (Champion & Hooper, 2003).

Unity of Command   A central and important feature of the police bureaucracy is **unity of command,** where each officer reports to one—and only one—supervisor. Each patrol officer reports to only one sergeant during his or her shift, and the sergeant then reports to only one lieutenant, and so forth up the chain of command. Although there certainly may be exceptions, patrol officers generally only report to the sergeant: They are not required to report to higher levels of the chain of command on a regular basis. Similarly, the higher levels of command, though ultimately responsible for all personnel below them, are not responsible for day-to-day supervision of personnel more than one level below them. For example, a lieutenant is responsible for the activity and behavior of patrol officers in his sector, but the lieutenant relies on the sergeant for the day-to-day supervision of those patrol officers. The clear unity of command ensures that line officers do not receive contradictory messages from different supervisors and also reduces the likelihood of duplicating efforts and wasting resources (i.e., since the lieutenant does not have to directly supervise patrol officers, he or she can engage in other important activities).

Span of Control   **Span of control** refers to the number of officers that a sergeant or other manager is responsible for supervising. A number of factors can help determine the most effective span of control, such as the amount of crime, the size of the department, the training of personnel, and the ability or performance of both supervisors and line officers. Traditionally, departments have tried to keep supervisors' span of control to just three or four officers, but technological advances—i.e., cellular phones, mobile digital terminals, video cameras in patrol cars, etc.—have allowed for larger officer to supervisor ratios (Champion & Hooper, 2003). Alternatively, the move to community policing and its emphasis on **decentralization** with fewer levels in the chain of command, as well as manpower shortages, has also led to increases in the span of control.

Rules and Regulations   The police bureaucracy is governed by an extensive list of rules, regulations, and policies that control and guide police behavior in a myriad of circumstances. The standard operating procedure manual (or SOP) can often be several inches thick and serves as a major point of emphasis in police academy training. Some police have argued that departments have becomes so rule-oriented that (1) it is impossible for a police officer to remember every single rule, regulation and policy; and (2) it is impossible for a police officer to go a single day without violating a rule or regulation in the policy manual. Nevertheless, written rules and regulations provide an important foundation for a police department that communicates the organization's expectations to its employees and also provides a level of protection against civil liability. As an illustration of the bureaucratic emphasis on written rules and regulations in policing, the Commission on Accreditation in Law Enforcement (CALEA) requires that agencies adopt over 440 written policies before they can become accredited.

Career Paths   Police bureaucracies have clearly defined career paths to be followed by those officers who are able to rise through the ranks. Departments vary in their procedures for promotion, but written tests, oral interviews, and review of performance in prior assignments are the primary elements of that process. Officers are typically required to serve a minimum number of years in patrol before taking a promotional exam, usually three to five years. Some departments treat the detective rank as a separate career path with different levels within that rank (the "gold" shield being the top rank), while other departments place all ranks in one career path. Also, the required level of education and other minimum requirements become more stringent as one proceeds along the department career path. Unfortunately, there is generally little room for advancement in police departments because of the limited number of supervisory positions.

Advantages and Disadvantages of the Bureaucratic Model for Police.   The bureaucratic model was applied to police departments in the early twentieth century as part of the professionalism reform movement, and the adoption of the bureaucratic model helped to advance policing in a number of important ways. Walker and Katz (2002) point to the differences between the police department in 1900 and the police department now to highlight those contributions. The political era police department lacked recruitment and selection standards, training, supervision, performance standards, accountability, written rules, and a sense of mission. As the professional reformers like Vollmer began to reshape their departments, the elements of the bureaucratic model facilitated that transformation. Moreover, the police bureaucracy was able to adapt to the increasing specialization of police departments and to accommodate the growing number of activities that resulted from that specialization (Walker & Katz, 2002).

Alternatively, there are a number of limitations or disadvantages associated with the bureaucratic model, especially when applied to police agencies. First, bureaucracies typically are very rigid and inflexible and are unable to keep pace with change (Walker & Katz, 2002). For example, police departments typically do not respond well to significant change, such as the adoption of community policing. Second, the flow of information in a bureaucracy will often break down and may lead to poor decision making. The adoption of a new policy can sometimes cause problems if line officers do not understand why a change is being made. Line officers possess a wealth of information about the areas they patrol, but supervisors who make department-level decisions may be unable or unwilling to tap the expertise of line officers before making those decisions. Third, bureaucracies—police included—

frequently are accused of not putting the needs of the client first and are seen as self-serving and isolated (Walker & Katz, 2002). For example, police are often reluctant to listen to the demands of business owners and residents. Fourth, bureaucracies tend to promote the status quo and de-emphasize creativity. Police officers are trained to think and act in a certain way and to handle situations in a prescribed manner. Creativity and innovation are typically not rewarded and are often resisted. Bittner (1970) said:

> Worst of all, we have good reasons to suspect that if some men are possessed by and act with professional acumen, they might possibly find it wiser to keep it to themselves lest they will be found to be in conflict with some departmental regulation. (p. 62)

Fifth, bureaucracies are rule-bound, and the proliferation of rules, policies, and procedures in policing has led some to argue that first-line supervision is rendered ineffective. More specifically, there are so many rules in the SOP that everyone violates one or more on a regular basis. When an officer is promoted to sergeant and becomes responsible for front-line supervision, the officers he or she is responsible for likely know about the new sergeant's transgressions (i.e., the dirty laundry). Depending on the nature and prevalence of those violations, the new sergeant's ability to supervise and provide accountability may be completely compromised (Skolnick & Fyfe, 1993).

Last, bureaucracies tend to be numbers-driven in terms of performance. Universities are driven by enrollments, businesses are driven by sales and profits, and police departments have traditionally been driven by their numbers: crimes, arrests, tickets, etc. Unfortunately, generating numbers in police work does not always equate with good performance. Recall that Peel believed that the true measure of good policing was the *absence* of crime. In any police encounter, not making an arrest, not issuing a ticket, and not using force may be the true sign of good policing. Skolnick and Fyfe (1993) argue that, outside of his or her immediate peers, the exceptional police officer may be completely invisible to the rest of the police department.

The basic limitations of a bureaucracy help to explain police resistance to abandoning the professional model, despite strong evidence indicating its ineffectiveness. New approaches such as community policing described in the last chapter require that officers adapt to change, communicate effectively within the department and with the community, think creatively, and put the needs of the community first. Not surprisingly, in-depth study of departments that have "adopted" community policing have sometimes found that little has actually changed beyond the rhetoric; alternatively, scholars argue that CompStat and zero tolerance policing are popular because they serve to reinforce many of the elements of the traditional police bureaucracy.

The Quasi-Military Style of Policing

Chapter 3 describes how Sir Robert Peel applied the quasi-military organizational style to the London police force and how U.S. police departments followed suit. The **quasi-military style** of U.S. policing consists of:

- Departments using rank designations (i.e., sergeant, captain).
- Police wearing uniforms.
- Hierarchical command structure.
- Authoritarian management style, with penalties for not following orders.
- Police officers carrying weapons and granted authority to make arrests and use force (including deadly force). (Walker & Katz, 2002)

The superficial similarities between police and the military, the influx of former military into law enforcement, and the popular rhetoric of "wars on crime and drugs" have facilitated the survival of the military model in U.S. law enforcement despite some critical problems with its application. These problems stem from several important differences between the police and the military that many argue make the use of the military model in policing inappropriate. For example, consider the implications of the following:

- The police serve a community of citizens while the military fights a foreign enemy.
- The police provide services to help people, and these services are typically requested by citizens. The military may, on occasion, engage in humanitarian operations, but its central mission does not involve service.
- The police are bound by law to protect the constitutional rights of the citizens. The military is not bound by the U.S. Constitution.
- Police officers possess tremendous discretion and wield a majority of the organization's decision making power. Soldiers exercise discretion much less often. (Walker & Katz, 2002)

Skolnick and Fyfe (1993) argue that the quasi-military model is improper for police and that officers should not be viewed as soldiers in a war. To illustrate their point, they review a speech from former Attorney General Richard Thornburgh at a national crime summit in the early 1990s:

> Let me turn once again to the example of Desert Storm and the great might that was brought to bear upon a threatening and violent enemy. Under brilliantly coordinated "command and control," the Gulf coalition forces made the best use of firepower guided by great ingenuity and relentless certainty. We had the weapons to do the job: "smart" weapons that worked with deadly effect against an enemy finally reduced to desperate encounter, ineffectual response, and abject retreat.
>
> Here at home in the fight against violent crime we should employ, to be sure, the same command and control, the same ingenuity and certainty. Only here we battle not with the weapons of the military, but with the far stronger weapon of our laws. We need to make certain that our laws are just as smart—just as efficient and effective against criminals—as those weapons that turned back the ruthless and violent intrusion by Saddam Hussein's forces. (Thornburgh, 1991)

Thornburgh's statement is compelling on its face, drawing upon patriotism and the "great might" of the United States military, but the analogy is weak at best.

Drawing a comparison between "smart" weapons that are designed to destroy foreign intruders and "smart" laws that are designed to define criminal conduct simply does not work. Police officers do not seek to destroy their enemy. Rather, police officers seek to prevent criminals from engaging in crime, and when that fails, they seek to arrest them for their illegal behavior. Skolnick and Fyfe (1993) also maintain that characterizing police as soldiers in a war is a primary cause of police misconduct because of police officers' inability to differentiate the enemy from others and because of the frustration that builds as a result of being in a war that cannot be won (see Chapter 8 for further discussion). "The view of police officers as soldiers engaged in a war on crime not only diverts attention from more effective strategies for crime control but also is a major cause of police violence and the violation of citizens' rights" (Skolnick & Fyfe, 1993, p. 115).

Skolnick and Fyfe (1993) also point to the central role of front-line discretion in policing as an indicator of the inappropriateness of the military analogy. Under the traditional bureaucratic model, the organization is pyramidal with multiple levels of command and decision-making power increasing at each level. Ultimately, the small few at the top of the bureaucracy make the important decisions about the organization. This model applies quite well to the military where generals make the critical decisions and foot soldiers carry out orders. In policing, however, it is the "foot soldiers" or patrol officers who hold tremendous **discretion,** engage in service delivery, and make the most important decisions. Clearly, the top levels of the police department make important organizational decisions, but decisions about freedom, life, and death are made by patrol officers. In this respect, police departments are more like hospitals, law firms, and universities than they are like the military:

> As in police departments, however, the big decisions related to direct delivery of services . . . are made by those on the front line. Doctors, not administrators, decide whether to operate or to medicate; professors, not deans, decide whether students' work is passing or failing; trial lawyers, not managing partners, decide whether to advise clients to settle or to go before juries; police officers, not chiefs, decide whether and when to shoot. (Skolnick & Fyfe, 1993, p. 118)

The location of power and authority at the bottom of the organization, rather than the top, has led police departments to create extensive SOP manuals in an effort to control the power of line officers. And, as mentioned previously, the copious SOP manuals produce their own problems, which Skolnick and Fyfe (1993) argue ultimately undermines front-line supervision by sergeants.

Civil Service

As described in Chapter 3, **civil service** emerged around the turn of the twentieth century as an effort to control the political influence of police personnel decisions. Civil service "is a set of formal and legally binding procedures governing personnel decisions . . . to ensure that personnel decisions are based on objective criteria, and not on favoritism, bias, and political influence" (Walker & Katz, 2002, p. 476).

Today, nearly every police department in the United States functions under a civil service system. The civil service agency, usually run by a committee of up to five people, works with the police department to develop policies, create job descriptions, develop recruitment and selection procedures, and to create criteria for promotions and terminations. Members are usually appointed to the civil service agency for a specified term by the city leadership (i.e., mayor, city council, etc.).

Although civil service effectively controlled political influence in police operations in the early twentieth century, many now argue that it is no longer useful and creates problems for police departments (Guyot, 1991). The biggest criticism of civil service is that it takes away departmental control of important decisions in three critical areas: hiring, promotion, and firing. In most police departments, it is not possible for a chief to make changes in existing personnel or promotional standards, or even to hire and fire at will (Walker & Katz, 2002). Guyot's (1991) study of the Troy Police Department highlighted a number of instances where the civil service agency interfered with the department's functioning. For example, the Troy Civil Service Commission thwarted the Chief's efforts to create and fill a departmental planner's position; it reduced punishments set by the Chief for officers engaged in misconduct; it hindered the hiring of female officers by maintaining height standards; and it prevented the termination of an officer who was an alcoholic but who refused to seek treatment (Guyot, 1991). Guyot (1991) argues that this type of interference limits the power of the police chief and negatively affects the functioning of the department. The problems described in Troy are not unique. In fact, the Civil Service League, an organization that helped draft the original Civil Service Act of 1883 (Pendleton Act) recommended in 1970 that independent civil service commissions be abolished. Nevertheless, the vast majority of police departments still operate under a civil service system.

Police Unions

The Unionization of the Police.   In 1894, a group of New York police officers who were concerned about working conditions and the welfare of police created the Police Benevolent Association (PBA), and in 1915, officers in Pittsburgh created the Fraternal Order of Police (FOP). In 1919, 33 police departments unionized with the American Federation of Labor (AFL) (Champion & Hooper, 2003). The unionization of police was challenged by management in most police departments. Boston provides an excellent example of the controversy that arose with the development of police **unions.** In August 1919, Boston police officers unionized because of poor working conditions such as:

- Officers were entitled only one day off every 15 days, and even then they were required to have their superiors' permission before leaving the city limits of Boston.
- A typical work week lasted anywhere from 73 to 98 hours.
- What off-duty time they received was often spent on standby duty in the back of precinct stations, which were infested with rats and insects.

- Standby officers had to share wobbly old bunk beds—two men to a bed.
- Promotions were often political, and some talented officers were either fired or ignored.
- Officers were often asked to perform nonpolicing duties such as delivering unpaid tax bills or promoting the mayor during elections. (Champion & Hooper, 2003, p. 88)

Shortly after receiving a union charter, the police commissioner ordered them to disband, and when they refused, the 19 leaders of the union were suspended. Within a month, nearly all of the 1,544 officers went on strike, and the city was overtaken by crime, violence, and rioting (Champion & Hooper, 2003). The officers were blamed for the violence that occurred, and all of the striking officers were fired.

Police Unions Today.   A police union "is an organization legally authorized to represent police officers in collective bargaining with the employer" (Walker & Katz, 2002, p. 477). Collective bargaining is the process by which the employer and employees determine working conditions. According to the 1997 LEMAS survey, officers in 73 percent of all municipal police departments are represented by a union. There are differences by size of the department: Nearly all large police departments have unions, but unionization is much less common in small departments (ten or fewer officers). Unions are often very powerful and play a strong role in advocating for police officers. Although there is no one police union (such as the United Automobile Workers or the Teamsters that represent all workers in their specific fields), the most common unions are the Fraternal Order of Police and the International Union of Police Associations (IUPA). The FOP represents several hundred thousand police officers throughout the United States, but in some jurisdictions it does not act as a police union, only as a fraternal association (Walker & Katz, 2002).

Police unions serve a number of functions for police officers. First, they represent officers in collective bargaining with the department. The principles of collective bargaining "are that (1) employees have a legal right to form unions of their own choosing, (2) employers must recognize employee unions, (3) employees have a right to participate in negotiations over working conditions, and (4) employers are required to negotiate with the union's designated representatives" (Walker & Katz, 2002 pp. 477–478). The chief and top management are typically not members of the union. The negotiation of a contract between the department and the union covers wages, work hours, and a host of other employment conditions. If the union and department cannot settle on a contract, an impasse exists and mediation or arbitration with an outside agent may occur. In private industry, an impasse can result in either a strike by the employees or a lockout by the employer. In large part because of the Boston incident described above, strikes by police officers are illegal in many states. Also, in the 1970s, police strikes in Baltimore (1974), San Francisco (1975), and New Orleans (1979) led to violence and large-scale disorder (Walker & Katz, 2002). The rationale for prohibiting police strikes is that they pose too great a threat to public safety, and even in states where they are not illegal, strikes are rare because of the public backlash against the action. However, police officers may often engage in other types of organized actions to send a message to management, including the "blue flu," where large numbers of officers call in sick at the same time, or they disrupt normal departmental functioning in some other way (i.e., writing no traffic tickets).

Second, the police union represents officers in grievance and disciplinary procedures. If an officer feels that he or she has been unduly treated by a supervisor, he or she can pursue action against the department with representation and support from the union. More commonly, the union provides representation, including legal representation, when disciplinary action has been taken against an officer. The vast majority of police unions have created formalized grievance and disciplinary procedures with their respective police departments to ensure that officers are given due process and are treated fairly. Some unions have created an Officer's Bill of Rights that lays out very clearly the due process rights of officers. These typically include the right to an administrative hearing, right to legal counsel, and the right to appeal disciplinary actions (Walker & Katz, 2002).

Last, unions give officers a voice in how the department is run through "shared governance" (Walker & Katz, 2002 p. 478). Police chiefs typically must notify the union and get its approval before making any changes in work conditions, such as switching to one-person patrol cars, mandating foot patrol, and rotating work shifts. Since work conditions are covered by collective bargaining agreements, any changes the chief wishes to make that are not specified in the agreement must received union approval. Failure to garner such approval can lead to the filing of formal grievances by the union (Walker & Katz, 2002).

Impact of Police Unions.   Unions have had a significant impact on policing in the twentieth century. First, unionization had led to significant improvements in officers' salaries, benefits, and other working conditions (Walker & Katz, 2002). Second, unions provide a degree of accountability for police chiefs, preventing them from making significant changes that negatively affect police officers and their working conditions. Third, unionization has led to the introduction of due process protections in grievance and disciplinary proceedings against police officers. Unions also often provide legal counsel to officers when needed. Last, unionization has led to more formalized and structured negotiations between management and the labor force.

However, there are also negative consequences associated with unionization. Many argue that unions have negatively affected police–community relations because unions typically resist affirmative action plans and other initiatives that seek to improve relations by changing some facet of working conditions (Walker & Katz, 2002). Unions also may draw criticism from the community because of their representation of officers who are accused of engaging in misconduct (brutality, corruption, and racial profiling, for example). Also, some argue that unions have served as a barrier to positive change. Unions have opposed incentive pay for college education, for example (Walker & Katz, 2002). Many of the improvements that occurred in professional policing were orchestrated by powerful and progressive police chiefs, such as August Vollmer. Today, police chiefs lack the power to make such sweeping changes without first getting approval from the union, and critics argue that unions generally oppose any effort that challenges the status quo.

FUNCTION AND STRUCTURE OF THE POLICE ORGANIZATION

Functions of the Police

The responsibilities of the police are numerous and extend far beyond the traditional objectives of crime control and law enforcement. The diversity and breadth of the functions of the police was first described in James Q. Wilson's groundbreaking research in the late 1960s. In his *Varieties of Police Behavior,* Wilson (1968) analyzed citizen calls to police and concluded that police have four major responsibilities:

1. Law enforcement: Applying legal sanctions to behavior that violated a legal standard.
2. Order maintenance: Controlling events and circumstances that disturb or threaten to disturb the peace.
3. Information gathering: Asking questions, doing paperwork, conducting interviews and interrogations.
4. Service-related: Assisting injured persons, helping those in need, animal control, community relations activities.

Wilson (1968) then determined how much time police spent on each of these responsibilities and his findings challenged conventional wisdom about the role of police in society. Specifically, law enforcement responsibilities comprised the smallest portion of time at just 10 percent. The other 90 percent of police officers' time involved service-related tasks (38 percent), order maintenance (30 percent), and information gathering (22 percent). Wilson's findings were groundbreaking because they challenged the image of police officers as engaged only in crime-fighting activities, a major tenet of the professional model of policing. Recall also the events that were occurring when Wilson's work was published: Riots were occurring in major urban centers throughout the country, Presidential Commissions were reporting that police played a contributing role in the disorder, and crime was increasing significantly. This early work by Wilson (1968) has been supported by additional research over the last three decades. In particular, the Police Services Study (PSS) examined more than 25,000 calls for service in three cities and found that: (1) 19 percent involved crime, and (2) only 2 percent involved violent crime (Scott, 1981).

    Wrobleski and Hess (2003, pp. 131–135) state that the police have five basic goals:

- *Enforcing laws:* Determining if a law has been broken and whether to enforce the law, conducting criminal investigations, apprehending offenders, and assisting in their prosecution.
- *Preserving the peace:* Intervening in noncriminal conduct at public events (crowd control), in social relations (domestic disputes), and in traffic control (parking, pedestrians) to maintain law and order.
- *Preventing crime:* Proactive efforts to eliminate potentially dangerous or criminal situations that include working with juveniles, educating the public, cooperating with other private and public agencies (private security, probation and parole), and providing visible evidence of police authority.
- *Protecting constitutional rights:* Police must carry out activities to meet their other goals (enforcing laws, preserving the peace, and preventing crime) in accordance with the U.S. Constitution; protecting civil rights and civil liberties is perceived by some as the single most important goal of policing.
- *Providing services:* Police are frequently called upon to provide a number of other services such as giving information, providing directions, counseling and referral, licensing and registering vehicles, working with neglected children, providing emergency medical services, dealing with stray animals, helping the homeless and mentally ill, and providing community education programs (i.e., DARE).

The American Bar Association (1980, pp. 1-31, 1-32) examined the police role in *Standards Relating to the Urban Police Function,* and they identified eleven different responsibilities.

1. Identify criminal offenders and criminal activity and, when appropriate, apprehend offenders and participate in subsequent court proceedings.
2. Reduce the opportunities for the commission of some crimes through preventive patrol and other measures.
3. Aid individuals who are in danger of physical harm.
4. Protect constitutional guarantees.
5. Facilitate the movement of people and vehicles.
6. Assist those who cannot care for themselves.
7. Resolve conflict.
8. Identify problems that are potentially serious law enforcement or government problems.
9. Create and maintain a feeling of security in the community.
10. Promote and preserve civil order.
11. Provide other services on an emergency basis.

A number of interesting issues emerge from examining the above list of responsibilities. First, in support of Wilson's (1968) earlier work, the list of responsibilities is diverse and only a few involve crime, crime fighting, and law enforcement. Second, a number of the responsibilities are vague (Walker & Katz, 2002). For example, what types of conflict should police resolve and how should they go about that? How can police promote civil order and a feeling of security in the community? What other types of services may they be called upon to provide on an emergency basis? Third, a number of the responsibilities above conflict with one another. For example, at a large demonstration that is blocking a major thoroughfare, which responsibility should take precedence: preserving the constitutional right to gather and engage in free speech or the maintenance of order and facilitating movement of people and vehicles (Walker & Katz, 2002)? The complex and sometimes contradictory roles of the police have important implications for how police performance is measured. Quite simply, how do we define good policing? This issue is addressed at length in Chapter 7.

Structure of the Police Organization

Despite the diversity among police departments with regard to size, jurisdiction, and approach (i.e., traditional, community policing, zero tolerance, etc.), the vast majority are structured in much the same way. This section describes the basic organizational makeup of a police department, including field services—patrol, traffic, and investigation—and administrative services—communications, personnel, training, records, research and planning, public information, and property. Issues surrounding supervision and leadership are also described.

Field Services

Patrol   Patrol is typically called the backbone of policing for a number of reasons. First, the majority of the department's personnel and resources are assigned to this task. Second, patrol represents the vast majority of service delivery—contacts with the public—for the department. As mentioned above, patrol officers wield the lion's share of departmental authority as this line level. Patrol serves three basic functions: (1) to deter crime, (2) to enhance feelings of safety among the community, and (3) to make officers available for service (Walker & Katz, 2002). Since patrol officers respond to calls for service, the actual nature of their work is determined by the needs of the community. Previous discussions of the Police Services Study (PSS) and other analyses of calls for service data described how much of their work does not involve law enforcement or crime control: The daily work of a patrol officer can involve tasks as diverse as delivering a baby, rescuing people from a burning building, searching for a lost child, and capturing a wild animal. The nature of a patrol officer's work will also be determined by the philosophy of the police department: Patrol officers may target low-level offenders and disorder (zero tolerance), engage in problem solving (problem-oriented policing), or meet with community residents and business associations (community policing).

The type of patrol can vary substantially in terms of approach and method. With regard to approach, the traditional method involves random patrol: Officers are assigned to a specific geographic area and move around that area in an unsystematic manner (Cordner & Trojanwicz, 1992). The rationale behind random patrol involves prevention and detection: By driving around randomly, police will appear to be omnipresent and will prevent potential criminals from engaging in illegal behavior. They will also be available to respond to calls for service and may detect crimes on their own. Directed or targeted patrol is different from random patrol in that officers focus on a particular area, such as a hot spot where crime and offenders are prevalent. This form of patrol is much more proactive, with police actively addressing a particular problem area, rather than simply riding around waiting for calls for service. **Directed patrol** often occurs after some degree of crime analysis that detects the problem, but it can also be more informal—with individual officers targeting areas on their beat without formal direction from their supervisors. Directed patrol may involve saturating a particular area with police for a specified period of time, with police aggressively enforcing laws, conducting random stops and frequent traffic stops. Directed patrol is frequently part of problem-oriented and zero tolerance strategies and is also employed in CompStat.

Methods of patrol can vary substantially. The traditional method under the professional model involves automobile patrol. As recently as 1997, the automobile comprised more than 80 percent of patrol activities nationwide (Bureau of Justice Statistics, 1997). Of course, the advantages of car patrol are that officers can cover more territory, and they can respond to call and emergencies more quickly. Automobile patrol can involve one- or two-person cars. Police unions have argued for two-person cars to improve officer safety, but the manpower shortage and need for efficiency have led many departments to move away from the two-person patrol car. Nearly 90 percent of cars today are single-officer vehicles (Walker & Katz, 2002). The chilling effect of car patrol on police–community relations was described in Chapter 3, particularly the isolation it imposed on police. Other vehicles are used for patrol, though far less commonly. These include motorcycles, all-terrain vehicles, helicopters, and in jurisdictions with waterways, marine or boat patrol. Some departments also use horse patrol.

The widespread adoption of community policing has led many police departments to adopt forms of patrol that allow for greater police citizen contact. The most common forms are foot patrol and bicycle patrol. The results of the Kansas City Preventive Patrol study and the foot patrol experiments in the 1970s bolstered the use of foot patrol, despite concerns about limited mobility. Foot patrol diminishes the isolation between police and the community and makes officers more approachable. It also increases the number of positive contacts between police and citizens, improves citizen attitudes toward police, and reduces fear of crime (see Chapter 3). Although most police departments use foot patrol (over 90 percent of large departments), less than 5 percent of all officers nationwide work on foot (Bureau of Justice Statistics, 1997). Bicycle patrol is seen as a compromise between foot and automobile patrol: Bike officers are still approachable and can engage with the public, but they are more mobile and have greater flexibility than officers assigned to foot and car patrol.

Patrol officers are not assigned uniformly across beats and shifts. O.W. Wilson in 1941 developed a formula for patrol distribution based on an analysis of calls for service and reported crimes (Wilson, 1941). There are generally three patrol shifts throughout the day: 7 am—3 pm, 3 pm—11 pm, and 11 pm—7 am. Some departments use different shifts, such as a 12-hour shift, with officers working the same amount of hours over a fewer number of days and getting additional days off. Also, most departments have moved away from using a swing shift schedule—with officers working different shifts throughout the month—because of research indicating the negative effects on officer health and well-being (Vila, 2000). Most serious crimes and disturbances occur overnight, so as a result, patrol is typically heavier on the overnight shift (Walker & Katz, 2002). Also, certain areas of a city are more crime-prone than others, so logically, patrol levels should be greater in those areas.

Response time remains an important part of patrol work, despite research indicating that most calls for service, even those involving serious crimes, do not occur quickly enough (i.e., victim delay in reporting) for police response time to make a difference with regard to arrest. Response time is important for noncrime related calls: accidents, fires, and health-related emergencies, for example. Patrol officers often are the first responders in these types of situations, and their ability to get to the scene quickly and administer first aid often can often save lives. Also, citizen satisfaction with police service is affected by response time. In other words, even if arriving quickly at the scene of a call for service does not affect the likelihood of arrest (in the majority of cases), citizens do expect that fast response and are upset when it does not occur (Furstenburg & Wellford, 1973).

Traffic   Although traditionally undervalued, traffic enforcement plays an important role in the activity of a police department. The primary goal of traffic enforcement is public safety, and this is accomplished through a host of functions:

- The elimination of accident causes and congestion.
- The identification of potential traffic problems and hazards.
- The regulation of parking.
- The investigation of property damage and personal injury from car accidents.
- Ensuring public awareness regarding safe use of automobiles and other vehicles.
- Ticketing and arresting offenders. (Thibault, Lynch, & McBride, 2001)

Traffic enforcement is unpopular among police officers for two reasons. First, traffic enforcement typically involves negative encounters with citizens who have violated some motor vehicle rule but who generally are not "criminals." There is often resentment on the part of the public, who view this activity is trivial ("Why are you bothering me about speeding when you could be catching real criminals?"). Also, police officers generally do not see these violations as overly serious, and in fact, they may often engage in the behavior themselves when off-duty (i.e., illegal parking, illegal turns, speeding, etc.). Second, traffic stops can be very dangerous for police officers. The officer generally knows very little about the individual being pulled over. In 1999, more than half of the officers killed in the line of duty were involved in a traffic stop (Onder, 2002). Both Timothy McVeigh and Ted Bundy were caught as a result of a traffic stop (Grant & Terry, 2005). Moreover, outside of the potential dangerousness of motorists, the nature of traffic stops is also dangerous, particularly if the stop occurs on a busy highway or street. Officers are out of their vehicles standing unprotected on a shoulder or side of the road, exposed to oncoming traffic.

Because of the difficulties and dangers of traffic enforcement, many departments have moved toward using technology to assist in this activity. The use of cameras, typically fixed to traffic lights, can show traffic violators, monitor traffic flow, and help with the tracking of specific vehicles. Traffic cameras were used in the search for the Washington, DC, area snipers in 2002 and played a crucial role in identifying potential suspects in the London subway and bus bombings in the summer of 2005.

Investigation   Once a crime has been committed and brought to the attention of the police, a criminal investigation begins. Although criminal investigation—including detective work and crime scene investigation—are the most romanticized elements of policing, these activities represent only a small portion of police work and they are surrounded by myths. For example, only 12 percent of all sworn officers in the United States are assigned to detective units (Police Executive Research Forum, 1981). Television and movies depict detective work as exciting and dangerous, with detectives possessing extraordinary skill and courage, capable of solving any crime if given enough time and resources (Walker & Katz, 2002). Similarly, the popularity of crime scene investigation on television has fostered the impression that all crimes can be solved within an hour through sophisticated scientific techniques, DNA, and fingerprints.

The realities of detective work are quite different from this portrayal. First, patrol officers, not detectives, make the vast majority of arrests (80 percent or more; Reiss, 1971). Second, research indicates that most detective work is neither exciting nor dangerous. A study by Rand in the 1970s found detective work to be "superficial, routine, and nonproductive" (Walker & Katz, 2002, p. 168). Most cases received a day or less of investigation, and the majority of investigative effort involved paperwork (Greenwood & Petersilia, 1975). Third, most crimes go unsolved. Although there is substantial variation by crime, the national clearance rate for index crimes is just over 20 percent (Federal Bureau of Investigation, 2000). Murder has the highest clearance rate, at 69 percent, but the rates for most of the other index offenses dip well below 50 percent. Fourth, the fancy techniques portrayed on crime scene investigation shows typically do not play a role in investigations. For example, fingerprints are rarely an important factor in criminal investigations: A study in New York City found police obtained a usable fingerprint in 10 percent of all burglary cases, and a fingerprint led to an arrest in only 3 percent of cases (Walker & Katz, 2002). Nevertheless, as technology continues to develop, these techniques of criminal investigation—particularly the use of DNA—will likely play a larger role (see Chapter 11 for more discussion of this topic).

Still, detective work offers a number of advantages over patrol for police officers. First, the assignment may involve a promotion and pay raise. Second, detectives have much more control over their work and are more independent. Patrol officers frequently race from call to call, while detectives are assigned specific cases and are given substantial latitude in investigating those cases (i.e., much less direct supervision). Detectives also have more normal work schedules and are able to work in civilian clothes as opposed to uniforms. Perhaps most importantly, detectives have a very clear measure of success: the arrest of a suspect. As discussed earlier in this chapter and in Chapter 7, patrol officers do not enjoy such a clear measure of their performance.

The size and resources of the department will dictate if there are specialized units for detective work and crime scene investigation. In small departments (and most departments in the United States are small, with fewer than ten officers), there may be one detective who is responsible for all investigations, or patrol officers may take on those responsibilities. Large departments have numerous detective units based on the type of crime, employ their own criminalists/evidence technicians, and may even operate their own crime laboratory. Typically, detective units are devoted to the major crimes: homicide, robbery, burglary, narcotics, and sex crimes. Units may also be devoted to vice (gambling, prostitution), gangs, juvenile, schools, and intelligence. There may also be specialized units such as K-9, emergency services or SWAT, transit, anti-terrorism, white-collar crime, and internal affairs. Again, the size and resources of the department often times determine the degree of specialization.

Administrative Services.   There are a number of administrative units within a police department that provide support and assistance for the field services. The personnel in these units are much more likely to be non-sworn since these units are not responsible for law enforcement, order maintenance and service delivery. The primary administrative service units are described below.

Communications/Dispatch   Peter Manning's (1988) description of the communications center belies its importance to the police department:

> My impressions of the communications center remain vivid and powerful. It was a smelly, smoky, poorly lit room reeling under the glare of harsh flickering fluorescent lights. Windowless, stuffy, with restricted exit and entry, few amenities. Nervous anxiety and worry was the prevalent tone. . . . I have rarely endured such an unpleasant field work experience. (p. xiii)

Communications is a critically important administrative function in police departments. This unit serves as the connection between the person in need of police assistance and the officers on patrol. Dispatchers who receive 911 calls must be carefully screened and properly trained so they can effectively respond to people in stress and adequately prioritize calls. Some larger departments may have separate operators who receive calls and then communicate with dispatchers to send patrol cars. Most departments, however, have one group of individuals receiving, processing, and making decisions about incoming calls. Also, the dispatcher serves as the only source of information for the patrol officer responding to the call, so it is imperative that the dispatcher get as much information as possible from the caller and that it be relayed accurately to the officer. If the call involves a car accident: What is the location? Are there injuries? How many cars are involved? Is the roadway blocked? If the call involves a reported crime: Are there injuries? Is the suspect still present? Is the suspect armed?

The dispatcher also serves an important screening role, making discretionary judgments about the nature of calls and whether a patrol car should be dispatched to the scene. Recall that most calls for police service do not involve a crime. Some areas have attempted to reduce this screening responsibility by developing separate 311 systems for non-emergency calls, but most jurisdictions throughout the United States do not have such alternative systems. Antunes and Scott (1981) state that the operator/dispatcher is "the key decision maker in the police bureaucracy" (p. 167). As a result, training of communications personnel is critical: Unqualified and/or improperly trained dispatchers represent a substantial civil liability if calls are screened inappropriately, information is not gathered accurately, and even if dispatchers are impolite or insensitive.

Personnel   The personnel unit functions as the human resources division of the police department. The unit is typically involved in a range of activities, including recruitment strategies; setting selection standards; maintaining personnel records; establishing standards of employee performance; administering health, safety, and benefit programs; processing applications for promotion, transfer, leaves of absence, and termination; and ensuring that the department adheres to local, state, and federal employment/labor laws (Grant & Terry, 2005). This unit plays a crucial role in the day-to-day functioning of the department and is particularly important for officer morale: It is the unit within the department that "takes care" of the officers in terms of their employment, benefits, health, and well-being.

Records   One of the biggest surprises for rookie police officers is the tremendous amount of paperwork involved in the job. Every police action generates paper. The records unit is responsible for maintaining and organizing this mountain of information and making sure that police have the ability to retrieve, examine, and cross-reference past and on-going cases. The records unit typically maintains information on a variety of police matters: arrest reports, incident reports, accident reports, juvenile reports, field interrogations, witness statements, suspect interviews, photographic records, fingerprint files, modus operandi files, warrant files, property damage reports, citizen complaints, and internal investigations (Grant & Terry, 2005). Maintaining accurate records is critical for successful prosecution of cases, especially in large jurisdictions when the trial may occur a year or more after the arrest. Quite simply, the officer will have to rely on his or her records, rather than memory, when testifying in court.

Training   The training unit is responsible for recruit training in the academy, as well as roll call and in-service training. The various forms and approaches to training are described in detail in Chapter 2. Large departments may operate their own training academy while smaller departments rely on a range of alternatives such as state-run academies and regional training centers. Training staff may be sworn personnel, college professors, or outside consultants. In-service training is a daily occurrence in most police departments and is usually performed "in-house." As stated in Chapter 2, training of police personnel is absolutely essential for fielding a professional police force.

Research and Planning   Many departments, both large and small, have created specialized units to assist with short-term and long-term strategic planning, as well as to stay on top of changes in law enforcements practices and standards. The research and planning unit may serve a variety of other tasks such as crime analysis, grant proposal writing, administering grants that have been awarded, as well as developing new law enforcement initiatives. The research and planning unit may also be responsible for following court rulings and disseminating changes in law to the rank and file through memoranda. Finally, the unit typically will research new tools and techniques and make recommendations to the department leadership or training staff (i.e., the adoption of a nonlethal alternative such as the Taser).

Public Information   The public information unit is responsible for communicating with the media and making information available to the public (Grant & Terry, 2005). A police department typically will have a spokesperson who speaks to media about an issue that is covered in the press (i.e., providing details about a crime that has occurred). The public information unit may also be responsible for holding press conferences, administering the department website, and releasing crime-related data. The media serves as the primary source of information about the police, so the public information unit plays the important role of managing the flow of information to the public.

Property   Police departments accumulate a tremendous amount of property: Evidence that is seized on every single case must be kept in a secure room until the case comes to trial (or is otherwise disposed of). This evidence can include any piece of property related to a criminal case, from DNA evidence to seized automobiles and yachts. "It is absolutely essential that all persons handling evidence be tracked and that evidence not be altered at any point when it is stored, handled, or transferred to court" (Champion & Hooper, 2003, p. 185). Problems with maintaining and documenting the chain of custody will seriously jeopardize ongoing criminal cases.

Supervision and Leadership

Supervision plays a vital role in the effective functioning of the police organization. In Chapter 3, the impact of lax or no supervision during the political era was described in some detail, and in Chapter 9, effective supervision is highlighted as a central component of a police department's internal response to police misconduct.

Core Features of Effective Supervision. Whisenand (2004) describes fifteen core responsibilities involved in the effective supervision of police personnel:

- Values: Values provide the character, courage, and consciousness for determining where the work unit is going and how it is going to get there . . . we supervise others and ourselves according to our value system.
- Ethics: Ethics focuses on moral duties and how we should behave . . . we also supervise ourselves and others according to our ethical standards. . . .
- Vision: A vision is individual values put into action, for supervisors are responsible for leading people in the creation of a vision statement for their work unit . . . without a vision, a supervisor will never be able to determine if he or she made a difference.
- Communications: Everything a police supervisor does involves communicating . . . the supervisor communicates to: be a leader, make decisions, and establish trust.
- Time Management: As we manage ourselves, we more effectively supervise others . . . there are five steps to effective management: develop a personal mission statement, identify your key roles, identify your goals, plan your week, and action and flexibility.
- Team Leadership: Successful team leaders . . . consistently (1) emphasize the positive, (2) know what's happening, (3) get your attention through a vision they have, (4) create meaning through communication, (5) build trust through positioning, (6) project positive self-regard, and (7) master change.
- Motivation: Supervisors are responsible for motivating their staff to accomplish the mission for the department . . . the reasons for having motivated workers are improved job performance and high job satisfaction.
- Empowerment: Delegation and participation lead to empowerment of personnel . . . empowerment enables us to claim our autonomy and commits us to making the organization work well.
- Team Training: The police supervisor is responsible for training a group of independently minded employees with all of their vast diversity and forging them into an interdependent team—one that is united, but not uniform . . . the main purpose for teamwork is, through alignment, to produce synergy within the work group.
- Vitality: The police supervisor is responsible for combating distress and maintaining vitality within the work group . . . too much or too little stress lessens our vitality.
- Organizing: The police supervisor is responsible for designing a work structure that facilitates all employees' making a maximum contribution to accomplishing the mission of the department.
- Performance: The supervisor's responsibility for an employee's job performance encompasses planning for it, setting specific objectives, and measuring their attainment.
- Conflict: The police supervisor is responsible for anticipating, defining, and solving personal, interpersonal, and group conflicts with precision and

compassion . . . it is up to the supervisor to convert dysfunctional conflict into productive energy.

■ Community and Problem-Oriented Policing: Community-oriented policing (COP) is a strategy for forging a partnership between the police department and its customers. Problem-oriented policing (POP) is a set of tactics for making it work . . . COP gives us a destination, while POP provides answers on how to get there.

■ Anticipation: The police supervisor is responsible for sensing, clarifying, and adapting to evolving trends in his or her work environment and career field.

Quite clearly, effective supervision goes far beyond simply checking up on one's subordinates to make sure they are not sleeping, "slacking off," or engaging in some sort of inappropriate behavior. Effective supervision is critical to efficient management of the department and its resources and is vital for the department to achieve its mission. Although Whisenand (2004) offers the aforementioned fifteen responsibilities that are likely to produce effective supervision and management, he is careful to point out that there is no preset list of methods that guarantee success: The diversity of the personnel in a department dictate which methods will work best.

Importantly, recent research also indicates that the style or quality of supervision can significantly influence behavior among patrol officers and that the degree of influence varies by supervisory style. Shepard Engel (2005) identified four different supervisory styles:

1. Traditional: Expect aggressive enforcement and "numbers"; emphasis is on control of subordinate behavior.
2. Innovative: Emphasis on developing relationships, less concern on enforcing rules and producing numbers; common in community and problem-oriented police departments.
3. Supportive: Emphasis on a protective role, serving as a buffer between line officers and management; less concern with enforcing rules and producing numbers; priority is to shield officers from "unfair" discipline.
4. Active: Lead by example; supervisor is heavily involved in fieldwork, thereby becoming both a street officer and a supervisor.

Shepard Engel (2005) found that the active supervisory style was more influential than other styles with regard to patrol officer behavior. "The findings suggest that to best influence their patrol officers' behavior, field supervisors must lead by example—the hallmark of an active style" (Shepard Engel, 2005, p. 138).

Two Cultures of Policing.   Reuss-Ianni (1993) argues that within the police organization there are actually two distinct cultures: the street cop culture and the management culture. These **two cultures of policing** are characterized by competing and often conflicting perspectives on police procedure and practice. Both cultures share the goals of combating crime and ensuring community safety, but they differ on how they define crime and community safety, as well as how they think those goals should be achieved (Reuss-Ianni, 1993). For the street cop, the job involves day-to-day interaction with the community. For the management cop, the job is a carefully planned and efficiently implemented program in which the individual patrol officer is a resource to be deployed.

The street cop culture talks of the "good old days," when the public respected the police, fellow officers could be counted on, and bosses were on the officers' side (Reuss-Ianni, 1993). Since all supervisors started out as patrol officers, they too were immersed in the street cop culture. However, a number of factors served to create the management culture, including escalating competition for scarce resources within the department (and among other city agencies), an increasing emphasis on management by the political leadership, and greater emphasis on accountability and productivity (Reuss-Ianni, 1993). As a result, the management culture focuses on maximizing the efficiency of the organization, rational decision making, cost-effective procedures, and objective accountability. These objectives often conflict with the objectives of the street cop culture, and street cops argue that the management cops have forgotten what it is like to be on the street (Reuss-Ianni, 1993).

The street cop culture functions under a complex set of rules, what Reuss-Ianni calls the "cop's code," that dictate police behavior and define the officer's relationship with peers and supervisors (see Chapter 8 for more discussion of this code). Rules that govern cop-to-cop interactions include:

- Don't get involved in another guy's sector.
- Don't leave work for the next tour.
- Hold up your end of the work. (Reuss-Ianni, 1993)

The rules that dictate cop-to-boss interactions highlight the divide between the two cultures:

- Don't give them too much activity.
- Keep out of the way of any boss from outside your precinct.
- Know your bosses.
- Don't do the bosses' work for them.
- Don't trust bosses to look out for your interests. (Reuss-Ianni, 1993)

Reuss-ianni (1993) argues that the existence of these two cultures and the conflict that occurs between them is a major factor in the increasing alienation of the street cop.

> While there is some uneasy accommodation between these two cultures, they are increasingly in conflict, and this conflict isolates the precinct functionally, if not structurally from the headquarters. The isolation produces disaffection, strong stress reactions, increasing attrition of personnel, and growing problems of integrity. (p. 4)

Whisenand (2004) and others argue that the divide between the street cop and management cultures can be overcome by adhering to the core principles of effective supervision laid out above.

CURRENT ISSUES IN POLICE MANAGEMENT AND ORGANIZATION

Alternative Organizational Models

Given the limitations of the traditional bureaucratic model described above, a number of alternative organizational models have emerged. A number of departments have attempted to create *flat* **organizations** by eliminating middle ranks and reducing excesses in the departmental hierarchy (Grant & Terry, 2005). A central theme of community policing involves decentralization, whereby police precincts operate almost as independent departments with little control exerted by headquarters. In the *functional structure* approach, specific units overlap in their purpose and responsibilities to facilitate cooperation and information sharing. The *matrix structure* approach,

> . . . creates a team problem-solving environment in which members of different divisions (i.e., detective bureau, patrol, vice/narcotics) are assigned to specific problem areas, such as counterterrorism, organized crime and so on. Matrix structures are like the task force model and are generally time limited based on a particular problem. Members return to their respective units upon completion of the project. (Grant & Terry, 2005 pp. 119–120)

The Hospital Model.   Guyot (1991) argues that police departments should move toward the **hospital model** and embrace the occupation as a profession. She argues that the lack of progress in policing is caused primarily by the occupation's reliance on the military organizational model, which is inappropriate for the police. The central feature of policing that allows for the application of the hospital model is discretion: Both patrol officers and doctors exercise tremendous discretion in handling their clientele.

According to Guyot (1991), an overview of the hospital model demonstrates how it can be applied to police departments. The typical hospital is run by two separate and distinct management systems: administrative and medical. The medical management system is comprised of doctors and other medical staff who make the day-to-day decisions regarding the treatment and handling of patients. Hospital administrators play no role in decisions related to the medical treatment of patients. Administrators are responsible for "the comfort of the hotel services, the efficiency of the records system, the maintenance of the buildings and equipment, the quality of nursing, the accuracy of lab work" (Guyot, 1991, p. 67).

> However, the central point is that the hospital's chief executive officer is responsible for overall policy and every decision that is not a medical judgment on an individual patient, whereas physicians are responsible to their clients, to themselves, and to their peers for the quality of their medical decisions. The controls on physicians come not from a hierarchy of supervisors but primarily from their own internalized standards, originating in their arduous recruitment and training. The peer review organization,

pathology review, and fear of malpractice suits are secondary controls. (Guyot, 1991, p. 68)

As illustrated above in Reuss-Ianni's two cultures of policing, the typical police department functions in much the same way as a hospital, despite application of the military model. The important day-to-day decisions involving clients are made by line officers (similar to doctors). Of course, the critical barrier confronting application of the hospital model involves replacing the punitive control and command management system with a supportive system that leaves officers free to make professional judgments. Consider how the hospital model would look when applied to a police department:

- Stringent recruitment and selection standards are employed (consider the standards for admittance to medical school).
- Rigorous training prepares officers for their profession, including academy training and a period of field training (for doctors, this involves four years of medical school and residency).
- There is no direct supervision or control of police officers carrying out their duties; performance is based on internalized standards (in a hospital, there are no "sergeants" who are responsible for checking doctor decisions on treatment).
- The management of the department is responsible for the overall functioning and efficiency of the organization, such as personnel, records, property, maintenance, etc., but does interfere with line officer decision making. Management would set general policies and procedures. Mid-level managers, if they existed, would play an administrative role only, with no supervision responsibilities.
- Questionable decisions by police officers would be examined by a peer review panel (the police version of the American Medical Association).
- Individual police officers could be sued for malpractice and would be required to get malpractice insurance.

Clearly, there are some limitations to Guyot's (1991) argument because of the fundamental differences between policing and medicine. For example, training of police officers can be measured in terms of weeks, not years. Police officers have tremendous authority, including the capacity to use force. Police officers are generally dealing with unwilling and uncooperative clients. Police have a wide range of complex and sometimes conflicting responsibilities. The history of police misconduct suggests that supervision is critically important to controlling police behavior. Nevertheless, Guyot's approach is compelling on a number of levels.

> Supplanting it [military model] with the hospital model is a starting point for rethinking fundamental questions, for almost never should police officers act like soldiers, but often they should act like physicians. To think of police work as human service akin to

that of medicine permits a bubbling up of new images, notions, possibilities, considerations, and approaches that do not arise within the confines of the police quasi-military tradition. (Guyot, 1991, p. 64)

Manpower and Resource Shortages

Currently, nearly all major urban police departments—as well as a good portion of mid-sized and small departments—find themselves understaffed and underbudgeted. Chapter 1 describes in some detail how departments are being forced to develop new, targeted recruitment strategies to draw diverse and qualified applicant pools. At the same time, budget constraints are forcing police departments to better manage and deploy their scarce resources. Three adaptations to these constraints that have emerged in recent years are discussed below: civilianization, consolidation, and contracting.

Civilianization.   Departments spend a significant amount of money to recruit, select, train, and outfit sworn police personnel. Yet, earlier discussions of the police workload indicate that most of the calls for service police receive do not involve crime and law enforcement. As a result, many departments have begun replacing sworn officer positions with non-sworn personnel, called **civilianization.** There are a number of roles on both the administrative and field services sides of the department that can be sufficiently filled by civilians, rather than the more costly and more hard-to-find sworn officers. These include positions in communications (i.e., dispatch), research and planning, crime analysis, crime scene investigation, traffic, and even calls for service where only reports will be taken (i.e., reports of stolen property). Recent research indicates steady growth in the use of non-sworn personnel, from 11 percent in 1960 to 18 percent in 1980 and 29 percent in 1997 (King & Maguire, 2000).

Walker and Katz (2002) note that there are several benefits to employing civilian personnel:

- They free sworn officers for critical police work that requires a trained and experienced officer.
- They possess needed expertise in such areas as computers or data analysis.
- In many cases, they are less expensive than sworn officers, thereby representing a cost saving. (p. 65)

Again, given that such a large percentage of the police workload involves service and information-gathering tasks, the use of non-sworn personnel allows the department to focus the efforts of trained police officers on crime-related tasks. In the 1970s and 1980s, the Santa Ana, California, Police Department (SAPD) implemented a department-wide civilian or para-policing program as part of its community policing initiative. Under this program, "para-police were trained semi-professionals who performed important, but more routine, preliminary or peripheral police tasks, usually connected with service to citizens" (Skolnick & Fyfe,

1993, p. 255). The civilian personnel performed a wide range of tasks: organizing neighborhood watches, presenting crime prevention seminars, taking crime reports, identifying and marking abandoned vehicles to be towed, conducting traffic accident investigations, recontacting crime victims, and even engaging in patrol in marked vehicles (through they were to call for sworn personnel if situations arose where authority or use of force was needed) (Skolnick & Fyfe, 1993).

The controversial issue surrounding civilianization is not whether it is a viable option (most agree that it is), but rather, how civilianized should the department become? Although civilians are generally paid less than sworn police, it is necessary to pay more for those with specialized skills such as crime analysts, computer experts, and crime scene investigators (i.e., natural science backgrounds). In many places, police unions have become wary of civilianization, viewing civilian personnel as a threat to their livelihood. "Cops are not independent and highly paid professionals, like doctors and lawyers, and so they see para-police not as heighteners of their status and professionalism but as potential union-busters" (Skolnick & Fyfe, 1993, p. 256).

As departments become increasingly civilianized, police chiefs must be cautious of the impact of civilianization on police officer morale: A divided police department with tension between sworn and non-sworn personnel does not create a healthy and productive work environment. Given the influence and power of police unions, the department should include union leadership in any planning and discussion of civilianization. If the police union is consulted, the department can fashion a civilianization plan that benefits the department in the ways described above, but that is also well received by the rank and file. For example, some departments have compromised by paying civilians with specialized skills the same as sworn personnel, but civilian employees are excluded from pension and benefit plans enjoyed by the sworn members of the department (Skolnick & Fyfe, 1993).

Consolidation.   The typical local police department is very small, with fewer than ten officers. The cost of operating a police department is significant, particularly for small jurisdictions across the United States. Given the tremendous number of small police departments and their burdensome cost, the National Advisory Commission on Criminal Justice Standards and Goals (1973) recommended that all departments with ten or fewer officers should be consolidated. The primary rationale for consolidation is that the cost of operating a police department could then be shared by several municipalities rather than just one. Moreover, a consolidated or regional police department will be larger and less fragmented than the alternative numerous small departments. As a result, **consolidation** should then lead to better communication and cooperation among police, better training (as the costs of additional training can be shared by jurisdictions), better police service, and less duplication of services. Research on the impact of consolidation is scant, but there are some indications that it can be effective. A study of a regional police department in Pennsylvania found that the consolidated force generated cost savings, better police services, and better coordinated responses to emergencies and crime (Krimmel, 1997). In the 1990s, the Charlotte, North Carolina, Police Department and the Mecklenberg County Sheriff's Department merged into one agency. However, Walker and Katz (2002) note that consolidation among large departments often creates numerous problems, as large bureaucracies are unwilling to give up their autonomy and may have very different standards, policies, and practices. Moreover, communities—both small and large—may resist consolidation because they are unwilling to give up their independence, or they feel that the consolidated force will be less responsive to the individual needs of their specific community.

Contracting for Police Services.   A third response to manpower and budget short-ages involves the **contracting of police services** from other law enforcement agen-cies. This strategy is particularly attractive for small towns who can buy police services from larger, contiguous towns, county sheriff's departments, and state police agencies. In rural parts of New Jersey, for example, many small towns contract with the New Jersey State Police for police service rather than operating their own police departments. The Los Angeles Sheriff's Department contracts with forty separate towns to provide police service (Walker & Katz, 2002). This type of contracting of services is relatively common in other areas of government, such as sewage, trash disposal, and water supply, as well as other areas of criminal justice (jails and emer-gency communication systems). The advantages and disadvantages of contracting for police services mirror that of consolidation. Advantages include cost savings, better coordination and response (i.e., less fragmentation), greater efficiency and less dupli-cation of service, better trained police, and generally improved police service. The disadvantages include a loss of sense of independence or autonomy, less identifica-tion between police and the community, and potential conflicts among communities sharing police service. Also, a community that disbands its police department in favor of contracting for services will be forced to fire their police officers (unless there is arrangement that they be hired by the other agency).

Militarization of the Police

Despite the widespread adoption of community policing across the United States, there is strong evidence to indicate a growing militarization of U.S. police depart-ments through the expansion of police paramilitary units (PPUs) (Kraska & Kappler, 2005). Police paramilitary units, such as SWAT and Emergency Response units, are unique from the rank and file of the department in a number of important ways:

- They are equipped with an array of militaristic equipment and technology, such as submachine guns, sniper rifles, automatic shotguns, and night vision goggles.
- They are equipped with numerous less-than-lethal weapons such as Tasers, stun devices, flash-bang devices, and beanbag guns.
- Their structure is modeled after military and foreign police special operations teams; they wear black "battle dress uniforms (BDUs)," combat boots, full-

body armor, Kevlar helmets; team members place a high premium on group solidarity and view themselves as "elite" officers.

■ There work has traditionally been very different from routine patrol, such as hostage and barricaded person situations, riots and disorder, and terrorism.

By the mid-1990s, nearly 90 percent of police departments responding to a survey indicated that they had a paramilitary unit; up from 59 percent in 1982 and 78 percent in 1990. Importantly, Kraska and Kappeler (2005) note that not only are PPUs becoming more common, but they are increasingly being used in more routine aspects of police work. During the 1980s, PPUs averaged approximately 13 call-outs per year, but by 1995, this number had quadrupled, and the majority of call-outs involved "high risk warrant work," typically involving drug houses (Kraska & Kappeler, 2005). Also, there has been a tremendous increase in the use of PPUs in patrol work (a 292 percent increase from 1982 to 1995). The following quote from an officer in a department well known for its community policing philosophy illustrates the point:

> We're into saturation patrols in hot spots. We do a lot of our work with the SWAT unit because we have bigger guns. We send out two, two-to-four-men cars, we look for minor violations and do jump-outs, either on people on the street or automobiles. After we jump-out the second car provides periphery cover with an ostentatious display of weaponry. We're sending a clear message: if the shootings don't stop, we'll shoot some-one. (Kraska & Kappeler, 2005, p. 469)

Kraska and Kappeler's (2005) research documents an increase in the number of paramilitary units, an expansion in their activities, and what they call a "normaliza-tion of paramilitary units into mainstream police work" (p. 471). Clearly, there are a number of negative consequences to these developments. First, the fundamental mil-itarism of these units "escalates to new heights the cynical view that the most expedi-ent route to solving social problems is through military-style force, weaponry, and technology" (Kraska & Kappeler, 2005, p. 472). Second, the popularity of these units within police departments, particularly the view that they are the elite or "best of the best," increases the likelihood that the rest of the department may seek out and adopt this militaristic view. Skolnick and Fyfe (1993) are quite clear and convincing in their argument linking the soldiers-in-a-war mentality to police misconduct. Third, and perhaps most importantly, the spread of these types of units raises questions about their threat to the safety of both officers and citizens. "Contemporary PPUs do not just react to pre-existing emergencies that might require highly trained teams of police officers; instead, most PPUs proactively seek out and even manufacture highly dangerous situations" (Kraska & Kappeler, 2005, p. 472). Quite simply, the more these units are called out—especially for routine police work—the greater the likeli-hood of injury to either police or citizens. Last, it is costly for a department to train, equip, and deploy a PPU. Especially in smaller departments, it is likely that a PPU that is properly trained and staffed will serve as a drain on the department's resources; alternatively, a PPU that is not properly trained represents a significant threat to the safety of the police and the community.

SUMMARY

This chapter examined a range of issues associated with the police department as a bureaucratic organization. The first part of the chapter described in some detail the bureaucratic and quasi-military style of the traditional police department. As a bureaucracy, the police share in common a number of organizational features with other bureaucratic institutions, including multiple tasks, a pyramid-shaped hierarchy, unit of command, and rules and regulations. The advantages and disadvantages of the bureaucratic model are examined as well. The quasi-military organizational style presents a larger problem for police, particularly because of the tremendous discretion and authority among line-level personnel. The important roles of civil service and unionization are also described.

The second part of the chapter focuses on the functioning and structure of the department itself. The chapter discusses in some detail the wide range of responsibilities left to the police and how those responsibilities sometimes are contradictory. There is remarkable similarity among U.S. police departments with regard to structure, including field services—patrol, traffic, and investigation—and administration. The vital role of supervision is described, with particular emphasis on the core features of effective supervision. The existence of "two cultures of policing"—one management and one street level—represents a challenge to the effective functioning of the department.

Finally, a number of current issues and controversies surrounding the police as an organization are discussed. A number of alternative organizational models have emerged, including flat or decentralized models, as well as the hospital model. Although intriguing, the likelihood of police adopting the hospital organizational model seems remote, given that is represents such a substantial change. The chapter also discusses the "three Cs" as responses to manpower and budget shortages: civilianization, consolidation, and contracting for police services. Each innovation brings with it advantages and disadvantages, and the challenge for a department is to strike a balance that is acceptable to both the rank and file of the department and the community. And last, the increasing militarization of U.S. police through paramilitary units is discussed. The growth of these units, and especially their "normalization" into routine police work, seems to represent a co-occurring and seemingly conflicting development to the spread of community policing.

KEY TERMS

Bureaucracy

Civil service

Civilianization

Consolidation

Contracting police services
Directed patrol
Decentralization
Discretion
Flat organizations
Functional structure
Hierarchical organization
Hospital model

Matrix structure
Quasi-military style
Response time
Span of control
Two cultures of policing
Unions
Unity of command

DISCUSSION QUESTIONS

1. Describe the core features of a bureauracy.

2. What are the advantages and disadvantages of the bureaucratic model for police?

3. Is the quasi-military organizational model appropriate for police? Why or why not?

4. What are the primary roles and responsibilities of police? Why do the police have an unclear mandate?

5. Describe the two cultures of policing, according to Reuss-Ianni.

6. Describe the hospital model and how it would apply to the police.

7. What are civilianization and consolidation?

REFERENCES

American Bar Association. (1980). *Standards relating to the urban police function* (2nd ed.). Boston: Little, Brown.

Antunes, G., & Scott, E.J. (1981). Calling the cops: Police telephone operators and citizen calls for service. *Journal of Criminal Justice, 9*(2), 167.

Bittner, E. (1970). *The functions of police in modern society.* Chevy Chase, MD: National Institute of Mental Health.

Bureau of Justice Statistics. (1997). *Law enforcement management and administrative statistics, 1997.* Washington, DC: Author.

Champion, D.H., & Hooper, M.K. (2003). *Introduction to American policing.* New York: McGraw-Hill.

Cordner, G.W., & Trojanwicz, R.C. (1992). Patrol. In G.W. Cordner & D.C. Hale (Eds.), *What works in policing? Operations and administration examined.* Cincinnati, OH: Anderson Publishing.

Federal Bureau of Investigation. (2000). *Crime in the United States, 1999.* Washington, DC: Government Printing Office.

Furstenburg Jr., F.F., & Wellford, C.F. (1973). Calling the police: The evaluation of police service. *Law and Society Review, 7,* 393–406.

Grant, H.B., & Terry, K.J. (2005). *Law enforcement in the 21st century.* Boston: Allyn and Bacon.

Greenwood, P.W, & Petersilia, J. (1975). *The criminal investigative process, V. 1 Summary and police recommendations.* Santa Monica, CA: Rand.

Guyot, D.G. (1991). *Policing as though people matter.* Philadelphia: Temple University Press.

King, W., & Maguire, E. (2000). *Police civilianization, 1950–2000: Change or continuity?* Paper presented at the American Society of Criminology meeting, San Francisco.

Kraska, P.B., & Kappeler, V.E. (2005). Militarizing American police: The rise and normalization of paramilitary units. In V.E. Kappeler (Ed.), *The police and society.* Prospect Heights, Ill: Waveland Press.

Krimmel, J.T. (1997). The Northern York County police consolidation experience: An Analysis of consolidation of police services in eight Pennsylvania rural counties. *Policing: An International Journal of Police Strategies and Management, 20*(3), 497–518.

Manning, P.K. (1988). *Symbolic communication: Signifying calls and the police response.* Cambridge, MA: MIT Press.

National Advisory Commission on Criminal Justice Standards and Goals. (1973). *Police.* Washington, DC: US Government Printing Office.

Onder, J. (2002). *Traffic safety.* Available at: www.sussexcountysheriff.com/traffic_safety.htm. May 15, 2005.

Police Executive Research Forum. (1981). *Survey of police operational and administrative practices-1981.* Washington, DC: PERF.

Perrow, C. (1972). *Complex organizations: A critical essay.* Glenview, IL: Scott, Foresman.

Reiss, A.J. (1971). *The police and the public.* New Haven: Yale University Press.

Reuss-Ianni, E. (1993). *Two cultures of policing.* New Brunswick, NJ: Transaction Publishers.

Scott, E.J. (1981). *Calls for service: Citizen demand and initial police response.* Washington, DC: Government Printing Office.

Shepard Engel, R. (2005). How police supervisory styles influence patrol officer behavior. In R.G. Dunham & G.P. Alpert (Eds.), *Critical issues in policing* (5th ed.). Long Grove, Ill: Waveland Press.

Skolnick, J.H. & Fyfe, J.J. (1993). *Above the law: Police and the excessive use of force.* New York: Free Press.

Thibault, A.T., Lynch, L.M., & McBride, R.B. (2001). *Proactive police management* (5th ed.). Upper Saddle River, NJ: Prentice-Hall.

Thornburgh, R. (March 4, 1991). Keynote address to the Attorney General's Summit on *Law enforcement responses to violent crime: Public safety in the nineties.*

Vila, B. (2000). *Tired cops: The importance of managing police fatigue.* Washington, DC: Police Executive Research Forum.

Walker, S., & Katz, C.M. (2002). *The police in America: An introduction.* New York: McGraw-Hill.

Westley, W. (1970). *Violence and the police.* Cambridge, MA: MIT Press.

Whisenand, P.M. (2004). *Supervising police personnel: The fifteen responsibilities.* Upper Saddle River, NJ: Prentice Hall.

Wilson, J.Q. (1968). *Varieties of police behavior.* Cambridge, MA: Harvard University Press.

Wilson, O.W. (1941). *Distribution of police patrol force.* Chicago: Public Administration Service.

Wrobleski, H.M., & Hess, K.M. (2003). *Introduction to law enforcement and criminal justice.* (7th ed.). Belmont, CA: Wadsworth.

■ ■ ■ ■ ■

SCHOLAR'S PERSPECTIVE

Restructuring of the City of Paterson, New Jersey, Police Department

Michael C. Walker*

Director of the Paterson (New Jersey) Police Department and Assistant Professor at the Passaic County Community College

THE CITY

The city of Paterson is located in the northeast part of the state of New Jersey, about ten miles west of New York City. The city was founded by Alexander Hamilton, the first Secretary of the Treasury, in 1791 as the first industrial city in the United States. During its industrial past, the city produced silk and textiles, the first Colt revolvers, steam locomotives, and the first submarine. Following the Great Depression many industries moved out of the city and, with the advent of the interstate highway system, many businesses and households followed their lead. Today, Paterson has a population of approximately 152,000 living within 8.4 square miles, making it one of the most densely populated cities in the United States and the third largest city in the state of New Jersey. According to the 2000 U.S. Census, the per capita income of Paterson's population is $13,257, and 22 percent of Paterson's population live below the poverty line. The demographic breakdown of the population is 31 percent white, 33 percent African American, while 50 percent of the population describe themselves as having Hispanic or Latino origins.

Paterson is governed by an elected mayor as chief executive and has a legislative body consisting of nine councilpersons, six elected to represent each ward in the city and three elected "at large."

*Michael C. Walker is the Director of the Paterson (New Jersey) Police Department and an Assistant Professor at the Passaic County Community College in Paterson, New Jersey. He retired from the police department with the rank of Police Captain and is a graduate of the 170th Session of the FBI National Academy. He holds a Master of Public Administration Degree in Criminal Justice Policy from the City University of New York, John Jay College of Criminal Justice.

THE POLICE DEPARTMENT

The police department of the city of Paterson is one of the oldest in the United States, having been established in 1866. It has an authorized strength of 450 sworn and is currently staffed by 410 sworn officers with an additional 33 recruits undergoing basic training. A police director is appointed by the mayor to oversee the policies and practices of the department, make personnel decisions such as hiring, firing, and promotion, and to administer the budget ($37 million in FY 2005). The day-to-day operations of the department are under the purview of the chief of police, who is assisted by two deputy chiefs, six captains, 26 lieutenants, and 66 sergeants. In addition to its patrol operation (discussed below), the department has investigative divisions including Criminal Investigations, Narcotics and Vice, Juvenile, and Internal Affairs. The patrol force is supplemented by a Traffic Division, a Special Operations Division, and a Street Crimes Unit. The department also manages one of twenty-three certified police academies in the state.

During 2004, the department responded to 197,675 calls for service and made 7,067 arrests. The FBI's 2004 *Uniform Crime Report* showed that Paterson experienced an 8.5 percent decrease in major crime from the prior year and, of the ten largest cities in the state, Paterson ranked ninth in crime per 1,000 population. This ranking was achieved despite the fact that the police department was ranked eighth among the ten cities in police officers per 1,000 population (at 2.65 per 1,000).

PATROL DEPLOYMENT TODAY

Currently the Patrol Division consists of two patrol platoons (A & B), each commanded by a captain and overseen by a Deputy Chief of Field Operations. Each platoon is responsible for providing police services throughout the city on the days that it is working. Policing in Paterson is conducted on a temporal basis with each platoon working for four consecutive days and being off-duty for the next four days. This is due primarily to the work schedule negotiated by the police union that requires that uniformed personnel work 11¼-hour tours for four days straight with the following four days off (referred to as the four-and-four schedule). Five squads are assigned to each platoon to ensure for police coverage for 24 hours. Command over, and responsibility for, crime and conditions in the city thus shifts from one captain to the other based on whose platoon is working. This has led to a lack of accountability and difficulties in communicating departmental priorities and strategies from the platoon going off-duty for the next four days to the one coming in. A lack of follow-through also results as one captain institutes a patrol strategy (such as park & walk or directed patrol) into a neighborhood during his time on, but which may not be maintained by the next captain. A basic command strategy that grew from this design was for commanders and supervisors to hope (and pray) that nothing really bad occurred during their "four days on" so that they can better enjoy their upcoming four days off. Responses to questions raised during CompStat meetings usually consisted of the commander's responding that the problem didn't exist while his platoon was working and that it was the other captain's issue.

Policing in the city is conducted by fifteen sector cars, each given responsibility for a segment of the city. These patrol sectors were established in 1975 and are unchanged despite significant demographic changes in the city, such as the demolition of high-rise, high-density housing developments and the construction of low-density housing throughout the city. The sector cars are supplemented by backup units and units assigned to directed patrol at the discretion of the patrol captain. The large number of calls for service (approximately 200,000 per year) combined with the public's demand for a rapid response to calls has resulted in the units running from one part of the city to the next to answer calls, with very little proactive policing and virtually no post integrity. Additionally, police officers are assigned to different units each day and thus are unable to get to know the various neighborhoods of the city and the people who live and work in them.

PROPOSED PATROL DEPLOYMENT

As illustrated above, the current patrol design hindered communication, accountability, and post integrity. Most strategies had a useful life of four days then died. Police officers had no ownership of their sectors since they would most likely be deployed to another sector the following day. Regardless, officers were rarely present in their own sector during their shift because they were being constantly pulled off to answer a priority call elsewhere.

The city is divided into six wards, each with a population of about 25,000. Some wards are more densely populated than others and, due to that as well as other factors, have a greater need for police services. Some wards are less densely populated and have a lesser need for intensive policing. The proposed patrol plan, which is geographical rather than temporal, will be to combine two wards, one with a greater need for policing along with one, contiguous to the first, with a lesser need, into a police district. Three police districts will be created, and each will be under the command of a police captain, four lieutenants, and 12 sergeants. Each district commander and his or her staff will be responsible for crime and the conditions that lead to it 7 days a week, 24 hours a day. Post integrity will be enhanced since each police officer will be assigned to a district permanently and his or her supervisors will ensure that, except for the most serious calls, he or she will remain within the district. District commanders will be permitted to assign their personnel in any manner they feel will be most effective in dealing with crime but will be held accountable for the result. This will help to ensure that patrol strategies last more than a few days and that a captain's vision for policing in his or her district is more enduring. Each district will have two platoons of officers, and three squads in each platoon will ensure coverage throughout the day.

One of the more interesting features of this initiative is that there will be a draft held to choose districts and the personnel assigned to each. Of the three captains, the one with the most seniority will choose which district he or she will command, and the others will then choose their districts. Then, again by seniority, the captains will choose their lieutenants, their sergeants, and the patrol officers to work for them. Similar to choosing sides for a neighborhood game of baseball, those officers with a greater work ethic will be chosen first and those with lesser values chosen last. Unlike the prior patrol plan, it will be unwise for a commander to choose a member of his or her team who is unlikely to achieve results, since the commander will be held ultimately accountable for what his or her district achieves or fails to achieve. "Slackers" will be less tolerated than they are presently.

Due to the existing union contract, officers assigned to patrol will still work the "four-and-four" schedule and are permitted to bid on their squad of choice (or work hours) by seniority. This will not change with the new plan but, hopefully, since the officers work in the same district and for the same captain, they will share his or her vision of policing in that neighborhood.

Technology will be utilized to bridge the gap between those officers who are off-duty and those who are working. BlackBerry® cellphones/PDAs are issued to each command-level officer in the department. These devices are used to give continuous updates on crime and conditions throughout the city. Both the Criminal Investigation Division and the Narcotics and Vice Division are mandated to post a crime and activity report on these devices by 9:00 am each day. By utilizing this system, police commanders are kept informed of the conditions in the city and in their district.

COMMUNITY POLICING

Paterson, like most cities, began to experiment with community policing in the late 1980s and throughout the 1990s. Community policing in Paterson mainly consisted of assigning a number of personnel to a community-policing division and having it, alone, responsible to address community concerns. As Dr. White states in this chapter, "many departments who 'adopted' community policing have found that little has changed beyond the rhetoric." This statement is true for Paterson. When one unit is given sole responsibility for any function of policing, it frees the other members of the agency from any responsibility for that function. When the task of working with the community is given to a 30-officer unit, the other 420 members of the department can say that it isn't their job to work with the community. Community policing in Paterson denigrated to the point where a couple of dozen officers basically hid in the community and performed virtually no police activity there. According to the broken windows theory, if police officers were to remedy quality-of-life conditions, the broader crime picture will shrink. In the city of Paterson quality-of-life offenses (public drinking, gangs, graffiti, public urination, and loud music) were rampant, but the members of the Community Policing Unit issued an average of less than one summons per month for quality-of-life violations. Due to the lack of productivity of the Community Policing Division, it was disbanded in January 2005. It is the hope of the administration that the new Police District Plan will make all members of the department accountable and responsive to the members of their community. This plan will make it easier for members of the community to identify the officers assigned there and to communicate any issues to the district captain and his or her staff. Additionally, district captains are tasked to attend all community meetings within their district where questions of crime or quality-of-life conditions may arise.

POLICE UNIONS

As Dr. White states in this chapter, "unions give officers a voice in how the department is run through 'shared governance'." This is also true in Paterson, and the above proposal reflected on some of the union issues involved with restructuring the police department (the four-and-four schedule and picks by seniority for tour hours). In addition, the contract between the city of Paterson and Paterson Police PBA Local #1 specifically states that "all major changes affecting an employee's health, welfare, working conditions . . . will first be discussed with the Association President prior to the decision being made to affect such change." As a result of this, the union had to be consulted regarding each and every element of this patrol plan. It is important to note, however, that even if interaction with the union was not mandated, police administrators would still make every effort to discuss major changes, such as this one, with the members of the agency and to get their input into the proposed change.

CHAPTER 6

POLICE FIELD WORK

The previous five chapters have dealt with a host of issues surrounding police officers and police departments, ranging from selection, training, and alternative philosophies of policing to the organization and administration of the department. In Chapter 5 we learned that the responsibilities of a police officer far exceed the traditional focus on crime and law enforcement; in fact, we now know that such crime control-related work represents only a small portion of their daily activity. This chapter delves into the actual work of police officers themselves, with particular attention paid to the current crime and order maintenance-related problems facing police today. The chapter begins by examining two critical elements that frame the work of police officers on the street. The first involves the law. Every action taken by a police officer must be in accordance with local and state law, as well as (and perhaps most importantly) the Constitution of the United States. The major legal issues that shape the work of the police are described, including the Fourth, Fifth, and Sixth Amendments, and recent Supreme Court rulings affecting the legal principles laid out in those Amendments. The chapter also discusses the U.S. Patriot Act and its implications for police and the law.

The second critical element of police field work involves discretion and decision making. Police exercise tremendous discretion in carrying out their duties. The chapter first defines discretion and traces its historical recognition by practitioners and scholars. The major factors that influence police discretion and decision making are also reviewed, including environmental, organizational, and situational variables. Last, the chapter describes alternatives for increasing the rationality of police decision making.

The final part of the chapter examines contemporary field work issues, which include some old and new problems. These include gangs, drugs and crime, domestic violence, the mentally ill, sex offenders, computer crime, identity theft, and terrorism.

POLICE AND THE LAW

The law plays a centrally important role in policing. In many ways, the law serves as a roadmap for police officers, providing guidance for appropriate and inappropriate behavior and serving as the primary tool for combating crime and disorder. The law also serves as a primary recourse for those who are victimized by police misconduct (see Chapter 10). There are three different types of law in the United States:

- **Criminal law:** Defines crimes and punishments.
- **Civil law:** Provides a means for controlling noncriminal relationships between individuals, businesses and organizations.
- **Administrative law:** Provides rules and regulations established by governments to control the actions of individuals, business, and industry. (Champion & Hooper, 2003, p. 377)

There are several different sources of law. First, police are responsible for enforcing local laws and ordinances passed by the jurisdiction in which they work. For example, city council may pass a new curfew law that prohibits children under the age of 16 from being out past a certain hour on school nights. The police will be responsible for enforcing that law. Second, the vast majority of crime-related work that police engage in involves state law—penal or criminal law that police rely on to determine if a crime has been committed, and if so, with which offense the individual should be charged. The third source of law is the Constitution of the United States, specifically the first ten Amendments known as the **Bill of Rights.** The Bill of Rights, passed after the Constitution was ratified, seeks to protect citizens from government abuses, and several directly affect police officers:

- First Amendment: Right to free speech, to peaceably assemble, and to petition the government for redress of grievances.
- Fourth Amendment: Protection from unreasonable search and seizures, no warrants for search and seizure issued without probable cause.
- Fifth Amendment: Protection from self-incrimination, double jeopardy (being tried for the same crime twice), and right to due process.
- Sixth Amendment: Right to an attorney, a speedy and public trial, right to confront witnesses.
- Eighth Amendment: Protection from excessive bail and cruel and unusual punishment.
- Fourteenth Amendment: Constitutional protections in state criminal cases.

Key Legal Principles and Issues from the Bill of Rights: Search, Seizure, and Arrest

Reasonable Suspicion.   Police officers cannot take legal action simply because they think a crime may have occurred. There are several standards of proof required to justify legal action by the police, and the lowest standard is reasonable suspicion. **Reasonable suspicion** is,

> the amount of knowledge needed to make an ordinary and cautious person believe that criminal activity is occurring. The knowledge must be specific and concrete, and the officer must be able to explain it clearly. (Champion & Hooper, 2003, p. 382)

Gut feelings or instinct are not enough to justify the police officer's taking action. There must be some available evidence that generates the suspicion of the officer and can be articulated. The facts from the *Terry v. Ohio* case offer an excellent example of the type of proof required to meet the reasonable suspicion standard. In that case, the officer witnessed several individuals hanging around a jewelry store and looking into the windows. The individuals moved up and down the street and repeatedly returned to the store. Believing the suspects were "casing" the store and were about to rob it, the officer conducted a field interrogation (detained them, pat-down search, and questioning). The suspects' actions were enough to reach the reasonable suspicion standard. Reasonable suspicion is necessary for stop-and-frisk field interrogations like the example above, but it does not permit the officer to conduct searches, seizures, or to make an arrest (probable cause is required for these actions, see below).

Probable Cause. **Probable cause** is the standard of suspicion required for the majority of formal police actions, including arrest, search, and seizure. Probable cause occurs when the available "evidence can lead a reasonable person to believe that a suspect has committed or will commit a specific crime" (Champion & Hooper, 2003, p. 382). Police can determine probable cause based on three sources of information:

- Officer's own observations: What the officer sees, hears, or smells (i.e., smelling marijuana during a car stop, or witnessing a crime occurring).
- Officer's expertise and circumstantial factors: The combination of the officer's expertise and circumstantial evidence (erratic driving that leads to a car stop and slurred speech of the driver).
- Information given to the officer by others: Information from other officers, witnesses, informants, and victims.

Probable cause can be articulated in an application for a warrant (search or arrest) that a judge will review and either sign or refuse. However, in most cases, police officers do not have the time to complete and submit a warrant application, and they are forced to make on-the-spot assessments about whether the available evidence reaches the probable cause standard. These on-the-spot decisions are then reviewed by judges at initial court appearances for the defendant and, to a lesser extent, by prosecutors who make decisions about the filing of criminal charges.

Searches and Arrests: With and Without Warrants. Whenever possible, it is best for police to obtain a warrant prior to conducting a search and/or making an arrest. This step allows for review of the available evidence by a judge and provides confirmation that the probable cause standard has been reached. In an application for a warrant, the officer presents all of the available evidence and swears the statement is true and accurate (affidavit). In a search warrant, the information must be detailed, including an exact address and the specific items to be seized. The search must then be limited to areas of the house where the specific items may be located. For example, if the items to be seized include large televisions, stereos, and automobiles, the officers are not permitted to search desk drawers and kitchen cabinets. If evidence not listed on the search warrant is found and the search has not violated the conditions of the warrant, the additional evidence can also be seized and is admissible. For example, if police are searching for firearms and they find drugs in an end table drawer, the drugs can be seized.

However, the nature of police work rarely allows police officers—patrol officers in particular—the time necessary to obtain a warrant. While detectives and officers in specialized units may have the time to apply for and obtain a warrant because they conduct longer investigations and have greater control over their caseload, patrol officers rarely know what each call for service will bring them. Imagine if every time an officer pulled over a drunken driver, the officer had to go back to the office, complete the warrant affidavit, deliver it to the judge, wait for the judge's decision, then drive back out to the scene and hope the driver is still there.

As a result, there are a number of important standards for police to follow when making warrantless arrests or searches. Police officers can make a warrantless search or arrest whenever they believe the probable cause standard has been reached and there are "exigent circumstances" that prohibit obtaining warrant (such as the suspect would escape or flee if the officer left the scene). Also, there are at least five different types of searches that an officer can conduct without a warrant:

- Search incidental to a lawful arrest: When an officer is making a lawful arrest, it is critical that the officer have total control over the person; therefore, the officer can make a detailed search of the person and the possessions that are within the arrestee's immediate control (i.e., if a suspect is arrested in his house, police can search the area immediately surrounding the suspect, but not the suspect's entire house).
- Search during a field interrogation: When conducting a field interrogation (i.e., *Terry* stop), the officer can conduct a superficial search of the individual's outer clothing.
- Search of automobiles: Police can search an automobile if they have probable cause to believe it contains criminal evidence (even if the driver has not been arrested), or if the suspect is arrested by or in the car (search incidental to a lawful arrest).
- Plain-view and open-field searches: Any evidence that is observed in plain view is open subject to "search" and can be seized (i.e., during a call for a noise complaint, the officer observes drugs on a end table by the door).
- Consent to search: If a citizen has voluntarily given the police consent to search, the police do not need a warrant to conduct the search.

Exclusionary Rule. Chapter 3 describes the U.S. Supreme Court ruling in *Mapp v. Ohio* (367 U.S. 643 [1961]), which established the **exclusionary rule.** This legal principle states that evidence that is seized illegally cannot be used in court. The illegal search violates the protections outlined in the Fourth Amendment (protection from unreasonable search and seizure), and thus is inadmissible in court. Since the original *Mapp* ruling, the Supreme Court has created a number of exceptions to the exclusionary rule where illegally seized evidence can be used in court:

1. Good Faith Exception: This exception holds that evidence is admissible when obtained from a seemingly acceptable warrant that is later determined to be invalid for reasons the police did not foresee.
2. The Inevitability of Discovery Exception: This exception holds that if evidence is seized illegally, but legal searches already in progress would have eventually found the evidence anyway, the seizure becomes legal because it becomes "inevitable" that it would have discovered.
3. Public Safety Exception: This exception holds that if police seize evidence illegally because of a threat to public safety, that threat outweighs the need to adhere to the rules and the evidence is admissible.
4. The Independent Source Exception: This exception holds that if evidence that is first seized illegally (and is inadmissible) is again seized with a proper warrant, it then becomes admissible.

The overriding theme from the exceptions that have developed over the last several decades is that the original principle laid out in the *Mapp* case was too broad—based on the opinions handed down by an increasingly conservative Supreme Court—and that there are cases where the violation of the Fourth Amendment protection against unreasonable search and seizure should not prevent the admission of evidence and hinder prosecution.

Importantly, available research strongly indicates that the police have adapted quite well to the exclusionary rule and its exceptions. Skolnick and Fyfe (1993) note: "Despite great interest by both objective scholars and partisan advocates, no study of the exclusionary rule . . . shows that exclusion of evidence results in dismissal of more than 1.5 percent of the criminal cases in any jurisdiction" (p. 194). In simpler terms, claims that the exclusionary rule—as well as other rulings from the due process revolution—have "handcuffed" police or in any way hindered their crime fighting ability appear to be unfounded.

Questioning, Interrogation, and* Miranda.**   Based on the U.S. Supreme Court ruling in *Miranda v. Arizona,* 384 U.S. 436 (1966) (see Chapter 3), police are required to read a suspect his or her rights once she or he has been arrested, or if the suspect's individual freedom to leave has been deprived. These well-known rights—the right to remain silent, right to speak with an attorney, etc.—must be read to a suspect (arrested or otherwise detained) before an **interrogation** takes place. However, if there is no arrest and interrogation, there is no need for police to read the ***Miranda **warnings.** For example, police officers are not required to read *Miranda* warnings during routine traffic stops for motor vehicle violations, nor when they are interviewing witnesses, citizens, and victims.

Once the officer has advised a suspect of his or her rights, the individual can either waive those rights and speak to police, or he or she can refuse and request legal counsel. Once a suspect asks for a lawyer, police must honor the request and end the interrogation immediately. Much like with the exclusionary rule, research shows that few criminal cases are lost because of problems with *Miranda*. Cassell and Hayman (1996) found that less than 4 percent of criminal cases were eventually overturned because of problems with reading the *Miranda* warnings. Additional research has shown that despite the *Miranda* requirements, nearly 80 percent of suspects waive their rights and speak to police without an attorney present (Leo, 1996).

Although the issues related to *Miranda,* custody, and interrogation seem straightforward, there have been a number of cases where the facts are unclear. For example, if the suspect is under the influence of drugs or alcohol, is mentally ill and in crisis, or does not speak English, how can the police be sure that the person understands his or her rights and has knowingly waived them? When has an individual's freedom to leave been sufficiently deprived so that *Miranda* warnings should be read? When has an interview become an interrogation? Consider the following: If a police officer calls a person on the phone and requests that he or she comes to the station to discuss an incident, does the officer have to read the *Miranda* warnings prior to the interview? Or, as part of an investigation, a detective is knocking on doors to interview potential witnesses. During a conversation with a neighbor, the officer begins to suspect that the neighbor is involved in the crime. Should the officer continue the "interview," or should the officer read the *Miranda* warnings and make known his suspicions? What if during the routine interview, the neighbor confesses to the crime without having been read his rights? Thus, the situations that arise may not always be clear-cut in terms of the critical issues related to *Miranda*. What is clear is that any information or confession obtained when the Court later determines that *Miranda* warnings should have been read—and were not—will be excluded. As a result, police officers are well-advised to read *Miranda* warnings in any case where they are unsure, or the facts are unclear.

Current Issues and Controversies Involving the Law

Pretextual Stops.   A **pretextual stop** occurs when a police officer stops an automobile for a motor vehicle violation (i.e., speeding) and uses that violation as a justification for investigation of more serious crimes (i.e., drugs). In *Whren v. United States,* 517 U.S. 806 (1996), the Court upheld the use of pretextual stops, calling them a constitutionally acceptable police tactic. In the *Whren* case, the officer pulled over Whren for a traffic violation, though his true intent was to investigate for drug-dealing activity. When the officer approached the car, he saw drug contraband in plain view and arrested the suspect. The Court ruled that, even though the traffic violation was only a pretext for the real reason for the stop, the officer had probable cause that Whren had committed the traffic violation. As a result, the stop was constitutional and the evidence seized (because it was in plain view) was admissible in court.

The controversy surrounding the use of pretextual stops involves its potential to lead to racial profiling (see Chapter 8). Most people commit some sort of traffic violation, whether it be speeding, not signaling when making a turn, or "rolling" through a stop sign. The concern is that police will then use other factors, most notably race, to decide who to pull over. The Court has also said that the law cannot be employed selectively (i.e., against minorities only) and that the officer must pull over the car for a specific motor vehicle violation (not just because he or she wants to "check it out"). Nevertheless, the use of pretextual stops, though constitutionally valid, can serve to worsen police–community relations, particularly among minority communities and if there are allegations of racial profiling.

Using Deception during Interrogations.   The U.S. Supreme Court has ruled in a number of cases that deceptive tactics during an interrogation are legal, within certain limits. Skolnick and Fyfe (1993) argue that deception and lying have become "the hallmark of the police interrogation trade" (p. 61). Examples include telling a suspect that he has been identified by an accomplice, presenting the suspect with faked physical evidence (i.e., fingerprints), and telling the suspect that he has been identified by a witness—all of which are permitted and commonly used police interrogation tactics. In *Arizona v. Fulminante,* 499 U.S. 279 (1991), an FBI informer coerced a fellow inmate into confessing to murder under the ruse of providing protection from prison violence. The Court upheld the conviction, noting that a coerced confession does not automatically require a conviction to be overturned.

A number of legal scholars have raised questions about the use of deception in suspect interrogations. Skolnick and Fyfe (1993) argue that lying in the interrogation room may send the message that lying elsewhere is acceptable. Others argue that deception can lead to confusion and possibly false confessions among the innocent. Richard Ofshe (1992), a social psychologist, states that deception can cause an innocent person to disbelieve his or her own recollection of events. Huff et al. (1986) estimate that there are approximately 6,000 false convictions each year in the United States and that the leading cause of improper convictions is false confessions. Yet, most police argue that the use of deception is a critically important tactic for conducting effective and successful interrogations. For the time being, the U.S. Supreme Court has agreed with police.

Curtilage.   How far do the protections of private property extend for a homeowner? Is the yard considered private? What about the walkway? What about a shed or detached garage? **Curtilage** is defined as "the area and outbuildings surrounding a house that are considered private property" (Champion & Hooper, 2003, p. 390). The Courts have handed down rulings in a number of cases that involve the protected areas around a house:

- A yard is always private property and receives Fourth Amendment protections, unless the owner has permitted public access to the yard.

- If a fence defines the perimeter of a house, the area inside the fence is generally considered to be protected, but if the fence is outside of the house's curtilage, the presence of the fence does not create an expectation of privacy.
- Garbage left at the curb for collection is not protected and can be searched without a warrant.
- Within a business, Fourth Amendment protections only apply to those areas not open to the public.

In *United States v. Dunn,* 480 U.S. 294, 301 (1987), the Supreme Court ruled that there are four factors to consider when determining if an area warrants Fourth Amendment protection: (1) the proximity of the area to the home, (2) whether the area is in the same enclosure as the home, (3) the nature of the use of the area, and (4) measures taken by the homeowner to protect the area from view. Alternatively, placing "no trespassing" signs and locked gates on areas that exceed curtilage does not create a reasonable expectation of privacy.

Technologically Enhanced Searches. New technological developments have allowed police to conduct searches in much less obtrusive ways, sometimes even without the knowledge of the individual. These types of searches involve aircraft (planes and helicopters), night vision and heat sensing equipment, and **wiretapping.** In *California v. Ciraola,* 476 U.S. 207 (1986), the Court ruled that police do not need a search warrant if they are in an aircraft and the area being searched is open to observation from the air, regardless of whether it is in property lines. The Court later extended this ruling to low-altitude helicopter searches (*Florida v. Riley*). The Court, however, has ruled that police must obtain warrants when using specialized heat seeking equipment to examine the interior contents of a home. In *Kyllo v. United States,* 121 U.S. 2038 (2001), the Court ruled that use of thermal imaging equipment to scan the outside of a suspected drug dealer's home (for high-intensity lamps used to grow marijuana) constituted a search and therefore required probable cause.

The Supreme Court has generally held that police must obtain a warrant prior to engaging in wiretapping (secretly listening to telephone conversations) or other forms of eavesdropping (surveillance over computers and electronic devices) (*Katz v. United States,* 389 U.S. 347 [1967]; *Berger v. New York,* 388 U.S. 954 [1967]; and *Lee v. Florida,* 392 U.S. 378 [1968]). In *United States v. White,* 401 U.S. 745 (1971), the Court ruled that police do not have to obtain a warrant if one of the parties in the communication consents to the eavesdropping. With regard to computers and the internet, the Court has ruled that computers are equivalent to "containers," and as a result, officers need probable cause to search them (see the section below on cyber crime). However, many of the rules and principles involving surveillance, eavesdropping, and wiretapping changed with the passage of the USA Patriot Act of 2001 described below.

The Patriot Act. In the wake of the September 11, 2001, terrorist attacks, the USA Patriot Act of 2001 was signed into law on October 26, 2001. The Act was criticized by civil libertarians because of the expanded powers it granted law enforcement, particularly with regard to wiretaps, search warrants, pen/trap orders, and subpoenas (Grant & Terry, 2005). A number of the more controversial provisions of the **Patriot Act** include:

- The FBI and CIA can now conduct nationwide roving wiretaps. Law enforcement is no longer limited to specific phones or specific computers. Instead, the government can issue one wiretap order that will allow investigators to extend the search to different phones and computers without having to prove in court that the information being access is specifically relevant to the investigation.
- The government can now receive all "noncontent" information voluntarily given to them by an Internet Service Provider (ISP) without the need for a court order or subpoena. Additionally, court order review is not required to access records of session times and durations and means and sources of payment.
- Simply by telling any single judge in the United States that the information collected would be relevant to an ongoing criminal investigation, the government can now spy on an individual's use of the Internet, including the key terms that person enters into search engines. This is regardless of whether the person being monitored is the target of the investigation.
- The Foreign Intelligence Surveillance Act (FISA) has been expanded, including less-stringent standards for searches that are based on counterterrorism measures.
- Where the standard of probable cause is not met for domestic surveillance, the U.S. Attorney General can obtain a FISA wiretap for the monitoring of an U.S. citizen. All information from the search can subsequently be shared with the FBI.
- The Act addresses money laundering and includes RICO-style provisions for the seizure of property and assets. (Grant & Terry, 2005, p. 180).

Proponents of the Patriot Act argue that the extended powers for law enforcement are essential to effectively combat terrorism in the post-911 era. President George Bush stated ("Bush signs law . . . , 2001, p. A17), "This government will enforce this law with all the urgency of a nation at war." Attorney General John Ashcroft stated ("Congress debates terror . . . , 2001, p. 3):

> We are not asking the law to expand, just to grow as technology grows. . . . Terrorist organizations have increasingly used technology to facilitate their criminal acts and hide their communications from law enforcement. Terrorists are trained to change cell phones frequently, to route mail through different internet computers in order to defeat surveillance.

Senate Banking Committee Chairman Paul Sarbanes ("Congress debates terror . . . , 2001, p. 3) describes the money laundering provisions of the Patriot Act as "the most significant money laundering legislation since money laundering was first made a crime" and "Osama bin Laden may have boasted 'Al-Quaeda includes modern, educated youth who are as aware of the cracks inside the Western financial system as they are aware of the lines in their hands,' but with [the Patriot Act], we are sealing up those cracks."

Critics argue that the Act was passed in haste and has unduly sacrificed the constitutional protections of U.S. citizens. They argue that the provisions outlined above violate protections in the Bill of Rights of the U.S. Constitution, including the Fourth and Fifth Amendments. For example, in 2001, the Justice Department issued a new regulation that allows itself to monitor inmate-attorney communications if there is reasonable suspicion that the communications are furthering or facilitating terrorism. The American Civil Liberties Union (ACLU) has protested the regulation, arguing that, under their code of professional responsibility, they are prohibited from communicating with clients if confidentiality is not ensured (Wrobeleski & Hess, 2003). Other critics have pointed to the potential impact on Muslim communities in the United States, drawing parallels between the current situation and Japanese internment camps during World War II. Despite the ongoing debate, many of the most controversial provisions of the Patriot Act were renewed in the summer 2005 by the U.S. Congress. Nevertheless, the debate will likely continue and will be shaped a great deal by the possibility of future terrorist attacks.

DISCRETION AND DECISION MAKING

> The modern policeman is frequently faced with the instant problem of defining an action as either legal or illegal, of deciding, in other words, whether to intervene, and, if so, what tactic to use. He moves in a dense web of social action and social meanings, burdened by a problematic, complex array of ever-changing laws. . . . Though a practitioner of legal arts, his tools at hand are largely obscure, ill-developed, and crude. (Manning, 1978, p. 15)

Defining and Discovering Discretion

Peter Manning captures quite well the difficulties that face police officers, particularly with regard to the role of **discretion** in their daily routine. Indeed, discretion is critically important to the police because the officer's tools are "obscure, ill-developed and crude," (Manning, 1978, p. 15) often forcing the officer to rely on his or her training, background, and judgment. In this context, the police officer's use of appropriately guided and controlled discretion becomes absolutely essential.

Any discussion of police discretion must first begin with defining the term and charting its historical recognition and acceptance in criminal justice. In general terms, discretion involves the ability to make a decision by choosing from several different alternatives. Police officers can choose from alternatives in a wide range of circumstances, from relatively minor incidents to those involving potential loss of liberty or life. Examples include issuing a speeding ticket, resolving a domestic dispute, handling an encounter with a mentally ill person in crisis, engaging in a high-speed automobile pursuit, using a less-than-lethal alternative such as mace or a Taser on a combative suspect, and using deadly force against a suspect.

Although discretion is widely accepted and considered an important part of policing today, this has not always been the case. Many scholars attribute the "discovery" of discretion in criminal justice to survey research conducted by the American Bar Association in the 1950s (ABA, 1956). Much of the early research and emphasis on discretion focused on its abolition; many argued that the decisions in criminal justice are too important to be made subjectively by criminal justice officials, including police. Law enforcement officials were especially reluctant to acknowledge the existence of discretion, arguing instead that laws were enforced consistently and equally all of the time (i.e, the myth of total enforcement). However, the President's Commission on Law Enforcement and the Administration of Justice (1967) argued that discretion is an essential element of criminal justice, and with regard to discretion in policing, stated that the "police should openly acknowledge that, quite properly, they do not arrest all, or even most, offenders they know of" (p. 106).

The Context for Police Decision Making

Police officers do not make decisions in a vacuum. Police decision making can be influenced by a wide range of factors involving the suspect, the officer, their encounter, the police department, and the external environment. Before examining the long list of factors that influence police discretion, one should consider more broadly the general context of police decision making. More specifically, there are several defining features of policing that provide an important backdrop for officers' use of discretion. Each decision a police officer makes occurs in the context of these important aspects of the occupation: the complex role, an inherent political influence, and a central role for the use of force.

The Complex Police Role.   Chapter 5 examines in some detail the complex—and sometimes conflicting—roles and responsibilities of the police, and it is difficult to fully understand police discretion without considering this complex role. Research has clearly demonstrated that the role of the police goes far beyond chasing criminals and solving crimes. The primary functions of the police also include a wide range of order-maintenance (or peacekeeping) and service-related tasks. "Police spend most of their time attending to order-maintaining functions, such as finding lost children, substituting as ambulance drivers or interceding in quarrels of one sort or another" (Manning, 1978, p. 107). The police have traditionally emphasized the crime-fighting element of their job, which has created a distorted image of their role (made worse by movies and television), exacerbated their role conflict, and devalued the other service and order maintenance elements of their role (Walker & Katz, 2002).

Police and Politics.   Chapter 3 details how one of the fundamental early differences between Robert Peel's London Metropolitan Police Department and early U.S. departments involved the role of politics. While London "Bobbies" were representatives of the Crown, U.S. police officers were tied to local politics. In many places during the last half of the nineteenth century, police functioned at the whim of local political leaders, leaving a legacy of poor performance, brutality, and corruption. In fact, one of the primary tenets of the Professional Reform effort—led by August Vollmer and others—centered on removing politics from policing. Many police scholars, however, argue that politics is an intrinsic part of U.S. policing (see, for example, Manning, 1978). As a result, the decisions made by police officers often occur in a political context.

Force as the Core of the Police Role.   Police officers have the legal authority to use force in certain situations including to protect themselves, to make an arrest, to overcome resistance, and to gain control of a potentially dangerous situation (see Chapter 8 for more detail on the central role of force). Research generally shows police use of force to be a rare event. A recent study by the Bureau of Justice Statistics indicated that police use some kind of force in 1 percent of all encounters with citizens (BJS, 1999). However, Bittner (1970) argues that force is the core of the police role. Accordingly, police use of discretion occurs in this context. Their ability to resort to force defines each police citizen encounter and shapes the decisions that citizens and police officers make during each situation.

The Factors that Influence Police Decisions

Over the last forty years, much research has focused on identifying the primary determinants of police behavior, and three sets of potentially influential variables emerge from prior research: environmental, organizational, and situational. *Environmental* variables refer to factors outside the police organization and can be separated into two basic categories: community-level characteristics that indirectly affect police behavior, such as variations in local levels of crime and violence; and direct external efforts to control police behavior (i.e., court rulings). *Organizational* variables refer to factors that are within the realm of the police agency, such as administrative policy, informal norms, and the police subculture. Last, *situational* variables refer to contextual factors specific to each police-citizen encounter. These contextual factors may involve the suspect (i.e. race), the officer (i.e., years on the job), or characteristics of the encounter (i.e., others citizens present). Each set of influential factors is described below (see referenced sources for more in-depth discussion).

Environmental Variables

- Formal action such as arrest and use of force appears more likely in minority neighborhoods. (Smith, 1986; Swanson, 1978; Wilson, 1968)
- The community's political culture helps shape police behavior. (Rossi, Berk, & Edison, 1974; Wilson, 1968; Wilson & Boland, 1978)
- Social class of a community affects police behavior. (Swanson, 1978; Westley, 1970; Wilson, 1968)

- The prevalence of community crime and violence affects police behavior. (Fyfe, 1980; Geller & Karales, 1981; Kania & Mackey, 1977; Mastrofski, 1981)
- Direct external efforts to control police behavior—such as changes in law and court rulings—can influence police behavior, if there is departmental support of those external efforts. (Skolnick & Fyfe, 1993; White, 2003)

Organizational Variables

- The departmental philosophy influences police officer behavior—i.e., aggressive crime fighting, community-oriented, order-maintenance. (Skolnick, 1966; Skolnick & Fyfe, 1993; Wilson, 1968)
- The size of the department can influence police officer behavior. (Brown, 1981; Mastrofski, 1981; Ostrum, Parks, & Whitaker, 1978)
- The degree of supervision and accountability that a department provides will affect police officer behavior. (Reiss, 1971; Walker & Katz, 2002)
- Organizational structure—such as the degree of bureaucracy or professionalism, adherence to the military model, rotating shifts and assignments, and patrol strategy—can influence police officer behavior. (Boydstun & Sherry, 1975; Brown, 1981; Murphy & Pate, 1977; Skolnick & Fyfe, 1993)
- Informal norms and rules affect police officer behavior (i.e., police subculture). (Brown, 1981; Reuss-Ianni, 1983; Skolnick, 1966; Skolnick & Fyfe, 1993)

Situational Variables

- Citizen hostility toward police increases the likelihood of formal police action. (Black & Reiss, 1967; Lundman, 1974, 1996; Reiss, 1971; Westley, 1970; Worden, 1989)
- Suspects in lower socioeconomic classes are more likely to be subject to formal police action. (Black, 1971; Black & Reiss, 1967; Reiss, 1971)
- Police tend to treat juveniles and the elderly more severely than middle-aged citizens. (Black, 1979; Friedrich, 1980)
- Some research has shown that minority citizens are treated more harshly than whites, though findings are mixed. (Black, 1971; Black & Reiss, 1967; Smith & Visher, 1981)
- Some research has shown that female citizens are treated differently than males, though findings are mixed. (Klinger, 1996; Smith & Visher, 1981)
- The degree of relational distance between suspects and complainants can influence police officer behavior—formal action is more likely when they are strangers. (Black, 1970; Friedrich, 1980)
- Seriousness of the alleged offense is an important influence on police officer behavior. (Black, 1971; Black & Reiss, 1967; Ricksheim & Chermak, 1993)
- Police may be more likely to act harshly toward suspects in public places than in private. (Friedrich, 1980; Reiss, 1971)

- Police often follow a polite complainant's wishes. (Black, 1971; Friedrich, 1980; Lundman, Sykes, & Clarke, 1978; Smith, 1984; Smith & Visher, 1981)
- The presence of others appears to affect police behavior. (Friedrich, 1980; Smith & Visher, 1981)
- Decisions made earlier in the encounter by the officer and citizen influence subsequent decisions—wielding a weapon or physically assaulting an officer will increase likelihood of a formal response. (Bayley, 1986; Binder & Scharf, 1980)
- Overall, officer characteristics—education, race, gender, attitudes—appear to exert little influence on police officer behavior. (Brooks, 2001; Fyfe, 1980; Geller & Karales, 1981; Worden, 1989)

Clearly, a wide range of both legal and extralegal factors have been linked to police discretion. Although it is difficult to assess or compare the relative importance of these factors, several overriding themes emerge. First, the police department itself plays a critically important role in guiding and controlling police officer discretion. The department can provide this guidance through a range of different means including official policies and procedures, training, effective supervision, and setting an overall organizational tone that officers will be held accountable for the decisions that they make. Second, police decision making appears to be affected by the environment in which officers work. Levels of community violence, socioeconomic status, politics, and even the level of disorder and disorganization all may influence police officer discretion. Quite simply, police officers are aware of and affected by their surroundings. Third, the police–citizen encounter is a fluid event with numerous decision points, and the decisions made by both participants at each of those points affect the final outcome. In many ways, the police–citizen encounter resembles a chess match with each participant making moves to which the other participant then responds. Any number of characteristics of the encounter—and either participant—can play a role in shaping how the incident is ultimately resolved.

Understanding the Complexity of Police Decision Making

Understanding how these kinds of factors explain or influence police discretion is complicated because of their interaction. For example, the influence of a high crime rate on police behavior may be confounded by the suspect's demeanor toward the police, as well as by organizational policies regarding patrol tactics in those high-crime areas. In a domestic violence incident, an officer may choose to arrest the batterer because the department has a formal mandatory arrest policy, because the victim requested that the batterer be arrested, and because the batterer disrespected the police officer. The officer's decision to arrest or not may also be affected by the presence of citizen bystanders, the socioeconomic class of the neighborhood, the suspect's demeanor, and any number of other factors. The overlap between these groups of influential variables makes it difficult for researchers to separate effects and evaluate their relative importance.

Clearly, there are no hard-and-fast rules for interpreting the importance of specific factors, as police–citizen encounters are complex. However, one critical element in determining the relative role of each set of factors is the perceived danger or threat facing the officer. Importantly, as the perceived danger in the encounter increases, situational factors tend to play a more prominent role and organizational and environmental become secondary. In encounters with low levels of danger, the officer is still influenced by situational factors, but the other characteristics become more influential. For example, the officer responding to a "man with a gun" call (typically a dangerous call) will be most influenced by the situational characteristics of the encounter: Is there an armed suspect? Formal organizational rules and environmental characteristics may still play a role in decision making (i.e., is this also a high-crime neighborhood?), but the relative influence of those factors will be mediated by the situational factors.

Alternatively, consider the domestic disturbance where the officer has control over the encounter and both the victim and batterer are compliant. Situational factors may come into play—victim's wishes/suspect demeanor—but organizational factors such as department policy and informal departmental norms become prominent in the decision-making process. The same dynamics tend to occur in the routine traffic stop: Once the officer perceives the situation to be nondangerous, organizational and environmental factors become more prominent influences on the likelihood of issuing a ticket (i.e., informal ticket quotas, neighborhood characteristics) and interact with incident level factors (such as suspect demeanor).

Building on What We Know: Increasing the Rationality of Police Decision Making

Police departments and police scholars have begun to think about ways to improve police decision making; that is, to reduce the likelihood that police officers will make bad decisions. Given their tremendous amount of discretion and the potentially devastating consequences of poor police decisions—strained police–community relations, riot and disorder, and even loss of liberty and life—it is critically important to think about ways to structure police discretion.

There are five major areas a police department can target to improve the rationality of police decision making. First, departments must be careful and selective in who they hire as police officers. A rigorous recruitment and selection process can weed out those who will be ill-equipped to make good decisions under pressure. In particular, candidates should be selected based on their ability to demonstrate good judgment, maintain an even temperament, respect and appreciate diversity, show creativity and problem-solving skills, think on one's feet, handle pressure, and show leadership skills (see Chapter 1 for more on officer recruitment and selection).

Second, departments must ensure that their officers are properly trained and adequately prepared for the situations they will encounter on the job. Police officers will be more likely to make rational and fair decisions if their training, both in the academy and while in-service, has prepared them to do so. Departments are increasingly using scenario-based training regimens and more seminar-based philosophies to bring the realities of police work into training (see Chapter 2 for more on police training).

Third, police departments should develop clear and understandable administrative guidelines for structuring police discretion in certain types of encounters. Davis (1971) argued that administrative rulemaking is the most effective method for controlling discretion, and research has supported his position in a number of critical areas of policing: use of deadly force, automobile pursuits, domestic violence encounters, handling the mentally ill, and the use of police dogs.

Fourth, administrative policies are meaningless if not enforced. Police officers must be held accountable for the decisions they make, especially if the decision violates departmental policy. When officers are not held to account for their decisions by management, the informal message sent to line officers is that, regardless of the decisions they make, their use of discretion is essentially unfettered (see Chapter 9 for more on the importance of accountability through administrative rulemaking).

Last, rational decision making by police is facilitated when there are mechanisms to supply systematic feedback (Gottfredson & Gottfredson, 1988). Traditionally, police officers know very little about the consequences of their decisions after the case or suspect moves further along in the criminal justice system. Did an arrest result in the prosecutor filing charges? Why did the case end in a plea bargain? Was there a conviction? Did the officer's decisions have anything to do with a negative outcome (case dropped, acquittal, etc.)? These are important questions that are typically not answered for police, but go to the central issue of whether the decisions made by police achieved the stated goal (Gottfredson & Gottfredson, 1988). Methods of systematic feedback, which can take any number of forms, can help clear up misconceptions, show an officer why a case was dismissed, improve communication between police and other system actors, and lead to changes in police practice that improve the rationality of decision making.

NEW (AND SOME OLD) CRIME PROBLEMS

As policing enters the twenty-first century, the profession is faced with a host of crime problems. Police have been struggling with some of these problems for several decades now, such as domestic violence, drugs and gangs, while other problems are new and emerging such as terrorism, computer crime, and identity theft. Taken together, the problems described below represent the most pressing crime-related challenges facing police today.

Drugs and Gangs

Drugs. Despite the massive efforts of the War on Drugs in the 1980s and 1990s, drug trafficking and possession still pose significant problems for the police. Although much of the violence associated with competition over lucrative drug markets has abated, the United States still spends approximately $12 billion per year on drug enforcement and interdiction, $4 billion on treatment, and $2 billion on prevention (Walker & Katz, 2002). Moreover, the effects of drugs and drug crime are still disproportionately felt among poor, urban minority communities.

Conventional wisdom regarding the most effective police response to the drug problem is that it should be multifaceted, incorporating prevention, treatment, and intervention/suppression components. Although the police themselves really play no role in drug treatment, the criminal justice system in general has been increasingly turning to substance abuse treatment as a response to drug possession cases, primarily through drug courts that provide judicial supervised treatment. Research on drug courts has generally shown them to be successful in reducing drug use and related crime among participants. With regard to prevention, the most popular strategy is ***Drug Abuse Resistance Education, or DARE.*** Developed by the Los Angeles Police Department in 1983, DARE consists of a series of one-hour lectures in elementary and middle-school classrooms conducted by sworn police officers (17 hours total). The sessions are primarily informational, focusing on the consequences of illegal drug use and building social skills to resist their use (Walker & Katz, 2002). DARE is enormously popular; by 1997, it was being used in an estimated 70 percent of public school systems. Despite its popularity, research examining the effects of DARE have consistently found no change in attitudes and drug use among those receiving the curriculum (compared to those who did not receive DARE). As concerns about the lack of evidence supporting its effectiveness have emerged, some jurisdictions have begun to abandon DARE for other evidence-based alternative models.

There are a number of enforcement and suppression strategies typically employed by police to combat drug trafficking and possession. More traditional strategies include buy–bust operations (i.e., undercover officers buying drugs and then making arrests), arresting low-level dealers and using them as informants to track higher level dealers, long-term undercover work, and crackdowns (mobilizing a large force in a targeted area for a relatively short period of time). Most scholars acknowledge that drug dealing and drug use have declined recently and that the police have played a role in this decline, but the exact nature of that role remains unclear (Walker & Katz, 2002). Enforcement efforts, particularly those that are targeted and employ problem-oriented and community-oriented approaches, seem to be effective—at least in the short-term—in reducing street level drug sales and use. In Chapter 4, see the discussions of targeted police efforts in Jersey City, Richmond (CA), and Boston that successfully addressed drug- (and gang-) related problems.

The primary criticism of drug enforcement efforts in the United States is that they may unfairly target poor, minority communities. National surveys of drug use consistently show that African Americans are only slightly more likely than whites to admit using drugs in any given month, yet African Americans are disproportionately represented among drug arrestees (Miller, 1996). Since much of drug enforcement is proactive work (rather than reactive responses to calls for service), many critics argue that police departments have unfairly targeted minority neighborhoods with their drug enforcement efforts. The law enforcement response to this criticism has generally been that police target their efforts where drug dealing and crime are most prevalent, and in many cases, this happens to be in poor, minority communities.

Although police have been combating the drug problem for several decades now, the types of drugs that are most prevalent has changed significantly in recent years. During the height of the War on Drugs, enforcement efforts focused almost exclusively on crack and powder cocaine. As crack use has decline in recent years, a number of other drugs have become increasingly common, including methamphetamine, club drugs such as ecstasy and GHB, and even heroin in some parts of the United States. These new drugs represent different challenges for the police in terms of enforcement and prevention, particularly because of how they are made and distributed and because of their appeal to a wider class of drug users (including younger children and middle- and upper-class youth). For example, much of the cocaine that was sold and used in the United States came across borders from South American countries, particularly Columbia. The cocaine and crack markets were controlled by rival gangs who often resorted to violence to gain a foothold and maintain control of those markets. Methamphetamine and club drugs are produced in the United States, often in homes or underground labs, and are shipped either locally or across state lines. Club drugs, in particular, are sold and used in night clubs, not on the street like cocaine.

Gangs.   Police have long struggled with gangs and combating gang violence, and in many parts of the country gangs continue to proliferate and create problems. The Chicago Police Department (n.d.) defines a gang as "a group of individuals with a recognized name and symbols who form an allegiance for a common purpose and engage in unlawful activity" (p. 1). Gangs are characterized by a number of elements including a leadership and organizational structure, associational patterns, territorial identification, criminal activity, symbols, and communication (i.e., graffiti). Gangs vary tremendously along these characteristics and tend to also be defined by race, gender, and type of criminal activity (i.e., predatory gang vs. drug gang) (Wrobleski & Hess, 2003).

Based on findings from the *National Youth Gang Survey* (National Youth Gang Center, 2000), there were an estimated 28,700 gangs and 780,200 gang members in the United States in 1998. Some gangs are informal and local, while others are organized and found across the United States (such as the Bloods, Crips, and a new Salvadorian Gang called MS-13). Although there are indications that the prevalence of gangs has declined slightly at the national level, research indicates that they continue to spread in rural and suburban communities, as well as smaller cities. There are a number of risk factors that contribute to youths' joining gangs, and perhaps the most important is the family. Quite simply, many children turn to gangs to fulfill needs they are not receiving in the home, such as caring, a sense of belonging, protection, and financial security. Other risk factors focus on the community (social disorganization, lack of access to legitimate opportunities), schools (academic failure, low commitment), peers (delinquent friends), and the individual (aggression, delinquency) (Howell, 2000).

Police generally rely on three methods of combating gangs and their related criminal activity: prevention, intervention, and suppression. This three-pronged approach, espoused by the Office of Juvenile Justice Delinquency and Prevention (OJJDP), is viewed as the optimal approach for reducing the gang problem. With regard to prevention, in 1991 the Phoenix Police Department created **Gang Resistance Education and Training (GREAT),** modeled after the DARE program. Much like DARE, GREAT involves a uniformed officer's coming into the classroom for hour-long lessons on conflict resolution, cultural sensitivity, and the consequences of gang participation and behavior. (GREAT is a nine-week curriculum). GREAT has since been adopted by the federal government and is administered by the Bureau of Alcohol, Tobacco, and Firearms (BATF). GREAT has not been studied extensively, although short-term results from one study indicated lower rates of delinquency and gang affiliation among those receiving the program. The long-term outcomes of those who participate remain unknown, however.

The second part of the police approach to gangs involves intervention: working with those already involved in gangs to pull them out. Much of this work involves the juvenile justice system, probation, and social services, but gang units in the police department play a critical role in member identification and initiating the intervention process (often through arrest). OJJDP places strong emphasis on community involvement and the development of collaborative partnerships as well, with a range of intervention approaches: counseling programs, mentoring, recreational activities (Police Athletics League, PAL), outreach programs, and court diversion.

It is widely recognized among government officials, scholars, and practitioners that a comprehensive gang strategy has both short- and long-term goals. Prevention and intervention generally involve longer term goals while, suppression—the primary activity of the police in this area—involves short-term goals. The Law Enforcement Management and Administrative Statistics survey (LEMAS) in (BJS, 1999) indicated that specialized gang units are becoming increasingly common: 56 percent of municipal departments with more than 100 sworn officers had gang units in place. One of the primary functions of the gang unit is intelligence: maintaining an accurate, up-to-date record of gangs, gang members, and gang-related information. Since gang units are typically small, a primary function of the unit is to collect information and make it available to the rank and file of the department. Members of the gang unit will often work closely with probation, prosecution, and social services to facilitate prevention and intervention efforts. Valdez (2000) says that a "full-service" gang unit should rely on prevention, intervention, and suppression to combat the gang problem. Oftentimes, gang units employ creative measures to address gang problems, such using civil injunctions and local ordinances—and even RICO statutes—to prohibit groups from engaging in certain activities. Fritsch, Caeti, and Taylor (1999) describe the overall strategy of the Dallas Police Department Gang Unit:

> Five defined target areas that were home to seven of the city's most violent gangs received over-time funded officers to implement several different enforcement strategies. The strategies included saturation patrol and aggressive curfew and truancy

enforcement. . . . The findings indicated that aggressive curfew and truancy enforcement led to significant reductions in gang violence, whereas simple saturation patrol did not. (p. 122)

Descriptions of the Boston Gun Project and the Comprehensive Homicide Initiative (in Richmond, CA) also demonstrate successful approaches to targeting gangs and gang-related crime.

Policing Domestic Violence

Police have traditionally underenforced laws prohibiting domestic violence. In 1967, for example, the International Association of Chiefs of Police stated in its manual that "in dealing with family disputes, the power of arrest should be exercised as a last resort" (International Association of Chiefs of Police, 1967, p. 1). The underenforcement of domestic violence laws by police stems from a number of issues, including traditional limitations on police arrest powers, particularly for incidents involving misdemeanor offenses, the fact that most domestic dispute calls do not involve violence, victim preference against arrest, lack of training, and the belief held by most police that domestic disturbance calls are more dangerous than other types of calls (making arrest a less attractive option).

The Changing Police Response to Domestic Violence. Over the last forty years, the police response to domestic violence has changed significantly. The first effort at changing the traditional police response to domestic violence occurred in 1965, when the New York City Police Department created the Family Crisis Intervention Unit (FCIU). Officers specially trained in conflict management and mediation were encouraged to take as much time as needed to negotiate the dispute and to make referrals to appropriate social service agencies (Bard, 1970). A number of police departments across the country followed suit and created specialized domestic violence crisis or mediation units.

The Shift to Mandatory Arrest During the late 1970s and early 1980s, a number of forces emerged that led to a shift toward **mandatory arrest for domestic violence offenders.** In the early 1970s, the feminist movement targeted spousal assault as a major women's issue, and by the end of the decade, hotlines and shelters for battered women had been established across the country. The perception that police were discriminating against women victims led to two class-action lawsuits against the police in New York City and Oakland (Sherman, 1992).

In 1978, the U.S. Supreme Court ruled in *Monell v. Department of Social Services of the City of New York,* 436 U.S. 658, that when a representative of an agency violates an individual's constitutional rights because of the agency's official *custom and practice,* the agency as well as the individual may be held liable (Skolnick & Fyfe, 1993). The ruling in *Monell* put local governments at risk of being forced to pay large civil judgments as a result of the behavior of individual officials (Skolnick &

Fyfe, 1993). In 1984, in *Thurman v. Torrington,* 595 F. Supp. 1521, the *Monell* ruling was applied to police behavior in domestic violence calls. The *Thurman* case extended police liability to acts of omission, indicating that failure to protect victims of domestic violence (arguably, the traditional police response) could result in civil litigation and large civil verdicts against the department and city (Skolnick & Fyfe, 1993).

Last, in 1984, results from the Minneapolis Domestic Violence study were published, which indicated that formal arrest led to significantly lower rates of recidivism among offenders (as compared to other less formal police responses) (Sherman & Berk, 1984). Within months of publication of the findings, "police departments across the nation began to adopt either mandatory or presumptive arrest policies for cases of marital assault" (Gelles, 1996, p. 30). Drawing heavily on the results from the Minneapolis study, the Attorney General's Task Force on Family Violence (U.S. Department of Justice, 1984) recommended that family violence be recognized and treated as criminal activity (Gelles, 1996).

Moving beyond Mandatory Arrest.   The National Institute of Justice funded replications of the Minneapolis experiment in six other cities, and results from the replications clearly challenged the Minneapolis findings; specifically, results in three studies indicated that arrest led to increased frequency of subsequent domestic violence offenses. Results from the original study and replications suggest that arrest has a differential impact on offenders, and Sherman (1992) argues that the impact of formal arrest is affected by the individual offender's stake in conformity: For those with much to lose (i.e., a good job, community standing, etc.), arrest serves as a deterrent; but for those with low stake in conformity (i.e., unemployed, criminal record, no high school diploma), arrest will NOT serve as a deterrent and may aggravate the offender.

A number of other problems emerged with the shift to mandatory arrest. First, inconsistent responses by prosecutors and courts is problematic for measuring the impact of arrest. Research shows that the majority of victims of domestic violence either refuse to make a statement or recant the statement later, often before the offender is charged. The lack of victim cooperation often causes prosecutors to drop the cases. Requiring police to arrest offenders when prosecutors do not file charges and courts do not impose sentences establishes a contradictory and frustrating mandate and likely severely limits the potential deterrent effects of arrest (Ferraro & Boychuk, 1992; Hirschel, Hutchinson, Dean, & Mills, 1992). Second, the shift to mandatory arrest has in some cases led to police reliance on dual arrest, where both participants in the incident are arrested. As a result, research indicates that, in many jurisdictions, the percentage of women arrested for domestic violence offenses increased notably following adoption of a mandatory arrest policy (Martin, 1997). Some jurisdictions have responded to this issue by adopting "primary aggressor" laws (where police must identify and arrest only the initiator or aggressor) and by modifying police training and policy.

Comprehensive Approaches to Domestic Violence. In several jurisdictions across the country, police have attempted to blend elements of each of these perspectives, employing mandatory arrest policies but also making an effort to establish a relationship with the victim and to connect her with a range of services that can help address her current situation. This approach often involves placing police officers with social workers as a crisis intervention team, with police focusing on arrest and building a case for the prosecutor while the social workers provide services to the victim including counseling, advocacy, shelter, support, and legal aid. Research on this type of domestic violence intervention has generally produced positive findings (Buzawa & Buzawa, 2001). Gamache, Edleson, and Schock (1988) evaluated community intervention projects (CIPs) involving coordinated police, judicial, and social service intervention in three suburban communities, and in all three communities, the intervention resulted in statistically significant changes in police and court responses, including an increase in arrests and the use of mandated counseling. More recently, White, Goldkamp, and Campbell (2005) reported that, following the implementation of a coordinated team response to domestic violence in Vacaville (CA), arrests for domestic violence declined significantly. Although Buzawa and Buzawa (2001) acknowledge that such programs can "dramatically affect the cycle of abuse" (p. 229), they note that the research suggests "there is a core group of abusers that are not, and apparently will not, be deterred."

Police and the Mentally Ill

Local criminal justice systems have a long history of dealing with individuals suffering from mental illness or disability. Because of their presence on the streets, the police represent the "front line" contact between criminal justice and the mentally ill or disabled citizens whose behaviors are disturbing to the community. Whether they "shoo" them away from the locations where they are not desired, put them in contact with assisting services, or arrest them and transport them to the lockup, the police aims are short term and generally involve moving them on to others to deal with their problems. Police involvement with the mentally ill is dictated by two legal principles: (1) their duty to protect citizens by removing dangerous people from the community and (2) their duty to help citizens who cannot help themselves (*parens patrie*) (Teplin, 1990). There are a number of reasons why the mentally ill are increasingly coming to the attention of the police and finding themselves in the criminal justice system, and these are detailed below.

Deinstitutionalization. The closing and downsizing of state psychiatric hospitals during the 1960s "was theoretically designed to improve the lives of severely mentally ill men and women by bringing them, and their care, out of state hospitals and into their communities" (Sigurdson 2000, p. 70). Predictably, the **deinstitutionalization** movement resulted in greater numbers of mentally ill persons residing in the community, and the relative failure to develop effective community-based mental health treatment networks in most jurisdictions left many of these individuals without appropriate resources and services (Lurigio & Lewis 1987). Without appropriate community-based resources, residents increasingly pressured police to respond formally (via arrest) to the problems and disturbances involving the mentally ill.

Mental Illness and Crime.   Although mental illness may be far more prevalent among nonviolent petty offenders, media attention (and public perception) focuses more often on the dramatic violent crimes that are occasionally committed by a mentally ill person (i.e., Hannibal Lector). In support of this perceived relationship between crime and mental illness, studies comparing crime among mentally disordered and nondisordered persons have consistently found higher rates for mentally disordered persons, particularly for violent crime (Belfrage, 1998; Hodgins, 1992). However, the relationship between mental illness and violence is far from clear. The majority of people suffering from mental illness do not engage in violence, and the majority of people who commit crime, particularly violent crime, do not suffer from mental illness (Swanson, Holzer, Ganju, & Jono, 1990). Some research, nevertheless, has identified certain risk factors, most notably substance abuse, that increase the likelihood that an individual with mental illness will become violent (Newhill & Mulvey, 2002; Steadman et al., 1998).

Mental Illness and Co-Occurring Substance Abuse.   Prior research has consistently reported the frequent co-occurrence of mental illness and substance abuse (Abram, 1990; Anderson, Rosay, & Saum, 2002). Hubbard and Martin (2001) note that "the significant statistical association between substance-related and other psychiatric disorders in the general and several clinical populations . . . suggest that these disorders may be causally associated with one another" (p. 5). Psychiatric and substance abuse problems also seem to co-occur in greater concentrations among populations of criminal offenders (Teplin, 1990).

The Contributing Role of Police Strategies.   The police themselves have engaged in a number of strategies that have unintentionally forced increased interactions with the mentally ill. First, given the frequent co-occurrence of mental illness and substance abuse, the law enforcement initiatives of the War on Drugs often brought the mentally ill to the attention of the police. Quite simply, street-level drug enforcement—the primary tactic employed in the War on Drugs—focused police attention on low-level buyers and sellers and necessarily increased the numbers of mentally ill persons being arrested by the police.

Second, because many of the people who are mentally ill and disabled become involved in fairly low-level criminal matters, more recent police initiatives such as community policing, zero tolerance policing, and even problem-oriented policing have increased the likelihood that substance-abusing mentally ill persons in the community will find themselves in the criminal justice system. These new initiatives often focus on the link between disorder and crime and typically target "quality of life" and low-level crimes—just the types of offenses often committed by the mentally ill.

The Police Response to the Mentally Ill.   Police officers have three basic options at their disposal when handling an encounter involving a mentally ill individual: arrest, hospitalization, and informal disposition ("shooing" them away from whoever called the police). The traditional police response to the mentally ill has been informal. Early work by Bittner (1967), later supported by Teplin (1986), showed that police resolve the majority of encounters with the mentally ill informally rather than taking the individual into custody or even initiating an emergency hospitalization. In Teplin's (1986) research, nearly 75 percent of calls were handled informally. The traditional informal response likely stems from a number of issues including a lack of training in how to properly recognize and respond to mental illness (until recently mental illness training involved just a few hours of academy training) and a lack of resources. Research shows that calls for service involving the mentally ill take significantly longer than other calls (Pogrebin, 1986), and in busy jurisdictions, police may lack the time to properly handle such calls. Also, in some cases, the mentally ill persons may be well known to police from many previous encounters (i.e., regular customers). The officer may know the person is not dangerous, that once or twice a month he or she stops taking his or her medication, and that a few kind words will resolve the situation.

There are also legal and treatment-related issues that affect police decision making in encounters with the mentally ill. The police can only involuntarily commit an individual if the person represents a danger to him- or herself or others (Walker & Katz, 2002). This is a difficult threshold to measure, and there is a significant amount of paperwork required to document that the threshold has been reached. Also, the services available for the mentally ill are typically very limited. Often, there are few beds available for involuntary commitment, and many service providers are unwilling to deal with individuals who are involved with criminal justice. "In some instances, police officers go from one agency to another looking for one that will accept the mentally disturbed person" (Walker & Katz, 2002, p. 140). In cases where informal disposition is not satisfactory—either because of the mentally ill person's behavior or the wishes of the complainant—police are left with few options and often resort to arrest.

The Debate over Criminalization of Mental Illness.   The increasing number of mentally ill found in the criminal justice system has fueled a debate over whether mental illness has been *criminalized;* that is, individuals who previously were treated in the mental health system are now being channeled to the criminal justice system. Abramson (1972) first noted that a disproportionate number of mentally ill individuals suspected of committing misdemeanors were being channeled into the criminal justice system through arrest (which he called *criminalization*). Researchers point to the increasing contacts between police and the mentally ill as evidence of that criminalization.

However, Shepard Engel and Silver (2001) challenge the criminalization hypothesis, arguing that the increasing number of mentally ill in the justice system does not necessarily suggest that police are inappropriately using arrest to handle encounters with the mentally ill. Shepard Engel and Silver (2001) argue that arresting the mentally ill is not always carried out with punishment as a goal: There simply may be no viable other alternatives (no services available except those in the justice system). Moreover, Shepard Engel and Silver (2001) argue that much of the research supporting the criminalization hypothesis did not control for legal and extralegal factors known to influence police discretion (see the earlier part of this chapter). In fact, their analysis of data from the *Project on Policing Neighborhoods* and *Police Services Study* shows that police are NOT more likely to arrest mentally disordered suspects than other suspects. As a result, whether the disproportionate number of mentally ill in the criminal justice system is a consequence of criminalization or other factors remains a subject of some debate.

Crisis Intervention Teams.   Many police departments around the country have developed new, innovative responses to mental illness. For example, the Memphis, Tennessee, Police Department has created a **Crisis Intervention Team (CIT),** comprised of officers who have gone through 40 hours of intensive training on appropriate responses to the mentally ill (Vickers, 2000). Two hundred thirteen of the 990 uniform officers in the department are CIT officers, and a CIT officer is dispatched to any radio call that has a mental health component (Vickers, 2000). Importantly, the CIT has a partnership with the University of Tennessee Medical Center, which provides emergency medical and psychiatric care 24 hours a day, seven days a week (Vickers, 2000). Officers can leave mentally ill individuals in crisis with the staff at the medical center and "be back on patrol within 15 minutes" (Vickers, 2000).

> The goals of CIT are to provide immediate response to and management of situations where the mentally ill are in a state of crisis; prevent, reduce, or eliminate injury to both the consumer and the responding police officer; find appropriate care for the consumer; and establish a treatment program that reduces recidivism. (p. 2)

Research indicates that, following the creation of the Memphis CIT, there have been significant decreases in injuries to officers and the mentally ill and an overall decrease in calls for service involving the mentally ill. The Memphis model has been adopted by a number of other police departments around the country including Los Angeles and Houston.

Identity Theft and Computer Crime

Identity Theft.   Modern technology has allowed our society to become computer and electronic-based but has also made us vulnerable to **identity theft.** Consider the following conveniences that are based solely on our identities: using a credit card at a restaurant or store that will be paid by the cardholder at some later date; using an ATM card to withdraw money from a bank account; banks shifting money electronically from one account to another; and paying bills online without hard copy checks or cash. All of these transactions are based on the financial identity of the consumer, and if another individual is able to represent him- or herself as that consumer, that person can make financial transactions in the consumer's name. This is identity theft.

Definition, Prevalence, and Impact   The NYPD defines identity theft as "obtaining and using an individual's pedigree information or credit card, bank account and phone-card numbers by way of fraud or deception, most often for economic gain." Identity thieves may also be motivated by non-financial objectives such as avoiding detection in the planning and commission of crimes and subsequently avoiding capture. Several of the 9-11 hijackers had committed identity theft to remain undetected in the United States. Identity thieves can obtain a person's identifying information in any number of ways, such as stealing records from an employer or business, hacking into computer databases and stealing data, rummaging through trash, stealing mail, stealing wallets, and "skimming" information from credit card magnetic strips. Once a thief has successfully assumed someone else's identity, the thief can go on spending sprees (cars, computers, even a house), open new credit card accounts, take out loans, establish cell phone service, and give the assumed name to police to evade arrest and further court processing (Federal Trade Commission, n.d.).

The Identity Theft Resource Center (2003) states that there are three main types of identity theft:

- Financial identity theft: Involves the imposter's use of personal identifying information, primarily the social security number, to establish new credit lines in the name of the victim.
- Criminal identity theft: Occurs when a criminal gives another person's personal identifying information in place of his or her own to law enforcement.
- Identity cloning: Involves the imposter using the victim's information to establish a new life.

Research indicates that identity theft is increasing exponentially. In 2003, there were 214,905 complaints filed with the Federal Trade Commission (FTC)—the federal agency designated to handle identity theft—an increase of 150 percent from 2001. The FTC estimates that approximately 11 million people are victims of identity theft each year, in 2004 costing more than $52 billion.

Although the victim may be unaware that his or her identity has been stolen for months or even years, the consequences of the crime can be severe and long term. Victims have lost jobs and job opportunities, been refused loans and mortgages, and have even been arrested for crimes they did not commit (Federal Trade Commission, n.d.). Once an individual's credit rating has been compromised, it can take months to clear away all illegitimate charges and unpaid debt. A study by the Identity Theft Resource Center (2003) estimates that victims spend, on average, 600 hours clearing their names after their identities have been stolen. The same study reports that the emotional impact of identity theft "has been found to parallel that of victims of violent crime . . . many of the listed symptoms [by victims] are classic examples of post-traumatic stress disorder and secondary PTSD (from secondary wounding)" (Identity

Theft Resource Center, 2003, pp. 4, 35). Although credit card companies and financial institutions do not hold victims accountable for the illegitimate charges made in their names, victims do suffer economic costs from the crime, particularly as they try to clear their names: postage, telephone, photocopying, travel time, lost time and wages from work.

Policing Identity Theft.   Several states have introduced legislation that makes identity theft a crime. In other states, officials rely on existing crimes that occur during the commission of identity theft such as fraud, traditional theft, and grand larceny. The NYPD for example, may count identity theft as a crime itself (it is covered under New York Penal Law sections 190.78–82, created in 2002), as grand larceny or as petit larceny, depending on the nature of the identity theft and the amount involved. Identity theft represents a significant challenge for the police for a host of reasons. First, victims may not realize that the crime has occurred for months or even years. Many victims do not report the crime to police, especially if credit card companies do not hold them responsible for the charges and the impact on their financial well-being is limited. For those who do report, police are often left trying to piece together the elements of a crime and find evidence months after it has occurred. Second, the nature of the crime means that victims may have no idea how or when the crime occurred. Their credit card may have been "skimmed" at a restaurant by the waiter, someone may have rummaged through their trash, or someone may have stolen mail out of their mailbox. Third, there is often little evidence left behind to form the basis of the investigation. If goods were purchased and delivered to an address known to the credit card company, the police department may often not receive this information.

There are two general types of identity thieves and each represents a challenge for police. First, some thieves work alone and often prey on acquaintances and/or family members. These types of cases tend to have a higher clearance rate because of the existing relationship between the offender and victim. However, the smaller scale of their crimes often makes these types of offenders more difficult to track. The second type involves large, organized identity theft rings that operate on a grander scale and victimize dozens, hundreds, or even thousands of people over a relatively short period of time. These rings may also be involved in other types of crime. In California, for example, investigators have discovered that there is a strong connection between identity theft and the drug trade.

Police also struggle with identity theft because many of the factors that contribute to the crime are out of their control. Credit card companies, financial institutions, and related companies are reluctant to implement security measures to address identity theft because the impact of the crime is relatively small—given their entire annual revenue—and they view the crime as a cost of doing business. Unless uniform changes were adopted across the market, companies will be fearful that the implementation of restrictive security measures will drive potential customers to competitors who have not implemented such measures. Consider some of the following issues and their potential impact on identity theft: discontinuing use of social security numbers as an individuals' identifiers (there are still some colleges and universities that use SSNs as student identification numbers and post grades in public locations by those numbers); requiring that credit and debit cards have photographs on them and requiring merchants to look at the photo before processing charges; stopping blanket mailings of credit card applications; and instituting security procedures to confirm identification when consumers call up to order new credit cards. Although many of the large banks, financial institutions, and credit card companies are now developing approaches to protect their customers, there has been a disconnect between those companies, their efforts, and the law enforcement community.

Perhaps the biggest challenge for police involves jurisdiction. Consider the following example:

> A computer hacker in San Francisco breaks into a business computer in Philadelphia and retrieves social security numbers of employees. The thief opens up a credit card in John Smith's name and uses the card to order computers and I-pods totaling $15,000, which are delivered to a warehouse in Seattle. Once the victim realizes that his identity has been stolen (when he gets his next credit card bill back in Philadelphia where he lives), where should he report the crime? Who has jurisdiction to investigate? If an arrest is made, where should charges be filed and which District Attorney's office should prosecute the case?

The victim's first response would probably be to report the crime to the Philadelphia Police Department (PPD). The PPD would likely tell the victim that since the crime did not occur in Philadelphia, it does not have jurisdiction to investigate. A call to the Seattle Police Department would likely generate a similar response. If the victim could determine that the hacker lives in California (which is unlikely), the San Francisco Police Department would also tell the victim it does not have jurisdiction. Because much of identity theft occurs across jurisdictional boundaries, it is often unclear who has the authority to receive a complaint and conduct an investigation. The NYPD will accept identity theft complaints from any New York City resident, regardless of where the crime occurred, because it relies on the victim's home address to determine jurisdiction. At a recent identity theft conference in California, investigators urged the California State Legislature to pass legislation authorizing the victim's home address as the determining factor for jurisdiction. However, because of inconsistencies across states, victims may be hard pressed to convince their local police department to even receive the complaint, let alone start an investigation.

The California Approach   The state of California has taken a unique approach to combating identity theft and protecting residents of the state. The Legislature passed a law authorizing the creation of five regional identity theft task forces throughout the state and providing $14 million per year to fund their work. The task forces involve district attorneys, local police, probation, and federal law enforcement. The task forces have developed strong relationships with banks and credit companies and often work with the private sector cooperatively to prevent and investigate crime. The task forces have specifically targeted the large, organized rings, hoping to get the most "bang for their buck" in terms of resources, making arrests, and protecting victims and citizens. The multijurisdictional approach addresses a number of problems that police have struggled with, including turf issues, lack of cooperation among different agencies (local and federal law enforcement, prosecutors, etc.) and the lack of knowledge and/or capability to handle the crime in many small departments. In fact, the task forces provide training to police around the region to improve their awareness and enhance their capability to respond to the crime (particularly the individual offenders, since the task forces focus on the organized rings).

Computer Crime.   The computerization of the United States and the creation and proliferation of the internet have created a host of new opportunities for crime, and as a result, a host of new problems for police. It is estimated that 50 percent of U.S. households have Internet access, and over $230 billion per year is spent on Internet commerce (Walker & Katz, 2002). As stated above, computers often play a central role in identity theft, but there are a number of other crimes related to computers and the Internet. The Computer Security Institute estimates that nearly 75 percent of major corporations have been victimized in the last year, costing at least $125 million per year. The FBI has developed a classification of "cyber criminals:"

- Insiders: Current or former employers who have knowledge about the company's infrastructure that allows them to steal information such as intellectual property, client lists, and marketing strategies.
- Hackers: Individuals who break into secure networks for the thrill of the experience or to make illegal financial transactions.
- Virus writers: Individuals who are not motivated by financial gain, but rather seek to infect networks with viruses to destroy data.
- Criminal groups: Groups who steal large amounts of information to sell for monetary profit. (Walker & Katz, 2002)

Carter and Katz (1996) state that **computer crime** is difficult for police to address for three reasons: computers allow criminals to use new, hard-to-trace methods to commit traditional crimes; computers allow criminals to cross jurisdictional boundaries electronically; and the evidence left by these crimes is little more than electronic impulses and programming codes (rather than physical evidence). Computer crime often falls within the jurisdiction of local law enforcement, but research indicates that the vast majority of police departments lack the personnel, resources, and expertise to investigate computer crime (Correia & Bowling, 1999). Some departments have created regional task forces to consolidate resources, efforts, and expertise. Other large departments, such as the NYPD, have created their own computer crime units. In 1998, the FBI took a leadership role and created the National Infrastructure Protection and Computer Intrusion Program (NIPCIP) to develop a national strategy for responding to computer crime (Walker & Katz, 2002). NIPCIP's mission is to:

> Continually assess the threat of computer crime in the United States; warn communities, corporations and individuals when they might be vulnerable to a computer-related

crime; and investigate incidents involving computer-related crimes that fall within the federal government's jurisdiction. (Walker & Katz, 2002, p. 189)

Cooperative partnerships among law enforcement and the private sector are also vital to effectively combating cybercrime. The technological expertise in companies such as IBM, Microsoft, and Apple is a critical resource for police to draw on when developing strategies for preventing computer crime, as well as effectively investigating crimes that already have occurred. Large private sector companies typically have their own security teams—often composed of former police officers—who are ideally suited for developing ongoing partnerships with police departments to combat cybercrime.

Terrorism

Police concern over terrorism predates September 11, 2001. From 1990 to 1998, there were domestic terrorist attacks every year; a total of 39 over that nine-year span (Federal Bureau of Investigation, 1999). Most notable among these is the attack on the World Trade Center in 1993, the attacks of the Unabomber (Ted Kaczynski), the attack on the Oklahoma City Federal Court building (Timothy McVeigh and others), and the attacks at abortion clinics and the Olympics in Atlanta in 1996 (Eric Rudolph) (Walker & Katz, 2002). Prior to 9-11, however, primary responsibility for preventing and investigating terrorist attacks rested with the FBI and various other intelligence agencies in the federal government.

Since September 11, 2001, terrorism prevention and investigation has become a core responsibility for some police departments and a concern for all in policing. Although the 9-11 attacks focused on major metropolitan areas—New York and Washington, DC—the terrorists lived in rural and suburban communities for months prior to the attacks. They attended flight schools in rural areas of Florida. The anthrax attacks that originated in small communities in New Jersey and Florida also demonstrate the need for vigilance and expertise among all police officers.

The first responders to a terrorist attack will include local law enforcement, local fire departments, and emergency services. The FBI and other federal law enforcement agencies have satellite offices in major urban centers, but they lack the manpower and resources to stage an immediate response to a terrorist event (with the exception of perhaps Washington, DC). As evidence of this, the first responders to the World Trade Center on 9-11 were the NYPD and NYFD: 343 New York City firemen and 23 New York City police officers lost their lives that day. The new and evolving role for responding to and preventing terrorism has important implications for police officers and the police department. Departments have been forced to revise training, deployment, and communication strategies and to create counterterrorism units within their departments. Police now provide extra patrol and guard around critical infrastructures such as power plants, food and water sources, and transportation hubs. Police departments now receive briefings from federal authorities in the FBI and Homeland Security about potential threats and terrorist plans garnered through electronic surveillance and interrogations of incarcerated terrorists. When the national terrorist threat level is raised (a color-based system: green = low, blue = guarded, yellow = elevated, orange = high, red = severe), local as well as state and federal law enforcement activate predetermined protective measures involving security, restricted access, surveillance, and contingency plans.

While many of these changes emphasize the activities of federal authorities and the military, their foundation rests upon proper planning and response at the local level. As a result, law enforcement and other local agencies have created special committees and task forces to train and prepare for, and ultimately to respond to, terrorist events. One example is described in detail to illustrate the central role of local level government—especially the police—in dealing with terrorism.

> Washington County, Oregon created an Anti-Terrorism Advisory Committee (ATAC) in November 2001 to place greater emphasis on the terrorist threat, improve information sharing and develop standards for countywide response. Washington County is mostly rural composed of three medium-sized towns: Hillsboro, Beaverton and Tigard. The ATAC includes members of law enforcement (town and county), emergency services, fire, local government, public health and hospitals.
>
> The ATAC has accomplished a number of objectives such as improving interagency communication, improved and standardized local response plans, and reduced duplicative efforts in the event of a terrorist attack. The Committee is also developing minimum prevention and response measures linked to common threat levels [like the national threat level system], a notification process to ensure the timely release of information to first responders, and decision-making procedures for the use of quarantines. (www.ocem.org; Grant & Terry, 2005)

Two final quotes are presented that highlight the central role of local police in combating terrorism, the first by Chuck Wexler, Executive Director of the Police Executive Research Forum (PERF), and the second by Bruce Glassock, former president of the International Association of Chiefs of Police (IACP). Wexler (2001) says that success in the war on terror will

> Require an improved relationship between local and federal law enforcement with respect to intelligence sharing and target hardening. . . . If we are to truly mount a major preemptive offensive then this relationship must evolve to one that recognizes the significant role of both local and federal agencies working collaboratively, sharing intelligence and developing joint strategies. (p. 1)

Shortly thereafter, Glassock (2001), then president of the IACP, sent a letter to the membership of the organization that stated:

> The United States has begun air and group strikes against the Taliban in Afghanistan, taking the war against terrorism home to its instigators. But the war against terrorism isn't limited to actions overseas, or even restricted to military actions. The fight against terrorism begins in our own backyards—our own communities, our own neighborhoods—and police chiefs need to prepare themselves, their officers, and their communities—the people they've sworn to protect—against terrorism.

SUMMARY

This chapter focuses on police field work and breaks down the topic into three major areas. First, the chapter considers police and the law, focusing on the most important legal issues arising from the Bill of Rights: reasonable suspicion, probable cause, warrantless searches, the Exclusionary Rule, and *Miranda* and interrogation. Current issues and controversies involving the law are also discussed, including pretextual stops, using deception in interrogations, curtilage and private property, technologically enhanced searches, and the U.S. Patriot Act. The major theme to be taken from this section is that the law is not static. Rather, it is constantly changing based on rulings from state and federal courts, and it is incumbent upon police to stay up to date on those changes.

The second major area discussed involves discretion and decision making. Police officers possess tremendous discretion and typically receive little guidance in how to make split-second decisions, sometimes involving such critical issues as liberty and life. The chapter reviews the important context of police decision making (politics, force, and a complex role), and presents the findings of research examining factors that influence police discretion. Those factors—environmental, organizational, and situational—interact in a complex sequence that is often dictated by the officer's perception of danger. Last, recommendations are put forth for improving the rationality of police decision making.

The final part of the chapter focuses on crime problems facing the police. These include some old problems—drugs, gangs, domestic violence, the mentally ill—and some new problems—computer crime, identity theft, and terrorism. Each crime continues to change and involve, forcing police to adapt and develop new strategies to effectively respond to the problems. Clearly, the job of a police officer continues to grow more complex in the twenty-first century: Consider that in addition to continuing to combat drugs and gangs, to resolving our domestic disputes and handling the mentally ill who are no longer institutionalized, we now also expect police to respond high-tech crimes involving computers, the Internet, and identity theft, and to detect, prevent, and investigate terrorist activity. It would seem that Vollmer's sarcastic quote presented in Chapter 2 regarding the unrealistic expectations citizens have of the police is becoming less sarcastic and more realistic!

KEY TERMS

Administrative law
Bill of Rights
Civil law
Computer crime
Criminal law
Crisis Intervention Team (CIT)
Curtilage

Deinstitutionalization
Discretion
Drug Abuse Resistance Education (DARE)
Exclusionary rule
Garg Resistance Education and Training
  (GREAT)
Identity theft

Interrogation
Mandatory arrest—domestic violence
Miranda warnings
Patriot Act
Pretextual stops
Probable cause

Reasonable suspicion
Terrorism
Warrants
Warrantless searches
Wiretapping

DISCUSSION QUESTIONS

1. What is the Exclusionary Rule? Discuss the various exceptions.

2. Describe the different types of searches police can conduct legally without a warrant.

3. Discuss the provisions of the U.S. Patriot Act that are seen as most controversial.

4. What is discretion? Describe the factors that research shows influence police discretion.

5. Discuss the evolving police response to domestic violence, from the early 1960s to present.

6. Discuss the reasons why the mentally ill are increasingly finding their way into the criminal justice system.

7. What is identity theft? Why is it so challenging for police?

8. Describe the role for local police in terrorism prevention and response.

REFERENCES

Abram, K.M. (1990). The problem of co-occurring disorders among jail detainees. *Law and Human Behavior, 14* (4), 333–345.

Abramson, M.F. (1972). The criminalization of mentally disordered behavior: Possible side-effect of a new mental health law. *Hospital and Community Psychiatry, 23,* 101–107.

American Bar Association. (1956). *American Bar Association survey of the administration of justice.* Chicago: Author.

Anderson, T.L., Rosay, A.B., & Saum, C. (2002). The impact of drug use and crime involvement on health problems among female drug offenders. *The Prison Journal, 82* (1), 50–68.

Bard, M. (1970). *Training police as specialists in family crisis intervention.* Washington, DC: U.S. Department of Justice.

Bayley, D.H. (1986). The tactical choices of police patrol officers. *Journal of Criminal Justice, 14,* 329–348.

Belfrage, H. (1998). A ten-year follow-up of criminality in Stockholm mental patients: New evidence for a relation between mental disorder and crime. *The British Journal of Criminology, 38* (1), 145–155.

Binder, A., & Scharf, P. (1980). The violent police-citizen encounter. *Annals of the American Academy of Political and Social Science, 452,* 111–121.

Bittner, E. (1967). Police discretion in emergency apprehension of mentally ill persons. *Social Problems, 14,* 278–292.

Bittner, E. (1970). *The functions of police in modern society.* Chevy Chase, MD: National Institute of Mental Health.

Black, D. (1970). The production of crime rates. *American Sociological Review, 35,* 733–748.

Black, D. (1971). The social organization of arrest. *Stanford Law Review, 23,* 1087–1111.

Black, D. (1979). *Dispute settlement by the police.* New Haven, CT: Yale University.

Black, D., & Reiss, A.J., Jr. (1967). *Studies of crime and law enforcement in major metropolitan areas, Vol. 2, Field surveys III.* Section 1. Patterns of behavior in police and citizen transactions. Washington DC: Government Printing Office.

Boydstun, J.E., & Sherry, M.E. (1975). *San Diego community profile: Final report.* Washington DC: Police Foundation.

Brown, M.K. (1981). *Working the street: Police discretion and the dilemma of reform.* New York: Russell Sage Foundation.

Bureau of Justice Statistics (BJS). (1999). *Contacts between police and the public.* Washington, DC: Government Printing Office.

Bureau of Justice Statistics (1999). *Law enforcement management and administrative statistics, 1997: Data for individual state and local agencies with 100 or more officers.* Washington, DC: Government Printing Office.

Bush signs law that expands police powers. (2001, October 27). Associated Press. *Star Tribune* (Minneapolis/St. Paul), p. A17.

Buzawa, E., & Buzawa, C. (2001). Traditional and innovative police responses to domestic violence. In R.G. Dunham & G.A. Alpert (Eds.), *Critical issues in policing* (4th ed.). Prospect Heights, IL: Waveland Press.

Carter, D., & Katz, A. (1996, December). Computer crime: An emerging challenge for law enforcement. *Law Enforcement Bulletin.*

Cassell, P.G., & Hayman, B.S. (1996, February). Police interrogation in the 1990s: An empirical study of the effects of Miranda. *UCLA Law Review, 43,* 860.

Champion, D.H., & Hooper, M.K. (2003). *Introduction to American policing.* New York: McGraw-Hill.

Chicago Police Department. (no date). *Gang awareness.* Chicago: Department of Human Service, City of Chicago.

Congress debates terror bill's effect on criminal justice. (2001, October 30). *Criminal Justice Newsletter,* 1–4.

Correia, M., & Bowling, C. (1999). Veering toward digital disorder: Computer-related crime and law enforcement preparedness. *Police Quarterly, 2* (2), 225–244.

Davis, K.C. (1971). *Discretionary justice: A preliminary inquiry.* Urbana: University of Illinois Press.

Federal Bureau of Investigation. (1999). *Terrorism in the United States: 1998.* Washington, DC: Author.

Federal Trade Commission. (no date). *ID theft: What's it all about?* Washington, DC: Author.

Ferraro, K.J., & Boychuk, T. (1992). The court's response to interpersonal violence: A comparison of intimate and nonintimate assault. In E. Buzawa & C. Buzawa (Eds.), *Domestic violence.* Westport, CT: Auburn House.

Friedrich, R.J. (1980). Police use of force: Individuals, situations, and organizations. *Annals of the American Academy of Political and Social Science, 452,* 82–97.

Fritsch, E.J., Caeti, T.J., & Taylor, R.W. (1999). Gang suppression through saturation patrol, aggressive curfew, and truancy enforcement: A quasi-experimental test of the Dallas Anti-Gang Initiative. *Crime and Delinquency,* 122–139.

Fyfe, J.J. (1980). Geographic correlates of police shooting: A microanalysis. *Journal of Research in Crime and Delinquency, 17,* 101–113.

Gamache, D.J., Edleson, J.L., & Schock, M.D. (1988). Coordinated police, judicial, and social service response to woman battering: A multiple-baseline evaluation across three communities. In G.T. Hotaling, D. Finkelhor, J.T. Kirkpatrick, M.A. Straus (Eds.), *Coping with family violence.* Newbury Park: Sage Publications.

Geller, W., & Karales, K. (1981). Shootings of and by Chicago police: Uncommon crises—part I, shootings by Chicago police. *Journal of Criminal Law and Criminology, 72*(4), 1813–1866.

Gelles, R.J. (1996). Constraints against family violence: How well do they work? In E. Buzawa & C. Buzawa (Eds.), *Do arrests and restraining orders work?,* pp. 30–42. Thousand Oaks, CA: Sage.

Glassock, B.D. (2001, October 16). *Letter to IACP colleagues.*

Gottfredson, M.R., & Gottfredson, D.M. (1988). *Decision-making in criminal justice.* New York: Plenum Press.

Grant, H.B., & Terry, K.J. (2005). *Law enforcement in the 21st century.* Boston: Allyn and Bacon.

Hirschel, J.D., Hutchinson III, C.D., Dean, C., & Mills, A.M. (1992). Review essay on the law enforcement response to spouse abuse: Past, present, and future. *Justice Quarterly, 9,* 247–283.

Hodgins, S. (1992). Mental disorder, intellectual deficiency, and crime: Evidence from a birth cohort. *Archives of General Psychiatry, 49,* 476–483.

Howell, J.C. (2000). *Youth gang programs and strategies.* Washington, DC: National Youth Gang Center.

Hubbard, J.R., & Martin, P.R. (Eds.) (2001). *Substance abuse in the mentally and physically disabled.* New York: Marcel Dekker.

Huff, C.R., Rattner, A., Sagarin, E., Macnamara, D.E.J. (1986). Guilty until proven innocent: Wrongful conviction and public policy. *Crime and Delinquency, 32,* 518–544.

Identity Theft Resource Center. (2003). *Identity theft: The aftermath 2003.* Washington, DC: Author.

International Association of Chiefs of Police. (1967). *Training key 16: Handling disturbance calls.* Gaithersburg, MD: IACP.

Kania, R.E., & Mackey, W.C. (1977). Police violence as a function of community characteristics, *Criminology, 15,* 27–48.

Klinger, D.A. (1996). More on demeanor and arrest in Dade County. *Criminology, 34,* 61–82.

Leo, R.A. (1996). Inside the interrogation room. *Journal of Criminal Law and Criminology, 86* (2), 266–303.

Lundman, R.J. (1974). Routine police arrest practices: A commonweal perspective. *Social Problems, 22,* 127–141.

Lundman, R.J. (1996). Demeanor and arrest: Additional evidence from previously unpublished data. *Journal of Research in Crime and Delinquency, 33* (3), 306–323.

Lundman, R.J., Sykes, R.E., & Clark, J.P. (1978). Police control of juveniles. *Journal of Research in Crime and Delinquency, 15* (1), 74–91.

Lurigio, A.J., & Lewis, D.A. (1987). *Toward a taxonomy of the criminal mental patient.* Unpublished manuscript, Northwestern University, Center for Urban Affairs and Policy Research, Evanston, IL.

Manning, P.K. (1978). The police: Mandate, strategies, and appearances. In P.K. Manning & J. Van Maanen (Eds.), *Policing: A view from the street.* Santa Monica: Goodyear Publishing Company.

Martin, M.E. (1997). Double your trouble: Dual arrest in family violence. *Journal of Family Violence, 5,* 51–64.

Mastrofski, S. (1981). Policing the beat: The impact of organizational scale on patrol officer behavior in urban residential neighborhoods. *Journal of Criminal Justice, 9,* 343–358.

Miller, J.G. (1996). *Search and destroy: African American males in the criminal justice system.* New York: Cambridge University Press.

Monell v. Department of Social Services of the City of New York, 436 U.S. 658 (1978).

Murphy, P.V., & Pate, T. (1977). *Commissioner: A view from the top of American law enforcement.* New York: Simon and Schuster.

National Youth Gang Center. (2000). *National youth gang survey.* Washington, DC: Author.

Newhill, C.E., & Mulvey, E.P. (2002). Emotional dysregulation: The key to a treatment approach for violent mentally ill individuals. *Clinical Social Work Journal, 30* (2), 157–171.

Office of Consolidated Emergency Management accessed on May 20, 2005. www.ocem.org

Ofshe, R. (1992, April 13). *The internalized coerced confession.* Lecture, Guggenheim Crime Seminar, Center for the Study of Law and Society, Berkeley, CA.

Ostrum, E., Parks, R.B., & Whitaker, G. (1978). *Patterns of metropolitan policing.* Cambridge, MA: Ballinger.

Pogrebin, M. (1986). Police responses for mental health assistance. *Psychiatric Quarterly, 58* (1), 66–73.

President's Commission on Law Enforcement and Administration of Justice. (1967). *Task force report: The police.* Washington DC: US Government Printing Office.

Reiss, Jr., A.J. (1971). *The police and the public.* New Haven: Yale University Press.

Reuss-Ianni, E. (1983). *Two cultures of policing.* New Brunswick, NJ: Transaction Books.

Ricksheim, E.C., & Chermak, S.M. (1993). Causes of police behavior revisited. *Journal of Criminal Justice, 21,* 353–382.

Rossi, P., Berk, R., & Edison, B. (1974). *The roots of urban discontent: Public policy, municipal institutions, and the ghetto.* New York: John Wiley and Sons.

Shepard Engel, R., & Silver, E. (2001). Policing mentally disordered suspects: A reexamination of the criminalization hypothesis. *Criminology, 39* (2), 225–252.

Sherman, L.W. (1992). *Policing domestic violence: Experiments and dilemmas.* New York: The Free Press.

Sherman, L.W., & Berk, R.A. (1984). The specific deterrent effects of arrest for domestic assault. *American Sociological Review, 49* (2), 261–272.

Sigurdson, C. (2000). The mad, the bad, and the abandoned: The mentally ill in prisons and jails. *Corrections Today, 62* (7), 70–78.

Skolnick, J.H. (1966). *Justice without trial: Law enforcement in a democratic society.* New York: John Wiley.

Skolnick, J.H., & Fyfe, J.J. (1993). *Above the law: Police and the excessive use of force.* New York: Free Press.

Smith, D. (1984). The organizational context of legal control. *Criminology, 22,* 19–38.

Smith, D. (1986). The neighborhood context of police behavior. In A. Reiss & M. Tonry (Eds.), *Crime and Justice: Annual Review of Research.* Volume 8. Chicago: University of Chicago Press.

Smith, D., & Visher, C. (1981). Street level justice: Situational determinants of police arrest decisions. *Social Problems, 29,* 167–178.

Steadman, H.J., Mulvey, E.P., Monahan, J., Robbins, P.C., Applebaum, P.S., Grisso, T., Roth, L.H., & Silver, E. (1998). Violence by people discharged from acute psychiatric inpatient facilities and by others in the same neighborhoods. *Archives of General Psychiatry, 55,* 393–401.

Swanson, C. (1978). The influence of organization and environment on arrest policies in major U.S. cities. *Policy Studies Journal, 7,* 390–418.

Swanson, J.W., Holzer, C.D., Ganju, V.K., & Jono, R.T. (1990). Violence and psychiatric disorder in the community: Evidence from the Epidemiologic Catchment Area Surveys. *Hospital and Community Psychiatry, 41,* 761–770.

Teplin, L.A. (1984). Criminalizing mental disorder. *American Psychologist, 39* (7), 794–803.

Teplin, L.A. (1986). *Keeping the peace: The parameters of police discretion in relation to the mentally disordered.* Research Report. Washington, DC: National Institute of Justice.

Teplin, L.A. (1990). The prevalence of severe mental disorder among male urban jail detainees: Comparison with the Epidemiological Catchment Area program. *American Journal of Public Health, 80,* 663–669.

Thurman v. Torrington, 595 F. Supp. 1521 (1984).

Torrey, E.F., Stieber, J., Ezekiel, J., Wolfe, S.M., Sharfstein, J., Noble, J.H., & Flynn, L.M. (1992). *Criminalizing the seriously mentally ill: The abuse of jails as mental hospitals.* Washington, DC: Public Citizens' Health Research Group and the National Alliance for the Mentally Ill.

U.S. Department of Justice. (1984). *Attorney General's task force on family violence: Report.* Washington, DC: U.S. Department of Justice.

Valdez, A. (June 2000). Put full-service gang units to work. *Police,* 54–55.

Vickers, B. (2000). *Memphis, Tennessee, Police Department's Crisis Intervention Team.* Practitioner Perspectives. Washington, DC: Bureau of Justice Assistance.

Walker, S., & Katz, C.M. (2002). *The police in America: An introduction.* New York: McGraw-Hill.

Westley, W.A. (1970). *Violence and the police: A sociological study of law, custom, and morality.* Cambridge: MIT Press.

Wexler, C. (2001, September). Terrorism and local law enforcement. *Subject to Debate,* 1–2, 4, 6, 11.

White, M.D. (2003). Examining the impact of external influences on police use of deadly force over time. *Evaluation Review, 27* (1), 50–78.

White, M.D., Campbell, S.P., & Goldkamp, J.S. (2005). Beyond mandatory arrest: Developing a comprehensive response to domestic violence. *Police Practice and Research: an International Journal, 6* (3), 261–278.

Wilson, J.Q. (1968). *Varieties of police behavior.* Cambridge, MA: Harvard University Press.

Wilson, J.Q., & Boland, B. (1978). The effect of the police on crime. *Law and Society Review, 12,* 367–390.

Worden, R.E. (1989). Situational and attitudinal explanations of police behavior: A theoretical reappraisal and empirical assessment. *Law and Society Review, 23,* 667–711.

Wrobleski, H.M., & Hess, K.M. (2003). *Introduction to law enforcement and criminal justice.* 7th edition. Belmont, CA: Thomson Wadsworth.

■ ■ ■ ■ ■

SCHOLAR'S PERSPECTIVE
The Police and Sex Offenders

Karen J. Terry, Ph.D.
Associate Professor, John Jay College of Criminal Justice

Despite the growing legislative priority to incapacitate sexual offenders in either prison or a hospital, the majority of known sex offenders are living in the community. The primary agencies in charge of supervising sex offenders in the community include the police, probation, parole, treatment providers, and victim service agencies, while other agencies such as prosecutors, social services, family and childcare services, health care providers, housing authorities, and employers may also play a role. In order to effectively supervise and manage sex offenders in the community, criminal justice agencies should work collaboratively to understand the risks and needs of the offenders and provide the appropriate level of supervision and treatment in order to protect the community.

In the past decade, the method of supervising sex offenders in the community has changed, and for no agency more so than the police. Prior to the 1990s, their duties consisted almost solely of investigating sex crimes once reported. However, there is now a sex offender registry in every state, and the police must now also work with other criminal justice agencies to monitor registered sex offenders. This includes duties specific to registration and community notification law statutes (RCNL), such as taking the offender's name and address and notifying the community of high-risk offenders, as well as responding to actions taken by the public as a result of high-risk sex offenders living in the community.

With regard to investigating sexual offenses, the police have many obstacles to preventing sexual crimes from occurring. Sex crimes most often occur within the home or another intimate setting, and the victims often delay reporting of the offense for months or even years. One study showed that of the known sexual offenses committed by Catholic priests against minors, 25 percent of the victims reported the offense within ten years, 50 percent reported within twenty years of the abuse incident, and 75 percent reported within thirty years of the abuse incident. This delay in reporting, which is associated with numerous factors such as age and gender of the victim, relationship between the victim and perpetrator, and nature and length of the abusive relationship, leads to a dearth of evidence. Some sexual crimes are violent attacks committed by strangers, yet these are not nearly as common as offenses committed by acquaintances or intimates, which account for approximately 90 percent of sexual offenses reported. Once the victim does report the crime, it is the duty of the police to investigate any allegations made and determine if there is probable cause to believe that a sexual offense did occur.

INVESTIGATING SEX CRIMES

There are three main sources of evidence in a sex crime: the victim, the suspect, and the crime scene. Many police departments have formed sex crimes units that are specially trained to investigate these offenses, and hospitals often now employ sexual assault nurse examiners (SANE) to gather forensic evidence of the sex crime, such as hair and semen samples. The police must collect information from the victim, including the identity of the offender (if known) and details of the offense. A delay in reporting a sexual offense diminishes the physical evidence available, but even among those victims who report immediately, many shower or change clothes so that some important evidence is gone.

Once the police identify a suspect, forensic evidence from him or her can be compared to that on the victim or at the crime scene. Unfortunately, while there may be fingerprints, bodily fluids, or trace evidence at the crime scene, on the suspect, or on the victim, this does not indicate whether an individual consented to a sexual act. Ultimately, many cases of sexual assault on adults depend upon the testimony of the accused and the victim rather than evidence if the suspect says the sexual act was consensual. The victim's statement and police report are also particularly important, as they are generally submitted in court, referred to in the development of the presentence investigation (PSI), and used in treatment for the offender. Once the offender is arrested and the case is passed onto the prosecution, the police work at the investigative stage is essentially complete.

MONITORING AND SUPERVISION OF SEX OFFENDERS

The other duty of the police in some states is to monitor registered sex offenders. This includes dealing with known sex offenders, particularly those who are classified as high-risk offenders, and controlling any disorder that results from the offender's living in the community (McGuicken & Brown, 2001). Some cities form specialist teams to handle the registration and monitoring of offenders, such as the Sex Offender Monitoring Unit (SOMU) in New York City. Because there are more than 4,000 registered sex offenders in the city, the specialized task force is necessary to handle the large volume of information collected on the offenders, as well as the continued supervision of the offenders themselves. Where possible, it is also helpful if the police can provide the community with education on the dangers (and myths) of sex offenders, who they target as victims, and their rates of recidivism.

Effective supervision of sex offenders requires an in-depth knowledge of each individual sex offender's high-risk situations and an ability to understand when the offender is nearing relapse. This can only be accomplished through collaboration between supervision agencies and treatment providers, who can coordinate surveillance, control, and treatment (Orlando, 1998). Before they can participate in effective collaborative management schemes, however, each agency must improve its own understanding of and duties toward this unique population, particularly the police, probation and parole, and treatment providers.

REFERENCES

McGuicken, G.K., & Brown, J. (2001). Managing risk from sex offenders living in communities: Comparing police, press, and public perceptions. *Risk Management: An International Journal, 3*, 331–343.

Orlando, D. (1998). Sex offenders. *Special Needs Offenders Bulletin.* Washington, DC: Federal Judicial Center.

CHAPTER 7

MEASURING POLICE
PERFORMANCE

The last two chapters have examined basic issues related to the business of police work, including the roles and responsibilities of police (Chapter 5) and the actual work in which officers are engaged (new—and old—crime problems, Chapter 6). This chapter examines two natural follow-up questions derived from the lessons of those chapters:

1. How does one tell if a police department is fulfilling its roles and responsibilities?
2. How does one tell if an individual police officer is handling his or her work well?

In simpler terms, how do we know if a police department—or individual police officer—is doing a good job? This chapter addresses these two very complex questions by first drawing upon our new knowledge of the complex roles of police and considering their implications for defining "good policing." The primary consequence of this hodge-podge of responsibilities is that the police have no clear mandate. The nature and consequences of an unclear mandate are discussed in detail.

With the unclear mandate of police as an important backdrop, the chapter next considers the traditional measures of police performance, which, at both the individual officer and departmental level, have focused on producing numbers: arrests, tickets, etc. Other traditional measures that are described include response rates, the Uniform Crime Reports, and clearance rates. The problems with each of these measures are also described. The chapter next turns to new measures of police performance, which to a large extent, are connected to the new philosophies of policing described in Chapter 4. Importantly, these new measures—NIBRS, peer evaluations, community satisfaction, decline in social and physical disorder, and expanded personnel evaluations—should not be seen as replacements for more traditional measures. Rather, the optimal approach to performance measurement involves supplementing these new measures with traditional ones and employing them together in a balanced manner that best reflects the mission and philosophy of the department.

THE UNCLEAR POLICE MANDATE

Most professions have a very clear mandate: college professors educate, car sales-men sell cars, and airline pilots fly planes. The fire department, the occupation con-sidered to be most similar to the police, also has a very clear mandate: to prevent fires and to extinguish as quickly and safely as possible those fires they could not prevent (Skolnick & Fyfe, 1993). But what is the mandate of the police? Given the diversity in responsibilities outlined in Chapter 5—specifically the findings of the ABA study and the research examining calls for police service (Wilson, 1968 and the PSS study)—the traditional response of preventing and controlling crime is inadequate. Manning (1978) says that the **police mandate** is a hodge-podge of conflicting duties and responsibilities that developed over time with little input from police. Despite their efforts during most of the twentieth century to focus on their crime control activities, it is clear that society expects and gets much more from the police.

The complexity of the police role developed mostly because of their availabil-ity, their quick response time, and their authority. Quite simply, there are no other agencies or businesses that provide police services—any of the eleven responsibili-ties on the ABA list—and are available 24 hours a day, seven days a week. As a result, many of the responsibilities have come to the police because there is no one else to provide those services, or all other avenues have failed. Westley (1970, pp. 18–19) says that police have assumed responsibility for all of these problems because polic-ing involves society's "dirty work," the tasks that no one else is interested in handling.

The complexity of the police role and their unclear mandate has a number of important consequences for police. First, police are sometimes put in situations where two or more of their responsibilities will conflict. This role conflict can be a source of significant stress and frustration for police officers, especially if they are given little guidance from the department in how to handle the conflict. Second, their unclear mandate has led to unfair and exaggerated expectations of the police on the part of the community (Klockars, 1980). Society has come to expect the police to respond immediately to our problems, to be courteous and compassionate when they arrive, and to solve the problem to our satisfaction. Klockars (1980) links this gap between expectations and what the police can realistically accomplish to misconduct (brutality, perjury, fabricating evidence, etc.). Frustrated by their inability to meet public expectations, police use illegitimate means to accomplish legitimate goals—what Klockars refers to as the "Dirty Harry" problem.

Last, the unclear mandate makes it very difficult for police to accurately meas-ure police performance, both among individual officers and the department as a whole. Police performance has traditionally been measured through crime levels and the "**numbers game**" (Skolnick & Fyfe, 1993). The performance of the police department is often seen as a function of changing crime levels: If crime decreases, then the police are performing adequately. However, given that police spend most of their time on other activities and that only a small portion of crime comes to the attention of police (i.e., because most crime goes unreported; see later in this chap-ter), using crime levels to measure police performance is inadequate. The same rationale applies for individual officers, whose performance is typically measured by how many numbers they generate (arrests, tickets, etc.). Quite simply, good policing may not involve an arrest or ticket in many cases. This focus on numbers then diminishes the role of prevention, which Peel emphasized (see the next section for more discussion).

There have been several suggestions for how the police can develop a more clear mandate. Manning (1978) has argued that the police should focus only on their crime-fighting responsibilities and that noncrime related tasks should be delegated to other city agencies. However, it is unclear who would perform these tasks and how much it would cost to delegate them (i.e., would a new agency have to be created?) Many departments have begun to hire greater numbers of non-sworn personnel (civilians) to handle noncrime related calls (see Chapter 5). Also, several cities have adopted 311 call systems to divert nonemergency and noncrime related calls from the 911 system. Last, Skolnick and Fyfe (1993) argue that the police should focus on the preservation of life as their primary mandate and that all other roles and responsibilities should be aligned with that overriding goal.

TRADITIONAL MEASURES OF POLICE PERFORMANCE

Recall that one of Sir Robert Peel's founding principles involved the measurement of police performance: specifically, that the *absence* of crime would indicate police effectiveness. As we know from Chapter 3, the U.S. version of Peel's London police model was, in many respects, very different from Peel's vision, and the issue of performance evaluation perhaps best typifies those differences. During the political era of policing, approximately 1850–1920, there was very little in the way of performance measurement at either the individual officer or departmental level. The police were tied very strongly to local politicians, and positions in the department were awarded to political supporters and friends. Given the political context and the lack of selection and training standards, it is no surprise that performance measurement was a nonissue for police departments.

However, the professionalism movement brought a wave of reform to U.S. policing, including freedom from politics, selection and training standards, and importantly, concern about police effectiveness and performance. The efforts by August Vollmer and other reformers to institute standards of evaluating police performance were intrinsically tied to their perceptions of the police role in society. Although the leaders of the professionalism movement recognized the diverse responsibilities of police—most notably the large portion of their work devoted to order maintenance and community-service-related activities—they sought to limit those responsibilities and focus solely on crime-control-related tasks. As a result, the initial conceptions of performance measurement that emerged during the early twentieth century focused on the crime and law enforcement-related components of police work.

The Numbers Game

Skolnick and Fyfe (1993) state that the police, like most bureaucracies, tend to measure their performance in quantitative terms. Given the renewed focus on crime control (see above), the early measures focused on counting numbers associated with crime: crime reports, arrests, tickets, and response time. The fundamental problem with these quantitative measures, according to Skolnick and Fyfe (1993), is that they do not account for quality.

> To use Herman Goldstein's term, the police are locked in a *means/end syndrome,* in which they tell us how often they employ the tools that have been provided to achieve their goals rather than whether the goals themselves have been achieved. It is as though doctors measured their performance by counting operations without bothering to determine whether patients were cured; as though lawyers counted their cases without regard to whether they won or lost for their clients. (p. 125)

In simple terms, arrest is not always the best course of action to resolve an encounter, and we learned in Chapter 6 that police officers exercise tremendous discretion in their daily activities. Oftentimes, police employ that discretion to *not* make an arrest. Consider the domestic dispute where the husband threatened his wife and could be arrested for misdemeanor assault. Yet, the wife is pleading with the officer to not make an arrest because they both were drinking, and it was a misunderstanding. She did not call the police; the neighbors called to complain about the noise. The husband is pleading with the officer because he says he will lose his job if he does not show up for work later that night. And there are three small children present watching the entire scenario unfold from the foot of the stairs. Is an arrest the best course of action in this situation?

Or imagine a police officer has been ordered by her sergeant to crackdown on drunken driving from an area home to numerous bars. The officer hides in an alleyway across from the bars and waits until patrons start coming out at closing time. The officer identifies a person staggering a bit toward his car and watches him get in and begin to drive away. The officer follows, and after observing him drive erratically, pulls him over and arrests him for drunk driving. The officer has accomplished the goal of making an arrest for drunken driving, making his sergeant happy, but the process of making the arrest has removed the officer from the street for several hours. Consider this alternative approach: The officer stands outside the bar at closing time and makes announcements to patrons as they leave about the dangers of driving drunk and how she will arrest anyone who appears intoxicated and gets behind the wheel. The officer also makes arrangements with a local taxi company to have half a dozen cabs waiting outside the bar to give rides to those who are intoxicated. At the end of the shift, the first officer has made an arrest and the second has not, but who has been more effective in combating drunk driving? The first officer has a "collar" to show her sergeant, but he has no idea how many people left the bars drunk during the several hours she was processing the arrest (or if those other drunk drivers endangered their lives or someone else's).

Skolnick and Fyfe (1993) recount a review of the NYPD's narcotics efforts by the New York State Commission of Investigation in 1970. The report showed that detectives made 7,266 purchases of heroin resulting in 4,007 arrests (NYPD policy was to make two buys before making an arrest). While these numbers appear impressive, the actual amount of heroin seized was just under 5 pounds, since most of the drugs purchased were only 4 to 12 percent "pure" (New York State Commission of Investigation, 1972). This investigative work produced some large numbers and involved a substantial amount of police work, but is that effective policing if less than 5 pounds of heroin was actually seized?

The preference for quantitative measures among bureaucracies in general and the police specifically derives from the remoteness of supervisors from the line where the work of the organization is carried out. Since policing is generally isolated and officers spend most of their shift outside of the observance of supervisors, it is difficult for those supervisors to measure performance and present it in a sensible way to the leaders of the department, as well as the community (Skolnick & Fyfe, 1993). As a result, "activity" becomes the standard measure of performance. Unfortunately, the good cop may not produce the numbers and may become invisible to the department, except for his immediate colleagues:

> Good cops always seem to identify the causes of problems and to come up with the least troublesome ways of solving them. Good cops think ahead and always leave a way out of any tough situation. Good cops rarely have to resort to the law to solve minor order maintenance problems like drunks and noisy kids on the street. Good cops spend their time finding out about the people and places on their beats instead of lurking at speed traps or near badly marked stop signs. Good cops know the people on their beats well enough to put an end to problems like double parking merely by telling store owners to warn customers against illegal parking. Local criminals know the good cops and stay away from their beats when they are working. Detectives know the good cops are tapped into the neighborhoods they patrol and frequently turn to them for information about serious crimes. (Skolnick & Fyfe, 1993, p. 127)

A veteran officer expressed this disconnect between headquarters and good street cops quite effectively:

> You know what they figure in headquarters? "Hey, nothing ever happens on this guy's beat. There's no crime, no traffic problem, no noisy kids. We put him out there and he shows us nothing. Never makes any arrests, no tickets. Nothing. Zip. What are we paying him for? Let's take him out of there and put him where he's needed. Let him help the guy on the next post. There's lots of crime there and no matter how many arrests and tickets we give out, the people still complain that they don't get enough protection. Isn't it funny how two streets so close to each other can be so different?" Hah! If the bosses ever came out to look, they'd see that the streets are the same, but the difference is the cops. The bosses can tell you what kind of numbers look good in a report, but they wouldn't know a good cop on a bet. (Skolnick & Fyfe, 1993, p. 128)

At the Department Level. *Maintaining Department Staffing Levels* Providing adequate police protection through proper allocation of patrol officers represents a basic measure of departmental performance. The allocation of police personnel can be measured in two ways. First, the **police–population ratio** is a standardized measure of police protection that allows departments to track their own staffing levels over time and to make fair comparisons between their levels and the levels of other police agencies. The ratio is calculated by dividing the number of sworn personnel by the population of the jurisdiction, then multiplying that number by 1,000. This formula provides the number of police officers per 1,000 citizens. For example:

> City A has a population of 1,500,000 and a police department with 7,000 sworn officers. The police–population rate is calculated as follows:
>
> $(7,000/1,500,000) \times 1,000 = 4.67$ officers per 1,000 citizens

The national average among local police departments is 2.3 officers per 1,000 citizens, although there is significant variation in that number. For example, the ratio in San Jose, California, is 1.6 per 1,000, while the ratio in Washington, DC, is 6.7 officers per 1,000 citizens (Walker & Katz, 2002). Generally, large police departments have larger police population ratios than smaller departments. Although the police–population ratio is related to crime, that relationship is not straightforward. Jurisdictions with serious crime problems will often respond by adding police officers, increasing their police–population ratio. However, adding more police does not necessarily result in better police protection, nor does it automatically result in decreases in crime. For example, Washington, DC, Baltimore, and Detroit all have police–population ratios well above the national average, but they all also have experienced among the highest crime rates in the country in the last decade or so.

The second way to measure police **patrol allocation** is more intensive and complex. Crime is not evenly spread throughout any jurisdiction, nor does crime occur evenly throughout a given day or week. Rather, there are specific areas of any city or town where crime is most prevalent, and almost universally, most calls for police service occur at night and on weekends. Also, a relatively small number of people generate a disproportionately high number of calls for service, including crime- and noncrime-related incidents. Research shows people with low income are the heaviest users of police services for noncriminal incidents, such as medical emergencies (Walker & Katz, 2002). As a result, police departments should take these factors into account when allocating patrol. O.W. Wilson (1941) developed a standard workload formula for patrol allocation, based on calls for service and reported crime. The department will be more effective in responding to and preventing crime if its allocation of personnel matches crime distribution over time and place.

Importantly, as time passes, police departments must reevaluate their workload formula to ensure that their coverage is still adequate. Over time (sometimes in surprisingly short periods of time), city population can increase or decrease, crime patterns and location can change, and patterns in calls for police service can change. For example, a 1987 report on the Philadelphia Police Department showed that their district (precinct) lines had not been evaluated in sixteen years, resulting in tremendous disparity in workload. Officers in the 35th district handled an average of 494 calls, including 38 for major offenses, compared to only 225 for officers in the 5th district (only eight major offenses). This type of disparity is likely to affect police officer performance, particularly in the very busy areas, as well as police officer morale.

Crime, Arrests, and Response Time   The primary measures for assessing the effectiveness of a police department have involved crime: reported crimes (published annually in the **Uniform Crime Reports [UCR]** by the FBI), clearance rates (arrests), and response time. Given the heavy emphasis placed on crime control by the professional reformers in the early part of the twentieth century, measuring departmental performance with crime-related indicators certainly seemed logical. However, as discussed in Chapter 3, a number of events occurred during the 1960s and 1970s that challenged the police role in crimefighting, and their ability to reduce crime. These include the large increase in crime in the 1960s, social research on the complexity of the police role, and the relative ineffectiveness of the reactive patrol model. In fact, a good number of researchers and scholars have argued for the last thirty years that police efforts have little effect on crime levels. However, the recent successes in New York, Boston, and other places would seem to refute that argument (see Chapter 4). Nevertheless, police departments—and consequently the public—have continued to focus on crime-related indices as their primary performance measure.

Setting aside the debate about whether the police can be expected to reduce crime, there are a number of important limitations with using crime-related measures to assess police department effectiveness. First, research has consistently shown that a large portion of crime never comes to the attention of the police. Often referred to as the **"dark figure" of crime,** these crimes are never reported to the police, and as a result, the police have no ability to investigate them and make arrests. There are a variety of reasons why victims choose not to report a crime, such as shame and embarrassment, the feeling that police can do nothing about it anyway, and a lack of trust or poor relationship with the police.

Recognition of the size and scope of the dark figure became evident as a result of the **National Crime Victimization Survey (NCVS),** a national-level survey of 49,000 residents conducted annually by the U.S. Census Bureau and the Bureau of Justice Statistics since 1972. The NCVS collects in-depth, self-reported data on victimization, and results show significant disparity with levels of reported crime. The NCVS indicates that only 39 percent of all crime is reported to the police; or alternatively, more than 60 percent of crime committed in the United States is not reported (and thus not investigated by police) (Bureau of Justice Statistics, 2003). For those who highlight crime control as the central role of the police, these data suggest that police are missing nearly two-thirds of their workload. Of course, the NCVS suffers from its own limitations, including reporting errors (accidentally or purposefully; not reporting crimes that do occur and reporting ones that did not) and "telescoping," or reporting that a crime occurred more recently than it actually did. Nevertheless, the annual survey results have consistently shown that a large portion of crime goes unreported, thus calling into question the use of crime-related indices as measures of performance evaluation for police.

In a related issue, the use of **response time** as a measure of police performance also presents problems. Response time is typically defined as the time it takes an officer to arrive at the scene of an incident from the time the call is received by dispatch, or from the time the officer received the call from dispatch. Results from the Kansas City Preventive Patrol Study (Kelling et al., 1974) and subsequent research (Bracey, 1996) show that very few calls for service involving crimes are actually susceptible to a rapid police response. In simpler terms, very few crime-related calls to the police—approximately 3 to 5 percent—involve incidents where the offender is still at the scene or has just left the scene, and a rapid police response will prevent an escape and result in an arrest. Of course, few would argue against the value of rapid response in certain types of noncrime related calls such as auto accidents, medical emergencies, and natural disasters, where the ability of the police to arrive quickly and administer first aid can save lives. With regard to crime-related calls however, Stephens (1996) argues that the emphasis on response time may actually have a negative impact on the department:

> Working to achieve a quick response is a drain on public resources that could be more effectively directed toward activities that might have an impact on the problem prompting the call. (p. 104)

The second limitation in using crime-related measures to assess police department performance involves the complexity of the police role. Chapter 5 describes the roles and responsibilities of the police, and results from numerous studies show that crime control activities represent a small portion of all police work. Wilson (1968) found that the police in his study spent about 10 percent of their time on law enforcement and crime-related activities, with the other 90 percent spent on order maintenance, service, and information gathering. The Police Services Study (PSS) examined more than 25,000 calls for service in three cities and found that: (1) 19 percent involved crime, and (2) only 2 percent involved violent crime (Scott, 1981). Again, these findings question the appropriateness of using only crime-related measures to assess police department performance.

The third limitation associated with using crime-related indices as measures of police department performance involves the central role of discretion in police work. Chapter 6 describes the vital importance of discretion to police, which underscores the point that, in many cases, police do NOT make arrests when they have legal authority to do so. This discretionary authority has been recognized and supported for more than thirty years, when the President's Commission on Crime and Justice (1967, p. 106) stated that "police should openly acknowledge that, quite properly, they do not arrest all, or even most, offenders they know of." If only a small portion of police work involves crime-related issues and in many of those crime-related cases it is proper for police to NOT arrest, then crime-related measures—particularly **clearance rates**—would seem to be an incomplete and inappropriate yardstick by which to measure police effectiveness.

Fourth, criminologists have been studying the causes of crime for years, and conventional wisdom suggests that many of the causes involve domains far out of the control of the police. In fact, this has been the argument of many who suggest that police can have no measurable impact on crime levels. These crime-causing domains include a combination of factors such as social disorganization, broken homes, poor parenting, poverty, lack of legitimate opportunity, poor education, peer influences, and emotional or psychological problems. If the major causes of crime involve the family, school, the neighborhood, and larger societal factors, how can the police reasonably be expected to prevent crime? Nevertheless, others have suggested that, despite the broad causes of crime, a good portion of crime can be suppressed or even prevented by the police, particularly crimes that occur in the street and are associated with gangs, guns, drugs, and drug markets. Recent research in New York, Boston, and Richmond (CA) indicate that police can be effective in taking guns off the street, in eliminating open air drug markets (and the crime they produce), and in reducing gang activities through arrest.

The Uniform Crime Reports (UCR)   By the end of the 1920s, the Federal Bureau of Investigation (FBI) began collecting crime data submitted to them by local police departments. In the mid-1930s, this crime recording and reporting function became formalized when the United States Congress mandated the FBI to compile national crime statistics called the Uniform Crime Reports (UCR) (Grant & Terry, 2005). Since that time, the FBI has collected crime and arrest data from police departments around the United States and has issued annual reports detailing the crime trends and statistics. Currently, the FBI collects data from over 17,000 local police departments, representing approximately 97 percent of the U.S. population (Maltz, 1999).

The UCR reports two major categories of offenses: Part I offenses, which include violent personal and property crimes—murder, rape, robbery, aggravated assault, burglary, larceny, motor vehicle theft, and arson (called the Index Offenses)—and Part II offenses, which include most other crimes (drug offenses, sex offenses, fraud, weapons offenses, prostitution, disorderly conduct, etc.). The annual UCR report presents national level data on the total number of crimes by category and type, crime rates (standardized by population), and clearance rates (by category and type). The report also presents similar data for states and cities.

Although the UCR has been used for more than seventy years as the major indicator of crime in the United States, it was clear by 1980 that it suffers from a number of problems. First, the UCR is completely reliant on reported crime, and as discussed above, the majority of crimes go unreported to the police. Second, the UCR reports only crime totals and standardized rates by population, failing both to capture the complexity of criminal events and the changing trends in crime over time, both nationally and at the local level (Grant & Terry, 2005). Third, the UCR captures only the most serious offense committed for each crime, through what is often referred to as the *hierarchy rule*. In this way, the UCR even underreports reported crime because it fails to document lesser offenses committed in multiple-crime encounters. For example, during a home invasion a suspect may commit a burglary (breaking and entering), robbery, and assault (of the homeowner), but only the robbery will be recorded by the UCR (Grant & Terry, 2005). The UCR is also unable to sufficiently record crimes that involve multiple victims and multiple offenders. Fourth, the definitions of crimes are determined by federal and state statute, and in many states, the legislated definitions of crimes do not match the definitions used in the UCR to record and report crimes. Fifth, the UCR does not collect and report data on minor offenses that are the central focus of new and emerging police strategies such as problem-oriented and community policing, zero tolerance policing, and CompStat. As a result, the success that a police department has in these types of minor offenses (turnstile jumping, loitering, etc.) will not be reflected in the UCR. Kelling and Coles (1996) state:

> Those of us who live, work and play in cities face an amalgam of disorder, fear, serious crime and urban decay: the problem does not begin with serious, or "index" crime. Conceiving of it and addressing it as such . . . leads to bad public policy, poor legal thinking and practice, and distorted criminal justice practices and priorities. (p. 5)

Last, the UCR is completely dependent on local police departments to submit accurate data in a timely manner. There have been numerous instances where police departments have submitted—either accidentally or intentionally (i.e., cooking the books)—inaccurate data that has been published in the annual UCR report (and has been used to calculate local-, state-, and national-level crime and clearance rates).

The FBI and Bureau of Justice Statistics (BJS) began a thorough evaluation of the UCR in 1982 and four years later produced a report titled *Blueprint for the Future of the UCR Program*. This report highlighted the major limitations of the current UCR—described above—and laid out a plan for revising and improving the reporting system (Grant & Terry, 2005). This report eventually led to the creation of the National Incident Based Reporting System (NIBRS), described later in this chapter.

At the Individual Officer Level

"'Activity' is the internal product of police work. It is the statistical measure which the sergeant uses to judge the productivity of his men, the lieutenant to assure himself the sergeant is properly directing his men, the captain to assure his superiors that he is capably administering his district, and the department administrators to assure the public that their taxes are not squandered." (Rubinstein, 1973, p. 44)

An earlier section of this chapter describes in some detail how police performance has been measured at the individual officer level. Called the "numbers game" by Skolnick and Fyfe (1993), police officers are assessed by the activity they generate. Traditionally, good performance means high levels of activity. Yet, often the best course of action to resolve a citizen encounter involves generating no activity: not making an arrest or not issuing a ticket. As Skolnick and Fyfe (1993) state, this means that the truly effective police officer may be invisible except to his or her co-workers. Rubinstein's quote above illustrates how the emphasis on "activity" flows from the street level all the way up to the department leadership.

All of the limitations of using crime-related indices to measure performance at the department level also apply at the individual officer level. These include:

- The dark figure of crime (most crime is not reported).
- The complex police role (much of an officer's time is devoted to noncriminal matters).
- Police discretion (officers often do not make arrests when legally authorized to do so, exercising discretion properly).
- The root causes of crime are outside of the individual officer's control.

Recall that Robert Peel, the father of professional policing, originally stated that police effectiveness is measured by the absence of crime. The absence of crime implies that police have prevented crime, but consider how "prevented crime" shows up in official police reports. Going back to an earlier example, the officer who addressed drunk driving by preventing it—standing outside of the closing bar and talking to exiting patrons, perhaps with half a dozen taxis waiting—may prevent dozens of drunk driving incidents (some of which may have ended in auto accidents), but on his or her daily activity log at the end of the night, it looks as if the officer has accomplished nothing (no doubt drawing the sergeant's ire). In the traditional department, the sergeant is more satisfied with the officer who arrested one drunk driver, but who let untold numbers of others go.

In addition to not accounting for the quality of police work (most would argue that the officer who prevented multiple drunk driving incidents above is the more effective officer), the numbers game also promotes an aggressive style of policing. If officers know their performance is measured based on activity, they will then focus on producing the numbers. This will result in a legalistic, arrest-oriented philosophy that may look good on paper (and in the UCR), but may not be perceived by its constituency as overly effective. This has several consequences. First, the arrest-oriented approach is likely to generate tension between the police and the community, especially the minority community where many of the arrests will be made. Officers who are constantly motivated to arrest with be less sympathetic and will be less likely to come across as understanding and tolerant. Also, as mentioned before, arrest is often not the best way to end a citizen encounter, so many incidents will be resolved under less-than-optimal circumstances. Second, Skolnick and Fyfe (1993, p. 115) argue that the numbers game is part of a larger "cops as soldiers" mentality that promotes aggressive police tactics against the "enemy" and "is a major cause of police violence and the violation of citizen's rights." Chapter 8 discusses the "cops as soldiers" problem in greater depth.

Problems with Traditional Performance Evaluations   Outside of their reliance on crime-related indices, traditional performance evaluations also suffer from several other problems. First, performance evaluations are often not completed at regularly scheduled intervals or are not completed at all. For example, prior to 1997, the Pittsburgh Police Bureau—one of the largest police departments in the state of Pennsylvania—did not conduct regular performance evaluations (Walker & Katz, 2002). As part of a consent decree (see Chapter 10) with the U.S. Department of Justice involving excessive force complaints in 1997, the Pittsburgh Police agreed to begin evaluating officer performance. Second, when carried out, performance evaluations have often been very subjective, with little in the way of meaningful content or constructive criticism. Supervisors often spend little time offering insights on how an officer might improve his or her performance.

Third, performance evaluations typically have not been taken seriously by supervisors. The reasons for the lack of care with this important task likely vary. In some cases, performance measurement has not been considered important at higher levels of the department, and sergeants sensing this ambivalence also give it only cursory attention. In many jurisdictions, sergeants and other supervisors are stretched thin by their regular duties and simply do not have time to complete rigorous performance evaluations. Also, as Skolnick and Fyfe (1993) suggest, sergeants are often compromised in terms of their supervisory capacity because they used to work with the men and women they now supervise, and the line staff know the sergeants' missteps and "dirty laundry." Consider these words about a new police chief trying to institute change; the same problem applies for front-line supervisors:

> He's a nice guy, but he'll never straighten out the department. He's been around it too long. The people he needs to push out of the way know about every free cup of coffee he took when he was a cop, every time he stole a half-hour from work, every time somebody went to bat for him when he was caught off base. If he does anything to hurt anybody in the department, he'll wind up being humiliated. Sure, he knows all the actors in the department, but his big problem is that they know him too. (Skolnick & Fyfe, 1993, p. 122)

The sergeant faces the same problems as the chief described above, but for the sergeant the free cups of coffee and stolen time are much more recent. The implication is that if a supervisor gives an officer a poor performance evaluation, the officer will then make known the sergeant's misdeeds.

Fourth, and in part for the other reasons stated above, performance evaluations have often been shown to be quite inaccurate. In its investigation of the LAPD, the Christopher Commission identified 44 officers who were disproportionately involved in excessive force incidents, and reviews showed that many of them had been given excellent performance evaluations by their supervisors. Michael Dowd was implicated in a misconduct scandal in the NYPD during the early 1990s (and is one of the most brutal and corrupt New York City police officers in recent memory), but his 1987 performance evaluation stated he had "excellent street knowledge" and could "easily become a role model for others to emulate" (Mollen Commission, 1994, p. 81).

Summary

Whether at the individual officer or departmental level, the reliance on crime-related indices to determine police performance is wrought with problems. In simple terms, police performance has typically been determined by measuring an activity where two-thirds of the work is missed, that represents only a small part of their overall responsibilities, that often does not involve the best course of action, and for which the causes far exceed their reach. This would be akin to measuring a doctor's performance by counting how many instruments he or she used during an operation, or a college professor assigning grades based on how often students came to class. That being said, students coming to class and instruments used in surgery are important, just as counting crime is important for the police. The important point to be taken is that, by themselves, these measures are not enough. How did the student perform on assignments and exams? Did the patient survive? Did the surgery accomplish its objectives (i.e., removing a tumor)? For the police, a number of other alternatives have been suggested in recent years to supplement and improve existing performance measures and to get to the elusive issue of quality. These are described in the next section.

NEW MEASURES OF POLICE PERFORMANCE

In the last decade, a number of new measures of police performance have become available at both the individual officer and department level. In some cases, these measures improve upon existing or traditional measures; in other cases, they represent an entirely new way of thinking about good police performance.

At the Department Level

National Incident Based Reporting System (NIBRS).   The **National Incident Based Reporting System (NIBRS)** was implemented in 1989 by the FBI as a means of improving upon the traditional UCR reporting system (described above). As the name suggests, NIBRS is an incident-based reporting system, with an incident defined as "one or more offenses committed by the same offender or group of offenders acting in concert, and at the same time and place" (U.S. Department of Justice, 2000). Importantly, this broad definition, and the manner in which information is recorded, allows for data to be collected involving multiple offenses, multiple victims, and multiple offenders (as well as multiple arrests) as part of one crime incident (Grant & Terry, 2005). This, of course, is a major weakness of the UCR reporting system. NIBRS also collects information on crime location, property, and separates completed from attempted crimes.

> The advantage of [an] NIBRS program is that it reports every crime that occurs instead of just the most serious crime of an event. For instance, under the UCR/Summary requirements if two holdup men rob 18 customers in a restaurant and then shoot and kill

the manager on the way out, you report just one murder. Under NIBRS you report one murder and 18 armed-robberies. (Hoffman, 2000, p. 31)

NIBRS divides crimes into two categories: Group A and Group B. Group A is composed of 22 offense categories involving 46 different criminal offenses. Group B is composed of arrest data on 11 different categories of crime. The offense categories (and specific offenses) in Group A are:

- Arson
- Assault offenses
  - Aggravated assault
  - Simple assault
  - Intimidation
- Bribery
- Burglary/Breaking and entering
- Counterfeiting/Forgery
- Destruction/Damage/Vandalism of property
- Drug/Narcotic offenses
  - Drug/Narcotic violations
  - Drug equipment violations
- Embezzlement
- Extortion/Blackmail
- Fraud offenses
  - False pretenses/Swindle/Confidence game
  - Credit card/ATM fraud
  - Impersonation
  - Welfare fraud
  - Wire fraud
- Gambling offenses
  - Betting/Wagering
  - Operating/Promoting/Assisting gambling
  - Gambling equipment violations
  - Sports tampering
- Homicide offenses
  - Murder/Non-negligent manslaughter
  - Negligent manslaughter
  - Justifiable homicide
- Kidnapping/Abduction
- Larceny/Theft offenses
  - Pocket picking
  - Purse snatching
  - Shoplifting
  - Theft from building
  - Theft from coin-operated machine

- Theft from motor vehicle
- Theft of motor vehicle
- All other larceny
- Motor vehicle theft
  - Parts/Accessories
- Pornography/Obscene material
- Prostitution offenses
  - Prostitution
  - Assisting or promoting prostitution
- Robbery
- Sex offenses, forcible
  - Forcible rape
  - Forcible sodomy
  - Sexual assault with an object
  - Forcible fondling
- Sex offenses, nonforcible
- Stolen property offenses
- Weapon law violations (Reaves, 1993, p. 1)

This comprehensive data collection strategy provides much more detail on the level and type of crime committed in the United States and offers better insight on crime trends over time. Trends in the numbers of victims and offenders can now be examined, not just offenses. It also facilitates the study of specific types of emerging crime, such as gang-related crime, bias (or hate) crimes, elder abuse, and terrorism (Grant & Terry, 1995). In terms of its practicality for local police departments, NIBRS allows a department to examine specific characteristics of offenders, victims, and crime locations, as well as property stolen. This detailed analysis can then be used to inform targeted police strategies and deployment.

Despite its significant improvement over the UCR system, NIBRS has experienced its own problems in implementation. Quite simply, it has not caught on as the FBI had hoped. Police departments are notoriously resistant to change, including change in crime analysis and reporting. The new system requires much more intensive reporting by local police departments. By 2003, fewer than 3,000 law enforcement agencies had adopted the NIBRS program; recall that over 17,000 report to the FBI for the UCR (Wrobleski & Hess, 2003).

Community Satisfaction Surveys. The widespread adoption of new philosophies of policing, especially community policing, has raised questions about what other outcomes, beyond crime, should be considered as important by the police. The tenets of community policing suggest that the police–community relationship itself should be considered a viable outcome worthy of measurement. As a result, a number of police departments have developed methods for assessing the degree of satisfaction among the community with regard to the police department. Brandl et al., (Brandl, Frank, Worden, & Bynum, 1994, p. 119) notes that many police departments have "come to see citizen support both as an important outcome in its own right and as an essential element in the 'co-production' of public safety." Surveys of the community can be performed in any number of ways, such as identifying residents at random and contacting them by phone or sending surveys in the mail or purposely contacting residents of certain neighborhoods. Questions can focus on the details and level of satisfaction of a particular encounter or on overall perceptions and views toward the police (i.e., getting a "pulse" on community concerns) (Champion & Hooper, 2003). For example, some police departments have instituted a regularized feedback mechanism where all (or some portion) of residents who have contacts with police are recontacted several days later to provide feedback on the encounter and their level of satisfaction with the outcome. Survey results can often indicate areas where police need to improve their community relations efforts; they can also serve to identify problem behavior among specific police officers. Champion and Hooper (2003, p. 547) list an excerpt from the Jefferson County, Indiana, Sheriff's Department community police survey, which asks residents to indicate their level of concern with a range of issues on a six-point scale (from not at all concerned—1—to extremely concerned—6):

1. My personal safety
2. Theft and burglaries
3. Juvenile problems
4. Gang activity
5. Buying and selling drugs
6. Prostitution
7. Vandalism
8. Abandoned cars
9. Loitering
10. Traffic violations or problems
11. Noise or disturbances
12. The safety of others
13. The overall crime rate.

Stephens (1996) states that, with the community satisfaction survey, the most important indicator of police performance becomes the level of change from one survey to the next. In Portland (OR), the city auditor's office conducts regular surveys of citizens to assess their perceptions of the quality of police service. In the 1996 survey, results showed that in one neighborhood, 20 percent of the residents knew the officer assigned to their neighborhood by name, while in another area only 11 percent of residents knew their neighborhood officer (Walker & Katz, 2002). Efforts to improve resident awareness of the police in the latter neighborhood can be evaluated by examining results from the next survey and looking for an increase in the percentage who know their neighborhood officer. Regardless of how it is structured, the community survey focuses on "the independent goals of public or customer satisfaction" (Alpert & Moore, 2000, p. 242).

Fear of crime among residents and the level of disorder in a neighborhood have also been suggested as possible outcomes for police to measure, and both can be assessed through the citizen survey. Kelling (1999), in particular, argues that quality of life is a principal goal of community policing, and as a result, issues associated with it should be measured as outcomes. As fear of crime and the level of disorder decrease (as a result of specific police strategies), quality of life should improve, and this improvement can be documented through regularized citizen surveys. Participation in community policing activities, such as police–community meetings, can also be viewed as a measure of police performance and serve as an excellent point of contact for police to conduct the citizen surveys. For example, as part of the evaluation of the Chicago Alternative Policing Strategies (CAPS) program, police examined the degree of citizen involvement in neighborhood beat meetings as an indicator of trust in the police department (see Chapter 4 for more discussion of CAPS) (Walker & Katz, 2002). The CAPS evaluation also involved telephone surveys of residents in 1997, 1998, and 1999. In each year, researchers used random digit dialing procedures to randomly sample phone numbers for the survey: In 1997, there were 3,066 respondents, followed by 3,071 in 1998, and 3,101 in 1999 (Skogan, 2004). The surveys, administered in Spanish and English, were carried out by researchers at the University of Illinois and included the following questions:

> How responsive are the police in your neighborhood to community concerns? Do you think they are [very responsive to very unresponsive]?
>
> How good a job are the police doing in dealing with the problems that really concern people in your neighborhood? Would you say they are doing a [very good job to poor job]?
>
> How good a job are the police doing in working together with residents in your neighborhood to solve local problems? Would you say they are doing a [very good job to poor job]?
>
> Indicate whether the following are "a big problem," "some problem," or "no problem" in your neighborhood:
>> Abandoned cars in the streets and alleys
>> Abandoned houses or other empty buildings in your area
>> Grafitti, that is, writing or painting on walls or buildings
>> Shootings and violence by gangs
>> Drug dealing on the streets
>> People breaking in or sneaking into homes to steal things
>> People being attacked or robbed (Skogan, 2004, p. 75).

The community survey does have its limitations, however. The results may not be scientifically valid, depending on how the surveys were conducted. Most police departments do not have experts in research methods to ensure that the sampling is done correctly, that the survey questions are constructed appropriately (e.g., unbiased), and that the results are interpreted correctly. Police departments can minimize this problem by partnering with researchers or professors from local universities to assist with the research. Brandl et al. (1994) cautions that citizens' perceptions may be skewed by their personal experiences with the police, by preconceptions, and/or by stereotypes. High-profile police scandals, even if they occur in other jurisdictions, can negatively affect peoples' perceptions of the police. By the nature of their work, police officers often deal with people who have had bad things happen, who are unhappy to see them, and regardless of the outcome, will be unsatisfied with the police response. For example, police officers are often mandated by department policy and state law to make an arrest in domestic violence calls, even when the victim expressly states that she (sometimes he) does not want the offender to be arrested. Also, many citizens have unrealistic expectations of the police, based on the idealized portrayals in televisions and the movies. Victims, in particular, may be unhappy with police response time, handling of the case, and the failure to locate the offender and make an arrest (which, depending on the type of crime, is fairly common).

Nevertheless, the citizen survey represents an excellent method for the police to tap into their performance in the noncrime related areas of their work. Most citizen interactions with the police involve service- and order-maintenance-related issues, which will not be captured through the crime-related indices described above. The citizen survey, if carried out in a regularized and methodologically sound manner, offers an important tool for assessing a community's satisfaction with police, for identifying areas for improvement, and for measuring change in satisfaction when new initiatives are implemented.

Identifying Measurable Outcomes.   Many of the new philosophies of policing described in Chapter 4 are perfectly suited for measurement of police performance. Problem-oriented policing and CompStat, in particular, involve problem-solving processes where specific issues are identified, potential solutions are developed and implemented, and assessments are conducted to determine if the problem has been solved. Alpert and Moore (2000) state that performance measurement can be enhanced by viewing "each problem-solving initiative as a particular program to be evaluated for its immediate impact" (p. 223). The original problem-oriented policing study in Newport News, as well as the research in Boston and Jersey City (all discussed in Chapter 4), represent excellent examples of how these strategies can be cast in terms of measuring police performance. Departments that have adopted CompStat hold weekly or biweekly meetings where new problems are identified and strategies implemented to address previous problems are assessed. By instituting a summary reporting mechanism, a CompStat police department can track its effectiveness internally, and if desired, it can produce reports for the community to document its level of success. "In this way, a file is created, activities are monitored, and results recorded and evaluated" (Alpert & Moore, 2000, p. 223).

The primary limitation of this method of performance evaluation is that the problems that a police department addresses can range in size quite dramatically. Police departments must be conscious of maintaining realistic expectations based on the size and nature of the problem. Alpert and Moore (2000) note that problems can vary by the police department resources that are committed to them; the amount of time required to solve them; the number of specialized resources required; the extent to which outside resources are required; and their importance and scale within the community. Based on these factors, efforts to address a problem may be short term or long term, may require the assignment of additional personnel, and may involve multiagency collaborations. When reporting results either internally or externally to the public, police departments may wish to develop a classification system that breaks down problems according to their scope, resource intensiveness, and time frame for solution.

Other Options.   Scholars, researchers, and police have discussed a variety of other potential measures of police performance. Alpert and Moore (2002, p. 223) state that police performance measures should also include:

■ Police-related and intergovernmental activities that improve the social fabric of the community.
■ Projects with the assistance of private industry that improve informal and formal social control in the community.
■ Fear of crime.
■ Victimization and police service programs that help promote community spirit in those neighborhoods where none existed.
■ The form and level of self-defense efforts by citizens.
■ The level of citizen trust and confidence in the police.

Skolnick and Fyfe (1993) argue that efforts to measure police performance will struggle until a clear mandate is developed.

> The most important consequence of failure to agree upon a statement of the police mission is that we do not have any way to tell when it is being done well. . . . The result is that it is difficult to distinguish good departments from those that are not; good officers from those who are not; good police work from that which is not. Instead, only the outliers at the negative end of the scale—officers whose records indicate violence-proneness; departments or units with histories of corruption—are readily apparent, while excellent performers are indistinguishable from the mediocre. (p. 243)

Skolnick and Fyfe (1993) do offer a number of suggestions for improving the current state of affairs with regard to police performance measurement. First, they argue that line officers should be involved in the definition of good policing. A major theme of their book is that line officers, much like doctors and lawyers, are the most important members of the organization. Any effort to define what is good policing must involve these line-level officers responsible for service delivery. Second, they point to accreditation with the Commission on Accreditation for Law Enforcement Agencies (CALEA) as a promising strategy for defining good policing (see Chapter 9 for a thorough discussion of CALEA). To achieve accreditation, a department must have in place more than 900 administrative standards in approximately 50 policy and operational areas. However, the primary effect of accreditation is to professionalize administration and management, with much less impact on line officers (Skolnick &

Fyfe, 1993). Nevertheless, accreditation offers an important baseline for departments to establish basic, minimum standards for police conduct and performance.

Third, Skolnick and Fyfe (1993) argue that protecting life should be adopted as the basic "acid test" for every police action: "Was the police action the best way to protect life?" (p. 245). There are a number of examples where police have achieved success when they have defined their effectiveness in terms of protecting life. These include deadly force and vehicle pursuit policies (see Chapter 9) and police hostage negotiations. With regard to police hostage negotiations, prior to the 1970s the lives of hostages were considered "already lost," and police efforts focused on apprehension of the suspects rather than saving the lives of the victims (Skolnick & Fyfe, 1993). However, following a number of high-profile hostage situations resulting in bloodshed (most notably, the New York State Police retaking of the Attica Prison in 1973), New York City police re-defined their role in hostage situations to protect life and created the first Hostage Negotiation Team (Skolnick & Fyfe, 1993). During the first ten years of operation, the NYPD Hostage Negotiation Team resolved more than 300 hostage situations without a single fatality to any hostage, hostage-taker, or police officer. Skolnick and Fyfe (1993) cite another example that illustrates the potential for protecting life as a starting point to define good policing:

> Skolnick once testified in a case where two highway patrolmen stopped a Mercedes-Benz going 65 miles an hour on a relatively deserted superhighway at 2 a.m. The driver, a tall black male, has passed the patrol car, which was traveling at 55 mph, the exact, but rarely observed, speed limit. The officers order the driver out of the car and asked to see his license. The driver opened his wallet and showed instead an emergency room physician ID card. He told the traffic cops that he was on his way to an emergency where someone was dying of bullet wounds.
>
> The highway patrolmen nevertheless insisted that he show his license. The driver said, 'This is nonsense. I'm a surgeon and a man is dying.' He then turned to return to the driver's seat. One of the cops grabbed him, choked him, and dragged him to the side of the road, half-conscious and in shock. He recovered about fifteen minutes later, subsequently suffered from neck pains and headaches, sued and won.
>
> Skolnick testified that protection of life was the primary responsibility of the police. The police, in this case, Skolnick said, should have allowed the doctor to drive to the emergency room (which happened to be only a couple of miles [distance]) and assisted in getting him there. (pp. 245–246)

At the Individual Officer Level

Over the last few decades, many police departments have also emphasized developing better, more accurate measures of individual police performance. Particularly in departments that have adopted community or problem-oriented policing philosophies, managers and supervisors have recognized that the numbers game—by itself—is no longer an appropriate measure of officer performance. Importantly, officers must have a clear mandate from the department with regard to how their effectiveness will be measured. Otherwise, line personnel will become increasingly frustrated with the performance evaluation process, which will lead to high levels of stress and could have a negative impact on their work. Some new initiatives for measuring individual officer performance are described below.

Expanding and Enhancing the Evaluation Process.   Traditionally, police officers have not taken seriously the department's evaluation of their performance. Police officer perceptions about the lack of utility of performance evaluation stems in large part from the fact that the evaluation process has typically focused on activities that do not reflect the real work that they do (Oettmeier & Wycoff, 2000). In simple terms, police officers know the numbers game and know it is not an accurate reflection of their performance. In many police departments, officers also know that the evaluations are often given short shrift by supervisors and are not taken seriously by upper level management. Yet, research highlights the importance of performance evaluation as a catalyst for initiating behavioral change among officers and, more generally, positive change throughout the department (see Wycoff & Oettmeier, 1993). "Performance evaluations can be used to alter the service expectations, policing styles and responsibilities of patrol officers" (Oettmeier & Wycoff, 2000, p. 398).

Expanding the Purposes and Assumptions of Performance Evaluation   Police departments have traditionally ignored the potential value of performance evaluation of their line personnel. Yet, there are a number of important reasons for a police department to evaluate the performance of its officers, each of which can lead to more effective and efficient police service:

- Administration: To help managers make decisions about promotion, demotion, reward, discipline, training needs, salary, job assignment, retention, and termination.
- Guidance and counseling: To help supervisors provide feedback to subordinates, assist them in career planning and preparation, and improve employee motivation.
- Research: To validate selection and screening tests and training evaluations and to assess the effectiveness of interventions designed to improve individual performance.
- Socialization: To convey expectations to personnel about both the content and style of their performance and to reinforce other means of organizational communication about the mission and values of the department.
- Documentation: To record types of problems and situations officers are addressing in their neighborhoods and the approaches they take to them. Such documentation provides for data-based analysis of the types of resources and other managerial support needed to address problems and allow officers the opportunity to have their efforts recognized.
- System improvement: To identify organizational conditions that may impede improved performance and to solicit ideas for changing the conditions. (Oettmeier & Wycoff, 2000, pp. 382–383)

The key for successful performance evaluation is that it accurately reflects the true work of police officers, although this is easier said than done. Frankly, police departments have been struggling with assessing their officers' performance since August Vollmer's time (almost immediately recognizing the weaknesses in the numbers game), and the shift to new philosophies of policing have only brought these questions back to the forefront. But the shift in philosophy, mostly involving the adoption of community and problem-oriented policing, has led to reexamination of some of the assumptions of the traditional performance evaluation model. For example, in a traditional model, officers are assessed at least once a year, and all are assessed with the same performance criteria, the same evaluation tool, year in and year out. Oettmeier and Wycoff (2000) suggest that these assumptions may be subject to change in a COP or POP department. Perhaps evaluation criteria should vary based on an officer's assignment, time on the job, and competency. Also, perhaps performance criteria should change over time, with the expectation that officer proficiency should improve with experience. And perhaps performance should be evaluated in phases consistent with individual development, rather than at preset times for everyone.

Moreover, the outcomes being measured must be greatly expanded beyond the activity an officer generates. Other potential outcomes include:

- Problem solving
- Nonaggressive behavior that reduces violence
- Citizen satisfaction
- Repeat business
- Displacement
- Indicators of neighborhood cohesion (i.e, occupancy rates, neighborhood groups)
- Having a sense of personal responsibility for an area and its people
- Believing in the importance of improving conditions in an area
- Accessing worthwhile information from citizens
- Collaborating with citizens to address crime and disorder problems
- Working with other agencies or community groups
- Using crime analysis data
- Strategic neighborhood planning
- Managing uncommitted time
- Developing/implementing/assessing neighborhood action plans (Oettmeier & Wycoff, 2000)

Spelman and Eck (1987) argue that outcomes must be conceived in broader terms and different degrees. For example, in the earlier discussion of alternative approaches to responding to drunk driving, both officers produced "effective" outcomes with their varied approaches (one officer produced an arrest while the other did not, but the second managed to arrange cab rides for numerous potential arrestees). Police effectiveness can be measured on a scale or continuum of different degrees such as total elimination of the problem, reducing the number of incidents created by the problem, reducing the seriousness of the incidents created by the problem, designing methods for better handling of the incidents, and removing the problem from police consideration by delegating it to another agency (Spelman & Eck, 1987).

Quite clearly, the sources that a police manager relies on for performance evaluation must be expanded well beyond internal activity reports and observations of the officer. Other members of the department may serve as an excellent resource for the manager, particularly detectives and investigators who may rely on the officer for his or her knowledge of the beat and the people who live and work in it (Oettmeier & Wycoff, 2000). The community is also an untapped resource for performance evaluation. Business owners, community and civic leaders, clergy, and apartment owners interact with the officer on a daily or weekly basis and can offer important insights on performance. And finally, the officer should be involved in his or her own performance evaluation. There should be a strong feedback system in which the officer can present detailed information about specific activities that may be unknown to the manager, and in which constructive criticism can take place (Oettmeier & Wycoff, 2000).

Importantly, the supervisors assigned the task of performance evaluation must be given enough time and resources to complete the officer assessments in a thorough and exhaustive manner. This task must come to be seen as a critically important function of supervisors (Oettmeier & Wycoff, 2000). Many of the mundane administrative functions may have to be delegated to other personnel so supervisors can focus their time on completing the evaluations. Or perhaps specific supervisors or groups of supervisors in each precinct can act as performance evaluation teams, with the sole responsibility of assessing individual officer performance by collecting data from the archival records, the officer, his or her co-workers, supervisors, and people from the neighborhood in which he or she patrols. In sum, the underlying rationale for an effective performance evaluation system is that it reflects the real work of police, that it is taken seriously by all members of the department (from the chief to line officers), and that the results produced by the system will help managers make important decisions regarding personnel that will improve overall police service.

Two Examples of Contemporary Performance Evaluation   As part of an effort to implement community policing, the Houston Police Department created a task force of officers to develop performance evaluation measures for officers involved in the new initiative. After many meetings and visits to police departments in four other cities, the task force produced a list of duties, roles, and skills necessary to be effective in the new community policing initiative (Oettmeier & Wycoff, 2000). This work led to the creation of a new, intensive performance evaluation tool for patrol officers. The assessment report, to be completed twice a year, includes four sections:

- Section I:
  - Work assignment: Changes in assignment, responsibilities or environment that affect officer's ability to complete tasks.

- Progress: Status of achieving objectives laid out in last assessment.
- Accomplishments: Successfully completed projects, notable actions, and significant deeds.
- Special recognition: Awards, letters of commendation, other recognition.
- Section II:
  - Supervisors are asked to rate the officer's professionalism, knowledge, relationships, and patrol management on a five-point Likert scale. Specific areas include:
    - professional appearance
    - adaptability and flexibility
    - initiative in improving skills
    - knowledge of laws and department policies
    - verbal expression
    - interaction with others
    - management of uncommitted time
    - identifying problems in his or her area
    - formulation of plans to address problems
    - management of calls for service
    - maintaining self-control in stressful situations
- Section III:
  - An open-ended area for the officer being assessed to add comments.
- Section IV:
  - Officer, supervisor, and superior officer receiving the assessment all sign the report. (Walker & Katz, 2002)

The New York Police Department (NYPD) employs a similarly intensive performance evaluation, completed annually for each officer (rookies are assessed at four and ten months in their first year). The evaluation requires that the supervising sergeant rate the officer on more than 25 different dimensions. These include:

- Performance Areas
  - Community interaction
  - Apprehension/intervention
  - Victim/prisoner interaction
  - Processing arrests
  - Vehicular offenses/accidents
  - Handling special offenses
  - Police interaction/notification
  - Vehicle operation/maintenance
  - Review and maintenance
  - Handling special cases
  - Vouchering
  - Report/clerical duties
- Behavioral Dimensions
  - Police ethics/integrity

- Comprehension skills
- Communication skills
- Reasoning ability
- Information ordering
- Problem recognition
- Visualization
- Spatial orientation
- Memorization
- Judgment
- Innovativeness
- Adaptability
- Drive/initiative
- Interpersonal skills
- Appearance/professional image
- Physical fitness/physical activities

The evaluation also includes qualitative assessments of officer performance on at least three of the dimensions, records the number of sick days and days lost, and assigns an overall assessment score and final recommendation (see the practitioner's perspective in Appendix 7A by Lieutenant Anthony Raganella, NYPD, for more discussion). The potential recommendations include continuing in present assignment, reassignment, additional training, performance monitoring for a specified time, and other.

In both cases presented above, the respective police departments have sought to expand the performance evaluation process beyond numeric measures to capture the "quality" part of police work. The departments have also worked hard to convey the message that the evaluations are a critical function of front-line supervisors and that advancement through the ranks of the department hinges on high-quality reports. Although neither performance evaluation system is perfect, each represents significant advancement beyond the traditional approach of documenting numbers through cursory and half-hearted efforts, with little consideration for either good quality or bad quality performance.

Peer Evaluations.   Many scholars have argued that a police officer's peers and co-workers are best suited to assess his or her performance on the job. There have been a number of studies demonstrating the viability of the **peer evaluation** approach. Bayley and Garofalo (1989) asked NYPD officers in three precincts to identify three officers who were highly skilled in handling conflict situations. Officers who received the highest ratings by their colleagues were then matched with comparison officers, and the researchers examined 467 potentially violent citizen encounters involving the officers (Bayley & Garofalo, 1989). Officers identified by their peers as highly skilled handled potentially violent situations differently:

> They were more likely to take charge of situations, less likely to simply stand by and observe, more likely to probe with questions and ask citizens to explain themselves, and more likely to verbally defuse situations. They were less likely to threaten the use of

physical force, more likely to request people to disperse, and less likely to order people to do so. (Walker & Katz, 2002, p. 444)

As a result, officers were quite able to identify the best performers among their ranks. Importantly, officers who were identified as highly skills by their colleagues also scored higher on departmental performance evaluations (compared to their counterparts), suggesting that the NYPD's evaluation process has merit (see discussion above) (Bayley & Garofalo, 1989).

The **Metro-Dade Police Citizen Violence Reduction Project** was designed to enhance officers' ability to defuse potentially violent situations by drawing on the work of Hans Toch, who has suggested "that the best ways of minimizing violence between police and citizens were to harness and articulate the overlooked expertise of street cops, the people most qualified by experience—and necessity—to prescribe guidelines for averting bloodshed" (Skolnick & Fyfe, 1993, p. 183). As part of this effort, the Metro-Dade Police Department (MDPD) created a task force of the most skilled police officers, detectives, supervisors, and trainers in the department. The task force then reviewed 100 police–citizen incidents that resulted in use of force, injuries to police, or citizen complaints against police. The task force reviewed the decisions made by the officers in those encounters to identify how the officers may have contributed to the outcome and to develop alternative decisions they could have made to minimize the risk of violence and injury (Skolnick & Fyfe, 1993). After reviewing the encounters, the task force produced a list of "dos and don'ts" for the most common types of encounters—traffic stops, suspicious vehicle stops, disputes, and responses to reported crimes—which were subsequently incorporated into a training program administered to all line personnel. In the year following the training, use of force, injuries to police, and citizen complaints against police all dropped from 30 to 50 percent (Skolnick & Fyfe, 1993). This project, like Bayley and Garofalo's (1989) in New York, tapped the expertise of skilled police officers and used their know-how to improve the performance of all line personnel.

Of course, the challenge for peer review is developing a system where officers are comfortable critiquing their poor-performing colleagues. In the Houston experience described above, the department decided against peer review because they felt officers would use the opportunity to "snitch off" other officers; that it would cause unnecessary conflict between officers; that many officers were not competent to engage in peer review; and that for some it would cause confusion over their roles (Oettmeier & Wycoff, 2000). Nevertheless, it seems clear that police officers themselves know a great deal about the abilities and performance of their co-workers and that they can offer valuable insights into the performance evaluation process. The challenge is to improve existing performance evaluations, perhaps like those described above from Houston and New York, and to supplement that with peer input in a way that does not create conflict or undue pressure for line personnel.

Community Satisfaction and Community Contacts. In the section above describing new performance measures at the department level, there was much discussion of **community satisfaction** as a new outcome worthy of consideration, particularly for departments that have espoused community policing. The same measure can be employed to assess an individual officer's performance. Supervisors can speak routinely with community leaders, residents, and business owners to gauge the performance of the officer or officers working that particular beat. This can be done informally over the phone or in person, or the supervisor could ask community members to put in writing their thoughts about the officer's performance. The supervisor could select community members at random, or he or she could contact people known to have had recent contacts with the officer (through calls for service). As indicated earlier, Skolnick and Fyfe (1993) argue that the good street cop knows the people and places on his or her beat and can engender their support and compliance simply by asking for it. As a result, the community itself represents an untapped resource for assessing individual officer's performance. Is the officer professional and approachable? Does the officer know the residents and business owners, and do they respect the officer? Is the officer responsive to their needs and concerns? How has the officer handled specific situations? Can community members document incidents where the officer successfully diffused a potentially violent encounter? How many informal citizen contacts does the officer engage in? Although the community represents an important resource for assessing officer performance, departments should not put citizens in a position where they are judging specific decisions made by the officer (Walker & Katz, 2002). Moreover, community input should not be the only or even most important measure of performance. Rather, community perceptions and attitudes can be added to the existing complement of assessment measures to produce a comprehensive appraisal of the quality of a specific officer's work.

SUMMARY

This chapter examined the often-overlooked question of how police performance should be measured, both at the departmental and individual officer levels. This discussion occurs in the larger context of the unclear police mandate. Specifically, police have numerous roles and responsibilities that sometimes conflict with no real clear mandate. Because police lack a clear mandate, it is very difficult to conceptualize methods for measuring "good policing." Police departments have traditionally relied on crime-related measures for evaluating their performance (called the numbers game at the individual officer level), but there are numerous limitations with this approach. In a nutshell, police performance is assessed by measuring an activity where most of the work is missed (unreported crime), that represents only a small part of their job (see Chapter 5), that often does not involve the best course of action (see Chapter 6, discretion), and for which the causes of the problem go well beyond their purview.

This chapter describes a number of new approaches to performance measurement currently being testing and/or employed across the United States. At the departmental level, these include NIBRS, community satisfaction surveys, and focusing on measurable outcomes. At the individual officer levels, new approaches include expanded performance evaluations, peer review, and community satisfaction. Importantly, there is no one best measure of police performance. The diverse responsibilities of the police prohibit the use of any single measure. Rather, the optimal approach involves employing a range of different measures that accurately reflect the diversity of police work, that tap into the "quality" of policing by drawing on citizens and officers' peers, yet still incorporates the more traditional measures associated with the numbers game.

KEY TERMS

Clearance rates
Community satisfaction
Dark figure of crime
Metro-Dade Police Citizen Violence Reduction Project
National Crime Victimization Survey (NCVS)
National Incident Based Reporting System (NIBRS)

Numbers game
Patrol allocation
Peer evaluation
Police mandate
Police-population ratio
Response time
Uniform Crime Reports (UCR)

DISCUSSION QUESTIONS

1. Explain why the police have an unclear mandate. What are the implications of this for performance measurement?

2. What is the "numbers game"? Explain its limitations for assessing police officer performance.

3. What are the primary limitations of crime-related measures of performance evaluation for police?

4. Discuss three new measures of police performance at the departmental level.

5. Discuss three new measures of police performance at the individual officer level.

REFERENCES

Alpert, G.P., & Moore, M.H. (2000). Measuring police performance in the new paradigm of policing. In G. Alpert & A. Piguero (Eds.), *Community policing: Contemporary readings* (2nd ed.). Prospect Heights, Il: Waveland Press.

Bayley, D.H., & Garofalo, J. (1989). The management of violence by police patrol officers. *Criminology, 27,* 1–25.

Bracey, D.H. (1996). Assessing alternative responses to calls for service. In *Quantifying Quality in Policing.* Washington, DC: Police Executive Research Forum.

Brandl, S.G., Frank, J., Worden, R.E., & Bynum, T.S. (1994). Global and specific attitudes toward the police: Disentangling the relationship. *Justice Quarterly, 11* (1).

Bureau of Justice Statistics. (2003). *Reporting crime to the police, 1992-2000.* Washington, DC: U.S. Department of Justice.

Champion, D.H., & Hooper, M.K. (2003). *Introduction to American policing.* New York: McGraw-Hill.

Grant, H.B., & Terry, K.J. (2005). *Law enforcement in the 21st century.* Boston: Allyn and Bacon.

Hoffman, J. (2000, January). National incident based reporting system: Still far from "national." *Law and Order, 31–34.*

Kelling, G.L. (1999). *Broken windows and police discretion.* Washington, DC: U.S. Government Printing Office.

Kelling, G.L., & Coles, C.M. (1996). *Fixing broken windows.* New York: Martin Kessler Books.

Kelling, G.L., Pate, T., Dieckman, D., & Brown, C.E. (1974). *The Kansas City preventive patrol experiment.* Washington, DC: The Police Foundation.

Klockars, C. (1980). The Dirty Harry problem. *Annals of the American Academy of Political and Social Science, 452,* 33–47.

Maltz, M.D. (1999). *Bridging gaps in police crime data: A discussion paper from the BJS Fellows program.* Washington, DC: U.S. Department of Justice.

Manning, P.K. (1978). The police: Mandate, strategies, and appearances. In P.K. Manning & J. Van Maanen (Eds.), *Policing: A view from the street.* Santa Monica, CA: Goodyear Publishing Company.

Mollen Commission. (1994). *The city of New York commission to investigate allegations of police corruption and the anti-corruption procedures of the police department: Commission report.* New York: City of New York.

New York State Commission of Investigation. (1972). *Narcotics law enforcement in New York City.* New York: Author.

Oettmeier, T.N., & Wycoff, M.A. (2000). Personnel performance evaluations in the community policing context. In G.P. Alpert, & A.R. Piquero (Eds.), *Community policing: Contemporary readings* (2nd ed.). Prospect Heights, IL: Waveland Press.

President's Commission on Law Enforcement and Administration of Justice. (1967). *Task force report: The police.* Washington, DC: U.S. Government Printing Office.

Reaves, B.A. (1993). *Using NIBRS data to analyze violent crime.* Washington, DC: Bureau of Justice Statistics.

Rubinstein, J. (1973). *City police.* New York: Farrar, Straus and Giroux.

Scott, E.J. (1981). *Calls for service: Citizen demand and initial police response.* Washington, DC: Government Printing Office.

Skogan, W.G. (2004). Representing the community in community policing. In W.G. Skogan (Ed.), *Community policing: Can it work?* Belmont, CA: Wadsworth.

Skolnick, J.H., & Fyfe, J.J. (1993). *Above the law: Police and the excessive use of force.* New York: Free Press.

Spelman, W., & Eck, J.E. (1987, January/February). Newport News tests problem-oriented policing. *NIJ Reports.*

Stephens, D.W. (1996). Community and problem-oriented policing: Measuring impacts. In *Quantifying Quality in Policing.* Washington, DC: Police Executive Research Forum.

U.S. Department of Justice. (2000). *National incident based reporting system. Vol. 1: Data collection guidelines.* Washington, DC: Author.

Walker, S., & Katz, C.M. (2002). *The police in America: An introduction.* New York: McGraw-Hill.

Westley, W.A. (1970). *Violence and the police: A sociological study of law, custom, and morality.* Cambridge: MIT press.

Wilson, J.Q. (1968). *Varieties of police behavior.* Cambridge, MA: Harvard University Press.

Wilson, O.W. (1941). *Distribution of police patrol force.* Chicago: Public Administration Service.

Wrobleski, H.M., & Hess, K.M. (2003). *Introduction to law enforcement and criminal justice* (7th ed.). Belmont, CA: Thomson Wadsworth.

Wycoff, M.A. & Oettmeier, T.N. (1993). *Evaluating patrol officer performance under community policing: The Houston experience.* Research in brief. Washington, DC: Police Foundation.

PRACTITIONER'S PERSPECTIVE

Measuring Police Officer Performance in the NYPD

Anthony J. Raganella*

Lieutenant, New York Police Department

Given the myriad of roles a police officer has, a clear-cut assessment to accurately and effectively measure job performance within the profession does not exist. Police departments have developed evaluation processes that attempt to take a very complicated measurement and simplify it into a measurable entity. Because of the variables involved in such a measurement, there is no perfect system or process by which to accurately measure performance. The NYPD has a system in place that hits the mark on many levels by taking this complicated measurement and converting into an understandable process that is manageable and as effective as possible, given the many complicated facets attached to such a difficult process.

In general, NYPD supervisors are tasked with rating the performance of subordinates assigned under them, in writing, once a year for the previous rating period of twelve months. The ratee is evaluated in 27 specific performance areas and behavioral dimensions, which are derived from a job analysis conducted specifically for the rank to establish specific standards of performance based on relevant job dimensions. Each area or dimension receives a response ranging anywhere from very low on the bottom end to extremely competent at the top. Then, the ratee receives an overall evaluation score that is commensurate with the individual areas and dimensions. For the rank of police officer, examples of performance areas for which ratees are evaluated include community interaction, processing arrests, vouchering, etc. In the behavioral dimension field, ratees are evaluated on dimensions such as police ethics and integrity, communication skills, memorization, drive and initiative, appearance and professional image, etc. Supervisors tasked with evaluating their subordinates work from a guide that is designed to assist them in the evaluation process by providing definitions, examples, and models for the individual performance areas and behavioral dimensions. This guide also gives the supervisors an understanding of how each area or dimension is defined and provides models of performance for which to use the rating scale and scores. Last, the supervisor writes comments on specific areas and/or dimensions, including a comment on the ratee's overall evaluation.

*Anthony Raganella, 10-yr. Veteran Lieutenant in the New York City Police Department, holds a BA in Behavioral Science from New York Institute of Technology

Once supervisors complete their evaluation of a direct subordinate, it is then forwarded to that supervisor's direct supervisor for review. This reviewer is responsible for ensuring that the evaluation is accurate and complete and may then make his or her own comments on the overall evaluation of the ratee. Additionally, there is an option for reviewers to prepare their own separate performance evaluations of the officer if the reviewer is in substantial disagreement with the rating supervisor. It should be noted that once the evaluation is completely prepared, it is shown to and discussed with the officer, who then signs it or has the option to place it into an appeal process if he or she disagrees with it. Also, supervisors have the option to conduct an interim evaluation on an officer at any time before, during, or after the rating period, which would be separate and apart from the annual evaluation. This interim evaluation, though rarely prepared, is by and large utilized for an officer experiencing difficulties meeting levels of competence when it would not be prudent to wait until the annual evaluation to document this. Furthermore, supervisors can recommend that substandard officers be placed into a performance-monitoring program where their performance is more closely scrutinized on a frequent basis. Continually receiving below standard performance evaluations places an officer at risk of being retrained, administratively transferred, or in the severest of circumstances, terminated from the department.

For obvious reasons, the use of performance evaluations to measure and monitor police officers' performance is an absolute necessity, given the gravity of responsibilities, accountability, and trust placed in officers. As a supervisor, the ability to monitor and measure performance of officers becomes a very important part of supervision and decision making. When tasked with personnel issues such as the movement or recruitment of officers from one area of the department to another, decision makers rely on these evaluations for officers whom they would otherwise know nothing about.

Despite the in-depth and broad range of markers for which officers are evaluated, there are some easily overcome inherent shortcomings in this otherwise sound process. First and foremost, it becomes difficult, if not impossible, to measure intangible areas of police performance. As an example, going about measuring how many crimes an officer prevented or how many bad situations that officer may have diffused is not easily attained. Furthermore, since the inception of the CompStat process and crime mapping, accountability and increased pressure to produce quantitative and qualitative enforcement activity has become a necessary element of the strategy in the new era of policing. As a result, more focus has been placed on the quantitative enforcement activity of officers in regard to arrests and summonses when evaluating performance. Additionally, this is an easily measurable component of the evaluation process. But, to measure how many "satisfied customers" the officer came into contact with during routine calls for service is a nearly impossible task.

Also of concern in a large department is the sometimes high turnover rate of officers and supervisors. It can be an obstacle to effectively measuring the performance of an officer over the course of a rating period if either the officer or supervisor has not been assigned his or her current position for a long enough period of time to get to know the ratee. Seldom seen, but still a possibility nonetheless, is the occurrence of personality conflict whereby the supervisor's ability to fairly rate a subordinate is hindered by some unresolved conflict or preconception of the ratee that negatively impacts the evaluation. Conversely, preparing an evaluation whereby the ratee is evaluated higher than should be can also be detrimental to the overall process and can serve to hinder an informed decision by other supervisors making decisions regarding personnel issues where it is necessary to take performance into consideration. Add to this that if two different supervisors were to rate the same officer with all other things being equal, they could conceivably end up with vastly different performance ratings. Despite these possibilities, the process has some safeguards in place to help avoid this. As previously mentioned, the rating supervisor must have his or her direct supervisor review and comment on the evaluation. Additionally, the ratee has an appeal option to an evaluation the officer believes is unjust, and the reviewing supervisor may prepare his or her own separate evaluation if in substantial disagreement with the rating supervisor.

Still another obstacle in the process involves supervisory complacency regarding administrative paperwork. Supervisors can sometimes find themselves inundated with volumes of paperwork and deadlines to meet. As a result, they can find themselves feeling that a performance evaluation is just another one of many pieces of paper that is overdue past its deadline and must be completed quickly. In turn, it is possible that overwhelmed supervisors, charged with evaluating squads of as many as a dozen or more officers, do not take the process seriously enough to effectively and accurately measure their subordinates' performance.

Supervisors charged with evaluating the performance of an officer can effectively and accurately accomplish this important responsibility by bearing some key factors in mind. First and foremost, the performance evaluations of police officers must be taken seriously, and the ramifications of their evaluations must be kept in focus. The importance of focusing intently on the process cannot be stressed enough. A supervisor's evaluation will dictate whether an officer is capable of advancing his or her career or moving into a specialized detail. Further, a detrimental evaluation will likely place an officer into special monitoring and will likely follow the officer for the remainder of his or her career. It could also place the officer in jeopardy of transfer or termination. Equally, evaluations where officers are undeservingly rated well above standards may allow them to be assigned to department units or details that they are not suited for or give personnel administrators a false read of the officer, thereby undermining the process. Second, and equally as important, the process of evaluating a police officer's performance is by no means a once-a-year event whereby a form is simply filled out and forwarded until the next rating period. Rather, to effectively and accurately paint a picture of an officer's performance on the evaluation, supervisors must rate their subordinates each day throughout the rating period. This requires a keen supervisor to constantly observe personnel on many levels. A good supervisor reviews officers' reports and observes their demeanor at 911 calls, as well as how the call was handled. Additionally, a thorough supervisor will periodically and randomly speak with complainants, prisoners, and other officers and supervisors for feedback on an officer's performance. In the event that an officer is newly assigned or the rating supervisor is new to the squad, it would be prudent for that supervisor to consult with the previous supervisor to gain insight and feedback as to the performance of the officer. Also, in addition to the performance areas and behavioral dimensions, supervisors should also take into consideration officers' sick records, civilian complaint records, E.E.O. guideline compliance, as well as their general enforcement activity when formulating overall performance evaluations.

While there is no one single determinative factor to accurately depict a police officer's performance, there are some informal litmus tests that can guide a supervisor when performing evaluations. As a supervisor, it becomes readily apparent very quickly who the "go-to" officers are in the squad. These are the officers that require very little supervision and guidance and show a wise use of judgment in varied situations. If a rating supervisor can honestly say that he or she would be comfortable with a particular officer handling a situation where his or her own family was involved, then that may serve as a good indicator of an officer who can be viewed as an example for others to follow. Given the nature of policing, a good overall officer is able to adapt to ever-changing situations, showing compassion and concern where necessary, or utilizing a strict zero tolerance approach when needed. Additionally, the role of front-line supervisors dictates that sergeants must be able to supervise at the same level as they teach their subordinates. The ability for officers to learn and build upon their experience is another area that rating supervisors should be in tune to when evaluating their officers. Last, supervisors should always be able to justify their ratings with documentation. Attentive supervisors should, whenever possible, document observations, minor disciplinary actions, and/or reward matters as they occur for use later on to justify their ratings of particular officers.

Overall, the performance evaluation process employed by the NYPD creates a checks and balance situation whereby officers are measured on and held accountable for their job performance, thereby creating a drive for them to meet or exceed performance expectations. In conjunction with the foregoing, it becomes incumbent upon rating supervisors to not only take the process seriously, but to remain objective and fair when preparing the evaluations. Yet, despite some inherent limitations in the process itself, the NYPD's process does as good of a job as any in measuring this difficult aspect of a police officer's work.

■ ■ ■ ■ ■ ▬▬▬

CHAPTER 8

POLICE MISCONDUCT

Police misconduct has a history as long as organized, professional policing itself. For example, despite Robert Peel's efforts to carefully select his officers, in the first three years of operation the London Metropolitan Police fired more than 5,000 officers and asked for 6,000 resignations, mostly for drunkenness (Germann, Day, & Gallati, 1985). Similarly, in the United States, every major police department has had at least one misconduct-related scandal in its history, and some departments have experienced them on an almost cyclical basis.

This chapter examines the major issues associated with police misconduct in the United States. The chapter is broken down into four parts:

1. Defining and Measuring Police Misconduct
2. U.S. Policing and Misconduct: History, Prevalence, and Consequences
3. Theoretical Frameworks for Understanding Police Misconduct
4. The Persistent Problems for Police

The first section defines and describes the major forms of police misconduct including police crime, occupational crime, corruption, and abuse of authority. With this background, the second section charts the long history of police misconduct in the United States, discusses its prevalence today and considers the consequences of misconduct for the police, the criminal justice system and the community. The third section explores the major theoretical explanations for police misconduct, focusing primarily on the rotten apple theory and structural causes. Given the long and persistent history of police misconduct, it is important to consider theoretical explanations for these problems to more fully understand why police engage in such behavior.

The final section examines the nature and prevalence of the most common forms of police misconduct, including abuse of authority (i.e., excessive force), corruption, and prejudice and discrimination, including racial profiling. The discussion of police problems is framed around the theoretical context, with specific emphasis on the contemporary controversies that have arisen with each problem. The specific police problems are highlighted through brief reviews of recent scandals that illustrate the depth and persistence of these issues for police and set the stage for subsequent chapters examining methods of controlling and preventing police misconduct.

DEFINING AND MEASURING POLICE MISCONDUCT

Defining police misconduct appears, on first glance, to be a rather simple task. Few among us have problems coming up with examples of police misconduct. Hollywood and television certainly provide clear-cut examples that would seem to epitomize police misconduct, such as Denzel Washington's portrayal of a narcotics detective in the movie *Training Day* and Michael Chiklis's character on the television show *The Shield*. Unquestionably, there is widespread consensus that certain activities constitute police misconduct.

Nevertheless, once we move beyond those few clear-cut examples of misconduct, the consensus disappears. We would all agree that taking bribes, sodomizing a suspect with a broom handle, and planting evidence at a crime scene constitute police misconduct. But consider the following examples. Given concerns about homeland security and terrorism, has an officer engaged in police misconduct if he stops a car of Middle-eastern men for no other reason than their ethnicity? Has a police officer engaged in police misconduct if he or she uses abusive language toward a citizen? Is it excessive force if an officer uses a Taser on a 6-year-old child? What if an officer accepts a free cup of coffee? Is that considered police misconduct? It has become clear that how one answers the above questions may vary considerably based on any number of factors including race, religion, gender, economic status, and political views (Walker & Katz, 2002).

Because of the complex and unique nature of the police role, there are a number of general categories of activities that constitute police misconduct. Kappeler, Sluder, and Alpert (1998, p. 20) provide perhaps the most comprehensive treatment of the categories of police misconduct, distinguishing between four different "variants." These are described below.

Police Crime

Kappeler et al. (1998) argue that not all crime committed by police officers should be considered **police crime,** or police misconduct (see also Sherman, 1978). For example, consider the off-duty officer who assaults his wife during a domestic dispute, or the off-duty officer who commits a burglary to support his drug habit. These criminal activities are unrelated to their occupation as police officers. Kappeler et al. (1998) state that the "factor that distinguishes police crime is the commission of the crime while on the job or by using some aspect of the occupational position to carry out the illegality" (p. 21). In simpler terms, unlike the off-duty officer who assaults his wife, the on-duty officer who assaults a suspect during an interrogation has committed a police crime. Other examples of police crime include:

- An officer who steals property while investigating a burglary.
- An officer who steals drugs or money from a known drug dealer.
- An officer who forces a prostitute to perform sexual acts in the back of the patrol car.

The defining feature of police crime—and the common element in the examples described above—is that the officer's position of authority plays some role in the commission of the crime. Police officers, just like everyone else, can commit crimes that have little or nothing to do with their occupation, and those criminal behaviors should be considered separate from police crime.

Occupational Deviance

Police **occupational deviance** refers to inappropriate "behavior committed under the guise of the police officer's authority" (Barker & Carter, 1994, p. 6). Occupational deviance may be either criminal or noncriminal conduct, but the key issue is that the behavior occurred as a result of the officer's authority (Kappeler et al., 1998). Examples of occupational deviance include:

- An officer who pulls over young female drivers for no other reason than to get their phone numbers.
- An officer who takes (and returns) impounded property for his or her own personal use (i.e., a car).
- An officer who sleeps while on the job.

Corruption

Goldstein (1975) defined police **corruption** as "acts involving the misuse of authority by a police officer in a manner designed to produce personal gain for himself or others" (p. 3). Although there is disagreement over the range of activities considered to be corruption, there is consensus on the two key elements: that it involves a misuse of authority and that it is for personal gain. Examples of corruption include:

- Accepting money to turn a blind eye to illegal activities such as gambling and prostitution.
- Taking money or property from crime scenes.
- Extorting money from suspects engaged in illegal activity (i.e., shaking down drug dealers).

Abuse of Authority

Abuse of authority is defined as "any action by a police officer without regard to motive, intent or malice that tends to injure, insult, or trespass upon human dignity, manifest feelings of inferiority, and/or violate an inherent legal right of a member of the police constituency in the course of performing 'police work'" (Barker & Carter, 1994, p. 7). According to Barker and Carter (1994), there are three types of abuse of authority:

- Physical Abuse: Brutality and excessive force, using more force than is necessary to accomplish the formal objective (search, arrest, etc.), and the unjustifiable use of force under color of the officer's authority.

- Psychological Abuse: Verbal abuse, harassment, or ridicule of a citizen by a police officer (i.e., the "third degree").
- Legal Abuse: Police officer violates a citizen's state, federal, or constitutionally guaranteed right (i.e., illegal stop and search as a result of racial profiling).

U.S. POLICING AND MISCONDUCT: HISTORY, PREVALENCE, AND CONSEQUENCES

The History of U.S. Policing and Misconduct

The development of professional policing can be traced to Robert Peel's London Metropolitan Police Force, created in 1829. Peel developed the basic foundations of modern policing, including careful selection of personnel, centralized administration, proactive patrol, prevention of crime as a central goal, impartiality, and adoption of a quasi-militaristic, bureaucratic organizational structure (Walker & Katz, 2002). U.S. police departments adopted the Peel model, though they did so selectively, and important differences emerged between London and U.S. police that led to widespread problems of police deviance in the United States (Miller, 1977). Most importantly, U.S. police departments were tied to local and municipal governments, and as a result, became tremendously influenced by local politics. Walker and Katz (2002) state ". . . politics influenced every aspect of American policing in the nineteenth century. Inefficiency, corruption and lack of professionalism were the chief result" (p. 29).

Historically, there were a number of efforts to reform the police, mostly notably the Progressives during the late 1800s and the professionalism movement led by August Vollmer in the early twentieth century. The professionalism movement in the early 1900s re-shaped the police into the contemporary model that is known today, with police as professional crime fighters, departments autonomous from political control with emphasis on administrative efficiency and specialization, and rigorous selection processes. Although the professionalism movement failed to meet many of its objectives, most scholars recognize that policing improved during the twentieth century (Fogelson, 1977; Walker, 1977).

Nevertheless, corruption and brutality scandals continued to plague most major police departments throughout the twentieth and into the twenty-first century. The NYPD has experienced a persistent pattern of misconduct, with blue ribbon commissions being organized about every twenty years since the mid-1880s (Anechiarico & Jacobs, 1996). In its report, the **Wickersham Commission** (1931) criticized the use of the "third degree" and condemned police for widespread brutality and misconduct. The National Advisory Commission on Civil Disorders (Kerner Commission) identified the police as contributors to many of the civil disturbances of the 1960s, focusing specifically on brutal and abusive behavior, poor training and supervision, and aggressive, impersonal patrol. In 1972, the **Knapp Commission** estimated that more than half of the New York City Police Department's officers had been engaged in corruption. More recently, police deviance has continued to make headlines: in the 1980s, New York City (Buddy Boys), Miami (the River Cops), Philadelphia, Boston, and San Francisco; in the 1990s, Los Angeles (the Rodney King case, Rampart CRASH unit), Milwaukee (Jeffrey Dahmer investigation), Washington, DC, New Orleans, and Pittsburgh.

How Prevalent Is Police Misconduct Today?

The question of how frequently police officers engage in misconduct seems to be relatively straightforward. However, the reality is that the answer to this question is quite complex and remains unknown. The problems in measuring the prevalence of police misconduct stem, in large part, from the lack of consensus in defining it. If we focus solely on the most serious forms of misconduct, the prevalence picture becomes clearer. In a recent report, Federal Bureau of Investigation (FBI) Director Louis Freeh stated:

> In recent years, the FBI has arrested police officers for corruption in every region of the nation, in large, medium-sized and small cities, towns and villages; from inner city precincts to rural sheriff's departments. From 1994 to 1997, a total of 508 persons were convicted in law enforcement corruption cases investigated by the FBI. (Hall, 1998, p. 20)

Nevertheless, given the huge number of police–citizen contacts in a given year, serious police misconduct is a statistically infrequent event. For example, since there were 663,535 full-time sworn law enforcement officers working in local and state agencies in 1996, the 508 convicted officers represents a tiny percentage of all police (less than one half of one percent). Similarly, a BJS survey of more than 80,000 people in 1999 found that police used some level of force in less than 1 percent of all encounters, and that one-third of 1 percent of all police–citizen encounters involved excessive force.

Citizen complaints represent another source for documenting police misconduct, and by all accounts, serious police misconduct appears to be rare. Research indicates that most citizen complaints against the police involve relatively minor infractions, most often rudeness and insensitive or derogatory comments. The simple fact is that the vast majority of police officers are honest, hard-working men and women who do not engage in serious misconduct. Yet, when one begins to consider lesser forms of misconduct such as those that form the basis for most citizen complaints—or behaviors that some departments prohibit but others do not, such as accepting gratuities—our estimates regarding the prevalence of police misconduct become much less clear.

The Consequences of Police Misconduct

The consequences of police misconduct can be severe and extend far beyond individual police officers and citizens. First, in many cases the misconduct is a crime, and "criminal activity by police officers undermines the basic integrity of law enforcement" (Walker & Katz, 2002: 323). Second, police misconduct can often involve the protection and support of other illegal activities (i.e., drug dealing). Third, police misconduct can undermine the effectiveness of the entire criminal justice system (Walker & Katz, 2002). In Philadelphia during the 1990s, police misconduct by officers in the 39th district (i.e., planting evidence, perjury) led to the review of thousands of criminal cases, with nearly 300 convictions being overturned (Human Rights Watch, 1998).

Fourth, misconduct can undermine the professionalism and effectiveness of the police department (Walker & Katz, 2002). Especially if the misconduct is widespread, accountability, discipline, and basic supervision become nearly impossible. Basic goals of the department, such as fighting crime and being responsive to community needs, are ignored when a portion of the police department is actively pursuing other illegitimate goals. Fifth, misconduct can cost taxpayers millions of dollars, either through having to directly pay police officer bribes and protection money (Burnham, 1974), or on the back end, having to shoulder the cost of civil judgments awarded to victims of police misconduct. For example, from 1986 to 1990, nearly $21 million in settlements and judgments was awarded to victims of excessive force by officers in the LAPD.

Last, police misconduct can undermine public confidence in the police and lead to strained police–community relations. Clearly, the police rely tremendously on the public to bring criminal activity to their attention. If large segments of the public resent the police and view them as an "occupying army," they will be reluctant to call for their help when crimes occur. In the extreme, police misconduct can lead to riot and civil disorder, as was the case in Los Angeles following the acquittal of the four officers who beat Rodney King.

THEORETICAL FRAMEWORKS FOR UNDERSTANDING POLICE MISCONDUCT

The Rotten Apple Theory

The **rotten apple theory** has traditionally been offered by police chiefs when an officer or group of officers engages in police misconduct. The rotten apple theory holds that the officers were involved in their deviant behavior on their own without the knowledge or support of their co-workers and superiors. Continuing the analogy, those officers represent a few bad or "rotten" apples in the barrel, and once they are removed, the problem is fixed—the rest of the apples and the barrel are fine. This theory offers the simplest and easiest-to-fix interpretation of police misconduct, which likely explains its attractiveness for police chiefs: By simply removing the "rotten apples" the problem is solved, and the organization is spared any real responsibility for the problem.

The Knapp Commission, investigating a corruption scandal in the New York City Police Department in the 1960s—made famous by the book and movie about Frank Serpico—took the rotten apple theory to task in its final report, arguing that it had, in many ways, prevented significant reforms from being implemented to address police misconduct. In their view, the rotten apple theory had reinforced the code of silence and prevented motivated police managers from starting reforms to correct the problem (Knapp Commission, 1972).

Others have argued that the rotten apple theory fails to explain why some departments have long histories of police misconduct or why it has become so pervasive in other departments (Walker & Katz, 2002). Also, the theory does not explain why an honest officer becomes corrupt. Back to the analogy, if there is nothing wrong with the barrel or the rest of the apples in the barrel, the theory would suggest that the apple was rotten beforehand. That is, the problem officer was susceptible to misconduct, or entered policing specifically to engage in misconduct, and the department's selection process failed to screen him or her out. Yet, research on police recruits indicates that they are not morally inferior and, in fact, that they enter policing for mostly altruistic and practical reasons (i.e., to help others, job security and benefits, etc—see Lester, 1983; Raganella & White, 2004).

There are many cases of police misconduct over the past two decades that seem to defy the rotten apple explanation. The Knapp Commission (1972) found corruption in the NYPD to be "widespread . . . with a strikingly standardized pattern . . ." (p. 1). Throughout the 1980s and 1990s, the Washington DC Metropolitan Police Department (DCMPD) suffered through a host of scandals involving corruption, mismanagement, deception, political cover-ups, and abuse of authority (Kappeler et al., 1998). In their discussion of the Rodney King beating, Skolnick and Fyfe (1993) argued:

> The dominance of this philosophy—in Chief Gates' terms, the "LAPD mentality"— suggests that King's beating could scarcely have been an isolated incident. More than 20 LAPD officers witnessed King's beating, which continued for nearly two minutes. Those who administered it assumed that their fellow officers would not report the misconduct and were prepared to lie on their behalf. In this respect, police brutality is like police corruption—there may be some rotten apples, but usually the barrel itself is rotten. Two cops can go berserk, but twenty cops embody a subculture of policing. (p. 12)

Yet, there have been cases that seem to support the rotten apple theory. Delattre (1989) argued that the Miami River Cops—involved in drugs and corruption in the 1980s—were rotten apples because there was no evidence of systemic corruption in the rest of the police department. In New York, the **Mollen Commission** (1994) concluded that the corruption was limited to a few officers only. Recent misconduct scandals in Los Angeles (Rampart's CRASH gang unit) and in Chicago also appear to be limited to several officers in specialized units (Barker, 2002). As a result, several police researchers now believe that complete dismissal of the rotten apple theory may have been premature (Barker, 2002).

Structural Explanations

Despite recent cases supporting the rotten apple theory, conventional wisdom among police researchers highlights **structural explanations of police misconduct.** That is, misconduct can occur with every profession, but the unique structural and organizational aspects of policing contribute to or even cause police misconduct. Quite simply, police officers face opportunities to engage in misconduct on an almost daily basis. Structural aspects that contribute to police misconduct are described below.

Legitimizing Police Deviance (The Law).   The police hold unique power because of their authority, and Kappeler et al. (1998) argue that "the special legal privileges accorded the police provide unprecedented opportunities to engage in deviance without arousing suspicion" (p. 61). Essentially, the police can engage in behaviors that would be considered criminal for ordinary citizens, such as use of deadly force, arrest, and search and seizure (murder, kidnapping, and burglary for ordinary citizens) (Kappeler et al., 1998). Moreover, the ambiguity of the law allows for situational application and permits officers to use the law to meet their own personal objectives (Ericson, 1981). For example, police officers can use minor violations to justify searches and interrogations and can garner cooperation by threatening more serious charges, whether warranted or not.

The criminal law may also be viewed as a contributor to police misconduct because it requires police officers to regulate activities that many believe are harmless and unworthy of police attention, such as gambling, alcohol, prostitution, and even drug use (Walker & Katz, 2002). When there is demand for a practice or service that is illegal, there is an increased susceptibility for police: Those who provide the service and those who desire the service will do what they can to get police to look the other way. Moreover, laws that are unenforceable can lead to misconduct if police officers begin to view and enforce the law arbitrarily (i.e., speeding).

Public Perception.   Public opinion polls have consistently found that most Americans are satisfied with the police, view them as honest and free from corruption, and that attitudes have been very stable over time. Kappeler et al. (1998, p. 66) argue that this perception makes detecting police deviance much more difficult because citizens "assume" police will be deviance-free. Manning (1997) states that the police are actively involved in the construction of this positive self-image, taking great care to publicize some of their activities while controlling access to other areas. This socially constructed perception, which hinges upon citizens giving police the benefit of the doubt, facilitates misconduct.

Isolation and Discretion.   Police officers, especially in suburban and rural areas, spend most of their shift alone. "Policing is low-visibility work" (Walker & Katz, 2002, p. 331). Also, many citizen encounters with police occur in isolation, reducing the likelihood that the encounter will be witnessed by others. At the same time, police officers exercise extraordinary **discretion** when carrying out their duties. Their broad discretion allows police officers to choose the time, location, and citizens that they will engage. As a result, officers interested in illegitimate activities can select times, locations, and victims (i.e., those engaged in criminal activity or those who are vulnerable) that reduce the chances their deviant behavior will be reported or observed by others (Kappeler & Vaughn, 1997).

Supervision.   Police officers generally work with no direct supervision (Walker & Katz, 2002). Police officers also value their autonomy and may resist efforts by supervisors to infringe on that independence (Reiss, 1971; Rubinstein, 1973). In many police departments, newly assigned supervisors receive little or no training for their new supervisory responsibilities. In many cases, an officer who is promoted to supervisor is working with his or her colleagues one day, and the next day he or she is their boss. Moreover, poor supervision serves a number of interests for the supervisor and the department, including reduction of personal conflicts with officers, insulation from deviant activities (deniability), and protection of the supervisors' own question-able activities (i.e., challenging officers about their conduct may result in "airing" of the supervisor's past deeds) (Kappeler et al., 1998).

Clearly, the lack of adequate supervision allows officers interested in miscon-duct to engage in illegal behavior with little threat of getting caught. Walker and Katz (2002) state, "Corruption flourishes in departments that tolerate it. Assuming that temptations or 'invitations' to corruption are prevalent in all communities, individual officers are more likely to succumb if they believe they won't be caught . . ." (p. 331).

Division of Labor/Specialization.   Most law enforcement agencies today are highly departmentalized with multiple areas of specialization: homicide, robbery, sex crimes, burglary, juvenile, gang, community policing, vice, narcotics, etc. Special-ized units are at greater risk of engaging in deviant behavior because of greater autonomy, limited supervision, greater secrecy, more discretion, greater access to resources with less accountability, and greater exposure to opportunities for corrup-tion (more interaction with individuals willing to avoid police involvement [Kappeler et al., 1998]). Specialized units also tend to develop their own group identity and a stronger-than-usual sense of solidarity, which can sometimes lead to the development of illegitimate goals.

Limited Career Mobility and Salary.   Opportunities for advancement in a police department—whether it has ten officers or 10,000—is limited, yet the only way to get a significant pay increase is through promotion (Walker & Katz, 2002). Structural elements of the promotion process can also frustrate officers. For example, most departments require officers to serve from two to five years at a given rank before becoming eligible for promotion. Promotions typically come at irregular intervals and are often postponed because of budgetary constraints. Last, there is little agree-ment on the best measures for identifying the most qualified applicants for a promo-tion (Walker & Katz, 2002).

The lack of opportunity for promotion clearly limits officers' ability to improve their salary and position in the organization. Although salaries have improved in recent years, starting annual pay is still below $30,000 in many areas, particularly for rural police departments. Officers who are unhappy with their pay may be tempted to seek illegitimate means to add to their salary, particularly if they believe that their performance has not been evaluated fairly. "When the means to achieve social and economic goals are structurally blocked, as they are in most police organizations, the potential for police deviance and corruption increases" (Kappeler et al., 1998, p. 76).

The Subculture. The existence of a distinct subculture among the police is well-established. Early work by Westley (1956, 1970) defined some of the key elements of the **police subculture** including an emphasis on secrecy, group solidarity, and reliance of violence. Niederhoffer (1967) stated that the police subculture is defined by cynicism and authoritarianism. Skolnick (1966) argued that the police develop a working personality shaped by the danger and authority of their work, and because of the potential for danger, they develop a "perceptual shorthand" to identify those who may represent a threat (the symbolic assailant). At the same time, police officers are constantly exposed to people at their worst: The police have been called because something bad has happened, or as Bittner (1970) puts it, "something-that-ought-not-to-be-happening-and-about-which-someone-had-better-do-something-now" (p. 1). Constant exposure to people in crisis can lead officers to become cynical and disillusioned.

The distinct "us vs. them" mentality is a common theme among the classic works on police subculture. Skolnick and Fyfe (1993) maintain that the "cops as soldiers" philosophy has served to deepen the "siege mentality" among police and contributes to police misconduct. Given that popular theories on the causes of crime emphasize factors that are well beyond police control (poverty, social disorganization, etc.), the analogy of police officers as soldiers has put them in the position of fighting a war they simply cannot win, and the consequences of that position can lead to police misconduct (Skolnick & Fyfe, 1993).

> When any soldiers go to war, they must have enemies. When cops go to war against crime, their enemies are found in inner cities and among our minority populations. There, in a country as foreign to most officers as Vietnam was to GIs, cops have trouble distinguishing the good guys from the bad. In this environment, the more cynical officers give up and do nothing or, worse, occasionally become corrupt. . . . There, some of the more passionate officers, who are not so easily discouraged from fighting the battles to which they have been assigned, and who typically are incorruptible, become frustrated and angry. (p. 116)

This frustration and anger that builds up in officers affects their perceptions of and interactions with the community. And for some officers, these emotions can boil over and lead to abusive and unjustifiable conduct toward the "enemy" (Skolnick & Fyfe, 1993).

Reuss-Ianni (1983, pp. 14–16) describes rules that guide the police subculture and shape the emphasis on secrecy, autonomy, isolation, solidarity, and bravery. A few of these include:

- Don't give up another cop (regardless of the seriousness of the transgression).
- Watch out for your partner first and then the rest of the guys working that tour.
- If you get caught off base, don't implicate anybody else.

- Don't get involved in another cop's sector.
- Protect your ass.
- Don't talk too little or too much; don't tell anybody more than they have to know.
- Don't trust a new guy until you have him checked out.
- Be aggressive when you have to, but don't be too eager.

More recently, Weisburd and Greenspan (2000) discovered the same emphasis on secrecy: 52 percent of officers surveyed said they thought it was not unusual for an officer to ignore the improper conduct of fellow officers; and only 39 percent stated that police officers would report serious criminal violations committed by colleagues.

Kappeler et al. (1998) offer an anthropological explanation for police misconduct, suggesting that police are part of an occupational subculture with a worldview that teaches them to distinguish between insiders and outsiders (us vs. them). This worldview is developed and maintained by a number of factors, including:

- Selection process: Those adhering to white, middle-class values are selected.
- Overemphasis on danger: Citizens are viewed as potential sources of danger.
- Authority: Police have legal authority to use force, violence, and coercion.
- Police perception of their work: Police see their work as the most critical of functions, as the "thin blue line" between order and anarchy.

THE PERSISTENT PROBLEMS FOR POLICE

Abuse of Authority

As defined above, abuse of authority can involve three different types of police actions: physical abuse, psychological abuse, and violation of a citizen's state, federal, or constitutionally guaranteed right. Although psychological abuse has been well documented in the past (i.e., the third degree), the most recent controversial cases have involved physical abuse and violation of one's rights. Oftentimes, these two forms of abuse occur simultaneously. For example, the four officers who beat Rodney King obviously engaged in physical abuse—the 56 baton blows—but they were eventually convicted in federal court for violating King's civil rights. The central issue with police abuse of authority involves their legally defined right to use force against citizens.

Police and the Legal Authority to Use Force. Police officers have the legal authority to use force in certain situations, including to protect themselves, to make an arrest, to overcome resistance, and to gain control of a potentially dangerous situation (Walker & Katz, 2002). Bittner (1970) argues that the capacity to use force is the central defining feature of the police role.

Whatever the substance of the task at hand, whether it involves protection against an undesired imposition, caring for those who cannot care for themselves, attempting to solve a crime, helping to save a life, abating a nuisance, or settling an explosive dispute, police intervention means above all making use of the capacity and authority to over-power resistance. (p. 40)

At the same time, police officers are mandated to use the minimum amount of force necessary to accomplish their objective: Use of force beyond this minimum standard is considered excessive. The **Commission on Accreditation for Law Enforcement Agencies (CALEA,** 1999: Standard 1.3.1) states that officers "will use only the force necessary to accomplish lawful objectives." In academy training, police officers are introduced to the use of force continuum. Although police depart-ments vary on the language and number of levels, the continuum typically involves a series of verbal and physical actions a police officer can take in response to actions by a citizen or suspect. As the suspect's resistance increases, the officer can employ greater degrees of force, and the officer can typically stay one level above the suspect. As a result, under most conditions, an officer can use nonlethal alternatives—such as pepper spray—on a suspect who is unarmed but is physically resisting. A police offi-cer is generally permitted to use **deadly force** in response to a suspect who is attack-ing with a knife, baseball bat, or automobile.

Despite its central importance to the police role, police use of force is actually quite rare. The Bureau of Justice Statistics (BJS, 2001) concluded that police used some kind of force in less than 1 percent of all police encounters. Specifically, just over 20 percent of the U.S. population (43,827,400) had a formal contact with the police in 1999, and 421,700 of the encounters involved some level of police force (BJS, 2001). The study also indicated that approximately two-thirds of the use-of-force incidents were appropriate, with the remaining one-third excessive (0.3 percent of all police citizen encounters involve excessive force).

Walker and Katz (2002) point out that, given 421,000 use of force incidents in a year, we can expect 1,100 incidents per day, of which 360 will involve excessive use of force. Other research, however, indicates that use of force is uncommon, and excessive force is rare. Reiss (1968) found that police used "improper" force in less than 3 percent of encounters with suspects; more recently, Worden (1995) found improper force was used in just over 1 percent of encounters. Alpert and Dunham (1997) calculated a force factor—the difference between the officer's use of force and the suspect's resistance—and found that: (1) in most cases, the officer's force matched the suspect's resistance and (2) officers followed the force continuum.

There is evidence, however, suggesting that some officers are more "violence-prone" than others. The Christopher Commission (Independent Commission on the Los Angeles Police Department, 1991) identified a group of 44 officers who were dis-proportionately involved in excessive force incidents. A fair amount of research has investigated whether violence-prone officers have characteristics that set them apart from other officers, and a number of factors stand out: 1) violence-prone officers tend to define their role narrowly, focusing on crime fighting and enforcement; 2) they believe they can perform most effectively when using their authority; and 3) they tend to view the public as unappreciative and hostile (Worden & Catlin, 2002). Clearly, there are important implications for controlling excessive force if the violence-prone officers can be identified; many departments have developed early warning systems to do just that (see Chapter 9).

The Consequences of Abuse of Authority.   Although police use of force appears to be rare, these incidents are controversial even under the best circumstances, and they can have potentially devastating consequences not only for the victim and the officer, but also for police department, the community, and their relationship (Fyfe, 1988; Geller & Scott, 1992). The National Advisory Commission on Civil Disorders (1968) concluded that the police were an "activating cause" of many of the riots that occurred during the 1960s (see also Skolnick & Fyfe, 1993: 78). More recently, riot and disorder followed the shooting death of a young black male by police in Cincinnati (2001), and police-community relations in New York City were strained by two incidents in the late 1990s: In 1997, Abner Louima was sodomized with a broomstick inside the 70th precinct house; and in 1999 four police officers fired more than 40 shots at an unarmed man (Amadou Diallo). And the acquittal of the officers accused of beating Rodney King sparked five days of rioting, taking more than 40 lives and costing more than $1 billion in property damage.

Contemporary Abuse of Authority Controversies.   *Less-Than-Lethal Weapons* Over the last two decades, technological advances have led to the development of a range of new alternatives to the traditional police weapons (i.e., gun and nightstick). These nonlethal or **less-than-lethal** weapons include tear gas, mace, oleoresin capsicum (pepper spray), impact weapons, ballistic rounds, foams, nets, and electronic stun devices (Wrobeleski & Hess, 2003). These weapons are intended to give police more options when increased use of force is required, but the situation has not escalated to the point where deadly force is necessary.

Despite their popularity and nearly widespread adoption, most of these less-than-lethal weapons have not been thoroughly examined in terms of their use, consequences, and effectiveness. One exception to this is oleoresin capsicum. Nowicki (2001) examined use of oleoresin capsicum and estimated its effectiveness at 80 to 90 percent. However, some problems have arisen when the weapon is fired inaccurately and police officers (or even bystanders) also get hit with the irritant.

The most controversial less-than-lethal weapon is the Taser. The Taser, an acronym for *Thomas A. Swift Electric Rifle* "is a conducted energy weapon that fires a cartridge with two small probes that stay connected to the weapon by high-voltage, insulated wire" (Hess & Wrobleski, 2003, p. 87). Despite its adoption by more than 6,000 law enforcement agencies in the United States (*Taser International* website, www.airtaser.com) there appear to be serious questions regarding its effectiveness and potential to cause serious injury or death, particularly when used against the mentally ill in crisis, those under the influence of drugs or alcohol, and those with heart and respiratory conditions. Recent incidents in Miami and elsewhere also raise questions about the circumstances when it is appropriate to use the Taser (i.e., against children or noncombative suspects).

On November 30, 2004, Amnesty International called for a moratorium on Taser use by police in the United States. According to the Amnesty International report, since 2001 more than 70 people have died after being shocked with a Taser. In a recently completed study by the United States Air Force, scientists concluded that the Taser may have unintended effects, but those effects are uncommon. *Taser International* maintains that its weapon has never been listed as a primary or direct cause of death (http://www.airtaser.com). And on December 7, 2004, the United States Department of Justice announced that it had begun to study the use of Tasers by police.

An increasing number of police departments have turned to dogs as a less-than-lethal option, particularly for capturing fleeing suspects and locating suspects who have hidden. Smith (2000) notes that "The courts have said the use of police service dogs can enhance the safety of officers, bystanders and the suspect. Police service dogs can also help prevent officers from having to resort to deadly force" (p. 36). Yet, problems have emerged with the use of police dogs also, particularly when dog bites occur. During a foot chase, it is not uncommon for fellow officers to be bitten if they do not heed the handler's instructions to stay behind him or her (Montoya, 2001). Also, in some cities, dogs have been disproportionately used on minority suspects. An examination of dog bite incidents in 1991 involving the Los Angeles Sheriffs Department determined that 81 percent of the victims were African American or Hispanic (Walker & Katz, 2002). Van Bogardus, a retired LAPD canine officer, argues that dog bites are similar to use of deadly force and that "find and bite" policies—where dogs pursue suspects and are trained to detain them with their teeth—are often excessive (Wylie-Marques, 2004). Bogardus developed a policy on when dog bites are appropriate:

> To protect the dog, the handler, or other officers only if the handler has probable cause to believe that such force is reasonable and necessary to prevent death or serious bodily injury to him- or herself or another person. (Wylie-Marques, 2004, p. 43)

Courts have also ruled that police dogs are a means of applying force and thus must meet the Fourth Amendment standards of reasonableness (Smith, 2000).

Hot Pursuits (Automobiles)   Alpert, Kenney, Dunham, & Smith (2000) define a **hot pursuit** as "a multi-stage process by which a police officer initiates a vehicular stop and a driver resists the order to stop, increases speed or takes evasive action, and/or refuses to stop" (p. 167). Police pursuits of fleeing suspects are controversial because of their risk of causing injury to the officer, suspect, and bystanders, as well as the potential for property damage. The National Law Enforcement and Corrections Technology Center reports that more than 70 percent of pursuits end with the successful apprehension of suspects, yet collisions occur in 32 percent of pursuits, property damage occurs in 20 percent, personal injury in 13 percent, and fatalities in 1.2

percent. Police Departments have traditionally given officers little guidance in when to engage in pursuits and when to break them off. At the same time, research indicates that most pursuits begin because of minor traffic violations and that those who flee are frequently under the influence of drugs and alcohol (Alpert, 2001).

There is also evidence suggesting that excessive force is more likely following a police chase. Alpert et al. (2000) found that the excitement and adrenalin associated with the pursuit affect the officer's actions after the chase has ended. Failure to stop and fleeing the police represents a direct challenge to the police officer's authority, and according to Van Maanen's (1978, p. 224) classification of suspects, these "assholes" are "most vulnerable to street justice." For example, the Rodney King beating took place after he led police on a seven-mile chase. Skolnick and Fyfe (1993) state:

> Younger cops, hotshot cops, aggressive cops relish the exhilaration of these pursuits. More than representing excitement, the high-speed chase dramatizes two crucial elements of policing: capturing daring criminals and meeting challenges to police authority. Anyone who speeds on a highway or, even worse, on city streets, imperils other drivers and pedestrians. Those who speed with the intention of eluding police are, by definition, audacious and dangerous. (p. 11)

As a result, police departments have been under increasing pressure to control officers' discretion in engaging in hot pursuits. A recent comprehensive study by PERF found that 91 percent of departments have a written policy governing pursuits, and nearly half have modified their policy within the last two years (of those, nearly 90 percent adopted more restrictive policies [Alpert et al., 2000]). Many departments have adopted policies that include a pursuit continuum, similar to a force continuum. Still, there is tremendous variation in pursuit policies, ranging from a total ban to allowing officers complete discretion (Wrobleski & Hess, 2003).

However, the risk of lawsuits resulting from property damage, injury, and death have increased recently, and departments can minimize the risk of lawsuits by establishing a clear and enforced policy "that balances the need to apprehend offenders in the interest of justice with the need to protect citizens from the risks associated with such pursuits" (Pipes & Pape, 2001, p. 16). In an effort to minimize risk, departments have also adopted a variety of other methods to end pursuits, with varying degrees of success. These include spike strips (to puncture tires), temporary barrier strips, GPS tracking systems, and the use of helicopters.

Deadly Force   The power to deprive citizens of life and liberty through use of deadly force represents the most extreme exercise of police authority. Although the decision to shoot clearly poses great risk to the suspect, the potential consequences of a police shooting far exceed the physical injury of one person. Police shootings have led to "riot and additional death, civil and criminal litigation against police and their employers, and the ousters of police chiefs, elected officials, and entire city administrations" (Fyfe, 1988 pp. 165–166).

By all accounts, police use of deadly force is a rare event (Geller & Scott, 1992; Reiss, 1971). Geller and Scott (1992) note that for the average officer to be statistically expected to shoot and kill a suspect, he or she would have to work 193 years in Portland, Oregon; 198 years in Dallas; 594 years in Chicago; 694 years in New York City; 1,299 years in Milwaukee; and 7,692 years in Honolulu. Although there were some indications that levels of deadly force increased during the late 1980s and early 1990s, the number of police shootings nationally has remained relatively stable over time (with variation in individual cities, of course [Geller & Scott, 1992]).

In the landmark case, *Tennessee v. Garner* (1985), the U.S. Supreme Court prohibited police officers' use of deadly force against fleeing felons unless there is an imminent threat to life. Prior to 1985, many departments allowed officers to use deadly force to prevent a suspect's escape, even when there was no threat. Given the potential consequences of deadly force, police departments have implemented strict administrative policies that meet the *Garner* requirement, and research has consistently shown that those internal policies effectively control deadly force (Blumberg, 1989; Fyfe, 1988; White, 2001). Numerous studies have also linked levels of deadly force to the prevalence of community-level violence (Geller & Karales, 1981; Kania & Mackey, 1977; Sorenson, Marguart, & Brock, 1993) and to situational-level factors such as the presence of a weapon and suspect behavior (Binder & Fridell, 1984; Binder & Scharf, 1980; Margarita, 1980; Robin, 1963). Also, shooting victims are disproportionately African American (Fyfe, 1981; Milton, Halleck, Lardner, & Albrecht, 1977; Robin, 1963; Takagi, 1974; White, 1999), although the causes of that overrepresentation are unclear.

It is clear, however, that police officers who use deadly force *miss* their intended targets far more often than they hit them (Geller & Scott, 1992; Matulia, 1985). Hit rates vary notably across police agencies, but rarely exceed 50 percent (Geller & Scott, 1992). Matulia (1985) stated that while Hollywood often portrays police officers as sharpshooters, "in reality many police officers have a difficult time meeting departmental qualification standards at the firing range, let alone during a combat situation" (p. 69).

Despite the relative inaccuracy of police officers, the rarity of police shootings, and departments' strict control over use of firearms, deadly force still represents a significant and controversial issue for police departments.

> Any experienced police officer knows the potentially devastating effects of even justified shootings by police—loss of life and bereavement, risks to an officer's career, the government's liability to civil suits, strained police–community relations, rioting and all the economic and social crises that attend major civil disturbances. (Geller & Scott, 1992, p. 1).

We again saw these consequences with the riots in St. Petersburg in 1996 and Cincinnati in 2001, and in the community outrage over the 1999 shooting death of Amadou Diallo in New York City.

Recent Abuse of Authority Cases. *The Philadelphia Police Department and the 39th District Scandal* The abuse of authority scandal in the 39th district of the

Philadelphia Police Department began to emerge in 1995. By 1997, five officers had been convicted of making false arrests, filing false reports, stealing money from drug dealers, and robbing drug suspects (Human Rights Watch, 1998). Because of the actions of the officers, by the end of 1997 nearly 300 criminal convictions were overturned and thousands more were under review.

One police officer was the subject of more than twenty citizen complaints before pleading guilty to robbery, obstruction of justice, and conspiracy to violate civil rights (Human Rights Watch, 1998). In January 1992, another officer observed a man urinating in an alley. The officer tackled the man, stepped on his groin, kicked him, and slammed him into the car. The officer was suspended for twenty days, but on appeal, the punishment was reduced to five days (Human Rights Watch, 1998). The city of Philadelphia has paid out more than $20 million in settlements arising from police misconduct cases in the 39th district.

Abner Louima and the New York City Police Department   On August 9, 1997, Officer Justin Volpe responded to a Brooklyn nightclub to disperse an unruly crowd. Volpe was struck in the head by a black man, who fled the scene, while Louima was arrested by another officer (Worden & Catlin, 2002). Volpe assaulted Louima while he was handcuffed in the back of the patrol car. In the lobby of the station house, Louima was stripped naked from the waist down, then escorted to a bathroom where Volpe used a wooden stick to sodomize Louima. Volpe then jammed the stick into his mouth, breaking his front teeth (Barry, 1997). Louima required surgery to repair a ripped bladder and punctured lower intestine. Shortly after the incident, two commanders were transferred, a desk sergeant was suspended, and 11 other officers were pulled off active duty. Five officers were criminally charged in the incident, and two, including Volpe, were sentenced to lengthy prison terms. Three officers were convicted of conspiracy for attempting to conceal details of the crime (Worden & Catlin, 2002).

Corruption

Types of Corruption.   As described earlier, the two key elements of corruption are the misuse of authority and personal gain. Stoddard (1968) outlined a variety of corrupt activities, termed "blue-coat crime," including:

- Mooching: Receiving free coffee, meals, liquor, cigarettes, etc., usually because officer is underpaid or for possible acts of favoritism later.
- Chiseling: Police demands for free admission to entertainment, price discounts, etc.
- Favoritism: Practice of using license tabs, window stickers, or courtesy cards to gain immunity from traffic arrest or citations (given to wives, friends, etc.).
- Prejudice: Minority groups receive less than impartial, neutral, objective attention.
- Shopping: Picking up small items such as candy bars, gum, or cigarettes at a store where the door has been accidentally left unlocked after hours.

- Extortion: Demands made for advertisements in police magazines or purchase of tickets to police functions, or the "street courts" where minor traffic tickets can be avoided by the payment of cash bail to the officer with no receipt required.
- Bribery: Payment of cash or gifts for past or future assistance to avoid prosecution. Bribery differs from mooching in the higher value of the gift.
- Shakedown: Taking expensive items for personal use and attributing it to criminal activity (burglary). Shakedowns differ from shopping because of the value of what is taken.
- Perjury: Fellow officers provide alibis for each other when one is apprehended for unlawful activity.
- Premeditated theft: Planned burglary. It differs from shopping because the act was premeditated (Stoddard, 1968).

A Corrupt Officer's Moral Career.   Sherman (1974) argued that corrupt officers go through a "moral career," engaging in increasingly serious misconduct over time. The moral career begins with the acceptance of minor gratuities, such as free meals and coffee, and the officer begins to see these gifts as a routine part of the job (Sherman, 1974). The second and third stages of the moral career involve more serious offenses, with the officer providing something in return for a gift or gratuity (Sherman, 1974). In exchange for the free meal, the officer allows the restaurant owner to serve alcohol without a license. The fourth, fifth, and sixth stages of the moral career are distinct in that the officer is no longer passively accepting what comes his or her way, but rather is actively and aggressively seeking out opportunities for corruption: The officer has become a **"meat-eater"** (Knapp Commission; Sherman, 1974). Activities at these later stages are more serious and involve larger sums of money (i.e., organized payoffs for not enforcing gambling or prostitution, narcotics trafficking, etc.)

Levels of Corruption.   There are different levels of corruption in police departments that, to some extent, mirror and expand upon the two different explanations of police misconduct offered earlier. The first level of corruption, Type 1, involves rotten apples and rotten pockets (Sherman, 1978). At this level, the corruption involves one or a few officers acting on their own without the support or knowledge of others in the department. The second level, Type II, involves pervasive unorganized corruption. At this level, the majority of the officers in the department are engaged in corruption, but there is little or no organization to the misconduct (i.e., there is no active cooperation among officers [Sherman, 1978]). The third and most serious level, pervasive organized corruption, involves highly organized misconduct that penetrates the highest levels of the department (i.e., the NYPD as described in the Knapp Commission report).

Current Corruption Controversies: Are Gratuities Low-Level Corruption?   One area where there appears to be disagreement involves the acceptance of gratuities: free coffee, meals, dry cleaning, movie tickets, etc. Some police departments have specific policies that prohibit officers from accepting gratuities, while others do not. Those in favor of police being permitted to accept gratuities typically argue that it is a "fringe benefit" or show of appreciation by a businessperson or resident. In some cases, police officers feel it is an insult to *not* accept the gift or service.

Those who argue against gratuities maintain that accepting the small gift can sometimes leave the officer vulnerable to more serious kinds of corruption. Also, some business owners may clearly expect something in return for the gift, such as increased patrols around their store or quicker response times to calls for service. Others argue that police officers because of their authority must avoid even the appearance of impropriety. The Knapp Commission (1972, p. 4) distinguished between **"grass eaters"** and "meat eaters," and suggested that the former—who passively accept what is offered and do nothing about it—represent the real problem because they foster the culture that corruption is "acceptable" (meat eaters are those who aggressively seek out opportunities for corruption). Twenty years later, former officer Michael Dowd developed what became known as the "Dowd test" by getting officers to accept small gifts, then engaging them in more serious acts (Dowd was convicted of drug trafficking).

Although police departments in the United States vary in this area, the model policy of the International Association of Chiefs of Police (IACP, Section 8, 1997) states that "officers shall report any unsolicited gifts, gratuities, or other items of value that they are offered and shall provide a full report of the circumstances of their receipt."

Recent Corruption Cases. *The New York City Police Department and the Mollen Commission Report* The Mollen Commission was created in 1993 to investigate allegations of corruption in the 75th precinct. Former police officer Michael Dowd testified before the Commission and detailed a range of corrupt activities including robbing crime victims, drug dealers, and arrestees of money and drugs, accepting money to protect illegal drug operations, and using drugs and alcohol while on duty (Frankel, 1993). Dowd acknowledged receiving approximately $4,000 a week to allow drug dealing and reported regularly snorting cocaine off the dashboard of his car.

The Rampart CRASH Unit of the Los Angeles Police Department (LAPD) In September 1999, former Rampart CRASH (Community Resources Against Street Hoodlums) officer Rafael Perez pled guilty to cocaine theft and was sentenced to five years in prison. As part of the plea bargain, Perez provided information on other officers in CRASH, and over a period of nine months, he detailed incidents implicating 70 other officers in misconduct ranging from bad shootings to drinking alcohol on the job (www.pbs.org/wgbh/pages/frontline/shows/lapd/scandal/cron.html). Perez told investigators how he and his partner shot, framed, and testified against gang member Javier Ovando, who was paralyzed as a result of the shooting. As a result of the Rampart CRASH scandal, more than 100 criminal convictions have been overturned, the CRASH unit has been disbanded, Ovando was awarded a $15 million civil judgment,

29 other civil cases totaling $11 million have been settled, and the LAPD was placed under a U.S. Department of Justice consent decree for a period of five years (www.pbs.org/wgbh/pages/frontline/shows/lapd/scandal/cron.html).

Prejudice and Discrimination

Prejudice and Discrimination Defined. Although **prejudice and discrimination** are terms often used interchangeably, they are actually quite different constructs. Prejudice refers to attitudes, beliefs, or opinions a person holds about something or someone; in other words, to "pre-judge" (Kappeler et al., 1998). Discrimination is an action or behavior that a person takes, based on a prejudice (Wilbanks, 1987). Importantly, a person can have prejudices, but not act on them. Although many of us typically think in terms of race when discussing prejudice and discrimination, any number of characteristics can serve as the basis for this type of police misconduct, including gender, age, sexual orientation, religion, appearance, geographic origin, and social class (Kappeler et al. 1998).

Discrimination by the police can be expressed on two different dimensions: officer rank and internal vs. external (Kappeler et al. 1998). In terms of rank, both patrol officers and administrators/managers can engage in discrimination, and their actions can be focused within the department (internal), or focused on the community (external). Examples of the four different categories of discrimination include:

- Patrol officer internal: Sexual harassment of female co-workers.
- Patrol officer external: Harassing minority youths or college students.
- Administrator internal: Placing minority officers in undesirable assignments.
- Administrator external: Failing to provide adequate police services to minority segments of the community. (Kappeler et al., 1998)

Current Discrimination Controversies: Racial Profiling. Although discrimination by police can occur in a number of different ways, the form that has received the most attention in recent years is **racial profiling** on highways: police officers pulling over motorists for no other reason than the color of their skin. Matthews (1999) defines racial profiling "as the process of using certain racial characteristics, such as skin color, as indicators of criminal activity" (p. 38). The traditional police argument in favor of racial profiling is that minorities are more heavily involved in crime, especially drug offenses, and racial profiling is an effective tool in fighting the war on drugs.

However, prevailing wisdom among police leaders and scholars is that racial profiling is not an appropriate or legal form of police work. The International Association of Chiefs of Police (IACP), for example, has recommended zero tolerance for officers who commit racial profiling, including their removal from positions of authority (Miller & Hess, 2003; Strandberg, 1999). Cohen, Lennon, and Wasserman (2000, p. 15) state:

racial profiling is inconsistent with the basic freedoms and rights afforded in our democracy. It erodes the foundation of trust between communities and public authorities. Worst of all, it inflames racial and ethnic strife and undermines America's progress toward color-blind justice.

Racial profiling represents a form of misconduct on two levels. First, racial profiling is a form of discrimination. It involves taking actions based on prejudice. Racial profiling is discriminatory, and discrimination is a form of police misconduct. Second, racial profiling involves a violation of one's constitutional protections against unreasonable search and seizure. Police officers must have reasonable suspicion to stop a car on the highway, meaning that the stop must be "sensible, justifiable, logical and based on reason" (Wrobleski & Hess, 2000, p. 325). That is, the officer must have a legal and legitimate reason for stopping the car (Miller & Hess, 2003, p. 178). Quite simply, the color of one's skin does not meet the reasonable suspicion standard.

How Is Racial Profiling Different from Other Forms of Profiling?   It is important to recognize that racial profiling is very different from other forms of profiling that are well-established and accepted, such as psychological profiling of serial murderers and rapists by the FBI. Swanson, Chamelin, and Terrieto (1984) summarized the purpose of psychological profiling:

> The purpose of the psychological assessment of a crime scene is to produce a profile; that is, to identify and interpret certain items of evidence at the crime scene which would be indicative of the personality type of the individual or individuals committing the crime. The goal of the profiler is to provide enough information to investigators to enable them to limit or better direct their investigations. (pp. 700–701)

Ressler et al. (1982) stated that the development of a psychological profile typically involves five stages:

1. A comprehensive study of the nature of the criminal act and the types of persons who have committed this offense.
2. A thorough inspection of the specific crime scene involved in the case.
3. An in-depth examination of the background and activities of the victim(s) and any known suspects.
4. A formulation of probable motivating factors of all parties involved.
5. The development of a description of the perpetrator based upon the overt characteristics associated with his/her probable psychological makeup. (p. 3)

Two very clear differences emerge between psychological and racial profiling. First, as Swanson et al. (1984) suggest, the psychological profile is intended to help detectives better direct their investigation, by either ruling certain people out or limiting their focus on specific types of people. Racial profiling, on the other hand, involves taking direct action against a person. Second, as Ressler et al. (1982)

suggest, the process of building a psychological profile is careful, intensive, and time-consuming. Racial profiling involves no such process and is based simply on the officer's preconceived notions of the motorist. In fact, a recent report by the Police Executive Research Forum (PERF) replaced the term "racial profiling" with "racially biased policing" to avoid confusion with other legitimate forms of profiling (Fridell et al., 2001).

How Prevalent Is Racial Profiling?   Is it very difficult to determine the true extent of racial profiling, in part because of data issues and problems with accounting for or ruling out other potential explanations for the police behavior. To address the data issue, an increasing number of police agencies are collecting racial information during traffic stops. By 2001, more than a dozen states required law enforcement agencies to record data on traffic stops; many other departments do so voluntarily (Wrobleski & Hess, 2003). Data collection is certainly an important first step, but careful analysis must follow. A primary problem with measuring racial profiling involves determining what the baseline measure should be. For example, it is simple to document the percentage of a population that is minority, and with agencies now collecting data, it is also simple to measure the race of those who are stopped by police.

Consider the following example. If 20 percent of the population of Town A is African American, and if 40 percent of those stopped by police in Town A are African American, can we conclude that the police are engaged in racial profiling? Clearly, African Americans in Town A are being stopped disproportionately based on their representation in the general population, but does that disproportionality equate to racial profiling? Are there other potential explanations? Perhaps black motorists are stopped at higher rates for other reasons, such as engaging in behavior that increases their likelihood of being pulled over (speeding, motor vehicle violations, criminal activity, etc.).

In simpler terms, the racial makeup of the population serves as a poor baseline measure for racial profiling, and, unfortunately, there is a lack of consensus among researchers regarding what is the best baseline measure. Other potential baseline measures include the percentage of minorities who drive in a given area, the percentage of minorities issued traffic or speeding tickets, and the percentage of minorities arrested for certain offenses. These baseline measures can be collected through official records or by observational research. For example, Lamberth (1998) documented the percentage of minority drivers who are eligible to be pulled over for speeding in New Jersey and Maryland by driving random sections of highways, at random times, while driving five miles over the speed limit. He then recorded the race of drivers who passed him to create a baseline measure of those eligible to be pulled over.

Driving while Middle Eastern—the New Form of Racial Profiling   In the wake of the September 11, 2001, terrorist attacks, the new form of racial profiling does not involve "driving while black" or "driving while brown," but "driving while Middle Eastern." Although the race, ethnicity, or religion involved in racial profiling may have changed, the legal issues remain the same: Police officers are still bound by the Constitution and constitutional law. Interestingly, public opinions regarding racial profiling have changed significantly since 9/11. Nislow (2001) states

> After years of enduring harsh criticism and suspicion from the public for alleged racial profiling practices, law enforcement in the aftermath of the World Trade Center disaster has suddenly found itself on the high road, as some who once considered the practice taboo are now eager for police to bend the rules when it comes to Middle Easterners. (p. 11)

Nislow (2001) further points out that, based on the PERF Model Policy, police can consider Arab ethnicity as long as requirements for reasonable suspicion and/or probable cause have been met. Nevertheless, as police leaders and researchers continue to struggle with documenting the prevalence of "more traditional" racial profiling against African Americans and Hispanics, we must now consider this new form of racial profiling against Middle Easterners.

Recent Discrimination Cases. *The Milwaukee Police Department and the Jeffrey Dahmer Case* The investigation of the sexual abuse of Konerak Sinthasomphone by officers in the Milwaukee Police Department represents a chilling and mostly unpublicized case of police discrimination. The following is a summary of the facts as recorded in the *Estate of Sinthasomphone vs. City of Milwaukee,* 785 F. Supp. 1343 (E.D. Wis. 1992). Konerak, a 14-year-old Laotian boy, was lured into Jeff Dahmer's apartment with the promise of money if he posed for photographs. Once in the apartment, Dahmer drugged, tortured, and sexually assaulted Konerak. When Dahmer left the apartment, Konerak managed to escape—drugged, naked, and bleeding from the rectum—and was discovered by two African American women, who immediately called 911. While waiting for emergency personnel, Dahmer returned and attempted to get Konerak back to his apartment. Nicole Childress and Sandra Smith, the African American women who found Konerak, prevented his recapture until police arrived.

Four Milwaukee police officers—all white males—responded to the call. Dahmer explained to police that he and Konerak were homosexual lovers, and that they had an argument. Childress and Smith repeatedly warned police that Konerak did not appear to be an adult, that he was intoxicated, and that he appeared fearful of Dahmer. Police entered Dahmer's apartment, and after a cursory investigation, left Konerak with Dahmer. Dahmer later testified that he killed Konerak shortly after police left, and Dahmer eventually killed at least four others before being arrested.

In a subsequent civil rights lawsuit, Konerak's family alleged that the MPD officers who handled the call "were the products of the department's discriminatory policies" (Kappeler et al., 1998). Essentially, the plaintiffs argued that the police showed deliberate indifference because Konerak was Laotian, the witnesses were African American, Dahmer was a white male, and the incident allegedly involved a homosexual relationship. The civil suit and a Mayor-appointed Citizen's Commission found significant evidence of externally and internally focused discrimination throughout the MPD. The Commission (Mayor's Citizen Commission, 1991) concluded:

> Victims and witnesses of all races and sexual orientations report examples of police officers as exacerbators of community tension and violence at scenes of incidents, rather than as peace makers. Our police officers seem to need improved and updated training in being peace officers: to resolve conflicts, to calm people who are hostile or distraught; to treat people as individuals, not as stereotypes; and to see members of the community as allies and aids, not as enemies. (p. 21)

The New Jersey State Police and Racial Profiling   Since the early 1990s, the New Jersey State Police (NJSP) had been accused of engaging in racial profiling, particularly on the New Jersey Turnpike (NJTP). The American Civil Liberties Union (ACLU) filed a number of law suits on behalf of citizens. In *State v. Soto* in 1994–1995, evidence presented showed that along a stretch of the NJTP, African Americans comprised 13 percent of drivers, 15 percent of vehicles speeding, and 46.2 percent of people stopped by the NJSP. In March 1996, the court ruled that state troopers were engaged in a state-condoned policy of racial profiling and that the NJSP had failed to monitor, control, or investigate claims of discrimination. In April 1999, then-Attorney General Peter Verniero admitted that motorists on the NJTP were stopped and searched based only on the color of their skin (http://www.aclu-nj.org/pressroom/aclunjwins775.htm). In the wake of the *Soto* case, a number of additional civil suits alleging racial profiling have been settled. In August 2002, the ACLU of Pennsylvania announced a $250,000 settlement in *White v. Williams,* and in January 2003, the state of New Jersey agreed to pay $775,000 to victims of racial profiling in *Morka v. State of New Jersey.* The New Jersey State Police was eventually the target of a consent decree by the Civil Rights Division, United States Department of Justice.

SUMMARY

This chapter covers the major issues associated with police misconduct, discussing the persistent problems of abuse of authority, corruption, and discrimination within both historical and theoretical contexts. Although defining police misconduct seems like a straightforward task, there is a lack of consensus among practitioners and scholars on basic definitions, and this lack of agreement has seriously restricted efforts to document the prevalence of police misconduct. Nevertheless, police misconduct has a history as long as professional policing itself, and, as history as shown, the consequences of misconduct can be devastating for the police department, the criminal justice system, and the community.

Given the persistence of police problems, significant attention has focused on theoretical explanations of police misconduct. Although popular among police leaders because of its simplicity, the rotten apple theory has generally proven to be insufficient in explaining police misconduct. Conventional wisdom has recently highlighted structural aspects of police work: that is, there are unique structural and organizational aspects of policing that contribute to or even cause police misconduct, such as the nature of the law, isolation and discretion, lack of supervision, specialization, limited career mobility, and the police subculture.

Finally, the chapter deals with contemporary controversies involving the major forms of police misconduct. Within abuse of authority, significant attention was devoted to the spread of less-than-lethal weapons (most notably the Taser), police pursuits, and deadly force. The discussion of corruption centered on its diverse forms and the controversy over accepting gratuities. Last, the chapter highlighted the current police controversies involving discrimination, most notably racial profiling. Although these problems are certainly not new for police, current issues involving police misconduct have evolved over time and now present significant challenges for the police departments of the twenty-first century.

KEY TERMS

Abuse of authority
Corruption
Commission on Accreditation for Law
   Enforcement Agencies (CALEA)
Deadly force
Discretion
"Grass eater"
Hot pursuits
Knapp Commission
Less-than-lethal weapons
"Meat eater"

Mollen Commission
Occupational deviance
Prejudice and discrimination
Police crime
Police subculture
Racial profiling
Rotten apple theory
Structural explanations of misconduct
Tennessee v. Garner
Wickersham Commission

DISCUSSION QUESTIONS

1. What are the major forms of police misconduct?

2. What are consequences of police misconduct for police, the criminal justice system, and the community?

3. Is the rotten apple theory a sufficient explanation for police misconduct? Why or why not?

4. What are the primary structural characteristics of policing that contribute to misconduct?

5. What are the key issues surrounding a police officer's decision to engage in a hot pursuit?

6. Should accepting gratuities be prohibited for police?

7. What is racial profiling? Is it an acceptable form of police work? Why or why not?

REFERENCES

Alpert, G.P. (2001). Managing the benefits and risks of pursuit driving. In R.G. Dunham & G.P. Alpert (Eds.), *Critical issues in policing* (4th ed.). Prospect Heights, IL: Waveland Press.

Alpert, G.P., & Dunham, R.G. (1997). *The force factor: Measuring police use of force relative to suspect resistance.* Washington, DC: Police Executive Research Forum.

Alpert, G.P., Kenney, D.J., Dunham, R.G., & Smith, W.C. (2000). *Police pursuits: What we know.* Washington, DC: Police Executive Research Forum.

Anechiarico, F., & Jacobs, J.B. (1996). *The pursuit of absolute integrity.* Chicago: University of Chicago Press.

Barker, T. (2002). Ethical police behavior. In K.M. Lersch (Ed.), *Policing and misconduct.* Upper Saddle River, NJ: Prentice-Hall.

Barker, T., & Carter D.L. (Eds.). (1994). *Police deviance* (2nd ed.). Cincinnati: Anderson.

Barry, D. (1997, August 16) Officer charged in torture in Brooklyn station house. *New York Times.*

Binder, A., & Fridell, L. (1984). Lethal force as a police response. *Criminal Justice Abstracts, 16* (2), 250–280.

Binder, A., & Scharf, P. (1980). The violent police-citizen encounter. *Annals of the American Academy of Political and Social Science, 452,* 111–121.

Bittner, E. (1970). *The functions of police in modern society.* Chevy Chase, MD: National Institute of Mental Health.

Blumberg, M. (1989). Controlling police use of deadly force: Assessing two decades of progress. In R.G. Dunham & G.P. Alpert (Eds.), *Critical Issues in Policing.* (pp. 442–464). Prospect Heights, IL: Waveland Press.

Brodeur, J. (1981). Legitimizing police deviance. In C.D. Shearing (Ed.), *Organizational police deviance.* Toronto, Canada: Butterworths.

Bureau of Justice Statistics. (2001). *Contacts between police and the public.* Washington, DC: U.S. Government Printing Office.

Burnham, D. (1974). How police corruption is built into the system—and a few ideas for what to do about it. In L. Sherman (Ed.), *Police corruption: A sociological perspective.* Garden City, NY: Anchor Books.

Christopher, W. (1991). *Report of the independent commission on the Los Angeles Police Department.* Los Angeles: City of Los Angeles.

Cohen, J.D., Lennon, J.J., & Wasserman, R. (2000, March). Eliminating racial profiling—A third way. *Law Enforcement News, 530,* 12, 15.

Commission on Accreditation in Law Enforcement. (1999). *Standards for law enforcement agencies.* (4th ed.). Fairfax, VA: CALEA.

Delattre, E. (1989). *Character and cops: Ethics in policing.* Washington, DC: American Enterprise Institute for Public Policy Research.

Ericson, R.V. (1981). Rules for police deviance. In C.D. Shearing (Ed.), *Organizational police deviance.* Toronto, Canada: Butterworths.

Fogelson, R.M. (1977). *Big-city police.* Cambridge, MA: Harvard University Press.

Frankel, B. (1993, September 28). Ex-NYC officer tells stark tale of cops gone bad. *USA Today,* p. A3.

Fridell, L., Lunney, R., Diamond, D., & Kubu, B. with Scott, M., & Laing, C. (2001). *Racially biased policing: A principled response.* Washington, DC: Police Executive Research Forum.

Fyfe, J.J. (1981). Who shoots? A look at officer race and police shootings. *Journal of Police Science and Administration, 9,* 367–382.

Fyfe, J.J. (1988). Police use of deadly force: Research and reform. *Justice Quarterly, 5,* 165–205.

Geller, W., & Karales, K. (1981). Shootings of and by Chicago police: Uncommon Crises—Part I shootings by Chicago police. *Journal of Criminal Law and Criminology, 72*(4), 1813–1866.

Geller, W., & Scott, M.S. (1992). *Deadly force: What we know.* Washington, DC: Police Executive Research Forum.

Germann, A.C., Day, F.D., & Gallati, R.R.J. (1985). *Introduction to law enforcement and criminal justice.* Springfield, IL: Charles C. Thomas.

Goldstein, H. (1975). *Police corruption: A perspective on its nature and control.* Washington, DC: Police Foundation.

Hall, D. (1998, December). Corruption report fails to raise ire among IACP chiefs. *Police,* 20–22.

Human Rights Watch. (1998). *Shielded from justice: Police brutality and accountability in the United States.* Available online at http://www.hrw.org, June 1, 2005.

Hess, K.M., & Wrobeleski, H.M. (2003). *Police operations.* Belmont, CA: Wadsworth.

International Association of Chiefs of Police. (1997). *Model policy: Standards of conduct.* Alexandria, Va: IACP National Law Enforcement Policy Center.

Independent Commission on the Los Angeles Police Department. (1991). *Report of the independent commission on the Los Angeles Police Department.* Los Angeles: Author.

Kania, R.E., & Mackey, W.C. (1977). Police violence as a function of community characteristics. *Criminology, 15,* 27–48.

Kappeler, V.E., Sluder, R.D., & Alpert, G.P. (1998). *Forces of deviance: Understanding the dark side of policing.* Prospect Heights, IL: Waveland Press.

Kappeler, V.E., & Vaughn, M.S. (1997). When pursuit becomes criminal: Municipal liability for police sexual violence. *Criminal Law Bulletin, 33*(4), 467–488.

Knapp Commission report on police corruption. (1972). New York: George Braziller.

Lamberth, J. (1998). Driving while black: A statistician proves that prejudice still rules the road. Washington Post, August 16.

Lester, D. (1983). Why do people become police officers: A study of reasons and their predictions of success. *Journal of Police Science and Administration, 11*(2), 170–174.

Manning, P.K. (1997). *Police work: The social organization of policing* (2nd ed.). Prospect Heights, IL: Waveland Press.

Margarita, M. (1980). Killing the police: Myths and motives. *Annals of the American Academy of Political and Social Science, 452,* 72–81.

Martin, S.E. (1980). *Breaking and entering.* Berkeley: University of California Press.

Marx, G.T. (1992). When the guards guard themselves: Undercover tactics turned inward. *Policing and Society, 2*(3), 151–172.

Matthews, J. (1999, November). Racial profiling: A law enforcement nemesis. *Police,* 38–39.

Matulia, K.J. (1982). *A balance of forces: A study of justifiable homicide by the police.* Gaithersburg, Maryland: International Association of Chiefs of Police.

Mayor's Citizen Commission. (1991). *A report to Mayor John O. Norquist and the board of fire and police commissioners.* Milwaukee: City of Milwaukee.

Meyers, S.L. (1993, October 8). Officers describe police watchdog agency as ineffectual. *New York Times,* p. A4.

Miller, L.S., & Hess, K.M. (2002). *The police in the community: Strategies for the 21st century.* Belmont, CA: Wadsworth.

Miller, W.R. (1977). *Cops and bobbies: Police authority in New York and London, 1830–1870.* Chicago: University of Chicago Press.

Milton, C., Halleck, J.S., Lardner, J., & Albrecht, G.L. (1977). *Police use of deadly force.* Washington DC: Police Foundation.

Mollen Commission. (1994). *The city of New York commission to investigate allegations of police corruption and the anti-corruption procedures of the police department: Commission report.* New York: City of New York.

Montoya, H.L. (2001, March). Dog hair and drool: Life in the front seat. *Police,* 31–34.

National Advisory Commission and Civil Disorders (1968). *Report of the National Advisory Commission on Civil Disorders.* NY: Bantam Books.

National Commission on Law Observance and Enforcement [Wickersham Report]. (1931). *Report on lawlessness in law enforcement.* Washington, DC: Government Printing Office.

Niederhoffer, A. (1967). *Behind the shield: The police in urban society.* Garden City, NY: Anchor Books.

Nislow, J. (2001, October 15). Are Americans ready to buy into racial profiling? *Law Enforcement News,* p. 11.

Nowicki, E. (June 2001). OC spray update. *Law and Order,* 28–29.

Pipes, C., & Pape, D. (2001, July). Police pursuits and civil liability. *FBI Law Enforcement Bulletin,* 16–21.

Raganella, A.J. & White, M.D (2004). Race, gender, and motivation for becoming a police officer: Implications for building a representative police department. *Journal of Criminal Justice, 32,* 501–513.

Reiss, A.J. (1968). Police brutality: Answers to key questions. *Trans-Action,* 10–19.

Reiss, A.J. (1971). *The police and the public.* New Haven: Yale University Press.

Ressler, R. K., Burgess, A.W., Hartman, C.R., Douglas, J.E., & McCormack, A. (1982). *Criminal profiling research on homicide.* Unpublished research report.

Reuss-Ianni, E. (1983). *Two cultures of policing.* New Brunswick, NJ: Transaction Books.

Robin, G.D. (1963). Justifiable homicide by police officers. *Journal of Criminal Law, Criminology and Police Science,* 225–231.

Rubinstein, J. (1973). *City police.* New York: Farrar, Straus and Giroux.

Sherman, L.W. (1974). *Police corruption: A sociological perspective.* Garden City, NY: Doubleday Anchor Books.

Sherman, L.W. (1978). *Scandal and reform: Controlling police corruption.* Berkeley: University of California Press.

Skolnick, J.H. (1966). *Justice without trial: Law enforcement in a democratic society.* New York: John Wiley.

Skolnick, J.H., & Fyfe, J.J. (1993). *Above the law: Police and the excessive use of force.* New York: Free Press.

Smith, B. (2000). Police service dogs: The unheralded training tool. *Police,* 36–39.

Sorenson, J.R., Marquart, J.W., & Brock, D.E. (1993). Factors related to the killings of felons by police officers: A test of the community violence and conflict hypotheses. *Justice Quarterly, 10* (3), 417–440.

Stoddard, E.R. (1968). The informal "code" of police deviancy: A group approach to "blue-coat crime." *The Journal of Criminal Law, Criminology, and Police Science, 59* (2), 201–213.

Strandberg, K.W. (1999, June). Racial profiling. *Law Enforcement Technology, 26* (6), 62–66.

Swanson, C.R., Chamelin, N.C., & Terrieto, L. (1984). *Criminal investigation.* New York: Random House.

Takagi, P. (1974). A garrison state in "democratic" society. *Crime and Social Justice: A Journal of Radical Criminology,* 27–33.

Taser International website, www.airtaser.com, June 4, 2005.

Tennessee v. Garner (1985) 471 U.S. 1, 105 S. Ct. 1694, 85 L. Ed. 1. Lower Court Rulings: *Garner v. Memphis Police Department,* 600 F. 2d 52 (6th Cir. 1979); *Garner v. Memphis Police Department,* Civil Action No. C-75-145, Memorandum Opinion and Order, slip opinion (W.D. Tenn. July 8, 1981); *Garner v. Memphis Police Department,* 710 F. 2d. 240 (6th Cir. 1983).

Tuch, S.A., & Weitzer, R. (1997). Racial differences in attitudes toward the police. *Public Opinion Quarterly, 61,* 642–663.

Uchida, C.D. (2001). The development of the American police: An historical overview. In R.G. Dunham & G.P. Alpert (Eds.), *Critical issues in policing* (4th ed.). Prospect Heights, IL: Waveland Press.

Van Maanen, J.V. (1999). The asshole. In V.E. Kappeler (Ed.), *The police and society: Touchstone readings* (2nd ed.). Prospect Heights, IL: Waveland Press.

Walker, S. (1977). *A critical history of policing: The emergence of professionalism.* Lexington, MA: Lexington Books.

Walker, S., & Katz, C.M. (2002). *The police in America: An introduction.* New York: McGraw-Hill.

Weisburd, D., & Greenspan, R. (2000). *Police attitudes toward abuse of authority: Findings from a National Study.* Washington, DC: National Institute of Justice.

Westley, W.A. (1956). Secrecy and the police. *Social Forces, 34*(3), 254–257.

Westley, W.A. (1970). *Violence and the police: A sociological study of law, custom, and morality.* Cambridge, MA: MIT Press.

White, M.D. (1999). *Police shootings in Philadelphia: An analysis of two decades of deadly force.* Ph.D. dissertation. Temple University (Ann Arbor, MI: University Microfilms).

White, M.D. (2001). Controlling police decisions to use deadly force: Re-examining the importance of administrative policy. *Crime and Delinquency, 47* (1), 131–151.

Wilbanks, W. (1987). *The myth of a racist criminal justice system.* Monterey, CA: Brooks/Cole.

Worden R.E. (1995). The causes of police brutality: Theory and evidence on police use of force. In W.A. Geller & H. Toch (Eds.), *And justice for all: Understanding and controlling police abuse of force.* Washington, DC: Police Executive Research Forum.

Worden, R.E., & Catlin, S.E. (2002) The use and abuse of force by police. In Lersch, K.M. (ed.) *Policing and Misconduct.* Upper Saddle River, NJ: Prentice Hall.

Wrobleski, H.M., & Hess, K.M. (2003). *Introduction to law enforcement and criminal justice* (7th ed.). Belmont, CA: Wadsworth.

Wylie-Marques, K. (2005). Canine (K-9) units. In Encyclopedia of Law Enforcements, Volume 1. L.E. Sullivan & M. Simonetti Rosen (eds.). Thousand Oaks, CA: Sage.

■ ■ ■ ■ ■

SCHOLAR'S PERSPECTIVE

Police Pursuit: Policies and Training

Geoffrey P. Alpert, Ph.D.*

Professor, University of South Carolina

The basic dilemma associated with high-speed police pursuit of fleeing suspects is deciding whether the benefits of potential apprehension outweigh the risks of endangering police officers, the public, and suspects in the chase. The issues addressed in a comprehensive National Institute of Justice (NIJ) study of police pursuit echo those discussed in research on police use of deadly force: On the one hand, too many restrictions placed on police use of pursuit could place the public at risk from dangerous individuals escaping apprehension. On the other hand, insufficient controls on police pursuit could result in needless accidents and injuries. Until now research on police pursuits has focused on [in-depth] studies of single agencies or studies based on limited data from multiple agencies. The recent comprehensive NIJ study included information from:

- A national survey of 737 law enforcement agencies, which yielded usable data from 436.
- More than 1,200 pursuits recorded by three police departments: Metro-Dade (Miami), Florida; Omaha, Nebraska; and Aiken County, South Carolina.
- Surveys of 779 officers and 175 supervisors—as well as selected interviews— in the above jurisdictions as well as in Mesa, Arizona.
- Surveys of 160 police recruits before training and 145 of them after training— as well as selected interviews—in South Carolina and Miami, Florida.
- Public opinion interviews with 300 people in Omaha and 255 in Aiken County.
- Interviews with 146 jailed suspects who had been involved as drivers in high-speed chases in Columbia, South Carolina; Omaha, Nebraska; and Miami, Florida.

*Professor, Department of Criminology and Criminal Justice, University of South Carolina. Ph.D. Washington State University.

Source: Alpert, G. P. (May 1997). *Police pursuit: Policies and training.* National Institute of Justice, Research in Brief. Washington, DC: National Institute of Justice, Office of Justice Programs, U.S. Department of Justice.

KEY FINDINGS

- Most agencies had written policies governing pursuit but many had been implemented in the 1970s. Of those that had updated them, most had made them more restrictive to control risk.
- Findings from both Metro-Dade and Omaha show the strong effects of policy changes. When Metro-Dade adopted a "violent felony only" pursuit policy in 1992, the number of pursuits decreased 82 percent the following year. In 1993 Omaha changed to a more permissive policy, permitting pursuits for offenses that had previously been prohibited; the following year, the number of pursuits increased more than 600 percent.
- As the severity of the crime increases, more law enforcement officers, supported by their supervisors and public opinion, said they are willing to risk the dangers of pursuit to chase suspects. In other words, the need to immediately apprehend a dangerous suspect is the most important concern for law enforcement personnel. Police said the most important risk factors to consider during a pursuit were traffic conditions and weather.
- Increasing the number of vehicles involved in police pursuits increased the likelihood of apprehension, but also the chance of accidents, injuries, and property damage.
- Pursuit-related injuries were found to occur more frequently when pursuits were conducted for felonies than for nonfelonies, when they occurred on surface streets rather than on highways or freeways, and when they happened in urban and suburban areas rather than in rural areas.
- More than 70 percent of suspects said that they would have slowed down "when I felt safe," whether the pursuit was on a freeway, on a highway, or in a town. Fifty-three percent of the suspects responded that they were willing to run at all costs from the police in a pursuit and 64 percent believed they would not be caught.
- There is a lack of initial and continuing training for law enforcement on the specific risk factors and benefits of pursuit driving. The survey of police recruits before and after academy training indicates that such education can have a major impact on attitudes.

CONCLUSION

Police pursuit driving remains a controversial and dangerous activity. For generations the conventional police wisdom was that effective law enforcement demanded that officers apprehend suspects, even at great social costs. The tragic accidents that have resulted from pursuits testify to their danger.

Policy

The study indicates the importance of perceived severity of offense committed by the fleeing suspect as the major factor in determining whether police should engage in or continue a chase. Therefore, policy might first focus on the type of offense and second on risks to the public, especially traffic patterns and congestion. A balance of these variables indicates that an appropriate policy would limit chases to violent felons. Specific rules and regulations would guide determination of the balance between risks of pursuit and the goal of apprehension of fleeing suspects. This study asked police for their responses to high- and low-risk situations. A policy would be based on formulating categories of risk and standards so officers could make distinctions during the heat of the chase. For example, criminal activities could be given a ranking, and risk factors could be scored in categories of high and low. From these scales, a chase matrix could be created that would give officers specific standards for [decision making] and rules for the beginning stages of a pursuit.

At the same time, more research is necessary to develop a thorough understanding of the impact of one variable on another. That is, univariate analyses of factors such as speed or type of vehicle being chased may mask the impact of other variables such as traffic and road conditions or the lack of training or supervision.

Training

Although many police officers and supervisors recognize the inherent dangers of pursuit and are making efforts to control them, this study reveals a lack of initial and continual training on the issues involved. A critical component of police training should be an analysis of the specific risk factors as well as the benefits of pursuit driving. This education requires careful training in departmental policies and the reasoning that underlies the more recent, restrained philosophies and policies.

CHAPTER 9

POLICE ACCOUNTABILITY
Internal Mechanisms

Traditionally, police departments have been responsible for policing themselves. Although there is a long history of external responses to police misconduct—external meaning from outside the police department—these efforts have been infrequent and almost always in response to a scandal. The Knapp Commission is a good example. In recent years, external efforts to control the police have become more common (i.e., citizen review boards), but primary responsibility for accountability still rests with the police department itself. This chapter describes the major internal mechanisms for controlling police behavior, including more traditional tools such as recruitment and selection, training, supervision, internal affairs, and administrative policy, as well as more recent innovations such as integrity tests and early warning systems.

With each internal mechanism, the chapter outlines its use over time, basic components, strengths, and weaknesses. Importantly, the author's perspective is that there is no one "magic bullet," or single best accountability mechanism. Each has its advantages and disadvantages, and the best approach for a police department is to employ a number of different mechanisms, each playing an important role in a comprehensive package of accountability.

INTERNAL CONTROL MECHANISMS

Careful Recruitment and Selection of Personnel

Although it is not always possible to identify potentially corrupt officers at the recruitment stage (i.e., see Mollen Commission, 1994), effective screening of applicants remains an important part of preventing police misconduct. Recent scandals in Miami, Washington, DC, and Los Angeles have been linked to "mass hirings," where departments hired hundreds of officers in a short period of time and did not conduct thorough background investigations. Careful recruitment and selection of personnel can serve to weed out many of those unfit for police work.

The History of Recruitment and Selection. Sir Robert Peel, considered the father of professional policing, was very selective in who was hired as a police officer. Peel looked for recruits who were intelligent, in good physical condition, and possessing an even temperament with a strong moral character (Miller, 1977). Unfortunately, early U.S. police departments did not follow Peel's lead. Since U.S. police departments were decentralized, they were generally under the control of local political leaders. Rather than selecting police personnel carefully, positions within the police department were often handed out as a reward for support of a local politician. The result was that, for much of the first fifty years of U.S. policing, departments used no recruitment and selection standards at all.

Beginning with the professional movement at the turn of the twentieth century, police leaders began to develop and employ selection criteria for police. These criteria set minimum standards for physical condition, intelligence, and moral character (i.e., no criminal record). These early efforts were re-inforced over the next seventy-five years, especially by the President's Commission report (1967), as local police departments developed and instituted selection standards.

Recruitment: The First Component of Accountability.   The goal of **recruitment** is to find or attract the best candidates for the position of police officer. Departments employ a variety of strategies to recruit job applicants. Common recruitment techniques involve posting fliers around the community, attending employment workshops at high schools and local community colleges and universities, and placing ads in newspapers, radio, and television. More recently, departments rely on posting job vacancies on their websites, in some cases, allowing potential candidates to download application forms. For example, the Los Angeles Police Department offers a special expedited recruitment and selection program for out-of-town applicants. Larger police departments may have an entire unit devoted to recruitment, but most departments do not have that luxury.

An effective recruitment strategy will reach a wide audience and draw a large number of qualified candidates. The larger the eligible applicant pool, the more selective the department can be in making its hiring decisions. To achieve this, the recruitment strategy should include a number of things. First, the recruitment effort should use multiple techniques for drawing applicants (outlined above), rather than just one. Casting a wide net is a necessary requirement for effective recruitment. Although there is a financial commitment up front in terms of paying for advertisements, sending officers to high school and college career days, etc., the department will recoup this money many times over in the long run. Second, an effective recruitment strategy will include special efforts to draw minority and female applicants. Many local police departments have **affirmative action** plans that require more active recruitment of minorities and women. Also, the **Commission on Accreditation for Law Enforcement Agencies (CALEA)** recommends that the racial makeup of the police department mirror the racial makeup of the community.

Third, the recruitment effort should effectively communicate the basic requirements for employment. Failure to convey these requirements will result in wasted time and effort as the department receives applications from people who are not qualified for the job. Last, the recruitment effort should highlight the benefits and advantages of being a police officer and present recruits with a realistic picture of what the job is like. Research consistently shows that people enter policing for practical and altruistic reasons: job security, benefits, and to help others (Ermer, 1978; Lester, 1983; Raganella & White, 2004). These factors should be emphasized in the recruitment effort. Recruiters should also convey to applicants a realistic picture of the job. Although there is a tendency to focus on the excitement and danger of the job, most police work is neither exciting nor dangerous. Applicants who enter policing with unrealistic expectations (as portrayed on television and in movies) will often become disillusioned and may be more likely to quit their jobs.

Selection Methods. Local police departments vary in their methods for selecting officers, but most hiring processes share several common elements (see Chapter 1 for a more in-depth discussion of these issues). All departments have basic requirements for employment: be of minimum age (usually 21), be a U.S. citizen, have a valid driver's license, have no prior felony convictions, and hold at least a high school diploma. An increasing number of police departments are requiring either two-year or four-year college degrees. Many departments will substitute military experience for educational requirements. Some departments have basic requirements regarding eyesight and hearing, as well as residency (officers must live in the community). Applicants are typically asked to pass a physical agility test, a written exam, an oral interview, a medical exam (including a drug test), and a psychological exam. Some departments will also ask applicants to submit to a polygraph test (lie-detector). Typically, police departments will conduct an extensive background examination that may include a criminal history check, credit check, and interviews of family members, neighbors, references, and former employers.

Police departments vary in how they rate and select applicants. In many cases, the selection process is considered as a whole with a recruit receiving an overall score based on performance in each stage. Other departments use initial stages as screeners, setting minimum performance standards that applicants must achieve to continue in the process. For example, many police departments ask applicants to first take a written civil service exam, and then select those who receive scores above a certain level. In recent years many departments have had to alter their selection processes so that females and minorities are not subjected to discrimination and so that the selection criteria are more related to the occupation (for example, eliminating basic physical requirements like pull-ups and push-ups in favor of more job-relevant tasks like "dummy pulls").

Again, the overall goal of the selection process is to identify those who are most qualified for the job and who are most likely to carry out their duties with honesty, integrity, and pride. A rigorous recruitment and selection process can weed out those who will be ill-equipped to make good decisions under pressure. In particular, candidates should be selected based on their ability to demonstrate good judgment, maintain an even temperament, respect and appreciate diversity, show creativity and problem-solving skills, think on their feet, handle pressure, and show leadership skills.

Police Training

Careful recruitment and selection must be followed up with effective training in the police academy, through field training programs, and through **in-service training** (see Chapter 2 for a more detailed discussion). The goal of **police academy training** is to provide officers with basic skills and knowledge necessary to become a police officer. The length and content of academy training varies significantly and may include up to 1,100 hours of training (Bureau of Justice Statistics, 1999). Many larger departments run their own police academies. Smaller departments tend to send their officers to regional, county, or state training centers. In some cases, departments require applicants to attend a basic law enforcement (BLE) training center prior to being hired. Once the BLE training is completed, the officer is hired and given additional department-specific training. Academy training covers a wide range of topics including (but not limited to) basic police powers, constitutional law, the criminal and civil justice systems, departmental policies and standards, physical training, use of force and firearms training, self-defense, emergency medical services, driver training, terrorism and disaster response, and proper handling of the mentally ill and domestic violence cases. Officers will also receive blocks of training on ethics and misconduct.

Following graduation from the academy, officers are typically assigned to a veteran officer for a period of field training. At this stage, the officer applies what he or she has learned in the academy under the guidance and supervision of a more senior officer. Most **field training officer (FTO) programs** are modeled after the original program developed in San Diego during the 1970s, where an officer is assigned to three different senior officers—each for four weeks—followed by a final two weeks with the original FTO (Walker & Katz, 2002). FTOs generally write daily or weekly reports on the rookie's performance and offer guidance and insights on the realities of policing. The FTO experience is intended to bridge the gap between the classroom environment of the academy and the "real world" of policing on the street.

The final form of training is called "in-service" and involves officers periodically receiving additional training on specific issues, such as handling the mentally ill, responding effectively in domestic incidents, or disaster response. Officers also are re-trained (and tested) in several areas to maintain proficiency, such as driving, firearms, and physical fitness. In addition, in-service training will be offered to police as new policies are developed and new tools are adopted. For example, an increasing number of police departments are issuing Tasers to their line officers as a nonlethal alternative. The adoption of a new weapon such as the Taser requires that officers be sufficiently trained in its proper use and handling. Also, there may be a need to make changes to department policy regarding its use, and officers may need to be retrained based on those modifications. As an illustration, in late 2004, the Miami-Dade Police Department drew criticism after two incidents where police officers used a Taser on children (in both cases, the use of the Taser was deemed appropriate according to departmental policy). In January 2005, however, the department changed its policy and now requires officers to consider the size, age, and weight of the individual before using a Taser (see Chapter 9 for more discussion of the Taser).

The overall goal of training at all three stages is to provide officers with the skills and knowledge necessary to carry out their responsibilities. Since most forms of police misconduct are either intentional or the result of "ineptitude or carelessness," officers who are properly trained are less likely than poorly trained officers to engage in police misconduct (Fyfe, 1995, p. 163).

Supervision

Policing is an isolated job. Most police officers, particularly in rural areas, will go through an entire shift having little direct contact with a supervisor. Nevertheless, routine supervision of police officers is a critical department task that serves as a foundation in the agency's effort to ensure officer accountability (Walker & Katz, 2002). Weisburd et al. (2000) reported that nearly 90 percent of police officers surveyed agreed that effective supervision prevents police officer misconduct.

The Critical Role of the Sergeant. Sergeants are primarily responsible for frontline supervision of police officers, and they typically engage in a number of activities to provide proper supervision. First, sergeants supervise their officers on a daily basis through face-to-face contact or radio communications (Walker & Katz, 2002). Some of these face-to-face interactions occur in the precinct house, others out on the street. Sergeants have different work styles, with some being more aggressive and hands-on while others are more laid back (Van Maanen, 1983). One study showed that sergeants spend about 30 percent of their time with officers and citizens, although they are more likely to be present if an arrest is made, an officer is assaulted, or force is used by police (Mastrofski et al., 1998).

Second, sergeants are responsible for reviewing and signing off on officers' reports (Walker & Katz, 2002). Officers must fill out reports for a number of formal actions including arrest, use of force, and pursuits. Sergeants review written reports to make sure they are completed accurately and to determine if the police officer acted properly. Third, sergeants are responsible for providing guidance and instruction to officers when their performance is unsatisfactory (Walker & Katz, 2002). Sergeants must make sure that their officers understand and comply with departmental policies and procedures. This may involve informal conversations in the station house, formal meetings and retraining sessions, and the filing of reports with Internal Affairs for violations.

Last, sergeants are responsible for completing performance evaluations of their officers. These evaluations are typically completed every six or twelve months, but departments vary tremendously in the nature of these evaluations. In some departments, the evaluation is very open-ended and informal; in other departments, the evaluation is formal and extensive. The NYPD, for example, uses an evaluation that asks supervisors to rate their officers on 27 different work-related dimensions. It is important that the performance evaluation not be a "rubber stamp" and that it be completed honestly and accurately. Unfortunately, this is not always the case.

Michael Dowd, a former New York City police officer convicted for a variety of criminal acts during the mid-1990s, received excellent performance evaluations from his supervisors prior to discovery of his illegal behavior.

Achieving Effective Supervision.   Effective **supervision** can be fostered in a number of different ways. First, the number of officers to be supervised by one sergeant should be 8 to 12 (Walker & Katz, 2002). Sergeants who have a "span of control" greater than 12 officers will likely find it difficult to provide sufficient supervision. The Special Counsel to the Los Angeles Sheriff's Department (1998) concluded that the high rate of police shootings among officers assigned to the Century Station was caused, in part, by inadequate supervision: Each sergeant at that station was responsible for 20 to 25 officers, two to three times the recommended span of control.

Second, new sergeants should receive proper instruction in their duties and responsibilities. Quite simply, good supervision can be and should be taught. New sergeants should receive extensive training from experienced instructors on proper methods of effective supervision. Third, effective supervision can be made easier if the sergeant not only punishes poor performance, but also rewards good performance (Kappeler, Sluder, & Alpert, 1998). Police departments tend to be punitively oriented, focusing on punishing poor behavior and not recognizing when officers perform well. By offering police officers incentives for following departmental guidelines, the supervisor can create an atmosphere where exceptional performance is valued and sought after.

Last, if feasible, sergeants should be transferred so they are not responsible for supervising officers who were very recently their peers. Many sergeants find it difficult to supervise officers they have recently worked with, either because officers do not respect their authority, they resent that the sergeant got the promotion and they did not, or because the officers may be aware of the sergeant's passed misdeeds (which may be relatively minor—i.e., taking sick days when not really sick—but still undermine the sergeant's authority). Kappeler et al. (1998) state:

> . . . A minor breach of authority can create serious problems for a new supervisor who chooses to accommodate his or her former equal over control responsibilities. Supervisors must establish a style that is acceptable to subordinates but also creates a working atmosphere that is healthy, productive, and conforms to accepted values. (pp. 222–223)

In sum, effective front-line supervision is the cornerstone of internal accountability. Goldstein (1975) stated that "corruption thrives best in poorly run organizations where lines of authority are vague and supervision is minimal" (p. 42). Quite simply, if officers believe they will be caught and punished for their transgressions, they will be less likely to engage in the misconduct (Klockars, Ivkovich, Harver, & Haberfeld, 2000). "Many officers face temptations everyday. . . . Management has the capacity and control to reinforce high integrity, detect corruption, and limit opportunities for wrong doing" (IACP, 1989, p. 53).

Administrative Guidance

Historically, police officers have received little guidance in how to carry out their duties, even with the most critical decisions. A review of **administrative policies** governing use of firearms in the 1960s (Chapman, 1967) showed that policies were ambiguous at best:

- Never take me out in anger; never put me back in disgrace.
- Leave the gun in the holster until you intend to use it.
- It is left to the discretion of each individual officer when and how to shoot.

Police have traditionally received little guidance in other critical areas, such as arrest, handling incidents involving domestic violence and the mentally ill, police pursuits, and use of lesser degrees of force. However, over the last thirty years, administrative rulemaking has emerged as the dominant form of discretion control in U.S. policing (Walker & Katz, 2002).

Administrative guidance in the form of policies, rules, and procedures communicate to the rank and file officers what the department expects, what is considered acceptable, and what will not be condoned (Kappeler et al., 1998). All three forms of administrative guidance play an important role in preventing and controlling police misconduct. The National Advisory Commission on Criminal Justice Standards and Goals (1973) described the difference between policies, rules, and procedures:

> Policy is different from rules and procedures. Policy should be stated in broad terms to guide employees. It sets limits of discretion. A policy statement deals with the principles and values that guide the performance of activities directed toward the achievement of agency objectives. A procedure is a way of proceeding—a routine—to achieve an objective. Rules significantly reduce or eliminate discretion by specifically stating what must and must not be done. (p. 54)

In other words, policies seek to guide officer decision making in certain situations, while rules tend to eliminate police discretion entirely. For example, most departments now have administrative policies governing high-speed pursuits that provide officers with guidance on when to and when not to engage in a chase. The policy will typically offer guidance to officers regarding the consideration of risk and benefits of the pursuit: weighing the competing goals of apprehension and public safety (bystanders at risk because of the chase). Similar policies exist for the use of nonlethal weapons, arrest, and even use of firearms. A rule, on the other hand, is more of a mandate prohibiting or requiring certain behavior. Many departments have rules prohibiting police officers from accepting gratuities or moonlighting with second jobs. Last, a procedure "is the method of performing a task or a manner of proceeding with a course of action" (Kappeler et al., 1998). A procedure mandates action in a situation: For example, the NYPD requires that all suspects who are struck with a Taser by police are to be transported to a hospital immediately for assessment and, if needed, medical care.

Both CALEA and the American Bar Association (ABA) recommend written rules and policies as an effective manner in which to structure police decision making. Carter and Barker (1991) argue that administrative rules play an important role in controlling police corruption because they serve six different purposes. Administrative policies:

1. inform officers of expected standards of behavior.
2. inform the community about those standards.
3. establish the basis for consistency in police operations.
4. provide grounds for discipline and counseling of errant officers.
5. provide standards for officer supervision.
6. give direction for officer training. (Carter & Barker, 1991, pp. 22–23)

Importantly, prior police research has demonstrated that administrative rulemaking can effectively control police officer behavior in a number of misconduct-prone areas.

Deadly Force.   Administrative policies governing deadly force give officers specific guidance on when it is appropriate—and not appropriate—to use their firearms. Deadly force policies must be in accordance with the U.S. Supreme Court ruling in *Tennessee v. Garner* (1985), 471 U.S. 1, which prohibits shootings of nonviolent fleeing suspects. Policies also may address the firing of warning shots, shooting from a moving vehicle, the destruction of animals, and when it may be appropriate to use deadly force to prevent the escape of a violent felon (see the IACP Model Policy on Use of Deadly Force, www.theiacp.org). Research shows that clear and enforced administrative policies can effectively reduce police use of deadly force, especially situations involving fleeing felons (Fyfe, 1979; Walker, 1993; White, 2001). Fyfe (1979) reported that the number of police shootings in New York was cut in half following the adoption of a restrictive deadly force policy. White (2001) and Fyfe (1988) both found that the number of police shootings in Philadelphia dropped significantly after the adoption of a restrictive administrative policy. Administrative policies demonstrated similar effects on police shooting behavior in Oakland, Omaha, Kansas City, Los Angeles, Dallas, and Memphis (Gain, 1971; Geller & Scott, 1992). Walker (1993) notes:

> These data support the conclusion that administrative rules have successfully limited police shooting discretion, with positive results in terms of social policy. Fewer people are being shot and killed, racial disparities in shootings have been reduced, and police officers are in no greater danger because of these restrictions. Officers appear to comply with the rules. This is an accomplishment of major significance and one that provides a model for other discretion control efforts. (p. 32)

High-Speed Pursuits.   Pursuit policies vary tremendously among police departments, with some prohibiting them altogether and others leaving the decision to the officer's discretion. Most policies, however, instruct officers to consider a variety of factors when deciding to engage in a pursuit, such as the nature of the violation, road conditions, the number of bystanders present, and other potential risks. The fundamental issue in a police pursuit is the tension between the need to enforce the law and arrest violators and the risk to public safety caused by the pursuit (Alpert, Kenney, Dunham, & Smith, 2000). Prior research has shown reductions in high-speed pursuits following implementation of administrative policies. Alpert (1997) reported that following the adoption of a restrictive policy in Miami, there was a reduction in the number of pursuits, the number of accidents, and the number of injuries (to police, suspects, and bystanders).

Use of Police Dogs (Canines).   In 1998, there were an estimated 7,000 police **K-9 (canine) teams** on patrol in the United States. Following the September 11, 2001 terrorist attacks, the use of canines in policing will likely increase tremendously (Wrobeleski & Hess, 2003). Police dogs perform several different tasks, including searching for concealed suspects, drugs, weapons, and explosives; crowd control; search and rescue; searching for evidence and dead bodies; and routine patrol. A study by the San Diego Police Department showed that a decrease in shootings of suspects and officers' injuries was proportional to the adoption and deployment of canine units (Wylie-Marques, 2005).

Although the advantages of police dogs are many, there have been problems with their use, most notably when suspects are bitten. Research has shown that, in some jurisdictions, minorities are disproportionately bitten by police dogs. In Los Angeles County in 1991, 81 percent of the dog bite victims (from canine units in the Los Angeles Sheriffs Department) were African American and Hispanic (Special Counsel to the Los Angeles Sheriffs Department, 1999). Court rulings and pressure from community groups have forced many departments to alter their use of police dogs. In *Mendoza v. Block,* 27 F.3d 1357 (9th Cir. 1994), the court ruled that use of a police dog is a type of force and, as such, is governed by standards of reasonableness (See also Robinette v. Barnes 854 F. 2nd 909, 6th Cir. 1988). In simpler terms, police dogs are similar to other forms of force—physical force, batons, mace, and Tasers—and their use must be appropriate based on the suspect's actions. So, for example, by 1999 the number of dog bites in Los Angeles (Sheriffs Department only) had dropped by 90 percent (though all of the victims were minorities) (Special Counsel to the Los Angeles Police Sheriffs Department, 1999).

Domestic Violence.   Police have traditionally underenforced laws prohibiting domestic violence (Buzawa & Buzawa, 2001; Sherman 1992). During the 1970s and 1980s, a number of forces led police to begin to adopt mandatory arrest policies in felony domestic disputes, including pressure from the women's rights movement, court rulings making departments civilly liable for failure to protect victims (*Thurman v. Torrington,* 595 F. Supp. 1521), and published research indicating the arrest reduced subsequent reoffending (Sherman & Berk, 1984) (see Chapter 7 for more detail). Although the results from the initial study by Sherman and Berk (1984) have been questioned, mandatory arrest policies (and mandatory arrest state laws) are very popular. Walker and Katz (2002) note that, although it is not definitive proof of the impact of mandatory arrest policies, research indicates that between 1971 and 1994 arrests for aggravated assault and misdemeanor assault increased at disproportionately high rates (aggravated assault by 140 percent, compared to just a 34 percent increase in arrests for rape and an 8 percent increase for robbery). This would seem to suggest that police began adhering to more restrictive administrative policies by more frequently arresting batterers in domestic disputes.

Limitations of Administrative Rulemaking.   Yet, department policies and rules, by themselves, are not enough to control police misconduct. First, it is impossible to create rules and policies for every possible situation (Walker & Katz, 2002). Ultimately, officers will still employ discretion. Second, in some cases, rules can lead to evasion or lying. For example, following the implementation of a restrictive deadly force policy in New York, Fyfe (1979) discovered a sizable increase in "accidental" shootings. Third, the adoption of many rules and policies can overwhelm officers and create a seemingly punitive environment where officers feel the department is "out to get them" (Walker & Katz, 2002). There may be a threshold effect as well. Standard operating procedures that are filled with policies and rules can become so overwhelming (sometimes several inches thick) that it is impossible to adhere to all of the rules and policies all of the time. This can, in turn, undermine the impact of the administrative rules as police officers begin to view them as unrealistic and unenforceable. A British constable described the department's rule book in very blunt terms:

> 140 years of fuckups. Every time something goes wrong, they make a rule about it. All the directions in the force flow from someone's mistake. You can't go eight hours on the job without breaking the disciplinary code. . . . But, no one cares until something goes wrong. The job goes wild on trivialities. (Manning, 1977, p. 165)

Last and most importantly, the rules must be supported and enforced by the organizational leadership. Administrative rules and policies become meaningless if violations are not punished. Officers soon learn what is acceptable not by what is written in the manual or posted on a bulletin board, but rather from the informal norms of the environment communicated by their peers and supervisors. For example, in Philadelphia during the early 1970s, the police department had in place a restrictive administrative policy governing use of deadly force. However, officers knew that the department leadership (i.e., Frank Rizzo) would support their use of firearms, regardless of the circumstances of the shooting (Skolnick & Fyfe, 1993; White, 2001).

> Appropriate departmental policies are the first step in creating an environment conducive to good decision making. They provide a statement of organizational values, structure discretion, and channel the use of power. If an officer is properly trained and internalizes those values and guidelines, he or she will be able to use discretion properly. (Kappeler et al., 1998, p. 220)

Internal Affairs

When we think about ways in which a police department monitors and investigates its officers' conduct, the first thing that usually comes to mind is the Internal Affairs Unit. Indeed, **Internal Affairs** (in some places, called the Office of Professional Standards or Responsibility) is the unit whose primary task involves investigating allegations of misconduct. This misconduct can involve violations of department rules, policies or procedures, or it can involve allegations of criminal conduct. Investigations by Internal Affairs typically are reactive: that is, the unit receives information about alleged misconduct and investigates to determine whether a violation has occurred. This information can come from a citizen complaint, official report, or from other police officers (supervisors or line officers). Although much of the work conducted by Internal Affairs is reactive, departments are increasingly using proactive investigations to identify problem officers, such as "integrity tests" (described below) or acting on unverified information about an officer's behavior (Walker & Katz, 2002).

The Challenges Facing Internal Affairs.   Although the Internal Affairs Unit is a standard component of nearly every police department's effort to ensure **accountability,** the unit confronts significant challenges from both outside of and within the department. External resistance to Internal Affairs has several different sources. First, many people simply believe that the police are incapable of policing themselves. This view is particularly common in communities where the relationship with the police is poor or where there is a history of police scandals. In fact, many people point to the long history of police misconduct (see Chapter 8) as definitive proof that internal mechanisms of accountability have failed and that external controls are needed. This is exacerbated by the fact that the vast majority of citizen complaints are not sustained. There are a number of reasons for this, but even in thorough investigations it frequently comes down to the officer's word against the complainant's (in part, because policing is an isolated occupation and many times there is no one else present at the scene). In sum, Internal Affairs must overcome the perception that its officers are biased in favor of the police because they are sworn employees of the same department as the officers whom they investigate.

Unfortunately, Internal Affairs investigators also face resistance and animosity from within the police department. Arnold (1999) states:

> Oftentimes unfairly portrayed in television crime dramas and police novels, internal affairs investigators have become the pariahs of fictional law enforcement agencies. Unfortunately some officers in real-life departments regard internal affairs investigators the same way. (p. 43)

Some officers feel that Internal Affairs investigators have broken "the code," or violated the "blue wall of silence." As discussed in Chapter 8, there is a strong sense of solidarity among police officers, in part because of the nature of the work and the constant threat of danger. Traditionally, there is also an "us against them" philosophy toward the community. Internal Affairs investigators are sometimes perceived as having violated the code because the nature of their work pits them against the rank and file and because they have "sided with" the complainant. The *Garrity* ruling, which states that officers can be disciplined or even fired for not answering questions from Internal Affairs, may have increased tension between line officers and Internal Affairs and fostered the belief that IA is biased against the rank-and-file (Walker & Katz, 2002).

The Keys for an Effective Internal Affairs Unit.   An effective Internal Affairs unit represents a critical component of a successful departmental response to police misconduct. There are a number of key issues that determine the effectiveness of an Internal Affairs unit. First, the unit must have the complete support of the chief (Walker & Katz, 2002). Kappeler et al. (1998, p. 230) state that the commander of Internal Affairs must also have "unlimited and direct access" to the chief. It is important for Internal Affairs to report directly to the chief, rather than other managers. Second, the Internal Affairs unit must be given sufficient resources and personnel to complete its tasks (Walker & Katz, 2002). There is no consensus on the optimal size of an Internal Affairs unit, and research has shown tremendous variation across departments. Sherman (1974) found ratios of one Internal Affairs investigator to 110 officers, and one investigator to 216 officers. Walker and Katz (2002) note that when Patrick Murphy took over as Commissioner of the NYPD in the early 1970s, he substantially increased the size of Internal Affairs, reducing the investigator-officer ratio from one to 533 to one to 64.

Third, officers assigned to Internal Affairs should receive proper training and instruction. Roles, responsibilities, and the nature of investigations in Internal Affairs are different from other assignments, and for officers to be successful in the unit, they must be adequately prepared for the challenges the new position presents. New challenges include dealing with fellow officers, dealing with citizens and their complaints, and investigating the conduct of officers rather than suspects.

Fourth, staff selection to the Internal Affairs unit is important. As Walker and Katz (2002) suggest, it is important for the officer to want the assignment; otherwise, it may be viewed as a punishment. If the officer resents the assignment, he or she may be less willing to work hard and conduct thorough investigations. Also, the selection criteria for Internal Affairs should, itself, be rigorous. Officers who have had problems in the past—whether it be an excessive number of citizen complaints, disciplinary action, poor performance evaluations—are not likely to make good Internal Affairs investigators. In some departments, the chief selects who is assigned to Internal Affairs, while in other departments the chief has no say at all (because of union contracts [Walker and Katz, 2002]). Some smaller and even mid-sized police departments rotate every detective and sergeant through Internal Affairs in an effort to eliminate tension between the unit and line officers (see discussion below). Under this approach, Internal Affairs investigators are not seen as "sell-outs" or "snitches" because officers know that everyone above the rank of patrol officer has had to put his or her time in the unit. Klockars et al. (2000, p. 1), highlighting the importance of making assignment to Internal Affairs a sought-after position, said the department must create "an environment in the police agency where assignment to IA is not regarded as a badge of betrayal but as a position of honor and responsibility." Often this can be achieved by tying promotion to serving in Internal Affairs.

Fifth, successful Internal Affairs will exist in a department where the informal environment promotes officers bringing information to the unit. Police officers represent a vital source of information about the behavior of their colleagues. However, because of the traditional solidarity associated with the police subculture, there is a reluctance to "turn in one of their own." Overcoming this **code of silence** is difficult but not impossible, and it begins with the chief's sending a message that misconduct—no matter how minor—will not be tolerated, and officers who report transgressions will be rewarded. Last, investigations conducted by Internal Affairs must be thorough and fair. If officers perceive that the unit is "out to get them," investigators will face nothing but resistance and opposition from line officers. Alternatively, if officers perceive that Internal Affairs investigations are weak and meaningless, they will assume that the department is not serious about rooting out misconduct.

Integrity Tests

As part of an effort to make the investigation of police misconduct more proactive, several police departments have begun conducting "**integrity tests.**" In an integrity test, the Internal Affairs unit creates a scenario that involves some aspect of routine police work and observes police officer behavior during the encounter. The key to the test is that the officer involved does not know he or she is being observed. This scenario may involve a number of things: a disabled car on the side of the road, a "citizen" who wants to file a complaint, or a traffic violator who offers the police officer cash to not write a ticket. Although such tests have become popular recently, the idea itself is not new. In fact, when Patrick V. Murphy took over as Commissioner of the NYPD in the early 1970s following the Serpico case and Knapp Commission hearings, he authorized Internal Affairs to conduct integrity tests by calling in phony complaints against officers to see if supervisors would ignore them (Skolnick & Fyfe, 1993). Murphy also created a "field associates" program where officers were anonymously recruited to report any misconduct they witnessed (Skolnick & Fyfe, 1993).

The New Orleans Police Department has been among the most active in conducting integrity tests. The Public Integrity Division (PID) conducts two types of investigations: directed, where the test is focused on a specific officer or unit; and random, which does not focus on anyone specific (New Orleans Police Department, 1997; Walker & Katz, 2002). The PID uses a variety of scenarios including staged car accidents and recovered personal property. In its 1997 report, the PID described results from 15 integrity tests, with 14 officers passing and 1 failing (New Orleans Police Department, 1997; Walker & Katz, 2002).

Punch (2000) argues that proactive integrity tests represent an important element of an effort to prevent police corruption, and he notes that police departments in Europe—including the Metropolitan Police in London—are also adopting such strategies. Officers who fail an integrity test can face a number of consequences, including additional training, suspension, and if serious enough, possibly even termination. As a result, police officers and police unions in several jurisdictions are opposed to such tests and view them as entrapment. For example, in January 2005, the announcement by the Vancouver (Canada) Police Department that it would begin using "honesty tests" was met with harsh criticism by the Vancouver Police Union, who argued that the tests were "misguided" and "offensive" (Roberts, 2005).

Early Warning Systems

Early warning (EW) systems have emerged in recent years as an additional proactive technique for preventing police misconduct. The goal of such a system is early identification of problem police officers before their behavior escalates to serious conduct. Essentially, EW systems are information systems that collect and analyze data on problem behavior, such as citizen complaints, sick days, resisting arrest charges, disciplinary incidents, and use of force incidents (Walker & Katz, 2002).

In the 1970s, a number of police departments began monitoring their officers' conduct in an effort to identify problem behavior, including Oakland, New York, and Kansas City (Walker, Alpert, & Kenney, 2001). Early warning systems were first endorsed in 1981 by the U.S. Commission on Civil Rights (1981) and later in 1996 by the U.S. Justice Department conference on police integrity (Walker & Alpert, 2002). The first EW systems were developed in the late 1970s by the Miami Police Department and the Miami-Dade Police Department (Walker et al., 2001). More recently, EW systems have been included in consent decrees placed on several police agencies by the Civil Rights Division of the Department of Justice (see Chapter 10). Walker et al. (2001) stated that, by 1999, 27 percent of police departments serving populations of more than 50,000 people have instituted an early warning system, with another 12 percent of departments in planning stages.

The Problem Police Officer.   The rationale for an EW system rests on the well-supported theory that a small number of police officers generate most of the department's complaints about problem behavior. Support for the problem police officer theory has been consistent:

- Houston, Texas (U.S. Commission on Civil Rights, 1981).
- Oakland, California, where Professor Hans Toch developed a counseling program for violence-prone officers—measured through use of force incidents (officers were counseled by peer officers) (Toch, Grant, & Galvin, 1975).
- Los Angeles, where the Christopher Commission identified 44 officers who averaged 7.6 complaints for excessive force, compared to 0.6 for the rest of the department (Christopher, 1991).
- Kansas City, where 2 percent of officers were responsible for 50 percent of all citizen complaints (*New York Times,* 1991).
- Boston, where 11 percent of officers were responsible for 61.5 percent of all citizen complaints (*Boston Globe,* 1992).
- Washington, DC (*Washington Post,* 1998).

In most of the cases cited above, the problem officers were readily identifiable, and "police managers ignored patterns of repeated involvement in critical incidents and failed to take any kind of supervisory attention to the officers with the worst records" (Walker et al., 2001, p. 201). Accordingly, if a police department can identify and intervene with its problem officers before their behavior escalates, the department can drastically reduce misconduct and problem behavior and significantly improve its relationship with the community.

Components of an EW System. An EW system has three basic components: the selection criteria, the intervention, and the post-intervention monitoring (Walker & Alpert, 2002). **Selection criteria** involve the behavior or "red flags" that identify a particular officer as being at risk. Police departments vary on the criteria used as red flags but some common indicators include citizen complaints, use of force incidents, involvement in civil litigation, departmental violations and sanctions, and excessive sick days (Walker & Alpert, 2002). Although some systems rely on only one indicator, Walker and Alpert (2002) recommend a system that uses multiple criteria:

> The use of multiple indicators provides a broader base of information than the sole reliance on a single indicator such as citizen complaints or use of force. Relying on a single indicator may result in failure to identify officers whose behavior legitimately requires intervention. Multiple indicators, by definition, are more likely than single ones to identify officers whose performance is problematic and may be in need of intervention. (p. 226)

The Miami EW system, one of the first ever developed, uses four categories of behavior as selection criteria: citizen complaints (five or more in a two-year period with a finding of sustained or inconclusive); use of force/control of persons (five or more control of persons incidents for the previous two years); reprimands (five or more reprimands for the previous two years); and discharge of firearms (three or more firearms discharges within the previous five years) (Walker et al., 2001).

The second component of an EW system is the intervention. Most EW systems are not punitive; rather, they seek to provide problem officers with the necessary counseling and training to change their behavior (Walker & Katz, 2002). The intervention stage is usually a two-step process: First, there is an informal meeting between the officer and his or her supervisor; and second—if deemed necessary after the first meeting—there may be a formal intervention (Walker & Alpert, 2002). This may include individual or group counseling and additional police training. In the Miami EW system, officers who are flagged by the system receive a performance evaluation from their immediate supervisor, who reviews all flagged incidents (Walker et al., 2001). The supervisor then decides if the officer requires formal intervention; if so, the supervisor drafts a memorandum recommending a specific intervention such as retraining, transfer, referral to an employee assistance program, fitness for duty evaluation, or dismissal (Walker et al., 2001). The memo is reviewed by the Internal Affairs commander as well as supervisors up the chain of command, and each supervisor must sign off on the recommendation (Walker et al., 2001).

The final component of an EW system is post-intervention monitoring, as the supervisor "keeps an eye" on the officer to make sure that the problem behavior does not continue. This monitoring can be informal and limited to the immediate supervisor, or formal with significant effort devoted to data collection and analysis, and internal review up the chain of command (Walker & Alpert, 2002). The New Orleans Professional Performance Enhancement Program (PPEP) employs a formal monitoring system, where supervisors are required to monitor officers for six months, including direct observation while on duty and written performance evaluations every two weeks (New Orleans Police Department, 1998; Walker et al., 2001).

Effectiveness of an EW System.   A national evaluation of EW systems concluded that the systems are expensive, complex, and high maintenance, requiring a substantial investment in "planning, personnel, data collection, and administrative oversight" (Walker et al., 2001, p. 213). The evaluation also found that while some systems are "symbolic gestures with little substantive content," others have proven to be effective in reducing citizen complaints, use of force, and other problem behavior: specifically, the number of complaints against officers participating in EW systems in New Orleans, Minneapolis, and Miami dropped by two-thirds in the year following the intervention (Walker et al., 2001, p. 213).

Walker and Alpert (2002) offer three recommendations—one for each component of the EW system—for a successful system: (1) multiple selection criteria across a broad range of performance measures should be used (rather than just one indicator); (2) the intervention should involve personnel and resources beyond the officer's immediate supervisor; and (3) post-intervention monitoring is essential to identify continuing problem behavior and to put both officers and supervisors on notice that they are being observed.

Accreditation

The Commission on Accreditation for Law Enforcement Agencies (CALEA) was created in 1979 by the four major law enforcement membership organizations: International Association of Chiefs of Police (IACP), National Organization of Black Law Enforcement Executives (NOBLE), National Sheriff's Association (NSA), and Police Executive Research Forum (PERF) (http://www.calea.org). CALEA has established a process where police departments can receive formal **accreditation** once they comply with the requirements for adoption of policies in a host of prescribed areas.

> The overall purpose of the Commission's accreditation program is to improve delivery of law enforcement service by offering a body of standards, developed by law enforcement practitioners, covering a wide range of up-to-date law enforcement topics. It recognizes professional achievements by offering an orderly process for addressing and complying with applicable standards. (http://www.calea.org)

The process is voluntary, and to be fully accredited, the department must develop policies and standards in 441 specific areas or topics. CALEA employs a team of assessors who evaluate the department's policies and procedures and determine compliance; the review process takes from three to five years (Skolnick & Fyfe, 1993). CALEA offers three different accreditation programs, in law enforcement, public safety communications, and public safety training. The Commission also offers a Recognition program, where smaller agencies can become credentialed by meeting 97 selected standards, rather than the 441 standards required for full accreditation (http://www.calea.org).

As of February 2005, approximately 550 local police departments, sheriff's offices, and county/regional law enforcement agencies have received full accreditation. Although this represents a small percentage of all law enforcement agencies in the United States, the process is viewed as important by most police scholars for professionalizing the administration of a department (Skolnick & Fyfe, 1993). CALEA states that "besides the recognition of obtaining international excellence, the primary benefits of accreditation include controlled liability insurance costs, administrative improvements, greater accountability from supervisors, increased governmental and community support" (http://www.calea.org).

Nevertheless, there are limitations to what can be accomplished through accreditation. For example, in an effort to allow departments to maintain their own independence, CALEA requires only that departments have policies in given areas: They do not specify what the policy should say (except with regard to the deadly force standard [Skolnick and Fyfe, 1993]). For example, CALEA requires that a department have a policy governing the use of nonlethal weapons, but CALEA does not offer any input as to what the policy should say. Skolnick and Fyfe (1993) view accreditation as a valuable tool but question its impact on street-level policing:

> In short, accreditation is directed at the tops of police organizations, rather than at the line. In addition, the primary focus of CALEA's assessors and commissioners is on documents, facilities, and general policies and practices rather than upon the actual quality of work or the reasonableness of specific police actions. Hence, and fittingly, CALEA is closely akin to the professional bodies that accredit hospitals, universities, and law schools. (p. 244)

Changing the Subculture

Some police scholars argue that to effectively control police deviance the department must break down the secrecy that defines the **subculture** (the "blue curtain"). The refusal of officers to turn in or testify against their colleagues who have engaged in deviance represents a serious barrier to anti-deviance efforts. A number of suggestions have been offered to break the code of silence, including punishing officers for withholding information or lying, rewarding officers for coming forward with information, punishing supervisors for the transgressions of their subordinates, and more generally, creating a working environment where deviance is not tolerated (New York Commission to Combat Police Corruption, 1996; Walker & Katz, 2002). The Mollen

Commission (1994) stated that, "Reforms must focus on making honest officers feel responsible for keeping their fellow officers honest, and ridding themselves of corrupt ones" (p. 5). The resistance to turn in fellow officers can be caused by a number of issues related to the informal culture, such as friendship, loyalty, even fear of retaliation, but in some cases, departments have formally punished officers for reporting misconduct. Following the Rampart scandal in Los Angeles, 90 officers sued the department for being demoted—or punished in some other way—for reporting misconduct (Chemerinsky, 2000).

The Central Role of the Chief

Success in changing the informal norms of the department—the subculture—centers on the attitudes of the chief. The Mollen Commission (1994) states that "commitment to integrity cannot be an abstract value. . . . It must be reflected not only in the words, but in the deeds, of the Police Commissioner . . ." (p. 112). Darryl Gates in Los Angeles, Frank Rizzo in Philadelphia, and Harold Breier in Milwaukee demonstrate how attitudes of the chief can send a message to line staff that abusive conduct is acceptable. Whether it was Rizzo's "spacco il capa"—to bust their heads—philosophy or Gates's "siege mentality," the message sent to line officers was the same: Misconduct will be ignored—in this case, brutality and excessive force—and the department leadership will support officers regardless of citizen's or suspect's claims (Skolnick & Fyfe, 1993). A U.S. Justice Department investigation of the Philadelphia Police Department concluded, "[Chief Golden] dismisses all suggestions of on-duty abuse as the product of perjured or fabricated testimony and media distortions. . . . Golden refuses to discipline or even admonish officers for 'bad' on duty shootings" (Golden was responsible for investigating all allegations of police brutality) (Thrasher, Tiefer, Fleetwood, & Lechner, 1979, p. 9).

Alternatively, Philadelphia after Rizzo (Morton Solomon), New York after Serpico (Patrick Murphy), and Miami after Liberty City (Bobbie L. Jones and Frederick Taylor) represent cases where meaningful, department-wide reform has occurred because of strong leadership that sent a clear message to line officers about what would be tolerated (and more importantly, what would not) (Skolnick & Fyfe, 1993). Murphy's actions following the widely publicized NYPD corruption scandal very clearly illustrate the potential influence of the chief:

> Murphy put in place systems to hold supervisors and administrators strictly accountable for the integrity and civility of their personnel. He rewarded cops who turned in corrupt or brutal colleagues and punished those who, although personally honest, looked the other way when they learned of misconduct. . . . Murphy used his authority to appoint and demote officers above the rank of captain to weed his department's 450-man executive corps of unresponsive dead wood and to advance promising young commanders quickly. . . . Murphy used his three and a half years in office to create an environment that loudly and clearly condemned abusive police conduct, those who engaged in it, and—equally important—those who *tolerate* it. (Skolnick & Fyfe, 1993, pp. 179–180)

Quite clearly, accountability and discipline are critical to a chief's efforts to effectively control police misconduct. The clear message coming from the chief's office that misconduct will not be tolerated must be followed by strict and swift discipline for those who commit violations. Kappeler et al. (1998) view a department's **disciplinary system** as a "critical reinforcer of its values, policies, and rules" (p. 224). The U.S. Commission on Civil Rights (1981) concluded, ". . .disciplinary sanctions commensurate with the seriousness of the offense that are imposed fairly, swiftly, and consistently most clearly reflect the commitment of the department to oppose police misconduct" (p. 158). When officers are not consistently punished for their transgressions, the informal message becomes much more powerful than the formal disciplinary system that is "on the books." The informal message is that the department is not serious about preventing and rooting out corruption, brutality, and other problem behaviors, and it is in this environment that such misconduct will flourish.

SUMMARY

This chapter began with recognition of two themes that are important to understanding the control of police misconduct. First, primary responsibility for preventing and investigating police misconduct—and punishing those who engage in it—still rests with the police department itself. Police departments employ a range of internal mechanisms in their battle against police misconduct; some are new innovations relying on technology and computers, others date back to the birth of professional policing. The major internal mechanisms include:

- Careful recruitment and selection of personnel.
- Proper police training that includes a period of academy training, field training with senior officers, and routine in-service training.
- Effective supervision of line officers by sergeants.
- Clear and concise administrative rules, policies, and procedures.
- An active Internal Affairs unit that
  - uses proactive integrity tests.
  - operates an early warning system.
- Accreditation through CALEA.
- Changing the subculture by breaking down the "blue wall of silence."
- Clear mandate from the chief, articulated through a consistent and effective disciplinary system.

The second important theme is that there is no single-best internal accountability measure, nor is there a measure that guarantees to prevent or eliminate all problem behavior. Each of the mechanisms above was described in some detail, illustrating both advantages and disadvantages. A police department's best defense against police misconduct is to employ a package of internal accountability mechanisms, beginning with a strong chief, effective line supervision, a clear and consistent disciplinary system, and an active Internal Affairs unit. These elements should be considered "the basic ingredients" that serve as the foundation of the department's anti-misconduct effort.

The next chapter will develop a third important theme in the area of responding to police misconduct: that the police department should not be left alone to police itself; external accountability mechanisms also play a central role in preventing and effectively reducing the prevalence of police problems.

KEY TERMS

Accountability
Accreditation
Administrative policy
Affirmative action
Code of silence
Commission on Accreditation for Law
  Enforcement Agencies (CALEA)
Disciplinary system
Early warning (EW) systems
Field training officer (FTO) programs

In-service training
Integrity tests
Internal Affairs
K-9 (canine) teams
Police academy training
Recruitment
Selection criteria
Subculture
Supervision
Tennessee v. Garner

DISCUSSION QUESTIONS

1. How a police department's recruitment and selection process can effectively combat police misconduct?

2. What are the three phases or stages of police training? Describe why each is important.

3. Why is the sergeant's role important for effective supervision of officers?

4. In what areas of policing has research shown administrative guidance to be an effective control of officer behavior? Describe the major findings in each area.

5. What are the keys for an Internal Affairs unit to be effective in combating police misconduct?

6. What are the main components of an early warning system?

REFERENCES

Alpert, G.P. (1997). *Police pursuit: Policies and training.* Research in Brief. Washington, DC: National Institute of Justice.

Alpert, G.P., Kenney, D.J., Dunham, R.G., & Smith, W.C. (2000). *Police pursuits: What we know.* Washington, DC: Police Executive Research Forum.

Arnold, J. (1999, May). Internal affairs investigation guidelines. *Law and Order,* 43–46.

Boston Globe (1992, October 4). Wave of abuse claims laid to a few officers.

Bureau of Justice Statistics. (1999). *Law enforcement management and administrative statistics, 1997.* Washington, DC: U.S. Department of Justice.

Buzawa, E., & Buzawa, C. (2001). Traditional and innovative police responses to domestic violence. In R.G. Dunham & G.A. Alpert (Eds.), *Critical issues in policing* (4th ed. June 20, 2005) Prospect Heights, IL: Waveland Press. http://www.calea.org

Carter, D.L., & Barker. T. (1991). Administrative guidance and control of police officer behavior: Policies, procedures and rules. In T. Barker & D.L. Carter (Eds.), *Police Deviance* (2nd ed.). Cincinnati, OH: Anderson Publishing.

Chapman, S.G. (1967). Police policy on the use of firearms. *The Police Chief,* 16–37.

Chemerinsky, E. (2000). *An independent analysis of the Los Angeles Police Department's Board of Inquiry report on the rampart scandal.* Los Angeles.

Christopher, W. (1991). *Report of the independent commission on the Los Angeles Police Department.* Los Angeles: City of Los Angeles.

Ermer, V.B. (1978). Recruitment of female police officers in New York City. *Journal of Criminal Justice, 6,* 233–246.

Fyfe, J.J. (1979). Administrative interventions on police shooting discretion: An empirical examination. *Journal of Criminal Justice, 7,* 309–324.

Fyfe, J.J. (1988). Police use of deadly force: Research and reform. *Justice Quarterly, 5,* 165–205.

Fyfe, J.J. (1995). Training to reduce police-civilian violence. In W.A. Geller & H. Toch (Eds.), *And justice for all: Understanding and controlling police abuse of force.* Washington, DC: Police Executive Research Forum.

Gain, C. (1971, December 23). *Discharge of firearms policy: Effecting justice through administrative regulation.* Unpublished memorandum.

Geller, W., & Scott, M.S. (1992). *Deadly force: What we know.* Washington, DC: Police Executive Research Forum.

Goldstein, H. (1975). *Police corruption: A perspective on its nature and control.* Washington, DC: Police Foundation.

International Association of Chiefs of Police (IACP). (1989). *Building integrity and reducing drug corruption in police departments.* Arlington, VA: Author.

Kappeler, V.E., Sluder, R.D., & Alpert, G.P. (1998). *Forces of deviance: Understanding the dark side of policing.* Prospect Heights, IL: Waveland Press.

Klockars, C., Ivkovich, S., Harver, W., & Haberfeld, M. (2000). *The measurement of police integrity.* Washington, DC: National Institute of Justice.

Lester, D. (1983). Why do people become police officers: A study of reasons and their predictions of success. *Journal of Police Science and Administration, 11* (2), 170–174.

Manning, P.K. (1977). *Police work: The social organization of policing.* Cambridge, MA: MIT Press.

Mastrofski, S.D., Parks, R.B., Reiss, Jr., A.J., Worden, R.E., DeJong, C., Snipes, J.B., & Terrill, W. (1998). *Systematic observation of public police.* Washington, DC: U.S. Government Printing Office.

Miller, W.R. (1977). *Cops and bobbies: Police authority in New York and London, 1830–1870.* Chicago: University of Chicago Press.

Mollen Commission. (1994). *The City of New York commission to investigate allegations of police corruption and the anti-corruption procedures of the police department: Commission report.* New York: City of New York.

National Advisory Commission on Criminal Justice Standards and goals. (1973). *Police.* Washington, DC: U.S. Government Printing Office.

New Orleans Police Department, Public Integrity Division. (1997). *Report.* New Orleans: City of New Orleans.

New York City Commission to Combat Police Corruption. (1996). *The New York City Police Department's disciplinary system*. New York: New York City Commission to Combat Police Corruption.

New York Times (1991, September 10). Kansas City police go after their "bad boys," page 1.

President's Commission on Law Enforcement and Administration of Justice. (1967). *Task force report: The police*. Washington DC: U.S. Government Printing Office.

Punch, M. (2000) Police corruption and its prevention. *European Journal on Criminal Policy and Research, 8* (3), 301–324.

Raganella, A.J., & White, M.D. (2004). Race, gender and motivation for becoming a police officer: Implications for building a representative police department. *Journal of Criminal Justice, 32,* 501–513.

Roberts, M. (2005, January 10). Vancouver police officers offended by plan to subject them to honesty tests. *National Post*, p. A-7.

Sherman, L.W. (1974). *Police corruption: A sociological perspective*. Garden City, NY: Doubleday Anchor Books.

Sherman, L.W. (1992). *Policing domestic violence: Experiments and dilemmas*. New York: The Free Press.

Sherman, L.W., & Berk, R.A. (1984). The specific deterrent effects of arrest for domestic assault. *American Sociological Review, 49*(2), 261–272.

Skolnick, J.H., & Fyfe, J.J. (1993). *Above the law: Police and the excessive use of force*. New York: Free Press.

Special Counsel to the Los Angeles Sheriffs Department. (1999), *11th semi-annual report*. Los Angeles: Los Angeles County.

Tennessee v. Garner (1985) 471 U.S. 1, 105 S. Ct. 1694, 85 L. Ed. 1. Lower Court Rulings: *Garner v. Memphis Police Department,* 600 F. 2d 52 (6th Cir. 1979); *Garner v. Memphis Police Department,* Civil Action No. C-75-145, Memorandum Opinion and Order, slip opinion (W.D. Tenn. July 8, 1981); *Garner v. Memphis Police Department,* 710 F. 2d. 240 (6th Cir. 1983).

Thurman v. Torrington, 595 F. Supp. 1521 (1984).

Thrasher, L.M., Tiefer, C.D., Fleetwood, M., & Lechner, S. (1979). *Report of investigation of misconduct of Philadelphia police force and recommendation*. U.S. Department of Justice, Civil Rights Division, internal memorandum to Assistant Attorney General Drew S. Days, III.

Toch, H., Grant, D.J., & Galvin, R.T. (1975). *Agents of change: A study in police reform*. Cambridge, MA: Schenkman.

U.S. Commission on Civil Rights. (1981). *Who is guarding the guardians?* Washington, DC: U.S. Government Printing Office.

Van Maanen, J. (1983). The boss: First-line supervision in an American police agency. In M. Punch (Ed.), *Control in the police organization*. Cambridge, MA: MIT Press.

Walker, S. (1993). *Taming the system: The control of discretion in criminal justice, 1950–1990*. New York: Oxford University Press.

Walker, S., & Katz, C.M. (2002). *The police in America: An introduction*. New York: McGraw-Hill.

Walker, S., & Alpert, G.P. (2002). Early warning systems as risk management for police. In K.M. Lersch (Ed.), *Policing and misconduct*. Upper Saddle River, NJ: Prentice-Hall.

Walker, S., Alpert, G.P., & Kenney, D.J. (2001). Early warning systems for police: Concept, history, and issues. In R.G. Dunham & G.P. Alpert (Eds.), *Critical issues in policing* (4th ed.). Prospect Heights, II: Waveland Press.

Washington Post (1998, November 15). DC police lead nation in shootings.

Weisburd, D., Greenspan, R., with Hamilton, E.E., Williams, H., & Bryant, K.A. (2000). *Police attitudes toward abuse of authority: Findings from a national study*. Washington, DC: U.S. Government Printing Office.

White, M.D. (2001). Controlling police decisions to use deadly force: Re-examining the importance of administrative policy. *Crime and Delinquency, 47* (1), 131–151.

Wrobleski, H.M., & Hess, K.M. (2003). *Introduction to law enforcement and criminal justice* (7th ed.). Belmont, CA: Wadsworth.

Wylie-Marques, K. (2005). Canine (K-9) units. In L.E. Sullivan (Ed.), *Encyclopedia of law enforcement. Volume 1 (State and Local)*. Thousand Oaks, CA: Sage Publications.

SCHOLAR'S PERSPECTIVE

Early Warning Systems:
Responding to the Problem Police Officer

Samuel Walker, Ph.D.*
University of Nebraska

Geoffrey P. Alpert, Ph.D.†
University of South Carolina

Dennis J. Kenney, Ph.D.‡
John Jay College of Criminal Justice

It has become a truism among police chiefs that 10 percent of their officers cause 90 percent of their problems. Investigative journalists have documented departments in which as few as 2 percent of all officers are responsible for 50 percent of all citizen complaints (*New York Times*, 9/10/91; *Boston Globe*, 10/4/92). An early warning system is a data-based police management tool designed to identify officers whose behavior is problematic and provide a form of intervention to correct that performance. As an early response, a department intervenes before such an officer is in a situation that warrants formal disciplinary action. The system alerts the department to these individuals and warns the officers while providing counseling or training to help them change their problematic behavior.

By 1999, 39 percent of all municipal and county law enforcement agencies that serve populations greater than 50,000 people either had an early warning system in place or were planning to implement one. The growing popularity of these systems as a remedy for police misconduct raises questions about their effectiveness and about the various program elements that are associated with effectiveness. To date, however, little has been written on the subject (Kappeler, Sluder, & Alpert, 1998). This appendix reports on the first in-depth investigation of early warning systems. The investigation combined the results of a national survey of law enforcement agencies with the findings of case studies of three agencies with established systems.

*Walker-Emeritus Professor, Department of Criminal Justice, University of Nebraska. PhD Ohio State University.
†Alpert-Same as insert for ch. 8.
‡Kenney-Professor, John Jay College of Criminal Justice. PhD Rutgers University.
Source: Walker, S., Alpert, G.P., & Kenney, D.J. (July 2001). *Early warning systems: Responding to the problem police officer.* Research in Brief. Washington, DC: National Institute of Justice, Office of Justice Programs, US Department of Justice.

HOW PREVALENT ARE EARLY WARNING SYSTEMS?

As part of the national evaluation of early warning systems, the Police Executive Research Forum—funded by the National Institute of Justice and the Office of Community Oriented Policing Services—surveyed 832 sheriffs' offices and municipal and county police departments serving populations of 50,000 or more. Usable responses were received from 571 agencies, a response rate of 69 percent. Approximately one-fourth (27 percent) of the surveyed agencies had an early warning system in 1999. One-half of these systems had been created since 1994, and slightly more than one-third had been created since 1996. These data, combined with the number of agencies indicating that a system was being planned (another 12 percent), suggest that such systems will spread rapidly in the next few years.

HOW DOES AN EARLY WARNING SYSTEM WORK?

Early warning systems have three basic phases: selection, intervention, and post-intervention monitoring.

Selecting Officers for the Program

No standards have been established for identifying officers for early warning programs, but there is general agreement about the criteria that influence their selection. Performance indicators that can help identify officers with problematic behavior include citizen complaints, firearm-discharge and use-of-force reports, civil litigation, resisting-arrest incidents, and high-speed pursuits and vehicular damage.

Intervening with the Officer

The primary goal of early warning systems is to change the behavior of individual officers who have been identified as having problematic performance records. The basic intervention strategy involves a combination of deterrence and education. Early warning systems also operate on the assumption that training, as part of the intervention, can help officers improve their performance.

Monitoring the Officer's Subsequent Performance

Nearly all (90 percent) the agencies that have an early warning system in place report that they monitor an officer's performance after the initial intervention. Such monitoring is generally informal and conducted by the officer's immediate supervisor, but some departments have developed a formal process of observation, evaluation, and reporting.

FINDINGS FROM THE THREE CASE STUDIES

Three police departments were chosen for the case study investigation: Miami-Dade County, Minneapolis, and New Orleans. The three sites were chosen for several reasons. Each has an early warning system that had been operating for at least four years at the time of the study. Also, the three systems differ from one another in terms of structure and administrative history, and the three departments differ in their history of police officer use of force and accountability.

Characteristics of Officers Identified by Early Warning Systems

Demographically, officers identified by the systems do not differ significantly from the control group [officers not identified by the system] in terms of race or ethnicity. Males are somewhat overrepresented and females are underrepresented. One disturbing finding was a slight tendency of early warning officers to be promoted at higher rates than control officers.

The Impact of Early Warning Systems on Officers' Performance

Early warning systems appear to have a dramatic effect on reducing citizen complaints and other indicators of problematic police performance among those officers subjected to intervention.

The Impact of Early Warning Systems on Supervisors

The qualitative component of the research found that these systems have potentially significant effects on supervisors. The existence of an intervention system communicates to supervisors their responsibility to monitor officers who have been identified by the program.

POLICY CONCERNS AND AREAS FOR FURTHER RESEARCH

Selection

A number of problems related to official data on citizen complaints, including underreporting, have been documented (Walker, 2001). Using a broader range of indicators is more likely to identify officers whose behavior requires departmental intervention.

Intervention

In most early warning systems, intervention consists of an informal counseling session between the officer and his or her immediate supervisor. Some systems require no documentation of the content of that session, which raises concerns about whether supervisors deliver the intended content of the intervention. Involving higher ranking command officers is likely to ensure that the intervention serves the intended goals. Further research is needed on the most effective forms of intervention and whether it is possible to tailor certain forms of intervention to particular categories of officers.

Post-Intervention Monitoring

Some systems rely on informal monitoring of the subject officers; others employ a formal mechanism of observation and documentation by supervisors. The relative impact of different post-intervention monitoring systems on individual officers, supervisors, and departments requires further research.

ONE TOOL AMONG MANY

An effective early warning system is a complex, high-maintenance operation that requires a significant investment of administrative resources. Some systems appear to be essentially symbolic gestures with little substantive content, and it is unlikely that an intervention program can be effective in a law enforcement agency that has no serious commitment to accountability. It can be an effective management tool, but it should be seen as only one of many tools needed to raise standards of performance and improve the quality of police services.

REFERENCES

Boston Globe. (1992, October 4). Waves of abuse laid to a few officers. Page 1.
Kappeler, V., Sluder, R., & Alpert, G. (1998). *Forces of deviance: Understanding the dark side of policing.* Prospect Heights, IL: Waveland Press.
New York Times. (1991, September 10). Kansas City police go after their 'bad boys.' page 1.
Walker, S. (2001). *Police accountability: The role of citizen oversight.* Belmont, CA: Wadsworth Press.

CHAPTER 10

POLICE ACCOUNTABILITY
External Mechanisms

Chapter 9 states that primary responsibility for accountability rests with the police, and the chapter reviews the major internal mechanisms for controlling police behavior. The overriding theme of this chapter, however, is that although police play a central role in controlling officer behavior, they cannot and should not be expected to do it by themselves. The long history of police misconduct (see Chapter 8) and the perception problem that police cannot effectively police themselves require that the accountability package include external mechanisms—efforts at controlling misconduct that are outside the purview of the police department itself.

This chapter describes the primary external tools for controlling police behavior. Some of these tools are well established and have been around since the start of professional policing, such as the criminal law, civil litigation, special investigations, and judicial intervention. Others are more recent innovations, such as U.S. Department of Justice consent decrees and citizen oversight. This chapter reviews each of these mechanisms, describing its history, basic elements, advantages, and disadvantages. Much like the last chapter, the author argues that there is no single-best external accountability measure, and the optimal approach for police departments and the communities they serve is to rely on a complete accountability package including multiple measures, both internal and external. The measures that make up an accountability package may vary by police department and community, and that is to be expected given the unique culture, environment, and history of towns and cities—and their police departments—throughout the United States. What becomes critical is that the police department and community view their roles in promoting accountability and preventing misconduct as equally important, and together, they work to identify the mechanisms of accountability that best suit their needs.

EXTERNAL CONTROL MECHANISMS

Criminal Law: Prosecuting the Police

Background. Brutality, corruption, discrimination, and other forms of police deviance typically involve a violation of state or federal law, and as a result, the offending officer can be prosecuted for the behavior. At the state level, police officers—like any other citizen—can be prosecuted for actions that violate the state penal code (Kappeler, Sluder, & Alpert, 1998). Officers convicted of serious offenses, such as assault, burglary, robbery, and even murder, often are sentenced to lengthy prison terms. Most states also have statutes that address directly the behavior of police officers and others acting in an official capacity when the violation occurs (i.e., official misconduct, abuse of authority) (Kappeler et al., 1998). At the federal level, Title 18 of the criminal code includes several sections that have been applied to police officers, including Section 242 (Criminal Liability for Deprivation of Civil Rights) and Section 245 (Violation of Federally-Protected Activities) (Kappeler et al., 1998).

Examples may help illustrate the role of criminal law in combating police misconduct. Following the brutal beating of Abner Louima, four NYPD officers were convicted and sentenced to prison. Justin Volpe pled guilty and received a 30-year prison sentence; Charles Schwarz received at 15-year prison sentence, and two other officers were sentenced to 5 years each for lying to federal investigators.

On March 3, 1991, George Holliday videotaped the beating and arrest of Rodney King by four Los Angeles police officers (with more than twenty other officers at the scene). On March 14, 1991, the four LAPD officers (Stacey Koon, Lawrence Powell, Timothy Wind, and Theodore Briseno) were indicted by a Los Angeles grand jury on state assault charges (Kappeler et al., 1998). Following their acquittal at the state trial—and the ensuing riots—the four officers were charged in federal court for violating King's civil rights. The jury in the federal trial found Coon and Powell guilty (Wind and Briseno were found not guilty), and they were subsequently sentenced to 30 months in federal prison.

Criminal Law as a Tool for Combating Police Misconduct.   Quite clearly, the criminal law and prosecuting the police for violations offer a number of advantages. First, criminal prosecutions allow for punishments that fit the seriousness of the offense (although it is certainly no guarantee). Former Jacksonville (Florida) Sheriffs' officer Karl Waldon, who was convicted of kidnapping, robbing, and murdering a convenience store clerk, received four life terms in prison for his crimes. Justin Volpe, the officer who sodomized Abner Louima, received a 30-year prison sentence. A civil judgment or dismissal from the police department would hardly seem proportionate to the crimes that were committed.

The nature of criminal trials at both the state and federal level offer a number of other advantages for providing accountability and responding to police misconduct. First, criminal trials of police officers accused of misconduct are public and typically receive significant media coverage. The publicity surrounding a criminal trial can send a clear message to the community that police misconduct is treated seriously, will not be tolerated, and those who engage in it will face serious consequences (this, of course, can backfire with an acquittal, or dismissal of charges). A criminal trial can also relieve the burden on the victim of the misconduct. Although questioned by many trial observers, Rodney King was not required to testify at the state criminal trial of the four LAPD officers. Alternatively, victims may find solace or a sense of closure by testifying as a witness at a criminal trial. Alternatively, the police officer accused of misconduct receives all the traditional protections of a criminal trial, including innocence until proven guilty, trial by jury of his or her peers, and the opportunity to confront accusers and testify on one's own behalf (of course, the officer can also choose to not testify).

Nevertheless, the criminal law is generally viewed as an ineffective tool in combating police deviance. Fyfe (1988) states that the criminal law is too vague regarding acceptable and appropriate behavior by police. Skolnick and Fyfe (1993) argue that "the criminal law remains so broad and presents so many enforcement problems that it cannot serve meaningfully as the parameters for any professional's discretion" (p. 197). They argue that, much like doctors, lawyers, and civil engineers, lay juries are ill-equipped to judge matters of professional conduct because they do not have the expertise necessary. Skolnick and Fyfe (1993) state:

> We are dead certain, for example, that a jury composed entirely of cops (from jurisdictions other than Los Angeles) would have rejected out of hand the defense argument that the officers who beat King were only following their training. Instead, in Van Maanen's terms, the King beating jury consisted only of *know-nothing* lay people who brought to court only their ignorance of police training and other professional police standards. (p. 196)

In fact, Skolnick and Fyfe (1993) point to the external review of doctors and lawyers by their professional associations—the American Medical Association (AMA) and the American Bar Association, respectively—as an effective means of monitoring and responding to official misconduct by doctors and lawyers (Skolnick & Fyfe, 1993). Criminal law is very rarely used in response to doctor and lawyer misconduct—some of which constitutes criminal conduct (i.e., unnecessary surgeries). The police have no similar professional association to review their conduct and hand down appropriate punishments, with the exception of Florida where the Florida Department of Law Enforcement (FDLE) can suspend an officer if an external review panel finds that officer engaged in misconduct. "When we try to use criminal law as a substitute for standards that should be applied *within* a profession or occupation, we almost invariably are disappointed with the results" (Skolnick & Fyfe, 1993, p. 198).

Going back to the state level, the criminal law is a reactive mechanism for controlling officer behavior that plays no practical role in preventing officer misconduct. Arguably, the criminal law could take on a deterrent aspect if it were applied successfully on enough occasions (i.e., certainty, severity, and celerity), but this is simply not the case, as illustrated above. Police officers are rarely prosecuted for their transgressions, and when they are, convictions are by no means guaranteed. As a result, criminal trials of police officers accused of misconduct likely have little deterrent value in terms of dissuading other officers interested in engaging in misconduct.

Finally, at the local level, there are a number of reasons why district attorneys (DAs) may be reluctant to prosecute police officers for violations of state law. First, district attorneys know that police misconduct cases are difficult to prosecute (for all the reasons stated above). Second, it is absolutely critical for continued functioning of the criminal justice system that the police and district attorney's office maintain a good working relationship. The DA's office, in particular, relies tremendously on police officers for successful prosecution of cases (physical evidence, reports, testimony, etc.). DAs may be hesitant to actively investigate and prosecute police misconduct for fear of the tension it might create between the two agencies.

Third, the political nature of the district attorney's position may affect the willingness to prosecute police (White, 1999). The DA is an elected position in most counties in the United States, and candidates running for the position are unlikely to receive an endorsement from the Fraternal Order of Police (FOP) if they have actively prosecuted police officers (White, 1999). The FOP endorsement can be critically important for a campaign, especially if the candidate is portraying himself or herself as "tough on crime." Also, in many jurisdictions, the district attorney's office often serves as a stepping stone to higher office (governor, senator, etc.), and as a result, the position is often held by people who cannot afford to alienate their political parties, the police, or the voters.

As an illustration, allegations of police misconduct in Philadelphia were rampant during the 1970s. In fact, in 1979 the U.S. Department of Justice filed suit against the Philadelphia Police Department (PPD) for tolerating brutality (the first time the Department of Justice had ever taken such a step). The District Attorneys in Philadelphia during the 1970s were Arlen Specter, who has served as a U.S. Senator for decades, and Edward Rendell, who has served as Mayor of Philadelphia, Chairman of the Democratic National Committee, and Governor of Pennsylvania. Neither could afford to actively investigate or prosecute police misconduct—and thereby taking on Frank Rizzo and the Philadelphia FOP—without jeopardizing their ambitions for higher political office.

At the federal level, the story of applying criminal law to police misconduct is not much different. The **Civil Rights Division of the U.S. Department of Justice** receives thousands of complaints each year alleging police violation of citizens' civil rights (U.S. Commission on Civil Rights, 1981). The federal trial (and subsequent conviction) of the four officers involved in the Rodney King beating is one example of this type of external intervention. Linda Davis, Chief of the Criminal Section of the Civil Rights Division, stated that her office receives approximately 8,000 civil rights complaints per year, 85 percent of which involve allegations of police misconduct (Epke & Davis, 1991). Of the complaints alleging police misconduct:

> . . . about one-third of these complaints are of sufficient substance to warrant investigations. . . . The Department of Justice is very select about the cases it pursues. Of the approximately 3,000 investigations conducted each year, it authorizes only about 50 cases for grand jury presentation and possible indictment. (Epke & Davis, 1991, p. 15)

The reasons for the lack of aggressiveness by the Department of Justice remain unclear. Skolnick and Fyfe (1993) point out that Justice's own analysis of its complaint data suggest that there are patterns worthy of investigation, most notably that there were several agencies that were producing a disproportionate number of complaints. Despite these patterns, federal prosecutions remain fairly rare, leading Skolnick and Fyfe (1993) to conclude that, "[the Department of] Justice plays virtually no active role in holding local police accountable . . ." (p. 211).

Civil Litigation: Suing the Police

Police officers can be sued in state and federal court for their actions or failure to act. Kappeler (2001) states "when police officers fail to perform their assigned duties, perform them in a negligent fashion, abuse their authority, or just make poor decisions, the possibility of civil liability exists" (p. 1). Many of the civil suits against police allege the types of misconduct described in some detail in Chapter 8, such as excessive force, corruption, discrimination, and abuse of authority. The incidence of **civil litigation** against police has increased significantly, from approximately 6,000 per year in the late 1960s to as many as 30,000 per year in the late 1990s (Kappeler, 2001; Silver, 2000). A report by the IACP (1976) found that one in every 34 police officers was sued.

Although the police have traditionally been successful in defending themselves against lawsuits, civil judgments can cost police departments and taxpayers millions of dollars. For example, Rodney King was awarded $3.5 million, and Abner Louima was awarded more than $8 million. In the 1990s, the City of Detroit was required to pay $124 million to victims of police misconduct, averaging nearly $10 million per year (Walker & Katz, 2002).

Police Officer Liability under State Law. Police officers can be sued in state court for a range of different torts. A **tort** is "conduct that interferes with the private interests of people or their property" (Kappeler, 2001, p. 18). Unlike crimes, torts are not punished by the state, but rather are redressed by monetary awards (Kappeler, 2001). Some state torts may also be crimes and may also involve criminal prosecution and punishment. Since torts involve civil actions, the burden of proof is a preponderance of the evidence, which is much lower than the beyond a reasonable doubt standard in criminal courts.

> In the typical civil suit brought against a police officer under state law, a plaintiff alleges that the officer owed him or her a legal duty, that the officer breached that duty, and that the breach caused the citizen to suffer some kind of harm, either physical or emotional. By suing the officer in civil court, the plaintiff usually hopes to recover monetary damages to compensate for the harm suffered (compensatory damages) or to punish the officer for his wrongdoing (punitive damages). (del Carmen & Smith, 1997, p. 225)

There are three general types of state torts: strict liability, intentional, and negligence. Strict liability torts involve extremely dangerous behaviors that the actor can be substantially certain will lead to damage or injury (Kappeler, 2001). Because of the nature of the behavior and the presumed likelihood of injury, the intent—or mental state—of the actor is not at issue (Kappeler, 2001). Police officers are rarely subject to strict liability claims. Kappeler (2001) points out two possible scenarios from the War on Drugs of the early 1990s that could lead to strict liability torts against police: (1) using military aircraft to shoot down airplanes engaged in drug trafficking (and causing the death of those on board) and (2) spraying chemicals from the air on drug crops, causing people on the ground to become ill or die. In each case, the police officers would have met the strict liability requirements: extremely dangerous behavior that is very likely to lead to injury or death.

With an intentional tort, the officer's state of mind is a central issue: The victim must show that the officer intentionally engaged in the conduct, and importantly, that the injury resulting from the behavior was likely and foreseeable (Kappeler, 2001). There is an important distinction in terms of intent. The plaintiff must only establish that the officer purposively engaged in the behavior; the plaintiff does NOT have to show that the officer intended to cause the injury. Like the strict liability tort, the officer is liable because the injury was "substantially certain" to occur as a result of the action. There are a number of intentional torts that are filed against police, including:

- *Assault and battery:* The officer intentionally places someone in fear of bodily harm without legal justification (assault), or intentionally and unlawfully touches the person (battery).
  - For example, a police officer who threatens someone inappropriately or uses excessive force.
- *False arrest and imprisonment:* The officer arrests someone without sufficient legal basis, then confines or detains the person (if the arrest was illegal, then the subsequent detention is also illegal).
  - For example, a police officer arrests a suspect without probable cause, and then detains the arrestee at the police station overnight.
- *Malicious prosecution and abuse of process:* The officer (1) initiates the criminal process through arrest, (2) the case is terminated in the victim's favor, (3) the officer did not have probable cause to make the arrest, and (4) the officer was motivated by malice or bad faith.
  - For example, a police officer arrests his ex-wife's new boyfriend without probable cause, as punishment for his relationship with the ex-wife.
- *Wrongful death:* The officer has intentionally and unlawfully killed someone, or has failed to prevent the death; the claim is brought by the victim's family to recover damages for pain and suffering of the victim and themselves, medical and funeral expenses, and loss of potential income.
  - For example, a police officer shoots a nonviolent, fleeing suspect who poses no imminent threat of danger to the officer or anyone else. (del Carmen & Smith, 1997, pp. 226–227)

The third and final type of tort is a negligence tort. In this type of claim, the officer need not have intentionally engaged in the behavior that produced the harm (del Carmen & Smith, 1997). Kappeler (2001) notes that the standard applied to negligence torts is "whether the officer's act or failure to act created an unreasonable risk to another member of society" (p. 23). Although the certainty or likelihood of the injury is lesser with the negligence tort than the intentional tort, the plaintiff must still demonstrate four elements to successfully prove negligence:

1. Legal duty: The officer had a legal responsibility to take action (or to not take action).
2. Breach of duty: The officer failed to meet his or her legal duty to act (or not to).
3. Proximate cause: The officer's breach caused harm to the victim.
4. Damage or injury: An actual harm occurred. (Kappeler, 2001)

Negligent claims have focused on a range of police duties and responsibilities, including operation of vehicles, failure to protect, failure to arrest, failure to render assistance, and negligent supervision (Kappeler, 2001). For example, an officer may stop an intoxicated motorist but only issue a warning. If the motorist then gets into a car accident after the officer lets him or her go, the officer may be liable for the injury caused by the accident (because of the failure to arrest, or protect). Also, police officers typically will speed when responding to a call for service. If the officer's driving is deemed to be reckless and causes injury to bystanders, the officer may be liable.

Police Liability under Federal Law. Although there are a number of federal statutes that can be used by citizens to sue police, the most commonly used statute is the Civil Rights Act of 1871 (Kappeler, 2001). Following the abolition of slavery, Congress passed the **Civil Rights Act of 1871** in an effort to control activities of the Ku Klux Klan and its members. **Section 1983** of the Civil Rights Act of 1871 provides civil and criminal remedies for those whose constitutional rights are violated by persons acting under state authority. Section 1983 states:

> Every person, who under color of any statute, ordinance, regulation, custom, or usage, of any State or territory, subjects, or causes to be subjected, any citizen of the United States or other persons within the jurisdiction thereof to the deprivation of any right, privileges, or immunities secured by the Constitution and laws, shall be liable to the party injured in an action at law, suit in equity, or other proper proceeding for redress.

In *West v. Atkins* (1988, p. 50), the U.S. Supreme Court specified the requirements for a Section 1983 claim: "Thus, generally, a public employee acts under color of state law while acting in his official capacity or while exercising his responsibilities pursuant to state law" (see also Kappeler, 2001).

Historically, Section 1983 was used very rarely as an avenue for responding to police misconduct. Skolnick and Fyfe (1993) argue that there were two reasons why Section 1983 was not used until the last thirty or so years. First, courts traditionally held that police officers could "be held liable only for actions that were unconstitutional but were authorized by the laws of their states" (Skolnick & Fyfe, 1993, p. 200). Thus, Section 1983 created a Catch-22: If the officer violated a person's constitutional rights and state law, the suit would fail because the officer's actions exceeded what was deemed permissible by state law (i.e., the officer was *not* acting under color of law; he was acting beyond it); if the officer's actions violated constitutional rights but not state law, the suit would fail because the officer could argue that he acted in good faith to follow state law (Skolnick & Fyfe, 1993). Either way, the lawsuit against the officer is dismissed. The second reason Section 1983 was not used more frequently involved the small civil awards one could win against police officers. Quite simply, civil rights lawyers, who usually work for a percentage of the civil award as their fee, were not overly interested in pursuing cases against poorly paid police officers who offered no prospects of a large monetary award (Skolnick & Fyfe, 1993).

Beginning in the 1960s, rulings in two cases broke down the resistance to filing Section 1983 suits against the police. First, in *Monroe v. Pape* (365 U.S. 167 [1961]), the Supreme Court held that the requirements of Section 1983 (under color of state law) are met whenever a police officer violates a citizen's constitutional rights, regardless of whether their actions also violated state law (Skolnick & Fyfe, 1993). This case involved Chicago police conducting a warrantless search of an individual's home, then interrogating the man for ten hours while he was held on "open charges" and denied contact with a lawyer. This ruling effectively eliminated the Catch-22 described above.

The second case, ***Monell v. Department of Social Services of the City of New York*** (436 U.S. 658 [1978]), originally had little to do with the police. Monell, a pregnant employee for the Department of Social Services, requested maternity leave but was informed by her supervisor that department policy was to deny such requests and require pregnant mothers to resign. Monell filed suit, arguing that she and other women were denied equal protection under the law because the Department of Social Services policy only affected female employees (Skolnick & Fyfe, 1993). The Court ruled in favor of Monell, stating that when an agency employee violates an individual's constitutional rights because of the agency's *custom and practice,* the agency as well as the employee may be held liable (*Monell v. Department of Social Services of the City of New York,* 436 U.S. 658 [1978]). Importantly, the Court defined custom and practice broadly enough to include whatever the agency does routinely, whether stated in official policy or not (Skolnick & Fyfe, 1993). The *Monell* ruling had dramatic implications for police, as it extended liability beyond poorly paid police officers to police departments and local governments. The plaintiff need only show that the officer's actions (which caused the constitutional violation) were part of a pattern of police behavior. Skolnick and Fyfe (1993, p. 202) state that the *Monell* case led to a dramatic increase in civil litigation against police because it "opened the deep pockets of government treasuries to civil rights plaintiffs." For example, from 1986 to 1990, the city of Los Angeles paid more than $20 million in civil litigation against police officers for excessive use of force (Independent Commission on the Los Angeles Police Department, 1991).

In 1984, in *Thurman v. Torrington,* 595 F. Supp. 1521, the *Monell* ruling was applied to police behavior in domestic violence calls. Torrington police officers typically did not make arrests in domestic disputes. Thurman had sought numerous restraining orders against her estranged husband and had repeatedly asked police to arrest him. Thurman filed suit against the police after she was stabbed numerous times and kicked in the head with the police present: In fact, the husband was not taken into custody until after he approached his wife again as she lay on a stretcher, bleeding from knife wounds to the chest, neck, and throat (Sherman, 1992). The Court, ruling in favor of Thurman and awarding her $2.3 million, extended police liability to acts of omission, indicating that failure to protect victims of domestic violence (arguably, the traditional police response) met the "custom and practice" standard and opened departments to civil liability (Skolnick & Fyfe, 1993).

The Advantages and Disadvantages of Suing the Police. Many police scholars argue that civil litigation against police is not only an effective avenue for victims of police misconduct to gain compensation for their victimization, but it also is an effective tool for fostering change in police departments. McCoy (1984) argued that the increasing costs of civil awards in police misconduct suits—and the associated dramatic increases in insurance—forced police departments to take steps to reduce problem behavior. Skolnick and Fyfe (1993) state that many departments have responded to this civil liability by adopting written guidelines and instituting training for officers, both of which decrease the likelihood of officer misconduct. As an example, the Los Angeles Sheriff's Department hired an attorney as special counsel "for the specific purpose of investigating problems in the department, recommending reforms and reducing the costs of misconduct litigation" (Walker & Katz, 2002, p. 368). Since the appointment of the special counsel, excessive force lawsuits have dropped from 300 per year in the early 1990s to just 77 in the late 1990s (Special Counsel to the Los Angeles Sheriff's Department, 2000).

There are also other advantages to civil litigation as a response to police misconduct. Proponents of civil litigation argue that "when the government takes on a responsibility to provide service or to protect the public, people injured by the government's negligent performance of those responsibilities deserve compensation for their injuries" (Kappeler, 2001, p. 11). Also, since the cases are heard in civil court and involve private claims against the police, district attorneys are not part of the process (thus, avoiding the problems associated with their involvement—see above). Moreover, civil cases do not involve vague criminal state statutes, nor are plaintiffs required to prove their cases beyond a reasonable doubt (preponderance of the evidence only). Given the substantial awards that can now be made (based on the *Monell* case), civil litigation offers a more promising avenue for receiving compensation for a wrong than the criminal process where convictions of police officers are difficult to obtain. Finally, and more generally, civil litigation allows the courts to draw the line between police conduct that is acceptable and that which is unacceptable (Kappeler, 2001).

There are a number of disadvantages to civil litigation as a response to police misconduct. First, and similar to the criminal prosecution of police officers, suing the police is an inherently reactive mechanism. Some scholars argue that civil litigation has done little to prevent future misconduct. Littlejohn's (1981) study of litigation against the Detroit Police Department during the 1970s found that it produced little in the way of police reform. A study of Connecticut lawsuits against police during the 1970s produced similar results (Walker & Katz, 2002). Skolnick and Fyfe (1993) note that most civil cases "are dismissed or settle before trial, and those that do make it to court usually result in no awards to plaintiffs" (p. 202) (though Skolnick and Fyfe suggest that this may be because police settle all but the most "hopeless" suits before trial).

Second, the costs of civil litigation go far beyond the awards that are made in specific cases. Police departments must obtain costly liability insurance, fund a legal staff (either within the department or pay for outside counsel), and pay other court-related expenses, in some cases including the fees of plaintiffs' attorneys (Skolnick & Fyfe, 1993). Ultimately, the costs of civil litigation are passed along to taxpayers. Finally, the prevalence of lawsuits against police can potentially have a negative impact on police officers. Simply put, there is anecdotal evidence suggesting that police have begun to avoid situations—or act differently—because they fear being sued. Termed by some as "litigaphobia," this fear can lead to confusion among police officers, leaving them with the "damned if you do, damned if you don't" mentality (Wrobleski & Hess, 2003). This mentality leaves officers susceptible to feeling unappreciated, and in some cases may even lead to increased tension between police and the community.

Judicial Intervention

The judiciary can play a role in defining appropriate police behavior in several different ways, depending on the jurisdiction and mandate of the specific court. Courts at all levels play a role in holding police accountable. At the local and state level, judges monitor police decision making at various stages of the criminal process, including bail hearings, preliminary hearings, and at criminal trials (Walker & Katz, 2002). Appellate courts at the state and federal levels review decisions made by lower courts with regard to police behavior and can issue injunctions that target specific police behavior. The U.S. Supreme Court also plays an important role in shaping police behavior through its interpretation of the Constitution and case law. Thus, judicial intervention has also served as a control on police officer misconduct. The impact of federal court injunctions and the U.S. Supreme Court are described in greater detail below.

Injunctive Relief. Courts can issue an **injunction,** which is "a court order that prohibits persons or organizations from engaging in some specific conduct" (Skolnick & Fyfe, 1993, p. 207). The injunction can also require that the targeted party engage in some specified behavior. There are several cases where plaintiffs have sought injunctive relief from the courts to change police practices.

In 1970, petitioners in Philadelphia filed two separate and important complaints against the mayor of Philadelphia, the police commissioner, and various other individuals (eventually called *Rizzo v. Goode*).

The central thrust of respondents' efforts in the two trials was to lay a foundation for equitable intervention, in one degree or another, because of an assertedly pervasive pattern of illegal and unconstitutional mistreatment by police officers. This mistreatment was said to have been directed against minority citizens in particular and against all Philadelphia residents in general. (*Rizzo v. Goode,* 423 U.S. at 366–67 [1976])

In the case, petitioners presented more than thirty examples of officer abuse to the District Court. Although the Court found that the evidence presented was not strong enough to support the respondents' claims of violated constitutional rights, the Court did find that the police department exhibited "a tendency to discourage the filing of civilian complaints and to minimize the consequences of police misconduct" (*Rizzo v. Goode,* 423 U.S. 362, 368–69 [1976]; also 357 F. Supp. 1289) and that the frequency of abuse prevented the occurrences from being dismissed "as rare, isolated incidents" (*COPPAR v. Rizzo,* 357 F. Supp. at 1319 [1973]). As a result, the District Court ordered the police department to develop and submit to the court a plan for recording and responding to civilian complaints (357 F. Supp. 1319). The Court of Appeals of the Third Circuit upheld the District Court's decision, but the U.S. Supreme Court later reversed the District Court and Court of Appeals rulings.

In *Lyons v. Los Angeles,* 461 U.S. 95 (1983), Adolph Lyons challenged the Los Angeles Police Department's use of the carotid control hold technique for subduing citizens in non-life-threatening situations. The Supreme Court, however, dismissed the injunction sought by Lyons. More recently, an appeals court dismissed a preliminary injunction that sought to compel the Los Angeles Sheriff's Department to demonstrate it was following its own policies and guidelines (*Thomas v. County of Los Angeles,* 9th Cir. 1991).

As a result, courts seem reluctant to use injunctions against police departments, thereby limiting their effectiveness as a control mechanism for police misconduct. Moreover, even when a court issues an injunction, its impact may still be limited if the police department leadership does not follow the rules laid out in the injunction (as was the case in Philadelphia during the *Rizzo v. Goode* case). Robinson (1984, p. 281) noted that the U.S. Supreme Court appeared to be limiting the use of injunctions by federal courts "as a means of social change," instead pushing for the more simple one-on-one civil claims described above (i.e., plaintiffs suing the police). Moreover, injunctions have one other important limitation: specifically, the mechanism does not offer compensation for the injury suffered by victims.

The U.S. Supreme Court.   The U.S. Supreme Court has played a critically important role in defining appropriate police behavior, particularly since the 1950s. As part of the **due process revolution,** the Supreme Court during the late 1950s and 1960s handed down a number of watershed rulings that affected police behavior and reshaped police accountability. In *Mapp v. Ohio* (367 U.S. 643 [1961]), the Supreme Court established the exclusionary rule, which states that evidence seized illegally cannot be used in court. The Court later established exceptions to the exclusionary rule—cases where illegally seized evidence can be used—including the public safety, inevitability of discovery, and good faith exceptions. In *Miranda v. Arizona* (384 U.S. 436 [1966]), the Court established the Miranda warnings and required that they be read to suspects prior to questioning. Over the last thirty-five years, there have been a number of challenges related to the Miranda warnings, but the Court has upheld its original ruling.

In *Terry v. Ohio* (392 U.S. 1, [1968]), the Court ruled that the authority to stop and frisk is governed by the reasonableness standard and that officers who are questioning people on the street may conduct a pat-down or frisk over the clothes. In *Tennessee v. Garner* (471 U.S. 1 [1975]), the Court ruled that police officers can use deadly force only to apprehend fleeing suspects who are "demonstrably dangerous (armed with a weapon; fleeing from a violent crime)" (Skolnick & Fyfe, 1993, p. 41). The Court argued that using deadly force to apprehend nonviolent fleeing suspects represented a violation of the Fourth Amendment's protection against unreasonable seizure. The Supreme Court has also defined police conduct in numerous other areas including searches of automobiles, searches with and without warrants, aerial searches, detention and interrogation, pretext/dual motive stops, surveillance, wiretapping, and entrapment, just to name a few (see Chapter 6 for more discussion of current issues involving the law and courts, including the Patriot Act).

The Impact of the Supreme Court as a Police Accountability Mechanism.   Police scholars disagree over the impact of Supreme Court rulings in controlling police behavior. Many argue that the impact of the *Miranda* ruling is limited because it is consistently undermined by both suspects and police: Studies show that 75 to 80 percent of suspects waive their *Miranda* rights and speak with police (Cassell & Hayman, 1996); other studies indicate that police frequently lie during interrogations (indicating that they have incriminating evidence when they do not) in an effort to obtain confessions (Leo, 1996). Research also consistently shows that few criminal cases are lost or dismissed because of problems with the exclusionary rule (Walker, 2001). Although some may argue that this suggests the exclusionary rule does not impact the police; one could also argue that police have adapted to the exclusionary rule—they follow the rule—and their adherence to the rule explains why so few cases are lost. With regard to use of deadly force, however, Tennenbaum (1994) found that the decision in the *Tennessee v. Garner* case produced a nationwide 16 percent decrease in fatal police shootings.

Yet, some argue that the impact of Supreme Court rulings have more general positive effects. First, Court rulings, especially those during the 1960s, established basic principles of due process, as well as the rights of the accused (Walker & Katz, 2002). The rulings in *Mapp, Miranda,* and other landmark cases during the due process revolution have guided police behavior for the last thirty or more years. Second, these Court rulings have also created penalties for violations committed by police, such as the exclusion of evidence (physical or a confession) or dismissal of charges (Walker & Katz, 2002). Third, the rulings have forced police departments to change their behavior and have led to reforms in recruitment, training, supervision, and management (Walker & Katz, 2002). This has occurred in part because police departments must act in accordance with the Constitution of the United States—as interpreted by the Supreme Court—and in part because of increased public awareness and expectations regarding police conduct (Walker & Katz, 2002).

Still, there are limits to the role of the Supreme Court in combating police misconduct. Walker and Katz (2002) point out five weaknesses or limitations of the Supreme Court as a police accountability mechanism:

1. The Court is unable to supervise day-to-day police behavior and cannot monitor whether individual police officers are following its rulings.
2. Most police work does not result in an arrest; as a result, most police behavior is never reviewed by a court (let alone the U.S. Supreme Court).
3. The police may often be unaware of recent court decisions; while large departments may have legal counsel that monitors the court and keeps police officers informed, officers in small departments (and the majority of police departments in the United States are small) often are on their own with regard to keeping up with changes in the law.
4. Some argue that court rules encourage evasion or lying by police; for example, officers may "interview" an individual without stating the *Miranda* warnings that are required during an interrogation.
5. The court rulings often are undermined by the actions of police and suspects (i.e., most suspects waive their *Miranda* rights).

Special Investigations

Special investigations or "blue ribbon" commissions have often been formed to investigate issues in criminal justice and policing, and specifically, in response to police misconduct scandals. "A commission is a group of individuals, generally appointed by a governor, mayor, or the president, who come together to investigate police misconduct" (Grant & Terry, 2005). These commissions typically hold hearings where witnesses, victims, experts, and police officers offer testimony, and a final report is produced and presented to the police department and city government. Blue-ribbon commissions have been used in response to police misconduct since the late nineteenth century. For example, in 1894, the New York State Senate formed a special commission—the Lexow Committee—to investigate allegations of corruption and brutality (Kappeler et al., 1998). The Lexow Committee found misconduct to be widespread throughout the department, leading to the appointment of Theodore Roosevelt as Commissioner of the NYPD.

Advantages and Disadvantages.   Walker and Katz (2002) argue that special commissions serve several important functions as an external accountability mechanism. First, a commission brings together the top scholars, experts, and practitioners in the field to think about police issues and make recommendations for improvements in the profession (Walker & Katz, 2002). Second, commissions often support original research conducted by scholars to thoroughly study the issues and produce new knowledge (Walker & Katz, 2002). Last, "blue-ribbon commissions are usually comprehensive in scope, addressing the full range of police issues, and not just a single problem" (Walker & Katz, 2002, p. 375). Special commissions also have a number of other advantages. They are typically well publicized, and because of that publicity, serve to place tremendous pressure on police to begin making reforms. Also, these types of commissions have had some success in breaking the "code of silence" and convincing police officers to offer testimony about the nature and extent of the problem. Frank Serpico's testimony before the Knapp Commission and Michael Dowd's testimony before the Mollen Commission are excellent examples of this point.

Special commissions also have disadvantages. First, these types of investigations are entirely reactive, formed *after* the misconduct has occurred. Moreover, typically the misconduct is either widespread and/or has erupted because of a publicized scandal before such a commission will be formed. In some cases, commissions have subpoena power, but often it is difficult to persuade police officers to testify during the hearing. And, of course, those called before the commission may assert their Fifth Amendment protection against self-incrimination. Also, in many cases, the special commissions can only make recommendations about reforms and have no power to require the changes to be made. Police departments can ignore the recommendations of the commission, although doing so may put them at risk of civil liability and result in substantial harm to police–community relations.

The Major Blue-Ribbon Commissions. *The Early Commissions Investigating the NYPD* A number of special commissions were formed throughout the late nineteenth and early twentieth centuries to investigate allegations of police misconduct by New York City police officers. As mentioned above, the Lexow Committee was formed in 1894 and heard testimony from nearly 700 witnesses (Kappeler et al., 1998). The Committee found that police officers routinely took payoffs and that "virtually every policeman in the department believed that payoffs were a [prerequisite] of police work" (Kappeler et al., 1998, p. 175). Less than twenty years later, another commission—the Curran Commission—also found corruption, payoffs, and protection of illegal enterprises to be widespread and systematic (Kappeler et al., 1998). In 1932, the Seabury Committee concluded that officers in the NYPD were receiving hundreds of thousands of dollars per year for protection of illegitimate businesses (i.e., gambling operations) and that vice squad officers were framing women for prostitution because they received a cut of the money paid by the women to bondsmen and lawyers (Fogelson, 1977).

The Wickersham Commission (1931) In response to the crime and social problems that arose during the Great Depression and Prohibition, in 1929 President Herbert Hoover formed the **Wickersham Commission,** formally called the National Commission on Law Observance and Enforcement. In 1931, the Wickersham Commission released a total of fourteen volumes that investigated social and crime problems and the criminal justice response to those problems (Grant & Terry, 2005). The Commission addressed a number of issues involving the police, but none received more scrutiny or drew more public outcry than the use of the "third degree." The Commission defined the third degree as "the inflicting of pain, physical or mental, to extract confessions or statements" and concluded that the practice was widespread throughout police departments in the United States (National Commission on Law Observance and Enforcement, 1931). Although there were numerous instances of physical torture, techniques that wore down the resistance of suspects were more common and just as troubling to the Commission. These techniques included long periods of questioning without breaks, withholding food and water, and using hot lights (Skolnick & Fyfe, 1993). The Commission also concluded that suspects were routinely held illegally and were denied access to lawyers and that corruption was widespread in many police departments.

The impact of the Wickersham Commission report was immediate. The report served to galvanize the police reformers of the professional movement, such as August Vollmer and Raymond Fosdick. Shortly after the Commission's report, appellate courts began excluding confessions that were obtained through use of the third degree, and in 1936, the U.S. Supreme Court in *Brown v. Mississippi* (207 U.S. 278 [1936]) excluded a coerced confession (Skolnick & Fyfe, 1993).

The Kerner Commission (1968)   Following the riots across U.S. cities during the 1960s, President Lyndon Johnson formed the National Advisory Commission on Civil Disorders—the **Kerner Commission**—to investigate the causes of the civil disturbances. In its report, issued in 1968, the Commission found that the causes of the riots were numerous and included larger societal issues such as prejudice, discrimination, inadequate social services, and unequal justice, but the Commission also noted that the police—and poor police–community relations—were a contributing factor. The Commission found that there was a "deep hostility between police and ghetto communities," and that several of the riots were sparked by police–citizen encounters (National Advisory Commission on Civil Disorders, 1968). The Commission highlighted a number of problem areas for the police that contributed to this hostility, including aggressive police tactics that targeted minority communities, brutal and abusive conduct by police, poor training and supervision of police, poor police–community relations and no effort by police to address this, and failure by police to hire minority police officers.

The Knapp Commission (1972)   In the mid-1960s, Frank Serpico—a five-year veteran of the NYPD—was transferred to a plainclothes unit in the Bronx responsible for enforcing gambling laws. Serpico quickly learned that little enforcement was being done and that officers in plainclothes units "throughout the city took part in long-established deals with gamblers in which, in return for a regular monthly payment, gambling operations . . . would continue unmolested" (Skolnick & Fyfe, 1993, p. 178). For nearly five years, Serpico refused to take the payoffs and tried to draw the attention of the police and city administration. Although he reached as far as the mayor's office, the corruption continued and Serpico finally contacted David Burnham, a reporter for the *New York Times* (Skolnick & Fyfe, 1993).

In the wake of the front-page story and resulting public pressure, Mayor John V. Lindsay appointed the **Knapp Commission** to investigate police misconduct. The Knapp Commission hearings were televised live, and Serpico—as well as other police officers—testified about the nature and extent of corruption (Al Pacino portrayed Frank Serpico in the movie *Serpico*). The Knapp Commission report concluded that corruption pervaded all levels of the NYPD and that the existing system of supervision and accountability was inadequate (Knapp Commission, 1972). Importantly, the Knapp report also dismissed the rotten apple theory of corruption and distinguished between "grass-eaters"—those who passively accept corruption or who know about it and do nothing—and "meat eaters"—those who aggressively seek out corruption. At the same time, Mayor Lindsay appointed Patrick Murphy as Police Commissioner, who immediately initiated a wide range of reforms that successfully reduced corruption and professionalized the NYPD.

The MOVE Commission   MOVE was a militant, revolutionary group created in Philadelphia during the early 1970s. The members of MOVE lived in a row-house, and their beliefs and lifestyle lead to numerous complaints by neighbors and confrontations with police. Although there were dozens of confrontations between MOVE and the police, including a standoff in 1978 that lasted more than 50 days and resulted in one police officer being killed, things came to a head in May 1985. In the early morning hours of May 13th, police officers raided the MOVE house with the intention of forcibly evicting the group. After an initial raid failed, nearly 500 police officers at the scene fired more than 10,000 rounds at the house, which had been heavily fortified. As the standoff continued throughout the day, the Police Commissioner approved a plan to use a state police helicopter to drop an incendiary device on the roof of the house to destroy a rooftop bunker and create an opening in which the police could fire tear gas. The explosion caused by the device immediately caused a fire that quickly spread to nearby houses. At the order of the Police Commissioner, the Fire Department did not attempt to put out the fire for nearly an hour. The fire quickly grew out of control, and by night's end, 61 homes had been destroyed (an entire city block), and 11 MOVE members died in the fire, including five children.

In the days following the incident, Mayor Wilson Goode appointed the Philadelphia Special Investigation Commission (**MOVE Commission**) to investigate the incident. The Commission heard testimony from a wide range of witnesses as well as the Fire Commissioner, Police Commissioner, and Mayor. Nearly six months later, the MOVE Commission issued its report and concluded:

- The barrage of 10,000 rounds was "excessive and unreasonable."
- Several police officers had observed MOVE members placing cans of gasoline on the roof in the days leading to the bombing, and the Mayor was aware of this fact.
- Once the fired started, the Fire Department could have quickly put out the fire. However, the Police Commissioner's decision to "let it burn" to force out the MOVE members was "unconscionable."

- At least two adults and four children tried to flee the MOVE house but were forced back into the burning house by police gunfire.
- Officers in the bomb disposal unit were not properly trained.
- The mayor was "grossly negligent" in his decisions and "failed to perform his responsibility as the city's chief executive by not actively participating in the preparation, review and oversight of the plan." (Philadelphia Special Investigation Commission, 1986)

In the wake of the MOVE hearings, both the Police and Fire Commissioners lost their jobs, and the mayor lost his reelection bid. The surviving MOVE members—including one woman and child who escaped the fire—sued the police department and city and were awarded $1.5 million. The city also rebuilt the entire city block at a cost of nearly $14 million.

The Mollen Commission   Nearly twenty years after the Knapp Commission, the NYPD again became involved in a widely publicized misconduct scandal. Following the arrest of six officers on drug charges, the Mollen Commission was created to investigate the misconduct. The **Mollen Commission** heard testimony from a number of witnesses, but no testimony was more disturbing than that of Michael Dowd, one of the arrested police officers. Dowd detailed incidents of beating drug dealers, stealing their drugs and money, selling drugs to other dealers and officers, and even using drugs while on duty—Dowd stated he snorted cocaine off the dashboard of his police car (Walker & Katz, 2002). The Mollen Commission found a link between corruption and brutality, mostly involving drug-related misconduct. The Commission concluded that the misconduct was able to occur over an extended period of time because of the strong code of silence that existed among the rank and file (reluctance to turn in a fellow officer), because the systems of accountability were inadequate, and because the department management did not thoroughly investigate complaints because they feared bad publicity from another scandal (Mollen Commission, 1994; Walker & Katz, 2002). Barker (2002, p. 8) notes, however, that unlike the widespread misconduct detailed in the Knapp Commission report, the deviance uncovered by the Mollen Commission was not systemic and was limited to "small groups of rotten apples."

The Christopher Commission   Following the beating of Rodney King, the Independent Commission on the Los Angeles Police Department—otherwise known as the **Christopher Commission**—was formed to examine the LAPD, its crime-fighting efforts, and its relationship with the community, especially the minority community. The Commission found evidence that racism and bias pervaded the LAPD (Independent Commission on the Los Angeles Police Department, 1991). The Commission reviewed 180 days of computer-based communications among officers (sent to and from officers in their cars on patrol and at station houses) and discovered a large number of messages containing offensive racial slurs and discussions of use of force. A survey of 960 police officers conducted by the Commission found that about one-quarter of responding officers agreed with the statement that "racial bias (prejudice) on the part of officers toward minority citizens currently exists and contributes to a negative interaction between police and community" (Independent Commission on the Los Angeles Police Department, 1992, p. xii). The Christopher Commission also (Independent Commission on the Los Angeles Police Department, 1991) identified a group of 44 officers who were disproportionately involved in excessive force incidents. The Christopher Commission concluded that there was a lack of accountability within the department and to the community and suggested that significant reforms were needed in management, structure, and recruitment to address the problems.

U.S. Department of Justice Consent Decrees

A **consent decree** is "an enforceable agreement reached between two parties involved in a lawsuit" (Ortiz, 2005, p. 93). The negotiation of the consent decree involves both parties in the suit, is approved by an officer of the court, and is binding and serves to settle the claim (Ortiz, 2005). If the party initially being sued complies with the consent decree, that party can then appeal to the court to have the decree dissolved; if the party fails to comply with the decree, the other party can appeal to the court for reinstatement of the original lawsuit (Ortiz, 2005).

Consent decrees have been used to settle disputes in a wide range of areas, especially conflicts arising between private companies and local governments (i.e., health care issues, pollution, etc.) (Ortiz, 2005). They have also been used to resolve disputes in criminal justice for some time, most notably claims related to treatment of prisoners. During the 1970s, consent decrees were used to settle a number of civil cases involving discriminatory hiring practices by police departments (Ortiz, 2005). The consent decrees typically required police departments to meet minority and female quotas for new recruits. For example, in 1975 the Milwaukee Police Department was placed under a consent decree requiring that 40 percent of new recruits be minority and 20 percent be female (Ortiz, 2005).

Pattern and Practice Lawsuits. The 1994 Violent Crime Control Act includes a section that allows the Civil Rights Division of the U.S. Department of Justice to bring lawsuits against police departments where there is a "pattern or practice" of abuse of citizens' rights (Walker & Katz, 2002). This section greatly expanded the use of consent decrees and allows their use as a mechanism for initiating police reform and accountability. Importantly, the Civil Rights Division is not filing suit to seek money from the police department. Instead, the government uses the **pattern and practice suit** to require court-ordered changes in police practices and management. Since the passage of the Violent Crime Control Act in 1994, the Civil Rights Division has begun fourteen "pattern and practice" investigations (Ortiz, 2005). By 2003, six investigations had been completed, resulting in five consent decrees and one memorandum of understanding.

Consent decrees have been put in place in Steubenville, Ohio; Pittsburgh, Pennsylvania; New Jersey (State Police); Los Angeles; and Detroit. The lawsuit against Columbus, Ohio, was dropped after the city agreed to sign a memorandum of understanding with the Justice Department (Ortiz, 2005). Consent decrees have been targeted at several different types of police misconduct. Officers in the Pittsburgh Police Bureau, LAPD, and Steubenville Police Department were allegedly involved in a range of illegal activities including use of excessive force, false arrests, and illegal search and seizure (Ortiz, 2005). In several cases, the citizen complaint procedures were also targeted by the consent decree. The consent decree placed on the New Jersey State Police addressed racial profiling (see Chapter 9). Finally, the lawsuit against the Detroit Police Department produced two consent decrees, one involving use of force and the other involving the handling of prisoners (Ortiz, 2005).

The requirements of consent decrees placed on these police departments are fairly similar and include required changes in a number of basic areas:

- Training: Cultural diversity, ethics and integrity, use of force, communication skills (de-escalating situations), leadership.
- Use of Force: Creation of a comprehensive use of force policy, use of force reporting system, and procedures for supervisory review of reports.
- Citizen Complaints: Creation of an open and restructured complaint filing process; allow complaints to be filed anonymously, by fax, email, phone, or third party; full investigations of all complaints in a timely manner.
- Early Warning System: Creation of a tracking system that identifies officers based on at-risk behavior; systems should include data on traffic stops, use of force, complaints, civil claims, arrests, searches, and personnel issues such as sick time, accidents, commendations, etc.
- Independent Monitor: Appointment of an independent authority to ensure that the department is meeting the requirements of the consent decree.

Consent Decrees as a Mechanism for Police Reform.   It is difficult to assess the impact of consent decrees as a vehicle for police accountability because only the Pittsburgh decree has reached completion (Ortiz, 2005). Nevertheless, early indicators suggest that departments have made significant strides toward complying with the requirements of the decrees. Ortiz (2005) argues that by the end of the decree "the Pittsburgh Police Bureau emerged as a national leader in personnel evaluation and monitoring, traffic stop data collection, and incident reporting policies" (p. 97). Similarly, the monitors involved in the consent decree against the New Jersey State Police note that the NJSP "have made significant strides to bring the organization into compliance with the requirements of [the] decree" (Lite, Greenberg, DePalma, Rivas, and Public Management Resources, 2001).

Yet, there are problems with relying on consent decrees as a form of police accountability. First, there is often a significant cost associated with implementing the changes required under the consent decree, such as data collection and creation of an early warning system (Ortiz, 2005). These costs can place tremendous pressure on police departments to meet their budgetary requirements. Second, being placed under a consent decree can have a serious negative impact on police officer morale and may even cause more tension between police and the community (i.e., from the negative national attention) (Ortiz, 2005).

Citizen Oversight

What Is Citizen Oversight?   Citizen oversight boards have emerged in recent years as a popular mechanism for maintaining police accountability. Walker (2001) defines **citizen oversight** as "a procedure for providing input into the complaint process by individuals who are not sworn officers" (p. 5). Although there are a variety of forms of citizen oversight (see below), the mechanism generally involves review of citizen complaints against the police by individuals who are outside of the police department. There is a long history of police problems in the area of receiving and investigating citizen complaints against individual police officers. For example, prior to taking his videotaped beating of Rodney King to the local television station, George Holliday first called the Foothill Station of the LAPD to offer the video to the police. The responding officer was not interested (Skolnick & Fyfe, 1993). The day after the beating, Paul King (Rodney's brother) walked into the same station to file a citizen complaint. He also was unsuccessful (Skolnick & Fyfe, 1993). The overall objective of citizen oversight is to "open up the historically closed complaints process, to break down the self-protective isolation of the police, and to provide an independent, citizen perspective on complaints" (Walker, 2001, p. 5). More specifically, citizen oversight boards have four goals: to deter future misconduct, to remove deviant officers, to satisfy individual complainants, and to improve and maintain public confidence in the police (Walker, 2001).

The History of Citizen Oversight.   Citizen oversight of the police has experienced significant growth recently. Currently, there are approximately 100 boards in the United States, and they are found in nearly 80 percent of big cities (Walker, 2001). However, the history of citizen oversight dates back to the early part of the twentieth century. Walker (2001) notes that the history of citizen oversight can be broken down into three distinct periods: the 1920s–1950s, when the idea first emerged; the late 1950s–1960s, when the idea became part of the demands of civil rights leaders; and the 1970s to present, when the mechanism has really taken hold. The idea of citizen oversight first appeared in 1928 in Los Angeles, when the local Bar Association created a committee of volunteers to receive and investigate citizen complaints against the police (Walker, 2001). In 1931, citizen oversight received a major boost when the Wickersham Commission (National Commission on Law Observance and Enforcement, 1931: 94) recommended the creation of a "disinterested agency" to handle citizen complaints. Following the second World War and the race riots of the early 1940s, there was a general push to improve police–community relations, and again, citizen oversight of police became a topic of discussion (Walker, 2001). Despite this shift in attitudes, early efforts at citizen oversight in Washington, DC, Philadelphia, and New York failed (Walker, 2001).

As discussed in other chapters, the police and their relationship to the community were identified as contributing factors in the racial tensions, riots, and disorder of the tumultuous 1960s. Civil rights leaders seized the idea of citizen oversight as a way to gain control of abusive police conduct. Their efforts were reinforced by the work of the President's Crime Commission (1967), which identified a number of problems in the training and supervision of police, and the Kerner Commission (National Advisory Commission on Civil Disorder, 1968), which again called for external review of complaints against police. Still, despite what appeared to be strong support for citizen oversight at the federal level, resistance by local police unions and departments, lack of legal standing, and lack of local political support hindered the spread of oversight boards.

Walker (2001) notes that two general shifts occurred during the 1970s and 1980s that allowed citizen oversight to re-emerge and gain popularity. First, the Watergate scandal and President Nixon's resignation significantly altered citizens' views of the importance of accountability (Walker, 2001). A number of other government-related scandals followed that served to reinforce the desire for control of government agencies (i.e., spying by the FBI, Iran-Contra, etc.) (Walker, 2001). Second, African Americans had begun to gain a larger voice in local politics, providing an important support base for citizen oversight of the police (Walker, 2001). As a result, citizen oversight boards were created, supported, and maintained in a growing number of cities, beginning with Kansas City, Berkeley (CA), Detroit, San Francisco, and Portland (Walker, 2001).

The Arguments For and Against Citizen Oversight.   Despite its recent growth, the idea of citizen oversight of the police is still quite controversial and the arguments for and against it are well defined. Walker (2001) succinctly summarizes the primary arguments among those on both sides of the issue. For proponents of citizen oversight, the need for outside review centers on the failure of police historically to objectively investigate themselves. The major arguments are:

- That police misconduct is a serious problem and internal police complaint procedures fail to address this problem.
- That citizen oversight will provide more thorough and fair investigation of complaints than those conducted by the police themselves.
- That citizen oversight agencies will sustain more complaints.
- That oversight agencies will result in more discipline of guilty officers.
- That more disciplinary actions will deter police misconduct more effectively than internal police procedures.
- That complaint review by oversight agencies will be perceived as independent and will provide greater satisfaction for complainants and also improve public attitudes about the police.
- That citizen oversight will help professionalize police departments and improve the quality of policing. (Walker, 2001, p. 12)

Those opposed to citizen oversight argue that it has historically failed to achieve its objectives, and in many cases, it has made things worse. The major arguments against citizen oversight are:

- That police misconduct is not as serious a problem as people allege.
- That police officers are capable of and do in fact conduct fair and thorough investigations.
- That police internal affairs units sustain a higher rate of complaints than do citizen oversight agencies.
- That police departments mete out tougher discipline than oversight agencies.
- That internal police disciplinary procedures deter police misconduct more effectively than oversight agencies.
- That internal police disciplinary procedures provide greater satisfaction to complainants and the general public.
- That external citizen oversight agencies harm policing by deterring effective crimefighting by police officers and also by undermining the managerial authority of police chief executives. (Walker, 2001, p. 12)

Many of the arguments on both sides of the issue would appear to have merit. For example, based on the long history of police misconduct and the traditional problems police have experienced in investigating themselves, a strong argument can be made in favor of citizen oversight. Yet, in the history of citizen oversight, the successes have been relatively few, with far more examples of failure. Moreover, there is no cookie-cutter approach to citizen oversight (see below), and the prospects for success would appear to be greatest when the police and community develop a plan together that best meets their local needs.

The Four Models of Citizen Oversight. Citizen oversight boards are organized in different ways, with varying degrees of independence from the police department (Walker, 2001). Boards have varied on at least four important characteristics: (1) who is responsible for the initial investigation and fact-finding, citizens or police; (2) who reviews the completed report, a hearing officer, the board or a police official; (3) the right of the complainant to appeal; and (4) who imposes the discipline on the officer (Skolnick & Fyfe, 1993).

Walker (2001) identifies four different classes of citizen oversight based on the degree of structural independence. Although there is tremendous variation within the four classes, these broad categories help flesh out the different approaches that have developed over time and location.

- *Class I* boards have the greatest degree of independence from police. Citizens file their complaints at the board office, which is physically removed from the police department. The board, which is composed of citizens, then conducts the investigation, and upon completion, makes recommendations to the police department. Examples include the Minneapolis Civilian Review Authority (CRA) and the San Francisco Office of Citizen Complaints (OCC).

- *Class II* boards typically receive the complaint at a location removed from the police department, but the complaint is then forwarded to the police, who then conduct the investigation. Once the fact-finding is done, the investigation is sent back to the board for review. The board then makes a recommendation to the police chief. The Kansas City Office of Citizen Complaints (OCC) is an example of a Class II board.
- *Class III* boards function as appellate review. The police department receives the complaint, conducts the investigation, and makes a final disposition of the complaint. If the citizen is unhappy with the outcome, he or she can then appeal the decision to the board. The board will then review the investigation and can either agree or disagree with the police finding. The board can refer the case back to the police department for further investigation. The Omaha Citizen Review Board is an example of a Class III board.
- *Class IV* boards function as an auditor system. The board does not receive or investigate complaints; those responsibilities are left to the police department. Rather, the agency has the authority to review, monitor, and audit the police department's complaint process. San Jose, the Los Angeles Sheriff, and Portland (OR) all have Class IV or auditor systems. (Walker, 2001, p. 62)

The Impact of Citizen Oversight.   Research on the impact of citizen oversight of the police is mixed, with some very clear success stories and even more clear failures (Walker, 2001). Historically, the early boards in Philadelphia, Washington, DC, New York, and Detroit failed. The efforts to evaluate the impact of citizen oversight boards have been plagued with a number of other problems. First, citizen oversight has suffered from unrealistic expectations. In many places, the mechanism was expected to immediately improve police–community relations and to be widely accepted by both parties. This has not been the case. Second, efforts to evaluate citizen oversight have overemphasized the **sustain rate** as a measure of success (i.e., what percentage of citizen complaints are found to be proven). Unfortunately, the vast majority of complaints cannot be sustained because the officer and complainant are often the only ones present during the incident, and the complaints boil down to "he said–she said" (Skolnick & Fyfe, 1993). Walker (2001) adds that there is no widely accepted "goal sustain rate," and there are a number of serious problems with the reporting and recording of complaint data that seriously undermine the sustain rate as a measure of success.

Yet, there are numerous examples where evaluations have demonstrated that citizen oversight has been successful. Walker (2001) notes that successful review boards "take a proactive view of their role and actively seek out the underlying causes of police misconduct. . . ." (p. 15) The successful boards also seek to institute organizational reform, rather than simply receiving and investigating complaints (Walker, 2001). For example, in San Jose, the Independent Auditor made 40 policy recommendations from 1993–1999, and 38 were adopted by the San Jose Police Department. Similar success has been witnessed in Portland, Oregon, Los Angeles (Sheriff's Department), and Minneapolis (Walker, 2001). However, there is no research that compares specific citizen oversight boards to internal affairs units or that compares the different types of citizen oversight systems (Walker, 2001). Until that research is conducted, the true impact of citizen oversight will remain unknown.

Finally, although most scholars and practitioners acknowledge that citizen oversight is not a panacea and will not put an end to police misconduct, there is consensus regarding some key elements that must be present to at least insure the possibility of success. According to Skolnick and Fyfe (1993) these core elements include:

1. A fully functioning civilian review agency needs to investigate complaints, conduct hearings, subpoena witnesses, and report its findings to the police chief and public.
2. Inadequate financing will devastate any system.
3. Civilian review agencies need to be staffed by competent, well-trained investigators who have the authority and the financial backing to carry out investigations.
4. It is simply not possible to have fair and effective civilian review when the hearing officers or panels are biased or less than competent. . . . Cops won't ever like civilian review, but they—and the public—are likely to find it more acceptable when investigations and hearings are conducted not by "representative" persons but by hardnosed, experienced investigators and fair and qualified hearing officers.
5. If a civilian review agency is to work effectively, without unreasonable delay, the oversight system must be afforded access to police witnesses and documents through legal mandate or subpoena power.
6. Both the accuser and the accused are entitled to know the outcome of the hearing and the reasons for the result. (pp. 227–228)

Finally, and this is the central theme of the last two chapters, citizen oversight should play a part in an overall system of accountability. To expect citizen oversight to by itself effectively eliminate police misconduct is unrealistic. Chances for success in combating police deviance increase considerably when a police department and community create a comprehensive package of accountability measures that includes a citizen oversight mechanism.

Public Interest Groups, the Media, and the Public

Public Interest Groups. There are a number of public interest groups that monitor police behavior and take action when misconduct is alleged. Both the American Civil Liberties Union (ACLU) and the National Association for the Advancement of Colored People (NAACP) have long histories of responding to police misconduct (Walker & Katz, 2002). The ACLU has played an especially important role, as a number of the organization's briefs have been the basis for groundbreaking U.S. Supreme Court cases (Walker & Katz, 2002). In 2004, Amnesty International issued a report on police use of the Taser and called for a moratorium on its use. Shortly thereafter, both the U.S. Department of Justice and the International Association of Chiefs of Police launched investigations into the Taser's use and potential to cause harm.

The Media and the Public.   Walker and Katz (2002) note that the media play an important role in police accountability. The television and print media report on police activity on a daily basis, keeping the public informed of police behavior. Crime and police investigations are often lead or front page stories. Kappeler et al. (1998) note that the news media played an important role in facilitating interest in reforming the police at the start of the twentieth century for this same reason: News stories about crime and the police generated interest in the police, uncovered problems, and provided an impetus for reform. Media coverage continues to serve this function today, as is often illustrated on the West Coast with the occasional high-speed chase that is captured live by television helicopters. Finally, in this role, the media can play an important part in exposing police misconduct. David Burnham's story in the *New York Times* led to one of the biggest scandals in NYPD history. Burnham's story led to the creation of the Knapp Commission and the appointment of Patrick Murphy as Commissioner, who then instituted dramatic reforms in the department. More than twenty years later, when the LAPD showed no interest in his videotape of the Rodney King beating, George Holliday delivered the tape to a local television station. By the next day, television media were showing the beating of Rodney King across the globe.

Ultimately, the police are accountable to the public they serve, and the public plays an important role in police accountability. As the public is kept informed by the media, the residents of a community have the ability to take action and demand change. Citizens and citizen groups can place pressure on police departments to initiate reforms, and just as importantly, the public can apply pressure on public officials in the city administration, such as the mayor and district attorney. As elected officials, mayors and DAs are hard-pressed to ignore citizen calls for reform without jeopardizing their political careers. Elected officials can initiate police reforms by replacing the police chief, setting up citizen review boards, creating blue-ribbon commissions, and aggressively investigating and prosecuting police misconduct.

However, there are limitations to the public and the media as initiators of police reform. Both tend to have short attention spans and to focus only on the most egregious cases (Walker & Katz, 2002). The media, in particular, often will cover only the most dramatic aspects of a scandal, such as focusing on those who become scapegoats (Walker & Katz, 2002). Highly publicized scandals will often produce extreme responses that may overshadow the root causes of the problem. For example, in the wake of a scandal, a police chief may get fired, and that will be the lead story on the news and in the newspaper. However, there will be little focus on the root causes of the problem before the media has moved on to the next big story.

SUMMARY

This chapter reviews the major external mechanisms for controlling police misconduct, including criminal prosecution (state and federal); civil litigation; judicial intervention; U.S. Department of Justice consent decrees; special commissions; citizen oversight; and the public, public interest groups, and the media. Each mechanism is described in terms of its historical context, its theoretical and practical foundations, its advantages and disadvantages, and examples of how it has been used over the past few years. Although each method of accountability has its advantages, criminal prosecution and judicial intervention seem to be the most limited in terms of their potential impact. Consent decrees, special commissions, civil litigation, and citizen oversight appear to hold the most promise as formidable external controls. Much like the discussion in the earlier chapter on internal mechanisms, the most promising approach for a police department appears to involve building an interrelated collection of accountability measures, both internal and external. Given the long history of police misconduct and the traditional failure of police departments to police themselves, these external elements represent a critical feature of police accountability that can have a significant impact on the public confidence in their police department.

KEY TERMS

Christopher Commission
Citizen oversight
Civil litigation
Civil Rights Act of 1871 (Section 1983)
Civil Rights Division, U.S. Department
of Justice
Consent decree
Due process revolution
Injunction
Kerner Commission

Knapp Commission
Mollen Commission
Monell v. Department of Social Services
of the City of New York
MOVE Commission
Pattern and practice suit
Special investigations
Sustain rate
Tort
Wickersham Commission

DISCUSSION QUESTIONS

1. Describe why the criminal law is not seen as an effective control of police officer behavior.

2. Why is the *Monell v. Department of Social Services of the City of New York* case important for controlling police officer misconduct?

3. What is a consent decree? Describe how they can be used to control police officer behavior.

4. Describe Walker's four classes of citizen oversight systems.

5. What are the main arguments for and against citizen oversight?

6. Explain how the courts have been used to control police officer behavior.

REFERENCES

Barker, T. (2002). Ethical police behavior. In K.M. Lersch (Ed.), *Policing and misconduct*. Upper Saddle River, NJ: Prentice-Hall.

Brown v. Mississippi, 207 U.S. 278 (1936).

Cassell, P.G., & Hayman, B.S. (1996). Police interrogations in the 1990s: An empirical study of the effects of Miranda. *UCLA Law Review, 43,* 860.

COPPAR v. Rizzo, 357 F. Supp. at 1319 (1973).

del Carmen, R.V., & Smith, M.R. (1997). Police, civil liability, and the law. In R.G. Dunham & G.P. Alpert (Eds.), *Critical issues in policing: Contemporary readings* (3rd ed.). Prospect Heights, IL: Waveland Press.

Epke, J., & Davis, L. (1991). Civil rights cases and police misconduct. *FBI Law Enforcement Bulletin, 60,* 15.

Fogelson, R.M. (1977) *Big-city police.* Cambridge, MA: Harvard University Press.

Fyfe, J.J. (1988). Police use of deadly force: Research and reform. *Justice Quarterly, 5,* 165–205.

Grant, H., & Terry, K.J. (2005). *Law enforcement in the 21st century.* Boston: Allyn and Bacon.

Independent Commission on the Los Angeles Police Department. (1991). *Report of the independent commission on the Los Angeles Police Department.* Los Angeles: Author.

International Association of Chiefs of Police (IACP). (1976). *Survey of police misconduct litigation, 1967–1976.* Fairfax, VA: Author.

Kappeler, V.E. (2001). *Critical issues in police civil liability* (3rd ed.). Prospect Heights, IL: Waveland Press.

Kappeler, V.E., Sluder, R.D., & Alpert, G.P. (1998). *Forces of deviance: Understanding the dark side of policing.* Prospect Heights, IL: Waveland Press.

Knapp Commission report on police corruption. (1972). New York: George Braziller.

Leo, R.A. (1996). Inside the interrogation room. *Journal of Criminal Law and Criminology, 86* (2), 266–303.

Lite, A.Z., Greenberg, B.D., DePalma, J.J., Rivas, A., and Public Management Resources (2001). *New Jersey monitors' fourth quarterly report.* Available: www.state.nj.us/lps/monitors_report_4.pdf, accessed June 17, 2005.

Littlejohn, E.J. (1981). Civil liability and the police officer: The need for new deterrents to police misconduct. *University of Detroit Journal of Urban Law, 58,* 365–431.

Lyons v. Los Angeles, 461 U.S. 95 (1983).

Mapp v. Ohio, 367 U.S. 643 (1961).

McCoy, C. (1984, January-February). Lawsuits against police: What impact do they really have? *Criminal Law Bulletin,* 53.

Miranda v. Arizona, 384 U.S. 436 (1966).

Mollen Commission. (1994). *The City of New York commission to investigate allegations of police corruption and the anti-corruption procedures of the police department: Commission report.* New York: City of New York.

Monell v. Department of Social Services of the City of New York, 436 U.S. 658 (1978).

Monroe v. Pape, 365 U.S. 167 (1961).

National Advisory Commission on Civil Disorder [Kerner Commission]. (1968). *Report of the National Advisory Commission on Civil Disorder.* Washington, DC: U.S. Government Printing Office.

National Commission on Law Observance and Enforcement [Wickersham Report]. (1931). *Report on lawlessness in law enforcement.* Washington, DC: U.S. Government Printing Office.

Ortiz, C. (2005). Consent decrees. In L.E. Sullivan & M.S. Rosen (Eds.), *Encyclopedia of Law Enforcement, Volume 1.* Thousand Oaks, CA: Sage Publications.

Philadelphia Special Investigation Commission. (1986). *The MOVE commission report.* Philadelphia: Author.

President's Commission on Law Enforcement and Administration of Justice. (1967). *Task force report: The police.* Washington, DC: Government Printing Office.

Rizzo v. Goode, 423 U.S. 362, 368–69 (1976).

Robinson, C.D. (1984). *Legal rights, duties and liabilities of criminal justice personnel.* Springfield, IL: Charles C. Thomas.

Sherman, L.W. (1992). *Policing domestic violence: Experiments and dilemmas.* New York: The Free Press.

Silver, I. (2000). *Police civil liability.* New York: Matthew Bender.

Skolnick, J.H., & Fyfe, J.J. (1993). *Above the law: Police and the excessive use of force.* New York: Free Press.

Special Counsel to the Los Angeles Sheriff's Department. (2000). *11th semi-annual report.* Los Angeles: Los Angeles County.

Terry v. Ohio, 392 U.S. 1 (1968).

Tennenbaum, A.N. (1994). The influence of the *Garner* decision on police use of deadly force. *Journal of Criminal Law and Criminology, 85,* 241–260.

Tennessee v. Garner, 471 U.S. 1 (1985).

Thurman v. Torrington, 595 F. Supp. 1521 (1984).

Thomas v. County of Los Angeles, No 91-56047 (9th Cir. 1991).

U.S. Civil Rights Commission. (1981). *Who is guarding the guardians?* Washington, DC: U.S. Government Printing Office.

Walker, S. (2001). *Police accountability: The role of citizen oversight.* Belmont, CA: Wadsworth.

Walker, S., & Katz, C.M. (2002). *The police in America: An introduction.* New York: McGraw-Hill.

West v. Atkins, 487 U.S. 42 (1988).

White, M.D. (1999). *Police shootings in Philadelphia: An analysis of two decades of deadly force.* Ph.D. dissertation. Temple University (Ann Arbor, MI: University Microfilms).

Wrobleski, H.M., & Hess, K.M. (2003). *Introduction to law enforcement and criminal justice* (7th ed.). Belmont, CA: Wadsworth.

■ ■ ■ ■ ■

SCHOLAR'S PERSPECTIVE

Supercession of the Camden, New Jersey Police Department

CARMEN V. LABRUNO, CHIEF*

HOBOKEN (NJ) POLICE DEPARTMENT

CAMDEN CITY

The city of Camden is located in southern New Jersey directly across from Philadelphia, Pennsylvania. It has a land area of 8.82 square miles and a resident population of approximately 80,000. A city of diverse cultures, it is predominantly African American and Hispanic with a 16 percent minority Caucasian population. The 2000 census reports the per capita income at $9,815 with approximately 35.5 percent of its residents in poverty status. It is the poorest city in the state of New Jersey and has been ranked as the fifth poorest city in the United States. The unemployment rate is in the high teens and the 2000 census has listed the median income of Camden at $24,612. Forty-nine percent of the population 25 years and older have less than a high school education and only 5.4 percent report having a bachelor's degree or higher. There are 29,769 housing units in Camden with a median value of $40,700 for owner-occupied units. One in eleven people in Camden will be a crime victim, and the 2003 and 2004 crime statistics have earned it the most dangerous city in the United States status. In 2004 the city averaged 102 nonviolent and 35 violent crimes per week. The city is governed by the Faulkner Act and elects a mayor and city council. Three of the past five mayors have been convicted of crimes ranging from embezzlement to laundering drug money and taking bribes.

CAMDEN CITY POLICE DEPARTMENT

The Camden Police Department is arguably the most studied police department in the state of New Jersey. The 2004 Uniform Crime Reports list the Camden police strength at 428 sworn police officers and 83 civilian employees. The city of Camden is divided into four geographic police districts based on size and crime statistics. Since 1987, the Camden Police Department has been subjected to four major management studies. The most recent study occurred in June 2002, which was preceded by studies in November 1998, March 1996, and the spring of 1987. A common theme

*Chief, Hoboken (NJ) Police Department. Ph.D. Graduate Center, City University of New York.

has triggered these studies—management failure to execute a plan to provide for the safety and security of the residents and visitors of Camden. Each study resulted in varying degrees of outside intervention and monitoring of the police department. For example, in 1987 the Attorney General assigned one of his senior employees as a police director to oversee the management and reorganization of the police department as well as the selection of a new police chief. The 1996 management study was in part a response to the alarmingly high statistics for crime, ranking Camden as having the highest number of index crimes per 1,000 population and the highest number of index crimes per police officer of the major urban cities in New Jersey. The 1998 management study was a follow-up of the 1996 study and came about as a result of public outcry over crime and the fear of crime in Camden. The number of crimes (Crime Index) was at 9,136 in 1997 and it was obvious to the Attorney General that the executive officer of the Camden Police Department failed to implement the recommended action plans of 1987 and 1996.

Additionally, the chief executive officer failed to comply with New Jersey State Department of Personnel hiring and promotion practices, and the Camden mayor had an unhealthy influence over the police department (he was subsequently indicted on 19 counts of political corruption and bribery and convicted). The new Attorney General appointed the Camden County Prosecutor as a "special monitor" over the police department. By 2002 the Camden Police Department was in a state of chaos, as virtually every aspect of the police department's operation was alleged to be mismanaged by the chief executive officer. A 2001 Office of Inspector General Audit Division report found the police department to be in material noncompliance with COPS grant requirements, expressing its frustration by citing as an example the Police Chief's inability to provide reliable budget and staffing data with respect to local funding and actual staffing of the police department.

The 2002 management study confirmed what most had suspected: Voluntary compliance was not working. The police department was not in compliance with the management studies of 1987, 1996, and 1998. This study once again found every aspect of the police operation deficient (it did cite an improvement of the 500 case backlog of Internal Affairs). Examples supporting the study's findings were the fact that 24 of the 41 communication officers were not certified; patrol deployment was inconsistent with criminal activity; 40 percent of the motor fleet was unavailable due to prolonged maintenance problems; General Orders did not exist to implement Attorney General–mandated procedures; and there was an almost complete absence of a working relationship between the police department and the city government. Additionally, it was revealed that the Chief of Police did not share the findings of the previous studies with his senior staff.

In the first quarter of 2003 the new mayor suspended the Chief of Police with the intent to dismiss him, citing the police department's failure to make meaningful progress in areas of concern noted in the 2002 Attorney General's management study. An agreement was subsequently reached and the chief resigned his position. The mayor's concern was well founded, as the crime rate for 2003 earned Camden the dubious distinction as the nation's most dangerous city. In March 2003 the mayor called for the supercession of the Camden Police Department by the Camden County Prosecutor.

SUPERCESSION

A management team consisting of a representative of the Camden County Prosecutor's Office, a representative of city government, and a representative of the Attorney General's Office assumed command of the police department. One of their first actions was to appoint an acting police chief and place him on the management team. The management team examined the four previous management studies; conducted its own needs assessment; interviewed police officers, business members of the community, members of the clergy, and residents. The end result of this collaboration was an action plan consisting of eight-two "action points." The action plan addressed the needs of the police department in every area of operation, including but not limited to communications, internal affairs, information technology, property and evidence management, patrol deployment, records management, rules and regulations, organizational structure, training, and motor fleet operations. Within six months of the promulgation of the action plan, all but five action points were completed. In March 2004, one year after supercession, a reorganization of the Camden Police Department was implemented. The reorganization was designed to place more police officers on the street in places they are needed, at times they are needed, and in relative proportion to their need. The Camden Police Department for the first time was engaged in proactive policing from CompStat-type meetings to computer analysis of crime data patrol deployment. It was acknowledged that success would not come overnight. The new police chief has partnered with county, state, and federal law enforcement agencies, and a concerted law enforcement effort is underway.

With the realization of management commitment, complacency and resistance to change, once a concern of management, was not a factor. The hard-working police officers of the Camden Police Department have taken ownership of the blueprint for success action plan. Many of these officers were embarrassed, yearned for change, and had a desire to be recognized as a force committed to improving the quality of life for the citizens of Camden.

Supercession, while viewed by some as drastic, was necessary to put the full force and authority of the state government behind the reform effort. It is unfair to assign total blame of Camden's difficulties on the police department. City government failures, as well as social and economics factors have significantly contributed to the city's decline. While it is difficult to quantify a successful police department supercession, benchmarks for success are crime reduction, citizen perception of safety, stabilization of the community, command accountability, and the removal of supercession status. Internally, the police department has committed to decentralization, geographic accountability, "despecialization," and collaboration.

In early 2005 a blue-ribbon panel of distinguished experts from the police and academic community was established to act as an advisory board to the police department. The advisory panel was charged with oversight of the police department and the production of a best-practices white paper designed as a blueprint for future policing in Camden. This confluence of action has resulted in an increase in morale among the men and women of the police department, a realistic partnership with the community, a 45 percent reduction in the homicide rate and an overall 18 percent reduction in crime in the first ten months of 2005. The fight to regain the streets of Camden has begun. A comprehensive plan is in place; county, state, and federal law enforcement agencies have partnered with the police department; rank-and-file members of the department are committed; and citizens are empowered and want their neighborhoods returned to them. The days ahead will be difficult but the effort worthy; time will reveal the success of the undertaking.

BIBLIOGRAPHY

Camden County Prosecutor's Office (March 8, 2003). Press Release.
Camden County Prosecutor's Office (March 18, 2003). Press Release.
Camden County Prosecutor's Office (September 11, 2003). Press Release.
Camden County Prosecutor's Office (March 19, 2004). Press Release.
Figueroa, E. (Chief of Police, Camden Police Department). (2005, November 8). Personal communication.
Figueroa, E. (Chief of Police, Camden Police Department). (2005, November 13). Personal communication.
Fisher, W. (2005, November 22). Personal communication.
New Jersey Division of Criminal Justice. (1987). *A management study of the Camden Police Department*. Trenton: Author.
New Jersey Division of Criminal Justice. (1996). *A management study of the Camden Police Department*. Trenton: Author.
New Jersey Division of Criminal Justice. (1998). *A management study of the Camden Police Department*. Trenton: Author.
New Jersey Division of Criminal Justice. (2002). *A management study of the Camden Police Department*. Trenton: Author.
New Jersey Department of Law and Public Safety. (2003). *Crime in New Jersey, 2003*. Trenton: Author.
New Jersey Department of Law and Public Safety. (2004). *Crime in New Jersey, 2004*. Trenton: Author.
Saponare, A. (Chief of County Investigators). (2005, November 23). Personal communication.
U.S. Census Bureau. (2000) Summary File 3, Matrices P37, PCT25, P52, P53, P54, P79, P80, P81, PCT38, PCT40 and PCT 41. Washington, DC: U.S. Census Bureau.

■ ■ ■ ■ ■

CHAPTER 11

TECHNOLOGY AND THE POLICE

This book focuses on the many current issues and controversies in local U.S. law enforcement today. Also, one of the primary themes of the book involves the central importance of history for understanding and framing the discussion of today's issues. Perhaps nowhere is this more important than with the discussion of technology and its impact on U.S. policing. Quite simply, technology more than any other phenomena has been the driving force behind change and advancement in policing. While aspects of technological innovation have been addressed throughout the book, this chapter focuses on several areas of law enforcement where technology has been integral.

The chapter begins with a discussion of Soulliere's (1999) stages of technological advancement, which loosely correlate with Kelling and Moore's (1991) eras of policing (see Chapter 3). The chapter then focuses primarily on two areas of policing where technology has been particularly influential: the development of forensic science and its impact on crime scene investigation and advances in crime analysis. With regard to forensics and crime scene investigation, particular attention is given to basic principles (i.e., Locard principle), developments in fingerprinting and DNA, and biometrics. The chapter also briefly touches upon profiling according to physical behavior and psychological makeup. The main thrust of the discussion on crime analysis involves the use of GIS and crime mapping, as well as geographic profiling. A number of other technological innovations are described, including the changing role of computers, closed circuit television, GPS, and imaging. The overriding theme of the chapter is that technological innovation has played a critically important role in enhancing the ability of police to accomplish their objectives. As we continue to progress through the twenty-first century, the role of technology is certain to remain important.

STAGES OF TECHNOLOGICAL ADVANCEMENT

Chapter 3 traces the development of professional policing in the United States from the mid 1800s through the start of the 21st century. Soulliere (1999) views that development with a different lens—one that is useful for this chapter—and that lens involves the stages of technological advancement. Soulliere (1999) describes four different stages of technological developments: first stage (1881–1945), second stage (1946–1959), third stage (1960–1979), and the fourth stage (1980 – present).

The First Stage: 1881–1945

The first technological stage of policing encompasses two of the eras described by Kelling and Moore in Chapter 3: the political and reform eras (Grant & Terry, 2005). In terms of technological advancement, the first stage involves the transformation of the police officer from the lone cop on foot patrol, completely disconnected from headquarters and responding only to what he sees or is brought to his attention by passersby, to the professional yet isolated officer on routine automobile patrol waiting for calls for service to come in to dispatch. The three critical advances in this stage that form the foundation of the reactive, preventive patrol philosophy are the automobile, the two-way radio, and the telephone. This stage is also defined by the other elements of August Vollmer's professional model including the first crime laboratory, fingerprinting, handwriting analysis, and the polygraph. Souillere (1999) notes that these advances had a number of important effects on policing including:

- Increased specialization within the organization (leading to more complex organizations).
- Increased mobility for officers on patrol.
- Increased officer safety (through better communications systems). (Grant & Terry, 2005)

The Second Stage: 1946–1959

Soulliere's (1999) second stage of technological advancement is the relatively brief period immediately following World War II when police departments became increasingly bureaucratic, in large part because of the innovations during the first stage. Also, there were important technological advances during this stage involving traffic enforcement, including the first speeding measures and early tools to assess levels of intoxication. These measures were the predecessors to radar and other automobile surveillance tools, as well as blood-alcohol measuring devices (Grant & Terry, 2005).

The Third Stage: 1960–1979

During this third stage, technology revolutionized the way police departments carried out their daily business. During the early part of this stage, police departments were lagging behind the rest of society with regard to technology, a major finding highlighted in the President's Commission on Law Enforcement and the Administration of Justice (1967, p. 125):

> The police, with crime laboratories and radio networks, made early use of technology, but most police departments could have been equipped 30 or 40 years ago as well as

they are today. . . . Of all criminal justice agencies, the police have had the closest ties to science and technology, but they have called on scientific resources primarily to help in the solution of specific serious crimes, rather than for assistance in solving general problems of policing. (see also Grant & Terry, 2005)

Despite the slow start, technology—especially computers—quickly became central components of policing in the late 1960s and 1970s. Examples include: the creation of the first 911 system in 1968; calls for service distribution centers; computerized databanks for criminal histories, warrants, offenders, and automobiles; computer-aided dispatch (CAD).

The Fourth Stage: 1980–Present

Soulliere's (1999) fourth stage is characterized by the enhanced access and use of information. Advances in computer technology, facsimile, the Internet, and telecommunications helped police departments store enormous amounts of information and allowed individual police officers to use that information is nearly real-time. Advances in **forensic sciences** have also redefined police investigations, particularly developments in DNA, fingerprinting, and imaging. Many of these technological advances will be described later in this chapter, but the earlier discussion of Comp-Stat in Chapter 4 serves as an excellent example. The NYPD stores enormous amounts of information about police activities in a centralized database and uses that information to chart trends in crime and disorder. The department then realigns its deployment of resources to address the trends and problems identified through the **crime mapping** analysis. In July 2005, the NYPD announced the opening of its **Real Time Crime Center (RTCC).** The Center, staffed by 26 highly trained officers, offers real-time support to detectives and patrol officers investigating crimes. The Center accesses enormous amounts of data: 5 million New York state criminal records; 20 million New York City criminal complaints, summonses, and 311/911 calls; 31 million national crime records; and 33 billion public records (www.nyc.gov/html/nypd). When a crime occurs, the RTCC provides support to detectives through 911/311 call review, location analysis (mapping), victim analysis, crime pattern analysis, and offender analysis.

CRIME SCENE INVESTIGATION

As of the fall 2005 television season, there were three *CSI* shows—Las Vegas, Miami, and New York—as well as half a dozen others involving coroners, forensic anthropologists, and forensic scientists. The romanticized and sometimes inaccurate depiction of crime scene investigation on television has led to an entire generation of would-be forensic scientists through the so-called "CSI-effect" (see Professor Michael Hallett's scholarly perspective in Chapter 12). In the real world of policing, forensic science has led to a slower but equally important revolution in police investigations.

Historical Perspective

Despite recent technological advances, crime scene investigation is not new. There are verified records of **fingerprints** being used as marks of authenticity in China more than 2,000 years ago (Gaensslen & Young, 2003). In the late nineteenth century, **Alphonse Bertillon** developed a system of criminal identification based on head size, finger length, and several other characteristics. In 1894, Juan Vucetich, employed by a police department in Argentina, wrote a book about the value of fingerprints as a means of identification of criminal offenders (Gaensslen & Young, 2003). In 1910, Thomas Jennings was arrested, tried, and convicted of murder, and fingerprints were the primary evidence against him. The professional reform movement, led by August Vollmer and others, placed a premium of using scientific methods of crime detection. During his tenure as Chief of the Berkeley, California, Police Department, Vollmer hired a Bertillon expert, urged the U.S. Congress to mandate the FBI to create a national fingerprinting bureau, hired a biochemist to operate a crime laboratory, and began handwriting analysis. Clearly, the seeds for forensic and scientific crime scene investigation were laid well before the turn of the twenty-first century.

The Locard Principle and Physical Evidence

The foundation of crime scene investigation rests on a single theoretical principle, called the **Locard exchange principle.** The Locard exchange principle states that:

> . . . whenever two objects come into contact, a mutual exchange of matter will take place between them. Linking suspects to victims is the most important and common type of linkage accomplished by physical evidence in criminal investigations. Linking victims and suspects to objects and scenes can also be accomplished by use of the physical evidence. (Miller, 2003, p. 116)

In simple terms, the principle maintains that criminal offenders leave behind trace physical evidence at the scene of the crime, through contact with either the victim or objects at the scene. This physical evidence can be any number of things, depending on the nature of the crime. The most common types of physical evidence and techniques for collecting it are described in the following sections.

Fingerprints. When a person grasps an item with reasonable pressure, grease oozing out of the pores under the ridges leaves latent fingerprints. No two persons have the same fingerprints, which are a combination of many possible patterns (i.e., arches, loops, and whirls). As a result, fingerprints left at the scene, once collected, can be compared to other known samples of fingerprints in an effort to identify a match. The comparison samples of fingerprints come from a variety of sources. Television and movies have shown us how people who are arrested are fingerprinted with the old-fashioned black ink and paper. Also, people serving in certain occupations are also fingerprinted either as routine, or as part of a background check (military, federal employees, teachers, etc.). In the past, investigators matched paper fingerprint cards from evidence collected at a crime scene with the fingerprints of persons previously arrested. While fingerprints provide clear and convincing evidence when a match occurs, the manual process of comparing fingerprints was extremely laborious and time consuming.

However, technology has dramatically altered this fingerprint matching process. First, in many jurisdictions the ink and paper approach has been replaced by digitized systems that scan the prints and store them in a computer. In 2000, the FBI began using the **Integrated Automated Fingerprint Identification System (IAFIS),** a national database of nearly 40 million criminals' fingerprints and their criminal records (Champion & Hooper, 2003). Many states also operate their own automated fingerprint systems. These computerized fingerprint systems have revolutionized the utility of fingerprinting, as now a fingerprint collected at a crime scene can be entered in IAFIS and compared to 40 million other prints in a matter of hours (usually a two-hour turnaround), rather than weeks or months.

Blood, Saliva, Semen, Skin.   Technological advancements in the last twenty years have greatly expanded how police can use physical evidence in criminal investigations, and perhaps the most important advances have involved deoxyribonucleic acid—DNA. **DNA** is essentially a genetic fingerprint: No two people have the same (with the exception of identical twins). In the mid-1980s, forensic scientists developed and began to perfect a method for amplifying small amounts of DNA, called polymerase chain reaction, or PCR (Champion & Hooper, 2003). This technique allows scientists to compare DNA samples collected from crime scenes to other known DNA samples. DNA can be extracted from blood, hair, semen, and saliva, and advances in testing—single nucleotide polymorphism (SNP) analysis and mitochondrial DNA analysis—have increased the accuracy of DNA testing to over 95 percent. DNA testing gained worldwide attention as part of the O.J. Simpson murder trial in the early 1990s, where blood evidence at the scene linked Simpson to the crime: There was one chance in 240,000 that blood at the scene was NOT OJ's, and there was one chance in 1.2 million that blood in O.J.'s home was NOT his ex-wife's (the murder victim). Of course, O.J. Simpson was acquitted of all criminal charges, in large part because of problems in the chain of custody of the blood evidence (see below).

DNA evidence collected from a crime scene is not useful unless there are samples for comparison. As a result, the FBI developed and maintains a **Combined DNA Index System, or CODIS,** which became fully operation in 1998. By the start of 2001, CODIS held over 440,000 offender profiles, and the FBI estimated that the system would hold over one million by 2005 (Champion & Hooper, 2003). To determine whether physical evidence collected from a crime scene matches an existing offender, the crime laboratory technicians compare the collected sample to the database. Since the system is computerized, the matching process occurs very quickly. Of course, the testing helps the investigation only if there is a match, producing a known suspect. Nevertheless, each collected sample is entered in CODIS, and since federal law now allows police to take blood samples from convicted felons, CODIS is continually growing.

Weapon. Technology has also improved the ability of police to investigate crimes by linking weapons to crime scenes and individuals. Perhaps the best known field in this area is **ballistics,** which studies the motion of bullets. When a weapon is fired, the bullet picks up tiny imperfections of the bore of the gun that it passes through. Scratches are caused by the imperfections in the lands and grooves placed in the barrel at the time of manufacture and also through use. Experts can then determine if rounds are fired by the same gun by matching the imperfections on the round collected at the crime scene to other known samples (again, from databases created by states and the FBI such as IBIS, the Integrated Ballistics Identification System) (Grant & Terry, 2005). Class characteristics of a firearm can also be determined from expended cartridges (the part of the round that held the bullet and is expended from the gun after firing). These characteristics include caliber, shape of the firing pin, location of the firing pin, size of the firing pin, and size of extractors and ejectors (and the geometrical relationship between the two) (Rowe, 2003). Once the make and model of the firearm is determined, investigators can focus their search for that specific type of weapon.

A second area of weapon investigation involves **tool marks.** Rowe (2003) states that there are three types of tool marks: compression (indented), sliding, and cutting.

- Compression tool marks result when a tool is pressed into softer material. Such marks often show the outline of the working surface of the tool, so that class characteristics of the tool (such as dimensions) can be determined.
- Sliding tool marks are created when a tool slides along a surface; such marks usually consist of a pattern of parallel striations.
- Cutting tool marks are a combination of compression and sliding tool marks. The cutting tool indents the material being cut and, as it does so, the working surfaces of the tool slide over the cut surface. (pp. 349–350)

Once a tool mark has been documented and collected from a crime scene, the tool mark examiner in the laboratory compares the tool mark with tools collected at the crime scene. The tool mark examiner can use a tool collected at the crime scene to make a *test tool mark,* and then compare the test tool mark to the mark collected at the scene using a specialized microscope. This type of tool mark analysis can be used to identify weapons used in serious person crimes, but it is also quite useful in identifying tools used to commit break-ins and to crack safes (Rowe, 2003). Successful tool mark comparisons put investigators one step closer to the criminal by identifying a potential link between the offender and the crime scene (i.e., if it can be determined that the suspect owns or possessed the specific tool in question).

Other Developments in Forensic Science. Beyond the most common types of physical evidence and techniques to collect that evidence described above, technology has also led to the development of a wide range of new fields in forensic science. These include:

- *Forensic Pathology:* Study of the deceased through autopsy to determine cause of death; forensic pathologists, typically employed as coroners, also review witness statements, medical history, and examine the scene (in addition to autopsy) to determine cause of death (accident, suicide, or homicide).
- *Forensic Toxicology:* Examination of all aspects of toxicity that may have legal implications; three divisions of forensic toxicology are postmortem drug testing, workplace drug testing, and investigation (identification) of contraband materials.
- *Forensic Odontology:* Application of dentistry to the legal system via identification of individuals through comparison of unique features of teeth (victims to dental records) and comparison of bite mark patterns.
- *Forensic Anthropology:* Application of theory and methods of anthropology to forensic problems, most commonly involving the recovery and identification of human remains.
- *Forensic Taphonomy* and *Entomology:* Involves determining the history of a body after death (often for identifying the time of death); includes the death event, the interval of bone exposure through modification of soft tissue (decomposition), the potential interval of bone modification, and the point of body discovery. Forensic entomology involves the study of insect activity and death, particularly flies and beetles.
- *Recognition of Bloodstain Patterns:* Using knowledge about the biological and physical properties of blood to interpret bloodstain patterns—such as spatter, castoff, and transfer—at a crime scene and assist with reconstruction of the crime.
- *Microanalysis of Trace Evidence:* Microanalysis of minor components of some evidence collected at a crime scene, such as glass, fibers, paint, and soil. The purpose is to determine whether an association of persons, places, and things can be established (i.e., can fibers found on a suspect's coat be matched to carpet fibers in the victim's house).
- *Forensic Footwear Evidence:* As someone walks, his or her shoes track over a variety of surfaces, acquiring dust, dirt, grease, residue, oils, blood, and moisture. This material is then redeposited on subsequent surfaces that are walked upon. The contact between the shoe and the surface results in this transfer of materials, which can then be collected and compared to a suspect's shoes. Shoe impressions can also be analyzed and provide information regarding shoe type, shoe size, and gait characteristics (i.e., limp). A match between the collected footwear evidence and the suspect's footwear can prove that the suspect was at the crime scene. The FBI maintains a database of thousands of shoe designs.
- *Forensic Tire Impression and Tire Track Evidence:* Tire impressions or tire tracks at a crime scene can be compared to the tires on a suspect's vehicle, linking the suspect to the crime scene. Tire evidence typically is not definitive

about a specific vehicle; rather it helps identify a specific type of tire and vehicle, which can suggest the suspect's presence at the crime scene.

- *Document Examination:* Forensic document examination can involve a comparison of handwriting and signatures, typewriters and printing devices, alterations and obliterations to documents, counterfeiting, photocopies, rubber stamp impressions, inks, and paper.
- *Fire and Explosion Investigation:* Applying knowledge of fire, including chemistry and physics, to identify the origin and cause of a fire or explosion. Once origin and cause are identified, the fire or explosion is classified as one of the following: natural act (lightning), accidental, incendiary (intentional), or undetermined (cause unknown).
- *Vehicular Accident Reconstruction:* Applying laws of physics (Conservation of Momentum and Conservation of Energy), physical evidence, eyewitness testimony, and engineering knowledge to determine the nature and cause of automobile accidents. (James & Nordby, 2003)

Basic Procedures in Crime Scene Investigation

There are a number of well-established steps or procedures that, collectively, attempt to establish the physical link between the offender and the crime scene or victim. These include securing the scene, the crime scene survey (or walk-through), documentation, searching for evidence, collecting and preserving evidence, and crime scene reconstruction. A brief discussion of each step follows below (see James & Nordby, 2003, for a complete discussion).

Securing the Crime Scene.   The first responder to a crime scene, almost always a patrol officer, has a number of important responsibilities, such as assisting the victim (i.e., emergency medical treatment), searching for and arresting the offender, and detaining and questioning witnesses. Another critical responsibility involves securing the crime scene. Based on the Locard principle (described earlier), anyone who enters the crime scene will alter and contaminate it by leaving additional evidence unrelated to the crime or by destroying evidence resulting from the crime (Miller, 2003). Thus, it is critical for the first officer on scene to block off the crime scene and control access to it. All movements into the scene and alterations to it should be recorded in a security log, and the crime scene investigator should review the security of the scene once he or she arrives (Miller, 2003).

Crime Scene Survey (Walk-Through).   This stage represents the first examination of the crime scene by the investigator. Miller (2003) cites six objectives for a complete and accurate crime scene survey:

1. Begin to prepare a reconstruction theory (i.e., how it happened).
2. Note any transient evidence requiring immediate protection and processing.
3. Take precautions if weather conditions may change.

4. Note points of entry and exit to crime scene.
5. Record initial observations of who, what, where, when, and how.
6. Assess need for additional personnel, equipment, or other agencies.

Documentation.   The documentation stage is perhaps the most important step in crime scene investigation. Documentation involves creating a permanent record of the crime scene and physical evidence as it currently exists (Miller, 2003). Once evidence is collected and processed, this documentation will represent the only existing evidence of the state of the crime scene upon discovery. Thus, this step is the most time consuming and laborious. There are four major tasks at this stage:

1. Note-taking: Emphasis on notification information (i.e., how the crime was discovered, time, etc.), arrival information (i.e., time, who was present), scene description, victim description, and the crime scene team (i.e., times of arrival and assignments).
2. Videotaping: No narration; should include the scene itself, surroundings, and the victim's viewpoint.
3. Photographs: Provide a still pictorial record of the crime scene and physical evidence; every photo must be recorded in a photo log; photograph everything.
4. Sketching: Assignment of units of measurement or correct perspective to the crime scene and the physical evidence within the scene.

Searching for Evidence.   The investigators then engage in a thorough search for evidence throughout the crime scene. There are a variety of search patterns that can be used to ensure that the entire scene is covered, such as the link, grid, zone, wheel, and spiral. Once evidence is located, it should be marked so it can be collected once the search is complete. No evidence is collected at this stage (Miller, 2003).

Collecting and Preserving Evidence.   The fifth stage of crime scene investigation involves the collection and processing of evidence. Transient or fragile evidence should be collected first, and one person should be assigned as the evidence collector to ensure consistency (Miller, 2003). Each piece of evidence should be collected and placed in a primary container, and the primary container should be stored in a secondary container. Each piece of evidence should be packaged separately, clearly marked, and sealed. Once all of the evidence has been collected and sealed, it can be transported back to the crime lab for analysis. The preservation of evidence and clear documentation of its transport, including all who are in control of it, is absolutely critical for maintaining the integrity of the investigation. Once this **chain of custody** is broken, the physical evidence is contaminated, and the defense counsel can challenge the validity of the evidence in court. This is what occurred in the O.J. Simpson trial and likely led to his acquittal. The blood evidence was overwhelming (statistics described above), but because of problems with the crime scene, collection of evidence, and handling of evidence at the scene and at the crime lab, much of the DNA evidence was considered suspect.

Crime Scene Reconstruction.   Crime scene reconstruction is the process of deter-mining or eliminating events that occurred at the crime scene. It is the theory of what occurred based on analysis of the crime scene and physical evidence, forensic labora-tory examination of physical evidence, logic, and experience and expertise of the crime scene investigator (Miller, 2003). The reconstruction process is both ongoing, beginning at the earliest stages of crime scene investigation, and fluid, changing as additional evidence is collected and analyzed. There are five basic steps to scene reconstruction:

1. Data collection: Organize and study all the evidence.
2. Conjecture: Formulate a possible explanation as the evidence is being studied.
3. Hypothesis formulation: Interpret the evidence and prepare a hypothesis about what happened.
4. Testing: Conduct additional testing to confirm/disprove the hypothesis (other alternatives are ruled out).
5. Theory formulation: Once the hypothesis is thoroughly tested and verified, establish the theory about what happened at the crime scene (Miller, 2003).

The Realities of Crime Scene Investigation

Although there is no question that technology has greatly advanced forensic science and crime scene investigation, the realities of the work are quite different from how they are portrayed on television (again, see Professor Hallett's scholarly perspective in the next chapter). First, it is a simple fact that crime scene investigation and forensic science are not relevant or necessary in many cases. This is perhaps best illustrated by the fact that patrol officers, not detectives, make the vast majority of arrests. When a patrol officer makes an arrest, it is usually because the suspect is still at the scene or the officer is given information about his or her immediate whereabouts (by the victim or an eyewitness). Also, keep in mind that most police departments are very small, with fewer than ten officers. These small police departments that dominate the land-scape of U.S. policing simply do not have the resources to employ criminalists and forensic scientists. Moreover, the vast majority of convictions occur as a result of a plea bargain (where the offender willingly pleads guilty), not a criminal trial where the details of crime scene investigation and physical evidence are discussed.

Second, the depiction of crime scene investigators on television suggests that they are "jacks-of-all-trades," both sworn police officers and scientists who can inter-rogate suspects and make arrests, as well as conduct laboratory tests in ballistics, blood spatter analysis, and DNA. Again, this is simply not reality. In small depart-ments, patrol officers and detectives often also act as crime scene investigators but lack the specialized skills to conduct laboratory analyses. In large departments, any number of models can be employed. Crime scene technicians who are civilian employees may be responsible for evidence collection and analysis. Specially trained detectives may serve as crime scene investigators, supplemented by crime scene scientists (in a laboratory) with superior skills and training. Many police depart-ments, small and big, contract with county and state crime labs rather than employing their own personnel. And within the crime lab itself, technicians specialize in one particular field (such as ballistics or DNA testing), rather than working in all areas of crime scene analysis.

Third, television would have us think that all the steps of crime scene investigation, analysis of the evidence, and investigation concluding in an arrest can occur in a matter of hours. In direct contradiction to this portrayal, there is a huge backlog of cases waiting for DNA testing at crime labs across the United States (estimated delays in some jurisdictions are up to 18 months). Also, in a typical case, there is often so much evidence that the technicians are forced to pick and choose what they analyze, leaving many pieces of evidence unexamined. Last, there have recently been questions arising about the accuracy of some aspects of forensic science. Some of these questions involve the science itself, others focus on the human element and the potential for human error: either making mistakes in the investigation process or in expert testimony in court. In sum, while quantum leaps have been made in recent years with regard to forensic science and crime scene investigation, there are still formidable challenges to the field and its successful application in law enforcement.

CRIME ANALYSIS

Historical Perspective

The notion of police departments analyzing crime trends to help direct their deployment is certainly not a new concept. In fact, two of Sir Robert Peel's early principles of professional policing dealt specifically with that issue:

- The distribution of crime news is absolutely essential.
- The deployment of police strength both by time and area is essential. (Champion & Hooper, 2003, pp. 61–62)

Crime analysis and targeted deployment were also emphasized by Vollmer (and others) as part of the professionalism movement in the early twentieth century. Finally, O.W. Wilson's formula for deploying police personnel (Wilson, 1941) is based on analysis of calls for service, and assignment of the greatest number of officers to those areas producing the largest number of calls. While the idea of crime analysis by police itself is not new, the tools available to conduct such analysis have changed dramatically in recent years. Computers, **geographic information systems (GIS),** and advanced statistical analysis have revolutionized how police departments can review crime and call for service data, and can then modify deployment to more effectively achieve crime prevention, suppression, and investigation.

Crime Analysis in the Twenty-First Century

Crime analysis is defined as "the collection and analysis of data pertaining to a criminal incident, offender, and target" (Canter, 2000, p. 4). Police departments routinely collect enormous amounts of information on crime incidents, offenders, and victims as part of their day-to-day operations. In fact, one of the biggest myths surrounding policing involves the tremendous amounts of paperwork and report writing the job entails (not typically portrayed on television and in movies). Crime analysis involves taking advantage of available data and analyzing it to inform the department's strategies and deployment. O'Shea and Nicholls (2003) state that crime analysis serves three basic functions for police:

1. Assess the nature, extent, and distribution of crime in order to efficiently and effectively allocate resources and personnel.
2. Identify crime–suspect correlations to assist investigators.
3. Identify the conditions that facilitate crime and incivility so that policymakers may make informed decisions about prevention approaches. (p. 8)

In simpler terms, crime analysis helps police with their efforts to prevent and investigate crime, as well as how to deploy personnel to best achieve those objectives. Canter (2000) states that the functions of crime analysis for police fall into two basic categories: strategic and tactical. Strategic crime analysis involves examining data over a long period of time, often using past trends to attempt to predict what will happen in the future. This type of forecasting can be used to estimate future changes in crime trends or to assess changes in the community dynamics such as socioeconomic status, racial makeup, community attitudes, or risk factors associated with crime (Grant & Terry, 2005). The second category of functions, according to Canter (2000), involves tactical crime analysis. This type of analysis examines recent or real-time data to inform immediate decisions about deployment. This type of analysis often focuses on pattern detection—multiple offenses involving the same characteristics—and hotspots—multiple offenses in a single area. Based on recent shifts in crime patterns (recent meaning over the past few days), officers are then reassigned to targeted areas to prevent/suppress and more effectively respond to crime incidents.

Although departments have long engaged in crime analysis, the development of computers and their integration into U.S. law enforcement has allowed police to analyze available data in much greater amounts and to do so much more quickly. A survey in 2000 indicated that approximately one-third of local police departments in the United States were using computers to engage in crime analysis (Hickman & Reaves, 2003).

Of course, there are limitations to the utility of incident, offender, and victim data for police departments. For crime analysis to be successful, there are three essential criteria for the data that will be analyzed: timeliness, relevancy, and reliability (Grant & Terry, 2005). With regard to timeliness, if a police department is going to modify its deployment to targeted specific areas identified through crime analysis, the data must be up-to-date and show problems that currently exist. In simple terms, old data is useless for police. The relevancy issue refers to the accuracy of the data: Do the data truly reflect what is occurring in specific neighborhoods within the jurisdiction? If police officers consistently make mistakes when filing reports and entering information into the computer, the error-prone data will lead to faulty analysis, which will then lead to inappropriately deployed resources. The final data issue is reliability, or consistency. "Would the same data, interpreted by different people at different times, lead to the same conclusions?" (Grant & Terry, 2005, p. 330). If two people analyze the same data using the same techniques and produce different conclusions, the limitations of the data for police seem obvious. Quite simply, police departments cannot alter their deployment strategies if the data are suspect.

Geographic Information System (GIS)

One of the more recent and most useful developments in crime analysis involves the geographic information system (GIS). GIS is an automated system that captures, analyzes, and displays data using computerized maps of given jurisdictions. The visual images of crime and arrest locations on computerized maps facilitate the analysis of crime, particularly short-terms trends that may involve patterns or hotspots. GIS benefits police departments in two basic ways:

> First, by deploying officers in a more intelligent fashion, police agencies will have more officers available for proactive work (such as problem solving). Second, by identifying crime patterns and inferring where crime is likely to develop, police can engage in preventive work to reduce their future workload. (Pelfrey, 2005, p. 217)

The NYPD was employing pin maps through GIS as early as 1990, and a study by the National Institute of Justice in 1999 indicated that 13 percent of all local police departments were using GIS on a regular basis (NIJ, 1999). GIS is a foundational component of CompStat, and recent studies indicate that CompStat and similar programs have been widely adopted (especially by large departments) across the United States (Weisburd et al., 2003).

The mapping process is quite involved and requires departments to go through a number of important steps (Pelfrey, 2005). First, the department must collect the data that will eventually be displayed on the computerized maps. These data typically involve calls for service, crime reports, and arrest reports. Departments routinely collect this information, and have for some time now, but for crime mapping it is critical that the data be computerized. The second component of data collection involves the actual computerized maps, which can be purchased from a number of sources. These detailed maps, which need to be updated regularly, encompass an entire city or county and include all streets as well as important geographic features (lakes, rivers, etc.) (Pelfrey, 2005). The second stage of the crime mapping process involves **geocoding,** reducing the crime events into geographic reference points. These reference points are typically the address of occurrence. For each event (call for service, arrest, etc.), an analyst must enter the address information into the GIS system so the event can be "mapped." This geocoding process can be tedious, but accuracy is absolutely critical. Mistakes that are made at this stage will result in crime events not being displayed on the maps because the GIS takes the available address and matches it with known addresses on the computerized map. If there is no known address for a match, the event will not be displayed. For example, an address geocoded as

"110 Main Street" will be successfully displayed, but "110 Mani Street" will not (unless, of course, there is a Mani Street and then the event will be mapped in the wrong location).

The third part of the mapping process involves layer assembly, or the matching of geocoded information with computerized maps. Mapping software, such as Map-Info, is used to facilitate this process. Pelfrey (2005) states that the best way to understand this process is to think about the maps as layers:

> Imagine a series of transparencies with pieces of information on each one. These transparencies can be layered on top of each other to produce different maps or coverages. The first transparency has an outline of the city. The second transparency might have an outline of all the major streets. The third transparency might have labels of these streets. A fourth transparency might describe the major geographic landmarks (rivers, forest, etc.). With these base maps, different datasets of information can be layered on top. A map of all the drunken driving accidents may be the next layer. (p. 221)

The final stage in the mapping process is the production of the actual map. Once the above steps are completed, the map can be produced for a given period of time, for given parts of town, and for given events. For example, the department could produce a map of all burglaries in the 35th precinct in the last seven days. The time frame, location, and event can be altered to produce comparative maps, assessing change in the levels of given events in the same location over time. Has the number of burglaries in the 35th precinct in the last seven days increased or decreased since the previous week? Of course, the visual depiction of events (burglaries) also allows police to examine locations to identify hotspots and/or patterns. The department can then modify patrol allocation based on the findings produced on the maps. Under the CompStat model, the NYPD uses the prevalence of crime reports over time to document whether particular strategies are effective: Did the strategy deployed last week result in a reduction of the number of burglaries in the 35th precinct? GIS systems vary in their degree of sophistication, in their styles and format, and in terms of available options for mapping data.

Pelfrey (2005) describes five uses of crime mapping for police departments:

- *Description:* The most common use of crime maps is to describe crime for a given area. A descriptive map can show the locations, times, and suspect description to an officer who might not have been on duty when the offense happened but may have knowledge about the offender or area.
- *Identification of Patterns:* An observant officer or analyst who views a series of descriptive maps is likely to start looking for patterns. Crime maps are especially useful in this endeavor. By layering offenses from different periods of time, one can conduct trend analysis [i.e., the CompStat model].
- *Interaction of Factors:* Identification of factors that are related to the production, or prevention, of crime. There are many obvious examples of correlated factors that most departments have already explored—the locations of bars and

drunk driving accidents, thefts and the locations of pawn shops, abandoned houses and drug markets.

- *Projective Analysis:* These projective, or inferential, analyses estimate where crime is likely to occur based on a series of factors. For example, if we know that drug sales are likely to increase as the number of rental properties increase in an area (as homeowners move out and slum lords take over), once a certain threshold has been passed, police can begin to pay special attention to an area to *prevent* the expected increases in drug sales.
- ***Geographic Profiling:*** Using a technique called Criminal Geographic Targeting (CGT), Kim Rossmo, a Canadian police detective and scholar, suggests that serial criminals are likely to commit their crimes in a specific pattern, which can then be analyzed to predict where they live. This technique does not produce specific addresses of offenders. Instead, it identifies neighborhoods from which offenders probably traveled to commit their crimes. (pp. 244–227)

There are, of course, limitations to the use of GIS for crime analysis. First, the maps and mapping software can be quite expensive. Police department staff must also be trained in all aspects of the mapping process. Second, the GIS mapping systems are only as good as the data that are entered. If departments do not collect or keep data in an organized and computerized system, it may require a significant amount of work just to institute data collection procedures that produce usable data. There are ethical issues as well, such as problems arising from making crime maps available to the public that show addresses where individuals were victimized (i.e., sexual assaults). Last, crime analysis using GIS is limited in its utility if the findings do not become available to officers on the street who can use the information. Otherwise, it may simply be an interesting academic exercise. From earlier discussions, it is clear that the NYPD, through its CompStat meetings, makes use of the information and develops strategies to address identified problems. Also, the Camden (NJ) police department has made crime maps available to patrol officers through desktop computers in the precinct and wireless laptops in patrol cars (Grant & Terry, 2005).

OTHER TECHNOLOGICAL ADVANCES

Computers and the Internet

Many police departments have become fully computerized, ranging from the collection and storage of calls for service and crime data, performance measurement and early warning systems, to laptops and mobile digital terminals (MDTs) in patrol cars. The use of computers has greatly expanded police departments' use of data, particularly for crime analysis, as well as the speed in which data analyses can be conducted. Like any other business, computers have helped police departments with regard to administration of the organization including management, personnel and resource allocation. Computers in patrol cars have become increasingly common, from just

5 percent of local police departments in 1990 to 40 percent in 2000 (Hickman & Reaves, 2003). MDTs allow police officers to carry out a variety of functions such as:

- Communications with supervisors and other officers.
- Preparing field notes and reports.
- Obtain information about people and places from existing databases such as vehicle records, driving records, criminal histories, and calls for service. (Stroshine, 2005)

These systems greatly enhance the information available to police officers and have led to more effective police work and increased officer safety. For example, a police officer who has pulled over a motorist for speeding can find out quickly if the car is stolen or if the person is wanted on a warrant or other charges. Rather than simply issuing a ticket, the officer can call for back-up (if needed) and take the person into custody.

Police departments, like society as a whole, have begun to use the Internet in their day-to-day activities. Many police departments, particularly larger ones, have created websites that provide a wide range of information about the departments. Websites typically include a list of personnel, especially command staff, "most wanted" pages, crime prevention information, and crime data. Some departments have made crime maps like those discussed above available via the Internet. Some websites also allow citizens to file crime reports, citizen complaints, and officer commendations online, and many have begun to use the Internet to help with recruitment. Some of the larger departments—Miami-Dade, for example—allow citizens to download application forms from the website. And last, police departments are also increasingly using email as a method for communication between officers and between officers and their supervisors. With the advent of wireless Internet and placement of computers in patrol cars, officers can email back and forth with headquarters while in the field.

Computers and the Internet have also allowed law enforcement agencies in surrounding areas—and around the country—to integrate their systems. The fragmented nature of U.S. policing, with thousands of police departments across the country who function independently, has limited the ability of police to track criminals across jurisdictional boundaries, and more generally, has hampered cooperation among different agencies. Innovations in computers have facilitated the development of "interjurisdictional communication technolody" such as offender databases and radio communications (Grant & Terry, 2005, p. 345). Examples include the NCIC (National Crime Information Center, a national criminal history database), IAFIS and CODIS (described above), and the Advanced Generation of Interoperability for Law Enforcement program (AGILE), which provides direct connections across radio systems of neighboring law enforcement agencies (Grant & Terry, 2005).

Global Positioning Systems (GPS)

Law enforcement agencies have begun using **global positioning systems (GPS)** in a number of ways, mostly notably in the tracking of offenders and officer deployment (Grant & Terry, 2005). Offender monitoring systems allow police to track the movements of parolees and high-risk offenders such as sex offenders, to prevent them from congregating near or traveling through sensitive areas (schools, etc.). Police departments have also used GPS to:

- Track stolen property and vehicles
- Track movement of patrol cars
- Provide aerial views of crime scenes
- Track suspect movelents at a crime scene (Grant & Terry, 2005)

Closed Circuit Television (CCTV)

England has implemented an extensive system of **closed circuit television (CCTV)** cameras, particularly in London, and many policd departments in the United States have begun to adopt similar public-surveillance systems. These systems are traditionally common around transportation hubs, such as airports and train stations, banks, and government buildings, but they are increasingly being placed in other public areas. Many cities have attached surveillance systems to their traffic signals, and since these camera systems feed into a central control area, they offer a comprehensive monitoring system for automobile and pedestrian traffic throughout the jurisdiction. When a crime occurs, police can then examine the feeds from the CCTVs in the area to identify potential suspects and vehicles and to track their movements. Investigators in London used CCTV footage to track the movements of suspected terrorists responsible for the subway bombings in July 2005. Although too late, federal investigators later tracked the movements of the 9/11 terrorists through footage from airport surveillance cameras.

There are limitations with CCTV and other public surveillance systems. First, it is unknown whether these systems have any preventive or deterrent effect on crime. Instead, their value lies in the evidence they provide of suspect movements *after* a crime has occurred. Second, civil rights advocates warn against a "big brother" or "Orwellian" effect, where right to privacy is threatened by such surveillance systems. Last, these systems are still prone to human error; technology can only take us so far. After studying CCTV control rooms in England, Goold (2001) concluded that the effectiveness of surveillance had less to do with technology than with the attitudes and working culture of the camera operators.

NIBRS

NIBRS is described in detail in Chapter 7, but it deserves mentioning here as well. The National Incident Based Reporting System (NIBRS) was implemented in 1989 by the FBI to improve upon the UCR system. NIBRS collects data for multiple offenses, multiple victims, and multiple offenders as part of one crime incident. The system also divides crimes into two categories—Group A and Group B—involving 46 different criminal offenses. In sum, NIBRS overcomes many of the limitations of the traditional UCR system and presents a much more detailed and comprehensive picture of reported crime and arrests in the United States. Unfortunately, law enforcement agencies have not been as willing to adopt NIBRS as they were to report under the UCR system. To date, only about 3,000 law enforcement agencies consistently report NIBRS data (out of the more than 17,000 agencies in the United States).

Biometrics

A **biometric** is a unique personal or physiological characteristic that is measurable and can be used to identify a specific individual. A biometric system "compares a known set of individual characteristics, which must be stored in what is known as the reference template, with the person's actual characteristics" (Champion & Hooper, 2003, p. 580). While the primary biometric used by police involves fingerprints (see above), there are a variety of other biometric systems available for use by police. These include:

- Hand geometry software that uses a three-dimensional scan and nine-digit code that accounts for finger length and palm shapes.
- Face recognition software that scans individuals in a given area and compares them to known suspects and offenders in a stored database.
- Retinal and iris scanning systems that illuminate unique features of the eye and compare the features to known individuals. (Champion & Hooper, 2003)

Civil libertarians have voiced concerns about some of these biometric systems, particularly face recognition systems that are deployed in public places with the general population. Cost and limited availability have also prohibited widespread adoption of these types of biometric systems by U.S. police departments, with the exception of fingerprinting, which remains a central feature of police investigations.

Cold Case Squads

Many police departments across the United States have developed **"cold case squads"** to reinvestigate crimes that occurred in the past (this topic too has been romanticized on television). In 2001, for example, the West Virginia State Police created a nine-person Cold Case Unit to reinvestigate murder cases and other serious crimes (Champion & Hooper, 2003). The rationale for these units is quite simple. When the cases were originally investigated, police did not have the repertoire of technological innovations, forensic science, and crime scene investigation tools that exist today. Cold case squads reopen these old investigations and pursue leads with the now-available technological innovations, such as DNA testing (as long as the evidence is still viable). Detectives in these units can now submit physical evidence for DNA testing and attempt to match that evidence against known offenders in CODIS. Champion and Hooper (2003) state that CODIS has provided investigative leads in over 1,500 cold cases.

Less-than-Lethal Weapons

Technology has led to the development of a host of non-lethal or **less-than-lethal weapons** used by police (described in detail in Chapter 8). The intent of this class of weapons is to provide police officers with viable alternatives to the firearm to control combative and assaultive suspects. These weapons seek to protect officers from injury by reducing the occurrence of physical confrontations with suspects and to protect suspects from serious injury or death that would occur if the officer was forced to fire his or her gun. There is wide range of weapons including tear gas, mace, oleoresin capsicum (pepper spray), impact weapons, ballistic rounds, foams, nets, and electronic stun devices. The most commonly used less-than-lethal weapons include the baton (original PR-24 or the newer extendable versions), mace/pepper spray, and the Taser. Little research has been conducted to study the impact or relative effectiveness of less-than-lethal weapons, with the exception of oleoresin capsicum (Nowicki, 2001). The Taser is now undergoing extensive testing because of concerns about how and when it is being used by police (i.e., against children) and because of 70 deaths that have occurred following its use (see Chapter 8). Despite the lack of research on their effectiveness, police have generally been very receptive to these new weapons and view them as an additional tool to protect lives and combat crime.

Imaging

Imaging is "the enhancement of optical capabilities for law enforcement personnel, as well as the recording and documenting of crimes as they occur" (Champion & Hooper, 2003, p. 582). Imaging serves three basic functions for police departments:

- *Accountability:* Recording and monitoring police officer behavior in the field.
- *Recording and documenting crimes:* Cameras that are placed in specific locations to record potential criminal activity or law violations (at traffic intersections to identify speeders and cars that "run through" red lights).
- *Illumination:* Night vision and thermal systems that enhance police officers' vision of potential criminal activity.

The most common type of imaging used by police involves mobile video systems, which are video cameras attached to police vehicles. These systems provide a variety of functions for police departments including increased accountability (because the police officer's behavior is recorded), documentation (the officer can activate an audio recorder and record information during a car stop or car pursuit), and as a training tool (to observe officer's behavior and offer constructive criticism). These video systems also present important evidence that can verify or contradict citizen claims in complaints against police. The video footage can serve as evidence, leading to the dismissal of false complaints, and can be introduced in civil litigation to support police officer claims (or can be subpoenaed by defense counsel to support the plaintiff's claims).

Night vision and thermal imaging devices, developed for use in the military, are now being used by police to aid in their investigations. These devices are often used during surveillance operations, and they can also be used during searches for suspects or missing persons in wooded or overgrown areas. In *Kyllo v. United States,* the U.S. Supreme Court ruled that the use of thermal imaging to examine houses for heat signatures (in this case, heat lamps used to grow marijuana) constitutes a search under the Fourth Amendment of the Constitution and thus requires a warrant. Finally, the radar flashlight is another form of imaging that can be used to detect the presence of a person behind brick, wood, plasterboard and concrete (up to 10 inches thick) based on the individual's respiration.

SUMMARY

This chapter examines the important—and often defining—role of technology in policing. Given that this book focuses specifically on current issues and controversies in policing, there are discussions throughout each chapter that highlight the importance of technological innovation. The chapter begins by describing the development of technology in U.S. policing, setting aside Kelling and Moore's (1991) model, and using Soulliere's four stages of technological advancement. The chapter then turns to a few areas in policing where technology has been absolutely crucial. These include forensic science and its impact on crime scene investigation, and crime analysis through GIS and crime mapping.

Although the seeds of forensic science were planted long ago, much of the discussion focuses on recent developments in fingerprinting, DNA, and weapons analysis. The Locard exchange principle, which serves as the foundation for crime scene investigation, states that any time two objects come together there is an exchange of matter. For the police, this exchange of matter means that offenders leave behind trace or physical evidence that can be examined and provide a link between suspects, victims, and crime scenes. The FBI now maintains computer databases holding millions of fingerprints, DNA samples, and tool marks that can be used for comparison against evidence collected at a crime scene. Importantly, technology allows these comparisons to be made in a matter of hours, rather than weeks and months. The chapter also describes the basic steps of crime scene investigation, highlighting the complex and scientific nature of the process. However, the portrayal of forensic science and crime scene investigation on television has produced many misconceptions and perhaps exaggerated the importance of their role in police work. Nevertheless, the utility of this merger of science and investigation for police has been greatly enhanced by technological developments over the last two decades.

The chapter also discusses crime analysis and the emerging role of GIS and crime mapping for police. Again, the idea of crime analysis is not new, but technology has changed the face of this effort in recent years. The development of GIS and crime mapping, in particular, has served to revolutionize the manner in which police use information and, specifically, how that information is used to determine deployment patterns. Crime mapping allows police departments to make better use of limited resources, and to assess the impact of specific strategies designed to affect crime in given locations. This type of analysis is the "engine" that drives the CompStat model, which originated in New York but has been widely adopted elsewhere (Weisburd et al., 2003).

Finally, the chapter closes with brief discussions of other innovations such as computers and the Internet, closed circuit television, NIBRS, less-than-lethal weapons, and various forms of enhanced imaging. In sum, the message of this chapter is that technology has played—and will continue to play—a defining role in U.S. policing.

KEY TERMS

Ballistics
Bertillon, Alphonse
Biometrics
Chain of custody
Closed circuit television (CCTV)
Cold case squads
Combined DNA Index System (CODIS)
Crime mapping
DNA
Fingerprints
Forensic science
Geocoding

Geographic information system (GIS)
Geographic profiling
Global positioning system (GPS)
Imaging
Integrated Automated Fingerprint Identification System (IAFIS)
Integrated Ballistics Identification System (IBIS)
Less-than-lethal weapons
Locard exchange principle
Real Time Crime Center (RTCC, NYPD)
Tool marks

DISCUSSION QUESTIONS

1. Discuss Soulliere's four stages of technological advancement.

2. What is the Locard exchange principle? Explain its importance for police.

3. Describe how technology has influenced the utility of physical evidence recovered at crime scenes, particularly fingerprints and DNA.

4. Describe the six stages of crime scene investigation.

5. Explain how police can use geographic information systems to assist in crime analysis.

6. Describe how police have used computers to run their departments more efficiently and effectively.

REFERENCES

Canter, P. (2000). Using a geographic information system for tactical crime analysis. In V. Goldsmith, P. McGuire, J. Mollenkopf, & T. Ross (Eds.), *Analyzing crime patterns: Frontiers of practice.* Thousand Oaks, CA: Sage.

Champion, D.H., & Hooper, M.K. (2003). *Introduction to American policing.* New York: McGraw-Hill.

Gaensslen, R.E., & Young, K.R. (2003). Fingerprints. In S.H. James & J.J. Nordby (Eds.), *Forensic science: An introduction to scientific and investigative techniques.* New York: CRC Press.

Goold, B. (2001). *CCTV in the United Kingdom.* Unpublished dissertation. Oxford, United Kingdom: Oxford University.

Grant, H.B., & Terry, K.J. (2005). *Law enforcement in the 21st century.* Boston: Allyn and Bacon.

Hickman, M.J., & Reaves, B.A. (2003). *Local police departments, 2000.* Washington, DC: Bureau of Justice Statistics, U.S. Department of Justice.

James, S.H., & Nordby, J.J. (Eds.). (2003). *Forensic science: An introduction to scientific and investigative techniques.* New York: CRC Press.

Kelling, G.I., & Moore, M.H. (1991). From political to reform to community: The evolving strategy of the police. In J.R. Greene & S.D. Mastrofski (Eds.), *Community policing: Rhetoric or reality.* New York: Praeger.

Miller, M.T. (2003). Crime scene investigation. In S.H. James & J.J. Nordby (Eds.), *Forensic science: An introduction to scientific and investigative techniques.* New York: CRC Press.

National Institute of Justice (NIJ). (1999). *The use of computerized crime mapping by law enforcement: Survey results.* Washington, DC: U.S. Department of Justice.

Nowicki, E. (2001, June). OC spray update. *Law and Order,* 28–29.

O'Shea, T.C., & Nicholls, K. (2003). *Crime analysis in America: Findings and recommendations.* Washington, DC: U.S. Department of Justice.

Pelfrey, W.V. (2005). Geographic information systems: Applications for police. In *Critical issues in policing* (5th ed.). Long R.G. Dunham & G.P. Alpert (Eds.), Grove, Waveland Press.

President's Commission on Law Enforcement and Administration of Justice. (1967). *Task force report: The police.* Washington DC: US Government Printing Office.

Rowe, W.F. (2003). Firearm and tool mark examinations. In S.H. James & J.J. Nordby (Eds.), *Forensic science: An introduction to scientific and investigative techniques.* New York: CRC Press.

Soulliere, N. (1999). *Police and technology: Historical review and current status.* Ottawa: Canadian Police College.

Stroshine, M.S. (2005). Information technology innovations in policing. In R.G. Dunham & G.P. Alpert (Eds.), *Critical issues in policing* (5th ed.). Long Grove, IL: Waveland Press.

Weisburd, D., Mastrofski, S.D., McNally, A.M., Greenspan, R., & Willis, J.J. (2003). Reforming to preserve: CompStat and strategic problem-solving in American policing. *Criminology and Public Policy,* 2, 421–456.

Wilson, O.W. (1941). *Distribution of police patrol force.* Chicago: Public Administration Service.

SCHOLAR'S PERSPECTIVE

Crime Mapping—A Tool for Law Enforcement

Jennifer B. Robinson, Ph.D.[1]

*Assistant Professor of Criminal Justice and Director
of the Crime Pattern Research Laboratory*

Northeastern University

Crime mapping is a natural tool for law enforcement agencies. By the mid 1990s, crime mapping became more widely used and accepted in large police departments, most notably by the New York Police Department (NYPD) and the Chicago Police Department (CPD). Crime mapping is a primary tool of CompStat, computer-aided statistical analysis, which was first introduced to policing in 1994 by the NYPD. CompStat has been heralded as a successful tool for law enforcement, leading to increased communication between departmental units and outside agencies. The use of CompStat by police is related to reductions in crime and improvement in community policing (Weisburd, Mastrofski, Greenspan, & Willis, 2004).

Improvement in the capabilities of desktop computers is a fundamental reason for increased use of crime mapping by the police. The basic component of crime mapping is the Geographic Information System (GIS). The GIS spatially codes (geocodes) data and attaches attributes to the features stored to analyze these data based on those attributes and to map the result. Since a GIS is able to organize data in a way similar to maps, it is an excellent tool for examining multidimensional and multifaceted crime problems. The GIS is able to clarify the spatial relationships that exist between general social indicators in an environment and the crime patterns that also exist there (Rich, 1995).

The GIS relies primarily (in crime mapping) on police calls for service data and arrest data, although other types of data (i.e., census data) can also be used. Computer-aided dispatch (CAD) data can be linked to GIS software to automatically record addresses of calls in a format that is recognized by the GIS software. This linkage reduces the number of errors in the data and allows for more accurate mapping.

The GIS is used by the police for crime analysis and resource planning (Craglia, Haining, & Wiles, 2000), intelligence dissemination (Ratcliffe, 2000,

[1]Assistant Professor and Director of the Crime Pattern Research Laboratory, Northeastern University. Ph.D. Temple University.

p. 315), and to inform residents about crime problems in their areas (Mamalian & LaVigne, 1999:3). Crime mapping is also used by police departments ". . . to support court testimony, to plan and monitor traffic flow, and to facilitate special operations and hazardous material transport . . ." (Travis & Hughes, 2002, p. 3).

A 1997 survey of law enforcement agencies in the United States found that of the departments who do not use GIS, 20 percent reported having budgeted funds to purchase hardware and software in the following year (Mamalian & LaVigne, 1999, p. 1). Of the agencies who reported using GIS to map crime, 91 percent reported mapping offense data and 52 percent reported mapping vehicle recovery data (Mamalian & LaVigne, 1999, p. 2).

By 1998, 75 percent of law enforcement agencies performed at least some crime analysis, but only 13 percent of those agencies used some form of crime mapping (Mamalian & LaVigne, 1999). In 1999, approximately 11 percent of small police departments (50 to 99 sworn personnel) and 32.6 percent of large police departments (100 or more sworn personnel) had implemented a CompStat-like program. Approximately 60 percent of departments with 500 or more sworn personnel had implemented crime mapping by 1999 (Weisburd, et al., 2004, pp. 6, 12).

Crime mapping is also used in criminological research to describe a number of different phenomena including, but not limited to, gang activity (Block, 2000; Kennedy, Braga, & Riehl, 1998; Thrasher, 1927), nonresidential burglaries (Ratcliffe, 2000), drug arrests and incidents (Olligschlaeger, 1998; Robinson & Rengert, 2005), police interventions (Robinson & Rengert, 2005), crimes of serial rapists (Hubbs, 1998; LeBeau, 1992), robbery (Block & Skogan, 1995), residential burglary (Rengert & Wasilchik, 1985; Groff & LaVigne, 2001), the home addresses of juvenile delinquents (Shaw & McKay, 1969), and home and work addresses of serial murderers (Rossmo, 2000).

Robinson's (2003) research on drug-free zones in Portland, Oregon, is an example of research that utilizes crime mapping. The research examined the effects of drug-free zones on changing spatial patterns of drug sales arrests in Portland from 1990 through 1998. The research first characterized the drug-free zone initiative as a situational crime prevention strategy with explicit geographic crime reduction objectives. It then considered how the intervention may have altered spatial patterns and levels of drug crime in Portland over time.

The analysis of possible effects of the drug-free zone strategy engaged a variety of methods, including mapping, clustering, and multilevel analytic techniques. Together, these methods were employed to identify hypothesized impacts of the drug-free zone intervention, in the context of the effects of temporal shifts and community characteristics, on drug sales arrests. This study found some support for the drug-free zones in changing both the locations and numbers of drug sales arrests in the targeted areas. Findings from the research suggest that future consideration be given to the relationship between drug-free zone status and law enforcement practices and to understanding the nature of the places where drug-free zones are employed.

For crime mapping to remain a truly useful tool for the police, the proper infrastructure to support it must exist, including an efficient method for distributing the information to the officers and management and databases that integrate accurate and useful information from a variety of sources (Manning, 2001, p. 93). The development of professional standards is also becoming important as more agencies use GIS to map crime. Funding is another key concern for the future. Funding should be increased in general in order to ensure that exposure to crime mapping and expertise in crime mapping continues to grow. Public access to crime maps and crime data is key to maintaining crime mapping as a useful tool for the police. Last, the development of methods to predict (forecast) crime patterns rather than simply display and explain current patterns will ensure that crime mapping continues to evolve and meet the changing needs of law enforcement.

REFERENCES

Block, R. (2000). Gang activity and overall levels of crime: A new mapping tool for defining areas of gang activity using police records. *Journal of Quantitative Criminology, 16,* 36–51.

Block, R., & Skogan, W.G. (1995). *Dynamics of violence between strangers: Victim resistance and outcomes in rape, robbery and assault: Final report.* Washington, DC: National Institute of Justice.

Craglia, M., Haining, R., & Wiles, P. (2000). A comparative evaluation of approaches to urban crime pattern analysis. *Urban Studies, 37,* 711–729.

Hubbs, R. (1998). The Greenway rapist case: Matching repeat offenders with crime locations. In N. LaVigne & Wartell (Eds.), *Crime mapping case studies: Successes in the field.* Washington, DC: Police Executive Research Forum (pp. 93–97).

Groff, E.R., & LaVigne, N.C. (2001). Mapping an opportunity surface of residential burglar. *Journal of Research in Crime and Delinquency,* 38(3), 257–279.

Kennedy, D.M., Braga, A.A., & Piehl, A.M. (1998). The (un)known universe: Mapping gangs and gang violence in Boston. In D. Weisburd & T. McEwen (Eds.), *Crime mapping and crime prevention.* New York: Criminal Justice Press (pp. 219–262).

Kyllo v. United States (99-8508) 533 U.S. 27 (2001).

LeBeau, J. (1992). Four case studies illustrating the spatial-temporal analysis of serial rapists. *Police Studies, 15* (3), 124–145.

Mamalian, C., & LaVigne, N. (1999). *The use of computerized crime mapping by law enforcement: Survey results.* Washington, DC: National Institute of Justice, Research Preview.

Manning, P. (2001). Technology's ways: Information technology, crime analysis and the rationalization of policing. *Criminal Justice: the International Journal of Policy and Practice, 1,* 83–103.

Olligschlaeger, A.M. (1998). Artificial neural networks and crime mapping. In D. Weisburd & T. McEwen (Eds.), *Crime mapping and crime prevention.* New York: Criminal Justice Press (pp. 313–347).

Ratcliffe, J. (2000). Implementing and integrating crime mapping into a police intelligence environment. *Policing: An International Journal of Police Science and Management, 2,* 313–323.

Rengert, G., & Wasilchik, J. (1985). *Suburban burglary: A time and a place for everything.* Springfield, IL: Charles Thomas.

Rich, T. (1995). *The use of computerized mapping in crime control and prevention programs.* Washington DC: U.S. Department of Justice, Office of Justice Programs.

Robinson, J.B. (2003). *Drug free zones, the police, locations, and trends in drug sales in Portland, Oregon, 1990–1998.* Doctoral dissertation submitted to the graduate school at Temple University.

Robinson, J.B., & Rengert, G. (2005, Fall). Drug free zones: The geographic perspective. *Western Criminology Review.* (Forthcoming).

Rossmo, D.K. (2000). *Geographic profiling.* Boca Raton, FL: CRC Press.

Shaw, C., & McKay, H. (1969). *Juvenile delinquency and urban areas: A study of rates of delinquency in relation to differential characteristics of local communities in American cities.* Chicago: University of Chicago Press.

Thrasher, F. (1927). *The gang.* Chicago: University of Chicago Press.

Travis, L., & Hughes, K. (2002). Mapping in police agencies: Beyond this point there be monsters. *Overcoming the Barriers: Crime Mapping in the 21st Century, 2,* 1–16.

Weisburd, D., Mastrofski, S., Greenspan, R., & Willis, J. (2004). *The growth of CompStat in American policing.* Washington, DC: Police Foundation.

CHAPTER 12

NEXT STEPS AND CHALLENGES FOR POLICE

Going back to the first pages of this book, two guiding principles were offered to serve as the backdrop for this discussion of current issues and controversies in policing. The first involves the central role of change in policing. One need only to consider Kelling and Moore's (1991) eras of policing (in Chapter 3) or Soulliere's (1999) stages of technological development (in Chapter 11) to understand this point. The second principle involves how we perceive or view that change. Specifically, history offers us a critically important context for framing the discussion of today's issues. Imagine trying to understand the shift to community policing without considering the isolated and disconnected nature of the professional model or its lack of effectiveness in dealing with crime. Imagine trying to understand prevailing trends in police training without considering the limitations of the traditional academy model. Quite simply, full understanding of today's police issues hinges on an awareness of where the profession has been and how it got to where it is today.

This final chapter is shaped by the aforementioned guiding principles as well as two final thoughts discussed in the preface. First, bear in mind that this book is NOT intended to serve as an introductory textbook to policing. As a result, there are likely topics in each chapter that did not receive coverage. Second, by its nature, parts of this book may soon be outdated or missing important topics. Because of the central role of change in policing, this is inevitable. However, in this last chapter I will try to address this issue by offering my assessment of where the future lies in the various areas of policing addressed in the previous chapters. These thoughts are simply intended to be my best guess about where the profession is headed over the next several years, but importantly, I continue to use history as my guide. Simply put, where the profession has been in the past will offer important lessons for understanding and meeting the challenges of the future.

THE FUTURE OF POLICING

Recruitment and Selection

Chapter 1 examined the history of police recruitment and selection, illustrating quite clearly how the profession has moved away from awarding positions based on political patronage and the "spoils system" to proactive recruitment and objective, standardized selection processes. A number of important themes emerge from that chapter that will define the future of recruitment and selection for police departments in the United States.

Active Recruitment.   Most police departments in the United States are facing manpower shortages and are having a difficult time filling available positions. A number of factors have contributed to the shortage of qualified applicants, including changes in basic requirements such as a college degree, low salaries compared to the private sector, and job opportunities in federal law enforcement. Unfortunately, the shortage of qualified applicants does not appear to be diminishing. As a result, police departments will have to become proactive in their recruitment efforts, "selling themselves" to potential applicants in a variety of ways. This may involve creating a recruitment unit or officer, utilizing the Internet and local media, attending local college and high school job fairs, and attending community events (many departments do these things already). Departments can no longer take a "wait and see" approach to recruitment: The future lies in drawing applicants by reaching out to the community through an organized and thoughtful recruitment strategy. Importantly, this strategy should be driven by knowledge regarding why people are motivated to become police officers and tailoring recruitment efforts to tap into those motivations.

Diversity.   Although policing has traditionally been an occupation dominated by working-class white males, the future of policing lies in **diversity.** CALEA recommends that a police department reflect the community that it serves: If the community is 30 percent Hispanic, so too should be the police department. Racial disparity between the community and police department has been linked to poor community relations and police misconduct (Skolnick & Fyfe, 1993). There is certainly no guarantee that building a representative police department will ameliorate police–community relations problems. However, it seems logical that a representative police department is more likely to understand the culture and views of the community and is more likely to be tolerant of those views. Given the history of poor relations in many communities, particularly poor urban areas, this can only represent a positive first step. The challenge for police departments, of course, is to identify ways to draw minority and female applicants, given the already thin applicant pool. **Affirmative action** offers a guide for police, but it is essential that police NOT go about hiring less-qualified applicants because of race or gender. The spirit of affirmative action rests on the notion that qualified minority and female applicants are available—departments may just have to look harder to find them. To do this, their recruitment efforts may have to be tailored to target those traditionally underrepresented groups.

College-Educated Police Officers.   There are persuasive arguments both for and against college degree requirements for police officers. Nevertheless, I believe that the future of policing should and will involve a continued move toward a college-degree requirement. The expectations placed on police officers today are greater than they have ever been before. We still expect them to prevent and solve crime, resolve our disputes, and respond with care and concern to our needs. Now we also expect police to employ sophisticated problem solving, to engage the community, and to protect us from the new threats of terrorism. Although the evidence linking college education to improved police performance is mixed, it seems clear that the new and emerging skills required to be an effective police officer in the twenty-first century are developed and enhanced through a college education.

Residency Requirements and Mass Hiring.   Available evidence suggests that the future of policing does NOT lie with either **residency requirements** or **mass hiring.** Given the well-documented shortage of qualified applicants and the relatively unconvincing arguments in its favor, residency requirements are likely to become less common over the next several years. Quite simply, such requirements unnecessarily limit the applicant pool and in many cases place an undue financial burden on police officers who may be able to live more economically in nearby or surrounding communities. However, as departments drop their residency requirements, they are well-advised to consider—and, if possible, evaluate—the impact of that change on police officer performance, citizen perceptions of police, and police perceptions of the community.

Budgetary concerns and issues often force police departments, especially in large cities, to go through extended periods of non-hiring, followed by a need to hire many officers at once. The causal link between such mass hiring practices and future deviance-related problems is relatively clear: When large numbers of officers are hired at once, the selection processes are strained and there is significant risk that poorly qualified applicants will slip through the cracks. Importantly, the need to hire police officers quickly cannot supercede the need for a deliberate and comprehensive recruitment and selection process.

The Selection Process.   Police departments should continue to embrace a structured and objective selection process that effectively "weeds out" unqualified and inappropriate applicants in accordance with legal and ethical standards. Extensive criminal history checks, oral interviews, physical fitness and psychological tests, and written tests should serve as the cornerstone of that process. Polygraph tests can be quite useful as well, when they are properly administered and their limitations are understood. Specific requirements regarding age, health, criminal background, work experience, and a range of other criteria described in Chapter 1 should be applied by departments as they deem fit. The diversity in departments, their needs, and the communities they serve mediate against trying to develop and institute uniform standards of any kind in these areas.

Training the Police

Chapter 2 charts the development of police training over the last 150 or so years, from no training at all to the highly structured and professional models employed today. Given the challenges facing police today—many of which are reviewed throughout this book—August Vollmer's tongue-in-cheek assessment of the skills required to be a good police officer is no longer a gross exaggeration (though admittedly still an overstatement!). These skills are transmitted through training, both in the academy and while on the job (in field training programs and in-service). It is through this training that the "Solomon/Sampson/Moses/Daniel/Good Samaritan/Alexander/Lincoln/Carpenter of Nazareth" police officer is developed. There are several themes that emerge in this area that should define police training for the foreseeable future.

First, the debate over whether policing is a craft or a profession is not important. In reality, it is a little of both. Yet, despite some obvious differences, the occupation of policing has many interesting parallels to the medical profession. Doctors and police officers both go through intense classroom training, followed by field training (though medical training is admittedly much longer). Both are in the business of saving lives, and when mistakes are made, lives are lost. For both occupations, proper and continued training improves performance and minimizes the likelihood of mistakes. Continuing with the doctor analogy, the key issue for police academy training involves making it more relevant—bringing the real world of police work into the classroom. For field and in-service training, the key issues center on reinforcing and building on the knowledge gained in the academy. The days of the veteran telling the rookie to "forget everything you just learned in the academy" must be over. The veteran now needs to say, "You just learned some really important things in the academy, now I am going to show you how to apply that knowledge and excel in your job."

Second, increasing the link between academy and field training will be facilitated by moving away from the traditional pedagogical model, by focusing greater attention on developing skills for critical incidents—problem-solving, handling the mentally ill, domestic disputes, counterterrorism—and by emphasizing the important skills required for effective day-to-day policing such as communication, writing, tolerance toward diversity, patience, and the rest of the Solomon/Sampson/Moses/etc. mix. Third, the militaristic, boot camp approach to police training is archaic and a direct contradiction to the current philosophies of policing. Police officers are not soldiers, and they are not in a war. The core elements of the boot camp approach that overemphasize danger and discourage independent thinking, while prepping officers for urban warfare against the enemy, foster the "us vs. them" mentality and is a major cause of police brutality (see Skolnick & Fyfe, 1993). Police training academies should emulate the Federal Bureau of Investigation (FBI) model, where physical conditioning is emphasized and critical skills are taught without the antagonistic, in-your-face boot camp mentality. Last, the training experience should be a three-phase program—academy, field training, and in-service—that is a career-long endeavor. In simple terms, effective training of staff is a core ingredient to good policing.

New Philosophies and Strategies

The traditional reactive police strategy—officers riding around their sectors waiting to respond to calls for service—has gone the way of the dinosaur. We now know that this approach is ineffective in preventing crime; that it contributed significantly to creation of the police subculture; that it isolated and disconnected the public from the police; and that it fails to recognize the other more prevalent—and in some ways, more important—responsibilities of the police (i.e., service-related tasks).

Which of the New Approaches Will Last?   There is a well-established history in policing for innovations to emerge, take hold for a short time, but then soon be replaced by a return to the norm. Will community policing, problem-oriented policing, zero tolerance, and CompStat-style approaches suffer the same fate? The answer will probably be different for each of the approaches. **Community policing** is perhaps in the greatest danger of fading away. While community policing became the police buzzword of the 1980s and 1990s, it never really took hold in many police departments. Community policing represents a philosophical shift in the department's mission and goals; yet, in many departments, community policing was relegated to a specific unit or group of officers. In many ways, community policing is a theory that has not been sufficiently tested because its full implementation has never been realized. The closest a police department has come to full implementation is the Chicago PD, though there were clearly some shortcomings in the process and outcomes (see Chapter 4).

Nevertheless, the community has always played and will continue to play a vital role in crime prevention. It is simply unfair for us to expect the police to handle the crime problem on their own, in part because it represents only a small part of what they do and because the primary causes of crime far exceed their purview. A good police officer knows the people who live, work, and hang out on his or her beat. The officer talks to them, and they talk to him or her. Whether you call this community policing or something else is not really the point. The point is that both the police and the community have a contributing role to play, and the best chances for combating crime involve a partnership that harnesses the resources and expertise of both.

While I do expect the term "community policing" to continue to disappear, problem-oriented approaches like **CompStat** hold great promise for the future. The extent to which these approaches are causally related to decreases in crime is still up for debate, but one issue that cannot be contested is that these strategies represent superior use and management of available resources. Terms like "data-driven," "innovative problem solving," "organizational flexibility," and "geographic organization" represent the future of U.S. policing. **Problem-oriented policing,** which is what I consider CompStat to be, centers on using information to identify specific problems, gathering the department's resources to develop solutions, implementing those solutions immediately, and then monitoring their impact. Importantly, the community plays a role in this process as an information resource (problem identification), as a partner in addressing the problem (informal social control), and as source for evaluating impact (has the problem been eliminated?). Finally, although **zero tolerance policing** has appeal because of its emphasis on disorder, the approach's failure to recognize and address the sources of the disorder and its potential negative impact on community relations represent a significant and possibly fatal flaw.

Organizational Issues

Police organizations experience the same advantages and disadvantages as other organizations espousing the bureaucratic model. On the downside, police organizations are traditionally overly rigid, inflexible, and unable to adapt to change. They tend to discourage creative thinking, overemphasize rules, and measure performance through numbers. Alternatively, the bureaucratic model has been central to the professionalization of policing, particularly through the development of standards in recruitment and selection, training, supervision, and performance measurement. Beyond this discussion of the bureaucratic model, there are a number of organizational issues that will shape the future of the police organization. First, as discussed above in the training section, the **quasi-military model** and corresponding "cops as soldiers" mentality has no place in twenty-first-century U.S. policing. Criminals are not enemies to be destroyed, plain and simple. The analogy does not work on both organizational and operational levels, given the location of police **discretion** (at the line level) and the importance of protecting life and constitutional rights. There are alternative models employed in federal law enforcement, and Chapter 5 also describes the hospital model. Second, the responsibilities of the police far exceed crime-related tasks, and these other responsibilities must become valued and recognized parts of the job. Many of the new philosophies of policing described in Chapter 4 seek to move the emphasis toward service and order-maintenance related tasks. Moving away from the militaristic style will also facilitate this shift. As part of this shift, departments will likely begin to deemphasize the specialization that has characterized the last fifty years of policing. The recognition that the patrol officer is the most important and valued member of the department brings to the forefront the need for officers to be generalists: skilled in many different areas, acting as the Solomon/Sampson/Moses, etc. that citizens expect.

Last, the future of policing in many parts of the country lies with the three Cs: **civilianization, consolidation,** and contracting services. Employing appropriately trained nonsworn personnel to handle non-emergency tasks frees up officers to engage in the targeted, problem-oriented strategies that represent the best chance to prevent and suppress crime. Given that the majority of police departments in the United States are small (fewer than 10 officers) and that the ongoing budget crises at the municipal level are not likely to disappear, jurisdictions are well advised to investigate the potential for creating regional police forces, or contracting with nearby larger agencies for services. Such approaches will naturally reduce the fragmentation that characterizes local law enforcement and will likely improve police services through better trained and better equipped police officers. Yet, some communities will resist losing the autonomy of having their own police department. It will be incumbent upon community leaders to assess the advantages and disadvantages of the three Cs vs. operating a police department and to ensure that the consequences—both positive and negative—are fully understood before decisions are made.

Police Field Work

Numerous themes emerge from the chapter on police field work that will continue to shape policing. First, the law plays a centrally important role as a roadmap for police officers, defining legal and illegal activity and serving as a primary tool for fighting crime. It is abundantly clear that the law is not static: New laws that affect policing are passed by local, state, and federal governments every day. Moreover, courts at the state and federal level, including the U.S. Supreme Court, hear cases and hand down rulings that have implications for police. Well-established principles such as reasonable suspicion, probable cause, wiretapping, and proper methods for interrogation are continually tested and, in some cases, modified by the judicial and legislative branches. The Patriot Act is a perfect example of this point. It is incumbent upon police departments to stay apprised of these changes. Larger departments can maintain their own legal staff, but the vast majority of police departments do not have that luxury. Instead, police officers must either stay abreast of law changes and court rulings themselves or rely on the leadership of the department to keep them informed.

Second, discretion is centrally important to police officers, and efforts to eliminate that discretion are usually destined for failure. Attempts to eliminate police discretion may work in the short term, but one of two things typically happens: Either police officers find ways around the effort and continue to exercise discretion, or police give it up and the discretion flows to other officials in the system. For example, mandatory arrest policies for domestic violence have been widely adopted, but little has changed in prosecution and conviction rates because of the decisions made by prosecutors (to not pursue cases, especially if the victim is uncooperative). We have known for some time that administrative policies that structure and guide discretion—and importantly, are enforced by police management—offer an effective avenue for reducing the prevalence of poor decision making. Recent examples of the effectiveness of administrative policy include deadly force, automobile pursuits, less-than-lethal weapons, and police dogs.

Last, the crime problems that police are facing today and that will challenge them in the future include a mix of old and new problems. Although crime and violence have decreased nationally, partly because competition over profitable crack cocaine markets has subsided, crime has increased in many cities. Gangs and related crime have reached a crisis point in many communities and have begun to flourish in suburban and rural communities. Police officers find themselves confronted with both domestic violence and the mentally ill on an almost daily basis. New approaches have emerged to address each of these more traditional crimes, and conventional wisdom suggests that the three-pronged model of prevention, intervention, and suppression offers the most viable strategy to address these problems. Alternatively, police today are also faced with crime problems that they have not had to worry about in the past, such as identity theft, computer crime, and terrorism. The fragmented nature of policing in the United States, with over 17,000 agencies, severely limits the development of effective responses to these new problems. Simply put, most small departments do not have the resources or expertise to investigate identity theft, computer crime, or terrorism. As a result, the future of policing in these areas rests with developing coordinated, multiagency partnerships or task forces, with a strong leadership role for federal law enforcement. These types of partnerships pool expertise and resources from many agencies, producing a more consistent and effective law enforcement response. Partnerships with federal leadership also offer an opportunity to provide necessary training, skills, and expertise to police officers in other departments so that an effective response can begin immediately once police find out about a crime.

Measuring Police Performance

Given my predictions above about the traditional reactive model of policing "going the way of the dinosaur," the **numbers game** approach to measuring police performance must be significantly modified. Activity, whether at the departmental or individual officer level, can no longer be the sole measure of police performance. The job is too complex, with too many other responsibilities, to rely on crime-related measures only. Regardless of the philosophy of the police department—COP, POP, zero tolerance, CompStat, and even the traditional reactive model—police officers spend the majority of their time involved in non-crime-related activities. Police departments must develop ways to measure performance in these other, non-number-producing activities.

The short answer to this problem is that there is no one "best" measure of performance, and departments should rely on a portfolio of measures to create an overall performance assessment. This portfolio must include crime-related activity, such as reported crimes, arrests, and tickets. But it should also take into account prosecution and conviction rates, which often (though not always) are a reflection of the work of police. There are also enhanced measures of crime-related activity such as NIBRS. Given the emphasis on police–community relations, it seems appropriate that community satisfaction surveys should be included in the performance assessments of departments and individual police officers. These surveys can tap into a range of social and community dynamics such as social and physical disorganization, fear of crime, street-level crime, perceptions of the police and satisfaction with their level of service.

Problem-oriented strategies and CompStat-like approaches produce natural, measurable outcomes, and the achievement of these outcomes can be used to assess performance on both a departmental and individual officer level. These approaches focus on problem identification, development of solutions, implementation, and assessment; a process that is perfectly suited to performance assessment. Moreover, **peer evaluations** can play a supporting role in performance evaluations. There is no question that police officers are the best judges of who among them excel in their work and who does not. The challenge for a police department is to develop an evaluation system that takes advantage of that knowledge, where officers are candid and honest about their assessments without creating conflict or undue pressure on line personnel. And last, several police departments have begun to employ intensive and detailed performance evaluation forms. For example, the NYPD's evaluation includes assessments on more than 25 different dimensions of performance, including routine aspects of the job and behavior dimensions such as reasoning ability, spatial orientation, and innovativeness.

However, the key to successful performance evaluation at the individual officer level hinges on the first-line supervisors who carry out the task. It must be viewed as a critically important part of the sergeant's job, and it may be necessary to eliminate other responsibilities to make sufficient time for performance evaluations. Another alternative involves creating performance evaluation teams who are solely responsible for assessing officer performance based on interviews with peers, supervisors, the officer, and reviews of available paperwork. The point is that assessment of line officer performance must be something that is taken seriously, given due time and resources, and represents an actual reflection of one's performance (i.e., good police officers receive good performance evaluations; mediocre officers receive mediocre evaluations, etc.).

Police Deviance and Responding to It

Clearly, police departments have come a long way in terms of reducing deviant behavior, such as brutality and excessive force, corruption, and discrimination. Given these successes, it would be nice—though unrealistic—to predict that the future of policing will not include additional instances of misconduct. However, as stated in Chapter 8, police deviance has a history as long as organized, professional policing itself. Despite the efforts of some of the top minds in policing and scholarly circles, many police departments continue to be plagued by deviance-related scandals in an almost cyclical nature. In New York, the incidents involving Abner Louima and Amadou Diallo occurred less than a decade ago. The New Jersey State Police is still under a consent decree for racial profiling on the New Jersey Turnpike.

Given the persistence of deviance in policing, departments would be well advised to think about building strategies to reduce the prevalence of misconduct, and to thoroughly investigate and eliminate it when it occurs. There are two general categories of police accountability measures, those that are within the police department itself (discussed in Chapter 9) and those that are outside of the police department (discussed in Chapter 10). First and foremost, there is no one best accountability measure that, by itself, will effectively control bad police behavior. Each measure has its own advantages and disadvantages, and the optimal approach is to employ a well-rounded package of accountability mechanisms. That being said, there are a number of mechanisms that, taken together hold great promise and should be fundamental elements of any anti-misconduct effort. These include:

- Careful selection of personnel
- Proper training
- Front-line supervision
- Guidance through administrative policy
- Internal Affairs unit

- **Early warning system**
- A clear message from the top of the department (accountability and discipline)
- Civil litigation (suing the police)
- Judicial intervention
- Consent decrees (pattern and practice lawsuits)
- Citizen oversight

It is unreasonable to assume that police departments can eliminate deviance altogether. Once again using history as our guide, there is a clear track record to refute that assumption. However, the department that employs a comprehensive accountability package including the measures listed above will likely substantially reduce poor decision making and bad behavior. At the same time, police officer performance and police–community relationships will improve significantly.

Technology

Chapter 11 states that technology, more than any other phenomena, has been the driving force behind change and advancement in policing. Consider the two-way radio, telephone, automobile, **fingerprinting, DNA,** toolmark identification, GIS and crime mapping, the Internet, less-than-lethal weapons, and geographic profiling. These innovations have, over the last seventy-five years, revolutionized policing. Consider the image of Joe Friday from the *Dragnet* television series in the 1960s and compare him to the characters of today on *CSI* and *Law and Order.*

Although the overriding message of Chapter 11 is that technology has played—and will continue to play—a defining role in U.S. policing, we must still be cautious about following technology "for the sake of technology." I am reminded of the old James Bond movies when Bond would enter M's laboratory and examine all of his new inventions, wondering about the relevance any of it had to his current mission (of course, Mr. Bond always found himself in positions where exploding pens, plastic explosive chewing gum, and cars that double as boats came in handy!).

Policing is still and will always be about talking to and helping people. Consider that much of the innovation that has been infused into policing over the last twenty years deals with crime and criminal investigation: fingerprints, DNA, imaging, crime analysis and mapping, forensic science. We must not forget that dealing with crime is a relatively small—though very important—part of the responsibility of the police. The majority of their work involves service and order-maintenance-related tasks where DNA and fingerprinting are simply not relevant (see Dr. Michael Hallett's scholarly perspective in Appendix 12A). Once again, it is important to use history as a guide: Technological innovation is largely responsible for the professional, reactive model of policing that emerged in the first part of the twentieth century. Let us not make the same mistakes again as we continue to advance technologically. If we do not lose sight of the core ingredients of effective policing, which center on talking to and helping people, technological innovation can continue to improve and advance the field of policing.

SUMMARY

This chapter serves as both a summary of the rest of the book and as a projected roadmap of where the profession of policing is headed in the near future. Some of the "guesses" about the future described above are almost "sure bets," while others are very much in doubt. One final thought I would like to add involves the central role of research and evaluation in the continued development of policing. More than any other area in criminal justice, research has played a central role in helping us to understand what police do, why they do it, how they do it, and how can we improve upon their current methods. Recall the early work on police discretion and factors influencing police decision making, the police subculture, police patrol (Kansas City Preventive Patrol Study), police response to domestic violence (original Minneapolis study and its replications), the success of administrative guidelines in controlling police behavior (deadly force, automobile pursuits, etc.), and the various successes and failures of COP, POP, zero tolerance, and CompStat. The future of policing should also maintain this central role for research. Quite simply, police and their constituents can guess about what works and what does not, but obtaining definitive answers to these questions will hinge upon both methodologically rigorous research and evaluation and then careful consideration of the implications of findings for their policy and practice. Despite being a relatively closed-off institution, the police have a long and distinguished track record of opening themselves to social researchers, and this continued openness is essential for the future.

KEY TERMS

Affirmative action
Civilianization
Community policing
CompStat
Consolidation
Discretion
Diversity
DNA
Early warning system

Fingerprinting
Mass hiring
Numbers game
Peer evaluation
Problem-oriented policing
Quasi-military model
Residency requirement
Zero Tolerance policing

DISCUSSION QUESTIONS

1. Describe the keys issues in recruitment and selection for the future of policing.

2. Describe the key organizational issues for the future of policing. Include in your discussion different strategies of policing such as COP, POP, zero tolerance, and CompStat.

3. Describe the key issues in police field work for the future of policing.

4. Describe the key issues in performance measurement for the future of policing.

5. Describe the key issues for police deviance—and controlling it—for the future of policing.

REFERENCES

Kelling, G.L., & Moore, M.H. (1991). From political to reform to community: The evolving strategy of the police. In J.R. Greene & S.D. Mastrofski (Eds.), *Community policing: Rhetoric or reality.* New York: Praeger.

Skolnick, J.H., & Fyfe, J.J. (1993). *Above the law: Police and the excessive use of force.* New York: Free Press.

Soulliere, N. (1999). *Police and technology: Historical review and current status.* Ottawa: Canadian Police College.

■ ■ ■ ■ ■ ▬▬▬▬▬▬▬▬▬▬▬▬▬▬▬▬▬

SCHOLAR'S PERSPECTIVE

COPS and *CSI:* Reality Television?

Michael Hallett, Ph.D.* University of North Florida

Not a week goes by, it seems, that I do not hear from a freshman or sophomore Criminal Justice student of their intention to do *crime scene investigations* professionally and, moreover, that they intend to "go federal" in their future law enforcement careers. I've learned to take this information in slowly before suggesting that students go to the *Sourcebook of Criminal Justice Statistics* and look up data on just how many federal versus state and local law enforcement positions there are in the United States. Most jobs in law enforcement, I explain, are at the local level—and most people get into law enforcement not to become crime solvers but because they wish to help people (Raganella & White, 2004). Most police work, in fact, involves helping people in trying situations and not crime fighting, I suggest, and probably the most rewarding jobs in law enforcement are at the local level.

For the *CSI* fans, I also keep on hand ready-made copies of several articles documenting the so-called the "CSI Effect," referring to how "on TV, it's all slam-dunk evidence and quick convictions," but in reality, criminal convictions based on forensic evidence alone are very rare (Roane, 2005). In real life, the empirical evidence on the utility of CSI is less than compelling. A recent study published in the journal *Science* notes that forensic evidence testing errors are the second leading cause of wrongful convictions—and that 63 percent of wrongful convictions can be attributed to such errors (Saks & Koehler, 2005, p. 892). According to this same study, 27 percent of wrongful convictions result from "false/misleading testimony by forensic scientists" (Saks & Koehler, 2005, p. 892). I explain to my young CSI wannabes (who plan to "go federal") that solving most crimes hinges on good basic police work—on what the local, frontline law enforcement officer does at the scene. In short, the particular version of criminal justice reality portrayed on television is invariably something less than authentic—even as one must respect the professional growth of a TV CSI investigator with a 98 percent clearance rate, but whose first calling was that of a professional nightclub dancer.

As the work of Peter Manning demonstrates, police have a special relationship to the mass media (Manning, 1977, 1997). Drawing on the work of Erving Goffman,

---

*Professor and Chair, Department of Criminology and Criminal Justice, University of North Florida, Ph.D. Arizona State University.

Manning documents how "the police self is shaped by mass media," particularly key elements of police subculture and police community relations (Manning, 2001, p. 153). In the aftermath of Rodney King, police departments became acutely aware of the importance of "controlling the message" through staff positions such as public information officers and official press conferences (Surette, 1998). Programs like *COPS*, in fact, portray only highly edited and stylized versions of police work selectively approved for broadcast by police officials. As a condition of access, the production company that produces the show *COPS* grants near full editorial control over all footage that ultimately gets broadcast, with police departments themselves referring to tapings of *COPS* episodes as "public relations opportunities" (Hallett & Powell, 1995). In research I conducted with a former colleague, officers filmed during the production of *COPS* episodes produced with Nashville Metropolitan Police Department revealed in survey research that they were simultaneously "happy with the portrayal of police work on *COPS*," but doubtful that the show offered either the "police perspective on the crime problem" or gave "an accurate portrayal of police work" (Hallett & Powell, 1995). So much for "reality television." Thus, in many ways, programs like *COPS* and *CSI* might rightly be viewed as public relations efforts or propaganda.

Unfortunately, we now exist in a media environment in which the media's portrayal of criminal justice "reality" is best characterized by what criminologist Ray Surette (1998) calls the "law of opposites":

> Whatever the media show is the opposite of what is true. In every subject category— crimes, criminals, crime fighters, the investigation of crimes, arrests, the processing and disposition of cases—the entertainment media present a world of crime and justice that is not found in reality. (p. 47)

Given that most Americans rely on media accounts of crime and criminal justice for their understanding of the crime problem, research suggests that many citizens are thoroughly misinformed about criminal justice policy and police work in particular. In our research on the show *COPS*, we concluded that overzealous and unrealistic portrayals of police effectiveness—portrayals of police as superhero crime fighters who always catch the criminal—in the end actually work to compromise our ability to fight crime and harm police by placing unrealistic expectations on them. However much we might want to believe that simply hiring more police and building more prisons to house their arrestees will solve the crime problem, long-lasting solutions to the crime problem clearly depend on addressing the underlying social problems that make police work such a challenging profession.

REFERENCES

Hallett, M.A., & Powell, D. (1995). Backstage with "COPS": The dramaturgical reification of police subculture in American crime info-tainment. *American Journal of Police, 14*(1), 101–129.

Manning, P. (1977). *Police work.* Cambridge, MA: MIT Press.

Manning, P. (1997). Media loops. In F. Bailey & D. Hale (Eds.), *Popular culture, crime and justice.* (pp. 25–39). Belmont, CA: Wadsworth ITP.

Manning, P. (2001). Policing and reflection. In R.G. Dunham & G. Alpert (Eds.), *Classical issues in policing.* Prospect Heights, IL: Waveland. (pp. 149–157).

Raganella, A.J., & White, M.D. (2004). Race, gender, and motivation for becoming a police officer: Implications for building a representative police department. *Journal of Criminal Justice, 32,* 501–513.

Roane K.R. (2005). The CSI Effect. *US News & World Report, 138* (15), 48.

Saks, M.J., & Koehler, J.J. (2005). The coming paradigm shift in forensic identification science. *Science, 309,* 892–895.

Surette, R. (1998). *Media crime and criminal justice: Images and realities.* Belmont, CA: Wadsworth ITP.

Abuse
  of authority (*See* Authority, abuse of)
  domestic, 187
  legal, 240, 247
  mentally ill and occurring substance, 186
  physical, 239, 247
  psychological, 240, 247
Academy training, 31
Accidental shootings, accountability for, 278
Accountability
  accreditation, 284–85
  changing subculture, 285–86
  chief, role of, 286–87
  due to unions, 137
  early warning systems (EW) for, 282–84
  importance of, 98
  integrity tests, 281–82
  Internal Affairs and, 279–81
  lack of, example, 160
  maintaining, 110
Accreditation, 284–85
Administrative law, 165
  limitations of, 278
Administrative services, 144–46
  communication/dispatch, 144–45
  personnel, 145
  property, 146
  public information, 146
  records, 145
  research and planning, 146
  training, 145–46
Advanced Generation of Interoperability for
  Law Enforcement program (AGILE),
  342
Affidavit, 166
Affirmative Action, 11–13, 270, 354
  plan components, 12
  reverse discrimination, 12
African Americans
  Affirmative Action and, 12
  brutality against, 92
  drug use, 180
  racial profiling, 258
  recruitment of, 10, 28
  use of force against, 252
  use of police dogs on, 277
Age, as requirement for recruitment, 4
Agency schools, 38, 61
Alcohol testing, 13
Alliance for the Mentally Ill, 54
Amendments
  Eighteenth, 77

Eighth, 165
Fifth, 80, 164, 165, 173, 308
First, 165
Fourteenth, 79, 165
Fourth, 81, 164, 165, 168, 170, 171, 173,
  306, 346
  knowledge of, 14
Sixth, 80, 164, 165
American Bar Association (ABA), 276, 296
  identification of police roles by, 139
  report on police roles and standards, 84
American Civil Liberties Union (ACLU),
  173, 260, 318
  of Southern California, 16
American Federation of Labor (AFL), 135
American Medical Association (AMA),
  296
Andragogy, 32, 40
  benefits of, 47–48
  definition of, 47
Anti-Terrorism Advisory Committee (ATAC),
  194
Anti-Terrorism and Effective Death Penalty
  Act, 56
Anti-war movement, 81–82
Arizona v. Fulminante, 170
Ashcroft, John, 172
Assault and battery, 300
Atlanta Police Department, health require-
  ments for, 5
Authority, abuse of, 237, 239–40, 247–53
  consequences of, 249
  controversies surrounding, 249–50
Authority, order of, 129
Automobile, 328
  patrol, 75, 77, 93

Background check, 8–9
Ballistics, 332
Barker, Ma, 3
Barrow, Clyde, 3
Battle dress uniforms (BDU), 154
Bean-bag gun, 56
Behaviorally anchored rating scale (BARS),
  44
Berger v. New York, 171
Berkeley Police Department
  and August Vollmer, 3
  reforms in, 75
Bertillon, Alphonse, 330
Betts v. Brady, 80

Bill of Rights, 165–69, 173
  exclusionary rule, 167–68
  legal principles from, 165–69
  probable cause, 166
  reasonable suspicion, 165–66
  searches and arrests, 166–67
bin Laden, Osama, 173
Biometrics, 344
Black, Donald, 82
Black codes, 70
Blue-coat crime, 253
Blue flu, 137
Blue-ribbon commissions, 307
  major, 308–12
Blue wall of silence, 279
Bobbies, 68, 70, 86, 174
Bogardus, Van, 250
Boston, Massachusetts
  Gun Project, 100, 183
  problem-oriented policing in, 100–101
  unions in, 135
Bow Street Runners, 68
Bratton, William, 112, 118, 119
Breier, Harold, 286
Broken windows theory, 93, 103, 106, 108,
    118, 120
  example of, 162
Brooklyn North Neighborhood Safety
    Project, 124–27
Brown v. Mississippi, 309
Brutality, 110, 205, 286
  against African Americans, 92
  in early twentieth century, 77
  during political era, 72–73
  in zero tolerance policing, 119
Bundy, Ted, 142
Bureaucracy, 128–38
  advantages and disadvantages of, 131–32
  career paths in, 131
  features of, 129–31
  rules and regulations, 130–31
  span of control, 130
  unity of command, 130
Bureau of Alcohol, Tobacco, and Firearms
    (BATF), 182
  creation of, 84
Bureau of Justice Statistics (BJS), 53, 175,
    210, 213, 248
Burnham, David, 309, 319
Bush, George, 172

California Psychological Inventory (CPI), 20
California v. Ciraola, 171
Call boxes, 72
Camden Police Department, supercession of,
    323–26
Capone, Al, 77
Centralization, of police, 73

Chain of command, 129, 284
Chain of custody, 335
Chicago Alternative Policing Strategies
    (CAPS), 108, 220
  findings of, 108–9
  program, 109–10
Chicago Police Department
  and crime mapping, 349
  and gangs, 181
Chief, role of, 286–87
Christopher Commission, 215, 248, 283,
    311–12
Citizen oversight, 314–18
  definition of, 314
  history of, 314–15
  impact of, 317–18
  models of, 316–17
  pros and cons, 315–16
Citizens, types of (Van Maanen), 105
Citizenship, as requirement for recruitment, 4
Civil disobedience, 81
Civilianization, 152–53, 358
Civil law, 165
Civil litigation, 299–304
  advantages and disadvantages of, 303–4
  police liability under federal law, 301–3
  police liability under state law, 299–301
Civil Rights Act
  of 1871, 301
  of 1871, Section 1983, 301
  of 1964, 5, 8
Civil Rights Division
  of the U.S. Department of Justice, 297, 312
Civil Rights movement, 81–82
Civil Service, 134–35
  Act of 1883 (*See* Pendleton Act)
  League, 135
Clearance rates, 212
Closed circuit television (CCTV), 343
Code of silence, 281, 285, 311. *See also* Blue
    wall of silence
Cold case squads, 344
College education, 354–55
  recruitment of students with, 75
  as requirement for officers, 16–19
College-sponsored training academies, 38, 61
Colonial America
  policing in, 69–70
  slave patrols in, 70
  vigilante committees in, 70
  volunteer system in, 69
  watch systems in, 69
Combined DNA Index System (CODIS), 331,
    342, 344
Commission on Accreditation for Law En-
    forcement Agencies (CALEA), 10, 38, 39,
    44, 64, 131, 222, 248, 276, 284–85, 354
  and recruitment, 270
  standards for in-service training, 46

Commissions
    Christopher, 215, 248, 283, 311–12
    Curran, 308
    Kerner, 49, 81, 83, 309, 315
    Knapp, 240, 242, 243, 254, 255, 269, 281, 308, 309–10, 319
    Mollen, 243, 255, 269, 285–86, 308, 311
    MOVE, 310–11
    Wickersham, 75, 77–78, 308–9, 314
Communication, 18, 144
    BlackBerry cellphones/PDAs, 162
    guidelines for effective, 55
    lack of system during political era, 73
    telephone, 75, 77
    training in, 55
    two-way radio, 75, 77
Community
    decline in sense of, 103
    satisfaction, 229
Community-oriented policing (COP), 14, 32, 46, 102–11, 107, 128, 141, 148, 213, 225, 357
    assumptions of, 111
    communication skills in, 55
    comparison with zero tolerance policing, POP, CompStat, 120–21
    core features of, 103–7
    diffusion of, 107–8
    example of, 162–63
    limitations of, 110–11
    and mentally ill, 186
    movements, 61
    organizational change, 104–5
    police-community partnership, 103–4
    problem solving in, 105–6
    programmatic elements of, 106–7
    research on effectiveness of, 108–10
    tenets of, 107
    theoretical foundations of, 102–3
    training in, 48–49
Comprehensive Homicide Initiative, 101, 183
CompStat, 93, 99, 112–18, 119, 128, 132, 213, 221, 234, 325, 339, 357
    background on, 112
    and Brooklyn North Neighborhood Safety Project, 126
    comparison with zero tolerance policing, COP, POP, 120–21
    components of, 115–16
    creation of, 87
    diffusion of, 116
    directed patrol as part of, 141
    example of, 160–61
    impact of, 116–18
    meetings, 53
    objectives of, 113
    stages of, 112–15
Computer crime, 192–93
Consent decrees, 312–14
    pattern and practice lawsuits, 312–13
    as reform mechanism, 313–14
    requirements for, 313
Consolidation, 153–54, 358
Constitution, 165, 259, 307
Contracting for police services, 154, 358
COPPAR v. Rizzo, 305
Cops as soldiers, 214, 246
Cop's code, 149
Corruption, 91, 110, 239, 240, 253–56
    current controversies, 254–54
    in early twentieth century, 77
    levels of, 254
    moral, 33
    during political era, 72–73
    recent cases of, 255–56
    types of, 253–54
Counterterrorism, 46
    training, 32, 56–57
Crime, 82
    absence of, Peel's definition of effective policing, 69, 132, 206
    blue-coat, 253
    computer crime, 192–93
    cybercrime, 193
    dark figure of, 210
    domestic violence, 183–85
    drugs, 179–81
    fear of, 108, 220, 222
    gangs, 181–83
    identity theft, 188–92
    mapping, 99, 329, 339, 340–41, 349–51
    and mentally ill, 186
    organized, 77
    patterns, 113, 117
    prevention, 69
    problems, 179–94
    reduction of by CompStat, 117
    sex, investigating, 202
    suppression, in Brooklyn North Neighborhood Safety Project, 124
    terrorism, 193–94
    triangle, 96, 102
Crime analysis, 337–41
    current, 337–39
    functions of, 338
    geographic information system (GIS), 339–41
Crime and Delinquency, 93
Crime fighting, 105
    as sole duty of officers, 74
Crime scene investigation, 329–37
    basic procedures in, 334–36
    blood, saliva, semen, skin, 331–32
    DNA, 331–32
    documentation, 335
    evidence, collecting and preserving, 335
    evidence, search for, 335
    fingerprints, 330–31

Crime scene investigation (*cont.*)
  forensic science developments, 332–34
  historical perspective of, 330
  Locard exchange principle, 330–31
  as portrayed on television, 365–66
  reconstruction, 336
  securing scene, 334
  walk-through, 334–35
  weapon, 332
Criminal Geographic Targeting (CGT), 341
Criminal identity theft, 189
Criminalization, of mentally ill, 187–88
Criminal law, 165, 295–99
  background, 295–96
  as tool against police misconduct, 296–99
Criminal Liability for Deprivation of Civil
    Rights, 296
Criminal record, as factor in recruitment, 5–6
Criminology program, founding of, 75
Crisis intervention team (CIT), 54, 188
  goals of, 55
Curran Commission, 308
Curriculum, for academy training program,
    40–41
Curtilage, 170–71
Cyber criminals, 192
  criminal groups, 192
  hackers, 192
  insiders, 192
  virus writers, 192

Dahmer, Jeffrey, 259–60
Daily observation report (DOR), 44
Dallas Police Department Gang Unit, 182–83
DARE. *See* Drug Abuse Resistance
    Education (DARE)
Davis, Linda, 297
Deadly force, 248, 251–52, 276
Decentralization, 130
Deception, use of during interrogation, 170
Decision making
  complex police role, 174
  context for, 174–75
  environmental variables, 175–76
  factors influencing, 175–77
  force in, 175
  organizational variables, 175, 176
  politics in, 174–75
  rationality of, 178–79
  situational variables, 175, 176–77
  understanding complexity of, 177–78
Deinstitutionalization, of mentally ill, 185
Department of Homeland Security
  creation of, 56
  and terrorism, 193
Detectives, 143–44
Developmental training, 64–65
Diallo, Amadou, 252, 361

Dillinger, John, 3
Directed patrol, 141
Disciplinary system, 287
Discretion, 134, 150, 178, 244, 358
  defining, 173–74
Discrimination, 256–60
  cases of racial, 259–60
  categories of, 256
  controversies in, 256–59
  definition of, 256
  internal *vs.* external, 256
  officer rank, 256
  racial profiling, 256–59
Dispatch, 144–45
District attorney, political nature of position,
    297
Diversity, 354
  in community, importance of, 50
  in police organization, 140
  in recruitment, 23, 28–29
  training, 49–51
DNA (deoxyribonucleic acid), 331–32,
    362
  evidence, 146
Dogs, use of, 250, 277
  bites by, 250
Domestic violence
  and accountability, 277–78
  changing response to, 183
  comprehensive approaches to, 185
  cycle of abuse, 187
  mandatory arrest, 183–84
  policing, 183–85
  training, 53
Dowd, Michael, 215, 255, 274, 308
  and Mollen Commission, 311
Driver's license, as requirement for
    recruitment, 4
Drug Abuse Resistance Education (DARE),
    139, 180
Drug Enforcement Agency (DEA), 84, 115
Drugs, 179–81
  houses, use of SWAT teams with, 155
  increase in use, 82
  testing, 13
  trafficking, 179
Drunk driving, 207, 225
Due process revolution, 79, 86, 305, 306
Dummy
  drag/pull, 19, 271

Early warning systems (EW), 282–84, 313,
    362
  components of, 283–84
  effectiveness of, 283–84
  function of, 292
  impact on performance, 293
  intervention, 284, 292, 293

officer characteristics identified by, 293
post-intervention monitoring, 284, 292, 293
prevalence of, 292
responding to problem officer, 291–94
selection criteria, 284, 292, 293
Education, as requirement for recruitment, 7
Emergency Response units, 154
Equal Employment Opportunity Commission (EEOC), 19
index, 10
Estate of Sinthasomphone vs. City of Milwaukee, 259
Evidence
chain of custody of, 335
collecting and preserving, 335
searching for, 335
Excessive force, 251, 286
in zero tolerance policing, 119
Exclusionary rule, 79, 167–68, 169, 305, 306
exceptions to, 168

False arrest and imprisonment, 300
Family Crisis Intervention Unit (FCIU), 185
Federal Bureau of Investigation (FBI), 115, 212, 213, 241, 356
crime laboratory, 3
development of, 3
National Academy, 47, 65
reforms in, 76
training academy, 3
Federal Law Enforcement Training Center (FLETC), 65
Federal Office of the Police Corps and Law Enforcement Education, 21
Federal Trade Commission (FTC), 189
Feelings-Inputs-Tactics (FIT), 52–53
Fielding, Henry, 68
Field services, 140–43
investigation, 143–44
patrol, 140–42
traffic, 142–43
Field training officer programs (FTO), 43–46, 63–64, 272
benefits of, 43–44
example of, 45–46
performance evaluation of rookies, 44
San Jose model, 43
selection of officers, 45
Field work, 164–95
future of, 359–60
Financial identity theft, 189
Fingerprints, 327, 330–31, 344, 362
early use of, 75
latent, 330
Firearms, Peel's beliefs about, 71
Flat organization, 150

Florida Department of Law Enforcement (FDLE), 296
Florida v. Riley, 171
Floyd, "Pretty Boy," 3
Force
deadly, 248, 251–52, 276
excessive, 251, 286
use of, 247–49
Foreign Intelligence Surveillance Act (FISA), 172
Forensic sciences, 329
developments in, 332–34
Fosdick, Raymond, 309
Fraternal Order of Police (FOP), 135, 136, 297
Freeh, Louis, 241
Friday, Joe, 79, 82, 362
Fulwood, Isaac, 21

Gang Resistance Education and Training (GREAT), 182
Gangs, 181–83
problem-oriented policing and, 100–101
risk factors for, 181
Gates, Darryl, 286
Gender, motivations for becoming police officer, differences among, 11
Geocoding, 339
Geographic crime analysis, 113
Geographic information system (GIS), 337, 339–41, 349
Geographic profiling, 341
Gideon, Clarence Earl, 80
Gideon v. Wainwright, 80
Glassock, Bruce, 194
Global positioning systems (GPS), 342–43
Goffman, Ervin, 365
Goldstein, Herman, 87, 93, 207
Goode, Wilson, 310
Gordon riots, 68
Grant, Heath, 27
Grant, Ulysses S., 2
Grass-eater, corrupt officer, 255, 310
Guiliani, Rudolph, 112, 118, 119

Hallett, Michael, 329, 362
Hamilton, Alexander, 159
Handwriting analysis, 328
Health, as requirement for recruitment, 4–5
Heat sensing equipment, 171
Height and weight, as requirement for recruitment, 5
Hierarchical organization, police as, 129
Hierarchy rule, 213
High-speed pursuits, 276–77
Hired guns, 71
Holliday, George, 296, 314, 319

Homes for Peace Officers and Firefighters, 16
Hoover, Herbert, 77, 308
  as creator of Wickersham Commission, 77
Hoover, J. Edgar, 3, 76
Hospital model of organization, 150–52
Hostage negotiation team, 223
Hot pursuits, 250–51
Hot spots, 113, 117, 155
Houston Police Department, performance evaluation in, 226

Identity theft, 188–92
  California approach, 191–92
  cloning, 189
  criminal, 189
  definition of, 189
  financial, 189
  impact of, 189–90
  jurisdiction, 191
  policing, 190–92
  prevalence of, 189–90
Imaging, 345–46
  functions of, 345
Immigration, impact of on society, 91
Independent Commission on the Los Angeles Police Department, 20
Injunction, 304
Injunctive relief, 304–5
In-service training, 31, 33, 46–47, 272
  in community policing, 46
  in counterterrorism, 46
  management, 47
  specialized, 46–47
Integrated Automated Fingerprint Identification System (IAFIS), 331, 342
Integrated Ballistics Identification System (IBIS), 332
Integrity tests, 279, 281–82
Intentional torts
  assault and battery, 300
  false arrest and imprisonment, 300
  malicious prosecution and abuse of process, 300
  wrongful death, 300
Internal Affairs, 279–81
  challenges facing, 279–80
  keys for effective, 280–81
International Association of Chiefs of Police (IACP), 38, 65, 183, 194, 255, 256, 284, 299, 318
International City Management Association (ICMA), 49
International Union of Police Associations (IUPA), 136
Internet, as tool, 341–42

Interrogation, 168
  using deception during, 170
Investigation, 143–44

Jacksonville Sheriff's Office, residency requirements for, 15
Jersey City, New Jersey, problem-oriented policing in, 100
Jim Crow laws, 70
Johnson, Lyndon B., 82, 309
Johnson v. Transportation Agency, 12
Judicial intervention, 304–7
  injunctive relief, 304–5
  U.S. Supreme Court, 305–7
Jurisdiction, in identity theft, 191

Kansas City Preventive Patrol Study, 85, 87, 93, 121, 141, 211
  levels of patrol, 85
Katz v. United States, 171
Kelly, "Machine Gun," 3
Kennedy, John F., 84
Kennedy, Robert, 84
Kerner Commission, 49, 81, 83, 309, 315
  problems identified by, 83
King, Rodney, 296, 311, 314, 366
  beating of, 20, 242, 243, 247, 251, 296, 297, 311, 314, 319
  civil litigation by, 299
King Jr., Martin Luther, 84
Knapp Commission, 240, 242, 243, 254, 255, 269, 281, 308, 309–10, 319
Kyllo v. United States, 171, 346

Law
  administrative, 165
  Bill of Rights, 165
  civil, 165
  controversies involving, 169–73
  criminal, 165
  curtilage, 170–71
  deception, use of, 170
  and police, 164–73
  police liability under federal, 301–3
  police liability under state, 299–301
  pretextual stops and, 169–70
  primary aggressor, 186
Law Enforcement Assistance Administration (LEAA), 7, 16, 83–84
Law Enforcement Education Program (LEEP), 7, 16, 83–84
Law Enforcement Management and Administrative Statistics survey (LEMAS), 182
Lawsuits, due to height discrimination, 5

Leadership
  in police, 146–49
  training, 33
Lee v. Florida, 171
Legal abuse, 240, 247
Legal counsel, impact of *Gideon v.*
    Wainwright on, 80
Less-than-lethal weapons, 56, 249, 345
  ballistic rounds, 249
  bean-bag gun, 56
  impact weapons, 249
  mace, 56, 249
  oleoresin capsicum (pepper spray), 249
  Taser, 56
  tear gas, 249
Lexow Committee, 74, 308
Lie detector. *See* Polygraph
Lindsay, John V., 310
Locard exchange principle, 327, 330–31, 334
London Metropolitan Police Department, 67,
    87, 174, 237, 240
  creation of, 67–69
  Metropolitan Police Act of 1829, 68
Los Angeles Police Department (LAPD)
  Affirmative Action and, 12
  and Christopher Commission, 215
  and DARE, 180
  excessive force in, 242
  psychological testing in, 20
  Rampart CRASH unit of, 255–56
  recruitment in, 270
  Rodney King beating, 20, 296–97, 311
  stress management training in, 52
  Vollmer as chief of, 92
Los Angeles Sheriff's Department
  contracting for services by, 154
  misconduct litigation, attorney for, 303
Louima, Abner, 119, 253, 296, 361
  civil litigation by, 299
Lyons v. Los Angeles, 305

Mace, 56
Malicious prosecution and abuse of process,
    300
Management
  culture, 148
  training, 47, 65–66
Mandate, police, 205–6
Mandatory arrest, 185
  moving beyond, 186
Manning, Peter, 173, 365
Manpower shortages, 152–54
  civilianization, 152–53
  consolidation, 153–54
  contracting for police services, 154
Maple, Jack, 112
Mapp, Dolree, 79

Mapp v. Ohio, 79–80, 305
  exclusionary rule in, 79, 167–68
Mass hirings, 21, 269, 355
McVeigh, Timothy, 142
Means/end syndrome, 207
Meat-eater, corrupt officer, 254, 255, 310
Media, 319
Memphis Police Department
  and crisis intervention teams, 54, 188
  handling mentally ill by, 54
Mendoza v. Block, 277
Mentally ill
  consumers, 54
  and crime, 186
  criminalization of, 187–88
  crisis intervention teams, 188
  deinstitutionalization of, 185–86
  hospitalization of, 187
  and police, 185–88
  substance abuse in, 186
  training in handling, 53–55
Metro-Dade Police Citizen Violence
    Reduction Project, 229
Metropolitan Police Act of 1829, and Peel, Sir
    Robert, 68–69
Miami-Dade Police Department
  health requirements for, 4–5
  use of Tasers in, 272
Miami River cops, 243
Militarization
  police, 154–56
  of training, 22, 42
Milwaukee Police Department, and Dahmer,
    Jeffrey, 259–60
Minneapolis Domestic Violence study, 186
Minnesota Multiphasic Personality Inventory
    (MMPI), 20
Miranda, Ernesto, 80
Miranda rights, 80
  knowledge of, 14
  questioning/interrogation with, 168–69
Miranda v. Arizona, 168, 306, 307
Misconduct, 146
Mobile digital terminals (MDT), 56
Mollen Commission, 243, 255, 269, 285–86,
    308, 311
Monell v. Department of Social Services of
    the City of New York, 185, 302
Monroe v. Pape, 302
Moral corruption, 33
Morka v. State of New Jersey, 259
Motorcycle patrol, creation of, 75
MOVE Commission, 310–11
Multicultural Close-Contact Training (MCC),
    50
Multicultural Law Enforcement, 50
Multicultural training, 49–51
Murphy, Patrick, 280, 281, 286, 310

National Advisory Commission on Civil Disorders, 240, 309. *See also* Kerner Commission

National Advisory Commission on Criminal Justice Standards and Goals, 153, 275

National Association for the Advancement of Colored People (NAACP), 318

National Commission on Law Observance and Enforcement (*See also* Wickersham Commission), 16, 77, 308

National Crime Information Center, 342

National Crime Victimization Survey (NCVS), 210

National Incident Based Reporting System (NIBRS), 213, 216–18, 343–44
    offenses, categories of, 217–18

National Infrastructure Protection and Computer Intrusion Program (NIPCIP), 192

National Institute of Justice (NIJ), 99, 266

National Law Enforcement and Corrections Technology Center, 250

National Organization of Black Law Enforcement Executives (NOBLE), 38, 284

National Sheriff's Association (NSA), 38, 284

National Youth Gang Survey, 181

Negligence tort, 300
    elements to prove, 301

Nelson, "Baby Face," 3

New Jersey Regional Community Policing Institute, training curriculum, 49

New Jersey State Police (NJSP), racial profiling by, 260

Newport News, Virginia, problem-oriented policing in, 99–100, 221

New York City Police Department (NYPD)
    appointments during political era, 71
    backgrounds checks in, 9
    basic training for, 37
    beating of Abner Louima, 253, 296
    and Brooklyn North Neighborhood Safety Project, 124
    comparison with London, 70
    and computer crime, 192
    corruption in, 240–41, 242, 286–87
    counterterrorism training in, 56–57
    creation of, 1–2
    creation of Family Crisis Intervention Unit (FCIU), 185
    Crime Control Model, 112
    and crime mapping, 349
    crime scene investigation in, 143
    factors for disqualification from, 6
    hostage negotiation team of, 223
    Internal Affairs in, 280
    Lexow Committee and, 308
    mandatory arrest for domestic violence by, 185
    measuring police performance in, 233–36
    and Mollen Commission, 255
    peer evaluations in, 228–29
    performance evaluation in, 227–28
    supervision in, 273
    use of CompStat by, 117
    use of zero tolerance policing in, 119–20

New York State Commission of Investigation, 208

Night vision, 171

Nixon, Richard, 84
    and Watergate, 315

Numbers game, 205, 207–15, 223, 224

Occupational deviance, 239

Office of Community-Oriented Policing Services (COPS Office), 48, 107

Office of Juvenile Justice Delinquency and Prevention (OJJDP), 182

Officer's Bill of Rights, 137

Oleoresin capsicum (pepper spray), 249, 345

Omnibus Crime Control and Safe Streets Act, 83

Organized crime, 77

Ovando, Javier, 255

Parker, Bonnie, 3

Pat-down search, 81

Paterson, New Jersey, Police Department
    community policing by, 162–63
    current patrol deployment, 160–61
    proposed patrol deployment, 161–62
    restructuring of, 159–63
    unions in, 163

Patience, as necessity for job, 33

Patrol, 129, 140–42
    allocation, 209
    bicycle, 141
    directed, 141
    foot, 86, 141
    formula for distribution, 141
    functions of, 140
    levels of, 85
    during nineteenth century, 72
    random, 140
    response time, 142
    saturation, 182
    targeted, 141

Pattern and practice suit, 312–13

Peace Officer Standards and Training (POST), 37–38, 62
    charges of, 62
    functions of, 38

Pedagogy, 47

Peel, Sir Robert, 67–69, 87, 132, 174, 206, 214, 237, 240, 269, 337
    beliefs about firearms, 71

and Metropolitan Police Act of 1829, 68–69
model of policing, 70
principles of, 68–69
Peer evaluations, 228–29, 360
Pendleton Act of 1883, 2, 71, 135
Pepper spray. *See* Oleoresin capsicum
Perez, Rafael, 255
Performance evaluation, rookies
behaviorally anchored rating scale (BARS), 44
daily observation report (DOR), 44
Performance evaluations, 234
contemporary examples of, 226–28
expanding purposes of, 224
outcomes for, 225
problems with, 214–15
reasons for, 224
Personnel, 145
Peterloo Massacre, 68
Philadelphia Police Department (PPD)
brutality in, 297
identity theft and, 191
and 39th district scandal, 252–53
Phoenix Police Department, gangs and, 182
Physical abuse, 239, 247
Physical agility, 8
Physical testing, during recruitment, 19
Pinkerton Detective Agency, 91
Pittsburgh Police Bureau, performance evaluations by, 215
Police
crime, 179–94, 238–39
discretion and decision making of, 173–79
field work, 164–95
and the law, 164–73
limited mobility and salary, 245–46
and mentally ill, 185–88
problems for, 247–60
professionalism, struggle for, 90–92
public perception of, 244
pursuit, 266–68
reform, consent decrees as mechanism for, 313–14
and sex offenders, 201–3
subculture, 246—247, 285–86
and technology, 327–47, 362
Police academy
agency, 38, 61
college-sponsored, 38, 61
regional, 38, 39, 61
traditional, andragogy in, 47–48
Police academy training, 61–63, 272
actions of effective program, 40
areas, 62–63
Centralize POST Academy, 39
Citizen Police Academy, 39
College/University Academy, 39

content areas in, 40
deficiencies in, 41–42
functions of, 39
historical perspective on, 36–38
limitations of, 35, 41–42
Municipal Police Academy, 39
Private Academy, 39
purpose of, 39
Sheriff/County Police Academy, 39
Specialized Academy, 39
State Police/ Highway Patrol Academy, 39
style and content of, 39–41
traditional model for, 38–41
types of, 38–39
typology of, 39
Police accountability
administrative guidelines, 275–78
citizen oversight, 314–18
civil litigation, 299–304
criminal law, 295–99
external mechanisms of, 295–320
internal mechanisms of, 269–88
judicial intervention, 304–7
media, 319
public interest groups, 318
recruitment, 269–71
selection methods, 271
special investigations, 307–12
supervision, 273–74
training, 272–73
U.S. Department of Justice consent decrees, 312–14
U.S. Supreme Court as mechanism for, 306–7
The Police and Minority Groups, 49
Police Athletics League (PAL), 182
Police Benevolent Association (FBA), 135
Police-community partnership, 103–4
purposes of, 104
Police Corps, 21–22
Police deviance, 361–62
legitimizing, 244
Police Executive Research Forum (PERF), 17, 38, 99, 194, 251, 258, 284
Police Foundation, 84
Police misconduct, 237–61
abuse of authority, 239–40, 247–53
consequences of, 241–42
corruption, 239, 253–56
criminal law as tool against, 296–99
defining, 238–40
history of U.S., 240–42
measuring, 238–40
occupational deviance, 239
police crime, 238–39
prejudice and discrimination, 256–60
prevalence of, 241

Police misconduct (*cont.*)
  rotten apple theory, 242–43
  structural explanations, 243–47
  theoretical frameworks for, 242–47
Police Officers Standards, 62
Police organization, 128–56
  administrative services, 144–46
  alternative models, 150–52
  bureaucracy in, 128–38
  civil service, 134–35
  field services, 140–43
  flat, 150
  functions of, 138–40
  goals of, 138–39
  as hierarchical organization, 129
  hospital model, 150–52
  management issues, 150–56
  manpower and resource shortages in, 152–54
  matrix structure of, 150
  quasi-military style of, 132–34, 154–56
  structure of, 140–46, 150
  supervision and leadership in, 146–49
  unions, 135–38
Police paramilitary units (PPU), 154, 155
Police performance
  clearance rates, 212
  community satisfaction surveys, 218–21, 229–30
  complexity of role, 205, 211
  at departmental level, 216–23
  effectiveness assessment, 209–12
  expanding evaluation process, 224–28
  identifying measurable outcomes, 221–22
  at individual level, 213–14, 223–30
  mandate, 205–6
  measuring, 204–31, 233–36, 360–61
  new measures of, 216–30
  numbers game, 207–15
  peer evaluations, 228–29
  police-population ratio, 209
  problems with traditional evaluations, 214–15
  response time, 211
  standard workload formula, 209
  traditional measures of, 206–15
  Uniform Crime Reports (UCR), 212
Police-population ratio, 209
Police Services Study (PSS), 138, 140, 211
  and mentally ill, 188
Police subculture, 78
Police work, nature of, 3
Policing
  community, 107
  as craft, 34–35
  cultures of, 148–49
  defining features of, 35
  definition of good, 222
  domestic violence, 183–85
  future of, 353–66

identity theft, 190–92
  limitations of academy training, 35
  organizational issues, 358
  philosophies of, 93–122, 356–57
  as profession, 35
  quasi-military style of, 132–34
  supervision issues in, 110
Policy, 275
Political era, 1, 71–73
  activities of officers during, 72
  corruption and brutality during, 72–73
  selection of officers during, 71–72
  street justice during, 73
Polygraph, 328
  creation of, 75
  tests, 19
Polygraph Protection Act, 19
Portland (OR) Police Department, surveys for, 219
Prejudice, 256
President's Commission on Crime and Justice, 211
President's Commission on Law Enforcement and the Administration of Justice, 7, 36, 38, 43, 62, 82–83, 174, 328
  recommendations of, 83
Pretextual stop, 169–70
Preventive patrol, 78
Primary aggressor laws, 186
Prior work experience, as requirement for recruitment, 7
Probable cause, 166
Problem-oriented policing (POP), 14, 32, 93–102, 148, 213, 221, 225, 357
  basic assumptions of, 95–96
  basic elements of, 96–98
  characteristics of, 98–99
  comparison with zero tolerance policing, COP, CompStat, 120–21
  diffusion of, 99
  directed patrol as part of, 141
  limitations of, 101–2
  and mentally ill, 186
  research on effectiveness of, 99–101
  SARA model, 96–98
  theoretical foundations of, 93–96
  training in, 48–49
Problem police officer, 282–83
Procedure, 275
Professionalism, 3, 74
  movement, 7, 240
Professional policing
  anti-war movement, impact of, 81–82
  Civil Rights movement, impact of, 81–82
  development of in United States, 70–71
  drug use, rise of, 82
  due process revolution in, 79
  fallout from 1960s, 86–87
  first fifty years of, 1–2

Gideon v. Wainwright, impact of, 80
Mapp v. Ohio, impact of, 79–80
Miranda v. Arizona, impact of, 80
national crisis and, 79–84
political era of, 1
recruitment, beginning of, 2–3
reform era of, 2–3
and research revolution, 84–86
riots, impact of, 81–82
Terry v. Ohio, impact of, 80–81
Professional policing model, 78, 128
development of, 67–88
origins of, 67–71
during political era, 71–73
problems with, 76–87
reform in early, 73–76
Progressives, 73, 91, 240
Prohibition, 77–78, 91
Project on Policing Neighborhoods, 188
Property Department, 146
Psychological abuse, 240, 247
Psychological testing, 5
during recruitment, 19–20
Public Enemy Number 1, 76, 82
Public interest groups, 318
Pygmalion effect, 42

Qualifications, for selection
age, 4
citizenship, 4
criminal record, 5–6
driver's license, 4
education, 7
health, 4–5
height and weight, 5
prior work experience, 7
residency, 6–7
veteran's preference, 7
Quality of life offenses, 103
Quasi-military style, of police, 132–34, 358
Quotas, 12

Race, motivations for becoming police officer, differences among, 11
Racial profiling, 78, 256–59
differences in, 257
of Middle-Eastern people, 258–59
by New Jersey State Police (NJSP), 260
prevalence of, 258
Real Time Crime Center (RTCC), 329
Reasonable suspicion, 165–66
Recidivism, 55
Reconstruction, crime scene, 336
Records, maintaining, 145
Recruitment, 1–30
active, 354
Affirmative Action, 11–13, 270

basic requirements, 13–19
beginning of, 2–3
challenge of, 27–29
component of accountability, 270–71
current issues and controversies in, 10–13, 20–22
diversity in, 10, 23, 28–29
education required for, 27–28
elements of, 3–10
future of, 29, 353–55
hiring decisions, using scoring system, 9–10
history of, 269–70
knowledge of foreign languages and, 14
mass hiring, 21
measuring performance, 20–21
motivations for, 10–11
police corps, 21–22
residency, 29
selection tests, 19–20
traditional approach to, 1–10
Reform, of police, 73–76
autonomy from political control as, 74
centralization as, 73
first efforts at, 73–74
of function, 74
partial success of, 76–77
Progressives role in, 73
second efforts at, 74–76
of selection process, 74
Reform era of policing, 2–3
training during, 37
Regional community policing institutes (RPI), 48
Regional police academies, 38, 61
Registration and community notification law statutes (RCNL), 201
Reiss, Albert, 82
Rendell, Edward, 297
Report on Lawlessness in Law Enforcement (*See also* Wickersham Commission), 77
Report writing, 18
Requirements, for becoming police officer, 13–19
alcohol and drug testing, 13
college education, 16–19
knowledge of technological advances, 13–14
residency, 15–16
Residency requirements, 6, 355
for recruitment, 6–7, 15–16, 29
Resource shortages, 152–54
Response time, 142, 211
Richmond, California, problem-oriented policing in, 101
Riots, 81–82, 138
cause of, 83
Watts, 81
Rizzo, Frank, 278, 286, 297

Rizzo v. Goode, 304, 305
Robinette v. Barnes, 277
Rookies, performance evaluation for, 44
Roosevelt, Theodore, 74, 90, 307
Rules, 275

San Diego Police Department (SDPD)
  dogs, use of in, 277
  problem-oriented policing in, 102
San Jose Police Department (SJPD)
  citizen oversight and, 317
  field training officer program, model of, 43,
    45–46, 63–64
Santa Ana Police Department (SAPD)
  civilianization of, 152–53
SARA problem-solving model, 96–98, 102,
  106
  analysis, 96
  assessment, 96, 97
  response, 96–97
  scanning, 96
Sarbanes, Paul, 172
Saturation patrol, 182
Schwarz, Charles, 296
Seabury Committee, 308
Searches, 166–67
  heat sensing equipment, 171
  night vision, 171
  open-field, 168
  pat-down, 81
  plain-view, 168
  technologically advanced, 171
  wiretapping, 171
  with and without warrants, 166–67
Search warrant, and *Mapp v. Ohio,* 79
Selection process, 284
  emergence of, 3–10
  minimum qualifications, 3–7
  for officers, 271
  tests, 3
Selection tests, 7–9, 19–20
  background check, 8–9
  oral interview, 9
  physical, 19
  physical agility, 8
  polygraph, 19
  psychological, 5, 19–20
  written, 8
September 11, 2001, 56, 193
  creation of U.S. Patriot Act, 171–73
  racial profiling after, 258–59
Sergeant, role of, 273–74
Serpico, Frank, 308, 309–10
Sex crimes
  forensic evidence, importance of, 202
  investigating, 202
Sex Offender Monitoring Unit (SOMU), 202
Sex offenders
  police and, 201–3

  supervision of, 201
Sexual assault nurse examiners (SANE), 202
Siege mentality, 246, 286
Simpson, O.J., 331, 335
Slave patrols, 70, 90
Social services, as duty of police, 72
Soulliere's stages of technological advance-
  ment, 327, 353
Span of control, 130
Special investigations, 307–12
  advantages and disadvantages of, 307–8
Specialization, division of, 245
Specialized training, 46–47, 64–65
Specter, Arlen, 297
Spoils system, 2
Standard operating procedure manual (SOP),
  130
Standards for Law Enforcement Agencies, 10
Standards Relating to the Urban Police Force,
  139
State-mandated training, 37
Street cop culture, 148
Street justice, 73
Stress
  external, 51
  internal, 51
Stress management, 28
  definition of, 52
  programs for, 52
  training, 51–53
Subculture, police, 78, 246—247, 356
  changing, 285–86
Substance abuse, mentally ill and, 186
Supervision, 146–49, 245
  and accountability, 273–74
  achieving effective, 274
  features of effective, 147–48
  problems with, 110
  sergeant, role of, 273–74
  of sex offenders, 201, 202–3
  styles of, 148
Supervisory training, 65–66
Supreme Court cases
  Arizona v. Fulminante, 170
  Berger v. New York, 171
  Betts v. Brady, 80
  Brown v. Mississippi, 309
  California v. Ciraola, 171
  COPPAR v. Rizzo, 305
  Estate of Sinthasomphone v. City of
    Milwaukee, 259
  Florida v. Riley, 171
  Gideon v. Wainwright, 80
  Katz v. United States, 171
  Kyllo v. United States, 171, 346
  Lee v. Florida, 171
  Lyons v. Los Angeles, 305
  Mapp v. Ohio, 79–80, 167–68, 305
  Mendoza v. Block, 277
  Miranda v. Arizona, 80, 168–69, 306, 307

*Monell v. Department of Social Services of
    the City of New York*, 185, 302
Monroe v. Pape, 302
Morka v. State of New Jerse, 259
Rizzo v. Goode, 304, 305
Robinette v. Barnes, 277
Tennessee v. Garner, 252, 276, 306
Terry v. Ohio, 80–81, 166, 168, 306
Thomas v. County of Los Angeles, 305
Thurman v. Torrington, 186, 277, 302
United States v. Dunn, 171
United States v. White, 171
West v. Atkins, 301
White v. Williams, 260
Whren v. United States, 169
Surette, Ray, 366
Sustain rate, 317
SWAT teams, 154, 155
Sylvester, Richard, 74
Symbolic assailant, 78, 246

Tallahassee Police Department, assessment of
    rookies by, 44
Tammany Hall, 2, 71
Tasers, 56, 146, 174, 238, 249, 272, 275, 318,
    345
Technology
  biometrics, 344
  closed circuit television (CCTV), 343
  computers and Internet, 341–42
  crime analysis, 337–41
  crime scene investigation, 329–37
  future of, 362
  global positioning systems (GPS),
    342–43
  imaging, 345–46
  less-than-lethal weapons, 345
  mobile digital terminals (MDT), 56
  NIBRS, 343–44
  and police, 327–47
  stages of advancement, 327–29
  training, 56
  use by cold case squads, 344
Telephone, invention of, 75
Television
  CSI effect on policing, 329, 365
  popularity of crime scene investigation on,
    143
  reality of shows on, 365–66
Tennessee v. Garner, 252, 276, 306
Terrorism, 193–94, 238
  anthrax attacks, 193
  national threat level, 194
Terry v. Ohio, 80–81, 306
  probable cause in, 168
  reasonable suspicion in, 166
Thomas v. County of Los Angeles, 305
Thornburgh, Richard, 133
Thurman v. Torrington, 186, 277, 302

Toch, Hans, 229, 283
Tool marks, 332
  test, 332
Tort, 299
  intentional, 300
  negligence, 300
  state, types of, 299
Traffic, 142–43
  cameras, use of, 143
  danger of stops, 142
  functions of enforcement, 142
Training, 31–60
  academy, 31
  and accountability, 272–73
  in America, 61–66
  basic law enforcement (BLE), 272
  central importance of, 32–34
  classroom, 35
  in communication, 55
  counterterrorism, 32, 56–57
  developmental, 64–65
  domestic violence, 53
  field training officer programs (FTO),
    43–46, 272
  future of, 66, 355–56
  in handling mentally ill, 53–55
  inadequacy of, 36
  in-service, 31, 33, 46–47, 272
  management, 47, 65–66
  multicultural/diversity, 49–51
  necessity of, 36
  police academy, 61–63, 272
  for police pursuit, 268
  post-hoc approach, 65
  regional community policing, 48–49
  specialized, 46–47, 64–65
  standards for, 38
  state-mandated, 37
  stress management, 51–53
  supervisory, 65–66
  in technology, 56
  topics covered in, 65
  types of, 37
  unit, 145–46
  in writing, 55
Troy Police Department, civil service,
    problems with, 135
Two cultures of policing, 148
  management, 148
  street cop, 148
Two-way radio, 75, 77, 328

Underlying conditions, 95, 96, 97, 98, 105
  definition of, 94
  in zero tolerance policing, 119
Uniform Crime Reports (UCR), 3, 160, 204,
    210, 212–13, 214, 216
  (2004), 323
  offenses, categories of, 212

Uniform Guidelines on Employee Selection
  Standards, 5
Unions, police, 135–38
  collective bargaining in, 136
  current trends, 136–37
  functions of, 136
  impact of, 137–38
  Paterson, New Jersey, 163
  unionization of police, 135–36
United States
  development of professional policing in,
    69–71
  policing in Colonial America, 69–70
  political era in, 71–73
United States v. Dunn, 171
United States v. White, 171
Unity of command, 130
Urinanalysis, 13
U.S. Commission on Civil Rights, 287
U.S. Patriot Act, 164, 171–73, 306, 359
U.S. Supreme Court, 304, 305–7. *See also*
    Supreme Court cases
  limitations of, 307
  as police accountability mechanism, 306–7
U.S. v. Weeks, 79
Us *versus them* mentality, 42, 82, 104, 105,
  246, 279

Varieties of Police Behavior, 85, 138
Verbal judo, 55
Verniero, Peter, 260
Veteran's preference, as requirement for
    recruitment, 7
Vigilante committees, in Colonial America,
    70, 90
Violence
  due to quasi-military style of policing, 134
  problem-oriented policing and, 100
Violent Crime Control Act (1994), 21, 107,
    312
Vollmer, August, 1, 3, 7, 27, 35, 51, 77, 87,
    90, 91, 92, 131, 175, 206, 225, 240, 309,
    330, 355
  assessment of police, 32
  and college education as requirement, 16,
    17–18
  and impact on unionization, 138
  as leader of reform, 74–76

progressiveness of, timeline, 75
  and technological advancements, 328
Volpe, Justin, 253, 296
Volstead Act, 77
Volunteer system, in Colonial America, 69

Walk-through (crime scene), 334–35
War on Drugs, 179, 181, 186, 300
Warrants, 166
  searches with and without, 166–67
Warren, Earl, 79
Washington, D.C., Metropolitan Police
    Department (DCMPD), 243
  academy training curriculum, 40–41
  mass hiring in, 21
  scandals in, 243
Watts riot, 81
Weapons
  analysis of, 332
  less-than-lethal, 345
  tool marks in, 332
West Point Military Academy, 47
West v. Atkins, 301
White v. Williams, 260
Whitman, Charles, 64
Whren v. United States, 169
Wickersham Commission, 77–78, 240,
    308–9, 314
  report, 16, 75
Wilson, James Q., 85, 138
Wilson, O.W., 74, 141, 337
Wiretapping, 171, 359
  and Patriot Act, 172
Women
  Affirmative Action and, 12
  recruitment of, 10, 28
Writing training, 55
Wrongful death, 300

Zero tolerance policing, 87, 93, 112, 118–20,
    132, 213, 236, 357
  comparison with COP, POP, CompStat,
    120–21
  directed patrol as part of, 141
  impact of, 119–20
  and mentally ill, 186
  problems with, 120